What Kind of a Thing Is a Middle English Lyric?

THE MIDDLE AGES SERIES

Ruth Mazo Karras, *Series Editor*

Edward Peters, *Founding Editor*

A complete list of books in the series
is available from the publisher.

WHAT KIND OF A THING IS A MIDDLE ENGLISH LYRIC?

Edited by
Cristina Maria Cervone
and
Nicholas Watson

PENN

UNIVERSITY OF PENNSYLVANIA PRESS

PHILADELPHIA

Published by
University of Pennsylvania Press
Philadelphia, Pennsylvania 19104-4112
www.upenn.edu/pennpress

Printed in the United States of America on acid-free paper
10 9 8 7 6 5 4 3 2 1

Hardcover ISBN 978-0-8122-5390-0
Ebook ISBN 978-0-8122-9851-2

A catalog record for this book is available from the
Library of Congress.

For Bernice K. Cervone and Alison Watson

"Frae the Greek o Sappho"

Doun gaes the muin hersel, an aa
    The Pleiades forbye.
Nicht is nearin her mirkest hoor
    And yet alane I lie.

Seldom it is that love will come weeping.
He comes most often silently creeping
To catch you unaware,
But never

Sleeping.

Tom Scott, "Frae the Greek o Sappho," from "Four Versions into Scots" (1953)
Bernice Kuenzig, from "Another Year Around," printed by permission of D. Donald Cervone.

Contents

Preface

The chapters and other materials in this book represent a coordinated attempt by a group of scholars and poets to rethink the Middle English lyric from the ground up, looking at this body of work from a range of new perspectives and methodologies current in medieval studies, lyric studies, and allied fields. Eleven chapters combine original research with reflections on what Middle English lyrics are, how they may be read and understood, and in what ways they mattered in the past and still matter in the present. They are followed by two chapters in which leading figures in the field of contemporary poetics respond to these reflections and by a series of new or recent poems written in medieval forms and in dialogue with medieval poetry. The chapters were written after extended conversations, initially at the Radcliffe Institute for Advanced Study at Harvard University and by various means later, which continue in the book itself, as the Introduction and cross-references in the chapter endnotes show. Some of the poems were also written for this volume. Although the bibliography has been updated to include a number of items published in 2020, it should be noted that the form of the book was already set in place before the many perturbations of that year.

While the Middle English period, conventionally understood to begin around 1150, is also conventionally understood to have ended a full three and a half centuries later, around 1500, the book takes the majority of its examples from poems written between the late twelfth and the late fourteenth centuries. This is the period in which poetry in England was being written in three major languages, English, Latin, and Anglo-Norman (also known as insular French, Anglo-French, or the French of England), either separately or together, so that a special richness of linguistic possibility intensifies the literary landscape. This was all the more so in those regions of the country with local textual communities writing in Welsh, Cornish, Hebrew, and more. We have reluctantly left the better-traveled terrains of the Old English period (eighth to eleventh centuries) and late Middle English period (late fourteenth to early sixteenth centuries) mostly to others.

The book is intended for students and scholars of medieval literature, as well as for those interested in poetry in general and current conversations surrounding the idea of lyric poetry in particular. As the book argues, this is a topic to which Middle English lyric has much to contribute.

*   *   *

With this book the editors honor Alison Watson, classicist and teacher, and Bernice K. Cervone, artist and poet, whose connection to our lyric project we hold in mind and heart. To each of them we say, in the words of the Radcliffe Song, written by Floretta Elmore '09, with music by Emily Coolidge '08, "For our strength and joy in living, love and praise to thee belong!"

Conventions

Contributors to this book use a range of Middle English editions, sometimes of the same poems, which may be based on different manuscript copies and represent these copies in different ways. Almost all modern editions lineate early Middle English poetry even when medieval scribes did not, as was most often the case in Middle English down to the late thirteenth century, following an Old English convention of writing poetry across the page in the same manner as prose. Many editors also use modern English conventions for punctuation, which articulates syntax where medieval punctuation tended to articulate sound. An exception tends to be in the treatment of the strong central caesura structural in alliterative poetry (and a few other meters), which editors often represent either with a common punctuation mark or as a space. Many editors also practice limited regularization of orthography. Middle English scribes made regular or occasional use of several letters derived from Old English scribal practice (and ultimately from the Germanic runic alphabet): thorn (Þ, þ) = *th*; eth (Ð, ð) also = *th*; yogh (ȝ, ȝ) = *y*, *ch*, etc., and less often wynn (Ƿ, ƿ) = *w*, and ash (Æ, æ) = short *a*. They also often represented modern *v* as *u* (and sometimes vice versa), *i* as *y*, and *w* as *uu*, as well as employing various abbreviations, such as versions of the ampersand. Modern editions vary in their treatment of these and other orthographic features, and this variation is carried over into the representation of Middle English in this book.

Chapters offer translations and marginal glosses of passages in Middle English and other languages as necessary. Unless otherwise stated, all these are the author's own.

In theory, all surviving poems in Middle English have been indexed in a series of publications, the most recent of which is the *Digital Index of Middle English Verse* (*DIMEV*: for a list, see the Abbreviations page following this). When appropriate, short Middle English poems are thus cited here with their *DIMEV* numbers, following standard field practice. *DIMEV* references for long poems are less likely to be cited. Like Middle English editing practice and a good deal else, indexing practice comes under scrutiny in these chapters but remains indispensable to attempts to keep track of the variety of forms in which Middle English poetry is preserved. Other systems and projects for cataloging and indexing that focus on medieval English lyrics more broadly, including those in Latin and French, are discussed in the relevant chapters.

Abbreviations

ANTS
Anglo-Norman Text Society. Oxford: Basil Blackwell for the Anglo-Norman Text Society, and London: Birkbeck College for the Anglo-Norman Text Society, , 1939–. Volumes designated O.P. from the Occasional Publications series. Others from Annual Texts Series.

DAMS
Digital Archive of Medieval Song. https://web.library.yale.edu/dhlab/medievalsong.

DIAMM
Digital Image Archive of Medieval Music. http://www.diamm.ac.uk/resources/sbs.

DIMEV
Digital Index of Middle English Verse. Published online as *The DIMEV: An Open-Access Digital Edition of the Index of Middle English Verse*. http://www.dimev.net. Based on IMEV and Supplement.

DMF
Dictionnaire du Moyen Français (1330–1500). ATILF–CNRS and Université de Lorraine, 2015. http://www.atilf.fr/dmf.

EETS
Early English Text Society. London: Trübner (1864–98), Kegan Paul, Trench, and Trübner (1898–1918); London, then Oxford: Oxford University Press (1918–). Volumes designated o.s. (Ordinary Series, 1864–) or e.s. (Extra Series, 1867–1921).

IMEV
Carleton Brown and Rossell Hope Robbins, eds. *The Index of Middle English Verse*.

MED
The Middle English Dictionary. Online at https://quod.lib.umich.edu/m/med/.

NIMEV
Julia Boffey and A. S. G. Edwards, eds. *A New Index of Middle English Verse*. London: British Library, 2005.

OED
The Oxford English Dictionary Online. Online at https://www.oed.com/.

Register   Carleton Brown, ed. *A Register of Middle English Religious*
               and Didactic Verse.
Supplement   Rossell Hope Robbins and John L. Cutler, eds. *Supplement*
               to the Index of Middle English Verse.
STC   *A Short-Title Catalogue of Books Printed in England, Scotland,*
               and Ireland and of English Books Printed Abroad, 1475–
               1640. Searchable as part of ESTC at http://estc.bl.uk. Full
               texts available via EEBO (Early English Books Online).
TEAMS   Teaching Association for Middle English Studies.

Introduction

Why stonde we? why go we no3t?

CRISTINA MARIA CERVONE AND NICHOLAS WATSON

Seoððe sone æfter þet;   com a king Blæðgabreat.
Seoððen þeos worle wes astolled.   ne cuðe na mon swa muchel of song;
of harpe & of salteriun.   of fiðele & of coriun;
of timpe & of lire.   gleomen him weoren deore;
he cuðen al þeos songes.   & þat gleo of ilcche londe;
Of him wes muchel speche.   3eond þas woruld-riche;
swa þat al þis mon-cun.   þat of him iherden tellen;
seiden þat he wes god.   of alle gleo-cræften.

(Then next after that there arose a certain king Blæðgabreat.
Since the world was established, nobody has ever known so much about
*   the art of song!*
Of the harp and the psaltery, of the fiddle and the bagpipe,
of the hand drum and the lyre. Musicians were precious to him;
he knew about all the songs and the music of every region.
There was so much talk of him around the whole world;
that all the people everywhere who heard him described
said that he was god of all the crafts of music.)

For the moore part they loughe and pleyde

King Blæðgabreat loved "gleomen," or so Layamon tells us in his history of early Britain, the *Brut* (ca. 1200),[1] and was honored for his knowledge of them. But who were these "gleomen," what was "gleo" and what were its "cræften"? Were "gleomen" musicians, as in our translation?[2] Or should we call them poets? composers? performers? entertainers? songmen? players? In Present Day English, "glee" generally means simply "extreme delight," "joy," or "playfulness," although if Layamon's first readers could travel through time they would discern elements of "gleomen" in members of present-day glee clubs. No doubt readers from several generations after Layamon would also acknowledge the music and poetry inherent to "glee." In Chaucer's *House of Fame*, "smale harpers with her glees" still "gape" upward at Orpheus, Orion, and the other greats on their plinths and try to imitate them "as craft countrefeteth kynde."[3] But while moderns in turn would no doubt recognize the work of "gleomen" if the time travel were to be reversed, the balance and boundaries of the word have grown elusive. Over the past hundred or so years, many of the categories and kinds of *gleo* as Layamon knew them have been poured into a single phrase, one whose meanings are no less vexed than those of *gleo*, "Middle English lyric."

Over the past century, a great deal of fine scholarship has been written about short poems in Middle English under the rubric of "Middle English lyric," yet we lack agreement on whether "Middle English lyric" is a literary genre or mode, a musical genre or mode, a combination of both, or something less definite altogether. Some might call "Middle English lyric" a utilitarian term, helpful to those who originated it for the purposes of producing anthologies, usually without music, but problematic for many who have encountered or used it since. Most scholars in the field have conceded that the category is unsatisfactory for a variety of reasons, while arguing, if they note that "Middle English lyric" is a taxonomic grouping of any sort, that the attempt to define its boundaries is impractical, since the works named by it are so scattered and diverse. Most of the time, we do not even know whether "lyrics" were spoken or sung. As a result, the phrase "Middle English lyric" does not presently make any clear claim, let alone a confident one, about the relationship between "Middle English lyric" and better-known bodies of works termed lyric, however much it dangles the possibility of such a relationship. This situation was one impetus for the conversations from which this book originated.

A great deal more has been written about the English lyric more broadly during the same period of time during which "Middle English lyric" has existed as a category. Here problems of definition have loomed large, ensuring both that debate must continue and that the terms of debate become part of the question itself. Is lyric indeed a genre, with point of origin, canon, and literary tradition? Is it a set of attributes, found in poems otherwise unconnected with one another? Is it a value system, based on those attributes? Or is it a modern category, based on that value system, that marks off certain texts as suitable for "lyric reading"? And what, if anything, does (singular) "lyric" now have to do with the (plural) "lyrics" that popular composers set to music? Despite widespread recognition that some shifting of the conversation is needed, not enough effort has yet been put into expanding the poetical bodies of work that provide the debate with its conventional frames of reference. Even with the recent advent of "global lyric," long-standing categories such as "Renaissance lyric," "Romantic lyric," "contemporary lyric," and a few others still largely reign supreme. Especially so far as the student anthologies that serve as the field's informal canon-makers are concerned, no sooner have the doors opened a crack to admit a few poems of new kinds or by new writers than they clang shut again. This impasse was another situation that prompted the writing of this book.

The editors' intention in initiating conversations among the scholars whose work appears in this book was to assess the state of current work on Middle English lyric and to explore its many difficulties and sources of interest, as well as to raise its profile in the study of lyric and of poetics more broadly: not by offering premade solutions to the problems of definition the phrase represents, but by providing doors into critical conversations surrounding the subject, doors we hope will in this case remain open. The chapters and other materials in this book thus reconsider, from a range of viewpoints, the challenging body of material loosely termed "Middle English lyric" at a point when the boundaries and essential nature of the topic under review have long been found difficult to grasp; when medievalists have largely sidestepped the implications of the keyword "lyric" even as such implications remain hotly contested by others; and when "Middle English lyrics" themselves have seldom been included in expansive debates over the nature of lyric.

Although our title question, "What kind of a thing is a Middle English lyric?," might seem simplistic or even naive, its terms are not. It is meant to act not only as a point of departure and a focus but as a puzzle and a lure. "A hauk to lure hasteth ful sone," John Capgrave notes in his *Life of Saint Norbert*.[4] We hope the same for those who encounter this book. The word "lyric" was known in Latin throughout the Middle Ages but arrived into English a good deal later than the poems discussed in this book, and considerably later than the once Greek noun from which "lyric" derives.[5] This is "lyre," first recorded in English in the passage of Layamon's alliterative *Brut* quoted above. The deceptively self-effacing word "thing," despite eliciting pushback in these chapters, carries multiple relevant senses. As we'll see, "kind" is a great deal more than a placeholder. And while the title does not use two related words that might seem inescapable, "form" and "genre," it deliberately picks up the naming or grouping not of our making that is problematical in several directions, "Middle English lyric."

At the inception of this project, the editors faced a choice. Would the project take a comparative approach to the topic, situating "Middle English lyric" in relation to other bodies of medieval poetry from Britain, the European mainland, or elsewhere in the world, or perhaps from different historical periods, ancient, modern, or contemporary? Although work of this type is not new, wider contextualization is now needed more urgently than ever. Or would it take a diagnostic approach, investigating "Middle English lyric" from diverse points of view as a phenomenon in its own right, as a point of disciplinary crossover between medieval literary studies and the study of poetics more broadly? We chose the second, partly because we wanted to begin with basic questions about "Middle English lyric" and how this category arose without revitalizing old paradigms that could too easily slip into our collective assumptions if we turned prematurely to comparative models. We also hoped a broadening of perspective on "Middle English lyric" would follow on from bringing scholars trained in various disciplines together.

The chapters of this book, the outcome of extensive collaborative conversations, respond variously to the title question, which they interpret in diverse ways and sometimes recast as they push outwards from its terms. But they build on a good deal of common ground. Among other points of agreement, the chapters presuppose that, although there is something interesting at stake in using the resonant word "lyric," "Middle English lyrics" are in significant ways different from many other bodies of poetry to which "lyric" is applied, medieval or modern. They agree that such difference, as well as being worthy of attention in its own right, has much to contribute to modern theorizing about lyric more broadly, not least in relation to a modern association of "lyric" with personal subjectivity and formal autonomy that comes under critique from a number of perspectives in what follows.

The chapters agree that Middle English lyrics—many of which are or remember songs, some of which are or remember dances—articulate sounds and movements as well as written words. They understand these works as intimately part of a social order, as well as of metrical and textual orders that demand close attention to internal structures and manuscript contexts. They also understand these poems as kinetic and self-reflexive vehicles for thought: word engines that generate meanings out of the rhythmical shaping of words, as well as out of the bodily metaphors that have now been shown to underpin human language and cognition, even when such metaphors go unacknowledged.[6]

More pointedly, although few of the chapters say so directly, they agree that, whatever else it may be, Middle English lyric is an expression, theory, form, or trace of "game" or "pley," in some of the mixed senses in which this word was, and still can be, used. When Chaucer says of the pilgrims' response to "The Miller's Tale" that "Diverse folk diversely they seyde, / But for the moore part they loughe and pleyde," differences of opinion and laughter are equally integral features of the tale-telling "game" in which everyone is involved and of the "holiday" of the pilgrimage that makes it possible.[7] "Pley" names activities specific to situations in which the tasks or protocols that govern ordinary time are suspended, including at holidays. Middle English lyrics sometimes use freedoms associated with holidays to stage escapes into private spaces that allow extraordinary encounters, conversations, and complaints: angry, desiring, mourning, exploratory. Alternatively, Middle English lyrics can be noisily celebratory in a public mode, as in the raucous story of the "Dancers of Colbek" from Robert Mannyng's *Handlyng Synne*, whose refrain, sung by carolers as they dance and sing in a forbidden churchyard, is used as the title for this introduction: "Why stonde we? why go we noȝt?"[8]

In these modes and others, the "pley" of poetry is a bodily activity, whether it involves singing, dancing, and joining hands in a group, or quiet, even subvocal reading, with movements of eyes, mouth, hands, and maybe feet. "Pley" is also therapeutic, arousing and releasing feeling; cognitive, aimed at reorienting the self in relation to society and perhaps the cosmos; and voluntary, involving choice both of the form of "pley" and of the game itself. Some forms of "pley" are even contemplative, serving to shape episodes of devout attentiveness Middle English texts called "meditacioun," "contemplacioun" or "eise."

None of this makes "pley" inherently ethical, benign, pleasurable, or free of violence. On the contrary, one role of "pley" is to create a space not only for misrule but also for strategic conflicts in which the social order of things can be redescribed or renegotiated. This is again clear in Chaucer's "Miller's Tale," which satirizes the way even small differences of status and type (as between the "clerk" Nicholas and the "parissh clerk" Absolon) produce acts of competitive aggression within communities. This process is so ubiquitous in *The Canterbury Tales*, and so compelling for poet, pilgrims, and readers, that the final "myrie tale," told by the Parson in penitential prose, "knytte[s] up al this feeste" by turning the game against itself, requiring all concerned to reflect on its ethical implications, and those of social living in general.[9] Even the Colbek carolers, whose lives are destroyed after they are cursed by a local priest to continue their dance for a year and day, reorganize the ethical framework within which *Handlyng Synne* initially places them, becoming an example less of the sin of sacrilege, as they dance over the graves of the dead at Christmas Eve, than of the abuse of clerical power: "Fellyche þou cursedest, and ouer sone," the priest's son, Aȝone, accuses his father, and Mannyng makes it clear that Aȝone is right.[10]

Mirroring poetry's own relationship with conflict, the body of writing we call "lyric" has long been an arena of contest, as modern scholars absorb and repurpose the rhetoric of praise and blame that powered millennia of odes, panegyrics, funeral poems, love songs, war songs, satires, flytings, and more. One ongoing set of debates, which engages our two passionate and brilliant respondents along with others, tussles over the definition and sway of the category of "lyric" in ways that are of special pertinence to our topic. Like scholars in other subfields of the discipline of historical poetics, Middle English lyric scholars also have their own areas of disputation.[11] Indeed, contemporary lyric studies and medieval literary studies derive points of contention from the same source: a tension between literary history and literary form drawn tight in the formative years of the discipline of English studies itself.

> . . . he looked upon me,
> And seyde thus: "What man artow?"

The phrase "Middle English lyric" is not the simple descriptor it may appear to be but a scholarly invention of the early twentieth century, framed to enable a particular kind of reading.[12] As several chapters below describe in more detail, the term first developed as a way to assemble a large but disparate body of short-form verse written in Middle English between the pages of edited anthologies, and so make them available to what was coming to be referred to as the "close reading" self-consciously being applied to other bodies of poetry at the same period.[13]

Significant as it is, there was nothing unusual about this process. The critical use of many genre terms goes back no further. The word "lyric" itself is a prominent case in point. "Lyric" first entered English in the 1580s: initially in discussions of Greek and Latin poetry sung to lyres and other instruments, described much as Layamon described ancient British poetry in the *Brut*;[14] then, more broadly, as a name for any monodic song, or in the plural ("lyrics") words set to music. Only during the first decades of the twentieth century, as English studies grew into an academic discipline with concerns that were increasingly interpretative more than rhetorical or philological, did "lyric" also become the preferred name both for short-form poetry in general and for certain aesthetic and ethical qualities, born within the patternings of verbal sound and meaning, that came be seen as embodied by the most successful of this poetry.[15]

To this day, the word "lyric" remains suspended in a matrix of usages. Indeed, the word's multiplicity of reference is an important engine of some of the most recent scholarly debates in the field. Musicologists (and some literary scholars) object to the exclusion of music from discussion of the term and the poetry it names.[16] Literary scholars are themselves divided into those who hold that there is "a thing called lyric" (however named) across periods, languages, and places, so that a transhistorical and transnational "theory of lyric" is possible, and those who argue that "lyric" in this sense is "a modern invention," serving less to categorize lyric than to produce lyric through reading poems *as* lyric.[17] While real disagreements exist in the mix, and while their stakes can be high, these views are not always as opposed as this brief encapsulation might suggest. Challenges to the implicit privilege of "the lyric *I*" as a construction wielded by some for gatekeeping purposes and left tacit by many, are also underway, from critics and poets alike. "Post-lyrics" and "anti-lyrics" speak back to "the lyric *I*" in the voices of one or another often racialized or marginalized *we*.[18] These developments may also hold potential for rethinking the postures of Middle English lyric, much of which is written in its own versions of a communitarian *we* and in the most localized of later medieval England's three written languages.

Our own use of "lyric" here is partly conventional but mostly strategic. Our title stakes a claim for a body of work produced across a period of several centuries to be included within a history of English lyric that is still often taken to begin only after the Middle Ages, as well as within the study of poetry more broadly.[19] We focus on Middle English lyric, acknowledging it as only a small part of a much larger body of medieval insular poetry written also in Old English, French, and Latin, as well as in medieval England's several other languages, including Welsh, Cornish, Norse, and Hebrew. Our title also stakes a claim for Middle English lyric to be included within the debates that have come to be associated with the term "lyric" itself, which have so far given them limited play. The book then sets out to make this claim cogent: not only to those who work on different bodies of lyric poetry, whether anglophone or not, by showing the intellectual and aesthetic interest and sophistication of the short poetry written in later medieval England, as well as its relevance to theorizing about poetry more broadly; but also to those who work in Middle English studies, by showing the value to this field of issues raised by the critical conversations that surround the term "lyric." Treating the term's multiple connotations as an opportunity, not a problem, the book seeks to offer alternatives to standard ways of carrying on intellectual business in medieval studies and in discussions of lyric poetry.

The book does this not by focusing on what Middle English lyric has in common with canonical lyrics from other times, places, or languages, although this approach has its merits. Rather, it investigates what makes these things distinctive, individually and as a baggy collective, in relation to the history of Western lyric more broadly, as usually told, and to the category of lyric, as commonly defined by those who understand it in aesthetic terms, as well as on the poems' own terms insofar as this is possible. This approach entails teasing out the very features of these poems that have been smoothed away by modern editors as part of a wider effort within literary studies to focus attention on what twentieth-century New Criticism taught students and teachers of English literature to call the "literary object," detached from its distracting material and cultural surrounds and contexts.

Here the "thing" of our title serves to emphasize how much Middle English short verse fails to meet the New Critical aesthetic ideal of this "well wrought" object:[20] through its embeddedness in specific performance situations, cultural and religious practices, as well as nonpoetic genres and media; through its lack of specific forms; through the anonymity of most (importantly, not all) of its authors; through the lack of a codified framework for its composition and of a consistent set of descriptors for its types; through the cold shoulder it apparently gives to earlier lyric traditions, including classical ones; and through its localism, provincialism, and vernacularity, among other qualities and circumstances. Indeed, we entertain the possibility that not only the word "lyric" but even the word "poem" might serve as a misleading limiter, inadequately describing some qualities of the works we are interested in. To inquire "what kind of a thing is a Middle English lyric?" is, then, to inquire into what, if anything, gives this material such specificity as it has, once it is removed from enshrinement in modern lyric anthologies, given the disparate functions it evidently served and the scattered ways in which it has come down to us.[21]

Recent comparative work on medieval poetry and song has shown just how scattered these ways were by the standards of other verse corpora contemporary with it.[22] The grouping of short poems of similar kinds into separated lyric anthologies, with or without music, was a relatively common feature of many medieval European literary cultures. It was also a feature of the literary culture of medieval England before the time of Middle English lyric. Although the practice of gathering spoken and sung poetry into collections may have been older, the earliest surviving anthology of short verse written in any European vernacular language is the Old English Exeter Book from the late tenth century: an expensively produced collection of about 120 short poems in unrhymed alliterative verse, old and new, including two famous homiletic soliloquies, *The Wanderer* and *The Seafarer*, and ninety Old English riddles.[23] One of the first Latin verse anthologies is the "Cambridge Songs," also from England but drawing on poetry from across Europe, copied about a century later.[24] A few books of Latin nonliturgical verse survive from the twelfth century,[25] and a profusion of anthologies of troubadour poetry in the langue d'oc (Provençal), and trouvère poetry in the langue d'oïl (French) from the thirteenth and into the fourteenth century, when they were joined by verse and song books in Italian, Catalan, Spanish, Portuguese, German, and Welsh, among others.[26]

Lyric anthologies of various kinds appear to have been the medieval rule, not the exception, in many European literary languages. It is therefore especially notable that there are no thirteenth- or fourteenth-century books of this kind dedicated to short poems in Middle English. One miscellany from the 1370s, the "commonplace book" of the Lincolnshire friar John of Grimestone, collects many poems and poetic fragments for the purposes of preaching.[27] Two other famous books include clusters of art poems among their contents, some of which could perhaps have derived from smaller, more cheaply produced chapbooks of short English or English, French, and Latin poems that have not come down to us, if such objects existed. What twentieth-century editors called the "Harley lyrics" form part of a large collection of religious and secular prose and verse in all three languages compiled in Ludlow (Shropshire), probably for a gentry household by their chaplain or parish priest, probably during the 1340s:[28] one of a small cluster of trilingual books that include short English poetry among their contents to survive from the late thirteenth and early fourteenth centuries.[29] What we now call the "Vernon lyrics," a collection of stanzaically elaborate religious poems, fill the last six folios of the more than four hundred that make up the huge Vernon manuscript, probably copied in the 1390s for an unusually wealthy aristocratic patron.[30] Although what counts as a Harley or Vernon lyric is a matter for discussion,[31] neither book includes much more than thirty poems in English (or some fifty in English, French, and Latin in the case of Harley) that could readily be regarded as candidates. The poems in these books show that in the fourteenth century there was a sophisticated, intergenerational and in many cases also multilingual community of English poets, aware of each other's work and interested in formal and generic experimentation.[32]

However, so far as the thirteenth and fourteenth centuries are concerned, these clusters of art poems are unusual. Many more lyrics from this period come down to us as single items in larger, often multilingual compendia of verse and prose: as quotations in works of Latin or French prose; as inscriptions on objects; and, commonly, inserted in blank spaces at the ends of manuscript gatherings, or in their margins, along with other occasional pieces (recipes, remedies, prayers, anecdotes). Individual works survive as scraps: scribbled as marginalia for no ascertainable reason, or awaiting planned or unplanned inclusion once they could be made to fit; inscribed or painted on material objects or architectural spaces, from the chantry chapel at Long Melford to Cooling Castle; recorded as snatches in Latin sermons.[33] Most of these works seem to have existed only incidentally as texts, whose written forms can best be seen as traces of the spoken or sung sounds and rhythms, and the associated breaths, gestures, and movements, of social artifacts that circulated orally within households and communities for whose members they were once as intimate as they are now remote from us. The artifacts suggest that qualities or aspects of Middle English lyric we find baffling might have been deliberate. Even perhaps the open-endedness of many examples could be purposeful and important in ways not transparent to us. No doubt it is significant that most of the Middle English terms used to describe short verses ("song," "lay," "carol," "proverb") highlight the communal flavor of this body of material, as do the poems themselves, often framed around *we* rather than *I*.[34]

The lack of anthologies largely persisted as late as Richard Tottel's *Songes and Sonettes* (*Tottel's Miscellany*) in the 1550s.[35] With partial exceptions, such as the carols of James Ryman gathered in Cambridge, Cambridge University Library MS Ee.1.12,[36] and one notable full exception in which French influence is clear—a collection of the English poems of Charles d'Orléans made for this long-suffering royal hostage soon before he returned to France in 1440[37]—fifteenth-century books that contain short English poems continued to resemble miscellanies more than anthologies. Most are organized around longer items, such as romances or chronicles, with the short poems filling up empty space at the end of quires or booklets. Important examples include the Findern Manuscript, notable for gathering poems copied by perhaps thirty gentry men and women from related families, and a miscellany compiled from a set of short books of materials often related to London in the early 1500s and later owned by the Elizabethan antiquarian John Stow (London, Lambeth Palace Library, MS 306).[38] Even when clusters of poems are grouped together apparently purposefully, as with the twenty-four political and moral Digby lyrics or with the poems of John Audelay (both early 1400s),[39] these books declare the social and generic embeddedness of Middle English more clearly than they do any notion of lyric autonomy.

Because medieval books were copied by hand with no central planning or documentation of the kind the Tudors obliged the Stationers' Company to keep of printed books, there is no way to be sure how far the books that survive to us are representative of what was once in circulation. Yet it seems unlikely that there were ever many English lyric manuscripts along the lines of the sumptuous continental collections of songs and short verses made for wealthy aristocrats, which survive in quantity because of their value as art objects. One possible factor here may have been the idiosyncratic character of England's musical scene.[40] Another may have been England's fluid and equally idiosyncratic linguistic situation. Between the twelfth and late fourteenth centuries, works written for the English aristocracy were not in English but Latin or French, a language learned nearly from birth by anyone of education. English was both a vernacular language, not used for a range of purposes that required Latin, and a socially particularized language, whose range of written uses was further restricted by the ubiquity of French, far the more common of the two written languages across the English twelfth and thirteenth centuries. By the end of the thirteenth century, however, as the chansonnier genre grew popular across Europe, the French of England was itself coming to be seen as provincial. Although works and books in this dialect circulated

in courtly settings alongside books of continental French into the 1400s, sophisticated English readers of French increasingly relied on imports from the
European mainland.[41] So, for cultural reasons, it makes a certain degree of
sense that the English aristocracy apparently did not commission chansonniers even in French language versions.

The relationship between French and English was beneficial to both
languages and eventually shifted decisively in favor of English. The Middle
English lyrics on which this book focuses were written, thrived, circulated,
and were read throughout a period of change significant for the English language. By the end of the fourteenth century, English had begun to assert
itself as the national language, or "moder tonge," and to represent itself as no
longer needing to exist in its former collaborative relationship with French, as
this language also gradually acquired a more pointedly national identity. The
disturbances of the Hundred Years' War and the Great Schism of 1378 to 1417
were factors in both cases.[42] As English displaced insular French from more of
its generic functions, it also continued its assimilation of many French words.
At the level of vocabulary, there is much to be said for the view that modern
English is the result of a rapprochement between English and French in the
late Middle English period. At the same time, French retained the high prestige it enjoyed everywhere in Europe, while English, now in competition with
French, entered a period of cultural self-consciousness from which it took
several centuries fully to emerge during the 1700s.[43]

Throughout this period (and later), English poets looked to Geoffrey
Chaucer as an originating figure, "Floure of poetes thorghout al Breteyne"
and eventually "the Father of English Poetry,"[44] canonizing not only Chaucer
himself, along with his contemporary John Gower, but an account of English
literature that begins in what (even now) is the middle: seven hundred years
into the history of writing in English, and near the end of the part of the
Middle English period on which this book focuses. In a mythological but
still consequential sense, much of the history of Middle English lyric as we
examine it here thus took place well before English literary history as such
has traditionally been framed as getting underway, with Chaucer.

Two further points are worth noting about this complicated situation.
The first is that the belief that there is a significant cultural gulf between
Middle English lyric and the short verse of the early modern period and
later—a belief often extended to the entirety of medieval literature—has val-
orized modernity and reinforced a notion of the medieval as different, in
some absolute sense, from later periods. Yet for that very reason, early English

poetry and its language have long been imaginatively powerful for later writers, who have viewed it as an important resource and have sought to play with it. From Thomas Percy's *Reliques of Ancient English Poetry* in 1765; to the pseudo–Middle English "Rowley" poems of the teenaged Thomas Chatterton from the same decade; to the early nineteenth-century fascination with "bardic" poetry; to the new poems that end this book: early English poetry has continued to function as a repository of forms, words, and stories, as well as a vehicle for the idea of the medieval in all its variety.[45]

While the direct influence of medieval English lyric poetry on the poetics of later periods is limited, a concept of what this poetry is, sometimes connected to a more general thought that there is something inherently lyrical about the medieval itself, powered lyric poets from Chatterton to Walter Scott and John Keats, and from Alfred, Lord Tennyson, and Christina Rossetti to W. H. Auden.[46] Today the varieties of global English are proliferating, enabling cultural alliances between bodies of poetry far distant in time and space, many of which acknowledge no debt to this canonical tradition. In this situation, Old and Middle English, like the Scots in the dedication of this book, have become vernacular all over again.[47] The relationships among nineteenth-, twentieth-, and twenty-first-century poems themselves, the emergent modern idea of lyric, and medieval lyric are in several ways thus more generative than first appears.

The second point is that the representation of Chaucer as the "lodesterre" of the English "language" and its poetry, which sweepingly confines all earlier poetry to what in the judgment of one early twentieth-century critic was merely "the twittering of birds before the dawn," is almost true in one sense but quite untrue in others.[48] The first of several Middle English poets who took their French and Italian contemporaries as models, Chaucer was innovative in his conception of English as a high literary language, in that he framed this notion overtly within his poetry in specific ways his predecessors and contemporaries did not.[49] Chaucer's project was in some sense conventional, since a key goal of writers of his and later generations was to make English more like Europe's other vernaculars, a project that did require a certain break with a trilingual national past.[50] Yet he and his poetic successors relied on existing English meters, forms, genres, and materials, including some with long roots back to Old English poetry.[51]

Chaucer acknowledges this fact in the shapely tail-rhyme romance that answers the Host's demand of him, "What man artow?" This is the "Tale of Sir Thopas," a poem that reaffirms the hybrid character of *The Canterbury*

Tales, in which neoclassical elements are only one part of a rich, "elvyssh" brew.[52] As we ask of Middle English lyric the same question the Host asks Chaucer, the differences between Middle English lyric and later bodies of short verse must therefore not be hypostasized to emphasize the "alterity" of the medieval past, however real these differences are. Indeed, one outcome of including Middle English lyric fully within the purview of lyric studies might be a realization that, throughout English literary history, informal, heterogeneous, and socially imbricated poetry that maintains a close relationship to song is normative.[53] While other outcomes are possible, as the chapters and poems of this book show, considering what *kinds* of things Middle English lyrics *are* remains a first step on the way to situating what *place* Middle English lyrics *have*, relative to literary history and the present day. So, it is with the kind of the thing Middle English lyric is that our lyric project has been most concerned.

Lyric Kinds: So comly a pakke of joly juele

Thy beaute com never of nature;
Pymalyon paynted never thy vys,
Ne Arystotel nauther by hys lettrure
Of carped the kynde these propertes.[54]

(Your beauty never came from nature;
Pygmalion never painted your face,
Nor neither did Aristotle, through his scholarship,
Speak about the nature of these properties.)

What, then, is *the kind* of the thing that is Middle English lyric? Like scholars today, medieval intellectuals analyzed literary and other entities through a variety of systems, most of them Aristotelian. An early one described a text's *circumstances*: "the life of the poet, the title of the work, the quality of the poem, the intention of the writer, the number of the books, the order of the books, the explanation," or "whom, what, why, in what manner, when, where, by what means," as a ninth-century *Life of Virgil* puts it, working with the lists of questions developed from Aristotle's *Topics*.[55] A later one, derived by twelfth- and thirteenth-century Latin Christian scholars from the *Posterior Analytics*, examined a work's *causes*: its material cause (source or subject), formal cause (form or structure), efficient cause (author or inspiration), and final cause (goal or rationale).[56] A third, developed from the *Praedicamenta* and used in the sciences and metaphysics, was organized around *categories*, generally listed as substance, quantity, quality, relative, where, when, posture, condition, action, and affection.[57] These are the "propertes" of "Arystotel" mentioned in *Pearl*, as the Jeweler wonderingly apostrophizes his dead but now glorified daughter, declaring that the erudition of the Philosopher himself would not be enough to distinguish the "kynde" of her transcendent "beaute," so far has it passed beyond the realm and capacities of the representational arts and natural sciences.

The question this book asks—both its title question and the "question in the guise of a term" implied by the phrase "Middle English lyric" wherever it is used in this book[58]—is in one sense all about categorization. But the categorical systems our medieval predecessors used for textual analysis pertained to texts that were taken to be authoritative within a particular discipline and whose authors were known, as is *not* the case in a body of verse that is largely anonymous and hard to place. Although a few of the poets discussed here were taken to be authoritative in this medieval sense (Richard Rolle, Geoffrey Chaucer, John Gower, perhaps William Litchfield), and although narrative poems such as *Pearl* are in some sense built around the topics, from a medieval perspective most Middle English lyrics are more easily describable as entities than texts.

Modern versions of all ten of Aristotle's categories can be seen at work in many chapters in this book, as these reflect on the Middle English lyric as a separated "thing" (substance) in relation both to other kinds of medieval literature and to other kinds of "lyric" verse; on its canon (quantity), essential properties (quality), and standing (relative); on its situation (where), place in history (when), and codicological contexts (posture); and on the varieties of its forms (condition), the purposes it served and serves (action), and the forces that shaped it (affection). Even so, in grouping the chapters, the editors do not present their arguments systematically. Instead, we offer many analyses, depictions, arguments, and performances here as variations and counterpoints on a single theme, taking in not only the chapters themselves but also the poems that follow.

One way to view this theme would be as *restoration*, which we adopt in a technical sense not derived from early modern humanism but from medieval Christian theology: specifically, from the twelfth-century polymath Hugh of St. Victor, for whom it optimistically names the diverse ways in which, from the origins of human history after the fall down to the present, "those things which had been impaired have been made better," first under the Torah, subsequently (so Hugh argues) under the "New Law" of the Christian church.[59] Hugh understands this program as divine in origin but human in execution, requiring the participation of all the arts and sciences and all the capacities of human selves and communities, intellectual, affective, moral, and creative.[60] "Restoration" as humanity must undertake it thus involves not only aspiring to the "lettrure" of Aristotle and imitating and admiring the artistry of "Pymalyon" but also cultivating the appreciative, if also provocative and costly, wonder of *Pearl*, and not necessarily privileging any one approach above any other. Another name for our theme, borrowed sidelong from Stephanie Burt, might be *admiration*, of a sort that is neither passive nor unproductive.[61]

In pursuit of this "final cause" in relation to our own miniature work of nontheological restoration, we have renounced categorical organization so that readers can experience the "pley" of our discussions as well as of our subject. Chapters that treat lyric as music (Butterfield, Fassler), lyric language (Cornelius, Gibbs), lyric meaning (Cervone, Nelson), lyric address (Zimbalist, Kumler), lyric canons (Cornelius, Fassler), lyric form (Cannon, Galloway), lyric dialogue (Nelson, Zimbalist), lyric setting (Butterfield, Albin), or lyric media (Kumler, Galloway), to name just a few relevant pairings, hail one another here across a distance measured in words. This introduction (Cervone and Watson) sets the dance in motion. Our respondents (Jackson, Burt) and the poets who have contributed to our chapbook (Burt, McCarthy, Keough, Revard, Arthur, Manhire, and Oberman), offer drumbeats, descants, refrains, but also cautions, reminding us that lyrics are understood in the mouth and the body as well as the mind, but also that the "lyric" is a contentious subject and that the work of the Middle English "lyric" within the discipline at large is partly a work of disruption.

We therefore present one view of our project now in the form of a *corona*, with the tail of each paragraph tied to the head of the next, rather as *Pearl* ties together its twenty sections in imitation of the eternal dance in which the "cumly . . . pakke of joly juele" join in heaven. We intend this arrangement, along with the chiaroscuro of approaches in the chapters and poems that follow, as an invitation to others to join this dance—scholars, teachers, students, poets, musicians, all readers—as you work out for yourselves *where best to begin in reflecting upon the complex "kynde" of the thing that is Middle English lyric.*[62]

Where to begin with the thing that is Middle English lyric? In Chapter 1, "Lyric Editing," Ardis Butterfield takes in several answers to this question before proposing her own. One way to begin is by defining the lyric corpus itself: no easy task, given how these short poems fail to amount to a tidily describable thing, even if one insists on the primary connection between lyric and song. The lyrics themselves are scattered, seldom travel with the music to which many were sung, are hard to distinguish from other stanzaic verse, and need to be studied as part of the multilingual literary culture of later medieval England, alongside French and Latin. This process is in its early stages, for reasons Butterfield elucidates by returning to the beginnings of modern lyric scholarship, to watch how twentieth-century catalogers, editors, and critics defined the lyric corpus in the opposite way, detaching lyrics from these same surrounds to make them available to close reading as literary objects. Arguing that this approach has proved a blind alley, Butterfield proposes a return to the beginning work of editing, to explore ways to offer "the whole song" to readers: words, music, variants, versions, and manuscript contexts. She ends with an intricate example from her forthcoming Norton edition of *Medieval English Lyrics*, taken from the beginning of the Middle English lyric tradition: "Seinte marie virgine," taught by Mary herself to the hermit Godric of Finchale in a vision. Intensive attention to the forms and contexts in which "Seinte marie virgine" survives, in this case less as a song for performance than as a reconstruction, "a narrative sketch of what the song was," illuminates *the work that Middle English lyric does*.

What is this work that Middle English lyric does? In Chapter 2, "Wondering Through Middle English Lyric," Cristina Maria Cervone offers an approach to this question by interrogating what sort of reading practices are prompted by the poems themselves. Would readers contemporary to Middle English lyric have shared the expectations present-day readers have of such works? Would they have approached these poems in ways we do? Medieval Christian belief was proudly built around two mysteries, the doctrines of the Trinity and the hypostatic union of God and human in Christ, whose unavailability to reason shuts down Dante's imaginative version of intellectual vision at the end of the *Paradiso*.[63] But even the created order as "paynted" by "Pymalyon" and "carpe[d]" by "Arystotel" was a source of wonder, revealing but also hiding its divine creator. Cervone suggests that Middle English lyric "*intends to prompt*" what she calls "the work of wonder": work that leads Aristotle to liken poets and philosophers. Like her chapter, this work entails speculative inquiry: a practice of feeling cognition carried out through lyric reading, whether by oneself or through the performative, participatory, and communal activities of song, or song and dance. Middle English lyric may draw us to wonder in different ways: sometimes through the surface conventionality of evocations of nature; sometimes in the manner of the "riddling lyric, one I do not understand," that receives special attention, "Summe men sayoun þat y am blac," where the polychromic possibilities hidden in the word "blac"—does it refer to clothing? To moral qualities? To complexion? To race?—constitute the riddle. In either case the conceptual category and experience of wonder can offer a bridge between present and past, suggesting an open-ended approach to reading historically distant poems that is aesthetically satisfying and aspires *to approach Middle English lyric on its own terms.*

How can we approach Middle English lyric on its own terms? In Chapter 3, "Lyric Romance," Christopher Cannon explores one set of these terms, as they relate to the topic of lyric *duration.* The "Harley lyrics," found in an omnibus trilingual book from Ludlow and one of the two largest surviving Middle English lyric collections from before 1400, has never been understood to include the "ballad-like" narrative poem that ends a cluster of English poems in the manuscript, the more than 1,500-line romance *King Horn.* Yet this placement suggests that the link between *King Horn* and short poems such as the one that precedes it, "Mayden, moder milde," was clear to the Harley compiler. This is partly because, in the fourteenth century, lyrics and romances might both be repertory items of the touring professional "menstralles" and "disours" who provided entertainment in large households, performing from memory with a level of variation vividly captured by the substantial but narratively insignificant differences between our three copies of *King Horn.* "Menstralles," the "gleomen" beloved by King Blæðgabreat in Layamon's *Brut,* represent yet another beginning for Middle English verse. But the circular narrative of *King Horn* is also lyric-like, patterned in ways that may either compress or distend time and movement, gesturing toward the temporal stillness of lyric, much as the Harley lyric "Annot and John" gestures toward the temporal progression of romance. *King Horn* is full of rhythms, repetitions, and refrains: "The se bigan to flowe / And Horn child to rowe." Despite the modern processes of lyricization that have categorized it otherwise, *King Horn* is a Harley lyric. *In its formal patterns, the poem itself tells us what it is.*

How do the formal patterns of a Middle English poem tell us what it is? In Chapter 4, "Language and Meter," Ian Cornelius discusses what we may learn about the "resonant meanings" distinctive to Middle English lyrics by attending to its fundamental building block, meter. The detailed workings of English meter are always tied to the sounds of English words and phrases. Yet this was never more true than during the intensive period of exchange among English, French, and Latin that was the thirteenth and fourteenth centuries, as English transformed from a Germanic synthetic language to a Romance-infused analytic language, with profound consequences for its morphology and syntax.[64] Moving through the metric changes that accompany this process, in which the earlier alliterative meter was partly replaced by the Latin septenary and the French *octosyllabe*, Cornelius focuses on this last, which in its English and insular French forms was based on beat, not syllable count, and which he calls a "dolnik." Technical slips in the *Index of Middle English Verse* as it has been written and revised over more than a century suggest that internalizing Middle English scansion may be yet harder than learning to wonder with Middle English lyric, given further shifts in the language and its phonology, orthographic and dialectal variance within the corpus, and the "fuzzy" relationship between words on a page and words in a mouth. But this is the discipline to which Cornelius summons us: to learn with our own mouths how the dolnik and other Middle English meters served to "bind" poetic "utterance . . . to itself," as a "verse object" capable of sustaining itself over time *as a bearer of meaning and value.*

What might be that meaning and value in the twenty-first century? In Chapter 5, "Lyric Value," Ingrid Nelson proposes an answer to this question that drinks from one of the founts that has watered lyric studies for a hundred years, I. A. Richards's *Principles of Literary Criticism* of 1924, but also seeks to redirect its flow. A psychologist as well as literary scholar, Richards saw the patternings of words, images, and meanings in lyric in idealizing ethical and utilitarian terms, reckoning its "value" in building the individualized and humane citizens the new Cambridge English faculty sought to fashion from its undergraduates. This program, grounded in ancient philosophical notions of elite personhood, was in complex reaction against near ancestors such as the program for building imperial citizens at "public schools" set in place by Matthew Arnold's brother Thomas.[65] Nelson urges both that "lyric value" merits recuperating and that it can be recuperated if it is introduced to a body of poetry Richards ignored, Middle English lyric: specifically, the dialogue poem, whose values are at odds with the "complex autonomy" his mode of secular humanism "championed." Far from celebrating personal autonomy or even its own autonomy as a "thing," Middle English lyric is social and porous, performing "difference, diversity, and plurality" through encounters framed as unresolved, respecting the contrasting or incommensurable view-points of the speakers, even when one of them is Christ. To insist that Middle English short poems are "lyrics" is thus to keep them porous to another open-ended dialogue that implies similar values: *a dialogue between past and present, where Middle English lyric may serve as still unenclosed common ground.*[66]

How may Middle English lyric serve as a common ground between past and present? In Chapter 6, "Cognitive Poetics of Middle English Lyric Poetry," Raymond W. Gibbs, Jr., looks at this question from the transhistorical and translinguistic perspective of cognitive science. Does abstraction exist in language? Can there be a linguistic utterance that indexes a concept directly, like a mathematical formulation, without passing through the material kingdom of the metaphor? Retreading an intellectual road journeyed long ago by Neoplatonic theorists, as they sought to build bridges of words between the world of things and the world of ideas, Gibbs presents a body of psycholinguistic research that is answering these questions with an increasingly confident "no." In this account of the workings of language, there is no "literal" level, except in some medieval senses of that term.[67] Here, metaphor and its vehicle, the material world, do indeed rule: their seat the speaking human body, this body a lifelong inhabitant of an entangled forest of analogic "simulations" that connect self and world. Gibbs inducts us into several of these analogues used in "everyday language" (ANGER IS HEAT; IMPORTANT IS BIG; MORE IS UP), then considers a poem, Chaucer's "Complaint unto Pity," whose "literary language" hews to the everyday with the subtlety common in Middle English lyric, beginning with its organizing metaphor, LIFE IS A JOURNEY. In this account, the kinds of verse we call "lyric," ancient, medieval, modern, are self-reflexive by-products of language itself. With their concentration of metaphor, these poems reflect the human fascination *in the unresolvable relationship language sustains between thought and thing.*

What relationships do Middle English lyrics sustain between thought and things? In Chapter 7, "Lyric Vessels," Aden Kumler moves us around and again around a group of English texts, proverbs, and short poems inscribed onto or cast as late medieval use-objects, especially drinking vessels and ewers. Gifted with written speech, these objects are social and moral actants. Vessel texts and verses are admonitory, recommending taciturnity and enforcing social hierarchy in the proverbial tradition of the late antique *Distichs of Cato.*[68] They are also kinetic, requiring the viewer to turn the object in the hand or, when the object is heavy, move this way and that around it with eye and body, sounding out the deciphered text in the mouth. Two copper-alloy and bronze ewers from Richard II's court, the Robinson Jug and the massive Asante Ewer—looted by British forces in 1896 from a royal collection in Bantama or Kumasi in modern Ghana, where it may have been for several hundred years—command special attention. Both are cast in such a way as to include intricately arranged short verses in English that remind servants and other members of Richard's *familia* to mind their place ("STOND UTTIR FROM THE FYRE" shouts one), and of the need to be wary of gossip or intrigue ("DEME THE BEST IN EVERY / DOWT" booms the other). Their use of English in a French-speaking court serves not only to emphasize their own respected but lowly social position and artisanal character but their plain-style determination to utter only "TROWTHE."[69] Inviting us to revisit our title question from the viewpoint of vessels literally "made of lyric," Kumler inducts us into a culture in which even objects are liable *to use the metric and sonic resources of lyric to reach out into the world, seizing attention and shaping behavior.*

How does Middle English lyric seize attention or shape behavior? In Chapter 8, "The Sound of Rollean Lyric," Andrew Albin evokes the rich soundscape of *Ego Dormio*, an intimate call to the life of contemplation by the hermit Richard Rolle in the form of a high-style prosimetrum, in which verse and prose are joined in antiphonal dialogue. "Hold þyn ere and hyre of loue," the hermit implores, opening a work of eroticized spiritual exposition in which stepped shifts between melodiously rhythmic prose and different kinds of verse mimic and aspire to induce parallel shifts between "distinct cognitive modes keyed to their reader's spiritual progress." Metric and rhyming patterns account for only part of the sonic effects here, important as they are to the work the lyrics carry out in transforming thought into feeling and feeling into thought, until the two meld into a verbal analogue of contemplative experience. Although "the sound of lyric utterance" can never *be* contemplative experience, it can be "an agent of readerly transformation" in other ways, through the reader's voicing of these verses and through the configuration of voices within the work itself, which requires the reader's voice to overlay, learn from, and be joined to two others: Rolle's own voice and that of the bride of Christ, who utters the words the hermit urges us to "hyre": "I slepe and my hert waketh" (Song of Songs 5:2). Even as *Ego Dormio* invites readers to use the ascending sounds of lyric praise as temporary vehicles of their own spiritual ascent, it also works *to build devout communities of the living and the dead as they sing the bride's song.*

How do lyrics spoken in the first person build devotional community? In Chapter 9, "The Lyric Christ," Barbara Zimbalist examines four poems written across two centuries that answer this question in developing ways. Each involves dialogue between Christ and a devout person: the Virgin Mary, a lyric narrator, two representative "men." In each, "Christ's speech incorporates readers within the devotional community it cultivates, and imagines the performance of readerly devotion it invites," providing readers with a "template" for their own devotions. But there resemblance stops, as the biblical Christ who speaks with Mary from the cross in "Stond wel, moder" is transformed into the fictive Christ of "In a valley of this restless mind," written in the form of a *chanson d'aventure*; then transformed again in the two late poems, into a figure who exists on the same diegetic level as readers, with whom he engages in a dialogue that is effectively a conversation. In these two "Complaints" (one of them by the London rector and preacher William Litchfield), Christ's penitent interlocutor, "man," *is* the community of readers who inhabit the mercantile and compromising world the poems evoke. In the earlier poems, readers enter the world of sacred history, interact with its central episode, the Crucifixion, then return to their daily lives with their devotional lives vivified. But in the later ones, Christ comes to them, moving through the poems into the civic space in which they circulate. Zimbalist's chapter shows how Middle English lyric itself remains constantly on the move, generating new approaches over time as it *draws on the rich resources of the multilingual lyric tradition that underlies it.*

   What resources do we ourselves need in approaching this multilingual lyric tradition? In Chapter 10, "The Religious Lyric in Medieval England (1150–1400): Three Disciplines and a Question," Margot Fassler gives an interdisciplinary account of the forms of religious lyric in Latin and insular French as well as English, the history of approaches to it, and the work that still needs to be done, issuing a call for more laborers even as she praises the vigorous state of the field. Musicologists have already cut through not only premature categorizations of these materials but also overly firm distinctions between liturgical and other poetry, as well as the limits of disciplinary viewpoints, especially those that disregard lyrics in languages other than English. The study of religious lyric before the fourteenth century is hampered by methodological and practical difficulties, often connected to low survival rates. Yet the canon of religious lyrics *from England* for this period still increases by an order of magnitude if we take lyrics in the Latin and French of England into account, even in the present state of knowledge. So, too, does our ability to investigate the poetic and musical traditions within which lyric in English developed through these centuries, before it proliferated exponentially in the fifteenth. Motivic and intertextual allusions across languages, genres, and types of song are subtle and dense, sustaining a "network of relationships" across centuries, as a case study of the sequence "Letabundus" and its numerous contrafacts illustrates. Despite the lacunae in the record, Fassler conjures up an England that, as far back as we can hear an echo, *was as filled with artful song as King Blæðgabreat's mythical ancient Britain.*

How did Middle English lyric arise in a land of artful song? In Chapter 11, "Theory of the Fourteenth-Century English Lyric," Andrew Galloway examines this question with an eye both to recent debates about the category of "lyric" and to what Middle English lyrics tell us about how poetic genres, even those resistant to narrative utility, can arise from broadly political and religious contexts yet also translate these into figural forms. Galloway navigates the topic of the aesthetic autonomy ascribed to lyric from the tricky perspective of lyrics embedded into longer works, while also pointing toward an emergent neoclassical theory of lyric in Chaucer and Gower. In the *Brut* chronicle's "Maydenes of Engelande," a taunting song sung by Scottish girls to lovers of the English dead after Bannockburn, a heavily overdetermined narrative sustains and theorizes a poem already strikingly aware of itself *as* a poem through its refrain. In versions of the macaronic dialogue "Vndo þi dore, my spuse dere," a passionate standoff between Christ and beloved, knight and lover, resists the narrative consummation toward which it drives, pointing to the interdependence of lyric with the "shared experience of worship, confession, and penitential communion" that was liturgy. In long neoclassical poems by Chaucer and Gower, where lyric interrupts narrative to become a complex literary event unto itself, we see the emergence of what might as well be Renaissance poetry from the thick social context typical of medieval short poems, still fragilely aware of the "new kinds of prestige and exclusion" neoclassicism entails. In these examples, *the "autonomy" of lyric is thus both an integral feature of lyric rhythm and voice and an idea in play in the poetry itself.*

Is lyric autonomy an idea necessarily in play in Middle English, or any other, short poetry? In Chapter 12, "Response: Old Lyric Things," Virginia Jackson surveys the ground covered in the first eleven chapters from a perspective at once theoretical and historiographic, bringing their discussion to bear on recent controversies over the term and idea of "lyric," and vice versa. Here, the "lyric" of contemporary criticism is the outcome of a double process whereby the term (as noun) swelled to encompass most forms of poetry even as its valence (as adjective) narrowed, threatening to subordinate all poetry to one hierarchy of value, with autonomy and subjectivity at its apex. Middle English lyrics (plural) as presented in these chapters complicate sacralized accounts of the lyric as part of a Hegelian march toward these supposedly core Western modern values, but also complicate claims that the "lyricization" of poetry is a work only of the past two centuries. The "medieval" in these chapters is more than a backdrop or Bakhtinian opposite to a process that gained momentum after the Enlightenment. For poets and readers contemporary to these works, lyric, considered as a distinct form not wholly subsumed within other categories such as song, is already present as one possibility amid a wider spectrum. Middle English lyric "contains contraries," not simply in its diversity but also in arguments and counterarguments that anticipate debates still current today. Middle English lyric *both can and cannot be separated either from the short English poetry of the centuries that follow* or from the ideological systems that have partly determined how lyric has come to be read and adjudicated.

How far are Middle English lyrics separable from the English lyrics of the centuries that follow? In Chapter 13, "Response: Hevy Hameres," Stephanie Burt suggests two answers to this question. First, she shows how specific features of Middle English lyrics singled out by earlier chapters anticipate later poems, some of them central to the modern lyric canon. We might take the parallels she adduces as a caution against exceptionalism, whether on the part of medievalists or scholars of lyric from other periods. Second, she qualifies her implied claims for long continuities in the history of English lyric, convergent evolution, or both, by suggesting more precise analogies between medieval and twenty-first-century lyric. Burt offers a series of these, including "extreme brevity," ambiguation of the relationships between speakers within poems or between poems and media or modes of performance, unclear generic markers and polyglotism, as potential bridges between contemporary experimentalism and English lyrics of the era before print. Often, connections she describes are traceable neither to historical continuity nor to revivalism, but (perhaps) to the desire to reembed and resocialize poetry on the part of modern poets reacting against "lyric autonomy," or to the rediversification of media in the age of the internet, or to actual parallels between the multilinguistic situations of Middle English and "world English."

Occasionally, however, these bridges are the result of a "medievalizing" of recent verse: an effect Burt explores not only through her account of Jos Charles's *feeld* but also by joining the editors in curating a selection of poems gathered for this book that take "medieval lyric" as their theme or point of departure. Written without knowledge of the chapters, and so bringing new readings, assumptions, and views to bear on our topic, these poems speak for themselves. But they, too, are integral to our collective attempt *to rethink the kind of the thing that is Middle English lyric.*

Conclusion: wiþ hevalogh . . . wiþ Rombylogh

Thus the rowing song sung by the maidens of Scotland to the maidens of England in the remarkable episode in the *Brut* chronicle discussed in Galloway's chapter, as they sing in humiliation of their enemies, their refrain an early form of "heave . . . ho," their words playing, obscenely and otherwise, on the several connotations of *pulling* and *heavy lifting*. Middle English lyric, so we have argued, is at one level a subset of the cultural keyword, idea, and practice of "pley."[70] Yet dance as they do in our imagined corona, the studies of lyric in this book also carry out a great deal of necessary work, undertaking their own kind of "hevalogh" and "Rombylogh" in an area of scholarship where, as several of them point out, heavy lifting has long been needed. How might we think about this the work these chapters do *together*, hauling, now, rather than dancing together?

"What kind of a thing is a Middle English lyric?" By way of concluding this introduction, we ask this question one more time, but this time also ask the chapters to offer, chorically, a set of partial answers that can be temporarily and loosely coordinated as a singular one. Break the corona, then, reorder it all, chapters and chapbook together—bearing in mind that many orders are possible—and call again on Aristotle and his categories to provide a frame.

- Middle English lyric is a small subset of a vast body of poetic and other texts in many languages that draw on the metaphors linking self to world that underlie human cognition and language, formalizing and intensifying them and making them intentional.

   (substance) *Gibbs: "Cognitive Poetics"*

- More specifically, Middle English lyric has been taken to be a still small and somewhat idiosyncratic subsection of a larger body of medieval English poetry in three languages, Latin, French, and English, but should not be isolated from that larger body because these genres and forms have their own interconnected histories.

(quantity) *Fassler: "Religious Lyric in Medieval England"*

- Like some other bodies of poetry, the fundamental basis of Middle English poetry is oral, consisting of the signature set of sound patterns we call meter. These patterns are distinctive within the period in which they were written, intimately shaped by spoken English, and kept in existence through recognition and repetition within the community of those who write, perform, hear, and know them.

(quality) *Cornelius: "Language and Meter"*

- Although the relations between modes of Middle English poetry are fluid, the poems we call "lyric" are also distinguished by larger patterns that privilege reflection over narration, including reflection on pattern itself. Given the primarily oral existence of Middle English lyrics, repetitions, which allowed even some longer narrative poems to be received as lyric, are also fluid, performed on different occasions with a degree of variance that does not compromise their coherence.

(relative) *Cannon: "Lyric Romance"*

- Many of the Middle English lyrics that come down to us survive either incidentally, because one version of them happened to be recorded, or within a larger setting. Lyric "close reading" here thus requires detailed attention not only to the shape of the verbal artifact itself but to the work it does within this setting.

(where) *Butterfield: "Lyric Editing"*

- This work may be systematic, as it always is within the genre of the prosimetrum, where verse offers a sound-rich and emotionally engaging opportunity for embodied reflection on passages of prose exposition, designed to assist readers in internalizing, or becoming, what they read, as well as in representing this transformation in literary form.

(where) *Albin: "The Sound of Rollean Lyric"*

- Or it may be indirect, playful, and ideological, as with the verses inscribed on courtly use-objects that require the viewer to undertake energetic decipherment in order to unriddle hortatory messages whose import is that all should know, and fearfully keep to, their place within the hierarchic household order.

(where) *Kumler: "Lyric Vessels"*

- Although Middle English lyrics are consistently artful and were occasionally gathered in collections that emphasize their existence as literary objects, their typical anonymity, availability to multiple uses in different media, and sometimes apparently casual survival in as many forms as there are copies, make it difficult to fit them into standard medieval methods of categorizing literary texts. Hence the term "thing," which names Middle English lyrics as entities, and the Aristotelian method of categorization by "kind" preferred here.

(posture) *Cervone and Watson: "Introduction: Why stonde we?"*

- These features are also the same qualities that make these poems revealingly difficult to fit into the generic category that is "lyric" itself. We could argue that the contingency of "Middle English lyrics," once we investigate these poems in their natural historical and codicological habitats, shows how vexed and problematic is this category as a whole.

(when) *Jackson: "Response: Old Lyric Things"*

- Or, we might make the more specific argument that these products of a preprint textual culture have recently found a new family, into which it is time to adopt them, in the experimental poetry of the late twentieth and early twenty-first centuries, as it plays with the categories it inherits from the modern lyric canon.

(when) *Burt: "Response: Hevy Hameres"*

- Or again, that Old and Middle English lyrics are still worth writing and imitating, their subjects, forms, vocabulary, and rhythms no longer familiar but recognizable and redolent, a permanent resource. "For out of olde feldes, as men seyth, /

Cometh al this newe corn from yer to yere" (Geoffrey Chaucer, *The Parliament of Fowls*, lines 22–23).

> (when) *Burt, McCarthy, Keough, Revard, Arthur, Manhire, and Oberman: "New Medieval Lyrics: A Chapbook"*

- Yet although Middle English lyrics typically ground themselves in the local, the communal, and the everyday, for example, working with liturgical language and practices that did not survive the Reformation, these patterned verbal entities are well able to distinguish themselves from the contexts within which they are embedded. Only with two vernacular "auctores," Chaucer and Gower, in the late fourteenth century, do they begin to separate themselves, uncertainly, into the exotic realm of literary neoclassicism in which Renaissance poetry would make its home.

> (condition) *Galloway: "Theory of Fourteenth-Century Lyric"*

- Alive to a sense of a broader world than their narrow confine, Middle English lyrics generate textual and devotional communities in dialogue with one another, and sometimes with Christ, whose voice in lyric frames devotional and responsive practices that are both distinctively of their time and envision a future moment beyond themselves. The interactions Middle English lyrics enable can turn *I* into *we*.

> (action) *Zimbalist: "The Lyric Christ"*

- The *we* of Middle English lyric enacts a reading experience of a sort quite different from that expected by the New Criticism. The intersubjective dialogue that lies at the heart of Middle English lyric underlines a sense of lyric value that does not valorize the solitary poet but draws on its audience for an active role.

> (action, affection) *Nelson: "Lyric Value"*

- That role must entail engaged participation, in part because Middle English lyric, whether by design or circumstance, often leaves so much unsaid, open-ended, to be pondered and interpreted. How much does Middle English lyric expect of us, and we of it?

(action, affection) Cervone: *"Wondering Through Middle English Lyric"*

Within Middle English lyric studies alone, many topics other than those covered by our chapters could benefit from intensive analysis: the stanza; the image text; the influence of insular French lyric; the macaronic, so distinctive a feature of medieval vernacular poetry, along with its cousin, aureation, and more.[71]

Going forward, as both our respondents in their different ways suggest, there also continues to be a pressing need for scholars interested in Middle English lyric to think expansively and teach more broadly, whether their disciplinary homes are in medieval studies, poetics, or other areas, by drawing Middle English lyric into conversations about poetry of all kinds. Most of the issues central to this book—cognitive, formal, critical, historical, editorial, and methodological—will have many analogies and equivalents not only across the full multicultural, multiracial, multinational, and multigeneric range of contemporary poetries in English, but also in other temporal and linguistic settings, many of them unrelated to the small archipelago on the western Eurasian littoral, one of whose less well-charted periods of literary production is our focus here. Indeed, to be worthy of Layamon's King Blædgabreat, he who "cuðen al þeos songes / & þat gleo of ilcche londe," and who we learn elsewhere "esteit tuz ens joius, / Unches ne fu fel ne irus" (was always joyful, never cruel or angry), such comparative work would need to be carried out with poetry written "ȝeond þas woruld-riche."[72] One long-term goal of this book is to bring this expansive project a step closer to realization.

Chapter 1

Lyric Editing

ARDIS BUTTERFIELD

Editing has a way of focusing questions, and not always comfortably. This book offers many brilliant and pleasurable ways of answering the book's central question—"what kind of a thing is a Middle English lyric?"—some abstract, some more technical, some centered on specific genres or methodologies. It might be said, though, that the very form of the question enables a certain provisionality of response. At bottom, as chapter writers we are engaging in a stimulating conversation not a decision. The hapless editor, however, has no such relief. Faced with the thousands of items of Middle English verse, now being cataloged more indefatigably than ever before, the business of trying to decide what kind of subset to pull from that catalog under the rubric of "lyric" is not only a question of semantics, or philosophy, or literary criticism, or "terminological hygiene,"[1] but a practical necessity. I write this chapter freighted (but also stimulated) by my perspective as editor of a new anthology of *Medieval English Lyrics* (Norton, 2023 [anticipated]).[2]

The "Thing": A Brief Modern History

Some comments first, on the "thing" called medieval lyric. It has had an unusual place in modern scholarship of the Middle Ages. From a popular perspective, lyrics provide an accessible, colorful, and often musical version of the Middle Ages. Professional singers and instrumentalists, backed up by the recording industry, have found a ready market for songs that seem to present an alluring aural link to a world of lovers and ladies, feudal castles, rich tapestries, and the glamour of chivalry. But this is an image of medieval song created by the troubadour and trouvère chansonniers and by medieval romance. In the field of medieval English literature some of this glamour has been borrowed, but only indirectly and largely inaccurately. Where continental chansonniers collect songs in lavish gilded technicolor, with artful author portraits, and (although patchily) with a great deal of music,[3] Middle English songs occur in plain and functional books with little illumination, most of the music having been lost or never committed to writing.[4] Items of text-only short verse run to well over two thousand, but apart from some isolated examples of purposeful sequencing in books of otherwise diverse contents, poetic anthologies are rare and hard to identify as such until the fifteenth century.[5] There are some thirty songs with Middle English texts before circa 1400 that survive with music, but again, largely sporadically; complete songbooks, where all the items have been copied with music and text together, are exceptionally rare and begin in any number only with the Tudor carol collections. Such patterns of survival (or should one say loss?) make it difficult to use the term "song" straightforwardly of English-language material; one finds oneself lurching instead from "lyric" to "short verse" to "poem" with uneasy vagueness.[6]

I start with questions about music because approaches to Middle English lyrics almost never do. I do so here to signal that lyric studies, and not only in the medieval period, have left music to one side to a degree that has impoverished and indeed misrepresented the object of study.[7] The modern history of Middle English lyrics has been a prime example of what Virginia Jackson has called "lyricization."[8] Writing of the reception of Emily Dickinson's poetry, she and Yopie Prins have influentially argued that the modern lyric arose through "a reading of poetry as lyric that emerged by fits and starts in the nineteenth century [and] became mainstream practice in the development of modern literary criticism in the twentieth century."[9] "Lyrics" came into being through the readers who wanted to read poems "as lyrics": in Jackson's pithy locution, "to be lyric is to be read as lyric."[10] Medieval lyric was likewise created by modern readers. From the use of the term "lyric" in the E. K. Chambers and F. Sidgwick anthology *Early English Lyrics: Amorous, Divine, Moral and Trivial* in 1907 to the heat of sixties and seventies New Criticism, lyric gradually became the poster child of medieval literature, exemplifying ambiguity, wordplay, and self-referentiality in the hands of Leo Spitzer and Stephen Manning with the same alacrity as were Robert Frost's "The Road Not Taken" or Charles Baudelaire's "Obsession" in those of Paul de Man or Herbert Tucker.[11] Short poems such as "I sing of a maiden" or

"Nou goth sonne under wod" gained iconic status through anthologies such as the 1974 Norton, in which each is presented with its own portfolio of exemplary close readings.[12]

Ironically, the very closeness of the fit between such lyrics and the lyric criticism of modernist critics then turned into a critical dead end. For although important scholarly research took place in the 1980s and 1990s, following the wider pattern of historicist scholarship in concentrating on specific questions of manuscript context and compilation, patronage and readership, society and politics,[13] critical commentary on lyric remained largely in a time warp, looking back to older studies by Peter Dronke (1965–66; 1968), Rosemary Woolf (1968), and Douglas Gray (1972).[14] A trio of brilliantly learned scholars deeply rooted in the literary and intellectual contexts for secular and religious lyric, their work was invested in staking out its aesthetic and formal qualities in relation to modern lyric, an approach that has remained dominant well into the current century. Remarkably, as if in recognition of the lack of fit between nineties' historicism and the relatively unchanged "New Critical" profile of medieval English lyric, there was no place at all for lyric in the 1999 *Cambridge History of Medieval English Literature*.[15]

And even as new work has begun at last to emerge again, there is some uncertainty about how to characterize both the approach and the object, an uncertainty one might see reflected in the title of this book. "Thing" has a quizzical and perhaps gently self-mocking aspect in the title that points us to the materiality of the object we are purporting to interrogate and is clearly a valuable and serious directive.[16] Yet the term also risks implying that there is a solid object of inquiry. The purpose of this chapter is to interrogate *that* on several grounds. First, staying closer to the pragmatic than the ontological, there has been a strange circularity between the modern criticism and the "thing" as an object to be read. A New Critical approach to the medieval lyric has required an object of inquiry that resembles the product of "lyric reading." And indeed this is exactly what one finds in modern anthologies: the medieval lyric (as thus described) stands on the page enveloped in the assumptions of old New Critical models of reading of the 1960s, that is, presented as a set of isolated items in thematic groupings that leave historical and manuscript scholarship on the margins.[17]

To grasp the "thing" means that one has to confront the nettle—there is no object to interpret that sits comfortably outside the hermeneutic act required to identify it. Editors of texts and musical pieces in any period are familiar with this conundrum in terms of the local matter of selecting and fixing details of a line or phrase; the Middle English lyric sharpens the case because there is no a priori genre in which to set the parameters of local editorial choice. To edit the Middle English lyric is to create the Middle English lyric. This is precisely what modern anthologists have done. But the point is not merely that medieval lyric is a "thing" created by modern editors, but that modern anthologies create a version of medieval lyrics that can only be read New Critically.

I will be arguing in this chapter and in the praxis of my edition, that the "thing" of Middle English lyric needs not so much a new definition, or even a new "new criticism," as a new kind of lyric editing. This new lyric editing holds numerous challenges, not all of which can be met in the current state of research. But its principles can begin to be outlined. These involve paying attention to the "whole" song: that is, to an object of study that not only includes music where that exists or can be posited, but a contextual landscape that takes account of the linguistic plurality in which Middle English lyric was composed, performed, and copied, and hence also to the many social and cultural environments of musical and poetic production in Britain during these centuries from circa 1150 to 1450. I use the phrase "the whole song" with a deliberate nod to the influential concept that drove a collection of essays on the medieval manuscript miscellany in 1996 edited by Stephen Nichols and Siegfried Wenzel: *The Whole Book: Cultural Perspectives on the Medieval Miscellany*. The notion of a "whole song" aspires to the bold reach of "whole book"; I offer it as another reason for interrogating the "thing-ness" of medieval lyric in asking what such a notion of wholeness might mean for lyric studies. The material object on the manuscript page is a surprisingly thin basis for apprehending the thing that is a song.

Cataloging the Lyric in Britain: Manuscripts, Languages, Literatures, Music

What follows gestures toward an outline of these environments. Matters are complicated in that "Middle English lyrics" occupy a place within several disciplinary fields. The terrain is not easy to map because research is incomplete and uneven across these different (yet overlapping) domains. It is also, unfortunately, carried out in fields that rarely cross-refer.[18] By far the most extensive work (unsurprisingly) has been carried out in Middle English, as I will detail shortly. However, this perspective has been partial. Even the deliberately uncontroversial description "Middle English short poem"[19] is misleading once we take a broader view: the "Middle English lyric" is not straightforwardly short, English, or poetic.[20] In fact its constituent features require an approach that thinks well beyond the confines of Englishness, of monolingualism, and of literature. Such an approach, however, is triply challenging: it requires some kind of grasp of the diversity, sheer quantity, and large-scale anonymity of the material and its material record; second, acknowledging its plurilingual character; and third, taking account of the survival of music. Each form of apprehension requires its own expertise in—respectively— the study of manuscripts, of the three principal languages and literatures of medieval England (English, French, and Latin), and of musical notation and form.[21]

Let me take these in turn. Some of these challenges can be seen most clearly by considering in more detail the contrast with continental European traditions. Various as the latter are, the transmission of continental lyric is characterized by large numbers of carefully compiled, theoretically and socially aware songbooks.[22] Song production in Latin and many vernaculars, notably French and Occitan but also German, Catalan, Flemish, and Tuscan, survives on a large scale with a great deal of music and an often fabulously luxurious and sophisticated focus on the material and conceptual images of song and its authors and consumers that is nowhere evident in insular manuscripts.[23] Insular lyrics, by contrast, occur in a highly diverse set of plainer manuscript contexts, from sermon and preaching material, moral, mystical, and penitential writing, liturgical books, books on law and medicine, romances, chronicles, political tracts, and drama to courtly poetic anthologies, commonplace books, and other miscellanies of prose and verse. Songbooks as such are rare until the fifteenth century.[24] The contrast is not just in diversity of book type, but in the lack of a similarly articulated or aestheticized format for lyric until at least the fifteenth century, and even then the types of anthologizing are far less ambitious or explicitly curated than they are in the troubadour and trouvère chansonniers, whose legacy is written all over the sophisticated complete oeuvre manuscripts by Guillaume de Machaut.[25] Anonymity is rife, indeed normal. Apart from the exceptionally early case of Richard Rolle in the mid-fourteenth century, and such rare survivals as the unusual personal preaching notebook of John of Grimestone, dated 1372, authorial attributions only start to appear in the fifteenth, including a handful of one-off manuscripts produced by lesser-known clergy or lay churchmen such as John Audelay and James Ryman, and the wider circulation of poetic anthologies that include poems by Chaucer, Hoccleve, and Lydgate.[26] Some individual items, such as Richard Caister's "Hymn," William Litchfield's "Complaint," or Lydgate's "Dietary," circulated with a name attached.[27] But there are also names about which nothing else is known, such as William of Shoreham, and hundreds of pieces of verse that cannot be attached to specific individuals in books of a very mixed character whose provenance is currently only sketchily tracked.

This brings me to a further dimension of this manuscript context for Middle English verse: language. Carleton Brown and Rossell Hope Robbins, the most important modern editors of medieval lyric, worked between the wars with around 450 manuscripts to edit a total of 750 items in English that they called "lyric," selected from well over 2,000. But (as it has now fortunately become truistic to affirm) England was a multilingual culture throughout the Middle Ages (and indeed well beyond), and until the later fourteenth century, it was literature in Latin and French that dominated intellectual, legal, administrative, and courtly circles. The last decade has seen a large-scale reorientation toward multilingualism in medieval literary studies, but that paradigm shift has yet to enter the basic research tools of insular lyrics. Brown and Robbins—and indexers after them—distort the notion of insular lyric by behaving as if only the items in English counted. Their catalog and the recent revisions of it are confined to material written in or predominantly written in English, and while this may seem obvious and forgivable, it means plucking English items out of what is often a densely bi- or trilingual context. As Susanna Fein, in particular, has strongly stated, the edition by G. L. Brook of the Harley lyrics was a classic instance of that selectivity masquerading as inclusiveness.[28] But it is time to go further and call for new indices that refer across the languages, manuscripts, and music. The work of the *New Index of Middle English Verse* (*NIMEV*) has been superseded in sheer extent and accuracy by that of the *Digital Index of Middle English Verse* (*DIMEV*) (which of course is able to access the crucial advantage of its online medium by being updatable), but the oddity of its focus on English items takes many forms. "Nou goth sonne" mentioned earlier, is a characteristic example. A beautifully meditative quatrain in English of just twenty-three words in total, it occurs in a thirteenth-century treatise by St. Edmund of Abingdon called in Anglo-French *Le merure de Seinte Eglise*. Over eighty manuscripts survive of this treatise in its various versions, Latin, French, and English.[29] In trying to ascertain the context of, for example, "Nou goth sonne" the *NIMEV* list of manuscripts mentions only sixteen (out of thirty-five) Latin and sixteen (out of twenty-eight) French manuscripts.[30] *DIMEV* had similar figures originally, but has been steadily adding manuscripts, and is now up to forty-one. To check whether the quatrain appears in English (or in Latin or French) in this widely transmitted treatise, one has to hunt out the individual manuscripts.[31] New online tools are urgent, especially for such basic needs as searchable indices of Anglo-French and Anglo-Latin texts, manuscripts, and music (for a prototype of such a tool, see the Digital Archive of Medieval Song [DAMS]).[32]

Moreover, these are revisions of an index of all surviving verse in English, not just "lyric."[33] Certain categories of information are supplied that one might use to define "lyric," such as author, title, subject, verse form, verse pattern, but none of them delimits the material in a way that would enable one to distinguish meaningfully between Chaucer's "Knight's Tale," Langland's *Piers Plowman*, the "Construciones artis gemetrie secundum Euclidem" (a didactic poem on the craft of masonry of 98 lines in couplets), an inscription on a brass church memorial, or the 39,674 lines of Thomas Castelford of Bek's *Chronicle of England*. There is no online equivalent for Anglo-French[34] or, for that matter, continental French verse.[35] The catalog of *Anglo-Norman Literature* (which includes all genres, not only verse) by Ruth Dean (completed with the aid of Maureen Boulton) is enormously helpful, but it inevitably leaves the border between "insular" and "continental" fuzzy, and is organized in ways that raise fresh questions about category.[36] Dean makes a major division between "secular" and "religious literature," and then subdivides each into further broad groupings, some generic, others topical: so under "secular" come "historiographical," "lyric," "romance," "lais and fabliaux," "satirical, social, and moral," "proverbs," "grammar and glosses," "science and technology," and "medicine." Under "religious" we have "biblical," "apocryphal," "hagiography," "homiletic," and "devotional." So the forty-five items listed as lyrics are categorized as secular not religious, which comes as quite a surprise in relation to the cataloging of English lyrics, of which Robbins famously remarked that "for every secular lyric there are three or four religious."[37] Items such as prayers or meditative poems that are described by scholars of English verse as "religious lyric" occur largely under "homiletic" and "devotional." But although Dean shuns the term "religious lyric," she allows "song" and "hymn."[38] As for music, Dean lists "lyrics with music" in a separate section at the start of "lyrics," followed by "lyrics without music"; however, she does not do the same for religious material, although there are cross-references to "devotional songs with music." No complete listing of manuscripts with music is provided.[39] The convenience of the layout and generous descriptions of each item mean that other details compensate for some of the idiosyncrasies of the larger categorization: instead of a blanket term "lyric" we are given a picture of specific genres, such as elevation prayers or instructions for levation, and can see at a glance that some are in prose, others in verse. In short, comparing the cataloging of insular French and English texts is instructive, not just about different disciplinary viewpoints but about the material itself, which is revealed in a broader perspective enriched by combining those differences.

Listing is one thing, editing is another, and taking account of trilingual contexts is a third.[40] To date, although brilliant pioneering studies have been made of specific manuscript collections and compilations especially of devotional and didactic material,[41] study of the lyric in England has largely proceeded along discrete disciplinary paths. In French, edited collections are few, and the most significant, apart from the early work of Thomas Wright, are just two: Isabel Aspin, *Anglo-Norman Political Songs* (1953), and David Jeffrey and Brian Levy, *The Anglo-Norman Lyric* (1990). For Latin, the absence of a coordinated and updated index of verse is a desideratum, though older resources such as *Analecta hymnica* or Szövérffy–Chevalier, *Repertorium hymnologicum novum*, are now available online.[42] Critically, Latin and French items have been drawn into discussions of lyrics in English in only piecemeal ways. Considerable work—scholarly and critical—remains in terms of gaining a larger view of how pieces were transmitted across all three languages and of the cultural and literary meaning of these relationships.

Music is a third challenge: little survives in comparison, again, with the Continent, where about a tenth (some 300) of troubadour and two-thirds (over 1,400) of trouvère song melodies survive for vernacular texts, compared to the handful of individual pieces with English texts (20–30) from the thirteenth and fourteenth centuries, and the fifteenth- and sixteenth-century songbooks.[43] That said, it depends what is being included, and also more survives in fragmentary form than this might indicate. The recent facsimile edition of *English Thirteenth-Century Polyphony* by William J. Summers and Peter Lefferts, which brings together most of the surviving polyphonic music from that period, contains "349 individual plates drawn from manuscripts with some sixty different shelfmarks" but most of these are unperformable fragments.[44] The so-called "Worcester Fragments" consist of the remains of nine or more codices and have proved to be a nightmarishly difficult jigsaw puzzle to try to reconstruct. But this is only polyphonic music, and the vast majority of it has

Latin texts. The monophonic music has until very recently been largely neglected by musicologists, in part because again so much of it has been lost or
survives in damaged fragments, but also (to put it crudely) because the musical
interest of pieces with several parts has been deemed greater.

Happily, two important new editions of music covering the periods circa
1150 to 1300 and 1380 to 1480 have started to change the picture. Helen Deeming has brought together and edited freshly (and in many cases for the first
time) 85 Latin songs, 14 in French and 16 in English. Most of these are monophonic, though pieces with two or three voices (and one up to six) have been
included.[45] David Fallows collects 124 songs, with a generous sense of the
links and transmission between the insular and continental pieces. His volume deliberately aims to fill the gaps left by the monumental editions by John
Stevens of Tudor music, largely carols.[46] As one can tell from the date spans,
the musical pickings for fourteenth-century song with English texts are virtually nonexistent. There is a great deal of new material assembled here, but
these efforts still represent only a starting point for the analysis and criticism
of insular song. Ironically such criticism must also reckon with the absence of
musical evidence. Conversely, literary and textual scholars do not usually take
musical issues into account, and even among music specialists, the pre-fifteenth-
century songs of England have received limited analysis.[47]

There has been just one book-length study to date of music and texts together (E. J. Dobson and Frank Ll. Harrison, *Medieval English Songs* [London:
Faber and Faber, 1979]), and this takes the form of an edition not a monograph. It was a pioneering yet controversial attempt to yoke the skills of literary and musicological editing.[48] As Stevens wittily remarked when it was first
published: "Few more curious books than this can ever have emerged from the
casual liaison of two learned men and a gramophone company."[49] The editors
provide a mass of philological and musical information, somewhat uneasily
harnessed and rationalized to provide performable song editions where the text
and music have both been subject to radical reconstruction.[50] In sum, the lyric
in England requires and awaits multidisciplinary research—primarily in English,
French, and music, but also in Latin and in the many fields that compose manuscript studies, including art history and sermon studies.

The picture I have presented thus far of the field calls for a multidisci-
plinarity that is still some way ahead of present scholarly capabilities and is
daunting for any single editor to contemplate. Nonetheless, if undertaken
within this framework, my goal in the new Norton anthology is to show that
a new approach to editing medieval English lyrics has the liberating poten-

tial to begin to uproot notions of "Middle English lyric" in ways that may have long-lasting consequences for a modern understanding of medieval culture, and perhaps more broadly still for lyric studies across periods. Before the fifteenth century, "medieval English lyrics" do not define themselves as such (and the term "lyric" is not used in English before the 1570s).[51] There is no single codex of English "lyric" before the fifteenth century.[52] By and large, insular manuscripts containing "lyrics" mix genres, languages, and registers to a degree that no modern anthologist of "lyric" has ever felt comfortable with reproducing except as facsimile objects.[53] What would happen if an anthology were to embrace rather than condense down that diversity and lack of predefined categorization?

The Methodologies of Modern Editions

The uncontrollability of the archive has not prevented the production of many modern anthologies of medieval English lyrics. By far the most extensive, and best, as well as one of the earliest, was carried out by Carleton Brown.[54] As part of his great labor in creating the *Index of Middle English Verse* (*IMEV*), he decided in the 1920s to publish a three-volume anthology of lyrics, from the thirteenth, fourteenth, and fifteenth centuries respectively.[55] His younger British colleague Rossell Hope Robbins, who helped Brown with the latter stages of the *IMEV*, then brought out two more volumes to supplement these: *Secular Lyrics of the XIVth and XVth Centuries* (1952; 2nd ed., 1955) and *Historical Poems of the XIVth and XVth Centuries* (1959).[56] The total number of items in all five volumes is 730: 91 in Brown's *English Lyrics of the XIIIth Century*; 135 in *Religious Lyrics of the XIVth Century*; 192 in *Religious Lyrics of the XVth Century*; 212 in Robbins's *Secular Lyrics of the XIVth and XVth Centuries*; and 100 in his *Historical Poems of the XIVth and XVth Centuries*. Unsurprisingly, given the scale of the undertaking, the rationale for each volume and for the project as a whole undergoes various instructive shifts. Brown, in the primal (and war-torn) stages of sifting the material, is often obscure; Robbins, from a slightly more distanced perspective, offers more.

It takes time to unravel what the scope of Brown's editorial project was. It was only in the preface to the fifteenth-century volume, the third of the three editions he published, that Brown explicitly (but with tantalizing brevity) announced that it had been a three-volume project: "the appearance of the present collection carries to completion the plan projected in the Spring of 1920 of a series of three volumes devoted to the Lyrics of the thirteenth, fourteenth and fifteenth centuries respectively" (4). It was not until Robbins's *Secular Lyrics of the XIVth and XVth Centuries* that more panoptic views emerged and help us to understand (in a way that perhaps Carleton Brown never articulated even to himself) why the earlier volumes take the shape that they do. We learn that since the *IMEV* was completed in two stages, first the religious and didactic verse (1916, 1920) and then the secular and political (1943), it was (implicitly) not possible for Brown to get to the secular material earlier. His three-volume plan was thus always incomplete. This is important because it shows, first, that Brown was primarily interested in the religious verse, and, second, how deeply the categories of "religious" and "secular" shaped his and therefore Robbins's presentation of "lyric development" through the centuries. What we are given is a series of volumes that carve out each century in separate but overlapping ways. The air of defensiveness in Robbins's introduction to *Secular Lyrics of the XIVth and XVth Centuries* seems to spring from this: he does at last provide a manuscript survey of Middle English lyric, but it is angled towards explaining the nature of his particular collection of secular poems, rather than towards presenting a full range of information about the editorial project as a whole. Such partiality is repeated in his next anthology of so-called "historical poems." These items are barely mentioned in the *Secular Lyrics of the XIVth and XVth Centuries* manuscript survey, and Robbins provides no further comment on their manuscripts in his separate edition.

The most useful information supplied by Robbins in *Secular Lyrics of the XIVth and XVth Centuries* has to be teased out of his introduction. One general observation is that the amount of material increases exponentially from the thirteenth to the fifteenth centuries. Robbins famously quotes his teacher G. G. Coulton that "for every page of English written in the thirteenth century, there would be 3 in the fourteenth and 10 in the fifteenth" (xxii). Another (which comes as no surprise) is the preponderance of religious material. Though the hard and fast division of "religious" and "secular" imposed by Brown and Robbins is problematic in many respects,[57] it is true that lyrics on the great themes of the trouvères—the sighs, frustrations, and jealousies of love, and the tight vocabulary of service, suffering, pity, and complaint—are relatively few. Other statistics provided by Robbins, especially in the light of the major revisions to the *Index* that have been carried out in recent years, notably in *DIMEV*, are less useful, though it is worth noting his calculation (mentioned earlier) that approximately two thousand "shorter Middle English poems of all types are preserved in 450 manuscripts, of which 35 contain 75 percent of all 'lyrics'" (xvii). I will return to this.

I have spent time on Brown and Robbins because theirs is the only modern editorial attempt to present the Middle English lyric as a field rather than merely a selection of highlights. Their work is also unsurpassed in its panoptic knowledge of several thousand Middle English manuscripts and the interconnections between copies of verse items, detailed with astonishing thoroughness in the notes to their volumes. The only other major editorial enterprise of a comparable scale is that of Richard Leighton Greene, who went in a different direction from Brown and Robbins and focused on a single genre, the carol, defined by him as "those lyrics which bear, in their regularly repeated burdens, the mark of their descent from the dancing circle of the carole."[58] His thoughts on the burden and on the connection with the *carole* are not uncontroversial, but of more importance here is that Greene's collection of nearly 500 carols has functioned as the nearest thing we have to a coherent repertory of "medieval English song," especially since he thickened it with a near book-length ninety-page introduction, an exhaustive presentation of variants, and a forty-five-page annotated list of manuscript sources. Interestingly, the larger generic question of how the carol and the rest of Middle English lyric connect or overlap has remained obscure.[59] Moreover, Greene's work on the texts of carols was itself a separate scholarly enterprise from that of John Stevens on the music. One peculiarity of the genre is that the books containing unnotated carol texts are quite different in kind from the songbooks in which a total of ninety carols are presented as art music with polyphonic settings that require trained singers. It is symptomatic of the different disciplinary approaches to the carol that Greene and Stevens made different decisions about language. Carols are notably bilingual, with nearly half structured around Latin tags.[60] Greene created his corpus by including only English-matrix texts, that is texts in which Latin was an ingredient; whereas Stevens included fully Latin songs in carol form as well as those with English texts. Once again, the notion of a medieval English song is misleading.

Brown and Robbins, while they present an unrivaled amount of verse and attendant scholarly information, make no attempt to be comprehensive. We need to delve a little further, though, into what precisely they selected to represent the field. It is important to note that they started from a position of compiling the *IMEV*. For this is the first crucial factor: the *IMEV* (and its subsequent iterations) set out to catalog *all* verse in Middle English. What, in that case, did Brown and Robbins decide defined the subcategory of "lyric" from within that catalog? Ian Cornelius has valuably helped us to focus on what "verse" might mean in this *Index*, an issue that, as he rightly points out, none of the indexers, remarkably enough, attempts to define.[61] But we are left with the question of whether "lyric" means something other than verse.[62] Brown's introduction to his fourteenth-century volume is not much help, since he uses "poem," "lyric," "song," and "verse" interchangeably throughout. Intermixed in his discussion are other terms such as "hymn," "translation," "prayer," "phrase." Robbins likewise moves without comment between "poem," "lyric," and "verse," but introduces "fragment," "little tags," and "scraps," and "quasi-doggerel" and "carol." Once he starts discussing fifteenth-century "commonplace books," many other terms appear: medical receipts, prognostications, charms, gnomic lines and saws, doctrinal and instructional verse, proverbs, book mottoes, epitaphs, weather rhymes, prophecies, punctuation letter, a church graffito. It is only in his *Historical Poems* edition that Robbins makes specific comment about a term: here he announces, with almost comic bathos, "'lyric' has been replaced by the wider term, 'poem'" (vii).[63]

On the face of it neither editor is much interested in a narrow definition of "lyric." (This has much to commend it.) For both of them there is a nebulous but overriding criterion of "literary value" and a desire to select "the best," but this is easily cast aside for other factors.[64] Robbins even discards the anthologist's often unspoken but golden rule of brevity: he includes nine "poems" longer than 150 lines because of their "importance," and notes several more that he wished he had had room for (*Historical Poems*, p. viii, n. 6). In short, what is more interesting than whether either of them defined "lyric" is the extent to which they allowed the manuscripts they worked with to color their selections. This is especially true of Robbins who, as we have just seen, strayed boldly into territory that no one before or since has called "lyric." He does so because, in a move typical of his cultural moment, he wanted to chase down a notion of the "popular."[65]

After Carleton Brown, editors have not only produced much shorter, single-volume selections.[66] They have also significantly changed his focus (as a cataloger) on the manuscripts and turned instead toward other ways of representing the material through themes and invented titles. Here are some examples of themes and categories: "Worldes blis," "All for love," "I have a gentil cok" (Luria and Hoffman); "Poems of Mourning, Fear and Apprehension," "Poems of Joy and Celebration," "Poems About Sex" (Hirsh); "Love Lyrics," "Penitential and Moral Lyrics," "Devotional Lyrics," "Miscellaneous

Lyrics," "Popular and Miscellaneous Lyrics" (Duncan).[67] They range from the overtargeted ("I have a gentil cok") to the blandly general ("Devotional Lyrics") to the odd yoking of not one but two quintessentially amorphous categories ("Popular *and* Miscellaneous"). Brown and Robbins came into their own with titles: "In Praise of Brunettes";[68] "A Henpecked Husband's Complaint I and II";[69] "I Repent of Blaming Women."[70]

Themes can of course be useful pedagogical tools and some of these anthologies have been excellent in that regard.[71] But they don't take us very far with the "lyric" question. It seems fair to say they have been used with understandable pragmatism as managing categories by editors to substitute for any major reopening of the fieldwork carried out by Brown and Robbins. They also reflect a practice of selecting lyrics according to what has become a modern canon of poems chosen for their potential as objects of New Critical readings. This leaves aside hundreds and hundreds of items.

Some New Editorial Goals and Principles

So what might a new edition do? The primary effort of my new edition of *Medieval English Lyrics* is to make some initial steps towards reintegrating close paleographical, linguistic, and musical studies of books containing lyric verse and modern critical approaches to lyric. The edition aims to present medieval English lyrics not from the perspective of modern thematic categories but rather from that of the medieval copyists. The original plan was to organize the edition around specific medieval books, but it quickly became apparent that the patterns of survival were too complex and piecemeal to carry this out systematically or even consistently. Nonetheless, its broad aim is to demonstrate, through careful selection of material, how the medieval lyric in England was recorded in writing across three and a half centuries from the early twelfth to the late fifteenth. Some principal types of copying context are provided, each with selections of the short verse contained within them. An effort is made, through specific case studies, to indicate the location of the item in its manuscript: whether it occurs in a group of other English language lyrics, or, as is more common in the first two centuries, alongside Latin and French items; whether it is set within—for example—a sermon, treatise, romance, chronicle, dramatic work, or saint's life; whether it occurs with music or with other items that are provided with musical notation; whether it occurs with verse or prose lineation, rubrics, enlarged initials, images, or any other form of visual highlighting. A final section broadens the copying context to include items recorded in media other than parchment: on walls and in stained glass, on tombs, in tapestries, and on domestic objects, clothing, drinking cups, and rings.[72]

The broadly chronological structure of the edition does not pretend to date lyrics (a largely impossible task to do at all precisely), but rather relies on the approximate dates at which the manuscripts were copied. But it also aims to show features of lyric composition that resist notions of chronology: the items (especially hymns) that were translated across languages and, in being copied and recopied over several centuries, gained new patterns of circulation and new forms of use. Insular lyrics show us very open instances of movement, transposition, and revision across French, English, and Latin. Some of the material aids the scrutiny of two opposing tendencies in the copying of short verse: instances where a scribe or compiler, occasionally even an author, plots a sequence of lyrics, and the examples of lyrics that seem to be genuinely isolated, the result of a desire to fill in a blank section of a page, to scribble a note in the margins, to jot down a melody or record a social encounter. It is possible to see at a glance, in other words, the kinds of lyric that lent themselves to being anthologized in their own time, and those that seemed to have a quite independent, fleeting circulation.

The more context one provides, the fewer items can be included.[73] But it seems important to do more than simply contextualize. Perhaps the key ambition of the edition is to question boundaries. The apparently innocuous choice of manuscripts rather than themes as the ground bass of the structure has the capacity to provoke a reader at every turn. To start with the largest category, my hope is that this anthology keeps in focus the fact that anthologies create peculiar conditions for reading poetry in any period. As Marjorie Perloff remarks, "the common practice of reading lyric poems in isolation—what we might call the anthology syndrome—presents a rather skewed view of the poetic process."[74] If she thinks this of modern poetry we might feel it all the more of medieval. Yet I want to turn this complaint around by using an edition to show the limits of "the anthology syndrome" while it indulges in it. A particular potential virtue of presenting a copying history is that it can highlight ways in which specific books themselves handle the process of anthologizing, and how that changes across three centuries. More specifically, by trying to provide a sense of how fully embedded many of the items are in larger textual and (where relevant) musical networks of the period, the edition, in short, fights its own generic limits.

This central propensity toward self-subversion may have the further merit of questioning certain organizing categories that are standard in most anthologies. The most obvious of these is, of course, the awkward pre- and postmedieval term "lyric" itself.[75] Readers are given the opportunity to enjoy the variousness of insular manuscript contents and see glimpses of short verse items that push sharply against any notion of lyric that focuses only on an examination of the first-person voice, love, questions of identity and self-referentiality, on time, apostrophe, or hyperbole. Here will pop up the medical instructions, recipes, charms, bookplates, sermon themes, word puzzles, and tomb inscriptions, precisely in order to attest to an inclusiveness in these medieval compilations that has been increasingly obscured since Robbins. I place these quirky items, resistant to conventional postmedieval notions of "the lyrical," up against those that do seem to express at least some of them, and thereby provoke new questions about "lyric" and "lyrical" that have a resonance with the questions being asked in the new lyric studies more widely. The shaping frameworks of individual manuscripts also enable new perspectives on authorship: understudied authors emerge, such as James Ryman, who set into relief the large numbers of items that are unattributed. In sum, the hope is that many items will cause readers to wrestle anew with the "work function" of medieval verse, especially in books where authorship is invisible.

An Example

I conclude with a specific case study to follow through these observations. It has been selected to show "lyric editing" in action. This means showing how lyric editing and lyric reading form the same axis in any effort to interpret the "thing" we are trying to create as we observe.[76] Not all of the items have this degree of complexity in the manuscript record. But some have more.

Godric's Songs

These open the anthology. I begin here for several reasons. One could argue (and many have, not least Bede himself) that "lyric" in English begins with Cædmon, but the multilingual environment of late eleventh- and early twelfth-century Britain was a different world from that of Cædmon's and is the one that the anthology is committed to.[77] Also Godric's songs happen, conveniently enough, to be "origin songs"—like "Cædmon's Hymn," they claim the special status of being inspired by God without the mediation of learning. The story of Cædmon, as told by the eighth-century Northumbrian monk Bede, is of a poor man, attached to a monastery near Whitby in the seventh century, who gained a reputation for composing beautiful songs. In his old age, illiterate, a nonsinger, dozing while taking his turn to look after the livestock in the night, Cædmon is commanded in a dream to sing of the creation of the world. He performs this song in the morning to the abbess, and it is agreed that God has given him a special gift. He composes many more and becomes a local phenomenon of devout musicality. This first God-given song is presented by Bede in a Latin translation, but also occurs in Old English in a remarkable number of copies of Bede's *History*.[78] The parallels with Godric are many, even uncanny. Like Cædmon, he was a layman and therefore without clerical education; his songs came to him in a vision. They also happen to be the earliest surviving songs in English *with music*, some three centuries after Bede, and four after Cædmon. Despite Bede's emphasis on music, "Cædmon's Hymn" does not survive with any. For the purpose of thinking about the whole song (as opposed to lyric) the manuscript record presents him, not Cædmon, as the ur-text/ur-author.[79]

Who was Godric? Born in Norfolk in the last quarter of the eleventh century, he spent the first part of his exceptionally long life traveling the seas as a merchant trader, perhaps even as a pirate, so one source claims. In the second part, seemingly to atone for his sins as a sailor and businessman, he settled down as a hermit near Durham and gained a reputation for extraordinarily self-punishing piety. Soon after his death, aged about one hundred, in 1170, some of the Durham monks wrote biographies of him. These relate the composition of the three songs and include not just the words but also the music. Like "Cædmon's Hymn," it is a miracle. Here, in three separate visions, he sees, first, the Virgin Mary who comes to Godric in a vision and teaches him a song about herself ("Seinte marie virgine"); second, his beloved dead sister Burcwen carried by two angels ("Crist and sainte marie"); and, third, St. Nicholas who, singing with choirs of angels, invites him to join them in their hymns of praise ("Sainte Nicholaes godes drud"). Godric's songs are puzzling in many respects. First, their musical record is oddly belated and patchy: in none of the manuscripts in which music survives do the songs occur where the narrative cues them.

Let me summarize how the songs are presented. The earliest biographies of Godric comprise an extensive and lively narrative by Reginald, who knew him personally, another by Galfridus (Geoffrey) of Durham, who also knew him, and a third that is anonymous but attributed elsewhere to one "Walter."[80] Versions of these narratives were then included in thirteenth-century chronicles from St. Albans Abbey by Roger of Wendover and Matthew Paris and in later lives of English saints by John of Tynmouth and John Capgrave, composing a total of twenty-five manuscripts that refer to the songs.[81] Just three manuscripts of his *Life* (London, British Library, Harley MS 322; Cambridge, Cambridge University Library, MS Mm.4.28; London, British Library, Royal MS 5.F.vii) contain musical notation for one or more of the songs. But in no case is the music supplied in a straightforward way. In the Cambridge manuscript (mostly twelfth century), a notated version of "Seinte marie virgine" has been supplied on an extra leaf in a thirteenth-century hand, evidently after the copying of the narrative; in Harley 322 (mid-thirteenth century), the music for "Seinte marie virgine" has been squeezed into the main text in the wrong point in the narrative (the different song text that was originally there has been scraped out and written over), and in the Royal manuscript (second half of the twelfth century) there is music for four items, not just three, all on a separate single thirteenth-century leaf bound into the booklet of Reginald's *Life*. In short, in none of the manuscripts in which music survives do the songs occur where the narrative cues them.[82]

For the music editor, since only one song, "Seinte marie virgine," occurs in more than one manuscript, the decisions are not entirely straightforward but manageable.[83] So that is one relief. But there are some other puzzles. The Royal manuscript has an extra item, "Sainte marie christes bur," following straight after "Seinte marie virgine." Dobson and Harrison thought this was a second stanza, but Deeming argues that it is a separate, different song. My own sense of the situation is a little different from both of these interpretations, but what Deeming's argument implicitly draws attention to is that both items are strangely formless, and differently so. They could only be stanzas of the same song if we were prepared to understand "stanza" in a quite different way from usual. Here is a second dilemma. Do I print the songs from the Royal manuscript? (See Figures 1 through 5.) It seems an obvious "yes," because it provides us with the largest number of songs. The problem is that it provides them as stand-alone items in an order that does not correspond to the narrative and with an extra one not cued in directly. But, as I have intimated, when we go back to the narrative to help determine their order, we find that there is only one manuscript in which the songs are placed according to the corresponding narrative cues, and this is a

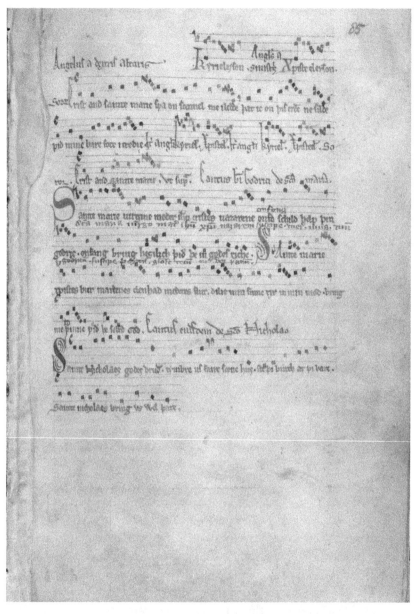

Figure 1. London, British Library, Royal MS 5.F.vii, fol. 85r.

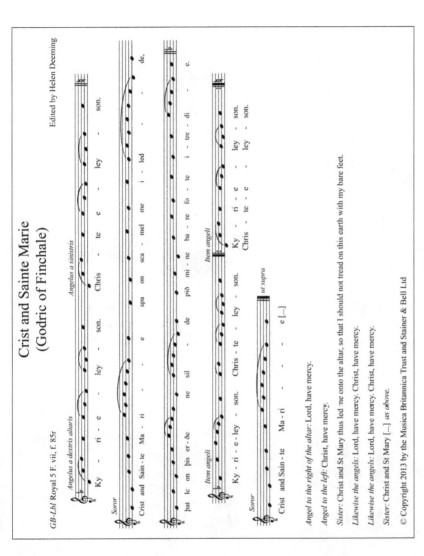

Figure 2. "Crist and Sainte Marie," from Deeming, *Songs in British Sources*, no. 31, p. 51. London, British Library, Royal MS 5.F.vii, fol. 85r.

Reproduced by permission of Stainer & Bell.

Crist and Sainte Marie
(Godric of Finchale)

GB-Lbl Royal 5 F. vii, f. 85r

Edited by Helen Deeming

Angelus a dextris altaris

Angelus a sinistris

Ky - ri - e - ley - son. Chris - te - e - ley - son.

Soror

Crist and Sain - te Ma - ri - e spa on sca - mel me i - led - de,

þat Ic on þis er - ðe ne sil - de pið mi - ne ba - re fo - te i - tre - di - e.

Item angeli

Ky - ri - e - ley - son. Chris - te - ley - son.

Item angeli

Ky - ri - e - ley - son. Chris - te - e - ley - son.

Soror

Crist and Sain - te Ma - ri - e [...]

ut supra

Angel to the right of the altar: Lord, have mercy.

Angel to the left: Christ, have mercy.

Sister: Christ and St Mary thus led me onto the altar, so that I should not tread on this earth with my bare feet.

Likewise the angels: Lord, have mercy. Christ, have mercy.

Likewise the angels: Lord, have mercy. Christ, have mercy.

Sister: Christ and St Mary [...] *as above.*

Figure 3. "Sainte Marie, virgine," from Deeming, *Songs in British Sources*, no. 32, p. 51. London, British Library, Royal MS 5.F.vii, fol. 85r.

Reproduced by permission of Stainer & Bell.

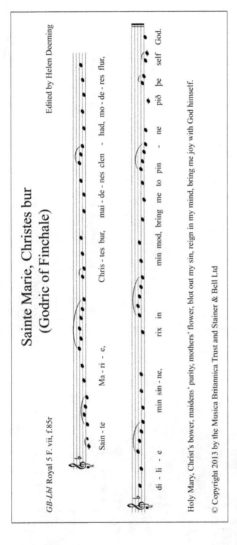

Figure 4. "Sainte Marie, Christes bur," from Deeming, *Songs in British Sources*, no. 33, p. 52. London, British Library, Royal MS 5.F.vii., fol. 85r.

Figure 5. "Sainte Nicholaes," from Deeming, *Songs in British Sources*, no. 34, p. 52. London, British Library, Royal MS 5.F.vii, fol. 85r. Reproduced by permission of Stainer & Bell.

further manuscript I have not mentioned yet (Paris, Bibliothèque Mazarine, MS 1716), because it has spaces for staves, rather than actual music.[84]

Where does this leave an editor? The principle of selecting a single manuscript (as far as possible) to indicate a helpful textual (and where appropriate, musical) context for the "lyric" is fundamentally disrupted by the surviving manuscript evidence. No one manuscript presents Godric's life with all the songs in the right narrative sequence. Harley is the only one that provides a narrative cue followed by a song with music. But it gives only one song, at a different point in the narrative from the others. The Royal manuscript leaf gives us four items, but not in context. The Mazarine manuscript gives us all the cues (for all four items), and hence all the narrative context, but no music.[85] One option would be to use the French text of the Mazarine manuscript inserting the music from the Royal page, but it seems to be a separate and subsequent tradition from the earliest Latin copies.[86]

There's still more. When we do go back to the biographies, we find that many of them provide texts of the songs in Latin, rather than English. Sixteen of the twenty-five give them in English. Seventeen of the twenty-five give them in Latin. (These figures are overlapping because eight manuscripts have both Latin and English.)[87] The Royal manuscript is an example of a manuscript that provides Latin only. The French translation of Reginald's biography in the Paris manuscript says that the Virgin sang "Seinte marie virgine" to Godric in Latin, and that Godric asked her to translate it into English: "Les parolles du chant furent en Latin mes par sa proiere li furent ensaingniees en anglois por ce que mieus conut la langue, et en tel maniere [en] rime et en chant comme vous ci poez veoir et oïr" (The words of the song were in Latin but at his request they were taught to him in English because he knew the language better, and in this form of rhyme and music as you can see and hear).[88] Matthew Paris, by contrast, announces the English text as "canticum illud Gallico ydiomate" (that song in the French language).[89] Both details offer fascinating insight into different perspectives on language in this period. For the editor interested not in isolating English texts but in conveying the wider cultural form of these songs, the main point is to show the way that Latin and French are involved in the presentation of these English songs as well as music.

What, then, might an edition of these songs look like? My lyric editing would like to include many features of the "whole" song that are excluded by a version of the texts alone. I would like to show, for a start, that the songs are musical as well as verbal. But it turns out that simply providing a transcript of the music alongside a choice of texts, selected by collating and weighing information from the various manuscripts, would not be sufficient. For both text and music are the product of narrative, and again this means more than that they are isolable items one can extract from a narrative. There are many reasons for this. First, they are narrated by a third person who casts his interpretative cloak over the songs. This might not in theory affect the nature of our transcript except that the premise of the narrative is that the songs are being uttered by someone who is illiterate, in music as well as language. The biographer is, as it were, transcribing the songs in his own words, in his own notation, and this immediately suggests that the written form of the songs is not, in any simple sense, Godric's. More than that, the particular type of literacy exercised by the biographer is plurilingual. The written form of the song texts—to put it simply—exists in more than language, and it is not simply a matter of choosing one over another because the songs' meaning is constituted by plurilingualism. It might be objected that the whole point of the narrative is to assert that Godric's songs are in English. But the nature of this English is not what it seems. It is formed by a monk whose first written language is Latin. This means that the English he writes is shaped by that education and is unlikely to be an exact transcript of what Godric sang. This may seem to be splitting hairs, but it turns out to matter a great deal once we attempt to interpret the meter and form of the songs. The Mazarine manuscript, moreover, demonstrates that the notion that Godric's English was an "original" version of the song would not be a monk's first assumption. Here the supposition is that the Virgin sang in Latin and Godric asked her to translate that into English (as cited above: "Les parolles du chant furent en Latin mes par sa proiere li furent ensaingniees en anglois por ce que mieus conut la langue" [The words of the song were in Latin but at his request they were taught to him in English because he knew the language better]). And for Matthew Paris it was clear the songs were in French ("That song in the French language").

When we delve a little further we find the written form of the music is not in any simple sense that of the biographer either. All the surviving music postdates the narrative. It seems likely the music we have is not the music Godric sang, but a later composition added to the biographies to strengthen his cultic impact within a new community.[90] As if these empirical considerations were not already complicated enough, the actual form of the songs offers another kind of puzzle. Quite simply, they are unexpectedly short. Here is the first, from Harley 322 (see Figure 6):

Figure 6. "Seinte Marie, virgine," from Deeming, *Songs in British Sources*, no. 78, p. 109. British Library Harley MS 322, fol. 74v.

Reproduced by permission of Stainer & Bell.

Seinte Marie uirgine
moder iesus cristes nazarene •
onfong • schild • help • þin go drich •
onfong bring heȝliche wiþ þe ine godes rych •[91]

(St. Mary the Virgin, mother of Jesus Christ the Nazarene, receive, protect, help your Godrich; receive him honorably with you into God's kingdom.)

Given their status as "origin songs," they are unassuming, perhaps even underwhelming, and hard to contextualize. Does closer consideration suggest anything different? If one goes back once more to their narrative context in Reginald's *Life*, then one finds that the songs are fully integrated into a visionary experience. When Godric is reported as seeing Mary and Mary Magdalene, he is addressed by name: "Nunquid Godrice, me cognosceris?" (Oh Godric, surely you know me?).[92] Mary, for so it is, assumes a personal relationship to him and engages him in conversation. The song has a much larger introduction than its few words might seem to warrant: it has a piercingly sweet odor that overwhelms him ("mellifluo odoris nectare domum totam inexplicabilis dulcedo replevit"), and he is taught it carefully so that he will remember and retain its melody: "harmonico cantu illud cum musico modulamine cantare docebat, quod ille saepius subsequenter post eam cecinit, et ipsius melodiae canticum cunctis diebus vitae suae retinuit" (in harmonious chant with a musical melody; he sang it many times after her, and he retained the tune of that song all the days of his life).[93] So much is said of this need to teach Godric that one wonders whether the song's words represent a mere fraction of the whole singing lesson. Reading back this passage and those in which the other songs are set or alluded to from the extraordinary scene in which Reginald and his young companion listen to Godric in the church (which I have discussed elsewhere),[94] we get the sense that the words in English provided in the narrative are a skeletal rather than fully bodied piece of performed music. Using language that, as Mary Carruthers has taught us, is typical of medieval descriptions of aesthetic experience, the powerful sensory effects on Godric of the song give it weight and substance that go beyond the words that are supplied.[95] My suspicion is that the music we find in later manuscripts is a later attempt to fill out this vision, and although it may bear some relation to reality, it is unlikely to be more than a faint outline of the kind of music Godric actually performed.[96]

In more detail, the text is riddling; the music almost too short to characterize (again, see Figure 6). The melodic phrases are similar to those we encounter in sequence-style pieces but with melismas on "Marie" and "virgine," as well as (in "Sainte marie christes bur") "sainte," "dilie," "in," and "pinne" (= "winne").[97] I quote now from the copy in Cambridge Mm.4.28, where the verse is followed by a Latin translation:

Sancte Marie virgine,
moder Jesu Cristes Nazarene,
onfo, scild, help þin Godric
onfang, bring hehtlic piδ þe i Godes riche.

Sancta Maria uirgo mater iesu Christi nazareni suscipe [tuere] adiuva
tuum • N • suscipe • porta • eternaliter tecum in Dei regnum •[98]

(Holy Mary, virgin, mother of Jesus Christ the Nazarene, receive, [protect], help your N, receive, bring [him] with you eternally into the kingdom of God.)

Textually, it divides into two halves and two people: the Virgin and Godric himself. Mary is named and identified, so is Godric, matching her request in the narrative. His name is revealed through rhyming wordplay: Godrich; God's kingdom. The shortness of the musical phrase on "piδ þe i Godes riche" articulates the rhyme, which sounds on "hehtlic" as well as "Godric." But other puns lurk less pointedly: the repeated "onfo (onfong, onfang)," which means to receive, to understand, to inherit, and perhaps also to receive a name, urges both the Virgin and Godric to do all four, so that he might be brought with her to the heavenly realm.[99] Each meaning plays on the other and on the forms of address in the song: by knowing and understanding his name, the Virgin will help Godric to know himself and know God, and receive the gift of God's honorable reception of him into his service, that is, inherit his kingdom. In Mm.4.28, this play on self-knowledge extends into these lines (see Figure 4):

Sainte marie christes bur
maidenes clenhad moderes flur •
dilie min sinne rix in min mod •
bring me ^to[100] pinne wiδ þe selfd God •

(St. Mary, Christ's chamber,
Virgin's purity, mother's flower,
blot out my sin, rule in my spirit,
bring me to joy with thee {with} God's self.)[101]

Once Godric knows himself his sin can be obliterated and his mind ruled by
"God himself." This line is compressed and obscure: at first reading the speaker
seems to be asking the Virgin to "bring me to joy with thee," but the phrase
"selfd God" interrupts this. The Latin translation offers "cum solo Deo," but
this knotted English could perhaps mean both the self that is God and the self
produced by God. God's rule is indeed Godric, a self formed by God, destined
for the joy that is God's self. And encompassing this in a beautiful embrace is
the Virgin, also God's self, enabling Godric's human identification with God.

The scene where his sister appears and the angels sing from either side
of the altar is especially dramatic: the veil between heaven and earth is made
transparent in music and brother and sister are reunited in this further intense experience of sweet melody. Once again, the passage suggests how the
music has been added in a cultic gesture: the quasi-liturgical setting with altar and dialogic angels comes to life in the notation not as a specific song but
as a dramatic interlude: a means of playing out this spiritual connection between Godric and his sister through the medium of music. Music, in other
words, is not an accompaniment to this vision so much as a way of embodying
it, and therefore making the experience transferable to a wider audience. It is
as if we have been given the neatly balanced core of the drama: repeated
"Kyrie eleison, Christe eleison" responses, followed by the sister's speech, all
repeated in the music. This at least is one way of explaining an otherwise
unattested structure, somewhere between a versicle response, liturgical respond, and strophic repetition.

The result is a song, yes, but more like a narrative sketch of what the
song was. Even the music, in short, is not music—it is a textual record of
something that had a quite different character in performance. The writing
it up changes it. It creates something new. The song is not a fixed object, or
even something that plays in real time. It is playing in historical time, in the
narrative that embodies it.

Editing the "Whole" Song

In conclusion, we are still at an early stage of viewing the "medieval English lyric" whole. Godric's songs, right at the alleged beginning of the tradition, illustrate how much is still undiscovered about insular lyric. New emphases of editorial perspective that use medieval compiling as their basis have the capacity to complicate, disrupt, and radically extend our sense of medieval lyric, indeed of lyric more broadly. Let me sketch some of the potential as I see it for a new "lyric editing." The process of shifting the field's Anglocentric focus toward a grasp and appreciation of the mobile linguistic world inhabited by English-texted songs liberates them from being treated as the fixed, isolable, "English" objects that they never were. Further analyses of the surviving music and its significance for the texts, as well as the significance of the words and their patterns for the music will shed new light on the composition and reception of song. A more connected, synoptic view of the place of English-language short verse in medieval copying practices will continue to undo certain kinds of categorization that have prevailed in so much criticism on medieval literature in general, but especially in lyric studies, notably such vague and misleading but determining dichotomies as "sacred" and "secular," "devotional" and "liturgical," "literary" and "functional," "Latin" and "vernacular," "prose" and "verse," "lyric" and "song." As the chapters in this book are beginning to demonstrate, there are many new kinds of focus that can help modern readers discern characteristics of this vast archive that have previously been obscured by anxieties and confusions over such overarching terms.

I would urge that lyric editing has the crucial function of encouraging any fresh research in this archive to be based firmly on material scrutiny. Manuscript study of medieval English lyrics has always been foundational. But the sheer number of manuscripts has been a bar to attempts to assess the books thoroughly yet broadly. Every manuscript, and every item, has the potential to yield rich networks of affiliation. Editing requires us to go back to the manuscripts; "*lyric* editing" shows that the whole song cannot be represented by a single text from a single manuscript, nor even from a single transcript chosen by means of collating information from several manuscripts. Instead, the post hoc copying of music and also text, often with different chronologies, and the multilingual complexity of a song's transmission (whereby music can circulate with texts in more than one language) present us with a "thing" that has not one but many forms of realization. Taking account of the music requires paying attention to the ways in which the writing is a partial and provisional link to a world of sound and action. As editors and readers we only get somewhere near the whole by juggling and juxtaposing transcriptions, until we realize that lyric reading is exactly about engaging with that moving process of assimilating simultaneous genres of information and not just with a flat and fixed text.

In that spirit I have offered here not one but several editions of Godric's songs: a facsimile of all four from the Royal manuscript (Figure 1); editions of each song by Helen Deeming from the Royal manuscript, including both text and music (Figures 2 through 5); a diplomatic text-only transcription of "Seinte marie virgine" from Harley MS 322 showing the punctum markings for the three verbs in line 3 (page 56); Deeming's edition of the music for "Seinte marie virgine" from the Harley manuscript (Figure 6); and a lightly edited version of the same lines from Cambridge University Library, MS Mm.4.28, with the Latin translation supplied by the copyist (page 57), followed by the Cambridge manuscript's version of "Seinte marie christes bur" (pages 57 and 58). If one had the French translation with the spaced out English lines also in one's mind's eye and ear, then one would have something like a resonant sonic history shaped by chronologies of writing in three languages and two musics.[102]

In that sense, the medieval lyric takes us "beyond parchment." It also does so quite unmetaphorically in the way that verses survive on many kinds of additional media, such as on church or manorial walls, in stained glass, on rings, tombstones, and jugs. English texted verse is again far from unique in this: and some hints in the texts of poems copied in manuscripts, such as those of the *Fasciculus Morum*, give glimpses of a domestic and imaginative sense of inscribed verse that has a rich counterpart in French, in such examples as the *devinailles* and tomb inscriptions in the prose Arthurian narratives or the *lais* of Marie de France, and in Latin. Once more, this brings us back to an understanding of verse as tied equally to tangible, visible, and auditory sensual experience as it is to the physical act of writing. All these kinds of sources for medieval verse take us back into contact with a historical past that demands to be understood in all its remarkable longevity. The pastness of medieval lyric, its tension between being a static, tangible object, a process of transmission of ultimately irretrievable but deeply illuminating complexity, and an experience of sound mysteriously shaped by words and music, is one from which lyric studies in any period has much to learn.

Chapter 2

Wondering Through Middle English Lyric

CRISTINA MARIA CERVONE

Beleeve, and leave to wonder!

———————————

I'm the little dark one,
the dark one.

They say darkness
is caused by sin
—you can't find that in me
and never will.

I am the rose without thorn
that Solomon praised:
nigra sum sed fermosa,
I shall be renowned.

———————————

Treating the shimmer of the black metaphor might seem to lend itself to
studying blackness as an abstraction rather than as a material condition
with real-world consequences.

Still understudied in both medieval and lyric studies (despite the increasing body of scholarship investigating them), the poems, or cultural phenomena, many refer to by the term "Middle English lyric" give those interested in them every reason to wonder about what they are and how they work. Nowadays most readers, including medievalists who are not specialists in this area, generally encounter them either in snippets within works of literary criticism or in modern anthologies of "Middle English lyrics" or of poetry or verse more broadly. In such places, these writings are stripped of their surroundings, reformatted to conform with contemporary poetic norms, and printed in a setting and in groupings that are foreign to them. Modern poetry anthologies are gatherings of a different sort from medieval manuscripts, designed for different uses. In the artifacts that preserve them, Middle English lyrics are seldom presented as poems in the modern sense; moreover, even though much writing in Middle English is in verse,[1] few English medieval compilations have what moderns would think of as a poetical focus. So, it is difficult to represent Middle English lyrics within modern settings that do not fundamentally change their context, and thus our responses to them, our readings of them. Beyond that, contemporary readers are distant from them in time and in culture—our knowledge of them is necessarily partial. Since how we read a piece of writing is inflected by the cognitive frameworks triggered by its presentation, I find myself wondering about medieval readerly expectations of Middle English lyric. In the absence of late medieval English treatises on poetry, what can be surmised about this issue must be teased out of the poems themselves, or their manuscripts or other vehicles of preservation. What shared notions of use do Middle English lyrics suggest? What do they ask us to bring of ourselves to them? What cognitive processes do they engage? These key questions may be summed up in one fundamental query: What sort of reading makes a "thing" like this productive?

Such a question implicitly acknowledges that in their native homes, these poems may draw on modes of reading that contemporary readers have not been trained in and that are not intuitive to us, and it is this possibility—even probability—that chiefly interests me here. My first epigraph quotes a lyric that poses a series of questions of its own, wonderings that prompt further thought about a Christian theological concept, the mystery of Christ's Incarnation, his becoming human while not relinquishing his divinity. The poem postulates that human thought might be incapable of imaginatively comprehending either that Jesus could be fully God and fully human or the virgin conception that makes that hypostatic union possible:

A God and yet a man?
A mayde and yet a mother?
Witt wonders what witt Can
Conceave this or the other.
                    (lines 1–4)

As I have argued elsewhere, this poem makes use of a range of meanings prevalent in medieval thought about aspects of the work of wonder (amazement, surprise, curiosity, puzzlement, admiration, speculation), and it does so while acknowledging a limit to human reason ("Witt wonders what witt Can" [line 3], or "only as far as wit can") until the enjambment of this same line briefly pauses on "can" as we linger over the thought that our thought *has* a limit, then makes the turn into the following line (4) that acknowledges the possibility of thought that *could* conceive of such a thing, generatively and comprehensively—an intelligence beyond the human.[2] In engaging diverse aspects of wonder, both by calling attention to the varied manners of working involved and by thinking through their implications, the poem ultimately moves beyond its own moment in an ambiguous call for a cessation that nevertheless impels further thought:

God, truth itselfe, doth teach it;
Mans witt senckis too farr vnder
By reasons power to reach it.
Beleeve, and leave to wonder!
                    (9–12)

While in one sense "believe and cease to wonder" carries a prescriptive force, the working of the poem to this point has habituated a sort of reading that ponders and opens up another possibility: "believe and allow (or even, *cause*) to wonder." The leave-taking of the poem thus does not foreclose thought so much as it opens up scope for it. A poem like this one invites readers to give of themselves as they ponder. Could this also have been true of lyrics that do not explicitly call on readers to do so?

Ruminating, then, on medieval writings about wonder and cognition, along with poems that explicitly call for readerly engagement of a challenging sort in and through time, I advance a thought experiment: what if Middle English lyric *intends* to *prompt* us to wonder, to bring part of the poem to it, as it were, even, maybe especially, when its meaning appears to be relatively straightforward? I do not mean we should generate complexity when it is not there, but rather propose to bring a mindset, in line with medieval ideas about the *work* of wonder, that anticipates scope for thought. In what follows, counterintuitively to much thought about the simplicity or straightforwardness of Middle English lyric, I situate verses alongside or within learned traditions that are inventive, literary, philosophical. Keeping an eye toward the sorts of reading and writing those who wrote or recorded these poems would have engaged in habitually in their practice or training, I consider Middle English lyric as potentially a medieval mode of *inquiry*. My interest is in how present-day readers' experience of such "things" may be affected if we presuppose that they expect us to approach them with interpretative agility even when—perhaps especially when—their concerns appear to be self-evident.

Wonderings

I begin not from direct evidence but from conceptualization. There is good reason, beyond my initial example poem, to consider the potential importance of wonder to the manner of working of these things. Ideas about and uses of wonder pervade medieval thought and culture.[3] In her influential presidential address to the American Historical Association in 1997, Caroline Walker Bynum categorized three types of medieval engagements with wonder: theological and philosophical; religious; and entertainment oriented. While all three are potentially in play for lyric, it is the first that primarily interests me here.

Some medieval writers draw attention to the cognitive underpinnings of wonder as leading to mental exploration (as against inaction or stupefaction). Their focus is on how wonder opens up lines of inquiry rather than on how questioning may cease once an answer is found. For instance, Augustine said, "Marvels are not 'against nature' but 'against *what we know* of nature,'" suggesting that more could be known.[4] While this line of thought developed in later periods into a results-oriented view of science (investigation can provide answers), for many medieval theorists, wonder epitomizes the productivity of being *in via*, a desirable state of seeking.

Moreover, in his *Metaphysics*, Aristotle laid the groundwork for connections later writers made between philosophy and poetry, saying that "it is owing to their wonder that men both now begin and at first began to philosophize . . . Even the lover of myth is in a sense a lover of wisdom, for myth is composed of wonders."[5] Commenting on Aristotle, Thomas Aquinas explicitly named wonder as the key link between poetry and philosophy: "the reason why the philosopher is compared to the poet is that both are concerned with wonders," because, Aquinas goes on to say, Aristotle noted that wonder prompts the one who wonders to seek a cause for what he does not understand.[6]

Aristotle, Aquinas, and others acknowledged that wonderment's inherent recognition of a lack or failure of knowledge incites those who wonder to seek to know more, and that such seeking could productively take written, generative form. What Aristotle and Aquinas meant by poetry might look more like Dante's *Commedia* (longer, narrative) than like my short-form English examples. Yet, Aquinas himself was a master of short-form (Latin, liturgical) verse that very much turned on the potential latent in human cognition for pondering, in and through poetic form itself, what is both ineffable and fundamentally incomprehensible. His *Pange lingua gloriosi*, the Latin hymn he wrote for the liturgical feast of Corpus Christi, is so tightly compressed in its sense, so skillful in its use of accentual rhythm, so reliant on its alternating triple rhyming that it cannot be adequately rendered into English without loss, as exemplified in what is perhaps its most challenging moment:

> Verbum caro panem verum
> > Verbo carnem efficit,
> Fitque sanguis Christi merum;
> > Et, si sensus deficit,
> Ad firmandum cor sincerum
> > Sola fides sufficit.[7]

To be sure, Aquinas was writing in Latin, not English. Yet for him, at least, short-form nonnarrative poetry offered precisely the means he needed to explore—and wonder through—a theological concept. Writers of Middle English, too, used poetry to work through an understanding of the mystery of Christ's Incarnation, as I have argued elsewhere.[8]

What if the work of wonder, in its various forms, *is* the work of Middle English short-form poetry? The valorization of close reading from the early twentieth century onward has led moderns to gravitate to lyrics that draw deeply on our capacity to wonder at what is wondrous.[9] Yet, even medieval short-form poems that seem less rich might flourish in a new way under intensified gaze when approached with an inquiring mindset, much as in film a close-up shot of something not obviously significant leads us to cast about for interpretation if the camera lingers. Perhaps, for instance, these sorts of poems may explore what is so familiar as to be overlooked, what is viewed but not seen. A. C. Spearing once said that many descriptors used by Chaucer and the *Pearl*-poet are ones moderns would term clichés—green as grass, round as a ball—and that poets used these comparisons for getting at the essential qualities of things.[10] Such imagery has come to seem too ordinary to be interesting, aligning too closely, perhaps, to what many think they already know. Nevertheless, for that very reason it can strike compellingly at the heart of a common experience of *things as they are*, or typically are. In simplicity, stripped down descriptive verse invites meditation on the nature of things, not necessarily or solely as a celebration of them, but also as a consideration of their qualities and interrelated workings.[11] Consider, for example:

Cantus occidentalis

Myrie a tyme I telle In may	*count/recount*
Wan bricte blosmen brekez on tre	*bright flowers*
þeise foules singez nyt ant day	*birds*
In ilche grene is gamen an gle[12]	*each; play; glee/joy/song*

The brief verse depicts a seasonal moment not attached to particularized experience. While post-Romantic aesthetics often value novelty of expression, on the evidence of texts, an aesthetic of *things as they are* would have been more salient for Chaucer's contemporaries than it is today. The verse does not cry out for deep attention. Nevertheless, it rewards deliberation. That "May" should be "merry" is a commonplace reinforced by poetic tradition and the usefulness of the alliteration, yet here the "telling [counting over] of a time" in alliterative tintinnabulation lends medial weight to a line that balances "Myrie" *against* "May" in a chiastic sound structure. That medial weight is retained in line 2 and draws attention to the action of the unfolding buds on tree branches, with the alliterating *b* sounds joined by the aspiration of the *gh* and the brightness of the *t* and *k* that "break" sonically to parallel how the buds break their confining and sheltering tightness when they unfurl into flowers, the *e* of "brekez" and "tre" lingering and settling. The "foules," presumably in those very trees, break into song as buds break into flower, night and day, for spring is a continuous process of growth and change through constancy, and this brief verse rounds out in the alliterative "gamen an gle" of birdsong in greenness and green space.

While on one level "Myrie a tyme" simply tells us, "it's spring!," lingering over the *how* of this poem—how listeners are shown and *hear* the spring in it—points up its aesthetic of *things as they are*. Stopping to consider the essential qualities of May, of buds, of birds, of song, prompts not only wonder at creation, and by extension if readers are so minded, its Creator, but also, perhaps, at our own place in things. That bringing of one's self to the reading may be prompted by the "counting over" and "recounting" signaled by "I telle" in the first line, where "I" is not attached to or generated by any particular character or persona but offers a shared yet individual experience through the "telling of time," each time the poem is recited or read. What is on offer in this brief stanza is not only a vision of spring, but a pausing to consider spring's recurrence, its generative qualities, even one's situation relative not only to this particular moment but to other connected moments and thoughts. The growth inherent to spring makes available, via a wondering mindset, a blossoming of interpretation.

For medieval Christian readers with monastic ties, a slow, ruminative reading process would be intuitive from *lectio divina*, a text-based practice involving reading of a sacred text, meditation, and prayer, with an eye less toward gaining knowledge than seeking wisdom, and that similarly encourages readers to extend their thought on the text into their thought on themselves.[13] While *lectio divina* is a specialized approach to sacred scripture, aspects of its methodology are found elsewhere, as in, for example, the liturgy for Mass, which draws together scriptural texts associatively for meditation, or in preaching itself, which unfolds from a specific set text. Such text-based habits of thought thrive on readers bringing something of themselves to their reading, beginning from but moving beyond what is written, often with an eye toward self-improvement. For comparison, a brief related lyric, "Mirie it is while sumer ilast," also found only in one manuscript,[14] contrasts summer with the coming winter, which leads to the personalized moralizing thought, "And ich wid wel michel wrong / soregn and murne" (and I with very many sins, sorrow and mourn). A poem like "Myrie a tyme" is ripe for such amplification and could perhaps have worked something like a script inviting further elaboration by the reader.[15]

I said "the verse does not cry out for deep attention," but "Myrie a tyme" survives only in a single manuscript, Cambridge, Pembroke College, MS 258, perhaps compiled by a parish priest of Lincolnshire, though not written by the same person who wrote out the rest of the page, a sermon, in Latin, for Palm Sunday (see Figure 7).[16] Why is the poem here? Does it fall into the class of Middle English lyric that without context seems secular but with the right context carries sacred significance? Or did the person who added it to the manuscript think it useful for insertion into a sermon, or meditation?

The three other English poems (there are also French ones) in this manuscript are similarly brief (one is a quatrain, one is two couplets, one is six lines long); among them is the well-known and much anthologized early Marian lyric, with its wonderful pun on sun/son and face/wood/cross:

Nou goht sonne wnder wode	*goes; tree/cross*
& me rewez marie þi bricte rude	*pity; face/cross*
Nou goz sonne vnder tre	*tree/cross*
& me rewez marie þi sone ant þe[17]	*and you*

"Nou goth sonne" was widely distributed in the Middle Ages, after appearing in many Latin, French, and English copies of St. Edmund of Abingdon's prolifically circulated *Mirror of Holy Church.* In the *Mirror* but not in Pembroke College MS 258, the surround of "Nou goth sonne" offers instructions for "Contemplacion biforen Midday" (meditation before the liturgical hour of sext, or noon), when, according to the *Mirror,* "þow schalt þenken of þe Annunciacion and of þe Passion," thus focusing attention on Mary's unique status in salvation history as well as her motherhood and, by extension, the special feeling a mother has on the loss of her only son.[18]

Considering the Annunciation and the Passion together was common. In the Roman rite the feast of the Annunciation was celebrated on March 25, the same date thought to be the day of Christ's Crucifixion and death (the Passion).[19] The liturgical association of the two moments—at Mass and in the liturgical hours—is important because they mark the beginning and ending of Jesus's earthly life. Both crucial events for salvation history are witnessed and experienced by Mary; moreover, the life history shared by mother and son is poignantly evoked in "Nou goth sonne."

Edmund advises readers to meditate on Mary's sorrow at the time of Christ's death and to recite "Nou goth sonne" in English, empathetically:

Þe selue heo seide in hire song of loue: "Ne haue no merueile þat i am **blo,** for þe **sonne** haþ discolurd me so." Þerfore seiþ **on English** þis in Maner of pite: "Nou goþ þe sonne bi þe wode . . ."[20]

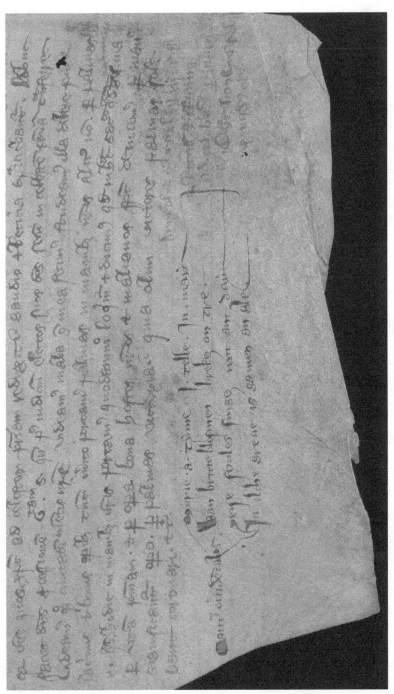

Figure 7. Cambridge, Pembroke College MS 258, fol. 141v (detail), "Myrie a tyme."

Reproduced by kind permission of the Master and Fellows of Pembroke College, Cambridge.

(The same one said in her song of love, "Do not be amazed that I am black/bruised/pale, for the sun has discolored me that way." Therefore say in English in this piteous manner, "Nou goþ þe sonne bi þe wode . . .")

Memes c'el tenure dit ele en la Chaunson d'Amur: "Ne vous emerveillez come jeo su brunecte e haulé, kar le **soleil** m'ad descoloree," *Nolite considerare quod fusca sim, etc.* E por ceo **en engleys** en tele manere de pité:
    Nou goþ sunne under wode . . . [21]

The idea that Mary's skin could be discolored by the sun because of sorrow is significant, a point to which I shall return in a later section. "Hire song of loue"/"la Chaunson d'Amur" refers to the Old Testament book of the Song of Songs; the discoloration comes in an early verse quoted in Latin in the French version (Song of Songs 1:5: "Do not consider me that I am brown, because the sun hath altered my colour").[22]

In the English but not the French, the invitation to meditate—including the translation of Song of Songs 1:5—initiates the sun/son pun further exploited by the poem (*soleil* can only mean "sun," but *sonne* can mean either "sun" or "son"). So, in the English *Mirror* but not the French one, the link between Song of Songs 1:5 and "Nou goth sonne" sited in the word *sonne* is enriched by Mary's unique position as mother to this particular Son. The *alteration* of color can be interpreted variously, but the color word *blo* is particularly apt for denoting the *alternation* of color one might expect from a mother anticipating and then witnessing her son's death: in Middle English, *blo* can mean "black," "blue," "dark," "bruised," "bruise-colored," "wan," and "pale," among other things.[23] It seems to have evolved this range from taking account of the varied colors, and perhaps the changes over time, in bruised flesh. The dark range of its signification is keyed to the dread and sorrow a mother might feel, the pale range the loss of blood following on that emotion. The surround of "Nou goth sonne" in English is thus doubly important to experience of the poem; omission of this context is a real loss for readers who lack it.[24]

Could "Myrie a tyme" also originally or elsewhere have had a surround—liturgical, meditative, or even preacherly—such as "Nou goth sonne" does in Edmund's *Mirror*? With or without such a context, is "Myrie a tyme" centered in a particular sort of learnedness, or even of contemplation? Indeed, learnedness is evoked by the *language* of the accompanying rubric, or perhaps title, "Cantus occidentalis" (western song, or possibly song of the West [Wind, i.e., Zephyrus]), a *Latin* tag to this vernacular lyric. For "Nou goth sonne," both versions quoted above indicate explicitly the poem is to be read in English, a guideline respected by translators who retain the Middle English. For "Myrie a tyme," too, the English of the poem stands out against the Latin rubric. That Latin provokes further thought, for in what way or ways is this a western song? "Song" might be a generic marker indicating a poem to be sung, or even just a short poem, or "lyric." Then again, would someone with knowledge of some other textual setting, such as the perhaps-priest who gathered it into Pembroke College MS 258, think "song" pointed to some other context, maybe even one associated with the Song of Songs? Or did he intend to incorporate it into a sermon, perhaps even a Latin sermon, such as the sermon for Palm Sunday written above "Myrie a tyme"? Did this person compose this poem on the spot, or did he simply take a fancy to a poem heard or read elsewhere and want to remember it? We cannot know, of course. Nevertheless, when placed within this manuscript's context rather than stripped of its surround in an anthology, even my example of simplicity is beginning to look a bit complex.

Ponderings

Close reading of the sort I have just offered presumes a leisure for rereading. What sort of reading process would medieval readers have used? Read through a wondering mindset, Middle English lyric invites participation, offering space within itself such that experience of time—of thought over time—is, indeed, part of its form. Such reading privileges pondering over comprehension, thought over quickness, drawing back over rushing ahead and is strongly salient in certain sorts of poems—witty poems that explore paradox or riddle, such as "A God and yet a man," or, looking to earlier medieval England, *The Dream of the Rood* or the Exeter riddles. While riddles share with Middle English lyric some modes of transmission, I am thinking in particular about circulation within learned communities and the participatory nature of solving puzzles.[25]

In recent work on the Exeter Book riddles, scholars of early medieval England have increasingly emphasized continuities with Anglo-Latin riddling traditions, situating the vernacular works within long-standing scholarly tradition while recognizing their distinct flavor and achievements. More-over, in her discussion of Old English riddles, Patricia Dailey postulates that the Exeter Book riddles, like other Old English poetry and prose, point towards what she calls "a culture of responsiveness" drawn on by writing that "cultivat[es] a wondrous response to the unknown." She is expressly interested in "what a response may effectuate, *in addition to* producing an answer."[26]

Dailey's attention to a response effect seems broadly applicable to Middle English lyric, and especially to lyrics' subtle evocations of community or com-munities. A riddle explicitly or implicitly poses the question, "who am I?," generating by extension a *we* of those clever enough to figure it out. "Who am I?" they ask, yes, but also, implicitly, "Are you one of us?"—"Are you in the know?" For readers immersed in such a mode, a poem such as "Myrie a tyme" might be thought of as prompting the question "How do you fit in here?" A piece of the answer must lie in how we read.[27] The verses on the jugs and ewers Aden Kumler discusses elsewhere in this book are similarly invested in implicitly asking those who encounter them *where do you stand?* with respect to "the social and political maintenance of distinction and hi-erarchy within elite communities." An object such as the Robinson Jug can "seem to rebuke and beckon at the same time." Ingrid Nelson argues that, for poems framed as dialogues, "the dialogue form itself encourages a po-em's audience to participate in intersubjective meaning-making." Barbara Zimbalist notes how certain fifteenth-century Christological complaint po-ems model how present and future devotional communities may be joined as "interpretive participation will allow [readers] to inhabit the final script of repentance and elicit divine forgiveness." Each argument, in a different way, touches on how lyrics evoke or make use of a sense of community that derives from readerly participation or posture.[28]

Aspects of Middle English lyric I wish to consider similarly include "communal" (socially and systemically), "cognitive," and "participatory." Whereas modern lyrics may privilege an individual voice, Middle English lyrics often leave space for "each of us" and "all of us" simultaneously to oc-cupy a voiced or implied *I* or *we*.[29] They invite a communal understanding of subjectivity, or what I have elsewhere termed "collective subjectivity," by which I mean a notably medieval way of working with a combined yet dis-tinct *I* and *we*, wherein the boundaries between *I* and *we* are deliberately overlaid and malleable. Such writing draws attention to collectivity just where we might expect individuality, without eliminating or overwriting either the general or the particular. While collective subjectivity is characteristic of Middle English lyric, it may be found in other sorts of writing, too.[30]

("Summe men sayoun . . .")

If, as I propose, the work of wonder *is* the work of medieval English short-form poetry, how much might such poems expect readers to bring of themselves to them? I want to engage this question and the implied communities it enacts—writerly and readerly, thus also medieval and modern—by looking at a more explicitly riddling lyric, one I do not understand, which begins "Summe men sayoun þat y am blac" (*DIMEV* 4966) (see Figure 8).[31]

   It occurs in one manuscript only, Cambridge, Gonville and Caius College, MS 383/603, which appears to be penned by an Oxford undergraduate, perhaps the "Wymundus London" whose name is written on several pages. Judging by the manuscript contents, he might have been a student at Magdalen.[32] This poem has hardly been discussed. While it carries no title in the manuscript, its first editor, Rossell Hope Robbins, called it "In Praise of Brunettes," which I think must be spectacularly wrong.[33] I do not believe this poem has anything to do with hair color; it is, on the face of it, a "black is beautiful" poem.[34]

Sum*m*e me*n* sayou*n* þ*at* y am blac		Some men say that I am black
yt ys a colour for my prow[35]		it is a color for my profit [suffering?][35]
þer y loue þer ys no lac		where I love there is no lack
y may not be so wyte as þou	*4*	I may [might?] not be so white as you
blac ys a col*ur* þat is god		black is a color that is good
so say y & many mo		so say I and many more
blac ys my hat blac ys my hod		black is my hat black is my hood [status?]
blac ys al þat longet þer to	*8*	black is all that belongs to it
blac wol do as god a nede		black will do as good a service
as the wyte at bord & bedde		as the white at table and in bed
& þer to also treu in dede		and as to that is as true in deed
and þer to y ley my lyf to wedde	*12*	and I pledge my life on that
Wynd & wat*ur* may steyne þe wyte		Wind and water may stain the white
y wis þe blac yt may nat so		truly the black it may not do

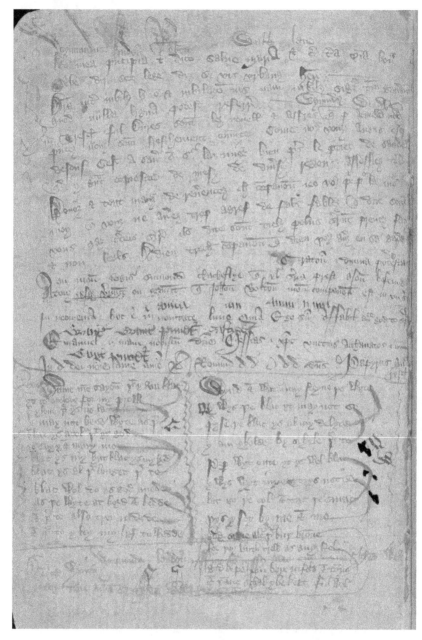

Figure 8. Cambridge, Gonville and Caius College MS 383/603, p. 190, with "Summe men sayoun."

[to] pre*yse*³⁶ þe blac ys al my delyte	to praise³⁶ the black is all my delight
y am yholde by schyle þer to 16	I am held by reason to that
Pep*er* wyt oute yt ys wel blac	Pepper on the outside is very black
y wys wyt inne yt ys not so	truly within it is not so
lat go þe col*ur* & tac þe smac	disregard the color and take the taste
þys y sey by me & mo 20	this I say with respect to me and more
god saue ale hem³⁷ þat buþ brou*n*e	God save all those who are brown
for þey buth trew as any stel	for they are true as any steel
god kepe hem boþe in feld & tou*n*e	God keep them both in field and town
& þan*n*e schal y be kept ful wel³⁸ 24	and then shall I be kept very well³⁸

The aesthetic achievement is high. This poem never rests in a statement; its shifting, puzzling, recursive treatment of blackness rewards pondering and raises many questions. What does the *I* mean by "blac"? Is the *I* black? (For many readers today, this will be *the* question.)³⁹ What does it mean to *be* white, as in line 4, and is that line ironic? How do wind and water stain the white—is this clothing of some kind, livery or a religious habit or academic gown, perhaps? Is the "hod" a hood, suggested by the "hat," or is it more of a condition, perhaps of melancholy, along the lines of Chaucer's man in black in the *Book of the Duchess*, who says "y am sorwe and sorwe ys y" (line 597)? What is the relationship of "blac" to the "broune" of line 21?⁴⁰ What does it mean to be kept very well?

Is the *I* female? Lines 9 and 10 suggest this; "bord & bedde" is a stock phrase used in marital vows and elsewhere to encompass generally all of a woman's duties in marriage.⁴¹ There might be a feminization in the sexiness of the pepper stanza, with "take the smack," and, maybe, in the "all the rest" that completes the second stanza's head-to-toe blazon. Or, does the steel comparison and "field and town" of the final stanza suggest that the *I* is male? While "I pledge my life" faintly conjures up a nongendered wedding vow, it has a hint of masculinity about it, along with "treu in dede" (11), which evokes an ethical and somewhat chivalric ideal.⁴² "Trew as any stel" (22) picks up the emphasis on fidelity and ethics from "treu in dede" while shading toward masculinity and offering a flash of white, perhaps, in that polished swords are "broun"—burnished, shining.⁴³ Does that mean "ale hem þat buþ broun" (21) are white, more than they are black?

My interest in collective subjectivity prompts other questions, too. Why do only *some* men say that *I* am "blac," and is there a possibility that they are wrong? Is the word "men" gendered? Why does the *I* presume the *you* is "so white" (4)? Who are the "more" in line 6 who say "blac ys god," and are they the same as the "more" in line 20 who are implicated in "lat go þe colur & tac þe smac" (19)? Do the *they* in lines 21 and 22 who are "broune" include the *I* or the *you*? Although this poem begins with an *I*, it engages throughout with variously conjured *we*'s of whom the *I* is a singular member within an implied larger whole, or various wholes.

"Summe men sayoun" overtly sets black and white in opposition in a fashion typical of debate poems, a common medieval genre, even as it hints at a variety of shared qualities that are presented indirectly. Stanza 1 introduces a dichotomy in which white is manifestly normative, as against a black the *I* will make a counterintuitive case for. The normativity of whiteness is reinforced by the ensuing stanzas and becomes a pivot point for the poem as a whole. The first words set out a paradox that is never resolved. If only *some* men say the *I* is black (whatever that might mean), perhaps the *I* is not black—yet the remainder of the poem champions blackness as if it is a given that the *I* is, in fact, and self-evidently, black. Is blackness physical (skin, hair, clothing) or metaphorical (melancholy, humanity), and is blackness habituated/perceptual (implied by line 1) or innate (perhaps implied by the rest of the poem)?

I began with a central question, what sort of reading process makes a lyric like this productive? "Summe men sayoun" takes a riddling stance that prompts us to consider who the *I* is and what "blac" means, of course, but the poem sustains other sorts of wonderings, too, and elicits far more questions than answers. What seems like it could be known—*things as they are*—slips under deliberate gaze, gesturing toward and sketching out implied questions— how do you fit in? are you one of us? If, as I am suggesting, Middle English lyric presupposes a deliberative or ruminative process of reading, much as monastic *lectio divina* does, though different from it, too, what happens when we slow down and ponder?

("blac, broun, and blo")

While "Summe men sayoun" does not meditate over lines of a biblical text in the fashion of *lectio divina*, there is more than a strong hint of the Song of Songs about that provocative and enigmatic first line, "Summe men sayoun þat y am blac." The Song of Songs context diminishes any likelihood the poem is a riddle of the kind that gives voice to nonhuman being, material objects, or abstractions.

Elliptically, the poem reimagines the words of the Bride, "Nigra sum sed formosa" (I am black and/but beautiful) (Song of Songs 1:4) or, in some translations, "Fusca sum et decora."[44] Even though a female *I* may thus be implied, the *I*'s gender is still obscure. Because exegetical treatments interpreted the Bride variously as (among other things) the soul or the Church and the Bridegroom as Christ, a devout *male* reader could (and often did) imagine himself in the Bride's position.[45] Yet, Christ (here, the Bridegroom) could himself be envisioned in this context as *female*, as in the following stanza from "In a valley of this restless mind," whose refrain derives from Song of Songs 2:8. The *I* is Christ; the "babe" is a soul, imaginatively both Christ's lover and his/her child who suckles at his/her breast; and the bedchamber is the womblike wound in his/her side:

> My love is in hir chaumbir. Holde youre pees!   *peace*
>   Make ye no noise, but lete hir slepe.
> My babe Y wolde not were in disese;   *I would not desire were*
>   I may not heere my dere child wepe;   *hear*
>   With my pap Y schal hir kepe.   *breast*
>   Ne merveille ye not though Y tende hir to:
>   This hole in my side had nevere be so depe,
>   But *quia amore langueo*.[46]   *because I languish for love*
>   (105–120)

While the *I* of "Summe men sayoun" sounds more like the Bride than the Bridegroom, the Song of Songs context heightens the poem's fluid ambiguity of reference with respect to both gender and color.

The Song of Songs might also help to explain an otherwise puzzling shift (if it is) from black to brown in the final stanza of "Summe men sayoun." In some translations of the Song of Songs, the Bride describes herself first as black (*nigra*) and then as dark or darkened (*fusca*); perhaps the modulation from "blac" (line 1) to "broun" (line 21) attempts fidelity to the biblical verse in this form.[47] For medieval commentators, the Bride was also interpreted as Mary, as in the Spanish lyric that heads this chapter, or in the meditation from Edmund's *Mirror*, many versions of which include "Nou goth sonne," where, as I noted earlier, Mary's darkness explicitly evokes the Bride. In Song of Songs 1:5, part of which is included in the French *Mirror*

given above ("Nolite me considerare quod fusca sim, quia decoloravit me sol"),
the Bride goes on to explain her "brown" coloration by saying "the sun hath
altered my colour" because she has been a "keeper in the vineyards."[48] The
color words in "Summe men sayoun" and in the English version of Edmund's
Mirror are especially tricky because *blac, broun,* and *blo* each can be translated as simply "dark," as well as at either end of the spectrum from Present Day English *black* to *white,* and (for *blo*) some colors in between (*blue,
blond*).[49]

Exploring dichotomies as overlays of one another is common in medieval thought. In poems of this period, a single referent may point to both
secular, erotic love (*eros*) and sacred, charitable love (*caritas*), or masculine
and feminine, or other seemingly contradictory categories, as "In a valley of
this restless mind" demonstrates.[50] Does the edge of an economic lexicon
touched by "prow" (if this manuscript reading is correct) and "lac" gesture,
in the context of loving without fault/without ceasing, toward a female
speaker in a fabliau vein, such as the wives in Chaucer's "Shipman's Tale"
and "Merchant's Tale," or even the Wife of Bath? Being able to read the *I* as
either/or, both/and, Bride/Chaucerian-sort-of-wife adds richness. Similarly,
a possibility I noted earlier, that line 4 might be ironic, also deserves consideration: not just "I *cannot* be as 'white' as you are" but also "maybe *you* are
not as 'white' as you *think* you are."[51] If that line *is* ironic, the inbuilt normativity of whiteness, which is present in the Song of Songs, too—I am black
but beautiful—gets breathtakingly turned on its head.

Amid such ambiguities, fidelity is central to the poem's strongest anxieties, as evidenced by its lingering and recursive recourse to truth claims that
persist throughout, insistently—*believe me, I'm telling the truth—no, really.*
That unease about being heard (or not), being believed (or not), being accurately recognized (or not) is of a piece with the foundational claim of au-
thenticity the poem situates in blackness, which comes to seem even more
"true" than normative whiteness. The poem begins by suggesting whiteness
represents purity, whether sexual or faithful ("treu in dede," 11), while the
rest of the poem sets about showing that being "true," a central focus for the
poem, is fundamental to being black, perhaps *more* fundamental than it is
to being white.

I have not yet directly confronted the question that for modern readers
is central: does "blac" refer to skin color?[52] Robbins, who called the poem
"In Praise of Brunettes," did not think so. However, the poem's contrast color
does not match for hair color: Middle English *white* would describe gray hair

but the poem is not interested in age. Present Day English *blond* would be Middle English *yelwe*, *gold*, *fair*, or possibly *blo*. Moreover, hair color does not explain many perplexities posed by the poem. Stanza 4, for example, begins with the image that seems least pertinent to *hair* color, "Wind and water may stain the white" (line 13), yet might evoke *cloth* (in line with the "hat" and "hood" of stanza 2) even as it more likely suggests the poet is talking about *skin* color, darkened by exposure to the elements over time.[53]

Beyond the ordinary effects of suntanning or weathering, medieval physiognomists believed that climate affected skin color, which was thought to be genetic but also environmentally and culturally or socially influenced.[54] For example, according to Albert the Great, moving to a colder climate could, over a few generations, turn dark skin light.[55] Skin color is also used in romance and elsewhere as an indicator of moral or ethical status, or even as a marker of Christianity. Some works whitewash black characters when they are converted to Christianity, so their skin turns from black to white, again reinforcing the normativity of whiteness, especially in a religious context.[56]

So, if blackness in "Summe men sayoun" does denote skin color in some fashion, a range of interpretations are possible: darkened by the sun (which corresponds with the Song of Songs), naturally dark (whether "racially" or otherwise), dark because of the humors (melancholic) or from sin. Skin color is not straightforward. Blackness frequently has a pejorative connotation in medieval commentaries on the Song of Songs and more broadly, since medieval writers often associate blackness with sin and the devil. Yet, Bernard of Clairvaux strikingly and positively envisions Christ as black, glossing Christ's blackness as his humanity.[57] There is also a long history of white male considerations of black female sexuality imagined in bodily terms, of which Bernard of Clairvaux's *Sermons on the Song of Songs* is only one example.[58]

These treatments were often misogynistic. The notion of a black woman doing "as good a service" as a white one at serving and in bed may look different in this light, especially given that the imagery links back to line 3 of the first stanza, where the *I* claims to be generous and not deficient in loving, even if/though? s/he is not white. But then the Song of Songs, however glossed, makes salient an approving reading—black is beautiful. In general, as Cord Whitaker says, "to be black is, in the European Middle Ages, to be other," while for Bernard of Clairvaux, as Bruce Holsinger puts it, "the color of salvation is white."[59] Bernard nevertheless went out of his way to describe Christ as black, where blackness positively represents Christ's humanity, which is, precisely, what makes *him* human, like *us*. Whitaker further shows how, in *The King of Tars,* "the black hound speaking 'in manhede' evokes Christ's Incarnation," his taking on humanity to become one of us.[60]

Wymundus London?

Thus far I have focused on close reading. What can we learn from this manuscript? As I noted earlier, Gonville and Caius MS 383/603 appears to be written by an Oxford student, perhaps Wymundus London. Richard Leighton Greene has suggested Wymundus London is "the 'London' and 'w London' whose name occurs regularly in the bursary books of Magdalen College, Oxford"; he cites A. B. Emden, *A Biographical Register of the University of Oxford to A.D. 1500.* Emden's entry in full is: "London, W . . . Magdalen Coll., demy in 1485 [Magd. Coll. Bursary Book, i, fos. 51v, 57; Bloxam, iv. 24; Macray, i.180]."[61] The first free grammar school in Oxford, Magdalen College School was founded in 1480.[62] First a chorister, then made a demy in 1485, this W. London might naturally have had an interest in song. A "demy" was a poor undergraduate scholar between the ages of twelve and twenty-five. The statutes of Magdalen College called for thirty of them; they were to become "competently instructed in reading, and plain singing" and would be taught grammar before proceeding to logic and sophistry.[63] While a Magdalen provenance would give useful context to the manuscript's focus on grammar, *dictamen,* and song, Greene's identification is tenuous, though tantalizing.[64] The poem might well have been composed earlier. There is no evidence that whoever compiled Gonville and Caius MS 383/603, especially if a student, was the poet, and very few manuscripts from this period are autograph (written out by the author).

Whoever copied these verses seems to have had a special interest in song. The manuscript's vernacular songs, especially the bawdy ones, have received the most attention, though the manuscript's grammatical material and specimens of letters (*dictamen*) have also been noted, particularly the specially legalized letters in French as well as Latin, and information on drawing up charters.[65] With the exception of "Summe men sayoun," the manuscript's English verses are all carols, written out as prose and packed tightly together on several pages scattered throughout the manuscript, with some indication of their music, whether by the first words of the song whose tune they would be sung to or where the music is written out (see Figure 9).[66]

Perhaps "Summe men sayoun" is a carol that is missing its refrain, since all the other lyrics, including the French one, are carols. Three of these carols are bawdy; all three have female subjects. The fact that the same person

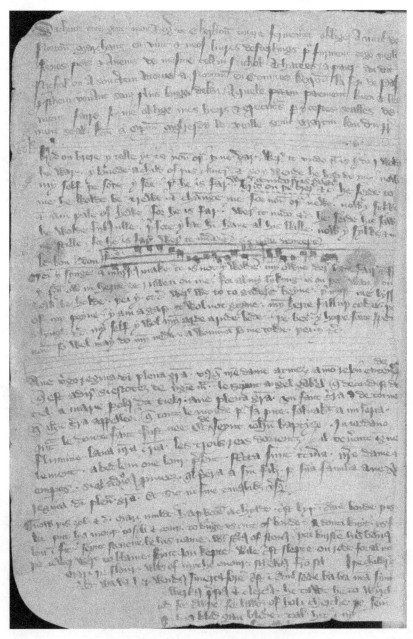

Figure 9. Cambridge, Gonville and Caius College MS 383/603, p. 210,
with "Bryd on brere."

Reproduced by kind permission of the Master and Fellows of Gonville and Caius College, Cambridge.

copied both these and "Summe men sayoun" might be evidence for a female subject for "Summe men sayoun," too, if this is a collection of a certain
sort.[67] Nevertheless, there are strictly religious carols in the manuscript,
as well.

What are we to make of the singularity of "Summe men sayoun," the
only poem on its leaf? Lines scribed above and below mark out its space,
with each line of verse occupying a line on the page. It is written in two
columns, with rhymes indicated and rubricated, except for that last stanza,
which is oddly positioned, so may have been added in later—while its rhymes
are indicated, they are not rubricated (see Figure 8). Since "Summe men sayoun" is isolated on its page, untypical in many ways, and enigmatic in its
message, it can be hard to know just how to place it.

("Pepyr be blac")

The poem's grammatical surround deserves attention, too. If the final stanza
is a late addition, the poem might originally have ended on the most memorable stanza, the pepper one. Stanza 5 elaborates on a proverb found in many
grammar school exercises for proper translation of Latin to English and vice
versa, as in, for example: "Thow pepyr be blacke hyt hathe a gode smake /
Niger rugosum quamvis piper est preciosum."[68] Though the English in extant examples is largely the same, the Latin varies considerably, which suggests the English proverb was used for the making of "Latins," improvised
Latin sentences generated from an English prompt.[69]

Given the proverb's ubiquity and fixed English form, it is notable that
the poem does something quite a bit more interesting, *rejecting* color—both
black and white!—in favor of taste ("smac"), whereas the grammar sentences
embrace the color. This rejection is worth setting alongside the strong de-
lineation of difference in debate poems. "Summe men sayoun" takes a stance
that seems oppositional in the manner of a debate poem (black vs. white),
creating *we*'s and *I*'s and *you*'s of communities and belongings in the process, but from its first line blurs dichotomies to question the very nature of
such oppositions. The poem elaborates on the rejection, introducing the
imagery of inner and outer, which might again suggest feminization and a
sexual context, reinforcing the normativity of whiteness (*don't worry—it's
white inside*) while elevating blackness (*it hath a good smac!*) and then dis-
missing them both (*forget the color!*), all the while giving the sense of a real
person saying something a bit saucy and breezily dismissive.[70]

The parallel structure of "without it is" and "within it is" takes the central position within the first two lines of the stanza, which give medial weight to the contrast. It would be easy to imagine these lines spoken by the Wife of Bath, though, again, nothing here inherently indicates the *I* is female. Moreover, the feminizing inner-and-outer language also parallels imagery used in devotional texts to model the experience of contemplation, often describing a walnut but sometimes fruit: peel back the dry outer husk to reveal the tasty inner meat.[71] The black-versus-white imagery is lacking in the walnut example, but the comparison would be salient for a certain kind of reader, much as the proverb would for another sort. Like stanza 1, this stanza reads quite differently if you are more steeped in the Wife of Bath than in devotional texts, and vice versa. It reads differently if it is the last stanza, too. It is worth recalling that the either/or-but-maybe-both/and sacred/secular quality is a hallmark of Middle English lyric, as against its continental contemporaries.

Moreover, the poem's treatment of "Thow pepyr be blacke hyt hathe a gode smake" is very like another sort of grammar school exercise, in which students are invited to elaborate on a concept or image rhetorically and inventively.[72] How delightful would it be for someone who knows the work of sweating your way through your *latinitates* to recognize the stanza's proverbial source, and that it had been played with and extended? In her discussion of the alliterative poem "A Complaint Against Blacksmiths," for example, Elizabeth Salter points to "a fifteen-line 'exercise' on the activities of blacksmiths engaged in the making of armour" in Geoffrey of Vinsauf's *Poetria Nova*, a passage, she notes, that "is designed to illustrate one of the 'difficult ornaments' of style: the metaphorical use of verbs by transposition from their original human context to that of inanimate objects."[73] Something similar might be happening here, too; the pepper stanza could readily be imagined as an exercise analogous to the elaborations students were asked to perform as they learned rhetoric, or the amplifications and alterations involved in riddle-making.

So, "Summe men sayoun" may have an academic playfulness of several types to it, born of a learned culture, much as Old English and Latin riddles do, though in another way. In its manuscript, it is found nestled among precisely the sort of grammatical texts that might have helped to produce it.

("y am blac")

Where does all this leave us? To return to the two questions I deferred, who is the *I* of this poem? We do not know, cannot know, and that may be part of the point. In part because "Summe men sayoun" is longer than "Myrie a tyme" and in part because of its more directly riddling stance, a poem such as this rewards deliberative thinking over and rereading through time. What sort of reading makes a thing like this productive? One that privileges multiplicity of sense, for one thing, and that also makes use of recursion. Look again at that second stanza:

> blac ys a colur þat is god
> so say y & many mo
> blac ys my hat blac ys my hod
> blac ys al þat longet þer to
>   (lines 5–8)

It is good poetry. Formalistically, this stanza balances itself through parallelism, alliteration, and a medial pause in the third line of the stanza ("blac ys my hat, blac ys my hod"). That medial pause itself would be particularly salient for someone who was working with proverbs, which often have this kind of formal balance: "Pepper is black, it hath a good smack." In its short, plosive syllable, "blac" punctuates the stanza, so that blackness seems to be everywhere, all around, and inescapable. Similarly, in stanza 4,

> Wynd & watur may steyne þe wyte
> y wis þe blac yt may nat so
> [to] preyse þe blac ys al my delyte
> y am yholde by schyle þer to
>   (lines 13–16)

the alliteration on *w* highlights "white" while "blac" holds the center of both inner lines (14 and 15), placing blackness foundationally in the middle of the stanza. This placement is made the more weighty by the potential enjambment of "y wis," which syntactically could be attached to either the phrase before or the one after it, and both picks up the *w* sound from line 13 and may effect a pause in line 14, highlighting the next stress word ("blac"). "Yholde" in line 16 speaks back to stanza 3's emphasis on fidelity and ethics. The balance of both these stanzas, their weight and ponder, suggests a composer used to the measure of Latin verse, perhaps.

A careful examination of this poem, stanza by stanza, can be both rewarding and exhausting. By contrast, there is a lightness to the poem when read without pause that lets it traverse wide ground without getting bogged down in details. The poem's technique—and the similar obliqueness of many Middle English lyrics, long and short—allows for isolated and immersive consideration of a wide range of topics in various configurations; topics may be engaged or left at will. The nonspecificity of "þer to," for instance, enables a fluidity that could go more than one way and in its vagueness widens the scope of its sense even as it suggests a sort of self-evidence and forward movement.[74] When you read the poem straight through, "blac" really is everywhere in view.[75]

My deeper look begins from blackness and everywhere moves outward to significations, diluting the compressed effect of blackness. The simultaneous tightness and looseness of how "Summe men sayoun" treats blackness, or "þer to," could usefully be considered temporal in a similar way to the "strophic" patterns Christopher Cannon elsewhere in this book discerns in *King Horn*. While there is less narrative impetus in "Summe men sayoun" than in *King Horn*, can we also say, in a way, that "events presented as if unfolding in time are also continually folded back on one another in language, as if their movement is not in fact progressive but the winding of a gyre"?[76]

The elusiveness of blackness in "Summe men sayoun," it seems to me, taps into a number of the ways in which Middle English lyric seems alien, harder to grasp the sense of than its medieval French or Italian and even many modern counterparts; less personal, while it seems assured and declarative, though what, precisely, it is declaring can sometimes be hard to say. "Summe men sayoun þat y am blac," we know, BUT, the poem seems to query, are you one of them? Or, channeling and perhaps feminizing Langston Hughes long before his time, are *you* black like *me*?[77]

Readings

Present-day readers cannot know how whoever wrote down "Summe men sayoun" in Gonville and Caius 383/603 read the poem (if this person was not the poet), nor what this person thought about it. Yet, this person had an evident interest in music and song, and perhaps we can glean further insights from that, insights that apply more broadly to my earlier suggestion that we might think of Middle English lyric as cognitive, participatory, and communal. In my close reading, I evoked the recursive aspect of ruminative interpretation, in solitude and silence, and it might seem like performed song would offer the opposite effect. Performance is a process in time; a carol, for example, when sung, must proceed from a beginning to an end. Yet, there will be elements of recursion; the joint singing of the refrain, most obviously, but others as well: musical, metrical, linguistic, thematic. A melismatic musical setting such as for the carol "Ther is no rose of swych vertu" may linger over some or all words, offering new and renewed opportunities to ponder relationships—between the first half of a verse and the second, between this line and that one, between a top melodic line and a bottom one, between one experience of a refrain and the next.[78] Such recursive elements engage what Seamus Heaney in another context termed the "law of increasing returns," because repetitions, instead of diminishing sense by emptying a refrain (for example) until it no longer holds any meaning, can enhance meaning by building on contexts layered over time.[79] Heaney's "law of increasing returns" would apply to recursions such as metaphor or the repeated use of a single word, underdetermined and therefore overfull, as is the case with "blac."

Experienced through communal dance and song, a carol is nevertheless generically predisposed to prompt carolers to *feel* the overlay of "each of us" and "all of us" because it is a *group* endeavor, kinetically enacted through breath and gesture.[80] Medieval reading was often similarly communal and voiced rather than silent and solitary, as Joyce Coleman and others have shown.[81] Roughly analogous modern practices might be poetry readings, performances, concerts. As the refrain to a different carol proclaims: "Nowel syng we bothe al and som!"[82] and the "al and som" of performed song may be most readily *felt* at the transitions into and out of the refrain, perhaps. Similarly, it seems to me, Middle English lyric opens up a space within itself for the experiential work of reading, such that experience of time—of thought over time, whether prompted by rereading or by recursions of performance or of song—is, indeed, part of its form.[83]

Such a mode of reading is prompted by a poem such as "Summe men sayoun" or "A God and yet a man," with which I began. As I noted there, this poem concludes with a line that predominantly—though not exclusively—suggests a closing down of thought: "Beleeve and leave [cease] to wonder!" Yet, this lyric deliberately and explicitly *opens up* a process of thought as it models wonderment itself. Even as it points toward the wondrous, the verse enacts and embraces a mode of reading that is intellectual and participatory:

Witt wonders what witt Can
Conceave this or the other.

The poem permits readers to wonder—indeed, prompts them to do so—even as it suggests a potential moment of thought in future in which we might begin to feel we could *know* rather than wonder about what we *do not* know. If part of the work of Middle English lyric is investigatory, in Aquinas's philosophical sense—a seeking of a first cause—that might help in part to explain why such a large number of these poems are devotional.[84]

My thought experiment proposed that we should read Middle English lyric as if we do not know when we come to such "things" what they are or what they mean to do. Present-day readers ought especially to seek to think them through, insofar as we can, on what might be their own terms. This approach ties in with medieval thought about wonder, one branch of which posits wonder as exploratory (while another posits that wonder prompts *admiratio*). Part of the working of these poems might be *that* we bring of ourselves to them. Perhaps these sorts of poems are not complete in themselves but require readerly participation, and readers contemporary to them would have known that. Experiential reading both brings present-day readers to a new understanding and can prompt admiration of how we got there. The deeper my reading of "Summe men sayoun," the more interpretative possibilities presented themselves. Increasingly it became evident that the poem has particular claims upon its reader—are you with me or against me?—that are framed rather subtly. These claims are not obvious without an inquisitive, participatory sort of reading, but they exemplify medieval interest in and use of collective subjectivity. The *work* of a poem such as this one lies in that experience of seeking, rather than in any singular solution to the riddle. This is true of riddle poems of all sorts, of course, yet it also seems to be true of Middle English lyric that is *not* a riddle, more broadly. Perhaps this is because the polyvalent potential of Middle English itself is exploited by these "things." Unlike in Latin, in Middle English it can be hard to tell what part of speech many words are, both within and out of context, let alone which of many possible meanings they point to, and skilled writers can amplify such ambiguities in their poetry or thought experiments. If, as I have suggested, the work of Middle English lyric is often the work of wonder, then we do well to be keenly alive to the ways in which Middle English words (*blac, broun, blo, leave*) slide and expand through further exploration. Rather than narrowing down meaning, they open it up when we give ourselves leave to give ourselves over to even subtle workings of such "things."

Chapter 3

Lyric Romance

CHRISTOPHER CANNON

What is the poem usually now called *King Horn* doing in the book now cata-loged as London, British Library, Harley MS 2253? This is not a question that book necessarily poses since it seems to have gathered writings of every kind. In fact, Harley 2253 is something like a survey of literary possibility in the early part of the fourteenth century in England, since it contains fa-bliau, satire, comic and biblical fable, debate, interlude, proverb collection, conduct guide, and pilgrim guide in all three of the literary languages in wide use (French and Latin as well as English).[1] For a long time literary his-tory ignored this whole, however, and from Joseph Ritson's *Ancient Songs, from the Time of King Henry the Third, to the Revolution* (1790) onward, only its short poems attracted real interest. Carleton Brown's *English Lyrics of the XIIIth Century* (1932) ensured that these short poems were foundational texts for the emergent category of the "English lyric."[2] G. L. Brook's se-lection of thirty-two of them for a slim edition transformed them into "the Harley lyrics" (1948), and from this point on these short poems also came to represent the Middle English lyric quintessentially.[3] Very large claims were made for the historical significance of these few poems (the "only substan-tial body of English secular love-poetry before Chaucer" that survives) and their "individualized voiced feelings" were praised as the closest Middle En-glish ever got to the "self-expression of subjective life" that Hegel had said constituted lyricism itself.[4] Thus, when the *Manual of the Writings in Middle English* arrived at its survey of the lyric as a Middle English genre, it did not even bother with the other short poems in the language but confined its survey to "the lyrics of Harley MS 2253" alone.[5] It is in the context of this slow but firm conflation of the Harley lyrics and that thing we now call Middle English lyric that it is surprising to find a poem as long as *King Horn* (at 1,544 lines, it is ten times longer than any of the poems in Brook's edition), sitting cheek by jowl with these lyrics in this manuscript's fifth "booklet," the gathering of the manuscript from which almost all of these lyrics were taken.[6]

But would the compiler of Harley 2253 have distinguished *King Horn* from the "Harley lyrics"? The *Manual of the Writings in Middle English* puts *King Horn* in volume 1 as "the earliest extant romance" of those that "seem to have been derived from Anglo-Norman models," and it is a poem that is generally said to be the "earliest Middle English romance" as such.[7] *Horn* was not, however, grouped with the other texts we now call "romances" in its day: it survives in two other manuscripts besides Harley 2253, and, in one of them, Oxford, Bodleian Library, MS Laud Misc. 108, it seems to have been included alongside the *South English Legendary* because, just like those saints' lives, it celebrates an exemplary figure.[8] Francis J. Child found the central episode of *Horn* (what he called its "catastrophe") in a ballad popular enough to survive in eight versions.[9] Although it was common enough both in antiquity and in Middle English to describe the recitation of any verse as "singing," because the lyric has always been particularly associated with music it seems a defining fact that the Harley lyrics describe themselves as songs (e.g., "I syke when Y singe" [2:270–73, *Digital Index of Middle English Verse* (*DIMEV*) 2279]), and yet, *King Horn* understands itself to be a song too ("Alle beon he blithe / That to my song lythe! / A sang ich schal you singe / Of Murry the Kinge" [1–4]).[10] And even though it unfolds for most of its length as the story of King Murry, his wife, and their extraordinary son, Horn ("King he was biweste / So longe so hit laste. / Godhild het his quen; / Faire ne mighte non ben" [5–8]), just like the Harley lyrics, *King Horn* begins in the first person ("ich schal you singe") before absorbing the "I" into the first person plural at the poem's end ("Yeve us alle His swete blessing" [1544]). In the intervening cyclical narrative Horn is banished from the kingdom of his birth (Suddene) by "Saracens," finds love in the kingdom of King Aylmer ("Westernesse"), proves himself in the kingdom of King Thurston (Ireland), and then returns to claim the hand of Aylmer's daughter, Rymenhild, but if, as Brook insisted, the "Harley lyrics" were characterized by their "expression" of the "characteristics" of "courtly love," this narrative is about nothing so much as "love," and the knightly endeavors that prove it, at "court" ("Horn in herte laghte / Al that he him taghte. / In the curt and ute" [247–49]).[11]

Brook was a collector of books himself, and so not unaware of the power of selection to make classifying claims, and he recognized from the start that "Harley lyric" was an awkward shorthand since "other Harleian manuscripts contain lyrics."[12] The "Harley lyric" is, nonetheless, a classic instance of what Virginia Jackson has called "lyricization," a process whereby "the notion of lyric [is] enlarged in direct proportion to the diminution of the varieties of poetry" that surround it, and an entirely "new concept" (the definition of the Harley lyric in this case) is "artificially treated to appear old," so that (again, in this case) the poems in booklet 5 of Harley 2253 other than its short poems are never even allowed to register as part of what is still presented as a historical category.[13] If the compiler of Harley 2253 put *King Horn* in the same gathering as what we have come to call the Harley lyrics because he saw it as somehow lyrical, then, the two questions I have so far posed necessarily contain two more. Even though "lyric" has been, both before and since the Middle English period, "the default term for short poems," could a Middle English lyric, like *King Horn*, be *long*?[14] This length might seem to be a function of the variety of actions the poem narrates, a characteristic Harley 2253 itself notices by describing it, in the rubric that precedes it, as a "geste" ("an action" or, by extension, "a poem about deeds").[15] In Hegel's formulation, lyric was defined by "inwardness" as opposed to "action," and recent definitions of the lyric have tended to define the form, as above all, "non-narrative."[16] But could a Middle English lyric, like *King Horn*, be *narrative*?

Literary history has already provided us with a number of categories to answer such questions if we want to do no more than say that *King Horn* resembled a lyric or manifested some of its qualities. There is, for example, the "lyrico-narrative," a term coined to describe the *Roman de la Rose* and other long poems that substitute "private, imaginative, affective experience" for "military and social exploits."[17] There are Paul Zumthor's *chant narratif* (narrative song) and *récit chanté* (sung narrative), the first referring to short poems that provide frames (*cadres narratifs*) for personal discourse, the second to sung stories such as the chanson de geste.[18] Although unique in using the term, *Aucassin et Nicolette* describes its own alternation of verse (in *laisses*) and prose as a "song-story," or *cantefable*.[19] As Andrew Galloway shows elsewhere in this book, the qualities we might attribute to lyric and narrative are often so tightly woven in medieval instances that it is impossible to disentangle them.[20] And the necessary correction to Brook's narrow definition of the "Harley lyric" might seem to have already occurred in scholarship on Middle English when Derek Pearsall described *King Horn* as a "lyric romance," "ballad-like" in its close "concentration on the dramatic moment, abrupt transitions, internally dependent repetition, and a cryptic allusiveness of episodic reference" that "demand the heightened alertness of response which one associates with song."[21]

I want to suggest in what follows, however, that, if the term "lyric romance" can expose some of the ways in which *King Horn* is like a lyric, it can also help us interrogate more deeply what we might understand (or define) both Middle English lyric and Middle English romance to be. *King Horn* may not have been included in booklet 5 of Harley 2253 because it was a song, but it fits there, I will argue, because Middle English romances are much more songlike than we customarily recognize when we view them as narratives. Placing a narrative of the particularly cyclical kind unfolded in *King Horn* next to the Harley lyrics shows, in a similar fashion, how difficult it is to distinguish poems by the quantity of their actions or the number of lines it takes to narrate them. Ardis Butterfield has observed that the sheer variety of medieval English texts that could be called "lyric" make the category something like an "ungenre," and I follow Butterfield here by insisting that the boundaries of "Middle English lyric" and "Middle English romance" alike have been drawn too narrowly.[22] "Lyric romance" is most useful as a term, then, not because it newly identifies some kind of Middle English text, but because it provides an analytic category that puts the modern distinction between two genres under scrutiny, as well as the characteristics thought to define and distinguish them.

Middle English Romance as Song

Paul de Man insisted that the "hermeneutics of the lyric" depend on the "phenomenalization of the poetic voice."[23] If so, then *King Horn* is a lyric to the extent that it begins, as I noted above, as a song ("A sang ich schal you singe"), but so too, as a rule, do most Middle English romances, since they are among the many kinds of texts that, as I noted above, also begin with this gesture. Even the closest Middle English analogue to *King Horn, Horn Childe and Maiden Rimnild,* begins with an *I* who proposes to perform the text that follows (adding a second person plural to that *I* immediately, thereby convening the audience who will attend to this performance):

Mi leue frende dere,
Herken & ȝe may here
& ȝe wil vnderstonde,

Stories ȝe may lere
Of our elders þat were
Whilom in þis lond.[24]

The other text uniformly characterized as a romance that accompanies *King Horn* in MS Laud Misc. 108, *Havelok the Dane*, also presents itself as an oral form:

Herkneth to me, gode men—
Wives, maydnes, and alle men—
Of a tale that ich you wile telle,
Wo so it wile here and therto dwelle.[25]

Such a stance must look rhetorical at this distance, but it almost certainly absorbed the performance conditions of these poems. As Joyce Coleman has shown us, "aurality" was a normal condition for the reception of Middle English texts of all kinds well into the fifteenth century, when authors, clerks, and both aristocratic women as well as men regularly performed or "prelected" them in public.[26] And, while it has been common to see minstrels as useful only when literature was performed for the illiterate, yielding fully to private reading when vernacular texts were circulated in writing, it is clear that minstrels were still disseminating Middle English romance well into the fourteenth century.[27] Indeed, the booklet of MS Laud Misc. 108 that contains *Horn* and *Havelok* resembles the kind of small volume a minstrel might have "packed into his saddlebag."[28] Whether or not Laud Misc. 108 was actually used in this way, the performances the poems it contains claim to record would have been authenticated by the minstrels who were clearly still at work performing poems around the time it was copied.[29] In fact, there were enough such minstrels at the beginning of the fourteenth century for Robert Mannyng to need to insist that his *Chronicle* (1338) was definitely not the production of such "disours."[30] John Gower is still imagining feasts in which a "menstral" and a "disour" perform at the end of the fourteenth century.[31] When describing *King Horn* as a "geste," the scribe of Harley 2253 may even have meant to identify it as a minstrel's production since William Langland says that what "japeris and jogelours and jangleris" recited were "gestes," just as Chaucer thought that it was "gestours" who recited "tales" in *The House of Fame* and "The Tale of Sir Thopas."[32] Middle English romances sometimes specifically identified the voices they phenomenalized ("As I here synge in songe") as those of "menstrelles that walken fer and wyde."[33]

Bibliographers have worked hard to identify more of the books such minstrels would have used, but, aside from Laud Misc. 108, only one other candidate has ever been found, Oxford, Bodleian Library, MS Douce 228, a small paper volume, so poorly produced that it seems to have been carried around by an owner who also wrote out its texts on its unruled pages.[34] Middle English romances are often so formulaic in their diction it has been suggested that they were composed orally.[35] But proof of that process is equally hard to come by, and where we have the sources for a heavily formulaic text such as *Bevis of Hamtoun*, it is clear that its author "was working with a written text before him."[36] Nevertheless, a text composed by writing could still have been transmitted orally by minstrels who learned it by heart, and the extant copies of even the most carefully translated romances bear all the hallmarks of such circulation.[37] A couplet in two different copies of the Middle English *Bevis* often conveys exactly the same meaning but in different words and with different rhymes. Here, for example, are the same two lines, first as they appear in the Auchinleck manuscript (Edinburgh, National Library of Scotland, MS Advocates' 19.2.1), next as they appear in Cambridge, Cambridge University Library, MS Ff.2.38:

> "God þe blesse, sire!" Beues sede,
> "Siȝe þe eni leuedi her forþ lede."

> "Crystys blessyng mote þe betyde
> Siȝe þe eni wumman þys way ryde"[38]

If these two versions of the text were dictated (or represent copies of versions that were dictated), either the decision to attribute the blessing to Bevis in the Auchinleck manuscript ("Beues sede") meant that the minstrel reciting that version had to say "lede" instead of "ryde" to complete the rhyme, or the minstrel reciting the version in the Cambridge manuscript, having stripped away the speech attribution ("sede"), had to alter "lede" to find a rhyme for "betyde." Whatever the direction of the changes—and these two versions may, of course, conceal alternative readings in copies now lost to us—they are not scribal misprision but invention; they do not misconstrue letter or word shapes but render the same meaning in entirely new words.

The divergences in the seven surviving texts of *Bevis* follow this logic to such a degree—cleaving to sense but varying by as much as every word in a given line—that Albert Baugh was clear that these texts could be nothing other than a record of "recitations of minstrels."[39]

Different copies of some of the other long romances from the early fourteenth century, such as *Guy of Warwick* and *Richard Coer de Lyon*, bear the same traces of oral transmission, but it is the three surviving texts of *King Horn* that are particularly marked by such traits. As James Hurt characterized these versions, "Although all three adhere closely to the same sequence of events, they differ so much in detail that it is hard to find a single line that is exactly the same in all three."[40] A set of witnesses that derive from very different copying traditions may produce such results. Joseph Hall believed that the extant texts of *Horn* descended from a common source that had been so corrupted in the process of transmission that each copy had to be "rewritten" by its scribe.[41] Hurt felt that the dating of the manuscripts made it unlikely that these texts were records of oral performance, since the copy in the Cambridge manuscript (University Library, MS Gg.4.27 or "C") was made fifty years after the copies in either Harley 2253 (L) or Laud Misc. 108 (O).[42] If no one minstrel could have dictated all three manuscripts, each one could still have been dictated by a *different* minstrel or the ancestors to any or all of the texts could have been transmitted orally. Certainly no relationship can be construed between these texts on the basis of common error: Hall proposed a stemma, but it serves no obvious purpose since extant manuscripts are only ever related to hypothesized progenitors, and Hall does not edit the text at all but, rather, prints all three texts in parallel.[43] As the following passage from these texts shows well, despite the significant variation in diction and line arrangement, the events of the narrative remain stable across all versions (here, as Horn and his companions are exiled after a Saracen invasion), as does the scaffolding of rhyme.[44]

L	O	C
þe children ede to þe stronde	Þe childre yede to stronde	Þe children hi broȝte to stronde
wryngynde huere honde	Wringende here honde	Wringinde here honde
ant in to shipes borde		In to schupes borde
at þe furste worde		At þe furste worde.
ofte hade horn be wo	Ofte hauede horn child be wo	Ofte hadde horn beo wo

ah neuer wors þen him wes þo.	Bute neuere werse þan þo	At neure wurs þan him was þo.
	Horn yede in to þe shipes bord	
	Sone at þe firste word	
	And alle hise feren	
	Þat ware him lef and dere	
þe see bygon to flowen	Þe se bigan to flowen	Þe se bigan to flowe
& horn faste to rowen.	And horn faste to rowen	& horn child to rowe;
(115–22)	(117–26)	(111–18)

There is one error that looks like a problem with transcription or a misreading ("be" for "wo") while all the consequential differences between these texts are at the level of the couplet, which seem able to wander *en bloc*. Some of that movement can be seen within the confines of the lines I have quoted, since the second couplet in L and C (rhyming "borde/worde") becomes the fourth couplet in O. But even the couplet that seems to vanish from O ("And alle hise feren / Þat ware him lef and dere") turns up again in L and C in more or less the same form a hundred lines later (as "& alle his yfere / þat him were so duere" [L 227–28] and "& alle his ifere / Þat were him so dere" [C 221–22]).

Such movement is exactly what we might expect of a minstrel who had memorized a text such as *Horn* in which rhyme yoked each line with another one while leaving any such pair free to wander in relation to all the other pairs, particularly to the extent that a couplet described a general rather than a particular action or setting. George Kane thought that "compression at one point and expansion at another" was one of the telltale characteristics of oral transmission. To these he added "a marked unevenness in the accuracy of production" of the kind, I think, we find on display in the passage below where the first and last couplets are reproduced "accurately" in each text but the "inaccurate" couplet between them conveys exactly the same information but in different words (and therefore with different rhymes).[45]

L	O	C
day is gon & oþer	Day igo and oþer	Dai hit is igon & oþer:
wiþ oute seyl & roþer	Wit uten seyl and roþer	Wiþute sail & roþer
vre ship flet forþ ylome	And hure schip suemne gan	Vre schip bigan to swymme

& her to londe hit ys ycome	And he to londe it wan	To þis londes brymme.
Nou þou myht vs slen & bynde	Nou men us binde	Nu þu miȝt vs slen & binde,
oure honde vs bihynde	Oure honden us bi hinden	Ore honde bihynde
(195–200)	(197–202)	(187–92)

Hall and Hurt would have to insist that the second rhyming pair in each of these texts is an error in transmission, but the differences never confound meaning and are often inspired (having a ship "swim" rather than "go," describing a journey as "winning" through to a destination, and a shore as a "brim"). The accumulation of differences of this kind across all three versions of *Horn* makes it generally true that these texts differ on the whole in treatment rather than meaning. Rhyme words provide the easiest way to trace this phenomenon comprehensively: C shares 658 of its 765 rhymes with both L and O and an additional 73 with one of the other texts; of the roughly 1,500 lines of the poem, 1,170 are shared across all versions. These could certainly be characterized as "radical divergences" between the texts (as Hurt describes them), but inasmuch as "all three [texts] adhere closely to the same sequence of events," these could also be described as a narrative convergence, as even Hall accepts, three very different ways of telling exactly the same story in rhyme.[46]

The extent to which *King Horn* was transmitted orally would have been invisible in any single copy the compiler of Harley 2253 had before him, and there is no reason to assume that he did not take his text from a written exemplar. But romances were clearly disseminated orally with enough frequency to authenticate any claim a romance might make to be an oral form. A French analogue for *King Horn*, the *Romance of Horn*, gestures toward the alternative since its very first lines insist on the written text, or the "parchment," that precedes the oral performance it pretends to be ("Signurs, oi avez les vers del parchemin, / Cum li bers Aaluf est venuz a sa fin" [Lords, you have heard the verses on parchment, telling how the noble Aaluf met his end]).[47] *King Horn*'s claim that it is a "song" was probably just as accurate an account of the way its lines made it onto the pages the compiler of Harley 2253 copied. It rightly begins by insisting it is a lyric because it was clearly, frequently, recited or "sung."

The Tempo of Narrative

Literary historians of French poetry have focused much more on the relationship between song and narrative than historians of Middle English because a host of thirteenth-century French texts are characterized by "lyric insertion," the embedding of recognizable lyric forms in verse narrative (rather than in prose, as with *Aucassin and Nicolette*).[48] Rather than a "crumbling of lyric into narrative," writers of such forms maintained a "keen sense of boundary" around these lyrics.[49] Modern theories of the lyric describe certain mixtures of narrative and lyric too, particularly in the dilation of dramatic monologue or the "lyric sequence . . . in which a broad narrative is discernable."[50] These distinctions also assume, however, that the lyric is generally a "still life" that captures a particular moment or state in which "movement is not consecutive but is, rather, heaped or layered."[51] Since sequential narratives in Middle English such as *King Horn* were sung, it also seems right to ask: could a Middle English lyric be such a narrative?

The distinction might even be said to turn on quantities of action whereby a "Harley lyric" is above all a song in which there might be some hint of activity but that activity is never detailed. "Annot and John," for example, fixes the "lady in a bower" ("burde in a bour"), and then, as an extended act of praise (or love) compares her static form, stanza by stanza, to jewels, flowers, birds, and, finally, to a sequence of famous women (2:120–23, *DIMEV* 2324). Such a lyric "pulls itself out of the narrative temporality of past event and into the distinctive space of lyric present," while *King Horn* puts an admired woman (Rymenhild) at the center of action that spans three kingdoms as she is wooed, abandoned, and then finally married off, while battles with a sequence of invaders (including a giant) rage round her.[52] There are, however, ways of thinking about the lyric present of a poem such as "Annot and John" that focus on the activity of *thought* it unfolds. Jacques Lacan called such activity "logical time" and illustrated it by means of a single, hypothetical event that was nonetheless prompted by the sequence of "comprehension," "meditation," and "conclusion" that, however quickly they followed one another, could only logically occur in succession.[53] A lyric such as "Annot and John" might be said to have a "resolutely non-narrative character" but still have something it is right to call a "non-narrative temporality," whereby what unfolds, stanza by stanza, may be the apprehension of an instant but is nonetheless also a sequence of thought in which a comparison of the woman's value to gems leads to a comparison of her body with the various colors of flowers, from which the speaker is led to the birds that give sound to the floral scene, and the smells of the spices that grow in it, and, finally, to complete the synesthetic tour (of sight, sound, and smell), to a list of the women who, like Annot, could be touched.[54] Neither Annot nor the speaker may move an inch in the course of this comparison, but, in this view, the ratiocination produces such detail as something like a story.

Narrative might also be understood as a function of the relationship between a "temporal dimension" (the span of time narrated) and a "spatial dimension" (the words required to narrate that span) whereby the distinction between a "Harley lyric" and *King Horn* is not to be understood as a function of the number of events narrated or even their quality but of what Gérard Genette called narrative "speed."[55] In this view, the temporality of any poem lies on a continuum from the full stop of a "descriptive pause" to the "durational realism" that Sartre likened to a "toboggan," hurling the reader into events that unfold on the page as if in real time.[56] This continuum can be neatly parceled up into four distinct modes: "We can say that a narrative, whatever it is, may tell once what happened once, n times what happened n times, n times what happened once, once what happened n times."[57] This scheme is complicated by mood (which allows for duration to be hypothetical) and progressive tenses (which allow events to be ongoing), but these gradations can substitute a much more nuanced ratio (of words to event) for a simple measurement of contents, collapsing the distinction we tend to make between lyric and narrative into a variety of narrative tempos.[58]

To see that narratives of any length may vary drastically in speed in this way also makes it easy to see how some of the Harley lyrics can be construed as narrative however slow the tempo of that narrative might be. The lyric usually called "Bytuene Mersh ant Averil" (2:122–27, *DIMEV* 842), for example, is punctuated throughout by the lyric pause of a refrain in praise of "Alisoun" ("An hendy hap Ichabbe yhent! / . . . / From alle wymmen mi love is lent / Ant lyht on Alysoun"), but it also posits a definite moment on the calendar in its first stanza ("bytuene Mersh ant Averil") and locates a set of events in that season (it is when plants sprout and birds mate); if the next stanza begins by dwelling on Alisoun's beauties in another lyric pause, it then extends its account far into the future should Alisoun fail to return the speaker's affection ("bote he me wolle to hire take") when he will give her up ("Ichulle forsake"); the third stanza moves through time iteratively, describing how the speaker feels every night ("nihtes"); and the last stanza moves into a future beyond the descriptive pauses of the first two stanzas and the iterative longing of the third, since the speaker now declares himself to be "worn out" ("forwake") by the passion in which the previous stanzas have fixed him (although he is still appealing to Alisoun to yield, he recognizes that he cannot suffer "evermore").[59] Genette would say that the first stanza of "Bytuene Mersh ant Averil" narrates what happens once once, the second and third stanzas narrate what happens *n* times once, the last stanza narrates what happens once once, and the refrain that interleaves itself between these stanzas narrates *n* times what happens once.[60] "Bytuene Mersh ant Averil" does tell a story then, putting even the most static description into sequence in time, "stretching" even the song's long pauses, as Butterfield aptly says of similar examples, into "semi-narrative."[61]

Viewed in these terms *King Horn* may actually appear *less* eventful on the whole than its length promises since its tempo is also variable, sometimes slowing to a stop as many lyrics do, "abbreviating" its song into something we might characterize as "semi-lyric."[62] This slowing is produced most effectively and most often by couplets that are repeated verbatim, usually at some distance from their first use, thereby insisting that a sequence of narrated events is in fact iterative. The plot of *King Horn* is, as I noted above, cyclical, with Horn passing from one kingdom (Suddene), to a second (Westernesse) then to a third (Ireland) before returning in triumph to Westernesse. The couplet that concludes the first of the passages I quoted in parallel above contains the whole of this cyclical pattern of travel in little but it also articulates key moments of this cycle: "The se bigan to flowe / and Horn child to rowe" occurs first at 121–22, when Horn is exiled from Suddene, with a small variation at 1105–6 when Horn returns to Westernesse ("He segh the se flowe / And Horn nowar rowe"), and again, a near repetition at 1517–18, when Horn returns to Suddene to claim his throne. Overlaying this pattern of repetition is a second created by a couplet that is equally summative in emphasizing Horn's achievement, between his travels, in royal courts, with significant changes in the narrative emphasized by the small differences that stand out from the repeated phrases: "The kyng com into halle / Among his knightes alle" (227–28) describes Horn's arrival in Westernesse, Horn's return home to the court after defeating the Saracen invaders ("He verde home into halle, / Among the knightes alle," 629–30), and the king's entrance when he gives Horn Rymenhild's hand and, with it, his kingdom ("The king com into halle / Among his knightes alle," 901–2). Genette would say that these repeated couplets refer *n* times to an event that occurs *n* times, but so self-similar are these couplets in their language that they also insist on the self-similar nature of the events they describe. Although a progression in time underlies each repetition, these couplets create what James Snead has called a "cut," a powerful interruption that turns progression into cyclicity, making it appear as if a narrative is doubling back on itself and therefore, rather than referring *n* times to *n* events, it is referring *n* times to an event that happened only once.[63]

A narrative that is so generally repetitive will, in other words, narrate the same event again and again, and so it might also be described as *strophic* to the extent that its narrative repetitions seem to be formal repetitions that segment a poem (again, as Snead might say, "cut" it) into a sequence of self-same units. The two strophic patterns created by the repeated couplets in *King Horn* overlap as if in a fugue (with the set of strophes on the court beginning before the first on the sea journeys has ended), and that overlap matches form to content, for if the strophes describing the sea journeys that spread Horn's actions across three kingdoms extend throughout the poem, the strophes that describe the court that is the stable center of all Horn's adventures sit at the poem's spatial center. There are, moreover, subsidiary repetitions inside each of these strophic patterns that further segment the narrative and retard its flow. Another pair of couplets provides a near repetition but is probably best described as the repetition of a rhyming pair:

> Ich here foyeles singe
> And that gras him springe.
> (133–34)

> The fole bigan to springe,
> And Horn murie to singe
> (597–98)

In fact, such repetition virtually defines this poem's rhyme scheme, since recurrent rhyming pairs highlight not only the recurrence of key events, objects, actions, and descriptive details, but also their collocation: a "honde" takes possession of the "londe" six times and "alle" enter the "hall" on five occasions (so, two more than in the couplet I have already mentioned). Twelve rhyming pairs occur three times:

anon/gon, borde/worde(s), herte/smerte, riche/iliche, schelde/(y)
felde, sente/wente, soghte/broghte, stille/wille, stonde/lond(e),
honde/stronde, tunde/grunde, there/yere.

And thirty-four rhyming pairs occur twice:

alone/mone, biseche/speche, blithe/swithe, bold/holde, dere/
(i)here, dere/stere, fere/here, feste/geste(s), flode/gode, funde/
grunde, furste/berste, hende/wende, hunde/fonde ("funde"),
husbonde/londe, ifere/dere, king/blessing, knight/mighte,
knighte/nighte, knighte/fighte, londe/stonde, lyve/wyve, nighte/
mighte, pleie/tweie, ringe/yonge, sitte/witte, sonde/londe, stonde/
honde, stronde/londe, turne/murne, two/tho, wende/ende, wende/
schende, wo/tho, yerne/werne.[64]

Such repetition in *King Horn* shows just how lyric Middle English romance
could be, ensuring that events presented as if unfolding in time are also continually folded back on one another in language, as if their movement is not in
fact progressive but the winding of a gyre. Set next to many of the rhymes in
a romance such as *Sir Orfeo,* which also understands itself as a song (a "lai"
made for a harp as "minstrelsy" [gle]), the rhymes of *King Horn* are unusually
repetitive. The composer of *Sir Orfeo* seems to have often understood rhyme
as an opportunity to extend the poem's range of image and topic so its couplets tend toward variety rather than repetition ("gle," for example, is rhymed
with "be," "y-se," and "tre"; "king" is twice rhymed with "thing" but also with
"lording"; "thing" is also rhymed with "harping" and "dancing"). The insistent
repetition of *King Horn* also helps us notice that even a Middle English romance capable of such variation such as *Sir Orfeo* also contains a high proportion of repeated rhyming pairs (alle/halle, blithe/swithe, game/name, thede/
yede).[65] As J. P. Oakden demonstrated long ago, in fact, recurrent phrases or
formulae not only characterize the style of almost all alliterative poetry of the
fourteenth century but of all the Middle English rhyming romances as well.[66]

The tempo of *King Horn* is slowed by repetition in language so much
that it could be said to put temporality itself under pressure. That is, its tendency toward stasis even seems to govern the language it uses to mark time,
so that temporal units may vary (from days to nights to years), but the number
of units is always the same. So, it takes seven years for Horn to mature (100),
he must wait seven nights before he is dubbed a knight (452), Rymenhild

feels seven years have elapsed while she waits of news about Horn (527), she must wait seven years for Horn before she can marry (736, 737), and Horn is away for seven years in the end (920, 926, 1150). If such narrative torpor makes it particularly easy to lose one's bearings in *King Horn*—since so many of the reference points that might be used to place one event in relation to others are exactly the same—it also shows particularly well how the narrative speed of a Middle English romance could slow to the narrative speed of "Annot and John," or "Bytuene Mersh ant Averil," or any "Harley lyric." To put this point even more mischievously, to notice all of the ways that the length of *King Horn* is only ostensible is to notice the extent to which the repetitiveness and tempo of a Middle English romance could render it, in formal and perceptual terms, short.

Refrain

"Lyric" is not a term Middle English had, and, as Ardis Butterfield has aptly put it, this ensures that a certain "torque" is usually necessary to use the term to describe any Middle English poem.[67] But, as has already become clear in my examples, Middle English texts that share many of the characteristics we now ascribe to lyric describe themselves as "lai" and "song," and, as Nicolette Zeeman has shown, this is part and parcel of the many ways that such poems were self-theorizing, in effect describing their own literary method in "imaginative" form.[68] Certainly *King Horn* embeds a very clear theory of the genres in which it participates, defining "rime" by means of an inset narrative recited by a giant, in which it is clear that the term refers to what we would now call "romance." As in our own accounts, such "rime" is a narrative replete with event, beginning with the characteristic appeal to listeners ("herkne" [hearken]), describing a martial contest for political power:

> A geaunt swthe sone,
> Iarmed fram paynyme
> And seide thes ryme:
> "Site stille, Sire Kyng,
> And herkne this tything:
> Her buth paens arived;
> Wel mo thane five
> Her beoth on the sonde,

King, upon thy londe;
On of hem wile fighte
Aghen thre knightes.
Yef other thre slen ure,
Al this lond beo youre;
Yef ure on overcometh your threo,
Al this lond schal ure beo.
Tomoreghe be the fightinge,
Whane the light of daye springe."
(808–24)

Later, *King Horn* defines "lai" and "song" as something very like what we now call "lyric," self-expressions of subjective life, voiced feelings both affecting and sufficiently distinct to reveal the disguised Horn's identity to Rymenhild:

Hi gunne murie singe
And makede here gleowinge.
Rymenhild hit gan ihere
And axede what hi were.
Hi sede hi weren harpurs
And sume were gigours.
He dude Horn in late
Right at halle gate.
He sette him on the benche,
His harpe for to clenche.
He makede Rymenhilde lay,
And heo makede walaway.
Rymenhild feol yswoghe
Ne was ther non that loughe.
Hit smot to Hornes herte
So bitere that hit smerte.
(1481–96)

If these were the alternatives the compiler of Harley 2253 had available to him—if *King Horn* can be said to provide us with the classifications he would have had to work with—then he includes *King Horn* in booklet 5 because he understood it to be more "song" or "lai" than "rime." Insofar as this is true,

G. L. Brook and all those who have excluded *King Horn* from the grouping we call "Harley lyrics" have simply failed to notice or follow the classificatory scheme provided in the very manuscript from which they claim to derive it.

The oversight is all the more significant insofar as the repeated couplets I highlighted above can be understood not only as devices that cut the narrative into strophes but as the *refrains* that medieval songs characteristically used for that purpose. Formally, the refrain may seem to be, above all, a mode of repetition, but it also retains elements of its roots in Latin *refringo*, *refringere*, "to break up," tending, in its repetitions, to parcel out a song into a series of self-same units.[69] The repeated couplets I have just called attention to do not fit this form, strictly speaking, but that is itself a characteristic of the medieval refrain, which has proved notoriously difficult to define in strict terms.[70] In the French tradition, refrains could be "part of a dance without being part of larger poems," and they occasionally survived independent of any textual frame.[71] Refrains could also be stripped away from the songs of which they were originally a part and embedded so fully in the texture of a much longer poem that they became its "subject," as if the refrain itself adumbrated the longer poem's whole narrative.[72] A refrain might also begin the poem, as in the case of the carol in booklet 5 of Harley 2253, "Ichot a burde in a boure bryht" (2:204–11, *DIMEV* 2325) so that it is not summative but generative (here, the urgency of the command, "Blow, northerne wynd, / Sent thou me my suetyng!") seeming to necessitate all that follows (here, another detailed account of a lady in a bright bower).[73] The term "refrain" has more recently been understood to describe a function rather than a form, a "retrograde motion" that "forms a closed circle" (as Gilles Deleuze and Félix Guattari put it), a pause in the unfolding of any subject matter wherein reference (as John Hollander has put it) "tends to collapse into a univocal sign (*That was full of meaning; now meaning stops for awhile and we all dance again*)."[74] As Eleanor Johnson has also noted, "each time a reader encounters a refrain in a lyric . . . forward narrative progress is halted" and the reader's attention is driven backward to the "structure of repetition" itself.[75]

The most summative of *King Horn*'s couplets, "The se bigan to flowe / And Horn child to rowe," could, in all these senses, be understood as the poem's refrain, and the other repeated couplet, "The kyng com into halle / Among his knightes alle," could be described as a "subrefrain," not least because both couplets produce a narrative tempo in which the forward motion of event in *King Horn* slows to something like a lyric pause. These repetitions could be thought to insist that *King Horn* also belongs among the

"Harley lyrics" according to the very principles of lyricization that might exclude it.[76] To be sure, many of the poems in G. L. Brook's collection lack refrains, and he takes short poems from booklets 4 and 6 that lack them too, but he also gathers every Middle English poem in Harley 2253 that *has* a refrain into the "Harley lyrics" and reaches into booklet 6 for two of the poems he adds to those in booklet 5 because those poems happen to have refrains too (the poems he calls "The Way of Christ's Love" and "The Way of Woman's Love").[77]

There are other Middle English narrative poems with refrains. The "citational repetitions" in *Piers Plowman* that often identify key thematic principles have been described in this way.[78] *Pearl*, a poem whose form has sometimes been seen as *sui generis*, has more recently been placed in a tradition of "pseudo-ballade" that includes lyrics—five of them from Harley 2253—that also have twelve-line stanzas with lines of four stresses as well as refrains.[79] But, if close attention to verse form tends to draw short and long Middle English poems together, the category of "lyric romance" acknowledges that conflation by placing romances in the literary culture in which poems of any length were understood as song. The category also makes it possible to say that what the repetitions and refrains in *King Horn* know better than literary history has so far is that this romance not only resembles a Harley lyric but is one. Simon Jarvis has argued for attributing exactly such thought to prosody, an understanding of the versification we normally subordinate to meaning *as* meaning, a recognition of the patterns of verse form as a "kind of cognition."[80] His most powerful example is Pope, whose verse, he argues, was "a form of knowledge whose furious pursuit of the rule (and thus of the felicitous transgression of the rule) internalizes, yet also exceeds and knows, the polish requisite to domestic luxuries and gentlemanly sociability alike."[81] It is more helpful to say that *King Horn* was aware of just how much it resembled the lyrics of booklet 5 of Harley 2253 rather than to identify those resemblances with an unnoticed principle of selection employed by the Harley compiler because it goes to the central question posed by this book, "What kind of a thing is a Middle English lyric?" The process of lyricization that began with the term "Harley lyric" and has since drawn such a firm line between short poems and long, "nonnarrative" and "narrative," has obscured the extent to which what we have been pleased to call a Middle English romance such as *King Horn* was *also* one of the kind of things the Middle English lyric was, and therefore still is.

Chapter 4

Language and Meter

IAN CORNELIUS

Previous chapters have begun to unpack the challenges that Middle English lyrics pose to readers. As Ardis Butterfield shows, these poems require us to read from several disciplinary perspectives simultaneously and they trouble the basic text-critical distinction between *Textträger* and the wider assortment of documentary witnesses that may sometimes attest to the former existence of a literary work without, however, transmitting *ipsissima verba*. Even when documentary records transmit the words and music of a Middle English lyric, we may retain a powerful sense that the thing itself has escaped, inapt to be carried on any substance except air. Subsequent chapters have explored the "polyvalent potential" of Middle English vocabulary and the polyvalent generic affiliations of verse technique. In different ways, Cristina Maria Cervone and Christopher Cannon show that the techniques of versification by which language is bound into a discrete thing also invest that thing with resonant meaning. Like these two previous chapters, the present one explores the intersection of verse technique and linguistic medium. My topic is the metrical shape of verse lines in Middle English lyric and the use of Middle English as a medium for verse composition.

Within the critical tradition to which we owe the term,[1] "lyric" has been centered on metered compositions, to which unmetered compositions are adduced by family resemblance. The advent of international free verse changed this field of play but has not yet neutralized the critical heritage, for which the most lyrical lyrics—the ones enlisted to exemplify the category—have embodied a metrical design.[2] Yet versification does not receive adequate attention in the standard reference tools available to students of Middle English lyric. Carleton Brown and Rossell Hope Robbins devoted only sporadic and incidental remarks to meter in their field-defining anthologies and bibliographical guides.[3] Progress has been made in recent decades, but much remains to be done.[4] To facilitate communication between lyric studies and prosodic studies, I shall employ a deliberately unrestrictive definition of "lyric," using this term to designate any "short composition in verse."[5] This is not a judgment against the contextual utility of richer definitions of lyric. My aim is just to get a clear and unobstructed view of my topic, versification. Illustrations will be drawn from the English verses sometimes embedded within the texts of Latin sermons and related preachers' books.

What Kind of a Thing Is Middle English?

Though I have adopted a minimalist definition of "lyric," the other element of our title question requires a fuller treatment at this juncture, for the varieties of English spoken and written between about 1150 and 1500 afforded historically delimited modes of metricality. For the term "Middle English" and this historical delimitation of it our book is indebted to philology and historical linguistics, the disciplines to which we also owe whatever may be known about the prosody of the language.[6] At its lower boundary, Middle English is distinguished from Old English by the reduction of weak final syllables. It is distinguished, too, by the diversification of local spelling systems in the surviving record, and by a massive assimilation of vocabulary items of Dano-Scandinavian and French provenance. The upper boundary is distinguished by comprehensive reorganization of the system of long vowels (the "Great Vowel Shift") and by progressive elimination of regional spelling systems developed in the Middle English period. These changes were distributed in time and place; the boundaries are clinal, not abrupt. Middle English nevertheless emerges as a robust object of inquiry, and the features by which it is customarily identified in historical linguistics have important implications for the use of the language in metered compositions.

In recognition of this linguistic framing, the adjective "English" refers in this chapter to a language, not a nation, culture, people, or territory. This specification could be construed to foreclose extra- and multilingual dimensions of our topic; on the contrary, it provides a foundation from which to approach the fact that Middle English verse developed within an intensely multilingual society and owes many of its distinctive features to that dynamic milieu.[7] Dano-Scandinavian speech communities had probably assimilated linguistically by the early twelfth century, ending some 250 years of English/Norse societal bilingualism.[8] Celtic languages remained a living presence; Welsh hosted a richly developed literature in prose and verse.[9] For a period of more than two centuries, ending in 1290, many English towns were home to communities whose formal written language was Hebrew. Ports at London and elsewhere afforded further language contact, with Dutch and Italian, for example. Yet enumeration brings its own distortions, tending to obscure the structuration of cultural practices: if one adopts a communicative perspective ("What languages did participants in literary culture expect their peers to engage?") one may describe the literary culture in late medieval England as trilingual, constellated from English, French, and Latin. Latin was the cosmopolitan language of learning, affording access to the widest spatiotemporal horizons. English was the principal demotic vernacular. French was at first a superposed vernacular: it was the spoken language of the Norman colonists. The chronology of Norman linguistic assimilation remains a matter of conjecture, but seems likely to have conformed to generational patterns attested in more recent immigrant communities. By the end of the twelfth century participants in literary culture (a rarified social stratum) would typically have spoken English in childhood.[10] During the same period of linguistic assimilation, and increasingly in the thirteenth century, French acquired the status of an elite or learned vernacular, employed in the domains of law, commerce, government, religion, and secular aristocratic literature. The result was a trilingual literary culture: during most of the Middle English period, most persons who could engage written English could probably also engage French and Latin, the two languages of social consequence. Literate habitus, as incorporated by boys in grammar school, was triune, and literate uses of English were shaped by the more prestigious and authoritative members of this unequal trinity.[11]

Sheldon Pollock, one of the greatest recent theorists of premodern literary cultures, would recognize this complex language situation as especially conducive to literary innovation: "literatures," Pollock remarks, "typically arise in response to other literature *superposed* to them in a relation of unequal cultural power."[12] Pollock's dictum is exemplified—though not neatly—

by the way that the English language acquired new metrical forms at the turn of the thirteenth century.

Verse Forms in Middle English: What and Whence?

The history is clear enough, at least in outline. At the beginning of the twelfth century, there was one basic way of writing poetry in English; this was the "alliterative" meter, inherited from common Germanic. Late in that century, at the dawn of the period we designate as Middle English, poets began to experiment with new English line types, modeled on the forms then current in the superposed Latin and French literatures. Accentual Latin verse, perhaps the goliardic meter, supplied a model for the English septenary line, as employed in *Poema Morale* (ca. 1170–90) and the *Ormulum* (ca. 1175). A century later, this line type was used in the *South English Legendary*, one of the first large works of Middle English poetic literature to circulate widely. About the same time that Orm and the *Poema Morale*–author were crafting their septenaries, other poets were taking cues from French *vers octosyllabe*. The result was a short English line with approximately alternating beat and offbeat, four beats to a line, and a good deal of variation around an eight-syllable norm. An early instance, probably from the end of the twelfth century, is the exposition of the Pater Noster in London, Lambeth Palace Library, MS 487 (*Digital Index of Middle English Verse [DIMEV]* 4305). By the end of the following century, the short four-beat line with alternating rhythm had become the most productive meter in Middle English. It is instanced variously in poems of religious instruction and biblical history (*Genesis and Exodus*, *Cursor Mundi*, *The Northern Homily Cycle*, *The Prick of Conscience*, and *Speculum Vitae*), romances (*Sir Orfeo*, *King Alisander*, and *Havelok the Dane*), works of literary fiction (*The Owl and the Nightingale*, *Pearl*, Chaucer's *Book of the Duchess*, and *The House of Fame*), and numerous lyric poems. In the fifteenth century this line type was eclipsed, incompletely, by Chaucer's invention, the five-beat decasyllabic line. That form, the progenitor of English iambic pentameter, was likewise inspired by verse in Romance languages.

This basic narrative is readily available in histories of English poetry, all of which are now rather dated.[13] In a recent bibliographic survey, Thomas Cable observes that "there is no general treatment of medieval English prosody that takes into account the discoveries made during the past forty years."[14]

The only book that might challenge Cable's assessment is Martin Duffell's *New History of English Metre*, billed as a single-volume update to George Saintsbury's *History of English Prosody*.[15] Duffell offers a valuable guide to modern linguistic metrics, and he excels in description of the English accentual-syllabic forms. Moreover, Duffell's *New History* is the first general treatment of English prosody to give more than perfunctory attention to the Latin, French, and Italian meters that influenced versification in Middle English.[16] His book suggests a small but important revision to received narratives of the genesis of Middle English meters.

At issue is the French *octosyllabe* and handling of it by English writers. By comparison with continental productions, the verse written in insular (or Anglo-Norman) French is not a true octosyllable. Fluctuations in syllable count were once construed as sloppy versification (or, alternatively, as pervasive scribal corruption), but Duffell holds that syllabic fluctuation expresses, accurately, a prosodic feature of the insular language. Continental varieties of French lost demarcative word stress in the High Middle Ages, and this development made purely syllabic meters a good fit for the linguistic prosody.[17] In Britain, however, the development of French was probably affected by a phenomenon designated by linguists as substratum interference.[18] When persons whose first language was English came to speak French, they projected English articulatory habits into the French language. That is, they spoke French with an English accent. Comparable substratum effects are responsible for the distinctive prosodies and phonologies of many present-day varieties of global English. In medieval Britain, the result of substratum interference was a variety of French that, by the second half of the twelfth century, had probably acquired, among other changes to the system of speech sounds, a "heavy expiratory word-stress."[19] As such, insular French was ill-suited to the purely syllabic meter employed by continental poets. Duffell contends that the short line employed in insular French verse is beat-counted, not syllable-counted, with four beats per line: poets in medieval England "versified in the same manner in two different languages."[20] The verse form appeared in insular French at the beginning of the twelfth century, fifty or seventy-five years before the earliest surviving instances in English—and with far greater assurance and accomplishment. The standard account of prosodic history therefore remains accurate in outline: the short English four-beat line was modeled on a superposed French form.[21] Yet the French form that served in this way as a model for new English productions probably owed its distinctive metrical configuration to the articulatory habits of an English substratum. Vectors of influence ran in both directions.

One would like to have a name for the short-line beat-counted meter that emerged from this field of French-English language contact. Duffell's name for it is "dolnik." Russian in origin, the term *dol'nik* was introduced into English metrics by Marina Tarlinskaja to name a meter that is beat-counted, in which weak positions are usually monosyllabic, but a significant minority are disyllabic and some are void.[22] The essential feature seems to be a "rhythmic pulse," or undulation of beat and offbeat, with twice two crests per line.[23] Derek Attridge has contributed a transhistorical survey of the English dolnik; his principal illustration of the form is the Middle English lyric "Nou goth sonne" (*DIMEV* 3742).[24] The poem dates from the thirteenth century and forms the opening item in Carleton Brown's anthology of the earliest Middle English lyrics. I quote from that anthology with typographical additions that aim to represent metrical structure:[25]

> **Nou** goth **son**ne / vnder **wod**<e>, —
> me **rew**eth, Marie, / þi **fai**re **rode**.
> **Nou** goþ **son**ne / vnder **tre**, —
> me reweþ, Marie, / þi **son**ẹ and **þe**.

My presentation marks the caesura with a virgule ("/") and places beat-bearing syllables in bold. The <e> at the end of the first line is an inflectional syllable omitted by the scribe whose spellings Brown reproduces in his edition of this lyric; the underdotted *ẹ* in the last line marks a graphic syllable elided with the following vowel. The prosodic shape of "Marie" could be queried, as could the syllabification of "reweth." Other scansions would be possible, as usual in English verse. Yet there remains ground for judgment, and Attridge rightly emphasizes that a foot-based scansion of this poem generates artificial difficulties. The lines could be described as a mix of iambs, trochees, and trisyllabic feet. Read the poem aloud, however, and you will hear a much simpler principle, consisting in "rhythmic doubling": "a beat is added to a beat to form a two-beat group ('nou goth sonne'); to this is added another two-beat group to form a four-beat group," or complete line; "to this is added another four-beat group, producing the first two lines of the poem."[26] This simple meter is employed in countless Middle English lyrics; I give a fuller description later in this chapter.

Tarlinskaja and Duffell apply the term "dolnik" equally to four- and five-beat verse. I shall instead follow Attridge in reserving the term for four-beat verse and the ballad measure to which it is closely affiliated. So defined, English dolnik is bordered on one side by the smoothly alternating octosyllabic meter first seen in English in John Gower's *Confessio Amantis*.[27] There, weak positions are invariably monosyllabic. On the other side, English dolnik is bordered by a line type with a higher proportion of disyllabic intervals, combined with a stronger caesura and more consistent patterning of weak syllables in the second half of the line. This line type is instanced by several of the Harley lyrics[28] and remains poorly understood. It is affiliated to the traditional alliterative meter, but simpler than that line type, with a more predictable rhythm.[29]

The historical relation between alliterative verse and the verse form I here designate as "English dolnik" is an area for future research. Older studies, including those of Tarlinskaja, confidently attribute the fluctuating syllable count of English dolnik to the influence of alliterative verse: English dolnik thus figures as the halfway house between the untamed alliterative long line and the politely syllable-counting verse of Chaucer and Gower. This account is plausible and may be correct, but there are difficulties. Studies that posit alliterative verse as the source of syllabic irregularities in English dolnik have thus far failed to appreciate the rule-governed syllabic patterning of alliterative verse.[30] They have also failed to take account of the multilingual literary culture. Received histories of Middle English versification should be revised to accommodate new understandings of English alliterative meter and of versification in insular French. What is clear is that English verse forms diversified prodigiously during the century after about 1170, and that English dolnik emerged as the most productive of the new forms.

Middle English Spellings

To describe the thirteenth century as a Cambrian explosion in English verse forms would be unjust to the stylistic range and accomplishment of prior English verse.[31] Still, the Middle English period witnessed a rapid diversification of metrical forms. The ground shifted, posing significant challenges to modern readers of medieval poetry, as it surely also did to some medieval readers of medieval poetry. Interpretative challenges are compounded by the brevity of lyric poems, for a short poem gives a reader little opportunity to work into the verse form, as she or he may do in a longer poem.

Medieval readers had one great advantage: Middle English was for them a living language. If they cared to read verse in this vernacular medium, they had probably grown up speaking the language in one of its regional dialect forms and they had probably absorbed English verse through the ear long before they came to read it in books.[32] Modern readers of this literature are in an inauspicious position, dependent on written records alone.[33] These records can be difficult to interpret. Middle English spellings are more nearly phonetic than those of the modern language, but the comparison is as likely to mislead as to enlighten. Speech sounds are underdetermined by the marks on the page, which presume a reader who knows the language and can select, at the speed of performance, among the array of possible speech forms fuzzily encoded by a given graphic form.

This reading experience is not wholly foreign to modern readers: when we read sixteenth- and seventeenth-century English poetry, we select between mono- and disyllabic forms of "heaven," "spirit," "ever," "never," and "over," for example, and between syllabic and nonsyllabic -ed. The operative form is often cued by meter, not spelling. Thus, "innocent" is trisyllabic in the line "That from the blood he might be innocent" but disyllabic, as "inn'cent," in "And fro me hid: of whose most innocent death."[34] The same principle holds in Middle English, where, however, poets and readers had a much richer field of variation at their disposal.

Many doublet forms had wide, overlapping geographical distributions. A good example is "without" and its trisyllabic variant "withouten": the Edinburgh dialect atlas shows that di- and trisyllabic forms of this word were available to poets and readers throughout most of the geographical ambit of Middle English.[35] Other syllabic variants were more restricted in geographical distribution. Syncopated, nonsyllabic forms of certain verbal inflections (namely, the second- and third-person singular present indicative) were already a feature of southerly dialects in Old English and continued to be an option in these areas in Middle English.[36] Chaucer used both the full and syncopated forms, *metri gratia*. Past participles with prefixed *i-* or *y-* (< OE *ge-*) are likewise a feature of southern dialects in Middle English: this verbal prefix was lost first in the north, where language change was accelerated by contact with Old Norse. Diatopic and diachronic variation intersect, and the linguistic situation is complicated further by the probability of differentiated sociolinguistic registers, some colloquial, others formal and conservative. In studies of literary Middle English, sociolinguistic register is increasingly recognized as an important dimension of linguistic variation, alongside and intersecting the dimensions of time and space.[37] Literary traditions may sustain linguistic repertoires differentiated from the surrounding language, and this consideration is probably relevant to one of the most important and difficult topics in Middle English prosody, namely, the status of weak final -*e*.

Much of the syllabic variation in lexical words in Middle English derives from the coexistence of relatively conservative and relatively innovative forms of the same word, differing in the retention or loss of weak final -*e*. This syllable had several sources and has been subject to numerous studies.[38] I supply a few exemplary illustrations. Some nouns ended in a weak vowel in Old English and retained a by-form with final -*e* in Middle English; thus, Middle English *herte* (< OE *heorte*) may be monosyllabic or disyllabic, whether or not the final -*e* is written. Other nouns, such as "gold," are monosyllabic by derivation, yet may acquire an inflectional -*e*, and thus disyllabic shape, when the object of a preposition. Some adjectives, of which *swete* (sweet) is an example, ended in a weak vowel in Old English and maintained a by-form with -*e* in Middle English. Other adjectives, of which "old" is an example, are monosyllabic by derivation, yet regularly acquire inflectional -*e* when modifying a plural noun or in definite usage. The verbal system is affected by a different series of considerations. The first- and third-person preterit singular indicative of strong verbs is always inflectionless, but most other verb forms had an inflection of some sort in Old English and could retain an inflectional syllable in the fourteenth century. Thus, the verb in "she drank" is securely monosyllabic, but the verb in "thei drunk" is entitled to an inflectional -*e* or -*en*. The form with -*en* is protected from elision. A historical grammar will indicate what form(s) one may expect for any given grammatical category and usage.[39] The poems examined later in this chapter will supply concrete illustrations.

Stepping back from this detail, one may say that literary English of the thirteenth and fourteenth centuries exhibits a degree of linguistic variousness unparalleled in later periods in this language prior to the twentieth century. Whereas the global diversification of English in the twentieth century has tended to favor the discontinuation of traditional poetic meters, linguistic variation in Middle English split significantly between the alliterative and accentual-syllabic traditions. Alliterative poetry tended to retain a conservative grammar of final -*e*, while the dolnik and other approximately accentual-syllabic verse made heavy use of forms without that syllable.[40]

Faced with this linguistic variation, some scholars have advocated an ambitious program of spelling correction in modern presentations of Middle

English poetry.[41] Per this policy, the manuscript spelling *neuer* would be emended to *ner* whenever the meter calls for a monosyllable; similarly, final -*e*'s would be added and deleted (always within the bounds established by historical grammar) to fix metrical form in orthography. Syllabic variants would be disambiguated, guiding the reader to the operative form in each case. Such treatment may be justified in student anthologies. It is harder to justify in scholarly editions, for it is not clear that the form *neuer*, written where the meter calls for a monosyllable, is an error, nor that an infinitive verb, written without its inflectional syllable where the meter calls for that syllable, is a scribal mutilation of a correctly spelled authorial text. The alternative possibility is that Middle English spellings are a fuzzy record of speech forms: they cue the word, leaving readers to select the operative prosodic form. This procedure was workable because poets and their scribes wrote for native speakers of the language, a fact that, again, places modern readers at a disadvantage. The metrical regularity of Middle English poetry is often perceptible only through the continuous activation of and selection between the array of variant forms available in the contemporary language as possible realizations of a given manuscript spelling.

The *Index of Middle English Verse*

In the preceding pages, I have sought to unpack what it means to say that Middle English served as a medium for composition of metered verse. In the second half of this chapter, I hope to demonstrate that the principal bibliographical reference guide for study of Middle English verse has not paid adequate attention to metrical form. Begun over a century ago and now available in five incarnations, the *Index of Middle English Verse* intends to supply a comprehensive bibliographical registry of the surviving archival records of verse composition in Middle English. Poems are listed alphabetically by first line, and each entry is assigned a unique bibliographic number; the medieval manuscript witnesses are listed, as are any printed editions. I here list the five iterations of the Index, together with abbreviated titles that I will use in subsequent discussion:

Register   Carleton Brown, ed., *A Register of Middle English Religious and Didactic Verse*, 2 vols. (Oxford: Oxford University Press, 1916–20)

IMEV   Carleton Brown and Rossell Hope Robbins, eds., *The Index
            of Middle English Verse* (New York: Columbia University
            Press, 1943)
Supplement Rossell Hope Robbins and John L. Cutler, eds., *Supplement
            to the Index of Middle English Verse* (Lexington, KY: University
            of Kentucky Press, 1965)
NIMEV   Julia Boffey and A. S. G. Edwards, eds., *A New Index of
            Middle English Verse* (London: British Library, 2005)
DIMEV   Linne R. Mooney, Daniel W. Mosser, and Elizabeth
            Solopova, eds., *The Digital Index of Middle English Verse: An
            Open-Access, Digital Edition of the Index of Middle English
            Verse*, http://www.dimev.net/.

By "Index," I refer to the whole enterprise, without discrimination between versions.

The Index is an indispensable research tool, enabling access to a corpus of poetry widely dispersed in surviving records and insusceptible to bibliographic organization by author, date, or title.[42] My criticism may be stated briefly: the Index never, in any of its iterations, states what it means by "verse." My argument to this point should establish that the category "verse" is not self-evident in Middle English. One may add that lineation—a feature of graphic presentation by which modern readers often distinguish verse from prose—cannot serve that discriminatory function in the records of medieval English. Scribes in early medieval England wrote their vernacular poetry in continuous format ("as prose"); lineated formats were adopted in the thirteenth century as part of a more pervasive reconfiguration of English literary culture under the superposed literatures of French and Latin, but continuous format remained an option for scribal presentation of English verse through the fifteenth century. A significant minority of surviving copies of Middle English alliterative poems are written in continuous format.[43] Continuous format is much more frequent, approaching the level of a presentational norm, for short English poems (alliterative or not) embedded in Latin prose.

Why has the Index been able to do without a definition of verse? Perhaps Saintsbury's *History of English Prosody* made the definitional question appear moot when Carleton Brown began work, for Saintsbury stated authoritatively that the earliest rhymed verse of the Middle English period already exhibits "*rhythm* of a kind roughly similar to that of English poetry as it has been known ever since"—or, more forcefully, that the "metrical rhythm" of the English verse of the twelfth and thirteenth centuries is "not distinguishable, except in accomplishment, from that of Lord Tennyson or of Mr. Swinburne."[44] These pronouncements would seem to absolve a bibliographer of Middle English verse from making any particular account of Middle English versification: acquaintance with the verse forms of modern English would suffice to guide judgment through the earlier materials. Only alliterative verse should present any challenge. Saintsbury acknowledged that alliterative verse is peculiar, and, true to Saintsbury's assessment, alliterative materials have provoked the Index's few remarks on verse definition.

In a preface to the *Register of Middle English Religious and Didactic Verse* (1916), Brown observed that "among the earliest compositions of this period it is not always easy to draw the line between irregular alliterative verse and prose" (vii). That difficulty called for special notice of editorial decisions: Brown reports that he excluded the early Middle English *St. Margaret, St. Juliana*, and *Sawles Warde* from the *Register*, for, though these works have a lot of alliteration, "they afford only slight traces of metrical form" (vii). "Metrical form" is here affirmed to be the sine qua non of verse identity, but treated as self-evident. Readers are simply expected to share Brown's unstated understanding. Brown and Rossell Hope Robbins offered no further discussion in their *Index of Middle English Verse*, published in 1943, nor did Robbins and John L. Cutler in their *Supplement to the Index of Middle English Verse* (1965). Versification resurfaces as a problem in the 2005 *New Index of Middle English Verse*, but the problem is once again posed in its narrowest form and accorded purely negative attention: "Some entries," Julia Boffey and A. S. G. Edwards remark, "especially ones added in the *Supplement* . . . seem to make gestures towards the alliterative line as part of a more general strategic use of alliterative prose" (xiii). As illustration, Boffey and Edwards point to a nine-line alliterative lyric intercalated into Richard Rolle's *Ego Dormio*, beginning "Al perisshethe and passeth þat we with eigh see" (*Supplement* 197.8, *DIMEV* 357). They are surely wrong to delete it.[45] More troubling is the fact that the category of "verse" continues to be treated as self-evident, even as successive editorial teams disagree about which Middle English items qualify. The chronological delimitation of "Middle English" is accorded due attention in the *Supplement* and *NIMEV*. Users are, however, provided no comparable discussion of the features that qualify a given Middle English text as verse.[46]

Nor, on closer inspection, can the Index's undertheorization of verse be construed as deference to Saintsbury. Saintsbury held that rhyme played a decisive role in establishing the modern English prosodic system. Brown,

Robbins, and their successors seem instead to have taken rhyme as a proxy for meter, and there are historical reasons why this should work. Like the French and Latin forms that inspired them, the new Middle English forms employed end rhyme, almost without exception. The persistence of rhyme-less alliterative verse during the Middle English period might have inspired poets to drop rhyme from their French- and Latin-derived meters, but in fact the opposite happened. Many alliterative poets adopted end rhyme, while almost no poets in the new forms dispensed with end rhyme. (The salient exception is the *Ormulum*.) Apart from alliterative verse, English poetry between circa 1170 and circa 1540 nearly always rhymes. This verse practice provided compilers of the Index with a clear and relatively simple modus operandi. Items without rhyme may be excluded from the Index, unless decorated with alliteration, in which case a finer discrimination becomes necessary. Items with rhyme are counted as verse and recorded in the Index, excepting very brief snatches of rhymed English embedded within Latin sermons. These are treated inconsistently, exposing weaknesses inherent in the failure of the Index catalogers to define just what they have been cataloging.

Verses in Sermons

Latin sermons and other preachers' materials from late medieval England not infrequently contain segments of English within their texture.[47] The English segments vary in extent, function, and overall aspect. Some are clearly verse, others clearly not verse, and others seem to place the category *en abyme*. Lineation is no help, for in these contexts English verse is typically written without line breaks, in continuity with surrounding Latin prose. Rhyme also fails as a criterion, for scholastic sermons typically analyze their thema into rhymed clauses, each expressing an aspect or implication to be elaborated in the main body of the sermon.[48] Rhymed sermon divisions are a regular feature of Latin sermons of the scholastic type; in sermons intended for delivery in English, the sermon division may be recorded in English, even when most of the remainder is recorded in Latin. These rhymed English sermon divisions have been the cause of much grief (should they be included in the Index, or excluded as prose?), but the problem has been posed too narrowly to admit solution. Absent a working definition of Middle English metrical forms, scholars have relied too heavily on rhyme to identify verse.

To spot the bugs in the code, it suffices to watch the criterion of rhyme in action, as it parses Latin text for embedded English verse. A good initial exhibit is the treatise *Fasciculus Morum,* a collection of *praedicabilia* compiled by an English Franciscan, probably early in the fourteenth century; twenty-eight surviving manuscript copies testify to wide circulation. The treatise has received exacting attention from Siegfried Wenzel in a series of publications, including an edition of the embedded English items.[49] These Wenzel divided into "verses" (of which he found sixty-one) and a smaller number of "other English phrases." Although Wenzel does not say so, his binary distinction relies on the presence of rhyme, and this alone, to distinguish verse from prose. That criterion decides correctly in all but a few cases.

One of Wenzel's "other English phrases" is a line of septenary verse.[50] I mark the caesura with a virgule and print the strong constituents in bold:

"**Who**-so **woll** noȝt **when** he **may** / he **schall** noȝt **when** he **wold**e."

A cycle of modal auxiliaries—"will," "may," "shall," and "would"—stake out the moral message and four of seven beats. A variant of this verse proverb is displayed in raised relief on the Asante Ewer (ca. 1390–99; *DIMEV* 1911), discussed by Aden Kumler elsewhere in this book.[51] In that version, a pair of infinitives sharpen the message of the proverb and swell it into a different metrical shape:

He that **wyl** not **spare whan** he **may**
He **schal** not **spend whan** he **wold**

The Asante Ewer version is probably best parsed as an unrhymed dolnik couplet: the infinitives "spare" and "spend" are each entitled to an inflectional syllable; if sounded, that syllable supplies an offbeat between the second and third beats in each line.[52] The absence of rhyme is odd, however, and the opening of the first line is metrically ambiguous. These peculiarities suggest that the ewer's couplet may go back to a form like that in *Fasciculus Morum*—a speculation that receives support from Bartlett Whiting's *Proverbs, Sentences, and Proverbial Phrases*, the standard reference work on this subject. Whiting records both forms of the proverb, but whereas the form in *Fasciculus Morum* is widely attested (W.275), the form on the Asante Ewer is recorded by Whiting only there (S.553).[53] It seems that someone involved in the making of the ewer recast a traditional proverb to address the problem of "wise measure in expenditure," as Kumler suggests.[54] Whiting also shows that the form of the proverb in *Fasciculus Morum* can be traced back, in that metrical shape, to the *Poema Morale*, possibly the first Middle English poem in the septenary meter.[55] In *Poema Morale* the line participates in rhyme, as expected. The version in *Fasciculus Morum* and the remetered version on the Asante Ewer are reminders that one cannot depend upon rhyme to identify poetry in Middle English.

False positives are more pernicious, for they inevitably cloud the category to which they are assimilated. Four of the rhyming English items in *Fasciculus Morum* instance no poetic meter that I can discern. Wenzel's number 55, a mnemonic on the *signa mortis*, may serve as an example.[56] Like the other English items in *Fasciculus Morum*, this one is usually written in continuous format; I reproduce Wenzel's lineation:

> When þe hede quakyth
> And þe lyppis blakyth
> And þe nose sharpyth
> And þe senow sta[r]kyth
> And þe brest pantyth
> And þe breþe wantyth
> And þe teþe rately3t
> And þe þrote roteliþ
> And þe sowle is wente owte,
> Þe body ne tyt but a clowte.
> [And after be hyt in þe pyte
> And with erth fast ydit.]
> Sone be it so steken*n*
> Þe sowle all clene ys for3eten*n*.

This text is recorded in *IMEV* (4035), *NIMEV* (4035), and *DIMEV* (6461), there designated as rhyming couplets. The first eight clauses exhibit what I would term local prosodic regularization, with reiterated xxSxSx or xxSSx stress contours: "And þe **lyppis blak**yth." These clauses could be construed as a peculiar spin-off of alliterative verse, but any narrower association would misunderstand how that meter works. Indeed, the most distinctive pattern here, besides the insistent feminine rhymes, is not prosodic at all, but syntactic: the drumming of parallel clauses.[57] The accompanying Latin text, for which this

English is a translation, is likewise marked by emphatic parallelism, isocolon, and feminine rhyme: "Quando nasus frigescit, facies pallescit, oculi tenebrescunt, aures surdescunt, nervi et vene rumpuntur, cor in duas partes dividitur. Nichil vilius vel abhominabilius cadavere mortuo."[58] As in the English, the staccato Latin clauses are arranged in couplets: first, a couplet with inflectional rhyme supplied by inchoative verbs of singular number, then the same in plural number; a pair of passive verbs supply approximate rhyme in the third couplet. How should we understand the rhymes in this pair of texts?

The use of rhyme in Latin prose was designated an aspect of the "Isidorian style" by medieval rhetoricians, who traced it to Augustine's *Soliloquies*.[59] Modern commentators have not adopted that term but agree that Augustine provided an important model and inspiration for the ornate Latin prose, rich in parallelism, isocolon, and figures of sound, crafted by some monastic writers in the twelfth century and exemplified especially in Bernard of Clairvaux's sermons on the Song of Songs.[60] Bernard and his followers crafted vivid evocations of spiritual experience, measured out in short, paratactic clauses. These stylistic preferences distinguished Bernardine devotional prose in the field of Latin letters and supplied an unusually apposite model for writers in vernacular languages: here was a Latin style that showed how parataxis and unsophisticated diction could be turned to advantage. Arrayed in parallel, cut to equal length, and ornamented with rhyme and alliteration, the clauses of English prose became a powerful communicative instrument, as exhibited in parts of the *Ancrene Wisse* and in the Katherine Group of saints' lives and devotional treatises.[61] These thirteenth-century texts should cast doubt on any judgment that Middle English prose was underdeveloped, or that ornate Latin prose could be rendered into Middle English only as verse. A prototype theory of categorization such as John Taylor's, endorsed at the outset of this chapter, would permit us to designate artful, emotional, and intricately patterned prose as lyric, but we should consider alternatives. Would the English clerics who composed and copied little blooms of rhymed English have thought of themselves as writing verse? What else might "When þe hede quakyth" be, if not a lyric, and why should it be recorded in *Fasciculus Morum*?

Fasciculus Morum is a preacher's reference book, consisting in an ordered repository of preachable materials, and it is accompanied in fully half of surviving medieval copies by a set of sermon outlines that show how its materials could be employed in sermons preached on specific days of the church calendar.[62] In the sermon outlines a preacher would find a thema, usually derived from the gospel or epistle lection for the day in question, a division of that thema, and precise cross-reference to appropriate materials in the *Fasciculus Morum*. The outlines are written in Latin, like *Fasciculus Morum* itself, but the sermons were probably delivered in English. This disposition of languages was evidently very common for sermons preached to the laity in England in the thirteenth, fourteenth, and fifteenth centuries: though preached mostly in English, the sermon text would be recorded mostly in Latin.[63] Sermon scripts and preachers' handbooks are texts susceptible to textual analysis, but they are also the written counterpart to a distinct semiotic performance, executed in another language and sited in the pulpit.

Modern linguistic anthropology has developed intricate conceptual frameworks for analysis of text-supported practices of oral semiosis like preaching a sermon or reciting a poem. I draw on this literature at the close of this chapter; my present argument requires only the traditional framework of classical rhetoric. From the perspective of classical rhetoric, a Latin script destined for vernacular delivery performs only *inventio* and *dispositio*: materials suitable for a sermon have been identified (that's *inventio*) and arranged into a workable sequence (*dispositio*). The resulting sermon structure could be highly intricate, but its verbal texture might be left in note form.[64] Only at exceptional moments, when the details of wording are too important to be left to improvisation, does the script descend to matters of *elocutio*, or the provision of wording in the language of delivery. English verse is often—not always—set down in English.[65] Sermon divisions are treated with the same care, and so are translations of biblical and patristic quotations. These elements are often recorded in English in sermon texts otherwise Latin. As Holly Johnson explains, a scribe may switch to English at points where "verbatim" wording is desired: preachers could generally preach "prose sections" from Latin notes "but could hardly be expected to generate Middle English rhymes on the spot."[66] This insight gets us halfway to an explanation of the bits of rhymed English that one finds embedded in Latin sermons. It tells us why these materials have been recorded in English. To explain what the bits of rhymed English are, we need a theory of Middle English prosodic forms.

As further illustration of the problem, I turn to a second bit of rhymed English, sometimes described as a Passion lyric. Though not in *Fasciculus Morum*, this second example circulated widely; I quote from Wenzel's edition and translation of a fourteenth-century bilingual sermon for Good Friday, on the biblical thema *amore langueo* (Song of Songs 2:5):[67]

Nam ista benedicta passio Christi isto die trahere debet lacrimas de oculis et singultus de corde cuiuslibet boni Christiani sicud testatur beatus Augustinus sic loquens de passione Christi: "Memoria passionis tue, o bone Iesu, lacrimas allicit, oculos confundit, faciem inmutat, et cor dulcorat."

Þe mynde of þy swet passion, Iesu,
>   teres it telles,
>   eyen it bolleȝ,
>   my vesage it wetes,
>   and my hert it swetes.

Et ideo sicut dicit idem Augustinus, "semper fit tibi fixus in mente qui pro te semel fuit fixus in cruce."

(For the blessed passion Christ suffered on this day should draw tears from the eyes and sighs from the heart of every good Christian, as Augustine witnesses when he speaks of Christ's passion: "The memory of your passion, oh good Christ, draws tears, clouds the eyes, distorts the face, and sweetens the heart."

The memory of thy sweet passion, Jesus,
>   it draws tears,
>   makes eyes run over,
>   bedews my face,
>   and sweetens my heart.

And as Augustine further says, "Let him always be fastened in your mind who was once fastened for you on the cross.")

The Middle English is recorded in *IMEV* and its successors, but has no metrical structure that I can discern: though the passage divides neatly into two-beat segments punctuated with rhyme, the patterning of weak syllables is rhetorical, not metrical. Wenzel, guided by rhyme, sets it out in lines as verse. For an alternative interpretation, one needs to look more closely at the Latin quotations that precede and follow, attributed here to Augustine. These feature parallel clauses and inflectional rhyme (*similiter cadens*). In the first quotation—the one translated into English—the four short clauses have been arranged such that the first two have verbs of the third conjugation, with *-it* inflection, and the second two have verbs of the first conjugation, with *-at* inflection. These are two couplets of prose clauses. The only stylistic difference between this Latin *auctoritas* and its English rendering is that the English employs full rhyme rather than inflectional rhyme, for the neutralization of weak final vowels in late Old English meant that repetition of inflections alone could not in English achieve the effect it did in Latin. (The spelling *telles* is an error for *Middle English Dictionary* [*MED*] "tollen, v.1," meaning "to draw, beckon, entice"; see sense 1[c].) The English translation is impressive, representing both the idea of the Latin text and its elegant expression. It is poetic, lyrical, and must have been valued by preachers, but it is not verse. It is instead a little pearl of rhetorical *elocutio*, a flower to be pinned into the oral text of a sermon preached on Good Friday. Some of the other flowers so recorded are indeed verse, but this one is just a flower.

For a Typology of Middle English Meters

The Index has operated without an adequate set of categories. This is evident from its treatment of rhymed English in Latin sermons; it is also evident in the notes supplied by the Index on the form of individual items. Rhyme scheme is duly recorded, as is the count of lines per stanzaic unit; if there is alliteration, its presence is often noted. Formal description proceeds no further: the field for "versification" in *DIMEV* makes no comment on the metrical structure of verse lines. So, for example, the Harley lyrics "Weping haueþ myn wonges wet" (*DIMEV* 6186) and "Ich herde men vpo mold" (*DIMEV* 2198) are recorded as having an identical verse form ("12-line alliterative stanzas" rhyming abababcdcd), yet their respective meters are not at all alike.[68] The lines of "Weping" alternate smoothly between beat and offbeat. The first eight lines of each stanza are standard Middle English dolnik, with four beats to a line; the last four lines of each stanza have three beats to a line. The lines of "Ich herde men" are uniformly four-beat, but the rhythm is more complex than dolnik: double offbeats are more frequent in this poem and disposed in accordance with the practice of alliterative verse.[69] Both poems employ alliteration, but only "Ich herde men" is alliterative. The two poems exemplify the differences in metrical design that hide behind an identical "versification" field in *DIMEV*.

By neglecting to distinguish one metrical design from another, editors of the Index place themselves in a poor position to distinguish metered from unmetered language. That problem cannot be fixed in the space of a chapter, but corrective efforts should probably begin with the Middle English dolnik, the most numerous line type in the surviving records. To that end, I here offer a metrical analysis of the English verses in the sermon *Amore langueo*. In an appendix I make a similar analysis of the English verses in *Fasciculus Morum*. The verses of *Fasciculus Morum* are more various than those of *Amore langueo*, and more instructive as well.

DIMEV records thirteen verse items in the copy of *Amore langueo* employed by Wenzel as his base text (Oxford, Balliol College, MS 149, fols. 31–38v).[70] This count includes two variant appearances of *DIMEV* 1367 but omits a second appearance (with slight variation) of *DIMEV* 1371. I have argued above that one item (*DIMEV* 5404, the translation of pseudo-Augustine) is not verse. I would also exclude *DIMEV* 880, which commemorates the seven torments of the Passion: "blod-[s]wetyng, hard byndyng, gret traualyng, smert betyng, long wakyng. Croys-beryng, scherp prikyng." These are rhymed cola, not verse lines. The remaining eleven items recorded by *DIMEV* in the Balliol copy of *Amore langueo* are all in a single meter, the ubiquitous English dolnik. The two versions of "For loue I morne & sorowe make" (*DIMEV* 1367) are an instructive quasi-exception: the version in the main text is severely compressed. In the bottom margin a later hand entered the full text of the lyric (virgules are my addition, marking the caesura; linguistic material in bold fills strong metrical positions; segments in italic are omitted in the compressed version of this lyric transmitted in the main text):

For **loue** I **morne** / *& sorowe make*
For morninge y **perische** / **for** þi **sake**
Though y perysche / y **hope** þi **grace**
My **lyue** *my hope* / ys **in** þi **face**

Repetition and grammatical transposition of the key words ("morne"/ "morninge," "y perische"/"y perische," "y hope"/"my hope") yields metrical verse; it also yields an elegant rendering of the concatenated Latin tags that precede this English item in the sermon: "Amore langueo . . . Langore pereo . . . Pereundo spero . . . Sperando reuiuisco." Given this Latin source, one should probably read "Y lyue" for "My lyue" in the final line.

The other English lyrics in the Balliol copy of *Amore langueo* give fifty-six lines of metrically homogeneous verse. Marginal or interlinear additions unique to Balliol twice spoil the meter.[71] Rhythmical alternation is the general principle and it operates most strictly at the close of the line. The interval between the third and fourth beats is monosyllabic in each line of the poem quoted above and in all but four lines in the other poems of *Amore langueo* (citations are to line numbers in Wenzel's edition of *Amore langueo*):

1. Wo and peyne and gret blame (459)
2. For þis day wondris he wroth (637)
3. Qwan þou scholdes þi liff lete (655)
4. Lorde þat lete oute blode of þi side (766)

In line 637 one might suppose that an auxiliary verb has gone missing; reading "For **þis** day **wondr**is / [**hath**] he **wroth**" would yield metrical verse.[72] At line 655 the four copies of *Amore langueo* show much variation; reading "þi liff [for]lete" would yield metrical verse.[73] In the two remaining lines above, the copy of this sermon in Dublin, Trinity College, MS 277 gives a variant reading with regular meter. For "gret" in line 459, Trinity has the disyllabic synonym "mekyll."[74] In line 766 Trinity omits "blode," correctly. The Balliol line must be read in context with the following:

Lorde þat lete oute blode of þi side
Watur and blode þat sprede wide

Somewhere in the transmission of these verses a scribe intruded "blode" into 766, in anticipation of following copy. The Trinity reading, omitting "blode" from line 766, yields better meter and better syntax. The word "sprede" may have inflectional *-e* in line 767, but that syllable is precarious, vulnerable to loss.[75] Trinity renders the meter more secure by adding a throwaway intensifier: "þat spred so wyde."[76]

On seven other occasions in the English lyrics of *Amore langueo*, Trinity has readings metrically superior to Wenzel's base text.[77] If we permit these Trinity readings to correct Balliol, then we may construct a metrical profile as follows:

- About half of the lines are headless, lacking a weak syllable before the first beat. The others begin with a single weak syllable; runs of consecutive weak syllables do not occur in initial position.
- One line in seven has a disyllabic interval (that is, two consecutive weak syllables) between the first beat and the second.[78] All others have a single weak syllable in this position. Since disyllabic

intervals are not restricted to headless lines, the feature cannot be reanalyzed as "trochaic substitution" or "initial stress inversion."

- About one line in five has a disyllabic interval between the second beat and the third; the disyllabic interval always straddles the caesura, with one weak syllable contributed from either side (an "epic caesura").[79] All other lines have a single weak syllable in this location; the weak syllable follows the caesura more often than it precedes it (the ratio is 3:2).
- The third and fourth beats are always separated by a single weak syllable. (Exceptions are lines 459 and 655, unless emended as suggested above.)
- I do not find convincing examples of stress clash anywhere in the line; nor of more than two consecutive weak syllables.

This description is based on too small a sample for numerical ratios to have authority. Moreover, some patterns not attested in the *Amore langueo* verses— stress clash and initial double offbeats, for example—occur as minority patterns elsewhere in Middle English dolnik, including the English verses of *Fasciculum Morum*.[80] Yet, the above metrical profile will at least serve to reiterate some theoretical features of my analysis, beginning with the question of footedness. The suitability of foot-based scansions remains an unsettled question in the specialist literature on medieval English meters.[81] I agree with the foot-prosodists that lines of Middle English dolnik are partitioned, but I see lines as dividing into two metrical cola, not four metrical feet. A foot-based analysis would always be possible, but presupposes greater structuration than I perceive in Middle English verse, and leads too easily into the conclusion that the verse is metrically sloppy.

My interpretation of the dolnik line as composed of two metrical cola may be controversial, but it is supported by poetic syntax. The midline division usually corresponds to an important syntactic break; among the verses of *Amore langueo*, the salient exception is line 195, where the caesura splits conjunctive "as" from the noun phrase it governs: "He syket as / a sorful man." The relevant patterns of poetic syntax become clearer at scale, when examined in a larger sample of verse. The 1,211 lines of *Pearl* contain numerous polysyllabic words—words that may, and often do, supply two metrical beats.[82] There are three possible placements within the line:

1. Of **cour**taysye, / as **sayt3** Saynt **Poul**e (457)
2. To **suche** is **heuenriche** arayed (719)
3. For **ho** is **Quen** / of **cor**taysye. (444)

When a polysyllabic word supplies two metrical beats, those beats may belong to the same colon, as in 1 and 3, or bridge the cola, as in 2. Line 719 is
the single instance of a midline polysyllable in *Pearl*, whereas 1 and 3 are represented by forty-three and seventy-six instances respectively. This distribution could be credited to *Pearl*'s intricate device of verbal concatenation,
which regularly places polysyllables at line end, but similar distributions recur at the level of the phrase. Consider, for example, the distribution of
noun phrases in which an attributive adjective immediately precedes the noun
it modifies, and the adjective and noun each supply one beat:

1. My **precious perl**e / **wythou**ten **spot.** (48)
2. He **se3** þer ydel / **men** ful **strong**e (531)
3. Ne **proue**d I **neuer** / her **prec**ios pere. (4)

The adjective and noun may be contained within a single rhythmical colon,
as in 1 and 3, or they may bridge the two cola, as in 2. *Pearl* contains just
eight instances of pattern 2, whereas 1 and 3 each occur over a hundred times.
Finally, one may note that the colon boundary coincides with the boundary
of a clause or a prepositional phrase in some 450 lines in *Pearl*—an average
of one line in three. Against this figure, one may place forty-three lines in
which a conjunction, relative pronoun, or preposition is divided from the
clause or phrase that it governs. An example is "I **entred in** / þat **er**ber **grene**"
(38), and this is the same type of mismatch that I flagged above, in a single
line of the *Amore langueo* lyrics: "He **syket as** / a **sorful man.**"

The numerical data admit opposing interpretations. One may interpret
rare mismatches of syntax and meter as evidence that Middle English dolnik lacks a caesura.[83] My preference is instead to interpret the mismatches
as complex realizations of a bipartite verse design: precisely because the
bipartite structure is so well established over long stretches of verse, poets can,
on occasion, place a major syntactic boundary after the first beat, or place a
word like *heuenriche* at midline, without damaging the legibility of their form.

Bipartite structure gives the line flexibility and perceptual clarity, allowing it to accommodate upward and downward deviations from normal syllable count. The meter admits least flexibility at its close, which is precisely

what comparative and general metrics leads us to expect: poetic meters tend to be defined most strictly at the right edges of metrical units.[84] The Middle English dolnik admits disyllabic intervals and stress clash up until the close, at which point the basic principle of stress alternation reasserts itself. Even in *Pearl*, where disyllabic intervals are very frequent at earlier points in the line, and trisyllabic intervals not infrequent, the interval between the last two beats is monosyllabic in somewhere between 85 and 95 percent of all lines.[85] Behind the fluctuating syllable counts in Middle English verse there are robust prosodic regularities.

A future iteration of the *Index of Middle English Verse* should employ a typology of metrical forms and classify verse items according to metrical type. As a step toward that end, we need better articulated positive descriptions of Middle English poetic meters. Despite much excellent work by prosodists, much Middle English poetry remains uncharted territory.

Conclusions

In a preface to the *Supplement to the Index of Middle English Verse*, Rossell Hope Robbins remarked that a disproportionate share of additions in that volume were "verse items of only two lines, including many preachers' tags and proverbs, gnomic sayings, and English lines in Latin stories"—or "short proverbial tags and shards . . . embedded in prose," as he put it a few pages later (xix, xxi). In subsequent decades, Latin preaching materials and other prose texts have continued to yield a steady stream of previously unrecorded Middle English, and this has rightly focused attention on questions of context. Scholars have inquired what English verses are doing in these manuscript and discursive contexts and how the textual ensembles worked. We have come to see embedded English items not as "shards" but as functionally integrated components of a larger bilingual construct. At the same time, increased access to archival documents has sharpened our sense that English verses in sermons are not much to look at on the manuscript page. They can appear to be dissolved in a bath of Latin. Most verse items in *Amore langueo* consist of a single couplet or quatrain, and the English verses in this sermon never hold forth for more than eight uninterrupted lines. The longest item, as indexed by *DIMEV*, is doled out, a quatrain at a time, over the last nine manuscript pages of the Latin text; individual quatrains punctuate, reecho, and ornament the preacher's exposition. From a visual standpoint as well as a semantic and functional one, lyrics are absorbed into their co(n)texts. All this has led in recent decades to some anxious questioning about the character and even the ontological status of Middle English lyric. If "For loue I morne & sorowe make" is a lyric, in what sense is a "Middle English lyric" a thing?

I have sought in this chapter to show what metrical analysis may contribute to that question. Context is not all: contextualization implies, as its dialectical counterpart, some grasp of the text as a unified thing among other things. Talk of the "unity of the poem" has become disreputable since the New Criticism, but we may benefit today from reflecting a bit on what, exactly, we seek to contextualize, and how those entities came into being. In performance studies and linguistic anthropology, one finds the term "entextualization" advanced as the technical counterpart to contextualization: contextualization names the ways that utterances accrue meaning from their discursive or pragmatic placement; entextualization names the ways an utterance binds itself to itself, and thus into an entity that may be repeated across multiple discursive and pragmatic placements.[86] Poetic meter is an important mode of entextualization in premodern literary cultures. If contextual analysis has tended to dissolve the presumed thing-hood of Middle English lyrics, metrical analysis shows that verses are robust enough to sustain that. Metrical structuration sets verse apart from its surround; it defines the verse object as a distinct entity, distinguished by a specifiable compositional craft.

Appendix: A Catalog of English Verse Forms
in *Fasciculus Morum*

Wenzel rightly describes the four-beat line as "the preferred verse form" in this collection; in a brief treatment, he also notices the presence of verse in a variety of other forms.[87] I offer an annotated catalog.

Four-beat lines (Middle English dolnik)

Fully half of the items designated by Wenzel as verse (32 of 61) conform to the metrical profile of Middle English dolnik.[88] Whereas the lyrics in *Amore langueo* avoid stress clash, those in *Fasciculus Morum* (henceforth *FM*) several times permit clashing stress at the caesura.[89] *FM* 43 makes especially effective use of this possibility:

That y ȝaf, / þat ys **myn.**
Þat I eet, / **þ**at was **myn**n.
That I **lefte** / behynde **me,**
Who **hit** schall **haue** / I **con** noȝt **se.**

This lyric begins with the sparest possible realization of the English dolnik. In my scansion, the first two lines have just six syllables each and just a single weak syllable per half-line. That scansion is open to doubt, and it claims little authority beyond the force of expectation: dolnik is the most frequent meter in *FM*, and thus probably the first meter a reader will try out upon a new and unknown bit of embedded English. One attempts to parse the material metrically—that is, to make it into verse—and the first two lines of this poem leave one uncertain whether one has chosen a plausible or fitting target form. The next two lines offer confirmation. The third line, while still headless, adds a syllable at the boundary between cola. In the fourth line the lyric arrives finally at the rhythmic contour normative for the English dolnik. A clipped, staccato stanza opening unfolds into a ponderous, deliberate stanza close. Contrastive stress between "ys" and "was" slows the pace at the end of the first couplet, syphoning prominence away from the rhyme word. The word "noght," in the last weak position of the last line, has a similar effect: it dampens the rhythmical bounce that would otherwise be afforded by the weak syllables in this line.

While closer to the dolnik than to any other form, eight lyrics have disyllabic intervals between the third and fourth beats, among other irregularities: *FM* 1, 10, 27, 32, 34A, 34B, 40, 48.[90]

Three-beat lines

The three-beat line type is instanced by *FM* 4, 52, 57, and 60 (the last line of 52 is irregular). I present *FM* 4 as an example.

Who-so **spekyth** [oft]
Of **þyng** þat **is** vn-**wrest**
Þouh hit **seme soft**
When he **spekyth mest**
5   He **schal** hit **heren** on l[o]ft
When he **wenyth lest.**

Line 3 "seme" is subjunctive, with grammatically justified weak -*e*. Line 5 "heren" is an infinitive, and the -*en* inflection written by the scribe of Wenzel's base text may be realized as the reduced endings -*e* or -∅. The meter cues a form without -*n*, yielding regular alternation of beat and offbeat.

The three-beat line is too short to admit much variation, but lines may begin with or without a weak syllable. The poems in this form in *FM* show a distinct preference for disyllabic rhyme, perhaps as a way of adding weight to a very short line.

*   *   *

With two exceptions, to be treated at the end, all remaining lyrics in *FM* are constructed by combining three- and four-beat units.

Six-beat lines (3 + 3)

The six-beat line is instanced by *FM* 15, 37, and 41B, the last of which serves as my illustration:

> Thys **word**le **vs** de**fy**lyþ / *and* **clan**syth **but** a **ly**te.
> Of **fil**þe þat **ys** þe**ryn**ne / **who** can **hym** best **quy**te?

Wenzel prints this item in short lines, though it rhymes only at the end. Line 1 *wordle* (world) is disyllabic, as probably also in 33.1; the spelling is rare but authentic. The adverb *þerynne* (< OE *þærinne*) is a favorite of Middle English poets, useful for its xSx stress contour and minimal semantic content.

The six-beat line derives from the fusion of two three-beat units. The resulting medial caesura becomes a flex point, exactly as in the four-beat line: note the extra unstressed syllable at the caesura in the first line above.

FM 41A and 41B form an instructive pair, consisting of four- and three-beat versions of the same material. At 41A.2 "world" is disyllabic again—or else transpose "fyle ys" to "ys fyle" as in three copies.

Septenary and ballad measure (4 + 3)

The septenary and ballad measure forms are instanced by *FM* 11, 13, 14, 39A, 39B, 54, and item C in Wenzel's "Other English Phrases." Rhyme alone dif-

ferentiates the short lines of ballad measure from the 4 + 3 units of septenary. One scribe turned 39A into ballad measure by introducing rhymes
(though ineptly) at the ends of four-beat units in that poem.

Five lyrics in *FM* are constructed from units of 4 + 4+3: these are *FM* 7,
16, 21 45, and 49.[91] *FM* 16 supplies my example; I have indented the three-
beat lines in accordance with conventions of modern print:

	Was þer neu*er* / caren so **lothe**	[SxS|xSxS]
	As **mon** when **he** / to **put goth**	[xSxS|xSxS]
	And **deth** has **layd**e so **lowe.**	[xSxSxSx]
	For **when** deth **drawes** / **mon** from o**þur,**	[xSxSx|SxSx]
5	Þe **suster nul** / not **se** þe **brother,**	[xSxSx|SxSx]
	Ne **fader** þe **sone** i-**knawe.**	[xSxSxSx]

Disyllabic "neuer" would not spoil the meter in line 1, but the monosyllabic
by-form "ner" is possible and I adopt it in my scansion. Later in the same
line, "caren" presumably represents *MED* "careine, n.," from Anglo-French
(= Mod. E. "carrion"). The word has etymologically justified *-e* and is so used
by Chaucer and Langland, scanning xSx. In this instance, however, final *-e*
would create an anomalous disyllabic interval in the second half of the
line. The word "put" (line 2) may acquire inflectional *-e* here, as the object
of a preposition. My scansion omits "þe" in line 6, where the article is grammatically superfluous and would contribute an anomalous extra syllable in
a three-beat unit. The second branch of a parallel construction permits terser
expression, optionally omitting particles understood from the first branch.
Scribes sometimes padded these constructions out, as if intending to clarify
syntax on the page.[92]

The four- and three-beat units in septenary and ballad meter behave as
expected. The four-beat units show the usual flexibility, with an extra syllable not infrequently appearing after the first beat or at the caesura. Exceptionally, there is an extra syllable at the head of 54.7. In 14 the four-beat units
have stress clash at the caesura.

Hybrid alliterative-dolnik

Wenzel rightly describes the form of *FM* 25 and 26A as "peculiar."[93] The second of these serves as my example:

Beholde myne **woun**des, / how **sore** I am **dyȝth,**   [xSxxSx / xSxxS]
For all þe **wele** þat þou **hast** / I **wan** hit in **fyȝt.**   [xxxSxxS / xSxxS]
I am **sore woun**det, / be**hold** on my **skyn.**   [xxSxSx / xSxxS]
Leue lyf, for my **lo**ue / **let** me comen **in.**   [SxSxxSx / SxxS]

Like the septenary, this is a long-line form with fixed caesura. The line always has two metrical stresses in its second half; these are typically separated by a disyllabic interval. Accentual patterning in the first half-line is more various, but there are usually two metrical stresses and at least one string of consecutive weak syllables. When a half-line has three stressable words it is often possible to read one as demoted. In 26A.4 I would demote "leue." The verse form is seen also in the alliterative Harley lyrics, noted earlier in this chapter. It developed in the thirteenth century, combining elements of the alliterative meter and the dolnik, and it continued to be used throughout the fifteenth century, most often for short poems. It represents a significant innovation in the history of English verse forms: in these poems the alliterative meter was simplified, shorn of its layered complexity, and reinterpreted as accentual-syllabic.

Chapter 5

Lyric Value

INGRID NELSON

> The arts are our storehouse of recorded values. They spring from
> and perpetuate hours in the lives of exceptional people, when their
> control and command of experience is at its highest, hours when
> the varying possibilities of existence are most clearly seen and the
> different activities which may arise are most exquisitely reconciled,
> hours when habitual narrowness of interests or confused bewil-
> derment are replaced by an intricately wrought composure.

So says I. A. Richards (1893–1979), the seminal literary critic who devised a
method of reading, "practical criticism," that in many ways inaugurated the
academic study of literature and made lyric poetry central to the English
literary canon.[1] In this passage from *Principles of Literary Criticism* (1924),
Richards links the "values" that a work of art preserves to an aesthetic model,
the "intricately wrought composure"; or, as his intellectual heir Cleanth
Brooks memorably puts it, a "well wrought urn."[2] Richards's method famously asked students to study and respond to a poem stripped of context—
without authorial attribution, date, or any sense of historical origin. Poems
best suited to this method tend to have certain formal features, particularly
brevity, rhetorical complexity, and language that is modern or modernizable.
They can be read as containers of complex meaning, made into bounded
wholes that reward contemplation by revealing layers of detail and depth. As
the poem, so the person: Richards developed what he called a "psychological theory of value" that privileged the development of complex, autonomous

subjectivity by means of the contemplation of poetry that shared these qualities. The aesthetic and ethical senses of "value" come together for Richards in this theory; good poetry makes good people.

Richards's use of the term "value" is not idiosyncratic. As we will see, his critical method arises in the early twentieth century alongside and in dialogue with a philosophical theory of value called axiology. Yet Richards's work is also in many ways a high-water mark in a history of lyric reading that has long privileged value, ethical and aesthetic. From Horace's insistence in the *Ars poetica* (ca. 19 BCE) on a rhetorical decorum that limited poetic genres to specific topics, to Sir Philip Sidney's sixteenth-century defense of the ethical and political values of poetry, valuing poetry has always involved defining and defending its values.[3] Yet valuing itself is a willful, ethical, and political act. Richards's privileging of the complex autonomy of the poem and of the person conduces to a humanist politics of universality that *under*values the diversity and difference of people's experiences within their social contexts and their places in a power structure. Likewise, Richards and his followers determined which poems to value at the expense of poetic "others" that did not conform to their aesthetic or social values. Virginia Jackson has referred to one aspect of this phenomenon as the "lyricization of poetry," the process by which the broad field of poetry has narrowed to comprise only verse writing that conforms to a normalized lyric form. The academic study of poetry now largely excludes, for example, "the riddles, papyrae, epigrams, songs, sonnets, *blasons*, *Lieder*, elegies, dialogues, conceits, ballads, hymns, and odes considered lyrical in the Western tradition before the early nineteenth century."[4] Yet as Jahan Ramazani has observed, poetry is in many ways the genre most open to absorbing and transforming other discourses, from news to prayer to song.[5] Medieval English poetry has especially suffered from these critical standards. At least since Bishop Thomas Percy's *Reliques of Ancient English Poetry* (1765), a collection of songs and ballads that their editor attributed to anonymous medieval bards, premodern poetry has been seen more as an object of antiquarian curiosity and sentimentality than of poetic analysis.[6] Thus Richards included the short poetry of Shakespeare and Donne, but not Middle English lyrics, among the anonymized texts he famously asked his students to analyze.

In short, even as Richards's theoretical work promoted the centrality of lyric poetry to English literature, he inaugurated a process of canon-making that increasingly neglected Middle English lyrics throughout the twentieth century.[7] Under the rubric of aesthetic and psychological "value" that Richards articulated, premodern poetry's literary and ethical potentials have been overlooked. Yet a genre is not, in and of itself, an ideology.[8] As I will argue in this essay, recovering and reimagining "value" as a framework for reading poetry can, in our own critical moment, reveal the value of Middle English lyrics.

My central claim is that if we examine the values of a particular group of medieval lyrics, the dialogue poems, on their own terms (so far as possible), these poems can serve as the foundation for a mode of lyric reading that promotes certain urgent ethical values at odds with the complex autonomy Richards and his followers championed. These are the values of difference, diversity, and plurality, in particular as they are represented and realized through the interactions between subjects. As I will show, premodern dialogue lyrics cohere more with modern phenomenology's concept of "intersubjectivity" than with Richards's post-Enlightenment concept of autonomous selfhood, even as the dialogue lyrics offer a more nuanced view of subjectivity and personhood than either theory. Yet even as I critique the values Richards assigned to poetry, I am indebted to his sharpening of the term "value" as a foundation for establishing a canon of poetry alongside a set of methods for reading it. And while many readers of poetry since Richards have rejected his values, few have done so by reintroducing Middle English poetry to their alternative lyric canons. Thus, "What do Middle English lyrics value?" is related to the question "What is the value of Middle English lyrics?"—a pair of questions that address this book's titular query.

To begin to concretize how Richards's concept of "value" might be refigured to apply to Middle English lyrics, let us employ his durable method, close reading. Consider the opening exchange in this anonymous thirteenth-century dialogue between Mary and Christ, set during the Crucifixion.

> Stond well, moder, under rode   *cross*
> Bihold thy sone with glade mode   *mood*
> Blithe, moder, might thou be.   *happy*
> Sone, how shulde I blithe stonde?
> I see thin fet, I see thin honde   *your feet; your hands*
> Nailed to the harde tree.[9]

If we approach these verses by asking what they value, certain aesthetic, formal, and thematic features come to the fore. These verses contain two voices, with equal space given to each; a lexis of emotion ("blithe") and beholding ("bihold"/"see") that connects affect with perception; a consistent rhyme scheme that, as we shall see, can be understood as couplets marked by internal rhyme. From these initial observations, which anticipate a more extensive discussion below, I posit that this poem values *porousness*. It moves across boundaries: between its speakers, between the external and the internal, within and across couplets. We might characterize the porousness of Middle English lyrics like this one in the words of a different poem, this untitled verse riddle from the tenth-century Exeter Book:

> A thing there is   strangely begotten,
> furious and fierce;   runs a violent course
> rages grimly,   moves over the ground,
> is mother of many   marvelous creatures.
> Moving beautifully,   it is ever striving;
> low-lying is its close grip.   None to another
> can fairly with wise words   describe its features
> or say how manifold   is the multitude of its kin.[10]

The commonly accepted answer to this riddle is "water." But taken proleptically, it might equally be "lyric": a genre strangely begotten, indescribable, the mother of many marvelous creatures. In the Middle Ages, texts, especially scripture, were often compared to water: quenching those who thirst for understanding, overflowing with meaning, shallow for the laity and deep for the learned.[11] Notwithstanding the dominance of "lyric" as a generic category, it has proven difficult to define: "None to another / can fairly with wise words describe its features" sums up the history of lyric theory.[12] This Exeter riddle suggests that a poem might be less a "well wrought urn" than its liquid contents. Brooks's evocative phrase alludes to John Keats's "Ode on a Grecian Urn," whose titular vessel inspires the speaker to declare, "Beauty is truth, truth beauty." But the Old English poem offers an alternative paradigm to the idea of the lyric as a bounded whole; instead, it imagines a force that is as ungraspable as it is powerful, as protean as it is indomitable.[13]

And while Richards's model of lyric as an "intricately wrought composure" reflected an ideal of complex and autonomous subjectivity, valuing the porousness of Middle English dialogue lyrics might rather encourage valuing plurality, intersectionality, and difference. By focusing on such lyrics in this chapter, I want to call attention to particular features of these poems that draw the reader or listener toward an exploration of difference. In par-

ticular, the plural voices of these lyrics express a condition of intersubjectivity, in which subjects define and refine themselves in relation to the other.
The making of subjectivity is thereby a social and communal process: *I* come
to understand myself through interactions with *you* and *us*. To decide to value
Middle English lyrics for their poetics and poetic theory is to acknowledge
a porousness between self and other that is at once psychological, in the sense
that *I* am constituted by not-*I*, and historical, in the sense that modernity is
constituted by premodernity. A lyric theory that values Middle English lyrics promises to illuminate how poetic forms and rhetorics of difference can
promote an ethics that values difference, too.

    The first part of this chapter explores an idea of value centered on the
place of lyric reading in academic institutions. The emergence of axiology
(the study of value and valuation) in the first decades of the twentieth century
coincided with that of academic lyric reading, linking economic and moral
values with humanistic thinking. I examine the implications of this intersection by considering the "psychological theory of value" Richards outlined
in his *Principles of Literary Criticism* and its influence on the development of
the English lyric canon and lyric theory. My focus is on decoupling Richards's actual theory of value from later American New Critical tenets, even
as I acknowledge how Richards's ideas sowed the seeds of this later school
as well as of more recent methods of reading poetry that actively refute the
canons and politics of the New Critics. I join a critical reassessment of Richards that examines how his theories have as much in common with contemporary anti-formalism as the theories and readings he inspired in later
formalists.[14] In particular, I demonstrate how Richards's argument for value
as a foundation for lyric reading can be reimagined to enable a critical re-
valuation of Middle English poetry.

    In the second section, I turn my attention to a selection of Middle En-
glish dialogue lyrics, reading for their values and their value. Such poems
frequently demonstrate what Thomas Reed, in his study of long-form medieval dialogue poetry, calls an "aesthetics of irresolution," articulating
plurality rather than consensus.[15] Thus these poems at once illustrate the
potentialities of intersubjective dialogue and its limitations. They progress
erratically, characterized by the misconceptions and intractability of much
human dialogue. However, the dialogue form itself encourages a poem's audience to participate in intersubjective meaning-making. By presenting readers,
listeners, and singers with multiple voices—voices that, as we shall see, are
grounded in a medieval rhetorical figure called *ethopoeia*—these dialogues

demonstrate the power of voice for a speaker as well as a listener and suggest that speaking and hearing are fragile but crucial activities, both for making meaning and for making ethical actors.

Theories of Value and Lyric Reading

In a 1916 essay, the American philosopher Ralph Barton Perry noted a conflict between the economic and moral valences of the term "value." Where economists prioritize the exchange value or cost of a commodity, moral philosophers privilege the life-enhancing values of an object or activity. He proposed that rather than dividing these meanings, we should understand these disciplines as part of a group of "value sciences."[16] Perry later codified his ideas in *General Theory of Value* (1926), in which he described a value as "any object of interest."[17] While the dual senses of "value" as merit and economic worth ("does this idea have value?"; "a thing of some value") date back to the Middle Ages, the philosophical and moral senses of "value" develop in the late nineteenth and early twentieth centuries ("these are my values").[18] Indeed, although Perry does not pursue the word's history further, we might note that the Middle English senses of "value," deriving from Latin *valere*, include a sense of merit specific to rank and status, as well as one pertaining to practical efficacy, for example, of medicinal herbs.[19]

Perry's work was seminal for the emerging branch of philosophy now known as axiology, the study of value and evaluative processes. A group of axiologists—notably G. E. Moore—influenced I. A. Richards. Richards studied moral philosophy and later psychology at Cambridge amid the flowering of the institution's brand of humanism, a secular idealism that embraced aesthetic experience as an ameliorating force in human life.[20] This interdisciplinary group of thinkers championed the potential for wholeness and goodness in humanity in their mortal lives rather than in a spiritual afterlife. One way of developing such wholeness was through aesthetic experience, an idea that Richards developed in the "psychological theory of value" he puts forth in his 1924 classic *Principles of Literary Criticism*. This theory, he hopes, will save criticism from two dominant critical paradigms: on the one hand, elitist and arbitrary judgments of "taste" and, on the other, a trees-over-forest philology.[21] Richards states that what he calls "high civilization" depends on, and indeed benefits from, the influence of the humanist values that literature promotes. Writing in the wake of World War I, Richards suggests that reading literature might heal and rebuild a people still suffering from the war's aftershocks.[22] He further claims that literature can repair human minds damaged by modernity and its instruments. "Mechanical inventions," Richards believes, are so disruptive to humanity "that our minds are, as it were, becoming of an inferior shape—thin, brittle, and patchy, rather than controllable and coherent." Poetry, as "the unique, linguistic instrument by which our minds have ordered their thoughts, emotions, desires," can strengthen our frail minds.[23]

A psychologist by training, Richards sought to replace both religious morality and scientific empiricism with a system of ethics based in a psychology that integrates the Freudianism and behaviorism of his era. In his psychology, infants demonstrate antisocial values and need to enter into "systematization" to become ethical social beings.[24] The primary ethical motivation for reading poetry is thus to make the reader's mind more normative and "civilized" in a postindustrial world that required "a more adaptable morality."[25] "We pass as a rule from a chaotic to a better organized state by ways which we know nothing about. Typically through the influence of other minds. Literature and the arts are the chief means by which these influences are diffused. It should be unnecessary to insist upon the degree to which high civilization, in other words, free, varied, and unwasteful life, depends upon them in a numerous society."[26] The values that Richards ascribes to reading poetry—expanding our emotional breadth, making us better members of society—emphasize the social aspect of what might otherwise simply be called ethics. While ethics have always been understood to have a social dimension, Richards's sense of "value" emphasizes the social repercussions of behavior and experience, even as it is grounded in the expansion of the individual psychology. But it is also important to note that Richards's psychological training produced certain assumptions about the human mind and its development that influenced his evaluations of particular poems and, as developed by his followers, the lyric canon.[27] In this model, the mind is fully autonomous and, when healthy, demonstrably normative or regular. It might be—indeed ought to be—influenced by other carefully selected minds, but primarily as indexes for a healthy normativity. Richards asserts, "What the theory [of value] attempts to provide is a system of measurement by which we can compare not only different experiences belonging to the same personality but different personalities."[28] The "system" helps to develop "civilized" minds.

What kinds of poems best accomplish this end? For Richards, as for many theorists, poetic value is determined by the mode of reading it encourages. The best poetry communicates to its reader an experience that is at once important and aesthetic, that is, conveyed with enough artistry and specificity to impart an equivalent (if not necessarily identical) experience. Sophisticated poetic language allows the reader to "construct an experience of equal value" in his own mind.[29] The valuable poem must not convey "stock conventional attitudes" but should rather introduce a new, more complex experience.[30] It does so by drawing on the "emotive" properties of language, "the effects in emotion and attitude produced by the reference it occasions."[31] Emotiveness is the bridge that language creates between minds. But just as all emotional experiences are not equally valuable to Richards, so too all uses of emotive language are not equally valuable. Thus Richards's theory of value ushered in a critical practice that focused on the details of poetic language, from sound and imagery to rhetoric and allusion.

Richards's theories influenced generations of critics in England and America. The group that came to be known as the American New Critics in particular promoted the idea that poems that produced complex and unusual experiences in readers' minds did so best by using complex and unusual language. Poems worth reading speak in "the language of paradox" that "unites the like with the unlike."[32] Irony, metaphor, and ambiguity in its many forms are features of language that particularly conduce to this kind of unity.[33] These elements lend themselves to "minute readings" whose purpose is the enrichment of the autonomous self.[34] Or, as a recent critic in the Richards lineage puts it, "The virtues of lyric—extreme compression, the appearance of spontaneity, an intense and expressive rhythm, a binding of sense by sound, a structure which enacts the experience represented, an abstraction from the heterogeneity of life, a dynamic play of semiotic and rhythmic 'destiny'— are all summoned to give voice to the 'soul'—the self when it is alone with itself, when its socially constructed characteristics (race, class, color, gender, sexuality) are felt to be in abeyance."[35] I quote Helen Vendler here not only for her clarity in summarizing the link between dense, complex lyric language and the self, but also to demonstrate the persistence of Richards's ideas for one of the most renowned and influential critics of poetry of our time. Here, Vendler resacralizes Richards's theory of value by asserting a post-identity ethic of poetic style. Rhythm, sound, and structure in poetry create a universal experience that expresses "soul" rather than, as Richards had it, building "mind." This soul is the most asocial and autonomous version of self, free of the burdens or pleasures of encounter with the other. It is no coincidence that Vendler upholds the canon of modern, first-person, introspective poetry as that best suited to literary study.

In short, Richards's contribution to axiology and to the academic study of literature was to link value with certain kinds of literary language. This, in turn, laid the groundwork for defining, especially in America, an English lyric canon that largely neglected Middle English lyrics. Richards's well-known pedagogical method—asking students to respond to anonymized poems short enough to be read and digested in a single session—privileged lyric poetry for its brevity, and modern (postmedieval) poetry for the invisibility of its historical specificity. That is, Shakespeare's and Donne's English is modernizable in a way that Middle English is not. Further, Richards's theory of emotional value privileged poetry whose language conveyed "emotional experiences" with precision and complexity. In this aesthetico-ethical value system, medieval lyric poetry is doubly disadvantaged: its language and substance are intentionally conventional. As a result, some defenders of medieval poetry have argued for the aesthetic, moral, or ethical value of their unadorned style as "intentionally anonymous" or "clear" and therefore universally assimilable.[36]

The reader may wonder why I have spent so much space on Richards and his values when for several decades many critics, and whole schools of theory and criticism, have rejected both. There are two reasons. First, many critics who champion the expansion of the poetic field beyond the Richardsian canon continue to overlook Middle English lyrics. Occitan troubadour poetry occasionally appears as a medieval forerunner of newer modes of poetic reading because it tends to serve late twentieth-century critical values more easily than medieval English lyrics.[37] Many of the most cogently articulated arguments for poetic forms that promote alternative modes of subjectivity, selfhood, or personhood center on the poetry of modernity or postmodernity. Theodor Adorno's classic 1957 essay "Lyric Poetry and Society" reads Goethe's "Traveler's Night-Song" to show how even an intensely inward-looking lyric "I" expresses his social conditions.[38] Adorno's essay has been seminal for critics who promote "anti-lyric" poetry as a critical object. Charles Altieri, for instance, describes what he calls an "anti-artefactual aesthetics" that read postmodern poems as processes rather than products.[39] Responding to Adorno, he suggests that "rather than accepting either romantic inwardness or versions of subjective agency as entirely constituted by social practices, this perspective emphasizes the range of expressive registers that agents bring into focus simply by manipulating and elaborating deictics."[40] Altieri's model for poetry as a record of "expressive registers" rendered in deictics is extremely helpful in thinking of mergings of form and value that depart from those posited by the New Critics and their followers. Yet Altieri, like many championing an anti-totalizing poetics of personhood, remains relentlessly presentist in his poetic corpus and, as such, reveals the latent influence Richards still exerts over critics who reject his values. An exclusive corpus must lead to an exclusive poetics.[41] It is as reifying to insist that only contemporary poems can speak to contemporary values as it is to refuse to historicize poetic reading.

The second reason for my extended discussion of Richards, however, is more recuperative. Among critics of poetry, he is the most explicit in his discussion of value. The axiological reading of poetry has far more to offer Middle English lyrics than it has to detract from them. Moreover, in taking "value" as a critical term we are restoring a conceptual category that was central to medieval culture. In a crucial sense, Richards's theory of value concerns how we value personhood: what elements contribute to a person of value, and how, conversely, we value cultural productions that effect such an increase in personal value. This was also important to medieval writers and thinkers, although they framed the discussion in different ways. In the later Middle Ages, we find abundant attestations of stock phrases that associate the term "value" with things of small worth, both financially ("grote") and proverbially ("flie").[42] These uses arise alongside others that emphasize positive financial and personal value(s), expressed in terms of commodity and of character. It appears, then, that the development of a language and concept of value in the later Middle Ages includes two important features: first, it includes its own negation; and second, it develops along distinct axes of economic value and personal value. These features of the value concept come together in what Peter Biller has called "medieval demographic thought," which includes a consideration of whether the kind of personhood represented by population, per se, has value.[43] Value was also an important concept for medieval poets, including Geoffrey Chaucer. As Robert Meyer-Lee has shown, Chaucer's *Canterbury Tales* contains an extended interrogation of literary value conducted through ideas of personal value as measured by social identity.[44]

A full exploration of medieval concepts of value is outside of the scope of this chapter. However, what I want to emphasize is that medieval axiology, like Richards's axiology, centers on a model of the value of personhood that is always in dialogue with the value of the encounters—cultural or interpersonal—that shape that person. Thus, if we decouple Richards's theory of "reading-poetry-as-value" from the particular values of complex autonomy that he promoted, we can see how values of personhood expressed in Middle English dialogue lyrics can offer the branch of contemporary poetics that has rejected the universalizing assumptions of Richards's model of personhood. With this in mind, let us turn to medieval lyrics and their intersubjectivity.

Intersubjectivity, Difference, and Middle English Dialogue Lyrics

I posited above that the poem "Stond wel, moder" values porousness. Indeed, the material witnesses of Middle English lyrics—that is to say, their original manuscript contexts—demonstrate the essential fungibility of these texts, which is perhaps their most striking feature by comparison with the modern printed (and frequently author-approved) texts of lyrics. Texts of Middle English lyrics survive in places that modern readers would not expect to find poetry: in sermons, among practical prose treatises, alongside prayers, in chronicles, and so forth. Further, they seldom appear with authorial attributions, much less titles, and often repeat each other's language.[45] As Ardis Butterfield puts it, Middle English lyrics demonstrate "a lateral, horizontal diffusion" across manuscripts, opening up the idea of lyric as a "network" rather than a node.[46] They have always been social texts. Only by imagining them as static artifacts have scholars been able to read them as conventional and doctrinaire scripts of official ideologies. In the terms of sociolinguistics, the surviving witnesses of Middle English lyrics demonstrate what is called *entextualization,* "the process by which circulable texts are produced by extracting discourse from its original context and reifying it as a bounded object."[47]

Readers of medieval literature have become increasingly interested in how such texts model forms of subjectivity that differ from literary constructions of distinct "characters" or "speaking subjects." A. C. Spearing and Julie Orlemanski have explored how aspects of textuality itself create new models of subjectivity from the self-referential function of grammatical features like pronouns and deixis.[48] Other accounts explore the collective implications of subjectivity in medieval literature. Elizabeth Fowler demonstrates how Chaucer's "Knight's Tale" evokes a "subjectivity-without-persons" "situat[ed] . . . in a kind of public 'being'" that allows works of art and literature to evoke common emotions in their audiences.[49] Cristina Maria Cervone's idea of "collective subjectivity" comprises "a combined yet distinct 'I' and 'we,'" while David Lawton's "public interiorities" describe how literary voice acts as a mediator between a text and its public(s).[50] And as Aden Kumler demonstrates, not only the language of lyrics but their material and practical contexts, for instance, when inscribed on ewers, determine how textual meaning is constituted within communal activities.[51] All of these ways of reading suggest that medieval poetry reflects and creates what we might call *transpersonal subjectivities*, where the understanding of self-as-subject is negotiated through one's social, material, and textual surroundings.

A specific form of transpersonal subjectivity occurs as interaction between persons, a concept that phenomenologists call intersubjectivity. In elaborating this concept, I follow the foundational work of Edmund Husserl (1859–1938) and Maurice Merleau-Ponty (1908–61), especially where it pertains to dialogue and communication. I turn to this framework as an alternative to the Richardsian model of subjectivity and in order to demonstrate the ways in which Middle English dialogue lyrics speak to both medieval and modern values. Husserl's seminal work *Cartesian Meditations* takes up and reimagines Descartes's method of beginning philosophical inquiry from an axiomatic premise (for Descartes, *cogito ergo sum*). Like his predecessor, Husserl finds an axiom in his awareness of himself as a thinking being. Unlike Descartes, he follows his inquiries not toward a proof of the existence of God but rather towards an examination of how the individual consciousness experiences the objects and others of a perceived external world; that is, toward the phenomenological. While Husserl takes the thinking self as the foundation of inquiry, he is concerned by the implied solipsism of this premise. Thus he argues for the existence of others with distinct subjectivities on a number of grounds. First, we perceive others as objects in an external world—that is, as bodies—but these bodies are animated by "governing" psyches. Further, these others and their respective consciousnesses combine to confirm the existence of an objective reality apart from any single consciousness, and it is only by admitting the existence of others that we can account for communal experiences and thereby discern that we exist in an intersubjective world. Finally, if we subscribe to an ethical sense, it is because we believe others to be distinct from ourselves. For all of these reasons, as individual subjects, we define ourselves with respect to the independent existence of others.[52]

Merleau-Ponty takes up and extends Husserl's account of intersubjectivity and, in particular, examines the role of spoken language and social interaction in subjective experience. According to Merleau-Ponty, the social world is not an object to contemplate, reject, or insert oneself into; rather, it is of a piece with the subject's existence. Social interactions, or what he calls "communication," are less about a self–other dichotomy than an articulation of certain shared qualities of existence that develop or refine the perceptual capabilities of each speaker.[53] Dialogue is an important mode of intersubjective communication: "In the experience of dialogue, a common ground is constituted by me and another; my thought and his form a single fabric, my words and those of my interlocutor are called forth by the state of the discussion and are inserted into a shared operation of which neither of us is the creator. . . . We are, for each other, collaborators in perfect reciprocity: our perspectives slip into each other, we coexist through a single world. . . . And even the objection raised by my interlocutor draws from me thoughts I did not know I possessed such that if I lend him thoughts, he makes me think in return."[54] It is less the individual's totalized language compositions that create thought and cognitive experiences than the shared production that is the dialogue. In other words, dialogue is an intersubjective mode that develops a sense of both difference and commonality as each speaker absorbs the other's words into an expansion of their own mental and affective experience. Commenters on Merleau-Ponty's ideas of communication extend these suggestions to sharpen the ideas of what it can accomplish. Frank J. Macke describes "intimate communication" as an encounter between bodies whose physical materialities facilitate an experience of intersubjectivity.[55] Further, as Nick Crossley emphasizes, for Merleau-Ponty speech is proof of the embodiment of thought; that is, the existence of thought as a physical expression rather than simply a mental operation. Intersubjective relations thus must include the physical and material environments in which they take place, as well as the social "fabric" that connects subjects, objects, and their situations.[56]

In short, speech occupies an important ontological space as the intersection of the mental and the physical, and dialogue creates a further intersection between speakers. The intersubjective experience of dialogue creates a temporary existential condition of not-self and not-other where meaning develops. Such a model is particularly apposite for understanding Middle English lyrics, a corpus that Ardis Butterfield has rightly described as follows: "No one poetic item, however crafted, stands alone to form an object of scientific inquiry. Each dissolves into an ever-expanding associational set of links. . . . This is a form of reading that is profoundly lateral: it is driven by words but clarified in practice."[57] These poems tend to rely on established idioms and commonplaces for their composition, with an apparent aim not of creating rhetorically unusual compositions but rather of elaborating on and selecting between the set of rhetorics and topics understood to fall within their purview.[58]

Thus, as a genre, these lyrics rely on a social model of language and its circulation. Medieval lyric dialogues perform, in many senses, the kind of intersubjective communication described by Merleau-Ponty and his commentators. As texts of performance, sometimes set to music, they create a temporal experience of difference for their speakers, singers, readers, and listeners: as one encounters each voice in the lyric, the performer or audience member has the opportunity to assimilate its words and ideas temporarily. The performance, then, is a kind of dialogue in Merleau-Ponty's sense among performer, audience, and text; each participant in the dialogue is altered by contact with the others. The medieval concept of voice facilitates this experience. As I have discussed in greater detail elsewhere, we should think of medieval lyrics as having voices, not speaking subjects.[59] By this I mean that the medieval lyric utterance reflects a particular set of circumstances as experienced by one utterer in time rather than the unique experience of a totalized speaking subject. A lyric voice is fungible in a way that a lyric speaker's utterance is not. The rhetorical form of *ethopoeia*, "ethos-making," informs these kinds of lyric voices. Isidore of Seville defines *ethopoeia* as follows:

> We call that "ethopoeia" whereby we represent the character of a person in such a way as to express traits related to age, occupation, fortune, happiness, gender, grief, boldness. Thus when the character of a pirate is taken up, the speech will be bold, abrupt, rash; when the speech of a woman is imitated, the oration ought to fit her sex. A distinct way of speaking ought to be used for young and old, soldier and general, parasite and rustic and philosopher. One caught up in joy speaks one way, one wounded, another. In this genre of speech these things should be most fully thought out: who speaks and with whom, about whom, where, and when, what one has done or will do, or what one can suffer if one neglects these decrees.[60]

In other words, the ethopoetic voices of medieval lyrics reflect material and social circumstances and speak from the conjunction of these factors at an imagined moment in time. They construct not a totalized psychology or subjectivity but a circumstantial utterance. Such a voice differs in important ways from the speaker of a dramatic monologue, a dominant paradigm of lyric genre as construed by many formalist readers. Dramatic monologues are spoken by characters with implied personal histories and continuous (if changeable) subjectivities and are "overheard" by a separate subject.[61] Ethopoetic utterances, by contrast, are universally assimilable. Speaking, reading, or hearing such a voice offers an opportunity to experience intimately its difference and potentially absorb it into one's own experience. Examples of such utterances are common in medieval treatises on rhetoric and poetics, from the set-piece speeches demonstrating figures of amplification in Geoffrey of Vinsauf's *Poetria Nova* to the sample explications collected in preachers' handbooks.[62]

Further, when two ethopoetic voices are put into dialogue, they to some extent perform the intersubjective experience that Husserl and Merleau-Ponty theorize. By voicing the intersection between the circumstantial and affective as responses to another ethopoetic voice, the speakers in these poems demonstrate a process of shaping their subjectivities with respect to another subject. To demonstrate how this works, I return to "Stond wel, moder." This dialogue between Mary and Christ on the cross adapts and translates the Latin sequence with the same setting, "Stabat iuxta Christi crucem." From the surviving music, we know that both the Latin and English versions are sung. However, the vernacular poem departs from its Latin source in significant ways. "Stabat iuxta Christi crucem" describes Mary's sorrow in the third person, explicitly presenting her emotional vicissitudes as a model for meditation. The English poem's first-person voice imparts a certain degree of empowerment to its female speaker, and perhaps to a larger population of women. As Sarah McNamer has demonstrated, "Stond wel, moder" is part of a cluster of English lyrics from the later Middle Ages that present laments in Mary's own voice, often protesting the violence and torture visited on Christ's body. This protest extends beyond the devotional to embrace the social and political anti-violence protests that medieval literature frequently associated with women's voices.[63] For Sarah Stanbury, the poem navigates the subtleties of gendered power relations by its representation of the female gaze: "Stond wel, moder" brilliantly tropes intersubjectivity, male and female gazes mingling in a shared and transformative touch."[64]

For Stanbury and McNamer, the dialogue form of "Stond wel, moder" opens a space for female subjectivity and agency. The first exchange establishes Christ's and Mary's relative affective positions:

Stond well, moder, under rode
Bihold thy sone with glade mode
Blithe, moder, might thou be.
Sone, how shulde I blithe stonde?

I see thin fet, I see thin honde
Nailed to the harde tree.

                         (1–6)

As I noted above, the opening expressly links the speakers' affective states to
their physicality and perceptions. Christ implores his mother to be "blithe"
(line 3), but she rejects his entreaty with an appeal to her senses: "I see thin
fet, I see thin honde / Nailed to the harde tre" (lines 5–6). Throughout
the dialogue this poem preserves the tension between Mary's perceptually
based sorrow and Christ's soteriological arguments against it. In their second exchange, Christ offers a theological commonplace:

Moder, do wey thy wepinge.	*dispense with*
I thole deth for monkinde;	*suffer*
For my gult thole I non.	
Sone, I fele the dedestounde,	*hour of death*
The swert is at min herte grounde	*bottom*
That me bihet Simeon.	*promised*
(7–12)	

Although Christ reminds her that his death redeems mankind, orienting the
scene in salvation time, Mary recalls them to the immediate moment of perception: "I fele the dedestounde" (line 10). She alludes to Simeon's prophecy:
"And Simeon blessed them and said to Mary his mother: 'Behold this child
is set for the fall and for the resurrection of many in Israel and for a sign
which shall be contradicted. And thy own soul a sword shall pierce, that,
out of many hearts thoughts may be revealed'" (Luke 2:34–35). The structure of Simeon's prophecy anticipates that of this poem, with the logic of
salvation theology acknowledging the immediate affective impact on Mary
and its connection to "many hearts."

   The dialogue between Christ and Mary both describes and legitimates
two very different affective responses to the same event. Remarkably, given
the weight of salvation theology and the authority of Christ's voice, this
dialogue never resolves the problem of individual suffering in the service of
community and cohesion. It concludes in a stalemate:

Moder, may I no lengore dwelle;
The time is come I shall to helle;

The thridde day I rise upon.
Sone, I will with thee founden;   *go*
I deye, iwis, for thine wounden;   *truly; your wounds*
So soreweful ded nes never non.   *death*

$$(49–54)$$

These stanzas posit equivalence between Mary's grief and Christ's death and resurrection. Mary's suffering is so great that she claims to die of Christ's wounds: "I deye, iwis, for thine wounden" (line 53). This renders the final line of the dialogue ambiguous: is the most sorrowful death ("So soreweful ded") Christ's or Mary's? This line suggests the intersubjective potential of affective dialogue, as sharing sorrow and pain through speech allows the other to experience it and perhaps set aside one's own pain or sorrow in an attempt at consolation.[65]

At the same time, voice is an intractable figure of difference. Many versions of "Stond wel, moder" conclude with stanzas in a third-person voice that assert Mary's "blisse" at Christ's resurrection:

When he ros, tho fell hire sorewe   *then*
Hire blisse sprong the thridde morewe   *arose*
Blithe, moder, were thou tho

$$(55–57)$$

These stanzas give the voice of an authorizing reader of the dialogue, perhaps for use in a sermon.[66] Yet the dialogue form itself works against the claims of these final stanzas, as it renders an intersubjective experience of sorrow through voice. Further, in what is arguably the earliest copy of the poem, the third-person ending is omitted.[67] Thus, it is possible that the dialogue as a stand-alone poem precedes the addition of the moralizing narration at the end. This aporia suggests an understanding of voice *as* difference, a concept elaborated by Jacques Derrida in his critique of Husserl's phenomenology. Derrida observes that phenomenology generally privileges an "interior" voice as the medium of self-presence, while writing is a degree removed from presence. Yet voice itself, he argues, is always already inscribed in a system of writing and difference. That is, utterance of one's interiority is predicated on the use of language, with its expression of what is absent. Far from the expression of a present and autonomous self, then, voicing acknowledges the absence and difference at the center of selfhood.[68] The voices of "Stond wel, moder" demonstrate just this absence and difference, as they destabilize any notion that experiences and affect are bounded within a single subject. Further, in a medieval context even the most seemingly intimate literary voices can anticipate public audiences, with all of their implications of interpretation and response.[69]

The equivalence between Mary's and Christ's perspectives is underscored by the music for this lyric that survives in some manuscript witnesses, where the same musical phrase repeats during Christ's words and Mary's.[70] The musical setting changes how we can understand the lyric's rhyme scheme. When copied or printed in stanzas, a convention I have replicated here, the poem appears to be constructed of six-line stanzas rhyming aabccb. Yet the music suggests that each set of three lines is a musical phrase, rendering the poem a set of long couplets with internal rhyme. Read in this way, the poem's strongest formal coherence is across the two voices, while the internal rhyme in each musical phrase asserts a porous sense of selfhood. In other words, like many Middle English dialogue poems, "Stond wel, moder" holds two strikingly different emotional and experiential subjectivities alongside one another. It represents a distinction between these subjects that integrates without merging them.

Equivalence of voice makes sense when the speakers are Christ and Mary. But many secular dialogue lyrics also survive, with very different content and valences than the devotional dialogues. One of the most well-attested groups of these in Middle English is the *chanson d'aventure*, or *pastourelle*. Commonly, these songs follow a narrative template: a speaker, often a knight, recalls a recent journey into the woods that begins in a state of pensiveness or playfulness. In the forest, he encounters a woman of lower birth. A dialogue commences, often her account of another lover's betrayal, that is inflected with erotic desire and frequently concludes in a dubious scene of consent.[71] Given this trajectory, these dialogues do not conform to the kind of intersubjectivity we might like to imagine, in which acknowledging the distinct consciousness of the other yields empathy and compassion. Yet it is striking that many of the Middle English *chansons d'aventure* express the constraints of women's desire and consent: their disappointment with their seducers, their limited socioerotic options. As Carissa Harris has observed, such lyrics "debunk some rape myths while perpetuating others," namely, by voicing female resistance but also its imagined attrition under the force of male desire.[72] In one such lyric, beginning "In a fryht as Y con fare, fremede" (In a wood as I, a stranger, did walk), the woman evaluates her options thus:

Betere is taken a comeliche yclothe,
In armes to cusse ant to cluppe,
Then a wrecche ywedded so wrothe
Thah he me slowe, ne myht I him asluppe!

(37–40)

(Yet it's better to accept one beautifully clothed
To kiss and to embrace him in arms,
Than be wed to a wretch so ill-tempered
That were he to beat me, I might not escape!).[73]

Such candor, if not enough to alter the inevitable ending, engages the reader or listener in the contingency and limitations of the woman's range of choices.

Formal features of *chansons d'aventure* can express the tension between the porousness of intersubjectivity and the class- and gender-based constraints that its underlying seduction/rape narrative implies. Nicolette Zeeman notes that, "as the *chanson d'aventure* comes to be used more widely, it offers a means of signaling not just the subjectivity of the lover or knight, but literary subjectivity and reflexivity per se."[74] Zeeman focuses on a congruence between the male speaker's subjectivity and the literary, but as Harris's work shows, the audience's and the woman's subjectivities are also woven into this matrix.[75] We can see this by examining a *chanson d'aventure* in carol form from the turn of the fourteenth century, known either as "Als me rode this endre day" or (as here) "Now springes the spray," given here in its entirety.

Now springes the spray,		*blooms; branch*
All for love ich am so seek		
That slepen I ne may.		
Als I me rode this endre day		*As; other*
5 O' my pleyinge		
Seih I whar a litel may		*maiden*
Began to singe,		
The clot him clinge!		*May the mud cling to him*
Way is him i' louve-longinge		*Woe*
10 Shall libben ay!		*always*
Now springes the spray, etc.		

Son I herde that mirie note,   *immediately*
Thider I drogh: *drew*
I fonde hire in an herber swot   *sweet*
Under a bogh,
15 With joye inogh.
Son I asked, "Thou mirie may,
Why singes thou ay?
    Now springes the spray, etc.

Than answerde that maiden swote,
Midde wordes fewe:
20 My lemman me haves bihot   *promised*
Of louve trewe;
He chaunges anewe.
If I may, it shall him rewe   *he will regret it*
By this day!
    Now springes the spray, etc.[76]

The lyric appears to conform to the *chanson d'aventure* structure. As Edmund Reiss points out, the initial, presumptively male speaker consistently misinterprets the woman's grief in the context of his own "pleyinge" (line 5): he perceives her "in an herber swot" (line 13) "with joye inogh" (line 15) even as she laments her lover's betrayal.[77] The meanings of this poem emerge, in part, through Merleau-Ponty's "shared operation" of dialogue as the man questions the woman: "Why singes thou ay?" (line 17). Here, the operation is not merely dyadic but multiple, mediated through the voices of the poem as well as those of singers and audiences in performance. Yet the poem does not indicate the gender of the first speaker, the rider.[78] Two women discussing their travails in love is not without precedent in medieval literature. Fabliaux and romances feature more experienced women counseling their innocent sisters on love and sex. It is even possible that there is a hint of otherworldliness here, with the spurned woman a kind of fairy who will wreak her revenge by supernatural means. Reading both speakers as female suggests a different dynamic between the two, with the second, more experienced speaker warning the first away from the pleasure she rode out to seek ("O my pleying," 5), a kind of reversal of the encouragement toward love we find in "Antigone's song" in Chaucer's *Troilus and Criseyde*. Although unexpressed in the poem, this reading suggests another type of shift that its dialogue facilitates, from innocence to experience.

Inasmuch as this poem dramatizes the potential misprisions of over-hearing, in "Now springes the spray" the audience also overhears an (imper-fectly) intersubjective exchange. The developments of successive strophes demonstrate a movement from overhearing to dialogue. The "litel may's" first utterances are in the ambit of what Husserl called "interior discourse," curses without context. When the rider asks her to explain her speech/song, she shifts to the more narrative mode of the third strophe: "My lemman me haves bihot / Of louve trewe" (lines 20–21). The dramatization of the dia-logue calls our attention to the social world of the speakers and of ourselves as sites of the continual reshaping of subjective experience. Importantly, its speakers are not what Merleau-Ponty called "collaborators in perfect reci-procity" but confounders of each other's meanings.[79] Recognizing the act of misinterpretation at the poem's center, the audience must decide whether to identify with a single subject position or attempt to accommodate multiple perspectives.

This poem's carol form develops multiple levels of mediation that mul-tiply its ethopoetic voices. In particular, its use of refrain draws singer and audience into the intersubjective matrix. In its first iteration, at the begin-ning of the lyric, the refrain is, simply, the song; that is, it stages an unme-diated performance of song. Throughout the poem, the refrain becomes increasingly metapoetic with each repetition, as the lyric calls attention to singing as a way of participating in the intersubjective dialogue. The first strophe frames the refrain as the "litel may's" song. Thus, the second per-formance of the refrain is in two voices, the maiden's and the singer's. The second strophe accretes another layer of mediation. The refrain that follows this verse is framed as the rider's resinging of the maiden's song. The final refrain is again the maiden's, this time bearing a specificity of experience not available to its earlier iterations. Again, Derrida's theory of the self-differentiating voice is helpful; the refrain's voicing is definitively not that of unmediated self-presence, but rather deploys the difference and absence of textuality. The refrain's accretive form models the "shared operation" of in-tersubjective dialogue even as the eccentricities of this *chanson d'aventure* un-derline the active participation and awareness necessary to such a dialogue.

Further, carols' refrains are bound up with their associated movement practice. Carols originally accompanied a round dance organized by a dance leader, with the refrain, or burden, sung by a chorus. Dancers typically moved around the circle during the strophes and danced in place during the burden, although this pattern could also be reversed. John Hollander has claimed that for the dancers in medieval carols, the strophe-burden shift delineated a break between meaning and movement: "Each occurrence of the danced-to burden increases its redundancy, and tends to collapse it into a univocal sign (*That was all full of meaning; now meaning stops for a while and we all dance again.*)"[80] Hollander argues that refrains' metapoetic potential only develops in modern poetry as the form moves away from its danced origins. Yet as scholars of the medieval carol have long observed, the carol poem began to lose its association with movement as early as the fourteenth century.[81] As Seeta Chaganti demonstrates, dance practice haunts the poetic form of the carol even without an accompanying dance, with "the dance world's push-and-pull between mastery and abandon" informing the accretive layers of meaning possible as a carol's burden repeats in performance.[82] As my reading of the refrain of "Now springes the spray" illustrates, the ethopoetic voices of medieval dialogue lyrics draw on the fixed form of the carol, suggesting the ways in which changing voices can modify the meanings of shared words. Put another way, repeating words is an active and social practice that encourages intersubjectivity, even as it preserves the difference of speakers and the possibility of disagreement.

The mediations and misprisions of "Now springes the spray" and "Stond wel, moder" demonstrate the necessarily active role of the audience in intersubjective dialogue. Dialogue, these lyrics suggest, is not inherently intersubjective, but requires attention and perception for mutual reshaping of each subject's experience, as well as that of the readers. I. A. Richards imagined that the different experiences found in a certain kind of lyric poem, voiced by a single subject speaking in the first person, contributed to a complex but normative ethical sense in the astute reader. At the same time, he foregrounded value as central to lyric reading. Middle English dialogue lyrics insist on the value of difference through their intersubjective voices, and this in turn is one of their values to lyric readers today. In "Stond wel, moder," Mary's pain is not subordinated to human salvation. It is expressed with dignity, legitimacy, and equivalence. The poem's dialogue form implies an ethics that recognizes both the importance of larger social goods and the individual experience within them. It promotes intersubjectivity rather than autonomy as a basis for ethical thought and action. The iterative form of

"Now springes the spray" demonstrates the imperfect process of intersubjective understanding, positioning its audience as active makers of meaning.

*   *   *

Any true ethic of difference must engage with, indeed value, the otherness of the past while acknowledging one's present self as its observer and interpreter. About twenty years ago, medieval literary studies engaged in a heated debate about the merits of applying psychoanalytic frameworks to medieval literature.[83] In a critique of historical empiricism, Aranye Fradenburg remarks, "The historicisms of our time remain largely committed to the alterity of the past. . . . [They ask,] How can we know an 'other' past if we ourselves are bound by the terms of our present?"[84] Fradenburg argues, however, that as interpreters of the past we must acknowledge the psychological and cultural forces that have formed our present selves. This earlier debate pertains to thinking about premodern short poetry in the terms set forth by modern theories of "lyric," a word medieval people rarely used.[85] The transhistoricism of much lyric theory has on the one hand encouraged valuing older and contemporary poetry equally, but on the other has erased or flattened historical difference by insisting on enduring values. In part, this is an attempt to grapple with a feature of poetic reading, the "experience" (*erlebnis*) of encountering a poem that brings the past into contact with the present.[86] We must assume that our situation as readers informs our reading, but this is no reason to avoid an engagement with the past, or to engage with it only on strict historicist—even New Historicist—terms. The past consists of multiple temporalities that have irreducible differences and surprising harmonies with the present.[87]

Pre-humanist Middle English dialogue lyrics offer a strange (odd, foreign, estranged) form that is surprisingly apposite to post-humanist values. As my readings have suggested, Middle English dialogue lyrics perform and model intersubjective experience for their audiences—readers and listeners, past and present. Further, the very willingness to include these lyrics in poetic canons that are not exclusively medieval constitutes an openness to difference. If we value Middle English lyric, we must do so by at once valuing its irreducible strangeness—in language, in culture, in textual form—and its ways of speaking to contemporary concerns. As John Michael puts it, "the social life of poetry implies a moment of reading—the intervention of the reader—that plays an essential but incalculable part in altering and defining the significance and efficacy of the text, whatever the context or intentionality that governed its moment of production may have been."[88] In the terms I have set forward in this chapter, we can understand Michael's "significance and efficacy of the text" as its aesthetic, ethical, and political value. Reading a poem, whether it was written yesterday or in the Middle Ages, brings the other near precisely by encountering its strangeness.[89] Choosing to value the formal, historical other that is the Middle English dialogue lyric is choosing to value difference, and to recognize the many voices in which it speaks.

Chapter 6

Cognitive Poetics of Middle English Lyric Poetry

RAYMOND W. GIBBS, JR.

The intellectual excitement and aesthetic pleasures we often experience when reading Middle English lyrics sometimes provoke us to wonder: what is it about these poems that is so interesting and appealing? There are myriad ways in which scholars collectively respond to this question. Some of us talk about the literary or linguistic qualities of lyrics or what these works reveal about Middle English history and culture, as well as what the production and interpretation of these lyrics tell us about the personalities and situational circumstances of their authors. We may also wonder about what Middle English lyrics suggest about poetic works and artistic creations, particularly as related to many enduring themes of great literature (e.g., love, religion, daily pleasures, symbolic life struggles).

More generally, how can some contemporary readers interpret lyrics written so many centuries ago, at a time when languages and human minds may have been quite different from our own? Of course, many Middle English lyrics are challenging, if not impossible, for readers to interpret and appreciate because of significant differences between Middle English and contemporary English, along with variations in their respective historical and cultural understandings of human beliefs and the world around them. Still, the minds of contemporary and Middle English speakers are not completely incompatible. In fact, our abilities to make sense of Middle English lyrics suggest that there are significant commonalities between contemporary speech and writing and the thoughts and literary expressions of Middle English poets from centuries ago.

This chapter explores these and other ideas regarding Middle English lyrics from the point of view of cognitive poetics. My primary argument will be that Middle English lyrics illustrate various ways of poetic thinking that motivate the creation of these literary forms and are deeply involved in how we interpret their meanings. These poetic figures of thought, the most notable of which are metaphor and metonymy, are not simply rhetorical flourishes, but are fundamental processes in everyday cognition and provide an important scaffold for many aspects of Middle English lyrics, including the specific words chosen, different grammatical constructions, print appearance, and sound patterns. Many of the metaphorical patterns evident in Middle English lyrics, for instance, reflect enduring embodied metaphorical concepts that are tacitly familiar to people past and present in different languages and cultures around the world. These shared cognitive, and mostly unconscious, mental structures provide one reason why Middle English lyrics can be appreciated by contemporary speakers and scholars. My response to the question "What kind of a thing is a Middle English lyric?" is that our experiences of reading, and singing, Middle English lyrics rely on shared unconscious cognition, a significant part of which recruits metaphoric concepts that are grounded in pervasive aspects of human embodied action. A close reading of Middle English lyrics, in fact, offers testimony to these enduring cognitive tendencies to think and speak in particular poetic ways that may be fundamental properties of human minds across time.[1]

The Rise of Cognitive Poetics

Cognitive poetics is an approach to studying literature and other expressive media through contemporary developments in the scientific understanding of human cognitive processes (e.g., how people come to cognitively know the world as seen in acts of perception, memory, reasoning, imagining, and language use). In recent decades, certain literary critics argued that literary creations and interpretations are significantly constrained by ordinary structures of human cognition.[2] Enduring metaphorical concepts, or "conceptual metaphors," are pervasive in abstract reasoning and language use and provide a motivated reason for exactly why human beings display metaphoricity through so many aspects of their linguistic and nonlinguistic expressive actions.

Most specific instantiations of poetic thought, as seen in Middle English lyrics, for example, are motivated by figurative concepts (e.g., metaphor, metonymy, irony) that are a fundamental part of the unconscious cognitive mind.[3] Although we correctly attribute great genius to brilliant writers, many of their creative language productions reflect underlying metaphoric concepts that provide a significant structure to the ways they, and all of us, think, reason, imagine, use language, and act in the real world.[4]

Consider, for example, the opening stanza of "Bytuene Mersh ant Averil" (or "Bitwene Mersh and Averil") from the collection of Harley lyrics in Middle English, Middle French, and Latin dated circa 1340.[5]

Bitwene Mersh and Averil
When spray biginneth to springe,
The lutel fowl hath hire will
On hire lud to singe.
Ich libbe in love-longinge
For semlokest of alle thinge:
He may me blisse bringe;
Ich am in hire baundoun!

An hendy hap ich habbe ihent!
Ichot from hevene it is me sent;
From alle wimmen my love is lent
And light on Alisoun.
            (1–12)

There are several embodied metaphoric concepts expressed in this stanza, most of which center on different experiences concerning love. For example, "Ich libbe in love-longinge" (line 5) is metaphoric because love is viewed as a substance or object that one desires in order to be fulfilled. Our understanding of this line is not abstract, but involves imagining, in a bodily manner, the inner subjective experience of physical longing as a desire to "live in" or "dwell in." When the narrator states, "He may me blisse bringe" (line 7), we understand the emotion of joy as a concrete object, in this case a gift bestowed upon him by his lover. This metaphoric idea is reinforced when the narrator states, "An hendy hap ich habbe ihent!" (line 9). The narrator's enthusiastic proclamation "Ich am in hire baundoun" (line 8) also reveals a different metaphoric conception of love as a kind of natural, powerful force of nature, perhaps sent from heaven, which constrains him in particular ways, as noted in the refrain, "From alle wimmen my love is lent / And light on Alisoun" (lines 11–12). The narrator actively withdraws his possible love from others to give over to Alisoun, an idea that we also experience as a taking away of something potentially valuable from the body.

Some of the coherence within this stanza emerges from the interconnected embodied, metaphoric ideas, yet the poem also expresses contradictory ideas about love. Cognitive poetic studies importantly demonstrate that people have multiple, sometimes contradictory, metaphorical perspectives on abstract concepts, many of which reflect different bodily experiences related to some concept, such as love. Contemporary English speakers employ diverse metaphors in talking of love (e.g., love is a journey, a natural force, a magical power, a plant that requires nourishment, a physical burden), similar to how Middle English writers express multiple, metaphoric, sometimes contradictory, views of love, as shown above. A cognitive perspective suggests that these complexities are not surprising as they are reflective of the flexible, multiple metaphorical ways of thinking about and speaking about many abstract concepts and experiences.

"Bytuene Mersh ant Averil" illustrates metaphor in action as a specific instance of the poetic mind during the age of Middle English. A long-standing view within the study of rhetoric and literature is that most linguistic metaphors are novel creations, reflecting the special individual talents of a select group of speakers and writers.[6] An accompanying assumption of this perspective is that most instances of metaphor that "litter" everyday speech are really "dead" metaphors that no longer convey vitally alive metaphoric thought. For example, the common expression "He was deeply depressed" conveys its meaning of sadness simply as a matter of convention, but not because of the motivating metaphor SADNESS IS DOWN (related to HAPPINESS IS UP).[7] Many language scholars, across many disciplines, view linguistic meaning as being represented in terms of abstract, disembodied thought, even if meaning may be shaped through cultural contexts and historical circumstances.[8]

These, and other, traditional views of literary language and thought have been challenged and sometimes discredited, given significant developments over the past forty years, initially largely from the fields of cognitive linguistics and psycholinguistics and more recently also from many allied fields, leading to the rise of cognitive poetics.[9] Cognitive poetics has become a major field of intellectual inquiry, as seen especially in the overlapping fields of cognitive linguistics, stylistics, literature, religion, law, and anthropology, to name a few. In fact, cognitive poetic principles have been applied to under-standing the language and underlying concepts that structure thinking and writing in a wide range of academic disciplines, including mathematics, bi-ology, computer science (artificial intelligence), and business/marketing.[10] Some cognitive poetic studies draw explicit connections to principles within classical rhetoric (e.g., the study of tropes), but again suggest that rhetoric, including most figures of speech (e.g., metaphor, metonymy, irony, oxymo-ron) are grounded in poetic modes of cognition and not just language.[11]

Three of the main conclusions from cognitive poetics, each of which are relevant to understanding the style and meanings of Middle English lyrics, are the following: (1) literal meaning is not necessarily easily identifiable or the most basic kind of meaning, (2) metaphorical meaning is not secondary and difficult to interpret, and (3) metaphorical meaning is grounded in re-curring patterns of bodily experience.[12] Metaphor is not just a specific lin-guistic device, but is more fundamentally a part of abstract thought in which people conceive of one topic or idea in terms of knowledge from a different domain of experience (i.e., a "conceptual metaphor" that typically underlies different "linguistic metaphors").[13] One of the most notable themes of cog-nitive poetics, then, is that we live by metaphor, given its necessity for pro-viding structure to many nonphysical and abstract ideas and experiences.

The original empirical evidence for conceptual metaphors comes from the systematic analysis of conventional expressions in different languages.[14] Consider the following ways that English speakers sometimes talk about their romantic relationships.

"We're headed in opposite directions."
"We're spinning our wheels."
"Our relationship is at a crossroads."
"Our marriage was on the rocks."

Cognitive linguistic analyses argue that these individual expressions are not clichéd idioms expressing literal meanings, but reflect, and are said to be sys-tematically motivated by, different aspects of the enduring conceptual meta-phor LOVE RELATIONSHIPS ARE JOURNEYS. There is a tight mapping according to which entities in the domain of love (e.g., the lovers, their common goals, the love relationship) correspond systematically to entities in the domain of journeys (e.g., the traveler, the vehicle, destinations). Each linguistic expres-sion above refers to a different correspondence that arises from the mapping of our familiar, often embodied, understanding of journeys onto the more abstract idea of a love relationship (e.g., difficulties in the relationship are conceived of as obstacles on the physical journey).

As mentioned earlier, love relationships can be understood via multiple conceptual metaphors (e.g., love can be magic, a natural force, a physical burden), which offer different insights about the complex nature of love relationships. For example, the idea expressed in "Bytuene Mersh ant Averil," that LOVE IS A SUBSTANCE OR OBJECT, is a metaphoric mapping underlying a wide range of systematically related modern English expressions, such as the following:

"I can't get a hold of my love for you anymore."
"My love for you overflows my heart."
"My heart is empty of love."

This conceptual metaphor actually combines with another conceptual metaphor, DESIRE IS HUNGER, to express ideas about physical longing for the substance of love and the love within the other person. Various conventional expressions are motivated by this metaphoric mapping.

"I am starved for your affection."
"I hunger for a new love relationship."
"There is no end for my desire for wealth and fame."

To take a different example, the idea that LOVE IS A NATURAL FORCE is another widely shared conceptual metaphor that motivates the following, and many more, conventional English statements:

"I was swept away by her intense love."
"Our love for each other is overpowering."
"I felt waves of passion any time I saw her."

The hypothesis that some concepts may be metaphorically structured makes it possible to explain what have been seen as unrelated conventional expressions or even "dead" metaphors. For example, linguistic expressions referring to the emotion of anger, such as "blow your stack," "flip your lid," and "getting pissed off," are all motivated by the vitally alive metaphoric concept ANGER IS HEATED FLUID IN A BODILY CONTAINER.[15] People do not just say "I blew my stack" for arbitrary reasons, but have tacit knowledge of the under-lying metaphoric motivation for the ANGER IS HEAT metaphor. The study of systematically related conventional expressions, including idioms, shows that many hundreds of conceptual metaphors are actively recruited both in the present and throughout the history of different languages.[16]

Cognitive poetic studies within cognitive linguistics have also demonstrated that many of the meanings of polysemous words are motivated by conceptual metaphoric mappings. For example, the meaning of "see" referring to knowing or understanding, as in "I can't see the point of your argument," is motivated by an enduring conceptual metaphor, UNDERSTANDING IS SEEING. Many instances of polysemy in all languages are historically derived from conceptual meta-phors that are still active parts of human conceptual systems.[17]

Not surprisingly, Middle English lyrics give evidence of polysemy that is motivated by enduring conceptual metaphors that are also grounded in pervasive patterns of bodily experience. Consider a small fragment of a lyric carol, from Robert Mannyng's exemplum "The Dancers of Colbek," in which the singing dancers, improperly using a churchyard, express the following refrain: "Why stonde we? why go we noȝt?"[18] What makes the refrain "Why stonde we? why go we noȝt?" so interesting, among other things, is that the use of "stonde" (stand) here is slippery between the literal and abstract. Readers may not understand the phrase "Why stonde we?" in purely literal terms, because "stonde" may also convey a metaphorical sense of making a temporary commitment (i.e., MAKING A COMMITMENT IS PHYSICALLY STANDING UP), as seen in "We took a stand against racism on our campus." In this manner, the physical meaning of "stonde" helps create a metaphoric interpretation, which gives the verse a polyvalent meaning, offering both richness and complexity to our very brief experience of this literary passage.

There is an even larger general principle at work when we interpret lit-erary expressions such as "Why stonde we? why go we noȝt?" We do not simply access bodily based meanings from the "mental lexicon" as part of our understanding of words like "stonde" when they convey symbolic, meta-phorical meanings. Instead, we come to an embodied understanding of "stonde" by specifically imagining ourselves engaging in the very actions mentioned in the language. One experimental set of studies demonstrated how people's varying physical experiences of standing enables them to infer the metaphoric meanings of "stand" in different discourse situations.[19] I ex-pand on this idea later on but for now suggest that polysemy often reflects bodily based understandings of metaphoric ideas.

Another major finding from cognitive poetics is that many novel metaphoric expressions do not express completely new source-to-target domain
mappings but are creative instantiations of enduring conventional conceptual
metaphors.[20] Consider the following lines from the medieval verse "Lenten
ys come with love to toune," written by someone unknown.

> Wommen waxen wonder proude,
>   So wel hit wol hem seme;
> If me shal wantë wille of on,
> This wynnë wele I wil forgon
>   And wight in wode be fleme.[21]
>   (32–36)

Several of these lines convey novel metaphoric expressions that are twists on
common embodied conceptual metaphors. First, the idea that "Women grow
amazingly proud" (32) is metaphorical precisely because emotions are abstract
concepts but still can be readily understood given the long-standing conceptual metaphor EMOTIONS ARE PHYSICAL OBJECTS, sometimes quite valuable
and worthy of show. When the narrator states "If I must lack the desire of
one" (34), he also refers metaphorically to the idea that EMOTIONS ARE PHYSI-
CAL OBJECTS, which we may not sometimes be in possession of. The line
"This wealth of joys I shall forgo" (35), may, possibly, relate to the narrator's
disappointment in losing some anticipated fortune in meeting and marry-
ing one of these women. However, we typically view the "wealth of joys"
as referring to the love he will not acquire, which again echoes the earlier
understood idea that EMOTIONS ARE PHYSICAL OBJECTS, and this specific instantiation, LOSING LOVE IS LOSING A VALUABLE OBJECT. This loss also has a
feel to it, an emptiness or a longing not fulfilled, which we experience because
of our bodily imagining of what is really a metaphorical action.

Although there are various verbal metaphors that express fairly novel
ideas (e.g., "Juliet is the sun"), the vast majority of linguistic metaphors are,
once more, motivated by common conceptual metaphors. Experimental studies
demonstrate that ordinary readers typically recruit conceptual metaphoric
knowledge when inferring the meanings of novel metaphors in poetry and
fiction.[22] Analyses of literary metaphors and novel metaphorical arguments
in expository writing offer additional evidence that many so-called "novel"
metaphors are grounded in conventional metaphoric mappings.

Since 1980, several hundred cognitive linguistic and psycholinguistic projects have demonstrated how systematic patterns of conventional expressions, polysemy, and novel metaphorical phrases reveal the presence of underlying conceptual metaphors.[23] These studies have explored a large range of target concepts and domains (e.g., the mind, concepts of the self, emotions, science, morality and ethics, economics, legal concepts, politics, mathematics, illness and death, education, psychoanalysis), within a vast number of languages (e.g., Spanish, Dutch, Mandarin, Hungarian, Persian, Arabic, French, Japanese, Cora, Swedish), including sign languages and ancient languages (e.g., Latin and ancient Greek), and have investigated the role of conceptual metaphors in thinking and speaking/writing within many academic disciplines (e.g., education, philosophy, mathematics, theater arts, physics, chemistry, architecture, political science, economics, geography, nursing, religion, law, business and marketing, and film).[24]

One reason why conceptual metaphors may be a prominent part of everyday language and thought is that they are often grounded in recurring patterns of bodily experience. For example, journeys frequently appear as source domains in different conceptual metaphors because of the regularity with which people take various journeys (i.e., starting from a source, moving along a path until reaching a goal). Similarly, people frequently describe good behavior in terms of cleanliness given the strong association between things that are clean and things that are good. Certain conceptual metaphors, known as "primary metaphors," have a greater universal appeal because they reflect pervasive correlations in embodied experience typically shared by all people, such as UNDERSTANDING IS SEEING (e.g., "I can't see what you are saying in that article"), INTIMACY IS CLOSENESS (e.g., "We have a close relationship"), IMPORTANT IS BIG (e.g., "Tomorrow is a big day"), MORE IS UP (e.g., "Prices are high"), and CAUSES ARE PHYSICAL FORCES (e.g., "They pushed the bill through Congress"). The combination of certain primary metaphors allows for metaphorical concepts without gaps. Thus, combining PERSISTING IS REMAINING ERECT with STRUCTURE IS PHYSICAL STRUCTURE provides for a conceptual metaphor THEORIES ARE BUILDINGS that nicely motivates the metaphorical inferences that theories need support and can collapse, and so on, without any mappings such as that theories need windows.[25]

Metaphors that are most common across different languages and cultures tend to be primary metaphors, given their relation to recurring correlations in ordinary bodily experience, but their concrete instantiation will often reflect cultural beliefs. For example, both English and Hungarian use metaphors related to the idea of LOVE IS A JOURNEY. But these two languages refer to this underlying conceptual metaphor in different ways that reflect varying cultural beliefs. English speakers talk of love journeys in which the lovers have strong personal agency (e.g., "We went our separate ways" or "Look how far we have come"), while Hungarians speak of love journeys in terms of what the world, or the road, forces them to do (e.g., "elváltak út-jaink" [our paths have separated]).[26] These subtle differences reflect cultural-ideological traditions, with American English adopting a more active stance in regard to relationships, and life more generally, while Hungarian embraces a more fatalistic attitude toward relationships and life events. My point is that conceptual metaphors, such as LOVE IS A JOURNEY, have different articulations in different cultures and language precisely because of the people's different cultural understandings about the embodied nature of journeys and the forces that shape them.

How do we know whether people, past or present, are really thinking in terms of embodied conceptual metaphors when they speak and write using metaphoric language, especially very conventional metaphors? People in different places and times may aptly employ metaphors as a matter of convention without necessarily engaging in active metaphoric thinking processes.[27] However, there is now a huge body of research from psycholinguistics, social psychology, and cognitive neuroscience that lends direct support to the claim that contemporary individuals, at the very least, routinely think in conceptual metaphoric terms in various ways.[28] For example, psycholinguistic studies show that people's speeded interpretations of idioms (e.g., "John blew his stack") recruit conceptual metaphors that are part of these phrases' underlying motivations (e.g., ANGER IS HEATED FLUID IN A BODILY CONTAINER).[29] People draw very specific inferences about the meanings of expressions such as "I hunger for fame" and "I craved her attention" in terms of the primary metaphor DESIRE IS HUNGER.[30] Readers also ordinarily interpret metaphors in texts by inferring conceptual metaphor themes that motivate and structure what these narratives mean (e.g., LIFE IS A JOURNEY, ARGUMENTS ARE WARS).[31] Studies also show that presenting arguments using certain metaphorical themes (e.g., TRADE IS CONVERSATION vs. TRADE IS WAR) influence readers' decisions on how best to deal with the topics of these arguments (e.g., addressing international trade dilemmas).[32]

A further development in the study of poetic cognition is research demonstrating how embodied conceptual metaphors shape the creation and interpretation of nonlinguistic expressive actions, such as gesture, music, film, and dance.[33] For instance, speakers can express metaphorical ideas using gestures even when their co-occurring speech is nonmetaphorical. One analysis of university students' discussions about honesty when taking exams showed one individual saying, "Like dishonest suggests, like, um, not truthful, the truth is what like." When saying "truth," the student made a flat-hand gesture with her left hand in the vertical plane, fingers pointing away from her body.[34] This gesture seems motivated by the conceptual metaphor of TRUTH or HONESTY IS STRAIGHT (e.g., "straight talk") even though nothing in the speech denoted this metaphorical idea.

Filmmakers also employ conceptual metaphors when they express different abstract concepts. The conceptual metaphor AN INTENSE MENTAL STATE IS AN UNSTOPPABLE FAST TRAIN is illustrated in Francis Ford Coppola's film *The Godfather*.[35] In one scene, Michael, played by Al Pacino, wishes to do better in his family's business and arranges a meeting with his primary opponents at a familiar restaurant. He earlier placed a gun in the restaurant's toilet, and when he goes to fetch the gun during the meeting, the soundtrack features a rumbling sound, readily understood as a moving train. As Michael walks back to the table, now carrying the gun, you continue to hear the train sound, but it stops when the camera pans to his opponents, only to begin again when the camera moves back to Michael. This sound effect suggests that Michael's present mental state should be understood metaphorically as AN INTENSE MENTAL STATE IS AN UNSTOPPABLE FAST TRAIN. Viewers may unconsciously apprehend the "something is rumbling" sound and map this auditory image to better apprehend Michael's disturbed state of mind.

This growing literature on nonlinguistic metaphor illustrates the extent to which poetic cognition, such as conceptual metaphors, are rooted in thought and not within language alone. In fact, social psychological studies offer compelling evidence that people routinely think in specific metaphoric ways even when they are not presented with metaphoric language per se.[36] Cognitive linguistics research has demonstrated that there is a widespread set of metaphors suggesting that GOOD IS UP and BAD IS DOWN, concepts that arise from good experiences being upward (e.g., being alive and healthy) and bad ones being downward (e.g., sickness and death).[37] Experimental studies have gone on to show that people evaluate positive words faster if these are presented in a higher vertical position on a computer screen and recognize negative words faster if they appear in the lower part of the screen.[38] Spiritual concepts are also conceived along vertical spatial dimensions. Thus, people judged words related to God faster when these were presented in the top half of the computer screen, with the opposite occurring for devil-related words. When asked to guess which people, based on their pictures alone, were more likely to believe in God, participants chose people more often when their pictures were placed along the higher vertical axis on the computer screen.[39] These findings are consistent with the idea that people conceive of good and bad as being spatially located along some vertical dimension. Furthermore, people also judge a fictitious person to be more important, and a better job candidate, when they make their evaluations while holding a heavy clipboard than when holding a lighter one, which surely reflects the common idea that IMPORTANCE IS WEIGHT.[40] People judge others to be more affectionate interpersonally after holding a warm, as opposed to a cold, cup of coffee, an expression of the basic correlation in experience of AFFECTION IS WARMTH.[41] These studies reflect only some of the large number of experimental results demonstrating how metaphoric concepts both spontaneously emerge from correlations in bodily experience and influence people's social reasoning and actions.

Another major development in cognitive science is the idea that people understand language through embodied simulation processes in which they imagine themselves, in distinctive bodily ways, engaging in the very actions mentioned in discourse.[42] Embodied simulations emerge from complex interactions between brains, bodies, and world. For example, part of the neural basis for embodied simulations is seen in the research on "mirror neurons." Studies have shown, with both humans and nonhuman primates, that motor areas of the brain are activated when individuals see other actors performing different bodily motions.[43] These findings imply that people tacitly imagine themselves performing the actions they perceive, which enables them to understand through simulations what other individuals are doing.

A variety of experimental research has observed that motor areas of the brain are activated when people hear action-related words (e.g., "run") and bodily related words in idioms (e.g, "kick" in "kick the bucket"). Psycholinguistic studies have shown that readers actively imagine themselves moving their bodies in particular ways when they see statements such as "John pulled open the drawer" (i.e., the movement of bringing something closer to the body) and "John closed the drawer" (i.e., the movement of pushing something away from the body).[44] Even conventional metaphorical phrases, such as "grasp the concept," are interpreted by one imagining grasping onto some objects, or the metaphorical object of a concept, that when held on to can be inspected and understood (i.e., why it makes sense to use "grasp the concept" and mean "understand the concept"). Thus, we do not understand language abstractly (e.g., by recovering underlying meaning propositions), but by embodying the actions, even when these refer to events that are impossible to perform in the real world (e.g., grasp the concept).

One implication of the embodied simulation hypothesis is that our experience of literature is also a matter of imaginatively projecting ourselves into the actions alluded to in texts, including those that are metaphoric and abstract. Reading Middle English lyrics should recruit automatic embodied simulation processes that sometimes dramatically, and sometimes subtly, alter our interpretive and aesthetic experiences of these artworks. Let's examine this idea in the context of one Middle English lyric, Geoffrey Chaucer's late fourteenth-century "Complaint unto Pity."

"The Complaint unto Pity:"
A Cognitive Poetic Analysis

This section offers a cognitive poetic analysis of Chaucer's "Complaint unto Pity" in terms of embodied metaphorical concepts and embodied simulation processes. There are various ways of adopting a "cognitive" approach to literary analysis, as seen, again, in the study of Old and Middle English poetry. But the perspective embraced here is specifically one that ties cognition to enaction. Our conceptual understanding of language, including poetry, is significantly grounded in embodied experiences in which we imaginatively project ourselves into the actions and thoughts of literary characters and events. Not all cognitive analyses of literature explicitly adopt this enactive view of thinking and linguistic interpretation. My aim here is not to offer a definitive reading of "The Complaint unto Pity," but to suggest a more detailed understanding of the embodied, imaginative processes that readers unconsciously rely on as they hear or read Middle English lyrics.

"The Complaint unto Pity" is an allegorical lyric about a frustrated lover who is hopelessly devoted to an unsympathetic lady. Written as a "complaint," the poem contains an unusual analogy in which the lady, personified as Pity, is discovered by the lover to be buried in a heart, surrounded by her many virtues, who are personified as the lady's guards. Most generally, the lover sets out to locate Pity and issue his complaint, only to discover that she is

dead, which reflects the metaphoric theme in which a person's inner psychological experience leading to some new idea or realization is understood in
terms of an outward physical journey of discovery toward some object or destination. This metaphoric theme naturally offers a concrete instantiation of the
common embodied conceptual metaphor LIFE IS A JOURNEY, which entails
the complex set of source-to-target domain correspondences shown below:

> travelers → people leading a life
> motion along the way → leading a life
> destination(s) → purpose(s) of life
> different paths to one's destination(s) → different means of
>   achieving one's purpose(s)
> distance covered along the way → progress made in life
> locations along the way → stages in life
> obstacles encountered along the way → impediments to achieving
>   life goals
> guides along the way → helpers or counselors in life

These correspondences are not simply a list of the features in common between LIFE and JOURNEY, precisely because conceptual metaphors help establish a more structured conceptualization of the target domain, which
people then speak of using mostly conventional words and phrases. For instance, experiences of LIFE and JOURNEYS do not share the features regarding travelers, paths, destinations, and so on. Instead, the mapping of JOURNEY
experiences onto the idea of LIFE creates the specific inferences that people
leading a life are travelers, problems in life are physical obstacles along a
path, and purposes in life are destinations.

Certain segments of "The Complaint unto Pity" make explicit reference
to some of these generic metaphorical correspondences, including the following lines:[45]

> Pite, that I have sought so yore agoo
> With herte soore and ful of besy peyne
>   (1–2)
>   (traveler → person leading a life)
>   (destinations → purposes in life, such as finding love,
>   obtaining pity)

And when that I, be lengthe of certeyne yeres,
Had evere in oon a tyme sought to speke
(8–9)
(distance covered along the way → progress made toward
goal)

I fond hir ded, and buried in an herte
(14)
(reaching destination → achievement of goal—or an
unfulfilled goal here)

But when I al this companye ther fond,
That rather wolden al my cause spille
(45–46)
(obstacles encountered along the way → impediments to
achieving goals)

For I have sought hir ever ful besely
Sith first I hadde wit or mannes mynde,
But she was ded er that I koude hir fynde
(33–35)
(destination → purpose in life)
(motion along the way → leading a life)

Readers' specific interpretations of these different segments are aided by their
entrenched embodied metaphoric knowledge of LIFE IS A JOURNEY, perhaps in
a more detailed manner in each case. For instance, the idea that love is a destination that one moves toward may be uniquely characterized depending on
our understanding of what that goal may be (e.g., toward the person Pity,
toward the lady's sense of pity toward the lover, and so on). These poetic segments also bring to mind the specific ways that this poem concretely elaborates upon this metaphoric concept in a novel manner. The metaphoric idea
LIFE IS A JOURNEY acts as a scaffold upon which more poem-specific and
history-specific meanings can be inferred as readers proceed through the lyric.
Later on, for example, the lover clearly finds Pity, and has attained his goal,
but rather than this being a success, it is a tragedy given that Pity is found
dead. Chaucer's poem is a novel literary creation, yet functions by offering

new historically and culturally specific twists on an age-old metaphoric theme. Part of the lyric's textual coherence stems directly from the way it elaborates in different ways upon a familiar metaphoric idea, as shown above.

Chaucer sets up a link between the lover's journey toward Pity and the general allegorical theme of life's quest for meaning as travel toward a desired destination or even several different metaphorical destinations (e.g., on the lover's sexual, romantic desires from Pity, his quest for pity) through the interesting slippage between "I" and "we" in the poem. The lover shifts from speaking, more specifically, of himself and his complaint to suggesting, more generally, that his concerns are relevant to all readers. As Cristina Maria Cervone suggested regarding this lyric, "the boundaries between an unspecified 'I' and 'we' of general human experience are deliberately overlaid and malleable."[46] Chaucer's genius is to provoke readers into pondering larger questions about the shared nature of pity, not just telling the tale of a specific person (i.e., the lover). Nonetheless, Chaucer's shifting use of "I" and "we" rests on a widely shared metaphor, often found in allegory, in which the GENERIC IS SPECIFIC. The GENERIC IS SPECIFIC metaphor allows us to understand a whole category of situations in terms of one particular case. One kind of figurative expression, proverbs, such as "The early bird catches the worm" and "Don't put all your eggs in one basket," typically functions via the GENERIC IS SPECIFIC metaphor, which provides a way of understanding a broad piece of received wisdom in terms of the concrete situation evoked by the proverb.

By describing the lover's plight and his complaint, Chaucer also elicits in readers the allegorical impulse in which people seek broader symbolic significance when interpreting language and other expressive artifacts. The impulse or tendency to perceive symbolic messages in mundane life experiences has also been shown to be a critical part of human unconscious thinking.[47] Readers cannot help but see themselves, and others, when reading about the lover's struggles and complaint. I will say more below about how this projecting of oneself into the lives of others is readily accomplished by embodied simulation processes. Once more, though, the slippage in the use of pronouns offers one linguistic device by which we draw general life lessons (e.g., what pity is and its function in life and love) from reading about one individual's particular life circumstances. A very interesting facet of "Complaint unto Pity" is Chaucer's perhaps playful portrayals of Pity as both a real woman and as a set of personifications, which include the emotion of pity.

Another poetic device within "Complaint unto Pity" is the extensive use of personification. Personification turns nonagents into agents. Not only is the lady (Pity) a personification of the emotion pity, so too are all of the lady's qualities or virtues given human form (e.g., Youth, Wisdom. Nobility, Beauty, Cruelty). These virtues are guides that keep the lover from reaching his lady, and they become "foes" of the lover (i.e., a manifestation of the LIFE IS A JOURNEY metaphor and the specific correspondence that guides are helpers, or that guards are protectors). Personification is a well-known figure of speech, but cognitive poetics research has suggested that "personification permits us to use our knowledge about ourselves to maximal effect, to use insights about ourselves to help us comprehend such things as forces of nature, common events, abstract concepts, and inanimate objects."[48] This cognitive poetic understanding of how personification works and its relations to metaphorical thinking must always be applied in specific terms given particular linguistic, as in Chaucer's own literary, texts. Of course, poets like Chaucer and Middle English scholars throughout the centuries are well aware of the complex ways personification can be employed to achieve various literary effects. My general argument, though, is that enduring poetic schemes of thought are critical to understanding what Chaucer, or any other Middle English lyric author, may have intended, as well as in explaining how readers, past and present, create meaningful interpretations of Middle English lyrics.

The personification of the lady's virtues is not surprising to see in two important respects. First, there is a common conceptual metaphor in which the self is understood as a container (i.e., SELF AS CONTAINER):

A person → the subject
The container → the self
Objects in the container → qualities of the self

We often see virtues, tendencies, beliefs, and knowledge metaphorically as objects, or sometimes substances, that can be added to, or taken out of, the bodily container that is the self (e.g., "I didn't think he had the courage in him" and "He has to push out all the anger he possessed"). The collection of the virtues as objects making up Pity is a perfect example of this kind of metaphoric reasoning.

Second, people's personal qualities, including their emotions, can also be metaphorically understood as different types of action. For example, beauty, nobility, jollity, cruelty, and so on are not just qualities that people possess, but specific actions which their personifications independently engage in for social purposes (i.e., to act beautifully, nobly, cruelly).

Consider some of the actions Cruelty performs in Chaucer's poem:

Now Cruelte hath cast to slee us alle,
In ydel hope, folk redeless of peyne
(26–27)

Then leve I al these vertues, sauf Pite,
Kepynge the corps as ye have herd me seyn,
Confedered alle by bond of Cruelte
(50–52)

And within the Bill of Complaint:

Shal Cruelte be your governeresse?
(80)

This is to seyne I wol be youres evere,
Though ye me slee by Crueltee your foo.
(113–14)

Cruelty is, indeed, a mistress, holding court center stage among the virtues (i.e., instantiating the conceptual metaphor is CENTER IS IMPORTANT—PERIPHERAL IS LESS IMPORTANT), working hard to keep away undesirable people "in ydel hope, folk redeless of peyne." The Bill of Complaint offers a clear attack on Cruelty's power to harm people, like the lover, by keeping them away from Pity and the human inclination toward pity. Of course, the lady, Pity, is herself a personification, who is also partly constrained by the multiple personifications of her virtues. As is the case with all personifications in this lyric, our knowledge of their individual talents, both positive and negative, enables us to create a complex portrait of not just a particular person (Pity), but of an important human ability to feel pity for others, which may be the central message of Chaucer's poem. We view Pity as one who possesses the positive virtues of beauty, yet also more negative virtues like Cruelty. The positive and negative personifications associated with Pity are not necessarily opposite but are paradoxically linked just in the way that a person's greatest strengths may also serve as motivation for their greatest weaknesses (e.g., one's beauty may also facilitate insensitivity, or cruelty, toward others). The lover's journey toward Pity and his encounters with different personifications of her emotions and attributes illustrate how people often have multiple conceptions of themselves. One reading of "The Complaint unto Pity" is to acknowledge the lover's struggle with the multitude of attributes in a desired person, a situation we all face at times in everyday life.

A more subtle form of personification is evident in Chaucer's repetitive use of "peyne." Notice how pain, like one aspect of the virtues, is something that humans experience, but it exhibits itself as a kind of action, similar to all personifications. For example, "peyne" is described as "besy," or gnawing, as if it were alive and eating away at the lover's soul and desire for Pity. When reading "Now Cruelte hath cast to slee us alle, / In ydel hope, folk redeless of peyne" (26–27), we envision pain as an agent that can offer guidance and wisdom to "folk." When the lover pleads his case in the "Bill of Complaint," and asks "For Goddis love have mercy on my peyne" (98), the lover's pain is seen as an affliction, but with a human face that God can show mercy upon. This leads the lover to ask "What nedeth to shewe parcel of my peyne?" (106). By raising this rhetorical question, the lover is essentially conceiving of his pain as its own person whose presence gives material evidence of the lover's torment.[49] The extensive use of personification, in all of its forms, is one of the lyric's most notable stylistic features and, indeed, is a notable characteristic of Middle English lyrics more generally.

Different conceptual metaphors that motivate "The Complaint unto Pity" are interesting by themselves and provide meaningful understandings of specific parts of the lyric. Of course, Chaucer's poem can be read globally as a whole, mostly focused on the general LIFE IS A JOURNEY metaphor and the lover's specific journey to Pity to deliver his complaint. The lyric expresses an allegorical theme about the need to both take pity upon others, particularly in the context of courtship, and to look more closely at pity as an important human quality, which may be too often neglected. Like all allegories, this lyric achieves its allegorical standing through the oscillation between the physical acts depicted in the poem and their metaphoric implications.

However, a cognitive poetic perspective also emphasizes the active embodied nature of poetic experience when reading "Complaint unto Pity." Readers do not merely interpret the lyric as a semantic puzzle, in which the meanings of the individual assertions must somehow be put together. Instead, people imaginatively simulate the actions referred to in the lyric as if they were engaging in these same activities. Note a few of the physical actions alluded to in this allegorical poem:

> Pite, that I have sought so yore agoo
> With herte soore and ful of besy peyne
> (1–2)

> To Pitee ran I al bespreynt with teres
> (10)

> Adoun I fel when that I saugh the herse,
> Ded as a ston while that the swogh me laste;
> But up I roos with colour ful dyverse
> And pitously on hir myn eyen I caste,
> And ner the corps I gan to presen faste
> (15–19)

Once again, as empirical research from psycholinguistics and cognitive neuroscience clearly demonstrates, we imagine ourselves participating in the very specific actions mentioned in the text. These embodied simulations are not generic, but are quite specific to the Middle English lyric and its poetic sensibilities. We unconsciously imagine ourselves searching for the lady with a sore heart and gnawing pain. We run, while weeping, to Pity. Upon finding Pity dead, we fall down, and do so as Chaucer instructs "Ded as a ston while that the swogh me laste," but then rise up with changed color and push our way toward the corpse. These particular imaginations are an automatic part of how we interpret linguistic meaning of all types. Language understanding is not a purely linguistic process but an embodied imaginative one. When we read about the lover falling down, or swooning, we imagine for ourselves what these specific actions may be like to perform. Thus, we do not just fall down, but swoon, dead as a stone.

A cognitive poetic approach to literary experience also extends to fine-grained sensory aspects of what we read or hear. For example, when listening to an oral rendition of "Complaint unto Pity," we perceive the dropping of the tongue from the roof of our mouths when hearing how the lover dropped to the floor "while that the swogh me laste," which enhances our understanding of the exact manner in which the lover fell, and stayed, down. When hearing different instances of "peyne," there is the tacit experience of our lips pursing together and pushing forward (e.g., "push," "punch," "punt," protrude"), which gives a precise embodied reconstruction of the way that "peyne" may gnaw or be "besy." Psycholinguistic studies indicate that people engage in these subconscious motor actions in very subtle but still significant ways when hearing speech, as well as when we subvocalize during silent reading.[50] These sensory experiences, rooted in the iconicity of language, are, once more, part of the embodied simulations we automatically create when listening to and reading Middle English lyrics or any other types of literary artifacts.

The process of creating embodied simulations enables us, as readers, to adopt the narrator's perspective as our own, even if only for a moment. We may embrace the lover's perspective and the larger symbolic motivations for his complaint, or ultimately reject it as naive and unrealistic. At the very least, people live the poem in specific ways, and experience enriched meanings given repeated readings, to create an embodied understanding of Chaucer's lyric. Psychological research shows that the embodied simulations people create, typically unconsciously, when engaging with literary texts can alter readers' personalities, their mood, feelings of empathy, and aesthetic liking, as well as their bodily sensations while reading.[51] These behavioral studies have all been conducted with naive readers, yet their results may still offer insights into the practices of literary interpretation.

Our embodied experiences of "The Complaint unto Pity" are, again, not a matter of putting together pieces of a semantic puzzle. Instead, we experience the lyric via embodied simulation processes and their cognitive and aesthetic products. As Cervone argued, part of our task as scholars is to explore, "getting at the essence of *pite*, not only as an ontological investigation of a concept, but as lived experiences at the moment of the reading of the poem."[52] In many respects, this is precisely what a cognitive poetic perspective aims to achieve.

It must be immediately acknowledged that our embodied experiences of literary readings are not always smooth sailing. We may easily ride the wave of systematically related metaphoric expressions in "Complaint unto Pity," given their common embodied roots in conceptual metaphors such as LIFE/LOVE IS A JOURNEY, and so forth. But as we have seen, not all journeys end successfully, a fact that Chaucer intended for us to infer, which may require additional cognitive effort for readers to interpret. Moreover, Chaucer's lyric is seen by some scholars as presenting an inconsistent allegory (e.g., the Bill of Complaint, written before the lover's journey, presumes she is dead, yet this is only understood once the lover reaches the lady, petition in hand, only to find her dead and buried in a heart, surrounded by her many virtues).[53] Scholars may debate the formal properties and aesthetic qualities of allegorical literature that appear to be consistent or inconsistent in their theme and style. However, inconsistency, in whatever way that is defined, is not necessarily an impediment to readers' appreciation of allegorical messages and may, in many instances, only enhance the interpretive diversity, and aesthetic pleasures, of complex literary forms, such as "The Complaint unto Pity."[54]

Implications for Studying Middle English Lyric Poetry

My advocacy of a cognitive poetic perspective on Middle English lyrics aims to situate another aspect of expressive literary language within the context of what is now known about human meaning construal within the cognitive sciences. Understanding what Middle English lyrics are, how they arose in specific historical and personal contexts, and how contemporary readers and scholars interpret and appreciate these works must recognize the underlying, mostly unconscious thought processes that play a fundamental part in human cognition and communication. The Middle Ages were obviously different from today, yet we now know the significant extent to which Middle English minds were also infused with metaphoric thinking rooted in embodied action and experience. At the very least, the study of Middle English lyrics offers additional, compelling evidence in support of this claim.

Literary critics do not simply interpret texts in an abstract manner, looking for deep transcendent meanings. Instead, similar to recreational readers, they understand texts, and write about texts and writers, in embodied ways. The critic Helen Vendler reminds us of this when she voices her own view of a critic's task when engaged in "close reading": "It's a view from the inside, not from the outside. The phrase 'close reading' sounds as if you're looking at the text with a microscope from outside, but I would rather think of a close reader as someone who goes inside a room and describes the architecture. You speak from inside the poem as someone looking to see how the roof articulates with the walls and the wall articulates with the floor. And where are the crossbeams that hold it up, and where are the windows that let light through."[55] Doing literary criticism "as someone who goes inside a room and describes the architecture" is, we might now say, creating embodied simulations to discover what it is like to "speak from inside the poem." Vendler described her preferred method for doing literary criticism in the following way: "I believe that poems are a score for performance by the reader, and that you become the speaking voice. You don't read or overhear the voice in the poem, you are the voice in the poem." Whenever literary critics "are the voice in the poem" and "stand behind the words and speak them as your own," as Helen Vendler once argued, they are engaging in exactly the same general process of embodied simulation that scientific studies have shown nonexperts construct during their readings of both nonliterary and literary language.[56] I do not in any way intend in this chapter to only reduce the act of understanding what Middle English lyrics are and how they function to a basic set of unconscious, poetic modes of cognition. Yet Middle English lyrics arise from and continue to be analyzed and loved in cognitive poetic ways of thinking that are widely shared among people from different times and cultures. Part of the answer to the question "What kind of a thing is a Middle English lyric?" is that this lyrical form emerged at a particular time and place given the widespread, yet mostly unconscious, understanding of embodied conceptual metaphors that are produced and experienced via psychological processes of the embodied imagination in action.

Chapter 7

Lyric Vessels

ADEN KUMLER

In this chapter I take up the question "what kind of thing is a Middle English lyric?" in relation to a series of vessels featuring brief, artfully fashioned texts.[1] In construing, at least for the space of this chapter, the brief inscriptions found on the objects I treat as lyrics, I take up the Middle English lyric as a question couched in the form of a (propositional) designation.

Medieval English lyrics have proven to be slippery creatures, eluding scholarly taxonomies. As Rosemary Greentree has written, "vexation comes from attempts to define the genre, to confine its members within a few descriptive sentences. Every statement can be questioned, every adjective is ambiguous, every category has exceptions."[2] Employing Julia Boffey's vigorously minimalist definition of Middle English lyric—"short poems in Middle English"—in this chapter, I am less concerned with current definitions of Middle English lyric, but rather wish to examine what happens to short poems in Middle English when they are integrated into the material form of an object other than a book and with materials other than ink on parchment or paper.[3] What effects are produced in and by an object when it is made of a brief Middle English poem, as well as wood, metal, or other material substances? How did short verse compositions in Middle English resonate when they had to be read in the round? In other words, how do Middle English lyrics read, sound, look, and feel when we encounter them not within the planar field of a manuscript's *mise-en-page*, but as poems volumetrically *mise-en-objet*?

Each of the poem-objects I examine is a vessel designed to contain and convey something: wine, ale, water, and, as I will explore, lyric. Fabricated with words as well as materials and nonverbal motifs, the concrete forms of these functional objects complexly engage with the issues of voice, address, and the artful patterning of language that we have come to see as the hallmarks of the lyric. Medievalists have long been aware that many artifacts, monuments, and the medieval built environment—writ large—featured texts in the Middle Ages. Anglo-Saxon inscribed objects and monuments have received increasing attention, with real consequences for how we think about imbrication of "text" and material form in medieval England.[4] By contrast, despite important forays in this direction in relation to the later Middle Ages,[5] not least in relation to Lydgate's "multimedia" works,[6] I would suggest that we have yet to really confront the extent and import of how poetry shaped the lived environment of late medieval England.[7]

In this chapter I examine a series of Middle English short poems crafted and encountered beyond the confines of the manuscript page in the form of functional artifacts—vessels—that effectively made lyric part of their substance, their pragmatic purpose, and their social and political functioning. *Pars pro toto*, these poem-objects invite us to consider what kind of thing lyric was, and what it could do, when it was *mise-en-objet* in late medieval England.

The "Voices" of Vessels

Mazers—turned wood bowls, usually fabricated from knots of maple wood—were used as drinking vessels by all social classes in late medieval Europe. The most elaborate mazers, made for elite milieus, feature metal bands at their rims, metalwork feet, and "prints," the medallions or knobs set in the bottom of the bowl's interior, featuring both sacred and secular motifs.[8]

One refined fourteenth-century English example, the Rokewode Mazer, incorporates an unusually long, rhyming inscription (Figure 10):

+ Hold ȝowre tunge and say þe best and let ȝowre neyȝbore sitte
    in rest
Hoe so lustyþe god to plese let hys neyȝbore lyve in ese[9]

The two rhyming couplets inscribed on the mazer's rim frame the drinker's imbibing with a piece of standard "good behavior" advice, well attested in late medieval courtesy literature and proverbs.[10] Each line is inscribed upon the cup's metalwork rim within an economically delineated banderole, a format often employed to signal the spoken word within pictorial space.[11]

Figure 10. The Rokewode Mazer. Maplewood with silver-gilt mounts.
Height 10.5 cm; diameter 16 cm. Circa 1380.
Victoria and Albert Museum, M.165-1914.

(Photo: © Victoria and Albert Museum, London.)

On the Rokewode Mazer, the two scrolls occupy a single circular metalwork band. To read (or voice) either couplet in its entirety, one must rotate
the cup. As the vessel turns, each couplet curves into and out of view. The
volumetric conditions of the poems' disposition on the exterior surface of
the mazer and the kinetics of reading this entails make seeing the inscribed
banderoles on the rim as "parts" to be voiced by two dining companions or as
the unitary "voice" of the vessel quite difficult. Instead, the poetry's *mise-en-
coupe* suggestively compels the user to follow the advice inscribed on the
mazer's rim. Inviting the "tunge" to drink, rather than to indulge in rash
speech, the silver-gilt rim of the Rokewode Mazer presents companionable
silence as, quite literally, golden.

The virtues of taciturnity are also lauded on the surface of another
fifteenth-century English mazer (Figure 11).[12] Now footless, the Cloisters Mazer features a wide metalwork rim-mount inscribed with a single rhyming
line of words separated by small spatular leaf forms:

Resun ❧ bad ❧ I ❧ schulde ❧ write ❧ th[i]nk ❧ micul ❧ t' ❧ spek ❧ lite[13]

The rhyming inscription has been rendered in modern English as "Loose talk is bad, I should write, think much, and speak little."[14] This may be a good credo for sober curators, but it seems to miss much of the play of the Cloisters Mazer's poetry. Rather than enjoining more studious scribal labor, I would suggest that the mazer's inscription conveys a first-person recounting of a personified Reason's injunction: "Reason commanded that I must write: 'think much and speak little.'"[15] And this is surely a sly piece of irony when read from

Figure 11. The Cloisters Mazer. Maple wood with silver-gilt mounts.
Height 7 cm; diameter 15.9 cm. Second half of the fifteenth century.
Metropolitan Museum of Art, Cloisters Collection, 55.25.

(Photo: CC0 The Metropolitan Museum of Art; www.metmuseum.org.)

the rim of the vessel: the mazer was, first and foremost, made to stop a drinker's mouth with wine, the proverbial loosener of reason.

As these two mazers reveal, inscriptions on some late medieval drinking vessels echoed contemporary advice literature by stressing the social value of restrained speech.[16] The Cloisters Mazer's attribution of this advice to "Resun" and its markedly indeterminate use of the first-person singular pronoun "I," however, play games with social convention. If we take the inscription to be a species of lyric, can we sustain an ascription of the "I" to the mazer itself? In the case of the Cloisters Mazer's inscription, we might conclude that it takes too much prosopopoetic exertion to imagine the cup itself as the inscribed (and apparently inscribing) "I" that should think much and speak less. But then again, for the diner who drank beyond reason perhaps it was indeed the wine (or wine cup) that did the talking?[17] What is more, other evidence suggests that vessels designed to hold liquids—both mazers and jugs—were frequently personified in at least two different ways in late medieval England.

In the second half of the thirteenth century English artisans began to produce ceramic vessels known today as "face-jugs" (Figure 12).[18] These vessels feature stylized male (only very rarely, female) faces and/or figures performing a range of gestures: beard pulling, grimacing, holding wreaths or rings with both hands before their chests. Undeniably lively, English "face-jugs" thematize a conception of the human body as a vessel and the sociability of dining. Inscribed language, however, plays no part in their performances. To the best of my knowledge, no surviving late medieval English anthropomorphic jug features an inscription of any kind (in distinction to other vessels for liquids and contemporary ceramics).

Other vessels—most notably mazers—were "personified" by different means in late medieval England. A 1328 inventory of silver plate in the refectory of Christ Church, Canterbury, lists 180 mazers; the majority of the cups are identified with reference to their size, material characteristics, the motif featured in the print, and/or their possessors.[19] A subset of the mazers are, however, "called" (*dicitur, vocatur*) by name:

Cuppa que dicitur bygge
Cuppe due cum uno cooperculo que vocantur angli.
C. cum rosa in fundo. qui dicitur Broke.
C. magnus qui vocatur austyn.
C. parvus. qui dicitur pylegrym
C. qui dicitur Hare.

Figure 12. Kingston-type ware face-jug. Height 11.5 cm; width 8.7 cm. 1270–1310.
British Museum, 1855,1029.11.

C. qui dicitur Denys cum circulo.
C. qui dicitur Lorechon.
C. qui dicitur Crondale cum circulo in fundo.
C. duo. qui dicuntur. Knoltoñ cum circul'.
C. qui dicitur Salamon sine pede cornu.[20]

Several of these names belong to venerated individuals (Austyn, Denys, Sal-amon); others seem to be either patryonymics or toponyms (Broke, Lorechon, Crondale, Knolton); yet others appear to be "nicknames" inspired by a dis-tinctive quality ("bygge") or from motifs employed in the cups' decoration ("angli," "Hare," "pylegrym"[?]). Notably, in this Latin-language inventory, mazers receive English or "englished" appellations.

The Christ Church community was hardly eccentric in its naming of drinking cups: the practice seems to have been widespread. In the will of Richard Le Scrop, lord of Bolton (1400 CE), we find "unum maser vocatum Spang."[21] The 1436 will of John Nawton, Esq., references "unam murram, quae vocatur cossyn," and a 1437 inventory of plate in the Frater of Battle Abbey (Sussex) includes "j magnus ciphus de murra qui vocatur fenix."[22] So too, "Herdewyke," "Abell," and "Beda" were counted among the mazers in Durham Priory's Frater in 1446.[23]

These records of named mazers disclose an onomastic mode of proso-popoeia that could, in cases, confer a quite individual human identity upon a given vessel. Considered together, the anthropomorphic jugs and the rec-ords of named mazers suggest that there was a lively tradition of imputing human qualities to the vessels employed at meals in late medieval England.[24] Among the varied effects of such "personification," certain vessels register a marked imputation of "voice."

A laver (a vessel employed to pour water for handwashing) in the collec-tion of the British Museum testifies clearly to this phenomenon and to its reverberation across linguistic registers in late medieval England (Figure 13). Featuring two lines of epigraphy—"+IE:SVI:APELLE:LAWR / :IE:SERF: TVT:PAR:AMVR CF" (I am called laver, I serve all with love CF)—the vessel names itself, in Anglo-French, as "laver" and claims for itself an affect-laden pragmatic vocation.[25] And other contemporary English lavers reveal that the British Museum vessel's auto-personification was not a "one off." A laver bear-ing the text "LAVE: SERF TVT PAR AMVR" in the Liverpool Museums' collection confirms that the imputation of affect, as well as a French vernacular "voice," enjoyed some currency in late medieval England.[26]

Figure 13. Tripod laver. Bronze. Height 25.8 cm; width 11.5 cm.
Early fourteenth century. British Museum, 1975,1001.1.

As I explore further below, the pragmatic and symbolic services performed by these and other vessels in the social-political choreography of elite dining form crucial occasions for the crafting and reception of their lyrics. Invested with language, these vessels participated by word and deed in the social and political maintenance of distinction and hierarchy within elite communities.

In the case of the two cast metal vessels that I examine in the remainder of this chapter, the cultural strategies I have touched on above—anthropomorphic form, naming, self-appellation and first-person "voice"—are not operative. Rather it is the short poems incorporated into the form and fabric of the vessels themselves that claim a participatory role for these vessels in the intersubjective politics of elite ceremonial. Attending closely to these two vessels, I pursue two interrelated questions: What does it do to a vessel to be made as much from Middle English lyric as from alloyed metal? And, by turn, what does it do to lyric to be given volumetric form, to be made of metal, and to be enlisted in the service of royal power?

The Robinson Jug's Lyric in the Round

Preserved today in the Victoria and Albert Museum, the Robinson Jug stands 38.5 centimeters tall without its now-lost lid, weighs 9.92 kilograms, and has a capacity of 9.5 liters (Figures 14–17).[27] The copper-alloy ewer features a pronounced spout, a bulbous belly, and a separately cast rope-work handle that terminates in an enclosed openwork quatrefoil. Raised relief Lombardic capitals encircle the jug's belly in three bands. Above these bands of text, the royal arms of England surmounted by a crown are cast in relief on the neck of the jug (Figure 15). A flat foot below the curve of the ewer's belly ensures that the hefty vessel can stand stably on a surface.

The form of the royal arms employed as a motif on the surface of the jug is that borne from 1340 to 1405, a period of time that spans the reigns of Edward III, Richard II, and Henry IV. Comparison of the Robinson Jug with the closely related Asante Ewer that features additional paraheraldic elements (discussed further below) has, however, allowed scholars to assign both jugs to King Richard II's household during the years 1390 to 1399.[28]

The three bands of raised relief letterforms on the Robinson Jug's belly pose a number of challenges to reading and interpretation. The published transcriptions of the vessel's text, as we will see, fail to convey both the form

Figure 14. The Robinson Jug. Bronze. Height 38.5 cm; diameter 26.0 cm; weight 9.92 kg; capacity 9.5 liters. Circa 1390–99. Victoria and Albert Museum, 217-1879.

(Photo: © Victoria and Albert Museum, London.)

Figure 15. The Robinson Jug. Bronze. Height 38.5 cm; diameter 26.0 cm; weight: 9.92 kg; capacity: 9.5 liters. Circa 1390–99. Victoria and Albert Museum, 217-1879.

(Photo: © Victoria and Albert Museum, London.)

Figure 16. The Robinson Jug. Bronze. Height 38.5 cm; diameter 26.0 cm;
weight 9.92 kg; capacity 9.5 liters. Circa 1390–99.
Victoria and Albert Museum, 217-1879.

Figure 17. The Robinson Jug. Bronze. Height 38.5 cm; diameter 26.0 cm;
weight: 9.92 kg; capacity 9.5 liters. Circa 1390–99.
Victoria and Albert Museum, 217-1879.

and the substance of the ewer's patterned language. This failure is, in itself, telling. By virtue of the technical process by which the Robinson Jug was made, and thanks to its specific design and plastic qualities, form and lyric substance are inseparable in the vessel's poetry. The inadequacy of verbal transcription to the ewer's seemingly slight poetry is an epiphenomenon of the object's facture as vessel *and* lyric.

A comparison of four published transcriptions of the Robinson Jug's text reveals considerable variation:

1. From J. Romilly Allen's notice in the *Reliquary and Illustrated Archaeologist* (1896):[29]

✛ GODDIS GRꝆCE   BꝆ IN ThIS
STOND VTTIR FROM   ꝆMꝆN PLꝆCꝆ
ON IVST COMꝆ NꝆRꝆ   ThꝆ FYRꝆ ꝆND

2. From the *Age of Chivalry* exhibition catalog:

+GODDIS GRACE BE IN THIS PLACE AMEN.+
STOND UTTIR FROM THE FYRE
AND LAT ON IUST COME NERE[30]

3. From the *Digital Index of Middle English Verse* (*DIMEV*):

STOND UTTIR FROM THE FYRE
AND LAT ON IUST COME NERE
+GODDIS GRACE BE IN THIS PLACE AMEN+[31]

4. From the Victoria and Albert Museum online collections catalog:
+GODDIS GRACE BE IN THIS PLACE AMEN.+ STOND UTTIR FROM THE FYRE AND LAT ON IUST COME NERE[32]

Representing the poetry in a completely consistent fashion at the level of individual words, the four transcriptions nonetheless present us with different texts. Whereas the Victoria and Albert Museum's online catalog entry (no. 4 above) transcribes the Robinson Jug's epigraphy as a continuous text divided into two sections, each signaled by the conventional epigraphic "in-cipit" marker of the cross, the transcription published in the *Age of Chivalry* exhibition catalog (no. 2 above) presents the text in three lines, implying that the signs of the cross serve as delimiting brackets for the first prayer-like line and that the two lines following form (at least implicitly) a semi-autonomous distich. The *DIMEV* (no. 3 above) likewise presents the text in three lines, describing it as "one couplet plus a one-line prayer," but signifi-cantly diverges from the *Age of Chivalry* by presenting the "one-line prayer" as the conclusion of the text, rather than its opening.[33]

Both the *Age of Chivalry* and the Victoria and Albert Museum's online col-lection catalog acknowledge that the ewer's cast poetry is *not* precisely as their transcriptions present it. The exhibition catalog observes how lines of text "are placed not in their proper order to read consecutively, but in sudden jumps,"[34] and the Victoria and Albert Museum's online description notes that "some of the letters on this jug have been placed upside down"; neither account acknowl-edges the transformation worked by its transcription.[35] Only Allen's 1896 transcription respects, if imperfectly, the epigraphic text as it appears in the ewer. Omitting one of the two signs of the cross occurring in the jug's relief text, Allen's transcription nonetheless allows his reader to see the curious ar-rangement of the text; an arrangement that seriously complicates continuous reading and one that all subsequent transcriptions emend beyond recognition.

In Allen's presentation of the text, an interval of space interrupts all three lines of the ewer's text, resulting in a two-column layout on the nineteenth-century printed page. Within this layout the reader must actively search out the unfolding of the text, a process that requires tracing a highly irregular path through the three bands of the epigraphic field, starting with "+GODDIS." In Allen's transcription, we must read from left to right in the first line and then, in a boustrophedon movement, continue reading from right to left in the second line, until we reach the intercolumnar blank space. This passage through the epigraphic field covers the opening rhymed text, "+GODDIS GRACE BE IN THIS PLACE AMEN." Already it is clear that Allen's transcription conveys formal properties of the epigraphic text that are effaced in other pub-lished presentations of the jug's poetry.

It is at this juncture, however, that Allen's transcription falters. For the flattening effects of the modern printed page, often lamented by medievalists, are felt acutely in even Allen's printed transcription. The problem is simple, but profound: the Robinson Jug is not a planar "support" for writing. The vessel's volumetric, plastic qualities play a constitutive part in its poetry.

When the vessel is viewed in profile with its pouring lip on the right, the uppermost line of the text begins with a cross placed just to the right of an interval of surface crossed only by cordons resembling ruled lines on a page (Figure 14). The "incipit" of the inscription in the top band is further emphasized by a crown motif in relief above the initial *G* in "GODDIS." This nonalphabetic element breaks the top line and visually echoes a larger crown placed at the base of the ewer's neck directly above, as well as a third crown, surmounting a shield bearing the royal arms, at the ewer's mouth. The sign of the cross not only signals the start of the poetic line but also formally integrates that incipit into the vertical axis of the three crowns, visually linking the upper edge of the vessel's form to the first letter of its text.

To continue reading we must rotate the ewer, or move ourselves, so that our eyes follow the letterforms as they curve around to the right (from this viewpoint), passing under the spout and the crowned royal arms. The alignment of the spout and the crowned, quartered shield defines a strong vertical axis when the jug is seen *en face*, as it were (Figure 15). The shield bearing the royal arms comes to a tapered point just above the uppermost cordon (the "ruled line" in relief) separating the first band of letterforms from the surface of the jug's neck. Immediately below the point of the shield we encounter the first of the rotated *S* letterforms noted in the Victoria and Albert Museum cataloging. This *S*, like every *S* that follows, is not, however "upside down" (as the Victoria and Albert Museum would have it). It is instead rotated ninety degrees to the right, a manipulation that transforms the otherwise horizontal segment of the Lombardic *S* into a vertical element subtly echoing the vertical axis of spout and shield above, thus extending that axis into the epigraphic field. A small relief lozenge following the *S*—a device employed inconsistently in the remainder of the epigraphy—signals the end of one word and start of another.

The jug's text proceeds smoothly in the first line, curving around the vessel until, having spelled out the word "GRACE," it reaches the point opposite its starting place on the other side of the jug (Figure 16). We have now (imaginatively) rotated the jug 180 degrees so that we see it in profile, with the spout facing to our left. And here the first line of poetry is interrupted by another hiatus of surface without letters, a spatial-material caesura that echoes the space on the left of the "incipit" cross where we began our reading on the opposite side of the ewer.

On the other side of this interval the line continues with the words "BE • IN" until the quatrefoil terminal of the jug's handle breaks into the epigraphic field, effecting another insistently material, plastic caesura (Figure 17). On the other side of the handle, the first epigraphic band resumes and ends in one word: "THIS" (Figures 17 and 14).[36] Taken together, the letterforms in this uppermost epigraphic band spell out "+GODDIS ◆ GRACE BE ◆ IN THIS" in two curving segments. Within these two curved bands nonverbal relief elements both structure the unfolding of the line and integrate it compositionally into the form of the jug as a whole.

To continue reading, as Allen's transcription alone indicates, our eyes must slide down the bulging slope of the jug's belly to the middle band of raised letterforms. But we do not need to rotate the jug, indeed we must not: the rhyming "prayer" continues with the word "PLACE," itself placed directly below the word "THIS" that terminates the first, upper line of the text Figure 14).

At this point the kinetics of reading required by the jug change dramatically (Figure 17). The second line of epigraphy involves us in a boustrophedon switchback motion, as we string words together moving from right to left ("PLACE," "AMEN"), even as the letterforms that compose each word are disposed in the customary left to right order. The handle's ornamental terminal again intervenes in the epigraphic line, in this case acting as a kind of punctus between the words "PLACE" and "AMEN" (Figures 17 and 16).

Viewing the jug in profile, with the spout facing left, we see that the word "AMEN" is quite isolated from the other words that fill the middle epigraphic band (Figures 16 and 17). A small interval of space divides it from the intruding form of the handle on its right; to its left occurs one of the two large hiatuses that separate one "stack" of curving segments of text from the other.

If we continue reading from right to left within the middle band, we produce the line "PLACE AMEN FROM VTTIR +STOND" (Figures 17, 16, 15, and 14). Clearly this will not do. At this juncture we must begin to look for a new point of departure from which the jug's text will again read sensically and perhaps poetically. We are cued to look for such a point of departure not only by the spatially isolated word "AMEN" but also, not least, by the sound of the text the ewer has thus far disclosed: "+GODDIS GRACE ◆ BE IN ◆ THIS PLACE AMEN." The rhyming of "grace" and "place" sonically binds the first six words into a diptych-like unit whose closure is sealed by the response of "amen." These formal effects, worked by the sound and conventional structure of the jug's opening words, are palpable; they should not, however, distract us from recognizing the spatial complexity of the textual *mise-en-objet*. A seemingly simple rhyming line is here fragmented across two bounded registers and made to turn back on itself. The jug's reader must actively search for the poetic line within the epigraphic field and break with a strong left to right reading habitus if the reader is to find poetry and sense on the vessel's surface.

That this complex disposition of the text cast into the jug was premeditated is, I think, demonstrated by the second deployment of the sign of the cross within the epigraphic field. Rotating the jug a half turn, so that we return to the place where we started, we find a second cross placed directly below the first (Figure 14). Here the "couplet" identified by the *DIMEV* begins with the words "+STOND • VTTIR FROM," which wrap around the front of the jug until they reach the "caesura" of smooth surface on the opposite side of the vessel (Figures 15 and 16). The middle band of the jug's epigraphy has now been read in its entirety; were we to continue reading across the surface of the vessel's belly we would return to the word "AMEN" (Figures 16 and 17).

To read to the end of the text we must move down the jug's belly to the third epigraphic band. In this lowest register, we have no sign of the cross to orient or cue our reading. If we repeat the boustrophedon motion required in the transition from the first to second registers—thus moving from the word "FROM" in the second band to the letterforms directly beneath it (Figures 16, 15, and 14)—we produce the phrase "FROM [/] NERE COME IVST ON," which can be wrestled into some kind of loose sense only with considerable exertion. If, however, we try a different kind of "leap" and move diagonally into the lowest epigraphic band on the right side of the interval, we produce a continuation of the line reading "FROM [\] THE FYRE • AND • LAT" (Figures 16, 17, and 14). This curving segment of epigraphy passes uninterrupted (from left to right, according to our imagined viewpoint) beneath the handle until it reaches at the smooth interval of surface on the other profile side of the jug (Figure 14).

Only one arcing segment of text remains: our way forward is clear. Picking up the poem on the other side of the caesura of smooth bronze surface we can easily read the words "ON IVST • COME • NERE" as they wrap around the ewer's front belly and conclude on the jug's other profile side, exactly opposite from where they started (Figures 14, 15, and 16).

As this labored close reading of the Robinson Jug's epigraphic surface reveals, poetry with three-dimensional form involves its beholder-reader-handler in a profoundly spatial, plastic, and even kinetic mode of encounter. The deliberately irregular arrangement of the Robinson Jug's short poems and the difficulty it poses to reading or sounding out the jug's poetry are integral to the jug's poesis. To piece together the vessel's poems requires considerable wayfinding across the object's material surface and listening not only to the sense but also to the sound of the words raised in relief upon that surface.[37] The division of the epigraphic field into two "stacks" of arcing segments of text is a foundational condition for the games the jug plays with word order, reading convention, and with sense. It was also, however, a condition stipulated by the technical process of fabricating the vessel.[38]

The Robinson Jug's makers understood what they were about. Employing a two-part mold to cast the jug, they were aware that during the casting process some amount of molten melt would seep out of the gap between each of the mold's two halves, leaving a slight raised ridge in the finished object. Accordingly, in disposing the letterforms and other motifs in the model for this mold, they anticipated how this eventuality, as well as the placement of the vessel's handle, would affect the forms cast in relief upon the surface of the object. From model, to mold, to the casting and finishing of the vessel, the making of the Robinson Jug involved considerable artisanal knowledge and skill; it was also a premeditated act of lyric-making.

The poem-object that resulted presents considerable challenges to its reader. Not least among them is the tension resulting from the spatial form given the short poems and their internal, textual-semantic coherence. The exterior surface of the jug is strongly organized into two primary aspects or volumetric fields. The vessel's frontal aspect is dominated by the ewer's pouring lip, by the crowned shield bearing the royal arms flanked by two smaller crowns, and by the uninterrupted curving bands of epigraphy below (Figure 15). The jug's rear aspect is dominated by the handle, flanked at the vessel's upper rim by two crowned displays of the royal arms, by two smaller symmetrically disposed crowns at the base of the jug's neck, and, further below, by the two epigraphic bands interrupted by the handle and the final, continuous text line below them (Figure 17).

The strong formal symmetries established between the frontal and rear aspects of the vessel also govern the layout of the poetry cast into the jug's surface. The stacks of segmented arcing text that curve across the front and back of the jug's belly abide by the vessel's bipartite format; a disposition of the jug's poetry that is reinforced by the "caesura" spaces that intervene between each "stack" of epigraphic bands when the vessel is seen in profile. As noted above, the compositional structuring of the jug into two primary aspects derives, in part, from the use of a two-part mold and the casting process itself. In the Robinson Jug the technological exigencies of the production process were taken as an invitation to cultivate structuring effects that physically and hermeneutically inflect the vessel's lyric substance.

The jug's bipartite compositional structure also responds intimately and directly to its function as a vessel designed for the pouring of liquids. Ewers like the Robinson Jug were primarily employed in elite households to hold and pour the water employed in the handwashing that opened and closed meals. Among the gentle servants of the royal household, the ewerer was responsible for preparing the water and for administering that water when the king washed his hands, an action that opened and concluded the social-political choreography of royal dining.[39] Bronze jugs, like the Robinson Jug, were thus intimately involved in honorific service, elite conviviality, and the maintenance of social-political hierarchy.

The form and features of the Robinson Jug—its pouring spout and handle, as well as its royal heraldic and paraheraldic motifs—clearly signal the vessel's role in carefully choreographed dining practices that were always, in form at least, socially and politically charged and intersubjective. The vessel's skillfully cultivated double aspect formally and functionally anticipates two beholders: a servant and one served. Although the weight and considerable capacity of the Robinson Jug may have made it an unwieldy vessel, it nonetheless clearly lays claim to a purpose: to hold the water supplied by the ewerer for the cleansing of the king's hands and the hands of honored guests.

The jug's function matters a great deal, I think, to how its lyrics read. The two short Middle English poems cast into the form of the ewer are part of its substance, but so too the material form and the function of the ewer are irreducibly part of this poetry. Although neither of the ewer's lyrics employs first-person pronouns, each is couched as an address that implicitly grants the vessel a lyric "voice." The formulaic language of the opening rhyming "prayer" ("Goddis grace be in this place. Amen.") performs a benediction—itself a speech act—implicitly addressed to all gathered in "this place." The occasion for this rhyming utterance is conjured only through a locative mode of deixis. "This place" is, presumably, any place where the ewer is, a kind of "everyplace" defined in relation to the vessel and its role in elite dining.

In the couplet that follows, the ewer's lyric "voice" shifts from benediction to social imperative: "+STOND ◆ VTTIR FROM [\] THE FYRE ◆ AND ◆ LAT ON IVST ◆ COME ◆ NERE." Couched as a direct address, the short poem "voiced" by the ewer also instantly conveys the occasional character of its lyric address. "Speaking" from its privileged position at a warm hearth, the vessel enjoins its addressee to cede their position so that the fire's warmth (and presumably the jug's company and contents) can be enjoyed by another. The jug thus actively articulates and maintains the rule of courtly hospitality by means of the poetry and practical function conjoined in its form.

The haptic forms of the vessel's poetry seem to rebuke and beckon at the same time. Addressed to anyone standing "nere" for too long, the jug "speaks" out of and into a situation defined only in relative terms. The "nere" that closes the couplet is a subtle yet effective deployment of lyrical deixis.[40] "Voiced" by the ewer, "nere" becomes the place where the ewer is and where "on ivst" should now come. Significantly, the vessel employs a lyric address in order to (re)assert the imperious rule of social-political order that organized royal feasting. Even as the feast created a situation of festive conviviality and talk, the ewer interpellates feasters in a regime of courteous submission to its lyric language of command.[41] A logic of conditional causality may thus effectively conjoin the ewer's two lyrics. Placed on the hearth so that the water it contains will be warmed, the ewer plays the part of a good host: encouraging one guest or member of the household to yield his or her position to another, thus making a place for just one to come near to the fire, and to itself, a vessel filled with warm water and, not least, lyric. Submission to the imperatives of royal hospitality, the vessel implies, will earn God's benediction.

Notably, the "voice" of the Robinson ewer does not employ the elite vernacular of French: the language favored at Richard's court and, as Froissart noted, by the king himself.[42] The choice of Middle English, rather than the French employed in other fourteenth-century poem-objects made in England, brings the language of the poem-object's makers—urban artisans—into the choreographed hierarchy of royal hospitality. Hardly "a self-humiliating script" like the "Maidens of England" lyric embedded in the English prose *Brut* examined by Andrew Galloway, the Robinson ewer nonetheless pointedly blessed and admonished elite diners in the language spoken by Richard II's populous and decidedly non-elite "affinity."[43]

The Asante Ewer's Lyric Substance

The Asante Ewer (Figures 18–24), a massive cast bronze vessel in the collection of the British Museum, is a close "sibling" of the Robinson Jug.[44] Retaining its original hinged lid, the Asante Ewer resembles the Robinson Jug not only in its form and in many of its details but also in its metallic substance; indeed, it seems quite likely that both vessels were produced in the

Figure 18. The Asante Ewer. Bronze. Height 43 cm from rim to foot (62 cm
with lid); weight 18.6 kg; capacity 15.8 liters. Circa 1390–99.
British Museum, 1896,0727.1.

Figure 19. The Asante Ewer. Bronze. Height 43 cm from rim to foot (62 cm
with lid); weight 18.6 kg; capacity 15.8 liters. Circa 1390–99.
British Museum, 1896,0727.1.

Figure 20. The Asante Ewer. Bronze. Height 43 cm from rim to foot (62 cm with lid); weight 18.6 kg; capacity 15.8 liters. Circa 1390–99. British Museum, 1896,0727.1.

Figure 21. The Asante Ewer. Bronze. Height 43 cm from rim to foot (62 cm with lid); weight 18.6 kg; capacity 15.8 liters. Circa 1390–99. British Museum, 1896,0727.1.

Figure 22. The Asante Ewer. Bronze. Height 43 cm from rim to foot (62 cm
with lid); weight 18.6 kg; capacity 15.8 liters. Circa 1390–99.
British Museum, 1896,0727.1.

Figure 23. The Asante Ewer. Bronze. Height 43 cm from rim to foot (62 cm with lid); weight 18.6 kg; capacity 15.8 liters. Circa 1390–99. British Museum, 1896,0727.1.

Figure 24. The Asante Ewer. Bronze. Height 43 cm from rim to foot (62 cm with lid); weight 18.6 kg; capacity 15.8 liters. Circa 1390–99.
British Museum, 1896,0727.1.

same workshop.[45] The repertoire of relief motifs cast into the Asante jug includes the royal arms (of 1340 to 1405), crowns on either side of the protruding surfaces of the pouring lip, two lions supporting the royal arms below this spout, and a symmetrical arrangement of three roundels enclosing falcons (or eagles?) on the ewer's neck.[46] On its lid, the ewer features single lions alternating with the motif of the hart couchant, a paraheraldic device employed by Richard II from 1390 to 1399 (Figure 24).[47]

As in the Robinson Jug, two short poems cast in raised letterforms and arranged in the "double stack" format appear on the Asante Ewer's belly (Figures 18 and 20). In the transcription provided by the British Museum, the Asante Ewer's lyrics read:

HE THAT WYL NOT SPARE WHEN HE MAY HE SHALL
NOT / SPEND WHEN HE WOULD DEME THE BEST IN
EVERY / DOWT TIL THE TROWTHE BE TRYID OWTE.[48]

The Asante Ewer is, however, a much larger vessel than its counterpart in
the Victoria and Albert Museum. Measuring 43 centimeters from rim to foot
(62 centimeters with its lid), weighing 18.6 kilograms, and with an extraordinary capacity of 15.8 liters,[49] the surface of the Asante Ewer's belly affords
a more expansive space for lyric than the Robinson Jug and it takes that larger
space as an opportunity to shape its poetry in ways that matter.

The kinetics and wayfinding required of the Asante Ewer's reader are
far less complicated than those demanded by the Robinson Jug. The diagram below transcribes the vessel's epigraphy from a bird's-eye view with the
ewer's pouring spout ([S]) on the left, its handle ([h]) on the right; the presence of one nonverbal motif ([m]) is noted in the top (innermost) band as
are the "ruled" expanses of surface ([rs]) in each of the epigraphic bands.[50]

Starting with the incipit cross in its lowest (outermost) band of text,
the Asante Ewer's poetry reads from below to above, always moving in a conventional (for English readers) left to right direction within each band (Figures 18, 19, 20, 21, 22, 23, 18). Although the ewer's two distichs share its
middle epigraphic band, their distinct rhyme schemes, as well as the intervention of one of the jug's "caesura" spaces, clearly disclose the shift from
the first to the second couplet in the middle epigraphic band (". . . he wold
["ruled" surface] deme the . . .") (Figure 20).

If the *mise-en-objet* of the Asante Ewer's lyrics is relatively straightforward, the vessel's poetry nonetheless challenges how we might think about
the "substance" of Middle English lyric.[51] Indeed, the material substance of
the Asante Ewer, as well as its form and function, significantly inflects its
poetry. So too, the lyric poems that form an integral part of the fabric of
the Asante Ewer situate the object within a larger literary field.

Although the *DIMEV* lists the Asante Ewer as the only witness to its
first couplet, "He that wyl not spare," the distich suggestively echoes a remark made by Dame Studie in the B-Text of *Piers Plowman*:

Elenge is the halle, ech day in the wike,
Ther the lord ne the lady liketh noght to sitte.
Now hath ech riche a rule—to eten by hymselve
In a pryvee parlour for povere mennes sake,

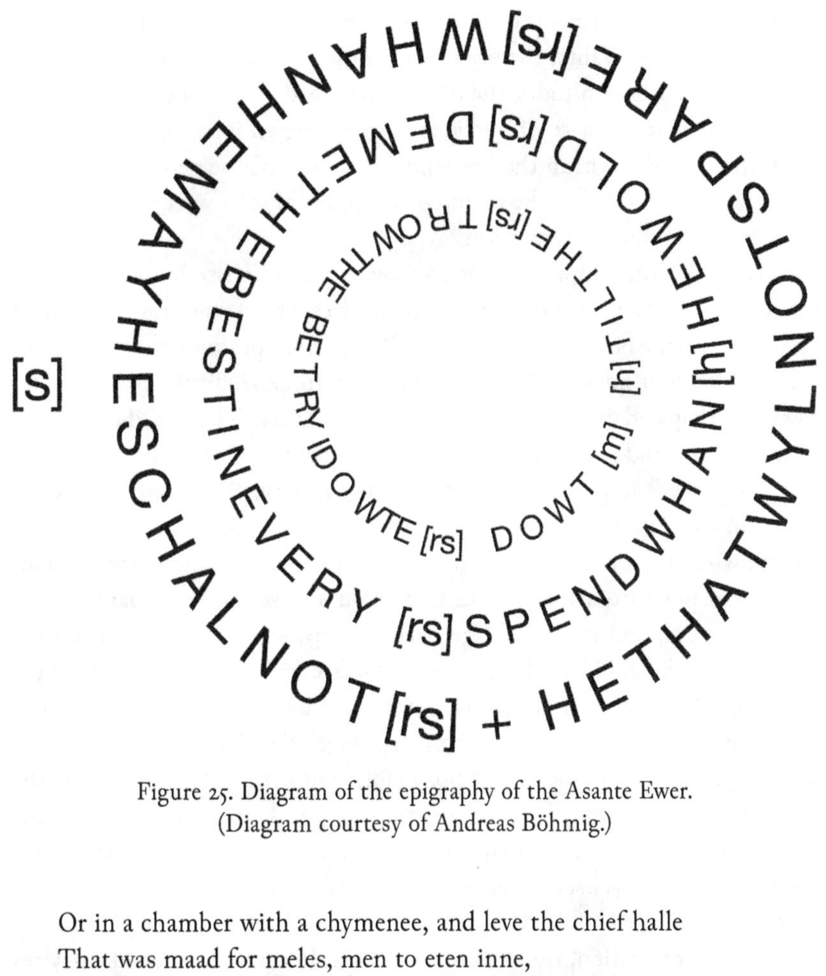

Figure 25. Diagram of the epigraphy of the Asante Ewer.
(Diagram courtesy of Andreas Böhmig.)

Or in a chamber with a chymenee, and leve the chief halle
That was maad for meles, men to eten inne,
And al to spare to spille that spende shal another.[52]

Condemning the sequestering of elite dining in "pryvee parlour[s]," Langland's Dame Studie contrasts this new, conspicuously private consumption and waste with the tradition of distributing excess food and drink as a form of aristocratic charity.[53] All those who today, "spare to spille," she claims, do so only so that they may "spende" in their own, uncharitable interest another day.[54]

Langland's critique invites us to think twice about the coupling of "spare" and "spend" on the surface of the Asante Ewer, an object designed to decorously supply liquids, that, if mishandled, might easily "spille." Indeed, the ewer would seem to turn the personification's point on its head. Emphasizing measured hospitality, the ewer commends a frugality that is prudential, not miserly. Although today the distich may read as an anodyne maxim, it was surely an acute piece of poetic apologetics when it was encountered in the form of a ewer within the household of a king whose perceived extravagance in dress, food, and the maintenance of his affinity were virulently decried as wasteful, even tyrannical.[55]

An object that impresses not only by its absolute size but also with its finely wrought facture and paraheraldic devices, the Asante Ewer may have served, in part, as a riposte to Richard II's critics. Speaking lyric in its own "voice," the ewer advocated for wise measure in expenditure even as it actively participated in the outflowing of hospitality. The specific material form, facture, and function of the ewer are salient to this reading of its poetry. The ewer's imposing size, remarkable capacity, sheer weight, and the ergonomics it entailed demanded special handling. Quite heavy when it was empty, when the ewer was filled it would have been unwieldy. Any attempt to lift and pour from the Asante Ewer would have required many hands, strained backs, and much spillage. Accordingly, scholars have conjectured that the vessel would have been set on a surface and its contents distributed by a ladle.[56] The person tasked with using the ewer would have been compelled to enact its first lyric maxim, "sparing" the liquid content of each ladleful, in order to "spende" it hospitably. Glossing this situation in the language of hospitality, largesse, distribution, and prudent judgment, the ewer's lyrics subtly rebutted contemporary critiques of regal extravagance: hospitality on a royal scale, the vessel asserted, *requires* decorous, measured extravagance.[57]

In this connection, the Asante Ewer's heraldic and paraheraldic devices take on added interest. These motifs have been discussed as marks of royal ownership; this is certainly correct. When these paraheraldic devices are considered in conjunction with the ewer's lyrics, however, they take on an added significance. Calling upon the beholder to practice the virtues of royal hospitality and largesse, the ewer prominently displays the royal arms and Richard II's hart couchant, marks of distinction that were, in the last decade of his rule, also (in)famous signs of political adhesion worn—often in the form of base-metal badges cast in relief—on the bodies of members of the king's affinity.[58] Simulating the badges and other tokens that Richard II distributed to his affinity, the stags that ornament the ewer's lid signal the vessel's allegiance to the king. Indeed, the accepted dating of the ewer makes it contemporary with the zenith of Richard II's recruitment and public signaling of his affinity by means of paraheraldic display.

Following his deposition in 1399 and death in 1400, Richard's aggressive and sophisticated use of such badges—and all that they communicated—became a topic of vehement critique, not least in the mode of poetry.[59] When the Asante Ewer was made for Richard's household, however, these heraldic and paraheraldic motifs were certainly not the stuff of satire or lament. Rather, they marked the jug as belonging to the king, both as an object and as a loyal adherent. In this respect, the ewer's first distich, inflected by its nonverbal motifs, supports Cristina Maria Cervone's proposal that "the work of Middle English lyric" is "cognitive, participatory, and communal."[60] The ewer's royal arms and paraheraldic "badges" honed this ethos to a partisan, political point. Identifying the vessel's place in the royal household and its participation in the political-military collective of the king's affinity, these motifs collaborate with the ewer's poetry to celebrate a politics of inclusivity articulated by marks of status, distinction, and loyalty that Richard disseminated and weaponized in the last decade of the fourteenth century. The Asante Ewer's lyrics may indeed have promoted the values of "intersubjectivity rather than autonomy" that Ingrid Nelson explores in her chapter, but they did so as part of a far-reaching show of collective force recruited to the king's service.[61]

But what of the Asante Ewer's second distich? Addressing the reader-beholder directly, the second short poem counsels "Deme the best in every dowt / Til the trowthe be tryid owte." As noted by the *DIMEV*, the distich circulated in a range of forms in late medieval England:[62]

1. Oxford, Bodleian Library, MS Rawlinson C.86, fol. 31r (SC 11951).

> Deame þe best in euery dowte
> Tyl þe trouthe be tryed oute[63]

2. Cambridge, Cambridge University Library, MS Ii.3.26, fol. 240.

> Deme the beste of euery dowte
> Tyll the trowth be tryed ooute
> A harde thynge hit is y wys
> To deme a thynge that vnknowen is
> Aqueyntanse of lordschip wyll y noght
> Ffor furste or laste dere hit woll be bowght[64]

3. London, British Library, Additional MS 31922, fol. 79v (where it is set to music and attributed to "J ffluyd [i.e., John Fflude/Flude/Lloyd]").[65]

4. London, British Library, Harley MS 1587, fol. 212 (where the couplet appears "copied many times as [a] pen trial; translating 'In dubiis servi . . .'").

Like so many lyrics, the couplet's brevity led it to be juxtaposed with other texts in manuscripts, thus opening the distich to a variety of intertextually and contextually inflected readings. If, or how, the couplet's permutation and circulation in manuscript might have inflected the "voice" of the vessel remains a question that has yet to be posed. As a preliminary observation, we can note that in Cambridge University Library MS Ii.3.26 (no. 2 above) the couplet is integrated into a short poem on the dubious value of "lordship," a treatment that would seem potentially relevant to its appearance in the Asante Ewer. As we have seen, on the surface of the Asante Ewer, "Deme the best" is "compiled" with a couplet emphasizing hospitable decorum and decorous (royal) expenditure. Given the "Deme the best" distich's opening stress on judgment, the juxtaposition of these two lyrics in the vessel invites further consideration.

Confronted with fear or uncertainty, we are counseled by the second distich to judge justly (or favorably?) until the truth of a matter can be proved. Easily dismissed as a "wise saw" that echoes other widely circulating adages, the distich was imbued with particular phenomenological and epistemological resonance when it was fabricated out of cast bronze.[66]

Bronze is a complex material. In the Middle Ages, as today, bronze was composed of several metals in varying proportions. Whereas in modern parlance "bronze" designates an alloy composed primarily of copper and tin, in the Middle Ages "bronze" designated an alloyed metal distinct from other alloys (e.g., silver, gold, pewter), but marked differences in the composition of bronze from one object or workshop to another resulted in bronzes made up of different combinations of copper with other materials.[67] The metallurgical diversity of bronze in the medieval period was further attenuated in late medieval England. There seems to have been little "from scratch" production of the alloy outside of Germany and the Lowlands in the medieval period. Accordingly, bronze objects were usually produced in late medieval England from imported metal, locally sourced scrap metal, and by melting down other bronze objects.[68]

The eye alone cannot securely determine whether an object is made of bronze rather than brass (an alloy of copper and zinc). The specific metals alloyed with copper to make bronze, let alone their relative proportions, elude even the closest noninvasive scrutiny. In late medieval England, where reliance on nonindigenous imports and recycled metals complicated matters considerably, the only sure way to "deme" the metallurgical truth of a bronze object was to substantially decompose it.

It was well known in fourteenth-century London that the appearance of copper alloy vessels could deceive the eye, with disastrous results. As the *Liber albus* attests, the problem of fraudulent alloys of copper was an acute problem: in 1316 the London potters (workers in copper alloys) brought a complaint to the mayor and aldermen of London, decrying how "many persons who busy themselves both with buying and selling pots of brass, and . . . buy in divers places pots of bad metal, and then put them on the fire so as to resemble pots that have been used, and are of old brass . . . and then they expose them for sale in Westchepe on Sundays and other festival days, to the deception of all those who buy such pots: for the moment that they are put upon the fire, and become exposed to great heat, they come to nothing, and melt. By which roguery and falsehood the people are deceived, and the trade aforesaid is badly put in slander."[69] As a remedy for this fraud, the mayor and aldermen ordered the potters to select four dealers in copper alloy vessels and four "most trustworthy and the most knowing" founders of copper alloys to make an assay that would determine the proper amount of lead to be alloyed in a hundredweight of brass "so all the workmen in the trade might from henceforth work according to such [standard]."[70] What the eye could not judge, fourteenth-century London legislation attempted to control.

Fabricated in the bronze of the Asante Ewer, the "Deme the best" couplet quite literally—that is, materially—epitomizes how hard it could be to "deme" rightly. The couplet's advice to "deme the best" until the truth be "tryid out" resonates acutely because of the punning character of the verb "tryen" worked into and read from the surface of a bronze object. The *Middle English Dictionary* identifies the first sense of "tryen" as "to separate out . . . ; ~ oute: . . . to separate metal from ore; refine (metal), purify by fire; extract (dross from gold . . .)."[71] The "truth" of the copper alloy from which the Asante Ewer was made thus confronted its beholder with a concrete exemplum of the indeterminacy of appearances and the difficulty of determining the truth without a thoroughgoing, even destructive process of "try[ing] owte."

The distich's seemingly clichéd advice becomes a particularly acute object lesson when it is offered in the form of a bronze jug. Addressing participants in a royal meal, the Asante Ewer not only enjoined them to "deme the best," but also concretely instantiated how much effort and difficulty was involved in ever really "try[ing] owte" the "trowthe." Definitively ascertaining the substantial, metallic "truth" of the ewer in fourteenth-century England would have required the vessel's destruction and, almost certainly, led to the making of yet another materially indeterminate object.

If the principal test of judgment staged by the Asante Ewer centered on how it was to be handled—decorously sparing or wasteful spilling of its contents—the vessel's material substance may, at least potentially, have also figured other "merciless" assayings of truth and their destructive consequences, not least the campaign mounted by the Appellants in 1388 to expose the hidden treachery of Richard's favorites: a judicial process that led to the deaths of many of the king's closest friends and advisers.[72]

Conclusion

In response to the question animating this book—"what kind of thing is a Middle English lyric?"—close consideration of the Robinson Jug and Asante Ewer provokes at least two counterquestions: "what kind of Middle English lyric is this specific thing?" and "how does this lyric read when it is this thing?"

The Robinson Jug and Asante Ewer offer particularly rich opportunities for asking questions of Middle English lyric. Virtuosic displays of bronze casting, the two vessels do things with lyric that reward close perceptual and hermeneutic attention. For this reason (and others could be adduced), these vessels may be imperfect cases from which to argue that the time has come for far-ranging, curious, and questioning engagements with Middle English lyric that energetically look beyond the pages of books. Indeed, in deliberately employing the term "lyric" throughout this chapter, I have been conscious that such usage amounts to a proposition. The poetry of the Robinson Jug and Asante Ewer might, arguably, be better characterized as "Ricardian public poetry," although such a designation would, inevitably, only open a different can of worms.[73]

"Lyric" strikes me as a good designation for the epigraphic poetry that I have discussed, not least because it is a term that is already porous, contested, and thus demands that we bring attention of an inductive rather than deductive kind to the works we study. From a tactical point of view, "lyric" strikes me as useful—precisely as a question in the guise of a term—to bring to many deployments of patterned language that took the form of objects, monuments, and architectural spaces in late medieval England. And I would further suggest that "lyric" is productive as a proposition, or a playful question brought to the objects I have examined, precisely because as a term of art and an artful practice, "lyric" was not codified, collected, or generically stabilized in late medieval England as it was on the Continent.[74]

Recent minimalist definitions of what "lyric" was when it was written in Middle English have licensed us to find and think in new, unfettered ways about late medieval England's rich production and consumption of short poems. Given this license, it would seem myopic to exclude the seemingly "modest" or "generic" short poems—in Middle English, but also in Anglo-French and Latin—incised into "posy" rings, the verse "tags" or *tituli* that appeared in textiles, murals, and in stained glass, as well as in epitaphs, brasses, and other commemorative monuments.[75] Why then would we want to treat lyric as a primarily "bookish" phenomenon when so many other extant objects and monuments (as well as those surviving only in the form of textual traces) clearly made lyric present, palpable, and sometimes public in late medieval England?

Countless objects and built spaces were made from Middle English lyric, just as they were fashioned from bronze, maple wood, pigment on plaster, carved stone, or the warp and weft of textiles in fourteenth- and fifteenth-century England. *Mise-en-objet* and encountered in monumental forms, lyric was an integral presence in the material culture of late medieval England and, in ways we are only beginning to discern, played an important part in shaping how people in late medieval England worked, encountered, and lived with poetry.

Chapter 8

The Sound of Rollean Lyric

ANDREW ALBIN

Toute poésie aspire en effet à se faire voix;
à se faire entendre.

—Paul Zumthor

Well known among scholars of medieval English literature and religion, Richard Rolle of Hampole (d. 1349) was likely late medieval England's most widely read author.[1] Writing primarily in Latin, Rolle is best remembered for the unapologetic sensory and affective enthusiasms of his mysticism, to which medieval England's subsequent mystical authors all respond in some fashion. Near the end of his career, Rolle wrote a number of works in Middle English, including a slender collection of lyrics noteworthy for their distinctive style and substantial impact on later devotional poetry in the English tradition.[2] These freestanding lyrics have much to recommend them; in this chapter, however, I consider a trio of inset lyrics in Rolle's *Ego Dormio*, a succinct vernacular epistle to a female acolyte seeking advice on advancement along the hermit's mystical path. Amid these instructive environs, Rolle's lyrics more readily reveal the method and measure of their operation, which depend on an often overlooked and poorly theorized dimension of lyric: its sound, not as the handmaiden of verbal meaning, but as a proper locus of meaningful experience in its own right.[3] In what follows, I seek to account for the efficacy of the sonorous matter these inset lyrics dispose toward their users,[4] in the interest not just of better understanding the Rollean lyric but also of expanding our sense of the kind of thing a Middle English lyric can be and the kinds of things lyric more broadly can do.

I slepe and my hert waketh

I start reading *Ego Dormio*, and it asks me, it asks my body, to listen. The text begins: "Ego dormio et cor meum vigilat. The þat lust loue, hold þyn ere and hyre of loue. In þe songe of loue I fynd hit written þat I haue set at þe begennynge of my writynge: I slepe and my hert waketh."[5] Citationally invoking the erotic dialogue of Song of Songs 5:2, a voice speaks in the first person, claiming an *ego* that declares in Latin that it sleeps. This somnolent condition belies the *ego*'s ability to speak; the speaking voice then indicates that its heart, something distinct from its *ego*, is attentive. I suspect that this heart is the source of speech, and as I do, the speaking voice turns to acknowledge me pronominally (*the*) in a more familiar tongue, putting off the idiom of learning and liturgy. I am drawn into attentiveness myself; through this rapid sequence of reorientations, *ego*'s heart begins a transit across bodies, from the breast of the biblical Beloved to my breast, so as to become my heart through an invitation into hearing: "hold þyn ere and hyre of loue." The gesture I am invited into is one of becoming ear, in which my hand cups my ear and become a second pinna, a prosthesis intended to augment my aural acuity and train my listening toward the voices and sounds *Ego Dormio* will shortly reveal. If I put my body into motion, if I put a hand to my ear and lean in and so make my body attentive, the text promises I will hear about the thing I want and will find reward in that hearing. Indeed, if I listen closely, I can already hear what I desire in the sounds of the words spoken to me: dialectally and scribally speaking, "lusting" (wanting) love is also "lysting" (hearing) love.[6] Depending on the tuning of my ear, then, in wanting love, I already hear love; love already speaks to me if I listen hard enough, even as I turn my ear to listen to the voice that wishes to tell me more about the love I want.

As I turn to that voice, its sound undergoes a noteworthy change. I lean in to listen for the love I have been promised and am met with "þe songe of loue," readily recognizable as the hallmark of Rolle's mysticism, a spiritual music I am most curious to hear—but this song turns out to be a written thing, twice over: in it, Rolle "fynd[s] hit written þat I haue set at þe begennynge of my writynge." The mystical "songe of loue" I desire turns out to be the scriptural Song of Songs I already know; the voice that spoke "ego" to me with such promise has been built out of borrowed, written language that can be lifted and "set" into another text, language Rolle immediately renders in the vernacular as if to demonstrate how readily scripture can be made to ring with his own voice.[7] This does not undo *Ego Dormio*'s vocal spell, scriptural *ego* giving easily onto Rolle's "I," but now the literary workings of that spell are exposed. *Ego Dormio* acknowledges that the speaking voice of its emerging I/thou relationship depends on that voice's writtenness as it rapidly shuttles and blurs the lines between speech and script in Latin and vernacular over its opening sentences.[8] With a mere twenty-five words, *Ego Dormio* thus coaxes me, inclines my body to listen to sounds that, before I even realize I am listening, are always and already half-silenced, half-animated by the written text in my hands.

Hold þyn ere and hyre of loue

When we talk about the sound of lyric, what we often mean is the schema of meters, rhymes, and rhetorical figures of sound against which poets dispose their verbal content: the formal design of lyric, as taxonomized in the catalogs of prosody. Yet the sound of lyric is not exhausted by poetic form. As Simon Jarvis argues, at its worst, scientistic prosodic analysis runs the risk of reducing a poem's "melodics" to an "acoustic carcass," an inert container lending the requisite strictures for art, and the criticism of art, to differentiate itself from mere verbal play.[9] In Jarvis's view, this approach to the sound of verse too easily resolves the enlivening tensions between narrative design and poetic line "into placid cooperation, a division of labour in which design supplies the idea and line its decoration."[10] When we regard the sound of verse as an artifice to which rational content must fit itself, or as an obeisant handmaid to poetic narrative, or as a mimetic effect poets employ to ornament verbal ideas, we regard a poem's melodics as unable to bear meaning in their own right, incapable of "sustaining the claim to a truth-content in a categorial regime built around the restriction of the dominant sense of truth to propositionality." We account better for the sound of lyric, Jarvis argues, once we start "thinking of the bodily, and of the musical . . . [as] vessels for a cognitive content" of a different order, allied with cognitive modes more familiar to philosophies of music than philosophies of language.[11]

Richard Rolle's *Ego Dormio* proves remarkably apt for exploring the embodied, melodic approach to the sound of verse Jarvis encourages, not the least because Rolle's text so emphatically invites us to encounter its self-consciously written discourse as the present audition of a speaking voice, or because it so frequently returns to the subject of heard sound over the length of its epistolary speaking. *Ego Dormio* hosts three inset lyrics, each formally distinct, each scripting idiosyncratic sonorous experiences in tension with their content and in relationship to their prose surrounds.[12] Each lyric invites its reader to experiment with different modes of devotional performance: the first scorns the imminent decay of the things of the world; the second scripts a Passion meditation and petition for Christ's favor; the third anticipates the sensory joys of contemplation and asks for death to speed the soul's heavenly homecoming. Functionally, these three poems chart devotional avenues for readers at various stages of a spiritual journey, avenues we are asked to discover with our ears instead of our eyes, as the presentation of the lyrics in manuscript attests: in contrast to common scribal practices of verse lineation in late fourteenth- and fifteenth-century Middle English books, no surviving copy of *Ego Dormio* lineates, brackets, or otherwise visually distinguishes the lyrics as poetry in contrast to their surrounding prose.[13] As text and in manuscript, then, *Ego Dormio* asks us to read and listen in order to detect its poems and their sonorous forms, out of which sounding spaces and aural experiences emerge to draw faithful readers into nonpropositional modes of cognition that may transform their capacity to sense, think, and become.[14]

In addition to sounding distinct cognitive modes keyed to their reader's spiritual progress, *Ego Dormio*'s three lyrics also formally organize the text, punctuating its treatment of and acting as poetic bridges between the three degrees of devout love in which Rolle seeks to instruct his reader. From one angle, then, *Ego Dormio* can be read as a miniature prosimetrum, an influential genre with which it shares many features.[15] Alternatively, from an angle suggested by its wooing overtures, which I elaborate below, the text can also be read as a kind of romance narrative, long a literary matrix for the recording of inset songs and lyrics.[16]

Across its verse articulations, the text may be parceled into four sections (Table 1). The opening prose section speaks to *Ego Dormio*'s addressee, traditionally understood to be a woman religious, perhaps a nun of Yedingham, perhaps

Table 1. *Ego Dormio*'s structure.

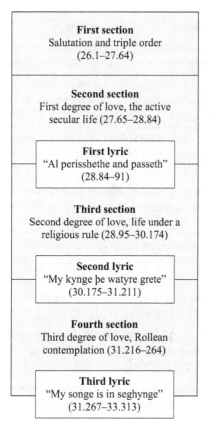

Rolle's protégé Margaret Kirkby, likely professed and striving to advance in her life of holy devotion.[17] Rolle's words carry a distinct air of familiarity; he colorfully enjoins his addressee to direct all her love to Christ and relinquish all care for worldly attachment, asserting her special aptitude. He then describes the angelic hierarchy's triple triads and maps this structure onto three ranks of heavenly reward, three degrees of devout love, three ways of life, and three stages of devotion through which the Christian soul may progress. This thoroughgoing tripartite order also maps onto the latter three sections of the text.[18]

In the second prose section, Rolle briefly considers the first degree of love, corresponding to the active, secular life. Devout layfolk, we read, ought to observe the Ten Commandments, avoid the seven deadly sins, affirm the doctrines of Holy Church, and prefer service to God over earthly satisfaction. This section concludes with the first lyric, then proceeds to a third prose section addressing the second degree of love, which corresponds to life under a religious rule. Here, Rolle exhorts his reader at length to forsake the world, forget family bonds, vow poverty, live in humility, and endure fleshly suffering. If she does so properly, worldly pleasures will lose their interest and spiritual goods will become her sole source of satisfaction. Because this conversion is unstable, however, she will need to renew her devotion to God constantly. The second lyric ensues; both it and the third lyric are built to be detachable from the text as practical devotions, packets of wrought language the reader can carry in memory and recite as needed during the lengthy work of spiritual dedication.[19] Should she execute this work well and God so grace her, Rolle's reader may be granted entry into the third and highest degree of love, the contemplative life, which occupies the text's fourth prose section. Here, Rolle describes the idiosyncratic sensory eremitism for which he was and is so well known. Removed from all worldly distraction, the contemplative's love for Christ and Christ's love for the contemplative abide unchangingly. Vice, sin, and sorrow are purged as the contemplative eagerly awaits his death day, constantly awash in the triple spiritual sensations that mark election to highest heavenly reward: inward heat, sweet savor, and angelic song. Finally, the third lyric closes the text.

From beginning ("þe songe of loue" [26.2]) to end ("I þi loue shal synge" [33.312]), angelic song, *canor* in Rolle's Latin, is omnipresent in *Ego Dormio*. This should perhaps come as little surprise: in a text so committed to inviting its reader to hear numinous, intimate voices in its text and to heed the sensuous, affective call of lyric sound, a phenomenon like *canor* lends itself as a compelling point of orientation. It is the goal toward which Rolle wants his addressee to strive, dubious though he is of her ability to achieve it. Once received, its effects are nothing short of metamorphic: inexpressible in words, music, or other media, heaven-sent and perceived directly by the soul without the sense organs' involvement, *canor* yet delights the soul through the corporeal senses, flooding them with so much stimulus as to screen them off from the lures of the world. The human form becomes a resounding instrument relaying melodious praise to God; the lines between the mystic, his experience, his angelic song-mates, and his God blur such that the distinctions between singer and song dissolve—the *canor*-graced contemplative becomes music, ontologically, as his thought transforms into melody. *Canor* thus hovers outside the text as the spiritual asymptote toward which lyric sound tends but which it can constitutionally never reach.[20]

Within this textual framework, *Ego Dormio* uses lyric sound to alter what and how a reader hears, says, reads, thinks, and sings as she scales the heights of contemplation. Attended carefully, *Ego Dormio*'s poems help reveal how Middle English writing could craft meaningful experience in and around sound that contributes to a reader's spiritual advancement. Over the epistle's length, vernacular text gives onto familiar voice, verbal pattern gives onto novel cognition, and loving affect gives onto angelic song, if God so wills it—a transformation reliant on the melodics of lyric sound. At the same time, *Ego Dormio* butts against the limits of lyric in pursuit of its aims; it thus is also a text about the failure of the melodics of lyric sound, written by a mystic who intimately knew the songs of angels and the inadequations of their verbal evocation. Heeded with well-attuned ears, *Ego Dormio* becomes a rare laboratory for lyric form and a daring experiment in lyric power—a sonorous *ars lyrica* that maps Middle English verse onto the soul that loves in listening and listens in love.

To þe I writ þis speciali

The first section of *Ego Dormio* is not punctuated by a lyric as the latter three are. This is informative in its own right, indicating that the text's lyrics are not simply struts in a literary architecture but have some constitutive role to play in the reader's advancement toward the third degree of love. Yet this is hardly to say that the text's opening is disengaged from the generation of meaningful sound. Rather, the first section of *Ego Dormio* plays a key role in the operation of the later lyrics, which I will here consider sequentially. It is the opening, though, that configures text and speech, voice and script, presence and absence, reading and hearing into an experiential latticework upon which the rest depends.

From its beginning, *Ego Dormio* builds out of language a participatory sounding environment founded on intimacy, virtual vocal presence, and affective charge that encourages readerly allegiance with the text's aural designs. We may account for each of these elements in turn. Rolle generates intimacy primarily in relation to the historical person, nameless though she be, to whom he addresses his text. Familiar first- and second-person pronouns, self-reflexive present-tense verbs, and gently urging imperatives talk to this woman as a known and cherished interlocutor throughout. He acknowledges her difficulties—"The thynk nowe peraduenture hard to gif þi hert fro al erthly thynges" (27.42–43)—but affirms his faith in her unique talent: "To þe I writ þis speciali, for I hope in þe more goodnes þan in anoþer" (26.33–34). He creates this text out of "a fondness between himself and his reader which already exists and is part of his reason for writing,"[21] embedding in the text the traces of a real relationship, a history of face-to-face verbal intercourse, of which *Ego Dormio* is the latest instance.

Ego Dormio's impression of vocal presence goes hand in hand with these overtures to personal intimacy. Across its length, the text wields literary techniques Patrick Diehl traces to later twelfth- and thirteenth-century developments in devotional writing that aimed to bring pious readers into temporal and spatial proximity with the events of sacred narrative: use of apostrophe; fluidity in pronoun reference, verbal person, and verbal tense; instability of narrative viewpoint; invitation to adopt the text as personal utterance; and cultivation of an inhabitable "I."[22] Initially growing out of innovations within the monastic Divine Office, these techniques later spread beyond the liturgy to shape religious lyrics and Passion meditations in both Latin and the vernacular, rousing "readers' desire to 'talk back' to the written works that were 'speaking' to them" in Christ's voice.[23] In combination with *Ego Dormio*'s vernacular idiom, its epistolary framing, its crafted rhetoric of intimacy, its retaining network of hearing, saying, and singing verbs, and a fourteenth-century literate culture that still predominantly expected reading to occur out loud, Rolle uses these same techniques to draw himself into vocal presence with his addressee.[24]

If these techniques aim principally at Rolle's addressee's ear, other ears still catch them. Readers unfamiliar with the living sound of Rolle's voice also encounter the textual features that generate the impression of authorial vocal presence, an effect the text anticipates and incorporates when it references "another þat redeth þis" (31.218), "þou or I or anoþer" (32.250). We read as if eavesdropping on the addressee's spiritual lesson at the same time that our overhearing is textually marked and remarked, with strange effect: the facticity of our presently reading selves evanesces into the text's speculative future—we are tucked away into the distal "anoþer" who will read *Ego Dormio* after the now of its epistolary exchange, in the manner of letters patent—at the same time that the text's epistolary discourse accumulates more palpable vocal presence through the deliberate textual efforts that lead to the impression of eavesdropping in the first place. Reader, addressee, and author encounter one another in an interstitial space the text constructs, a virtual space where orienting referents of temporality, presence, and sensory perception destabilize.[25] It is from within this space that Rolle enjoins his reader—his addressee, but also his future readers—to bring *Ego Dormio*'s words into actual sounding space by reciting its lyrical devotions.

It is also within this virtual space of sensory encounter that *Ego Dormio* launches its project of affective solicitation with an early, memorable turn of phrase. "Forþi þat I loue þe, I wowe þe, þat I myght haue þe as I wold," Rolle boldly declaims in the text's opening paragraph, "nat to me, bot to my Lord. I wil becum a messager to brynge þe to his bed . . . for he wil wed þe if þou wil loue hym" (26.6–10).[26] Such an overture arcs with erotic voltage, a stunning surprise that is carefully set up. The seeming-exegetical thrust of *Ego Dormio*'s opening sentences falls off as the slumbering first person of Song of Songs 2:5 slips into a dream state beyond biblical remit: "Mich loue he sheweth þat . . . is euer his loue þynkynge, and oft sithe þerof dremynge" (26.3–6)—and then out from desultory oneiric space leaps Rolle's indiscreet proposal. These are not the kinds of words one uses lightly; rather, they are the kinds of words that attract bodies, voices, and desires out into the open. Rolle's beckoning repetition of *I* and *the*, his wooing language and suggestiveness at the bedside draw out an erotic frisson he then channels toward the promised Bridegroom. This is masterful affective legerdemain, reliant as much on Rolle's charismatic persona as on his addressee's devotional fervor. It crystallizes early on the dreamlike environment within which the remainder of *Ego Dormio* unfolds, an environment tailored to enhance the sound of lyric utterance as an agent of readerly transformation.

Poysoned in a swet morsel

> Al perisshethe and passeth þat we with eigh see;
> hit vansheth in to wrechednesse þe wel of þis world.
> Robes and richesses roteth in þe diche;
> pride and peyntynge slak shal in sorowe.
> 5   Delites and dreries stynke shal ful sone;
> har gold and har tresour draweth ham to deth.
> Al þe wiked of þis world dryueth to a dale
> þat þay may se har sorowynge; þer wo is al þe rabil.
> Bot he may synge of solace þat loued Ihesu Crist,
> 10   when al þe wreches fro wel falleth in to helle.[27]
>
>   (28.84–91)

Ego Dormio's first lyric is easy to miss. The section of the text it punctuates lists the basic habits and beliefs expected of medieval Christians in conversational prose only to give onto the short alliterative lyric without warning, a feature all the more palpable in manuscript: with the exception of two deluxe copies, no witness to *Ego Dormio* visually signals the first lyric to the reader's attention.[28] Indeed, a survey of the manuscripts reveals significant ambiguity around where the lyric ends and begins. Systematic use of scribal pointing, paraph marks, and rubrication reveal that more than half of the surviving manuscripts do not consider lines 9 and 10 to be part of the verse.[29] The beginning of the lyric is equally contested. More than half of the manuscripts indicate it as here, but a substantial minority of them also include the preceding sentence, which flirts with the sound patterns of an alliterative line that soon sets in in earnest:

Men thynke hit swet to syn, bot har hire þat is ordeyned
for ham is bitterer þan galle, sowrer þan attyre,
wors þan al þe woo þat men kan þynke in erth.[30]
(28.82–84)

Nor is this the only instance of alliterative flirtation in anticipation of the lyric's first line. In the midst of his didactic prose, Rolle offers a simile that compares the "venymous synnes . . . [that] sleeth þe soule" (27.75–28.76) to confections soaked in poison: "As a man poysoned in a swet morsel taketh venym þat sleeth his body, so doth a synful wrech in lykynge and luste[31] destroieth his soule, and bryngeth hit to deth withouten end" (28.79–82). For an attuned ear, the brisk double *s*'s and *l*'s of "so doth a sinful wrech in lykynge and luste" also yield a sudden burst of alliteration akin to what we hear in lines 5 and 7 of the lyric proper.

Yet most readers of *Ego Dormio* do not come to the text with ears already perked for the sound of verse. Rather, the text seems to ease the reader into hearing its lyric, letting slip snatches of consonantal percussion, stitching alliterative half-lines into the surrounding prose until we find ourselves in the midst of bona fide alliterative lines. Scribal disagreement over the lyric's beginning and end effectively witnesses this easing-in. In this way, the first lyric seeks to enact the gesture *Ego Dormio* invites us into at its outset: it draws our ears into greater attentiveness, using verbal sound, not verbal sense or visual presentation, to help us realize we are reading something different from the prose we thought we were.

This invitation to trust in our ears chimes with the first lyric's content. The lyric begins by identifying how the perishing world we ought to eschew is full of lures "þat we with eigh see" (1). The eye likewise perceives the woe that this material infatuation earns: the repeated "Al" and "se(e)" of "Al þe wiked of þis world dryueth to a dale / þat þay may se har sorowynge" (7–8) points back to "Al . . . þat we with eigh see" in line 1, reiterating the poem's scorn for visuality.[32] As the lyric phases in and out of alliteration over its last lines, it replaces the thingful world's visual regime with a sonorous regime of spiritual affection: "Bot he may synge of solace þat loued Ihesu Crist" (9). Open song replaces visual allure, a shift toward euphony indicated by the internal "wel" / "helle" rhyme of line 10, the first such rhyme in *Ego Dormio*.

Still, this is an ominous rhyme to end the lyric on, one that bodes little better for sonority than visuality. The first lyric's sound is doing more complex work here than first meets the ear, work that traces back to the simile out of which flirtation with alliterative verse first arises. Sin is like an envenomed sweet morsel, its poison untasted by the tongue; it has already done its damage by the time it is detected. The lyric repeats this deception in sound: hidden to eye and initially to ear as well, lyric insinuates itself into the reader's hearing undetected until it is too late and she catches herself already delighting in its patterned sound. The style of verse is likewise significant: rather than meter, a matter of stress, or rhyme, a matter of vowels, Rolle chooses alliteration, a matter of consonants, to govern the sound of these lines. The reader discovers her mouth engaged in the work of teeth, lips, tongue, and palate, of hisses, liquids, stops, and taps, over and above sustaining vocalic flow. The alliterative lyric, here a corporeal lyric, takes alluring bodies that will not endure as its subject matter; once our readerly ear recognizes the pleasurable presence of a lyric where it did not expect one, we rummage through the body of the text to discover the span of its verses, which we cannot in the end determine with certainty. At the same time, then, that the first lyric invites us to make our ear attentive, it seduces our curiosity and our pleasure in sounding bodies. Sonority is not, of itself, redemptive. We must, *Ego Dormio* insists, go further.

Loue ledeth þe rynge

My kynge þe watyre grete, and þe blod he swete;
Sethen ful sore bet, so þat his blood hym wette,
When har scourges met.
Ful fast þay can hym dinge, and at þe piller swynge,
His faire face fouled with spetynge.
The þorne crowneth þe kynge; ful sore is þat prickynge.
Alas, my ioy and my swetynge is demed for to henge.
Naillet was his hand and naillet was his feet,
And þurlet is his side, so semly and so swete.
Naked his white brest, and rede his blody side,
Wan was his faire hewe, his woundes depe and wide.
In fyve stiddes of his fleisshe þe blode kan doun glide

As stremes done on þe stronde; this peyn is nat to hide.
To þynke is grete pitte, how demed he is to deth,
15   And nailled on þe tre, þe bright angels brede.
Dryvyn he is to dele, þat is oure gostly good,
And fouled as a fole, in heuyn þe halowes food.
A wonder hit is to se, who-som vndrestood,
How God of mageste was deynge on þe roode.
20   Bot soth þan is hit said þat loue ledeth þe rynge:
þat hym so low hath leyd bot loue hit was no thynge.
Ihesu, receyue my hert, and to þi loue me brynge;
Al my desire þou art, I couait þi comynge.
Thou mak me clene of syn, and let vs neuer twin.
25   Kyndel me fyre within, þat I þi loue may wyn,
And se þi face, Ihesu, in blis þat neuer may blyn.
Ihesu, my soule þou mend; þi loue in to me send,
þat I may with þe lend in ioy withouten end.
In loue þou wound my thoght, and lift my hert to þe;
30   þe soul þat þou haste boght, þi louer make to be.
Bot þe I couait nat; þis world for þe I fle.
Þou art þat I haue soght; thy face when may I se?
Thou make my soule clere, for loue þat chaungeth chere.
How longe shal I be here? When may I cum þe nere
35   Thi melody for to hire?
Of loue to hyre þe songe þat is lestynge so longe?
Wil thou be my louynge, þat I þi loue may synge?
                                        (30.175–31.211)

The problem the first lyric brings to the fore is the ease with which our attentive ear turns to the pleasures of the world in preference to those of the
soul.[33] While forgivable for those stationed in the first degree of love—active
folk are expected to fall into and atone for their aesthetic miscalibration—
the entanglements of the secular life cannot be abided among those intent
on a life of devotion. It is the job of the second lyric to train *Ego Dormio*'s
more ambitious readers, its addressee first among them, to turn their ear in
the proper direction and correct their will's inclination so they escape the
lures of the world, the flesh, and the devil (29.150–30.168). It accomplishes
this reform by re-sounding lyric form: by fathoming lyric anew as a site of
nonpropositional cognition; by crafting new, and newly powerful, patterns

of verbal sound; and by incorporating into lyric's design the iterative, spoken devotional practices Rolle enjoins his reader to adopt.

In the section preceding the second lyric, Rolle challenges his addressee to embrace the spiritual life, enjoining her to "gyf þe myche to say psalms of þe psauter and pater noster and auees" (29.129–30), not "blaber[ing] on þe boke" (29.135–36) but praying with serious devotion. Through the proper performance of prayer and devotion to the Holy Name, the aspiring contemplative can direct all her thought to Christ, who will protect her mind from the deceptively sweet morsels of sin encountered in the first lyric: "he shal reue hit to hym, and hold hit fro þe venym of worldis besynesse" (29.137–38). Her efforts will be in constant need of renewal, however, in order to prevent her affection from cooling and her will from slipping into the idleness of *acedia*: "þou shalt haue euer fightynge whils þou leuest . . . þat þou fal nat in il delite ne in il thoght or in il word and in il werke" (29.151–53). The second degree of love is thus characterized by a constant labor of aesthetic, cognitive, and affective rededication, conducted through meditative prayer understood primarily as spoken verbal practice.

It is to this work that Rolle refers his reader in the sentences immediately preceding *Ego Dormio*'s second lyric. "I wil þat þou neuer be ydel," he writes, "for be euer other spekynge of God, or wirchynge some notable werke, or thynkynge in hym, and principaly þat þi thoght be euer hauynge hym in mynde. And thynke oft[34] of his passione" (30.170–74). Even before the lyric begins, these prefatory instructions mark out the arena within which the lyric's sonority will operate. Rolle invites his reader to perform three activities to avoid idleness, "spekynge," "wirchynge," and "thynkynge," which he subsequently gathers into one collective activity, "thoght." Within this gesture lies an important if implicit claim: that the human enterprise called "thoght" subsumes these three activities, "other . . . or . . . or . . ." indicating their coordination as much as their difference. Bookended with clear instructions to "thynke oft" (30.174, 31.212), the second lyric is thus foregrounded as a verbal environment where the modes of cognition ("thynkynge") arising from the sound of spoken verse ("spekynge") will be potently in operation ("wirchynge").[35]

Affect is the cognitive currency of the second lyric. As its preface indicates—"thynke oft of his passione"—the lyric offers a Passion meditation, a devotional genre that expects readers to envision vivid entry into the affectively hypercharged scenes of Christ's death.[36] No stranger to the genre, Rolle paints a vivid picture of the Crucifixion in the lyric's first seventeen lines, but something unusual occurs at line 18: the Passion meditation breaks off and the lyric self-reflexively comments on the verses it has just offered as an object of "wonder" (30.192).[37] It then switches devotional genres: lines 22 through 37 offer a love complaint addressed to Christ. The second lyric thus involves an affective shift from sober wonder, where the brute sensory presence of Christ's crucified body captures the reader's seeing "I," to petitionary love-longing, where the Beloved's absence motivates utterance to a "þou" who only becomes addressable after the generic switch at line 22. This mirrors the turn from an alluring visual world to the devout spiritual rededications of the second degree of love. Closer attention to the lyric and its patterning of sound reveals how this affective shift is not just accomplished in but directly constituted by lyric sound.

Unlike the first lyric, the second is immediately detectable: marked off with a decorated initial or marginal note in the majority of manuscripts, the five monorhymed, near-metrical half-lines comprising lines 1 through 3 are difficult to miss.[38] The rhetorical techniques of intimacy, virtual vocal presence, and affective charge *Ego Dormio* employs more generally remain in operation here, though with a difference: the text's vernacular first person singular is elsewhere distinctly marked as Rolle's authorial *I*; here, the hermit must take a step back to make space in that *I* for the reader, since this *I* marks their point of imaginative personal entry into the scene of the Passion.[39] This is not to say that Rolle's strong *I* entirely recedes; rather, it hybridizes with the *I* of the reader's meditative prayer, adumbrating that prayer with the authority of his mystical experience and symbiotically sustaining his virtual vocal presence. The voice the reader hears in this lyric, the voice with which she speaks this lyric, is thus both her own and not her own.[40]

This hybrid, inhabitable first person is put into potent relation to the crucified Christ. The rapid, rhymed, past-tense verbs of lines 1 through 3— "grete," "swete," "bet," "wette," "met"—hammer out the chronological and memorial distance across which the reader's devotion to the suffering Christ reaches. Over the next sequence of monorhymes in lines 4 through 7, the power of this affective relation begins to close the temporal gap. By line 4, the five verbs' firm past tense gives way to potential present tense ("Ful fast þay can hym dinge"); by line 6, we observe the crown of thorns and iron nails piercing Christ's flesh in the here and now of the present tense. The intensity of Christ's suffering and the strength of the reader's compassion make chronology and geography navigable through the vehicle of the lyric's *I* as affect attracts the two figures from distant into proximate, present relation through the meditation's end.

Put another way, love brings bodies together by means of the lyric, an effect the poem makes explicit in lines 18 through 21, an interlude that separates the opening Passion meditation from the ending love complaint. Here as well, grammatical subject and verb tense are highly mobile. In the absence of an *I*, the reader finds easy habitation in the lyric's indefinite grammatical subjects, and the interlude's temporally fluid verb tenses echo the collapsing distances of the Passion meditation's opening. More crucially, the lyric here folds back on itself like a Möbius strip: "wonder hit is to se . . . [Christ] deynge on þe roode" (18–19) names precisely the affective impact the lyric's Passion meditation aims to effect in its reader. The poem thus metatextually identifies the truth of its own emotional impact, at the same time that it affirms the loving truth of Christ's sacrifice—two "soths" (20) profoundly intertwined and sponsored by affect's convergent attractions.

A third "soth" lies embedded in these lines that directly connects these truths to lyric sound. Denotatively, the second lyric's "soth" is a proverb: "loue ledeth þe rynge" (20). The "rynge" referred to here is a *carole*, a popular social song performed by a group linked in a circle or chain who sing and dance the refrain, in alternation with strophes sung by a soloist or solo group, who dances in the middle of the circle or leads the open chain.[41] That is to say, a "rynge" is a dance coordinated through the sounding performance of lyric; a "rynge" draws bodies into proximity and, however fleetingly, knits communities together, putting feet into rhythmic movement through the organizing structuration of sound.[42] The temporal, spatial, affective, and cognitive convergences the second lyric's Passion meditation sponsors are here emblematized: distances contract, gaps are bridged, desiring humans come into contact, choreographed by the dance leader Love, a divine Love whose wedding "rynge" Rolle wishes to secure on his reader's behalf at the very outset of *Ego Dormio*. In the proverbial ring dance and in the devotion the second lyric both scripts and is, Love teaches us the steps, Love sings the lyric's verses, and Rolle's readers join the chorus, embodying the lyric as moving song, as motion and emotion, not as solitary singers but as thoughtful actors in loving relation to others with whom they have come close. It is to this love that the second lyric seeks to incline our will and around which it pivots. Love's "soth"—the "soth" of the lyric, the "soth" of Christ's sacrifice, the "soth" of Love's "rynge"—indicates that lyric sound is the force that achieves this affective shift.

Indeed, we can observe this achievement once we return to the matter of how the second lyric patterns verbal sound into new poetic form. Rolle composes the second lyric with a compound line, each half-line usually

containing three stresses—the rhythm often resembles iambic trimeter—
observing both medial and terminal rhyme. His rhyme schemes fall into
one of two types. The first type (1a) is characterized by monorhyme at medial and terminal positions; at two points in the poem, a tercet of this type
(1b) lacks the second half of its third line. The second type is characterized
by differing rhyme at medial and terminal positions. One variation (2a) lacks
rhyme altogether at one of these positions, usually the medial; the other (2b)
rhymes at both medial and terminal positions, though the medial rhyme usually changes every two lines. The rhyme scheme for the entire lyric may be
diagrammed as in Table 2, with slashes indicating line breaks, *x* indicating
nonrhymes, and brackets labeling the rhyme schemes. I have started a new
line to distinguish Passion meditation, four-line interlude, and love complaint.[43] Though not exact, the alignment of rhyme scheme with content is
noteworthy. The rapid-fire monorhymes of type 1 rhyme schemes mark the
shift from Passion meditation to love complaint, from one lyric genre to another. Viewed mimetically, this phonic resurgence formally represents the
lyric's pivot; viewed performatively, it prompts that pivot.[44]

Table 2. Rhyme scheme for *Ego Dormio*'s second lyric.

⌐ 1b ¬⌐ 1a ¬⌐ 2a ¬⌐ 2b ¬			
aa / aa / a / bb / xb / bb / bb / xc / xc / xc / xc / xc / xc / dx / dx / ef / ef			

⌐ 2b ¬
gf / gf / hi / hi

⌐ 2b ¬⌐ 1a ¬⌐ 2b ¬⌐ 1b ¬⌐ 1a ¬
ji / ji / kk / kk / xk / ll / ll / mn / mn / mn / mn / oo / oo / o / pp / qq

Yet the inexact alignment of rhyme scheme and switched genre and the
later resurgence of rhyme scheme 1a in the lyric's closing lines resists these
assessments; a better explanation emerges when we revisit the lyric's dynamics
of affect. After the interlude signals and channels the awful wonder of the
lyric's Passion mediation into Christ's loving subjection,[45] newly introduced
vocatives and second-person imperatives addressed to Jesus draw us into a new
affective state, one articulated around absence instead of presence, longing
instead of fascination. From a reader's perspective, in the freshness of first
reading at least, this unanticipated turn demands acclimation to a new literary

genre, discursive mode, and affective texture. The recurrence of rhyme scheme type 1a, I argue, signals this acclimation's taking hold. Where mimetic and performative readings of the second lyric would anticipate a more square alignment of sound with literary form or genre, sound instead aligns here with the setting in of affective orientation, signaling the completed shift from sober wonder to love-longing. If we were curious about how quickly Middle English authors expected readers to catch up with a text's emotional twists and turns, we have here a possible answer: about two lines of verse.

Moreover, as readers lift the second lyric out of *Ego Dormio* and commit it to memory as a prayer they "thynke oft," lyric sound goes beyond registration of affective orientation to become the structure of affect directly. As the prayer is performed over and over, the familiar shifting of rhyme schemes becomes habituated not as an artifice of alignment but as the familiar shifting of affect itself, such that the two become reflexes of one another, too enmeshed to tease apart.[46] In this way, the second lyric realizes the claim to a truth-content outside propositionality that Jarvis's melodics proposes, to striking effect.

What to do with the third appearance of monorhyme, though, in lines 33 through 37? No new devotional genre appears here, no new demand that the reader reorient her affective state. A turn of a different sort occurs here, one that recalls the songful conclusion of the first lyric and anticipates an entirely different order of cognition. Up until now, the second lyric's sensory emphasis has been almost exclusively visual and tactile. Here, though, a "chaunge" (33) occurs, and the poem suddenly throngs with petitions for new sounds: "When may I cum þe nere / Thi melody for to hire? . . . Wil thou be my louynge, þat I þi loue may synge?" (34–37). "Loue" who formerly "[led] þe rynge" (20) suddenly "chaungeth chere" (33), and the lyric's *I* requests a concomitant change in itself: clarity of soul that yields onto the next life, onto everlasting melody, onto fullness of love for Christ, onto the singing of the song of love. The verbs that drive these lines—"make," "chaungeth," "be," "cum," "hire," "hyre," "is," "be," "synge"—outline a transformative itinerary whose endpoint is both vocal and aural, perceptual and spiritual, musical and ontological. In other words, the second lyric concludes with a petition for *canor*, a sound that the lyric is incapable of providing, the sound that Rolle does his best to declare in the final section of *Ego Dormio*.

Who shal to my leman say

My songe is in seghynge, my lif is in langynge,
Til I þe se, my kynge, so faire in þi shynynge.
So faire in þi fairhede, in to þi light me lede,
And in þi loue me fede; in loue make me spede,
5 That þou be euer my mede.
When wil þou cum, Ihesu my ioy, and keuer me of kare,
And gyf me þe, þat I may se, hauynge for euer more?
Al my coueitynge ware comen, if I myght to þe fare;
I wil no þynge bot only þe, þat al my wilnes ware.
10 Ihesu my sauyour, Ihesu my confortour, of fairnesse þe floure,
My helpe and my sokour, when may I se þi toure?
When wil þou me kalle? Me langeth in to þi halle
To se þe and þyn alle. Thi loue let hit nat falle;
My hert peynteth þe palle þat stiddeth vs in stalle.
15 Now wax I pale and wan for loue of my leman.
Ihesu, both God and man, thi loue þou lered me þan
When I to þe fast ran; forþi now loue I can.
I sit and synge of loue langynge þat in my brest is bred.
Ihesu, Ihesu, Ihesu, why ne ware I til þe ledde?
20 Ful wel I wot þou sest my state; in loue my þoght is stedde;
When I þe se and dwel with þe, þan am I fild and fedde.
Ihesu, þi loue is feste, and me to loue þynketh best.
My hert, when may hit brest, to cum to þe, my rest?
Ihesu, Ihesu, Ihesu, to þe is þat I mourne;
25 Forþi, my lif and my lykynge, when may I hethen tourne?
Ihesu, my dere and my drery, delites art þou to synge;
Ihesu, my myrth, my melody, when wil þou cum, my kynge?
Ihesu, my hele and my hony, my quert, my confortynge,
Ihesu, I couait for to dey when hit is þi paynge.
30 Langynge is in me lent, þat my loue hath me sent.
Al wo fro me is went, sethen þat my hert is brent
In Criste loue so swete, þat neuer I wil lete,
Bot euer to loue I hete, for loue my bale may bete,
And to my blisse me brynge, and yif my desyrynge.
35 Ihesu, my loue swetynge,

Langynge is in me light, þat byndeth me day and nyght,
Til I hit haue in sight, his face so fayere and bryght.
Ihesu, my hope and hele, my ioy euer euery dele,
Þi loue let hit nat kele, þat I þi loue may fele,
40   And won with þe in wele.
Ihesu, with þe I bigge and belde; leuer me ware to deye
Þan al þis world to weld and haue hit in maistry.
When wil þou rewe on me, Ihesu, þat I myght with þe be,
To loue and loke on þe? My sete ordayn for me,
45   And set þou me þerin, for þan may we neuer twyn,
And I þi loue shal synge þrogh syght in þy shynynge
In heuyn withouten endynge. Amen.
                                        (32.267–33.313)

Immediately after the second lyric, *Ego Dormio* urges its addressee to memorize the poem and incorporate it into her private devotional life beyond the text. In return, Rolle promises, she will receive ample spiritual reward: "If þou wil þynke þis euery day, þou shalt fynd gret swetnesse, þat shal draw þi hert vp, and mak þe fal in wepynge and in grete langynge to Ihesu; and þi þoght shal be reft abouen al erthly þynges, abouen þe sky and þe sterres, so þat þe egh of þi hert may loke in to heuyn" (31.212–15). Abundant spiritual sweetness, the heart's uplifting, supermundane thought, and the opening of the heart's eye are all hallmarks of Rollean sensory contemplation—that is, they mark entry into the third degree of love. Yet access to the third degree of love is limited to an elect spiritual elite: "I wot neuer jf many men be in suche loue, for euer þe hegher þat þe lif is, þe fewer folowers hit hath here" (27.58–60). Recitation of a lyric, however great the reciter's devotion, can hardly be sufficient to open the contemplative gateway. Having stirred up his reader's hope, Rolle promptly walks back his promise, placing the determination over who receives spiritual heat, sweetness, and song squarely in God's hands: "And þan entres þou in to þe þrid degre of loue, in þe whiche þou shalt be in gret delite and confort, if þou may get grace to cum þerto. For I say nat þat þou, or another þat redeth þis, shal do hit al, for þat is in Goddis wille" (31.216–19). The second lyric is thus quickly pointed up as insufficient for attaining the "melody" and "songe" it petitions at its conclusion. The reason for this insufficiency becomes clear as *Ego Dormio* describes the third degree of love in its last prose section. Rolle's firsthand experiential account of this highest affection begins explicitly with sound, or rather, with the absence of sound: "This degre of loue is cald contemplatif lif, þat loueth to be onely withouten ryngen or dyn and syngynge and criynge" (31.224–25). The obstreperous soundscape Rolle describes is obviously that of the secular world, but it is also, upon reflection, that of *Ego Dormio* up until now: true contemplative life cares little for the lyrical feet of the dancing "ryng," for the "dyn" of the first lyric's alliterative verbal percussion, or for lachrymose Passion meditation, guaranteed to "mak þe fal in wepynge" (31.213). All outward "syngynge," sacred as much as secular, drowns out the spiritual melody one should seek to hear instead, an aural incompatibility Rolle insists upon at multiple points across his writings.[47] It is here we begin to detect the limitations and failures of lyric sound for *Ego Dormio*'s overall project: entrance into the third degree of love demands departure from the resounding world and the sonorous practices the text has explored so far, because the outward, material sonority of those practices fundamentally interferes with the inward, spiritual musicality of *canor*.

This being so, *Ego Dormio*'s third and final lyric can only occupy a vexed position. As the lyric that caps off the final prose section and the text as a whole, it ought to guide us into the Beloved's melody and complete the transformation of "thoght" into song that the third degree of love promises (31.231–33). Yet as a scripted, outward, vocal utterance, it is incompatible with the divine music it positionally suggests it will make available, both because the outward sound of speech distracts the sense of hearing from its proper spiritual object and because human modes of expression are incapable of capturing *canor*. The lyric acknowledges the insufficiency of its utterance in its opening lines, which immediately draw attention to their failure of a songfulness that is projected into a refulgent future the poem's *I* does not yet occupy: "My songe is in seghynge, my lif is in langynge, / Til I þe se, my kynge, so faire in þi shynynge" (1–2). As we continue to read, the third lyric remains strikingly static, ending almost exactly where it begins with verses that closely echo the content, language, futurity, and even rhyme of the opening lines: "And I þi loue shal synge þrogh syght in þy shynynge / In heuyn withouten endynge" (46–47). There is no generic shift, no affective reorientation to be found here; the only substantial change lies in the kind of song the lyric addresses. At its opening, the lyric recognizes itself as deficient song, as windy "seghynge," a term that homophonically conjoins the "saying" of verse with the "sighing" of unsatisfied desire.[48] At its close, the lyric anticipates genuine song beyond its bounds, discarding outward "seghynge" for a heavenly "syghtynge" that relinquishes lyric saying for the ontological singing of angelic *canor* at the same time that it transvalues and redeems the visuality the first lyric so derogates.[49]

Rolle's verses thus provide us with a term, "seghynge," for the unmusical, earthbound melodics of love complaint that characterizes the end of *Ego Dormio*'s second lyric and the entirety of its third. The sound of this "seghynge" melodics becomes more apparent once we map the third lyric's rhyme schemes. Though the third lyric is more diverse in its sound effects, employing alliteration more liberally than the second,[50] its rhyming patterns strongly recall those of the earlier love complaint with spans of type 1 monorhyme and type 2 alternating rhyme occurring in turn, in a kind of prosodic inhalation and exhalation. Type 2 rhyme schemes expand their first half-line from three to four stresses, usually with internal rhyme on the second and fourth stress, to yield an approximation of ballad stanza, spans of which I have bracketed in Table 3. By contrast with the second lyric, monorhyme predominates here; functionally, it registers not transitional affective acclimation but the poem's stagnated affective state of "langynge," a term that recurs refrain-like in lines 1, 12, 18, 30, and 36.[51]

Table 3. Rhyme scheme for *Ego Dormio*'s third lyric.

aa / aa / bb / bb / b / xxc / ddc / xxc / adc / eee / ee / ff / ff / ff / gg / gg / gg /

aah / xxh / iih / jjh / kk / kk / xl / xal / xxa / xxa / xxa / mm / mm / nn / nn /

aa / a / oo / oo / pp / pp / p / xqr / qr / ss / ss / tt / aa / a

Rather, it is the type 2 rhyme schemes, the spans of ballad stanza, that stand out here and ask for notice against the third lyric's prevailing monorhymes. In the third lyric, it is these sounds that mark out a difference: appearances of the Holy Name (indicated in Table 3 in boldface) multiply in and around them. Rolle's enthusiasm for and association with Holy Name devotion is well documented;[52] when he advocates it in *Ego Dormio* as a practice proper to the second degree of love, he writes that it prepares the devout for mystical ecstasy: "If þou loue hit right and lestyngly . . . þou shalt be rauyst in to a hegher lif þan þou can couait" (29.145–47). While this is not the Holy Name's first appearance in *Ego Dormio*'s verses—it appears three times in the second lyric's love complaint—the nineteen repetitions of "Ihesu" across the third lyric build a verbal and affective force of their own in competition with the lyric's rhyme schemes, whose nonrhyming disruptions almost all co-occur with the Holy Name's appearance. At lines 19 and 24, the Holy Name repeats three times in immediate succession, a feature one manuscript records and underlines with bright red ink in a noticeably oversized script.[53] This is clearly a new, noteworthy feature of Rolle's lyric composition in *Ego Dormio*; given its disruptive effect on the third lyric's formal patterns, it asks a reevaluation of lyric sound.

In fact, lyric sound seems to reach a dead end here: the third lyric's disruptions and insistences urge us to leave its static "seghynge" behind and turn to the Holy Name instead in pursuit of the third degree of love. Indeed, if we turn back to it, Rolle's prose description of the third degree of love centrally features the Holy Name, which appears immediately alongside his description of melodious cognitive transformation that occurs at contemplation's apex: "for heynesse of þi hert, þi praiers turneth in to ioyful songe and þi þoghtes to melodi. Þan Ihesu is al þi desire, al þi delit, al þi ioy, al þi solace, al þi comfort, so þat on hym wil euer be þi songe, and in hym al þi rest. Þan may þou say, I slepe and my hert waketh. Who shal to my leman say, for his loue me longeth ay?" (31.231–32.236).[54] The Holy Name devotion recommended for the second degree of love becomes an anaphoric spilling out of totalizing affect in the third ("Ihesu is al þi desire, al þi delit, al þi ioy, al þi solace, al þi comfort"), Rolle's iterative fivefold refrain rhetorically anticipating the mystical state in which "on hym wil euer be þi songe." His simple copula, "Ihesu is al . . . ," leaves unspecified, and so fruitfully openended, what "Ihesu" actually is: person and name, word and Word, sound and song, all of which "Ihesu" seems to encompass in a manner that exceeds devotional meditation. Clearly, the Holy Name—or, at least, what the Holy Name becomes in the third degree of love—is more closely allied to the audition of *canor* than anything we have encountered so far.

The nature of this tie emerges in the subsequent sentence. From within this state of permanent restful song in "Ihesu," the contemplative will at last be able to authentically utter the verse of the "songe of loue" that spurs *Ego Dormio* in the first place: "Þan may þou say, I slepe and my hert waketh." The internal cross-reference is difficult to miss. In the heart of his account of the third degree of love, Rolle returns us to the beginning of his text where we first encountered these words (26.2–3). There, the "songe of loue" referred to the biblical Song of Songs; here, it refers to the mystical song of *canor*. It is unlikely that Rolle understands biblical book and spiritual music-making to be the same thing—though scripture is the Word of God, it is still a thing in the world, a text recited by human mouths, and thus it hits the same material and sonorous wall as lyric—but it does appear that he understands the Song of Songs, the most lyrical of biblical books and source of so much impassioned mystical creativity, to stand in privileged relationship to angelic song.[55] Here, perhaps, is the closest lyric sound can come to its asymptotic limit within the mystical project: the sound of the Word speaking words of intimate love and supplying loving words to His beloved through the Song of Songs, rendered not in the sacralizing Latin of ecclesiastical ritual and biblical authority but in the intimate vernacular of Rolle's lyrical corpus.

It is in this regard that Rolle extends his vernacular re-citation of Song of Songs 5:2 with a lyric refrain, readily recognized as such by its courtly love topos, metrical regularity, and rhyme: "Þan may þou say, I slepe and my hert waketh. Who shal to my leman say, for his loue me longeth ay?"[56] Otherwise unattested and so perhaps purpose-built for *Ego Dormio*, this rogue lyric irrupts into the epistle unannounced, springing from the Song of Songs as if to identify the biblical book as the well of lyric origin.[57] Poised at the farthest reaches of transcendent lyric utterance, it directly queries the limits of saying: "Þan may þou say . . . Who shal to my leman say?" The question the rogue lyric asks is not rhetorical; it worries that no one, not even I, is capable of properly saying "my love" to my Lover, hoping to the contrary but anticipating a negative answer, precisely because saying, which is to say "seghynge," is the province of devotional thought, of the second and third lyrics. The contemplative firmly stationed in the third degree of love is thus able to utter the Song of Songs as lyric to the extent that her utterance interrogates and undermines its own utterability. If she were able to say her love to her Lover, that love would be inadequate. Only the Word speaking Love through the Song of Songs can suffice; only Ihesu can properly be the song that Rolle's lyrics seek to train us toward.

Now I write a songe of loue

Like the second, the third lyric is prefaced with instructions that point out the poem as a distinctive packet of sounding language that Rolle's addressee should put to independent devotional use. "Now I write a songe of loue," the hermit addresses her, "þat þou shalt haue delite jn when þou art louynge Ihesu Criste" (32.265–66). In many ways, this prefatory remark prepares the way for the lyric that follows: it reminds the reader of Rolle's authorially marked *I* that will sustain its hybridized hold, somewhat more strongly this time, on the lyric's inhabitable *I*; it reiterates the writtenness of the lyric at the same time that it underlines Rolle's virtual vocality with present-tense verbs and pronouns of direct and familiar address; it locates the reader's affective reward, her "delite," in a potential future tense just as the lyric locates the true song its "seghynge" cannot provide in a future the lyric's *I* does not yet inhabit.

At the same time, though, Rolle calls the third lyric "a songe of loue," the same phrase he uses to refer to the song of *canor* and the Song of Songs in *Ego Dormio*. While the indefinite article is important—the lyric is *a* song, not *the* Song—the turn of phrase asks us to think hard about what Rolle understands "songe" to be, and, more basically, what sound in fact *is* in his text. Obviously, sound is a physical phenomenon *Ego Dormio* is finely attuned to with its intricate patternings of verbal material, but sound is also a cognitive phenomenon operating outside the boundaries of propositional reason, an experiential phenomenon the text designs to construct and reconstruct its reader, and a spiritual and ontological phenomenon that stands in utter opposition to these, well beyond the reach of any text or utterance one can conceive or perform. The "songe of loue" is many things, not all of them mutually reconcilable, though all conceptualized as apprehensible through the human capacity to hear, broadly conceived. Investigation of Rollean lyric sound thus not only augments our sense of what kind of a thing a lyric is (script, sound, Holy Writ, Holy Name, structures of thought, reflexes of affect) and what kinds of things lyrics can do (seduce, incite, direct, transform, fail, redeem). It also reveals the enmeshment of the study of Middle English lyric and the project of historical sound studies, which seeks to investigate embodied listening practices, sound's discursive contexts, and the lived aural experiences of historical hearers.[58] Heeded in this manner, Rollean lyric calibrates our modern ear to a delicate and otherwise muted medieval sound art, one that uses text to sculpt aural space and experience through a disposition of sonic material that stands to transform those who hear, those who utter, and the world around them.[59] By listening closely to *Ego Dormio*'s lyrics, then, we interrogate and expand our understanding of what sound was and how listeners heard in the late medieval past.

A close listening to *Ego Dormio* ultimately yields a clearer sense of the nuanced and potent work lyric sound is capable of, not as an adjunct to verbal content but as affecting literary material in its own right, within the domain of Middle English devotional writing. At the same time, Rolle's text reveals the limitations of this sonorous work for his contemplative project by exposing its three inset lyrics' asymptotic failure of the ideal lyric, the Holy Name, under whose auspices Song of Songs 5:2 discloses its rhyming refrain. In this respect, we do well to heed *Ego Dormio*'s repeated summons back to its opening as it approaches its close. "Ego dormio et cor meum vigilat. The þat lust loue, hold þyn ere and hyre of loue": instructions of hearing, and also of not hearing. Is Rolle asking us to hold a hand to our ear so as to hear better, or to hold a hand over our ears so as to hear truly?[60] The one attends to the delight of lyric sound; the other attends to the delight that lyric sound fails of. As modern listeners to Middle English lyrics, *Ego Dormio* invites us to adopt both postures at once. As *Ego Dormio* taught its devout medieval reader, the accomplishment of love hangs upon the difference.

Chapter 9

The Lyric Christ

BARBARA ZIMBALIST

Christ speaks with a particular intensity in the Middle English lyric. Usually, he speaks in the first person, and while occasionally he quotes or echoes his own biblical speech, most often his speech is vernacular and original to the poem in which it appears. Sometimes, he comforts his mother from the cross as she grieves his passion. At other moments, he laments mankind's disobedience in solitude. Still elsewhere, he offers advice to anonymous interlocutors with contemporary concerns. Despite the ubiquitous presence of Christ's lyric speech within medieval poetry, however, scholarship of the Middle English lyric has no particular designation for it. Such poems are usually assigned to Rosemary Woolf's somewhat generic category of "Passion lyrics": lyrics in Christ's voice, addressed to "mankind" from the cross, that direct the human interlocutor to respond with compassion and repentance.[1] This designation highlights the affective qualities of Christ's lyric speech that have been long recognized as one of the central means through which Middle English poetry encouraged devotional response from readers.[2] Yet such affectivity constitutes only one valence of Middle English lyrics. Christ's lyric speech also engaged readers through rhetorical and formal innovations that generated other responses and effects.[3] By interrogating how Christ's speech elicits response in lyric poetry, this chapter responds to what Ingrid Nelson terms "the difficulty of placing Middle English lyrics in the long history of the lyric genre."[4] It shows how within Middle English religious lyrics, Christ's speech invited intellectual interpretation and, in some cases, verbal imitation. I argue that through rhetorical, formal, and structural tensions, both resolved and unresolved, "the lyric Christ"—by which

I mean the Christ who speaks within lyric poetry in order to elicit a response from a reader or readers—creates a distinct devotional community through the Middle English lyric.

The devotional community created by the lyric Christ is also, of course, a community of readers. As we will see, the lyric Christ speaks in poems from different centuries and in different narrative modes—in dialogues, dream visions, love laments, and complaints. It is this very difference that emphasizes the core function of the lyric Christ: it establishes what might be termed a "collective subjectivity" both within the poem's form, structure, and rhetoric, as well as beyond the poem's formal parameters, within the devotional community. As Cristina Maria Cervone has argued, this type of "collective subjectivity" in medieval poetry encourages self-conscious consideration of communal identity through the rhetorical and deictic formulations of the poetry itself.[5] I suggest that the lyric Christ creates such collectivity by inviting interpretive response from diverse readers, and in doing so (to borrow a phrase from Brian Stock), formed those readers into new textual communities of shared devotional concern.[6]

The collective, communal responses invited by the lyric Christ created a distinctly Middle English devotional community. The religious literature of late medieval England exhibits what James Simpson terms an "anagogic sensibility": a spiritual impulse both ongoing and participatory that imbricates readers within the imagined future community that is envisioned by the text, then left to its readers to enact.[7] As he argues, one example of this sensibility might be Julian of Norwich's claim near the end of her *Revelation of Love* that "this book is begun . . . but is not yet performed."[8] Read through Simpson's anagogic lens, Julian's claim suggests that the work of her text must be carried out by its readers. Middle English devotional prose such as the *Revelation* engages readers hermeneutically in ways like this by urging them to individual acts of devotion that vary widely. Within the Middle English religious lyric, however, the lyric Christ asks for reader participation through shared responses shaped by the specific rhetoric, structure, or form of his speech. The lyric Christ thus creates devotional community through both a shared hermeneutic activity as well as a common formal response. For this reason, the lyric Christ generates formal tensions that any individual lyric can only ever partially resolve, even as it unites its readers through shared response beyond the text. In this way, the lyric Christ projects the community of readers into the imagined future by evoking imitative, interpretive response beyond the poem. At the same time, the lyric Christ provides devotional models and scripts for this type of response, thus bringing the imagined future into being. The formal and poetic qualities that make the Middle English lyric what it is, then, also constitute the devotional function of the lyric Christ.

By tracing the role of the lyric Christ in medieval devotional poetry, this chapter responds to recent calls for reassessing the formal, structural, and hermeneutic difference of premodern poetics.[9] Two long-standing generic criteria for lyric poetry—the understanding of lyric as an expression of an individual subjectivity and the understanding of lyric as short-form poetry—prove especially difficult to apply to medieval poetry.[10] Middle English religious lyrics, particularly lyrics that contain or consist of Christ's speech, fit uneasily within these categories. Lyrics in Christ's voice do express an individual subjectivity, of course, but that subjectivity is divine rather than human; or, because it is Christ who speaks, his voice is both divine *and* human. Furthermore, the lyric Christ almost always speaks in dialogue with a human interlocutor; and that interlocutor eventually comes to stand in for the reader, expanding the function of Christ's speech beyond the formal parameters of the lyric that contains it and into the future devotional practice of the reading community. Finally, lyrics consisting of Christ's speech often far exceed any definition of a "short" form as conventionally understood, as Christopher Cannon discusses elsewhere in this book:[11] the shortest poem examined here runs to sixty-six lines, the longest to more than seven hundred. Yet as we will see, the central poetic qualities of the lyric Christ function to complementary devotional ends despite differences in length, century, or narrative mode.

The rest of this chapter examines four examples of the lyric Christ that highlight not only its common function across the Middle English lyric tradition but also the different imitative and interpretive practices it introduces into Middle English devotional reading. Early Middle English lyrics offered readers templates for devotional imitation. The thirteenth-century "Stond wel, moder, under rode" dramatizes the Crucifixion through eleven stanzas of alternating dialogue between Christ and his mother, then concludes with a template for devotional speech in imitation of that dialogue.[12] The fourteenth-century "Quia amore langueo" (or "In a valley of this restless mind," hereafter "Valley") embeds the lyric Christ within the generic and narrative frame of dream poetry.[13] Through fourteen stanzas steeped in the discourses of courtly love and the Song of Songs, an anonymous narrator tells of his encounter with Christ, who laments because of the cruelty of his beloved.[14] Unlike "Stond wel," "Valley" constructs a rhetorically complex vision of Christ that requires both interpretive and imitative engagement from readers. Despite their different identities as dialogue and dream vision, these two early lyrics share a similar manuscript context. Both appear in compilations of religious lyrics: "Stond wel" in London, British Library, Harley MS 2253, and "Valley" in London, Lambeth Palace Library, MS 853. Fifteenth-century lyrics offer more expansive accounts of the lyric Christ while demanding more participatory interpretive response. In the "Complaint of Christ," Christ repeatedly complains about humankind's persistent ungratefulness for eleven twelve-line stanzas before "mankind" repents and asks for mercy in a single concluding stanza.[15] Like "Stond wel," the "Complaint of Christ" offers readers a template for devotional speech; but unlike that earlier poem, that template responds to Christ rather than imitating him. Finally, the "Complaint of God" by the fifteenth-century preacher William Litchfield (sometimes spelled "Lichfield" or "Lichefeld") also places readers into the position of Christ's addressees; unlike other lyrics, however, this long lyric dialogue between Christ and an anonymous "man" elicits a participatory reading practice that expands the devotional community established by the Middle English lyric beyond the imitative scope of the earlier poems.[16] Like the early lyrics, the two Complaints also share a manuscript context, circulating together in at least two instances.

The material history of the lyric Christ reveals his widespread presence within Middle English poetry. Though fewer exemplars of the earlier lyrics survive, all survive in multiple manuscripts. "Stond wel" appears in part or whole in six manuscripts ranging from large collections of lyric poetry to prose compilations.[17] While in a manuscript such as Harley 2253 the poem may simply function as part of a collection of known lyrics, in more thematically coherent manuscripts—such as Oxford, Bodleian Library, MS Digby 86—it figures as one of several poems focused on Christ. "Valley" survives in only two manuscripts: a compilation consisting of both lyric and narrative poetry and a compilation consisting entirely of devotional and didactic lyric poetry.[18] In both cases the poem appears alongside religious lyrics praising Christ. The material history of the Complaints suggests that later, longer versions of the lyric Christ appealed to an even wider range of audiences. The "Complaint of Christ" survives in ten manuscripts ranging from compilations of lyrics to miscellanies of devotional, political, and moral texts; Litchfield's "Complaint of God" survives in twelve manuscripts and one early printed edition.[19] The manuscript diversity of the two Complaints suggests an increasingly broad audience, both real and imagined.

Read together, these poems show how the lyric Christ invited Middle English readers to became a devotional community in two specific ways. First, imitating Christ and his lyric interlocutors united readers into a textual community through a common verbal response. Second, interpreting Christ's lyric speech shaped readers into devotional community united by shared hermeneutic action. By reading the lyric Christ across multiple narrative and formal structures from different centuries, we can see a recurring movement from individual to collective devotional concerns, and a corresponding formal expansion that destabilizes easy generic categorization. Through these conjoined formal and hermeneutic developments, the lyric Christ models and elicits verbal devotion in vernacular engagement with the divine speaker. In what follows, I look first at Christ's speech, then briefly at the speech of his lyric interlocutors, and finally at the speech imagined and even provided for the readers of these poems. Together, these speakers demonstrate the devotional function of Christ's speech in the Middle English lyric.

Christ's Speech

Christ's lyric speech takes on different style and form depending on the lyric mode within which he speaks. In early Middle English lyrics Christ speaks with historical or biblical interlocutors about scriptural events and he models how to understand or interpret them. Later Middle English lyrics depict Christ in conversation with an increasingly general interlocutor, sometimes an allegorical persona, sometimes an abstract personification referred to as "Man" or "Mankind"; these poems tend to focus on more contemporary spiritual concerns. This section looks first at Christ's dialogue with the Virgin Mary in "Stond wel," then at his combined invitation and lament in the visionary "Valley," and finally at the "Complaint of Christ." While his speech takes on different formal and conceptual qualities in each of these poems, in all of these lyrics Christ's speech invites a collective responsiveness by creating narrative tension between the devotional speech contained within the poem, on the one hand, and the speech suggested, invited, or even modeled by the poem—but not included within it—on the other. And while the lyric Christ consistently generates this tension more broadly, it is generated in different ways and resolved to varying degrees depending on the particular lyric's devotional purpose.

"Stond wel" puts Christ in dialogue with the Virgin Mary.[20] While their conversation, framed by the Crucifixion during which it occurs, has long been recognized as affective, its devotional aspect has received less attention.[21] I suggest that its dialogic form creates tension between individual and communal devotional needs, while its repetitive structure generates tension between repeated form and expanding content. The first nine stanzas consist entirely of dialogue between Christ and Mary in a repeated pattern:

> "Stond wel, moder, under rode,
> Byholt thy sone with glade mode;
>   Blythe moder myht thou be."
> "Sone, hou shulde Y blithe stonde?
> Y se thin fet, I se thin honde
>   Nayled to the harde tre."[22]
>   (1–6)

The consistent structure of repetitive dialogue maintained by each stanza frustrates expectations of conclusion or closure, fostering a sense of indeterminately expansive conversation. In each stanza, Christ tries to comfort his mother, first explaining the salvation his passion will elicit, then reassuring her of her sorrowful unity with all human mothers, and finally proclaiming her the intercessor for humanity. Yet Mary counters each new explanation with her own rationale for refusal and her consistent rebuttals continue to necessitate Christ's additional explanations. Thus, as the initial exchange in stanza 1 establishes the dialogic pattern for the remainder of the poem, the repetition in each subsequent stanza continues to highlight the difference between individual and communal desires.

Throughout the course of the poem's first nine stanzas, Christ's rhetoric transforms at the same time that it enacts transformation. First, his addresses to Mary transform from command to explanation to request. The first four stanzas begin with direct instructions: "Stond wel, moder, under rode / Byholt thy sone with glade mode"; then "Moder, *do wey* thy wepinge"; and finally "Moder, thou *rewe* al of thy bern!" (1–2, 7, 19, my emphasis). Each of these commands attempts to control Mary's response to the Passion, yet she remains resistant. In response, Christ's speech transforms from command to instruction in stanzas 5 and 6. He explains first that "Betere is that Ich one deye / Then al monkunde to helle go" (26–27) and then that "Yef Y ne deye, thou gost to helle" (32); still, neither command nor logic prevails upon his mother to cease her lamentation. Finally in stanza 3 he begins to plead, asking

Moder, merci! Let me deye,
For Adam out of helle beye,
Ant his kun that is forlore.
(13–15)

As it transforms from command to instruction to pleading, Christ's speech
moves from Mary's individual sorrow over his passion to the greater spiritual benefit his passion will gain for the entire Christian community. At the
same time that Christ's speech transitions from individual to communal concerns, moreover, it transforms his interlocutor. In response to Mary's repeated refusal to be comforted by his commands and explanations, Christ
first connects her individual pain with the pain of all mothers. In stanzas 7
and 8 he tells her

Moder, nou thou miht wel leren
Whet sorewe haveth that children beren,
Whet sorewe hit is with childe gon
(37–39)

and

Moder, rew of moder kare,
For nou thou wost of moder fare
Thou thou be clene mayden-mon.
(43–45)

These lines transform Mary not only from individual maternal sufferer into
communal participant in the sorrow of human motherhood but also into the
intercessor par excellence, available to all in the Christian community who
pray to her for help. The variation contained within Christ's repeated dialogue
thus expands Mary's individual concerns into communal spirituality, just as
within the individual suffering of the crucifixion Christ intercedes for all.[23]

While the lyric dialogue of "Stond wel" presents Christ in conversation
with a recognizable historical figure, in the visionary lyric "In a valley of this
restless mind" he speaks with more vaguely allegorical figures. Both poems
gradually move from individual to communal devotional concerns through
repetition, but "Valley" intensifies that potential collectivity. The poem's

stanzaic structure and repeated refrain suggest stability and continuity, even as its rhetoric challenges such expectations through subjective and deictic indeterminacy. Moreover, the generic structure of dream vision dissolves over the course of the poem while the formal structure of stanza and repeated refrain remains intact. As a result, "Valley" foregrounds Christ's speech, rather than any particular generic and formal quality of the Middle English lyric, as the poetic element that unites readers into a devotional community.

In "Valley," Christ speaks initially with an anonymous Dreamer. Later in the poem, he speaks with multiple allegorical figures. The poem enlarges the devotional scope of the dialogue lyric by multiplying Christ's conversationalists as he speaks within multiple narrative modes: the dream vision and the love lament. This doubled narrative mode immediately complicates any individual narrative subjectivity and establishes a communal rhetoric. The first two stanzas begin conventionally, as the anonymous narrator describes the dream state within which he encounters Christ:

> In a valey of this restles mynde,
>   I soughte in mounteyne and in mede,
> Trustynge a trewelove for to fynde,
>   Upon an hil than Y took hede:
>   A voice Y herde—and neer Y yede—
>   In huge dolour complaynynge tho:
>   "Se, dere Soule, how my sidis blede,
>   *Quia amore langueo.*"
>
> Upon this hil Y fond a tree,
>   Undir the tree a man sittynge;
> From heed to foot woundid was he,
>   His herte blood Y sigh bledinge:
>   A semeli man to ben a king,
>   A graciouse face to loken unto:
>   I askide whi he had peynynge:
>   He seide, "*Quia amore langueo.*"[24]
>   (1–16)

While Christ replies initially to the dream narrator, his speech quickly turns into a long love lament that literally takes over the poem. After these first two stanzas, the rest of the poem consists entirely of Christ's speech. As in

"Stond wel," then, in "Valley" the lyric Christ establishes a conversational structure only to transcend that very structure within later stanzas.

After speaking to the anonymous Dreamer, in "Valley" Christ addresses allegorical biblical figures. Despite the relative stability of Christ's consistent first-person speaking position throughout "Valley," he gradually takes on an increasingly plural subjectivity as he repeatedly addresses different interlocutors. While the poem begins with his courtly voice, in stanza 14 Christ characterizes himself through maternal imagery, insisting that

> My babe Y wolde not were in disese;
> I may not heere my dere child wepe;
> With my pap I schal hir kepe.
>
> (107–9)

By the last stanza he is speaking as a loving husband to the "dere Soule" he refers to as "myn owne wiif" (126, 121). As Susanna Fein has suggested, these multiple subjectivities gesture toward Christ's theological identity as the desired object of each Christian soul, available rhetorically and conceptually to multiple interlocutors.[25] Furthermore, while this multiple address introduces multiple identities within the narrative voice of a single speaker, it also gestures toward a corresponding plurality within the devotional community to whom he speaks. Though Christ speaks within multiple discourses to multiple interlocutors throughout "Valley," then, he speaks to all of them about the love humankind owes to God. Anyone might respond to his lament, repeated in refrain at the end of each stanza.

In "Valley," the intertextuality of the repeated refrains brings diverse subjectivities together into a devotional community.[26] All sixteen stanzas conclude with Christ's Latin refrain, "Quia amore langueo." Each repetition attributes the refrain to Christ as part of his love lament, overheard within the dream. Most immediately, the refrain evokes its source text, the Song of Songs.[27] However, while within "Valley" it is always Christ who utters the love-lament, in the original biblical context this lament is spoken by the Bride searching for the absent Bridegroom. This intertextuality associates Christ with both the lover and the beloved, as the female lover searching for her cruel beloved in the biblical context and the male sufferer languishing from his beloved's neglect and abuse within the poem. As Ann Astell observes, in "Valley," "Christ incorporates all these features in the *historia* of his passion and death as a way of expressing his Incarnation, his full identification with the humanity symbolized by the Bride."[28] The doubled gender suggested by the refrain's biblical intertextuality further expands the potential for multiple dialogic participants. Furthermore, the refrains in "Valley" establish an unresolved tension between rhetoric and structure that amplifies the potential for responsive plurality established by multiple narrative modes: Christ repeatedly invites response while that very repetition indefinitely forestalls the possibility of response within the poem. In this way, the lyric Christ suggests that the devotional community beyond the poem might provide the response "Valley" invites but does not provide. At the same time, the lack of any concluding narrative frame curtails any potential transformation of Christ's refrain beyond repetition. The tension generated by Christ's repeated refrain, between recursive, formal repetition and rhetorical and intertextual expansiveness, gestures toward the larger devotional function of the lyric Christ: to address and thus instantiate a devotional community that must resolve the poem's tensions both *in* as well as *beyond* the moment of reading.

Finally, Christ's repeated refrains transform his speech from singular to plural by creating a devotional community that functions beyond its particular poetic context. As a citational refrain, "quia amore langueo" not only gestures to an origin text outside of "Valley"; it also shares its intertextual refrain with other contemporary lyrics. As Ardis Butterfield has demonstrated, the citational variability of such shared refrain, which she terms "cross-contextuality," characterizes the medieval lyric specifically.[29] That variability suggests a common, shared set of possible refrains—not original to any one poem but always cited in quotation from another source such as scripture—which function not through novelty but through familiarity in order to establish an expected meaning and elicit a common response. The Latin refrain in "Valley" functions in precisely this way: in addition to quoting the Bible, it appears as the refrain to the contemporary lyric "In a Tabernacle of a Tower," the Marian lyric consisting of Mary's love lament for Christ often paired with "Valley" in critical accounts because of their shared refrain and stanzaic structure, common imagery, and adjacent manuscript placement.[30] Both poems include "quia amore langueo" as the repeated refrain of a divine or holy speaker: in "Valley," Christ; in "Tabernacle," Mary. The intertextuality and cross-contextuality of Christ's repeated refrain thus evokes common knowledge of Christ's love for humankind and an interpretive community with a shared understanding of devotional speech, precisely through the narrative depiction of the individual speaker. Whereas the dialogue of "Stond wel" presented Christ's speech as a powerful, exemplary,

completed conversation with the Virgin Mary, the later "Valley" presents
Christ's speech as subjectively plural and formally indefinite. Both lyrics present Christ speaking in dialogue, but in different ways and to different devotional ends. While in "Stond wel" Christ's speech transforms his mother
into intercessor for the devotional community, in "Valley" the lyric Christ
creates a collective responsiveness by invoking multiple potential respondents
within the devotional community. This movement, from *speaking on behalf
of* the devotional community to *speaking to* the devotional community,
emerges with further intensity in the "Complaint" lyrics of the next century.

In fifteenth-century Complaints, the lyric Christ speaks in dialogue with
general personifications of humanity, in less intertextual and more entirely
original shape. As in "Stond wel" and "Valley," Christ's varied complaints and
repeated refrains highlight the difference between individual and communal
devotional concerns; yet unlike those earlier lyrics, the later complaints from
the very first lines invite an explicitly collective responsiveness that gestures
toward a devotional community both atemporal and contemporary. In the
"Complaint of Christ," Christ's conversation with "Mankind" gradually
combines the historical community with the contemporary community. Even
before he begins the long catalog of human disappointments and failures
that constitute the majority of his speech, his rhetoric establishes a plural
interlocutor:

> This is goddis owne complaynt
>   To euery man þat he haþ bouȝt,
> And þus he seiþ to hem ataynt,
>   *"Myne owne peple, what han ȝe wrouȝt*
> Þou þat to me art so faynt,
>   And y þi loue so fer haue souȝt?
> *In þine answere no þing þou paynt*
>   *To me; for whi, y knowe þi þouȝt.*
> Haue y not doon al þat me ouȝt?
>   Haue y left ony þyng bihynde?
> Whi wraþþist þou me? y greue þee nouȝt;
>   Whi art þou to þi freend vnkinde?"[31]
>   (1–12, my emphasis)

Christ's direct questioning of "Myne owne peple" (4) commands a spoken
answer. He demands verbal transparency and cautions against deception or

exaggeration in future prayer ("In þine answere no þing þou paynt / To me,"
7–8), immediately establishing a general, atemporal, collective addressee. His
rhetorical questions remain carefully vague; asking "Haue y not doon al þat
me ouȝt? / Haue y left ony þyng bihynde?" (9–10) allows any interlocutor to
question what "ouȝt" to have been done or what "þyng" might have been left
behind. This repeated mode of questioning figures "Mankind" as a devotional
community while acknowledging the potential variety of the individual members of that community.

     Christ's questions alternate between asking about the historical, biblical
things he has done for the Christian community and the things he has done
personally for individual believers. As the poem proceeds, however, his rhetoric focuses increasingly on contemporary, communal concerns. By gradually expanding the identity of his addressee from a historical "Man" to a
contemporary "Man," the "Complaint of Christ" joins historical and contemporary community identities. The complaint begins with a catalog of
the ways in which Christ has helped, promoted, and comforted man throughout biblical and eschatalogical history: he made man in his image and delivered him from Egypt (stanza 2); he sustained the Israelites in the wilderness
and was crucified for man's sins (stanza 3); he ordained for mankind a place
in paradise (stanza 4). After this detail of his historical mercies, Christ directly addresses a contemporary, communal interlocutor in the present tense
in stanza 5. He poses a series of rhetorical questions, asking "O Man, y loue
þee! whom louest þou?" and "I am þi freend; whi wolt þou feyne?" (49–50);
he then proceeds, throughout all the subsequent stanzas, to accuse this
general, contemporary addressee of failing to love him enough. Stanzas 6
through 10 contain almost no biblical imagery or reference (with the exception of Christ's reference to his crucifixion), instead consisting almost entirely of contemporary complaints such as "euery day þou woundist me
newe" (stanza 7, line 74) and "þou me temptist from day to day" (stanza 8,
line 86), followed by divine exhortation to "biþinke þee what þou art" (stanza
10, line 109). This increase in Christ's direct address in the contemporary
moment over the course of the poem's second half has the effect both of
foregrounding the poem's expanding temporal collectivity and of reorienting
the devotional community created by the lyric Christ within the contemporary
moment.[32]

     The structure and rhetoric of the lyric Christ functions variously in
poems from different centuries; yet in each of these lyrics Christ's speech in-
stantiates a collective responsiveness. Moreover, while that responsiveness

differs from lyric to lyric, it consistently creates a devotional community, both in the poem as well as beyond it. The nature of that community changes from poem to poem, yet it remains the effect of the lyric Christ. As we will see in the next section, the lyric figures and personas who reply to Christ's speech further develop that devotional community.

Christ's Addressees

In each of the lyrics examined here, Christ addresses interlocutors named and anonymous, implicitly and explicitly; sometimes the poems include their responses and sometimes they do not. Yet in all of them Christ's speech creates his addressee; that addressee, in turn, confirms the power of Christ's speech to articulate the necessity for the devotional community to respond beyond the limits of the poem. In this way, while Christ's speech establishes narrative tension within the Middle English lyric between the poems and their readers, his interlocutors dramatize the devotional function of that tension. In the variety of their responses, they demonstrate that the devotional effect of Christ's lyric speech extends beyond the formal limits of lyric to shape the conceptual space of reading. This section compares the earliest and latest lyrics examined here to show the ways in which Christ's addressees both model and shape the devotional community elicited by his speech. In "Stond wel," Christ speaks with Mary, who does respond, but not in the way he asks her to. In William Litchfield's "Complaint of God," however, the allegorical "Man" responds obediently to Christ, but does not completely demonstrate the repentance he asks for. In what follows, I show the different ways in which these addressees evoke the possibility—even necessity—for a collective response to the lyric Christ. Taken together, these lyrics demonstrate an increasingly responsive, participatory devotional community, initially within the conceptual space of the lyric but eventually beyond the formal parameters of the poems themselves.

Early lyrics both anticipate and dramatize how Christ's addressees exceed formal parameters to devotional effect. Often, the spoken response of Christ's early addressees does not adequately respond to the lyric Christ's requests. In "Stond wel," for example, Christ repeatedly addresses the same historical figure: his mother Mary. She responds throughout the poem within the repeated dialogue structure, and her responses draw attention to their own devotional incompleteness.[33] Whereas Christ's speech transforms and is transformed through repeated dialogue, within that same structure the speech of his addressee—Mary—remains resistant to full transformation. While her speech initially remains consistent with her intensely personal sorrow, as in her stanza 6 insistence that "hit is my kynde / That Y for the this sorewe make" (35–36), even this lament introduces the larger concept of communal human nature, or "kynde," thus gesturing toward the potential communal efficacy of her speech. In stanza 8, she responds to Christ's articulation of her new intercessory identity by requesting

> Sone, help at alle nede,
> *Alle* tho that to me grede
> Maiden, wif, ant fol wymmon.
>   (46–48, my emphasis)

This speech functions as intercession, demonstrating the power of Christ's speech to transform his mother from individual human mother to the Mother of All, whose speech functions devotionally for others as well as herself. Mary's transformation remains incomplete, however; her final speech in stanza 9 reverts to her personal lamentations in refusal of her son's requests:

> Sone, Y wil with the founden;
> Y deye, ywis, for thine wounden.
> So soreweful ded nes never non!
>   (52–54)

Mary's dialogue thus establishes the need to expand the poems' devotional community from Mary and her son to all Christians, even as her own dialogue fails to complete that expansion. In early lyrics, then, the structure, rhetoric, and form of the lyric Christ's addressee raise the possibility of (and necessity for) a devotional community, even though the addressee does not model that expansion. In later Middle English lyrics, however, Christ directly addresses more abstract, general interlocutors with an explicitly communal identity from the very beginning of the poem. As a result, even though these poems create devotional community through their addressees like earlier lyrics do, Christ's fifteenth-century addressees more explicitly project responsive speech beyond formal parameters and into the future of the devotional community they imagine.

William Litchfield's "Complaint of God" significantly expands the rhetorical, dialogic, and devotional role of Christ's addressee. Christ identifies communal response as the site of sin and failure as well as repentance and salvation. As in "Stond wel," Christ repeatedly speaks to a reluctant interlocutor. He remarks,

> Man, I am more redy alway
> To forȝeue þee þi mys-gouernaunce
> Þan þou art mercy for to pray.[34]
>
> (713–15)

Elsewhere in the poem, Christ compares the sinful contemporary speech of "Man" with his more successful, imagined future speech, cautioning that

> In wordis and in veyn spekynge
> what euere þu waastist, þou myrie art;
> Of such y wole haue rekenynge
> On doomysday . . .
> Þanne schalt þou ȝeue acountis ful streite.
>
> (273–77)

Christ's description of past and future speech suggests that the devotional speech promised and even partially performed by "Man" does not fully respond to his request and that only future promised speech will. Indeed, Christ warns man that at the last judgment

> Þanne wole not helpe to plete ne pray
> þerfor, as riȝt wole, þanne deme schal y:
> And þerfore, man, whilis þou may,
> Man, make amendis or þou die.
>
> (289–92)

This demand that "Man" reply before mortal time runs out articulates a poem's new narrative tension. Christ's speech creates an expectation of response, and the addressee repeatedly—but only partially—meets that expectation within the poem's dialogic structure. At the same time, the repetitive nature of the dialogue and the communal, plural construction

of the addressee extends the performance of "Man's" response into the atemporal future of the devotional community imagined by the poem.

Finally, the fact that Christ's addressee in Litchfield's poem shares
Christ's repetitive refrains emphasizes the devotional purpose of tensions created and only partially resolved by the poem's rhetoric and structure. The
repeated, yet always-incomplete, verbal response of "Man" performs contrition and confession:

> A Cristen soule conceyued with synne
>> Receyued in conscience þis compleynt;
> Fallyng doun flat with doolful dynne,
>> And seide, "lord, mercy, moost souereyne seynt!
> I, moost unkynde wretche of mankynne,
>> Y knouliche y am þi traitour atent;
> Þis wickid lijf þat y lyue ynne,
>> Y may it not from þi knowynge gleynt:
> I want wordis and also witt;
>> Of þin kindenes to carpe oon clause;
> Al þat y haue, þou ȝaue me it
>> Of þi goodnesse, wiþ-outen cause;
> Þouȝ y haue greued þee, & do ȝitt,
>> Þou þi benefetis not wiþdrawis;
> I haue deserued hellë pitt,
>> So haue y lyued aȝens þi lawis.
> . . . .
> Sore me repentiþ my mys-lyuynge,
>> For, merciful lord! y schal amende."
>> (165–80, 195–96)

The reply of "Man" blends contrition and confession in the past and present
tenses ("Y knouliche . . . y lyued aȝens þi lawis," 170–80) with the future
promise of speech ("y schal amende," 196). And because these replies are
repeated within a dialogic structure, the poem's recurring refrains consistently project "Man's" communal response into the future. In this way, the
addressee's present-tense speech responds to the lyric Christ even as it raises
the possibility of future devotional speech that does not belong to this particular addressee, and is not contained within the poem, but will be articulated by the future devotional community of readers. While Christ's addressees

formulate expected-yet-incomplete devotional response in the anagogic mode, then, the completion of that devotional response is left to the future devotional community of readers. The next section will show further how the speech of Christ's addressees models the shared response of the devotional community it imagines for the imitative participation of readers.

Christ's Readers

As we have seen, the lyric Christ's dialogue with different addressees elicits a collective, communal responsiveness. Although that responsiveness functions in markedly different ways, it consistently invites readers' participation. The structure, genre, and form of Christ's speech (as well as that of his addressees) suggests that the devotional work of these lyrics remains incomplete without additional speech, extending the communal response beyond the parameters of the poem—and into the future moment of reading. In this way, the lyric Christ offers imitable models of devotional speech through vernacular reading and prayer. In the Middle English lyric, then, Christ's speech incorporates readers within the devotional community it cultivates, and imagines the performance of readerly devotion it invites. This section shows how the lyric Christ imagines readers first in imitation of Christ and then as interpreters of his speech, then in imitation of his addressees, and finally as self-regulating members of the devotional community.

"Stond wel" creates both conceptual and dialogic templates for collective devotion that extend formally beyond the speech of Christ and his addressee. The first-person, present-tense discourse of both speakers facilitates readerly imitation: readers might imitate Christ's pleas to his mother for mercy, Mary's expressions of compassionate sorrow, or both. At the same time, the curious irresolution of the dialogue between mother and son (Mary's refusal to be comforted) evokes a sense of incompleteness that demands continuation beyond the parameters of the poem's formal structure. In this way, the formal aspects of the poem's generic structure—the dialogue—suggests the need for ongoing devotional work through conversation in which the reader might participate.[35] The final two stanzas provide opportunity for that readerly participation by transforming dialogue into a template for prayer that encompasses the needs and concerns of the entire devotional community.

Stanzas 10 and 11 of "Stond wel" transform from the first-person speech of Christ and Mary into an anonymous third-person voice, first in address,

then in praise, and finally in supplication. This narrative shift constitutes
the most important devotional moment in the poem:

> When he ros, tho fel hire sorewe;
> Hire blisse sprong the thridde morewe:
> > Blythe moder were thou tho!
> Levedy, for that ilke blisse,
> Bysech thi sone, of sunnes lisse;
> > Thou be oure sheld ageyn oure fo.
>
> Blessed be thou, ful of blysse;
> Let us never hevene misse
> > Thourh thi suete sones myht.
> Louerd, for that ilke blod
> That thou sheddest on the rod,
> > Thou bryng us into hevene lyht!
> > > (55–66)

As a prayer for intercession, these final stanzas perform the devotional speech
modeled by Christ earlier in the poem, but remain separate from the rhetorical position of either Christ or Mary.[36] When the anonymous narrative
voice petitions Mary to "be *oure* shield ageyn *oure* fo" (60, my emphasis), it
offers readers an immediately available example of vernacular prayer. The repetition of "oure" invites readers to join the devotional community it elicits.
Additionally, the transformation of dialogue into petition continues the rhetorical work left incomplete by the earlier stanzas, as the poem's dialogic
incompleteness and generic fluidity imbricates readers within its devotional
ambit.[37] By performing the intercession Christ commands earlier in the
poem, the final stanzas confirm Mary's acceptance of her son's death and her
role as intercessor. At the same time, they suggest that each reader enters
into the conversation and completes Christ's persuasive task through the very
act of petitioning Mary in imitation of his lyric speech. The transformation
of dialogue into petition thus transforms readers into participants in the creation of Mary as the blessed intercessor of all.

Furthermore, in the final two stanzas of the poem the formal shift from
first-person dialogue to third-person petition signals the expansive nature
of dialogue that the community of readers will continue. The final two stanzas
provide readers with a template for devotional speech that allows them to

imitate Christ's repeated pleas to his mother and, through that imitation, participate in the dialogue they have just read. In this way, "Stond wel" creates a devotional script for readers and invites them to enter the devotional community it proposes. Tellingly, the transformative final stanzas survive in only half of the manuscript versions of the poem.[38] Both their presence and absence suggest an awareness of the poem's potential devotional utility, the possibility of later additions to the poems, and perhaps even an unease with the participatory power its dialogic construct suggests for vernacular devotion. Yet their survival nonetheless reveals a readerly desire for the conclusion to such dialogue. Ultimately, "Stond wel" unites vernacular readers within a suggested communal response that engages with Christ through the very prayer it offers. The poem is unique in this regard; later lyrics also imagine readerly participation but do not include anonymous, third-person templates for devotional response available for immediate imitation. Instead, later Middle English lyrics require an interpretive mode of participatory devotion.

While in "Stond wel" Christ speaks in dialogue that eventually incorporates readers, "Valley" invites readers to interpret as well as imitate Christ's speech. Through its grammatically and rhetorically plural addressee, "Valley" opens the subjectivity of both witness and beloved to readers who encounter Christ's speech in direct address, intensified by the rapidly shifting rhetoric. In ascertaining which position he or she occupies, each reader entertains the possibility of occupying either or both, and in this way inhabits— even momentarily—the rhetorical position as Christ's beloved. In this way, though the language of nominalization remains elusive, the poem creates a rhetorical intimacy in which the reader eventually receives the full force of Christ's imperative, direct address: by stanza 16 the frame narrative has disappeared, and the "dere soule" that is the object of Christ's speech has merged with the addressee to become any "soule" reading the poem.[39] The reader thus becomes the recipient of Christ's concluding exhortations and commands that recommend specific types of devotional activity.[40] In this way, Christ's rhetorical and subjective plurality draws readers into the poem's devotional work by necessitating interpretive activity.

In "Valley," Christ's multivalent subjectivity further facilitates the reader's participation within the devotional community it invites. Sarah Stanbury has shown, for example, how shifting gender, sexual, and familial speaking positions widen the poem's potential addressees.[41] In combination with the disappearance of the framing narrative voice in "Valley," this multivalent subjectivity requires a hermeneutic response: the quoted speaker never explicitly identifies as Christ except as a "Truelove that fals was nevere," while the narrator describes him as "a semeli man to ben a king."[42] The reader must identify Christ as the speaker for him- or herself, by correctly interpreting clues such as the description of "My sistyr, Mannis Soule, Y loved hir thus" (18) and "In my side Y have made hir neste. / Loke in: how weet a wounde is heere!" (57–58). In "Valley," then, the lyric Christ encourages interpretive reading as a mode of devotional activity. That hermeneutic response, in turn, unites the devotional community.

In contrast to the earlier lyrics, in the fifteenth-century complaints Christ speaks directly to the readers, incorporating them within the poems' communal addressee as he repeatedly demands answers in an increasingly urgent rhetoric. Complaint poems borrow the structural and generic parameters of the dialogue lyric to elicit this shared participatory hermeneutic from readers; and in doing so, they provide vernacular templates for future devotional speech. While as in their predecessors "Stond wel" and "Valley," the Christological complaint poems present Christ in conversation with an interlocutor, in both the "Complaint of Christ" and Litchfield's "Complaint of God" Christ's interlocutor remains corporate and anonymous. Rather than Christ directly addressing a narrative persona within the poem, the subjectivity evoked from the very beginning of complaint lyrics allows Christ to speak to the contemporary community of each reader. As a result, the fifteenth-century complaints most clearly demonstrate how the lyric Christ incorporates the reader within the devotional community. Further, they suggest that as that devotional community became more clearly defined over time, as the lyric Christ appeared in longer, more expansive lyrics, the "anagogic" quality of the devotional community—to borrow James Simpson's word—became not only more visible, but more essentially a part of the experience of reading the lyric Christ in Middle English poetry.

The "Complaint of Christ" more clearly projects the devotional community it imagines into the future by emphasizing the difference between Christ's repeated refrains and the imagined but forestalled responses to those refrains. As we saw in the first section of this chapter, the poem's repeated refrains gradually situate the contemporary reader, rather than the allegorical addressee, in dialogue with Christ.[43] The final stanza then reconfigures Christ's repeated refrain into the addressee's long-expected response in the form of a petition for mercy:

A! lord, aȝens þee wole we not plete,
    For as þou wolt, it is, & was;
We han deserued hellë hete,
    But now we ȝeelde us to þi grace.
We wolen bowe, & þou schalt bete,
    And chastice us, lord, for oure trespace,
And lete merci for us entrete,
    Þat neuere no feendis oure soulis chase.
    A! blissid lady, fair of face,
       help! for wee be fer bihynde;
    Þat wee wiþ weepynge moun crie, alas!
    For that we were to oure freend vnkinde."

                        (121–32)

The verbal repentance of "Mankind" imitates the versification, meter, and rhetoric established by Christ in the previous nine or ten stanzas; perhaps most significantly, "Mankind" concludes the poem by formally participating in the repetition of Christ's repeated refrain. The "Complaint of Christ" thus imagines a far more accessible devotional response than that imagined by either "Stond wel" or "Valley."[44] Rather than inviting readers to imitate the lyric Christ, the "Complaint of Christ" invites them to imitate Christ's addressee. Here, it is through the particular construction of the addressee (rather than Christ) that the poem projects that devotional response into the future, beyond the moment of reading. As Christ comments in his final refrain, "*if þou wolt, þou maist* be kynde" (120, my emphasis): he invites his interlocutors, both inside and outside of the poem, into an ongoing devotional process initated by reading.[45]

Furthermore, the lyric Christ of the complaint poems imagines the future devotional community as self-regulating. Readers must recognize themselves as the "mankind" Christ's complaints address, whose interpretive participation will allow them to inhabit the final script of repentance and elicit divine forgiveness. Yet the lyric's repetition appears, initially, to discourage the very repentance it claims to invite. As we have seen, the poem establishes an expectation of response from the first stanza, yet stanza after stanza continually frustrates that expectation with repeated accretion of Christ's accusatory complaints rather than rhetorical examples of mankind's repentance. In this way, Christ's speech elicits repeated hermeneutic engagement, establishing habits of interpretive activity and devotional practice even as it delays their performance. The poem repeatedly asks readers to imagine themselves as the sinful mankind, inculcating interior habits of repentance and contrition in response to the lyric Christ. As we will see in Litchfield's "Complaint of God," the lyric Christ continues to foster this self-regulating devotional hermeneutic for readers by providing an expanding script of dialogic response.

Litchfield's "Complaint of God" combines the dialogue structure of "Stond wel" with the general, appropriable addressee of "Valley" to extend the devotional response of the "Complaint of Christ" in the contemporary moment of reading into the future moment of speech. Unlike the "Complaint of Christ," Litchfield's "Complaint of God" portrays the replies of "Mankind" to each of Christ's complaints, offering readers multiple templates for devotional response. At the same time, the repeated refrains intensify the sense of urgency established by the "Complaint of Christ" and double the sense of necessary response established by "Stond wel." As in those lyrics, the poem's form and structure allows readers to occupy the first-person position of repentant speaker. Here, however, the reader receives multiple templates for devotion from which to choose. "Mankind's" first reply exemplifies penitential and confessional speech:

> A Cristen soule conceyued with synne
>   Receyued in conscience þis compleynt;
> Fallyng doun flat witt doolful dynne,
>   *And seide,* "lord, mercy, moost souereyne seynt!
> I, most vnkynde wretche of mankynne,
>   *Y knouliche* y am þi traitour atent."
>   (165–70, my emphases)

After repenting verbally, "Mankind" protests that "I *want wordis* and also witt; / Of þin kindenes *to carpe oon clause*" (173–74, my emphasis). This vocabulary describes the failure to profess belief in Christ's goodness and mercy specifically as a verbal failure. "Mankind" goes on to declare that "Sore me repentiþ my mys-lyuyng, / For, merciful lord! y schal amende" (195–96), providing an orthodox model of devotional speech appropriate to any context requiring contrition and repentance. This entire stanza thus presents the speech of "Mankind" as a devotional act: as spoken repentance available to any vernacular reader. Throughout the rest of the poem, each of the replies of "Mankind" offers a new variation on this repentance, providing readers with multiple templates to inhabit in the moment of reading or to imitate beyond the reading moment. And because each of these replies focuses on a sinfulness specific to the context of medieval London, Litchfield's "Complaint of God" reveals a contemporary preference for devotional speech as a useful, practical response to universal concerns of sin and human failings. Readers can regulate their devotional activity by inhabiting the responses appropriate to them, exercising choice in their practice of lyric devotion. And even as the sheer length of the "Complaint of God" encourages a selective use of these templates for devotional speech, the repeated repentance of "Mankind" locates the habit of devotional response in the contemporary community.

Finally, emphasis on the contemporary community in the "Complaint of God" maintains focus on future devotional practice. "Mankind" not only models devotional speech through repeated reply to Christ, but also speaks in a subjunctive tense that encourages readers to practice that devotional speech beyond the moment of reading.[46] The final response of "Mankind" begins, like previous responses, with a direct request for forgiveness: "Graunte mercy, ihesu, crop & roote / Of al frenschip, for þou neuere failis" (741–42). The stanza quickly moves beyond the temporal moment of reading and into the projected future of earthly life; mankind explains that

> als ofte as me yuel aylis
> I wole fallë flat to þi foot
> to helpë me in goostli batailis.
>   (744–46)

The action described in these lines does not take the form of forgiveness or repentance of the dialogic speakers; instead, the action is the promise of "Mankind" to perform future devotional speech when evil ails him. The final lines then blur the attribution of that speech between the first-person speaker ("Mankind") and, once again, a collective, communal responsiveness:

> How my3te *y* of þi merci mys,
>   Siþen to helpe man þou art so hende?
> Now, ihesu, lord, þou weel *us* wisse,
>   And, whilis *we* lyue, such grace *us* sende

Þat *we* may bide wiþ þee in blis,
　And wiþ aungils, world wiþouten eende,
Þat to be chosen, ordeyned ys
　To leeue al synne, & hem amende.
　　　　　　(765–72, my emphases)

Over the course of this final stanza, the poem's *I* becomes *we* and *us,* explicitly expanding the devotional speech modeled by the dialogic speaker to the
community of vernacular readers. When combined with the deictic shift from
individual to corporate, this final shift in temporal frame results in increased
hermeneutic demands. "Mankind" offers a model of verbal devotion, but not
the specific script requested in earlier stanzas. As a result, the reader must
apply this verse dialogue to his or her individual situation, requesting Christ's
grace during devotional reading and practicing interpretation during future
devotional speech and thought beyond the text. In response to the lyric
Christ, then, these final lines institute a self-regulating hermeneutic that
unites readers into a devotional community through shared response to the
Middle English lyric.

Conclusion

My focus on the formal construction and devotional effects of the lyric Christ
resonates with suggestions elsewhere in this book that the most productive
strategy for approaching genre must include not only an assessment of specific formal qualities but also an investigation into their potential effects for
readers. Much critical discussion has been devoted to defining the genre of
lyric poetry, and my intention here has not been to rehearse that history.
Rather, I hope to have shown that paying attention to how Christ's speech
functions within medieval religious poetry demonstrates the ways in which
Middle English lyric both inheres within and departs from larger narratives
of genre. The devotional community created by the formal, structural, and
generic tensions of Christ's speech demarcates the Middle English religious
lyric from the lyrics of later eras, even as it both resonates with and resists a
deeply familiar, transhistorical view of the lyric mode.[47] The lyric Christ reveals a particularly Middle English moment in the history of the lyric: a
collective impulse within a genre long viewed as the height of individual expression; an expansive, varied formal structure that engenders the transfor-

mation of the individual into the collective; and a fundamental tension, manifested both formally and conceptually, that impels devotional practice beyond the moment of lyric reading and into the imagined future. Within the Middle English lyric, then, Christ's speech activates a hermeneutic that functions beyond the formal or narrative limits of any one poem. Instead, it becomes a "lyric tactic" common to the Middle English lyric and a distinct feature of the devotional spirituality of medieval English readers.[48]

Chapter 10

The Religious Lyric in Medieval England
(1150–1400)
Three Disciplines and a Question

MARGOT FASSLER

What is wanted at this point in the study of lyrics is not more antholo-gized groupings but rather a letting-go of the categorical terms by which we have laid canonical claim to them.

—Susanna Fein

Lyrics imported into or composed in medieval England may be strewn through the pages of a staggering variety of sources or may exist in planned anthologies and liturgical books. Many examples were penned in three prin-cipal languages, Middle English, Old or Middle French, and Latin (and not infrequently in two of these languages).[1] They clearly served multiple pur-poses, from preaching to meditation, from religious ritual to scatological musings, from singing, dancing, and the drama to private recitation. And their production occupied a range of persons, the majority of whom remain unidentified. Add to these unsettling situations the losses of much of the material to time and deliberate destruction, and epistemological, method-ological, and pedagogical problems can seem overwhelming. Indeed, these difficulties have too often stymied the study of the lyric in medieval England, as the scholarship with its multiplicity of often unrelated approaches and serious lacunae testifies. Even basic parameters remain unquantified, as

Thomas C. Moser notes: "Another limitation on our understanding, beyond the small number of surviving early Middle English lyrics, is our inadequate sense of the lyric poetry available in England's two dominant literary languages between 1150 and 1350."[2] The varied nature of the page on which many lyrics may exist can strike a chord with postmodern sensibilities, played out on crowded computer screens.[3] The collection of chapters gathered in this book attempts the necessary work of recontextualizing and repositioning the lyric, not through a greater narrowness, but from the multiplicity of disciplinary viewpoints the subject demands.

Our group of authors recognizes that new approaches now challenge former ways of working, and accordingly our studies are informed by the fruits of labors appearing in the last twenty years or so.[4] Here I work from out of the scholarship and sources central to answering the various questions posed by the corpora of religious lyrics from medieval England as organized and studied by scholars from three different disciplines, briefly examining and comparing their taxonomies: liturgical, musicological, and finally literary. By so doing, I have moved from the question "What kind of a thing is a Middle English lyric?" to the overlapping but more general question "What is the religious lyric in medieval England?" Accordingly, the broader purpose of the present chapter is to place overviews of three basic fields of study under one roof, thereby laying a foundation for interdisciplinary exchange.[5] This study concentrates on the transformative centuries immediately after the Norman Conquest; it is in this period that transitions took place in language and culture and that records were made of new repertories of texts and music reflecting this change. From around 1100 to 1400, experiments in language and form were ongoing, and the mixing of languages and styles was great. After this brief tripartite overview, I offer a concluding section that examines one particular piece, the Latin sequence "Letabundus," a lyric found in sources fundamental to each discipline. Even though it appears in several guises, all are dependent on remembrance of the foundational text and its distinctive melody. In addition, just as the melody was retexted in various languages, so too aspects of its formal structure were introduced into a variety of genres. The work is also much studied, by liturgiologists, musicologists, and literary scholars, and so provides a touchstone for several differing approaches.

Underlying the overview presented here is the idea that the religious lyric in England can well be treated as part of large, intertextual, multilingual complexes of material. Middle English lyrics existed alongside and often joined with their counterparts in Middle French and especially in Latin;[6]

they are found too alongside treatises and sermons in other languages. One lyric or group of lyrics may be modeled upon another, perhaps even existing as deliberate contrafacts, that is, as retexted versions of preexisting melodies. A symposium on the art of the contrafact in Basel, "'Contraffare'—Alte Melodien, neue Texte" (November 2017), assembled a group of scholars whose work features the art of retexting, perhaps the most significant compositional process for the sung lyric throughout the Latin Middle Ages and, until recently, little studied. The process of contrafacting is basic not only to the lyric and its development, but also to the medieval motet, whose texts are, after all, commonly lyrical in nature. Ardis Butterfield has studied contrafacture as elemental to creating multilingual relationships within repertories of lyrics in medieval England: "cross-hatched interlinked examples show the persistent mobility of the 'English' medieval lyric. Its textual dynamism works across French and Latin as well as English, and it often makes little sense to try to decide which is the 'original' version."[7] Just as the repertories are entwined in many of the sources and in practice, so too should our approaches be, at least as we try to suggest new ways of thinking about the religious lyric in this period and geographical region. My own assignment for this book is to add the Latin sequence to the mixture and see what happens when we do this to our broader understanding of development within the lyric in England. Of major importance to this effort is the scholarship of both David Hiley and Helen Deeming, whose names appear frequently in the notes to this chapter.

Ingrid Nelson's book *Lyric Tactics* has also been especially useful for my study, laying out as it does the distinction between "tactics" and "strategies" when thinking about the Middle English lyric. Here I extend these ideas to other types as well, especially to the sequence. In the first part of my study, that devoted to the sequence, I move from tactics to strategies as the repertories grew and were standardized for the liturgy in the thirteenth and fourteenth centuries, suggesting that having some strategic liturgical collections of lyrics in the same period that nascent tactical Middle English lyrics are starting to appear can be useful. In the second and third sections, I deal first with sung lyrics not in liturgical collections, especially as recently edited by Helen Deeming (whose work is crucial throughout) and then more briefly, as it is not my expertise, with early numbers of Middle English lyrics without music; in these repertories, "tactics" predominate. Nelson, in reviewing the distinction between the tactical and the strategic in her chapter on Herebert's hymns, for example, says: "Because of the complexity of the fraternal use of lyrics, it may be helpful at this point to recall the distinction between strategies and tactics. Both of these terms refer to modes of relation to institutional forms and standards. A strategic relationship to these forms follows their prescribed usages. By contrast, a tactical relationship to these forms is ad hoc and improvisatory, often involving unauthorized hybridization, recombination, or merging of discrete form or categories."[8] My chapter addresses one major question: Of all the forms and genres that existed in the Latin liturgical repertory, which one was of greatest interest to those who were setting the first lyrics to music "tactically" in the period 1150–1400? This question is subsequently broken into two interrelated parts: What happened to this form when greater numbers of lyrics were written in the vernacular, in the late medieval and early modern periods? And what happened in movements across institutional boundaries to the tactical and strategic understandings and use of this way of creating sung lyrics or lyrics based on earlier forms?

The Sequence in Medieval England

Because the English language was in a state of fluidity across the late eleventh and twelfth centuries, we might expect there to be greater continuity with the past in Latin repertories of religious lyrics than we find in writings in English. What happened to the sung Latin lyrics that were collected and performed in early medieval England, at least inasmuch as records of these survive? It is clear that major transformations were afoot in the twelfth century through the fourteenth century in English sequence repertories, and this in spite of the fact that the late Anglo-Saxon liturgy had been already deeply shaped by influences from the Continent.[9] Several genres of religious Latin lyrics were produced and copied in England through this time, including offices, hymns, tropes, and sequences, and all of them were developing not only because of the tastes of the new and mostly foreign-born leaders of the English church but also because liturgical Latin poetry itself was undergoing dramatic change throughout Europe. For example, whereas many uniquely English offices survived from before the Conquest to be recopied and sung in later English books, there were many new offices composed as well, and in the new style that featured syllable counting, rhyming, accentual poetic strophes. The poetry of the office for Thomas Becket (d. 1170) is often seen as watershed, written as it was in the late twelfth century for a saint who was of Norman descent and who came to surpass even the Anglo-Saxon Dunstan in popularity.[10] The repertory of hymns inherited from pre-Conquest liturgies for the office likewise was witness to change, and there is more work to be done on this lyric genre as well.[11] Repertories of proper tropes for the Mass liturgy in England, the most important of which was that of Winchester, were dropping away and were retained in only the most conservative institutions, as far as can be told from surviving sources.[12] Of all the repertories of liturgical Latin lyrics, however, the sequences were among the most telling for understanding this period of change, for the repertories of them were significant both before and after the Conquest and to a degree that change can be measured and accounted for over several centuries. Because of their form, sequences demand an interdisciplinary approach, and although quite a bit of work has been done on English sequence repertories, there is much more to learn.

As a lyric form, sequences are like none other, for they are shaped very much by their music. Sequences are long chants, sung at Mass before the intoning of the Gospel. They are through-composed, that is, the music changes strophe by strophe, and so they are constructed in double versicles, so that each poetic strophe breaks in half, the music repeating for the second half. Late medieval sequences often have rhyming, accentual trochaic texts, laid out in half strophes, which are paired by the use of common music for each half. The first strophe of the sequence "Stabat iuxta Christi crucem" can serve as an example:[13]

1.1   Stabat iuxta Christi crucem
       Stabat vite videns ducem
       Nitens valle facere:
1.2   Stabat mater, nec iam mater
       Et qui sit eventus ater
       Novo venit funere.

(She stood beside the cross of Christ, she stood seeing the leader of life, struggling to bid farewell: the mother stood, not now a mother, and what might be a terrible ending arrives with new closing ritual.)

The poetic lines of late medieval sequences are shaped by syllable count, with powerful end rhymes marking out the strophes.[14] Typically the ending of the eight-syllable line is a paroxytone, a word whose accent falls on the next-to-last (penultimate) syllable, commonly represented by 8p. The third, or final seven-syllable line of the three-line half strophe ends with a proparoxytone, a word with the accent on the antepenultimate syllable (two from the end); it is commonly labeled 7pp. The whole half strophe is expressed as 8p + 8p + 7pp, a pattern predominating in "Stabat iuxta Christi crucem" as in countless other late medieval sequences. The music for 1.1 and 1.2 is the same, creating a tight musical structure that places the first half of the strophe in an intertextual relationship with the second half and linking them even more powerfully through the rhyming cadence of the final lines of each half strophe. This procedure governs the entire work, giving this, and hundreds of other sequences, the musical form AABBCCDDEE, and so on. Because of their rhythms and regularity, late sequences stood out in vivid contrast to the flowing, elaborate chants juxtaposed with them in the Mass liturgy. The two chants surrounding the sequence in the Latin liturgy were the gradual and the alleluia. Both of these chants are responsorial and feature melodies in which long passages were sung to a single vowel sound (melismatic). Sequences, on the other hand, are basically syllabic.

Sequences were composed for centuries beginning with the ninth, when the poetry was different in style from (although related to) that exemplified in "Stabat iuxta Christi crucem." The well-known collection of works by Notker Babulus of St. Gall forms a benchmark for the early medieval sequence.[15] These earlier works also employed a double-versicle format, but there was more variation in line lengths, and the sharply accentual, rhyming rhythmic trochees that characterize the twelfth-century Parisian/Victorine sequence had not yet come to predominate in the form employed for these texts and melodies in later periods.[16] Many late sequence melodies were extremely popular and were set multiple times, opening up the possibility for great numbers of contrafacted works, as was the case with the vernacular settings of "Stabat iuxta Christi crucem" to be examined below.[17]

The sequence in England has been much studied by David Hiley, whose scholarship is fundamental for the discussion to follow.[18] As reflected in discussion here and in Table 1, there are essentially three stages in development of the liturgical sequence in England, and these unfold against the backdrop of the political upheaval that drove changes in a variety of realms including in the liturgy, in architecture, and of course, in music and music copying.

Stage 1. There are three sources that preserve the sequence repertory from the first stage in pre-Conquest England, two from Winchester and a fragmentary one from Exeter (see Table 1, pp. 277–78). Hiley includes several tables

containing these works in his various studies, one comprising a simple list of
all the pieces found in all three manuscripts together: ninety-six works, fifty
for the temporal and forty-six for the sanctorale.[19] There is a divide in the
character of the texts versus those of the melodies. When it comes to texts,
"there is no doubt that new texts were composed in abundance, about half the
total number, in fact: a striking if not quite Notkerian proportion."[20] That is
to say, there were significant numbers of new Latin lyrics being written in
Anglo-Saxon England to supplement the sequence repertory. The sequence
melodies are quite another story, however, with the great majority having
been imported from the Continent and reset with texts written at Winchester.[21] To reset sequence melodies was a common practice, so this does not
show a lack of interest or creativity; rather it is clear that poets in Winchester
were eager to fashion their own lyrics for their liturgical practices, and the
sequences afforded a "soft spot" in the liturgy for them to work.[22]

Stage 2. The substantial numbers of Latin lyrics penned for English repertories before the Conquest did not jump the gap between Anglo-Saxon liturgical practices and those that came at the hands of the Norman invaders.
Of course, as is well known, and as the sequence repertories that survive from
the eleventh century make clear, the liturgical practices of England had been
heavily influenced by those of the Continent, especially of northern French
territories, long before 1066. Still, the manuscripts show a highly significant
number of native sequence texts in the eleventh century, nearly all of which
disappeared from the later sources: "Little of the Winchester repertory passed
into the post-Conquest repertory of other English churches."[23] The failure of
this substantial body of poetry to survive in liturgical practices relates to the
specific ways in which Anglo-Saxon saints themselves jumped the gap to take
their places at the table of celebration in the twelfth and thirteenth centuries.
In recent decades, scholars have come to believe that there was not a dramatic
loss of Anglo-Saxon saints' cults, but rather continuity through various strategies for reshaping older materials. Although there is still much to learn, it is
clear from the scarce twelfth-century sources that remain that this was a period of transition in the development of the liturgy in general and of sequence
repertories in particular in England.[24] The sequences of northern France were
already of major importance in the Anglo-Saxon repertories preserved from
Winchester and Exeter.[25] This changed in the course of the twelfth century
in the wake of the liturgical reforms of Norman churchmen and the cantors
who implemented them and saw to it that new books were copied. But this
change occurred at a time when liturgical chant in general was undergoing

major transformations throughout Europe through the slowly increasing use of rhymed, accentual verse for newly composed liturgical music, especially as evidenced in the sequences and in new offices, as well as in the *conductus*, a kind of strophic song with moral or religious content. The twelfth century was a time of great diversity and transformation for the liturgy in England and for poetics within liturgical forms.

Stage 3. The twelfth century, from which but a handful of relevant sources survive, was followed by another change, one that would be equally transformative: the early thirteenth-century development of a streamlined and fairly uniform liturgical practice at Salisbury Cathedral, one that would slowly win acceptance throughout much of England. As Richard Pfaff says: "By the third quarter of the thirteenth century there is a clearly understood entity known as *usus Sarum*"; by the time of late fourteenth century, the Sarum use had extended "throughout most of southern England."[26] David Hiley has studied what this transformation meant for sequences in England (although including sources from after 1400), and in his overview he cites the 236 rhymed sequences appearing in the English sources he studied from the later Middle Ages, works that were newly composed after the Conquest and many of which were of continental origin. Of these, 70 percent have only one English witness; 14 percent have two witnesses; and 10 percent have six or more witnesses. "This means that many of the collections have an original and independent flavour, to put it no more strongly."[27] Hiley also speaks of the lack of a tendency—so prominent on the Continent—for the reuse of sequence melodies: "The English seem generally to have preferred to invent new ones for each new text."[28]

There were two main strains of sequences operating in late thirteenth- and fourteeth-century England: those sequentiaries belonging to Benedictine houses, and those that were of the use of secular churches and cathedrals. The sequentiary of the Sarum books evolved into the most conservative and uniform in character of all the books compiled during the fourteenth century, but even it was subject to change in regard to a large influx of Marian sequences. The differences between the repertories can be observed through the study of Hiley's numerous tables, which not only divide the sequentiaries by Benedictine and "other" sources, including those of Sarum, but also suggest geographic and institutional points of origin.[29] A late thirteenth-century sequentiary, the so-called Dublin Troper or troper-proser (Cambridge, Cambridge University Library, MS Additional 710) has been edited in facsimile.[30] Although it is essentially a Sarum book, Hiley points out that this source includes several short sequences, similar in style to those edited by Deeming and described below.[31] The sequentiary from the nuns of Barking can be reconstructed from the early fifteenth-century ordinal and customary (Oxford, University College, MS 169), which provides textual incipits only.[32] In the same period of time that the sequences of the Sarum use were settling into particular number, the nuns of Barking were celebrating a liturgy with more than one hundred works, several of which repeated for different liturgical occasions. This exuberant repertory contains many works not otherwise known or recoverable because of the scant number of surviving sources from Barking and from other Benedictine houses. Clearly, however, the genre was beloved in medieval England and was undergoing various kinds of transformation in the thirteenth through the fifteenth centuries.

A major change taking place in later English sequence repertories, both secular and Benedictine, is an explosion of new works in honor of the Virgin Mary. Large supplements of Marian pieces were added both early (in the thirteenth-century Salisbury noted missal now in the John Rylands Library) and in several fourteenth-century collections. Other features of the sequences as sung in England include frequent dividing of them into small units and singing them in other places in the liturgy, most commonly at the offertory and at vespers (as at Barking).[33] The desire for such works may help account for the kinds of pieces found in Cambridge, Cambridge University Library, MS Additional 710. The form and its several varying collections point to much further study; still, this overview gives a sense of the great popularity of these lyrics in several modes of liturgical practice. So, although there was a hardening of the musical arteries as English sequence repertories were standardized and promulgated through the widespread adaptation of Sarum, new Marian works were coming in to spark interest in the genre.

Sung Lyrics in Nonliturgical Sources: The Double-Versicle Form

To look at the state of the lyric in medieval England in the centuries immediately after the Conquest, it is necessary to turn to sources with music that are not part of liturgical collections, these works providing a foil for the hundreds of lyrics constituting the liturgical sequence repertory the parameters of which are outlined above. Fundamental to the work is one edited collection: Helen Deeming's *Songs in British Sources*, which covers the period

Table 1. Sequences in Surviving English Liturgical Sources

(Those with asterisks are cataloged in the Clavis Sequentiarum [Calvin M. Bower], online at CANTUS)[34]

Siglum	Origin	Type/materials	Century
Stage 1: Pre-Conquest Sources			
Cambridge, Corpus Christi Coll. 473**[35]	Winchester Old Minster	Cantor's book	1020s–30s
Oxford, Bodl. 775**	Winchester Old Minster	Cantor's book	ca. 1050
London, BL, Harley 2961	Exeter	Collectar/hymnary/sequences (Leofric Collectar)[36]	1050–72
Stage 2: Late Eleventh- to Twelfth-Century Sources			
Durham, UL, Cosin V.V.6[37]	Canterbury/Durham	Sequences added to gradual	12th, 1/4
London, BL, Royal 2.B.iv[38]	St. Albans	Troper and gradual (imperfect)	late 12th
Shrewsbury, XXX	Haughmond (Augustinian)	Incipits/noted	12th
London, BL, Cotton Cal.A.xiv**[39]	Worcester	Noted sequentiary	mid-12th
Stage 3: Thirteenth- to Fifteenth-Century Sources			
Benedictine:			
Worcester Cathedral Chapter Library F.160	Worcester	Liturgical compendium Sequence incipits text/music	13th
London, BL, Harley 5289[40]	Durham (monastic)	Missal (texts)	14th
Oxford, Bodl. UC 169	Barking	Ordinal (textual incipits)	early 15th
Cambridge, UL Ll.1.10	Cerne	Sequentiary (texts)	late 14th–early 15th

Siglum	Origin	Type/materials	Century
London, BL, Egerton 3759	Croyland	Gradual	13th
Duke of Northumberland	Sherborne	Missal (texts)	ca. 1399–1407
London, Westminster	Westminster	Lytlington Missal (texts)	14th
Oxford, Bodl., Rawl.lit. b.1	Whitby	Missal (texts)	15th
Cambridge, St. John's, D.27	St. Mary's York	Missal (texts)	ca. 1400

Others (Non-Benedictine):

Siglum	Origin	Type/materials	Century
London, BL, Harley 622	Ronton (Augustinian)	Gradual	14th
Oxford, Bodl. UC 148	Chichester	Sequentiary (noted)	13th
Oxford, Bodl., Lyell 9	Breamore (Augustinian)	Texts	late 13th
London, BL, Harley 3965	Hereford	Gradual	14th
Oxford, Bodl., Lat.lit.b.5**	York	Gradual	14th
Manchester, Ryland Lat. 24[41]	Salisbury	Noted Missal/Sarum	13th
Cambridge, UL, Add.710**	Dublin	Sequentiary/Sarum	13th–14th
London, BL, Add. 37519	Oxford	Missal (texts)/Sarum	14th
London, BL, Add. 11414**	Lincoln	Missal (texts)/Sarum	14th
Oxford, Bodl., Don b.5	Adderbury (Worcester)	Noted/Sarum missal	late 14th
Paris, Arsenal 135[42]	London?	Noted sequentiary/Sarum	13th
Cambridge/Pembroke 226	Gilbertine Ordinal	Incipits only	14th–15th
New Haven, CT, Yale University, Beinecke Ege 1026.1988	Norwich (Altstatt)	Gradual/Sarum	ca. 1500

1150 to 1300; the older anthology *Medieval English Songs* with extensive notes and commentary by E. J. Dobson and F. Ll. Harrison is sometimes consulted as well in the discussion to follow.[43] Musicologists think of lyrics as sung phenomena, that is, as songs. In her edition of songs in British sources, Helen Deeming defines "song" broadly as a short work with a poetic text and copied out of liturgical context (although the piece in question may have a liturgical context in another source).[44] She does not include song texts for which no music survives; nor obviously does she include melodies without words. She excludes all fragmentary pieces that are previously published and, likewise, many previously published works in general, thus leaving out the younger Cambridge songbook and several other pieces as well.[45] Still, the works she has collected and edited are a window onto the imaginations of those who sang lyrics and who wrote them down as they thought of them, sometimes with no apparent rhyme or reason, and other times because something in the texts nearby triggered a correspondence, either for the person who copied the song or for the compiler.

The goal of such an edition is "to bring to light a wealth of new pieces never previously published, and to re-establish the musical content of pieces that have long been known, in an attempt to recreate as much as can be recovered of the song culture of high medieval Britain."[46] All of the sources for these songs, in chronological order, are studied in some detail on Deeming's website, with discussion of musical notation included and copious bibliography.[47] The sources that Deeming has drawn upon and described demonstrate a kind of progression, willy-nilly, through the history of the sung lyric in England (exclusive of liturgical sources) for about 150 years. The most dramatic trend is for there to be more lyrics in general and more in Middle English, in particular, as time goes on, but the forms of the songs demonstrate both experimentation and variability. The most common form of all is that of the sequence, a through-composed double-versicle chant, coming out of the liturgy to be experimented with in Latin works, in English works, and even in a work in French.[48] The *conductus* is frequent as well, especially in the later thirteenth century, but the terminology and the form are in transition, as I will discuss further below. Yet another form appearing in this collection is the lai, notoriously difficult to define.[49] Of great interest are those works with refrains, either of text or of music, and I will mention several in discussion to follow. Deeming's chronological work allows for tracing development in the "tactics" employed by composers and poets who experimented with form over a period of 150 years, the very time during which liturgical composers were incorporating their sequences into new kinds of collections for singing.

Deeming's category "Songs 1150–1200" is poor in numbers of pieces. The great majority of these are Latin sequences, well-known works, and to understand them more completely, it would be essential to locate their melodies and their variants and see how many were *unica*, or if not, from what tradition they might have emerged. These are works that illustrate lyric tactics: nearly all have been copied on stray leaves, often in hit-or-miss fashion, and copied usually by hands extraneous to the core sections of the book, and apparently merely to make use of blank parchment. Yet there is often a loose connection between the content of the piece and the nature of the collection. The song attributed to St. Godric of Finchale, for example, is found with an excerpt from his vita in Cambridge, Cambridge University Library, MS Mm.4.23;[50] and the sequence "Interni festi gaudia," a well-known work for Augustine, is found in a collection that includes a copy of Augustine's *Confessions* (Cambridge, Corpus Christi College, MS 253). A collection of six Marian sequences found in Oxford, Trinity College, MS 34, a book that apparently belonged to the Cistercian abbey of Kingswood, Gloucestershire, contains nothing to connect the six sequences to the treatise in the manuscript (two long treatises, Berengaudus on the Apocalypse and Cassiodorus's *Institutions*); rather, the Marian theme unites the group of sequences themselves. The sequences are not, however, in liturgical order. As Cistercians did not in general sing sequences in their liturgies, this collection may well have originated elsewhere; sequences often circulated in *libelli* shipped from place to place, and were used not only for the liturgy but also for a variety of devotional purposes.[51] Deeming has written about the importance of music "heard" and recreated in the mind, especially for prayer and devotion. Her study of "Dulcis Jesu memoria" should be of great use in future analyses of lyrics with known melodies (whether actually notated or not).[52]

English-language songs in Deeming's second section (1200–1250) are triple in number from her first, but only because the four twelfth-century songs attributed to Godric of Finchale fall into this manuscript grouping; without them, the number of early works would stand at two. Songs with English texts were not yet being copied in significant numbers with their music in this period; instead, Latin lyrics were still what was sung, or at least being copied, in England in the first half of the thirteenth century. Sequences still prevail, but the *conductus* had also become popular, a form frequently offering lugubrious critiques of religion and society, and very different in

character from the celebratory nature of the sequence. The formal characteristics of both the sequence and the *conductus* are fundamental to songs in
the vernacular in this category.

The differing approaches of Deeming and Dobson and Harrison point
to another kind of decision that editors of notated medieval English lyrics
must make. The question is often asked if music can be located through intertextual relationships. That is, if a similar and related text is set to music,
can this same melody, then, be assumed for yet another text? Maidstone,
Kent, Maidstone Museum and Art Gallery, MS MA.13, a collection of sermons and some lyrics, includes one Middle English lyric with music, "Man
mei longe," Deeming no. 41 (p. 60); the work is edited by Dobson and
Harrison as well: no. 6a (p. 122). Although Maidstone MA.13 contains the
only surviving example set to music, "Man mei longe" exists in three other
manuscripts besides Maidstone MA.13: Oxford, Bodleian Library, MS Laud
Misc. 471, and the closely related London, British Library, Cotton MS Caligula A.ix, and Oxford, Jesus College, MS 29. In addition, the text is quoted
in several sermons, and so was clearly known and "in the air" in the late
thirteenth and fourteenth centuries.

The sole copy with music (Maidstone MA.13) has been transcribed both
by Deeming and Dobson and Harrison, and it is clear that the person who
scratched out this copy was not a professional, but rather "an inexperienced or
unaccustomed writer of music."[53] For knowing song culture, then, this is a
fine example: it is attested multiple times, in multiple sets of circumstances,
and music is only one of the dimensions of this miniature sermon in song.[54]
The music is of the form: ABABA'CDEA'B' with the CDE lines forming a
departure, both in tonality and in range, and here too the text is often at its
most dramatic and warning, for the sermon is about the delusions of the
world and the turning of the wheel of fortune (only with indirect allusion). In
both British Library Cotton Caligula A.ix and Oxford Jesus College MS 29,
"Man mei longe" is followed directly by another lyric, closely related in theme,
"On hir is mi lif ilong." Dobson and Harrison note not only this juxtaposition,
but also the fact that both English songs have the same form and the same
number of stanzas, as well as the same theme, and some common phrases of
text. "In fact it proves possible to set the words of 6b ('On hir is mi lif ilong')
to the tune recorded for 6a ('Man mei longe'), as our settings show, with only
the slightest variations, most of which consist of no more than a modification
of the method of underlaying the words."[55] And so, through this method,
another English song with music has entered this rare repertory.[56]

The later songs in Deeming's edition, 1250 to 1300, are substantially greater in number. An explosion of works cast in the double-versicle form of the sequence is perhaps the most significant development taking place in the sung insular lyric in the second half of the thirteenth century; related to it in form are both the lai and the lament.[57] When it comes to sung lyrics in this geographical region in the second half of the thirteenth century, the majority in this category demonstrates that those who copied and sang works in the genre were experimenting with double-versicle form, developing "tactics" for the manipulation of poetry and music, in the midst of a slow transformation in taste and style. One of the most telling examples is perhaps also the most famous, the thirteenth-century sequence "Stabat iuxta Christi crucem" (of probable English origin) with its vernacular contrafacts (a work quoted above). Deeming uses various methods in editing this complex of material, beginning with consultation with the edition of the Latin sequence in *Analecta hymnica*,[58] and then moving the three vernacular settings, each of which presents special difficulties for the edition (Deeming 66a and b, 90, and 110).

The setting of the lyric found in Cambridge, St. John's College, MS E.8 features both the Latin ("Stabat iuxta Christi crucem") and the Middle English ("Stond wel, moder"), the texts copied one below the other to the same music (Deeming 66a and b). But this double-texted song is incomplete, breaking off at the end of strophe 5a (it probably continued on a now-missing page). The setting of the same vernacular version found in London, British Library, Royal MS 12.E.i, fols. 193r–194v, is also incomplete although the text is all there, and so Deeming supplies the music for the rest of the text from the Latin sequence found in the late thirteenth-century or early fourteenth-century English gradual, Paris, Bibliothèque de l'Arsenal, MS 135.[59] The third version, found in Oxford, Bodleian Library, MS Tanner 169* (Deeming 110), is a different English contrafact of "Stabat iuxta Christi crucem," but complete only in its last strophes. Deeming has provided the Latin for the opening from the sequence, but the English of the opening strophes of this piece are lost. A picture of the page containing the song is found in the Digital Image Archive of Medieval Music (DIAMM): https://www.diamm.ac.uk/sources/3888. The copies of the songs (Deeming, 66a and b and 110) are on extraneous flyleaves; Deeming 90, however, is part of a smaller collection of poems copied at the end of one of two books bound together. All copies are late thirteenth or early fourteenth century; Paris, Arsenal 135, which contains the Latin sequence, is usually dated to the second half of the thirteenth century (although dated to the fourteenth century in *Analecta hymnica*).

To make a better guess as to when this Latin sequence first was appearing in England, we turn to the fulsome tables constructed by David Hiley of English sequences, which, as we have seen, divide the sources into those from Benedictine establishments and those from other kinds of monasteries and secular churches.[60] Only one Benedictine liturgical collection contains "Stabat Iuxta Christi crucem": St. Mary's of York, Cambridge, St. John's College, MS D.27 (late fourteenth or early fifteenth century); however, the piece was found in five non-Benedictine collections, including Paris, Arsenal 135. The earliest witness is Manchester, John Rylands Library, MS Latin 24, a gradual dated to the mid-thirteenth century.[61] Such information is helpful in situating the vernacular lyrics based on this Latin sequence: they were set to a melody that was quite new to the liturgy, relatively speaking, and that was favored in nonmonastic (non-Benedictine) circles. The Latin lyric, which was sung in some places to celebrate Mary at Eastertide, depicts Jesus and Mary at a time of intense suffering and confusion. Mary experiences the intense pain she forewent in childbirth, and then the final strophes of the sequence move to the joy of Easter. The poem creates a place for Mary in the transition from death to life celebrated in the season. The two contrafacts for the Latin sequence are very different from each other. The fragmentary Deeming 110, the incipit of which is not known, is a paraphrase of the Latin original. But "Stond wel, moder" is a miniature play at the foot of the cross, relying on the use of dialogue that becomes popular in late sequences on the Continent as well.[62] Several other songs in Category C, Deeming's third category (1250–1300), take up this subject, some of them in the vernacular: Deeming 74, "Jesu Christes milde moder," is a polyphonic sequence with an English text; "The milde Lomb," a strophic song, explores the relationship between John the Evangelist, Mary, and Jesus at the cross. Themes of passion and repentance, crucial to the preaching of members of the Franciscan order (see below), are frequently found in lyrics contained in Deeming's chronologically latest group of works.[63]

Many further adaptations of the double-versicle form of the late medieval sequence are at play in the songs from 1250 to 1300; clearly experimenters in both Latin and the vernacular were seeking ways to adapt this form to their purposes. The lai is a highly flexible form in this repertory, with varying line lengths; the number of times a line repeats varies from piece to piece as well. The lament is also sequence-like in its form, but not in its subject matter.[64] Several lyrics were set in very short double-versicle forms, with the appearance of shortened sequences, some with refrains. These works are among the forerunners to the cantilena, a double-versicle polyphonic genre, most typically with text for the Virgin Mary. These and other short double-versicle works may have been intended as substitutions for the sequence in the liturgy and for other chants as well. In an excellent overview of English music from the period and its formal characteristics, Peter Lefferts describes the many reasons that new works for the Virgin Mary predominate in fourteenth- and fifteenth-century repertories, saying that these works, and their lyrics, must be seen in the context of "the dramatically increased veneration of Mary in England in the thirteenth and fourteenth centuries, a new devotional fervor that has left us interrelated evidence from architecture, liturgy, and music. The musical evidence [is] testimony to the increasing ostentation and frequency with which services for Mary were performed."[65] This Marian fervor found in liturgical celebration was the cause of an explosion in composition of new sequences in the thirteenth and fourteenth centuries, a development that helps contextualize the rise of the sung Middle English lyric in the fifteenth century in the carol literature, at least as far as a Marian emphasis is concerned (see below). John Caldwell has pointed to reasons for studying the cantilena and the carol side by side, although their forms are quite different.[66]

There is no collection like that of Deeming for sung lyrics in England in the fourteenth and fifteenth centuries, doubtless because there is much more to account for in the manuscripts, and the great majority of lyrics that survive with music have Latin texts, with the exception of the carol.[67] The series Polyphonic Music of the Fourteenth Century (PMFC) (Paris and Monaco, Éditions de l'Oiseau-Lyre) has four volumes dedicated to English repertories, music with Latin, French, and English texts, much of it religious in character.[68] Related to the propensity for double-versicle structure is the cantilena, several of which appear in PMFC 14 and 17. So even here, as in Deeming's edition, one finds the double-versicle form of the sequence front and center, indeed several of works in PMFC are sequences proper, set polyphonically.[69]

The great interest demonstrated in study of Helen Deeming's edition of the sung lyric bears out in study of the liturgical sequence as well. In fact, this is the one genre that allows for study of both the tactical and the strategic: sequences dominated in both ways as an exceedingly popular way to import lyrics from other regions, to write new lyrics both for preexisting melodies and for newly made ones. This domination leads to a major question: if the sequence was the favored genre for poets and musicians in thirteenth-century England, then what happened to this form as a source for vernacular lyrics in England of the fourteenth century?

The Literary Perspective Through Around 1400

Thomas Duncan's volume *A Companion to the Middle English Lyric* contains an excellent and representative overview of the sources of the Middle English lyric by Julia Boffey.[70] Boffey divides the materials into categories by the natures of authorship, by institutions, by types of anthologies, by those existing as part of sermon collections and other professional uses, by songbooks, commonplace books, and as sporadic additions. It will be noted, however, that much of the body of lyrics is very late, from the second half of the fifteenth century and even from the early sixteenth century. As a literary scholar with a particular assignment in *A Companion*, what Boffey cares about are lyrics in Middle English. This is not necessarily to be expected, as many literary scholars work across languages, as demonstrated in *What Kind of a Thing Is a Middle English Lyric?* Boffey's focus means that the context of the lyric as she presents it is fairly narrow, although the quantities of the surviving verse, the later one goes, are increasingly substantial, making this a project of the early modern period as much as it is late medieval.[71] This chronological divide is only one of the problems standing in the way of interdisciplinary study of the religious lyric in England. I apologize for using Boffey's essay and *A Companion to the Middle English Lyric* as a kind of straw man to advocate for the broadening out that many colleagues in *What Kind of a Thing?* not only endorse but also put into practice. Boffey's essay is an excellent overview, yet its taxonomy is very useful to ponder and is one that has been in place for generations, though it is now being modified.[72]

There is no detailed discussion of music and the lyric in Boffey's overview, nor in the entire *Companion* except for the few mentions of it in Karl Reichl's excellent essay on the carol (see below). Indeed, in general there have been few studies of the subject in any scholarship that mention both the textual and musical dimensions of the insular lyric in tandem, giving equal or at least substantial weight to both.[73] The anthology *Medieval English Songs*, with extensive notes and commentary by E. J. Dobson and F. Ll. Harrison, is a masterful overview with edited examples for performing. Yet here, too, the work is divided between comments and notes by a literary scholar and commentary and notes by a musicologist, with the edition bringing the knowledge of both together. The perpetual dividing of the spoils makes the work of Ardis Butterfield of highest importance.[74] Her fruitful partnership with Helen Deeming, whose recent edition is the subject of discussion above, also points toward what can be gained from multidisciplinary engagement. The ways that Boffey thinks about the lyric and her methods of categorization are different from the ways in which sung lyrics have been edited and studied by Deeming, who has rather chosen a chronological mode of categorization. Deeming's *Songs in British Sources* covers a relatively narrow chronological span (1150 to 1300), yet even then the organization in this collection is by time period, as that is where the sources are.

In Boffey's particular overview, major emphasis is given to individual authors and the manuscripts that contain their writings. This is an emphasis that those who work on sung manifestations of the lyric in England cannot share, as seen in Deeming's studies by contrast: there is no English troubadour from the twelfth century, no trouvère from the thirteenth, and no English composer from the fourteenth century of known name who can rival Machaut. Another major emphasis is given not only to individual authors and the manuscripts that contain their writings but also to manuscripts that contain lyrics, many of which have no known poets or even are miscellanies of various types.[75] The fruitfulness of such focused study can be seen in a collection of essays on the Auchinleck manuscript edited by Susanna Fein, exemplary for its breadth of coverage and for the new ideas that emerge in its pages.[76] Here the study of the vernacular lyric in later periods has more in common with the methods used for study by Helen Deeming, whose work is concentrated on sources that are not dedicated to lyrics. But the differences in time periods between the two emphases are great and stand in the way of transdisciplinary work.

A third area to discuss when it comes to the fourteenth century is how one evaluates the role of the Franciscans in the development of the Middle English lyric. Several of the people known by name and involved with the production of lyrics in England in the fourteenth century were Franciscans, of that there is no doubt. The English bishop Richard Ledrede of Ossory (d. 1360) reworked texts in the vernacular into Latin versions, his process the opposite of other lyric poets mentioned below. These Latin lyrics were edited three times in the same year (1974), each scholar exhibiting idiosyncratic strengths and weaknesses, and only one knowing about (and able to incorporate) the conclusions and methods of another.[77] Ledrede's Latin lyric collection is a set of probable contrafacts, Latin religious poetry, replacing secular lyrics for the tunes of carols and music for dramatic revelry.[78] The works in the collection reveal a great deal about the formal characteristics of vernacular lyrical verse in the mid-fourteenth century among a group of Franciscan clerics, suggesting that in the first half of the fourteenth century the verse was primarily strophic and syllable counting and featured refrains; that is, not unlike the carol. In addition, Ledrede's work testifies to the great quantity of lyrics and their popularity with these clerics and also, presumably with the populations they served, a repertory that is greatly lost to us, although its underlying formal concerns can be divined from the recastings of these works. The work proves the popularity of the form, in the vernacular or in Latin, of the carol, a short strophic work with a refrain.

Although the subject of Franciscan influence on the development of the English lyric is somewhat fraught, there is no question that a major role was played by the friars in the development of the carol in fourteenth-century England. Kathleen Palti, who has digested much of the work on the carol in recent decades in her excellent thesis, says, "The evidence is not sufficiently extensive to support bold conclusions, but Herebert and Grimestone's books do show that Franciscans found it useful to write these kinds of songs down and to experiment with ways of doing so."[79] As Siegfried Wenzel has pointed out, and many other scholars joined in the fray, one of most important "ways" was to ingraft the lyrical within preacherly modes of discourse, and many of these attempts show up in collections that were either produced by or influenced by Franciscans.

Carols, however, are frequently treated separately in literary studies. This happens, for example, in *A Companion to the Middle English Lyric* with a separate chapter by Karl Reichl on the carol.[80] Reichl summarizes the scholarship on the carol up to around 2005 when his discussion was published. Clearly much always goes into defining it, pointing out that the term is problematic, and that the word "burden" for refrain was essentially an invention of Richard Greene. One of the greatest difficulties is trying to figure out the antecedents of this form, for although we know it was sung, music only commonly exists for it in the fifteenth and early sixteenth centuries, by which time it has become an art song. Reichl rather points, as many other scholars have done, to parallel phenomena, manifestations of a common drive to write religious, paralitugical songs with refrains in the vernacular, especially as inspired by the Franciscans: the *lauda* in Italy and the *villancico* in Spain, thus underscoring fruitful ways to look across to the Continent for further contextualization of the first strata of carols in England.[81] But there are other popular texted musical genres well established in the thirteenth and fourteenth centuries in England that could have formed the basis of new kinds of works, especially the sequence. Why did that not happen?

Franciscans, Sequences, and Carols

An overview of the lyric in medieval Britain from three perspectives suggests that greater interdisciplinary conversation concerning the subject may well prove fruitful for the future. And indeed such approaches are beginning to inspire new ideas about the lyric in medieval England.[82] There are things that can be learned from bringing the three disciplines together, even in an overview such as this one, and especially now that so much careful scholarship has appeared on the sources themselves in recent decades. The liturgical collections of sequences found in the first section above offer a host of strategies for lyrical forms, whereas the sequences discussed in the second section reflect a variety of lyric tactics: can the interplay between the two bring new understanding?

A major question arises immediately from this review of form and formal structure, given that sequences—and double-versicle forms more generally—loom large in the music and the sung lyrics in Britain in the thirteenth and fourteenth centuries. There were many examples of interest in sequences, in the edition of Helen Deeming, in the demonstrable experimentation with the form in liturgical collections, and an influx of new works as well in the fourteenth century, most significantly the cantilena. Why, then, are the lyrics that adapt liturgical forms and are found among the works of Herebert, Grimestone, and Ryman—to give an overview of three Franciscan lyricists—not related in major ways to the sequence either formally or thematically? Clearly, inasmuch as they were interested in other liturgical models, the sequence was not favored.

It is not hard, however, to think why the sequence as a lyric genre of great influence and well-established importance in thirteenth- and fourteenth-century England was not destined to be the liturgical genre of favor for the development of the vernacular lyric, especially at the hands of Franciscan poets and preachers. Although several of the collections of sources containing lyrics in the fourteenth through the early sixteenth century in England are related to the activities of friars, the list of sequence manuscripts found in Table 1 above contains no liturgical manuscripts produced by and/or used by communities of English Franciscans, either male or female. Why would this

be so? It is true that the liturgical books of the friars in England were especially devastated in the reforms of the sixteenth century; given that houses
of friars were often urban, they were especially easy to plunder. According
to the calculations of Nigel Morgan and others, at their suppression in the
1530s, the number of English friaries was vast, and there were six houses of
nuns as well, yet the number of their archives and liturgical books is painfully small: only twenty-four liturgical books are known to have survived to
the present time, and among them only a handful of books preserving the
Mass and Office liturgy (see Table 2).[83]

Table 2. Surviving Franciscan English Liturgical Books

(Adapted from Nigel Morgan, 2017; not including Books of Hours and Calendars)[84]

Siglum	Type/materials	Century
Books with Material for the Mass:		
Brussels, Bibl. des Bollandistes 692	Missal, prepared for a friary in Scotland	ca. 1275–1300
Cambridge, University Lib., Hh.I.3	Bible; missal, abbreviated	ca. 1262–1275
Liverpool, Cathedral Lib. 27	Psalter with hymnal; votive Masses[85]	ca. 1290–1300
London, BL, Harley 2813	Bible with missal texts[86]	ca. 1230–1250
Oxford, Bodl., MS Lat.liturg.f.26	Portable missal[87]	ca. 1260–1275
Oxford, Bodl., MS Tanner 334	Portable missal[88]	ca. 1325–1350
Paris, BN, lat. 1332	Portable missal[89]	ca.1320
Office Books		
Cambridge, University Lib., Dd.5.5	Made in Paris for Marie of Saint-Pol[90]	ca. 1330
Cambridge, University Lib., Add.7622	Most complete breviary to survive	ca. 1280–1300
Vatican, Bibl. Apostol., Ottob. Lat.91	Martyrology	ca. 1450
London, Dr. Williams Library, Anc.6	Psalter with some collects	ca. 1330
London, University Coll., lat.6	Breviary (fragments)/ French missal; bound together later	ca. 1280–1300
Oxford, Bodl., MS liturg.407	Early Psalter bound with a Franciscan hymnal	ca. 1200; 1300–1350

The reason that these sources have not been tabulated by David Hiley is that apparently none of them contain sequences. This lack is not surprising. Franciscans, unlike their mendicant counterparts, the Dominicans, were not initially mandated to sing sequences in their Mass liturgies. In fact, the choice as to whether to have them or not varied, and was somewhat idiosyncratic, depending on region.[91] The liturgical rules implemented by Haymo of Faversham for the use of Franciscans mentions but a handful of sequences, and these sometimes only in versions that were promulgated in particular regions, as witnessed to by the surviving copies.[92] The General Chapter at Metz in 1254 stipulated that if the brothers wished to sing sequences, they might sing them only on certain duplex feasts: "Letabundus," "Verbum bonum," or "Hodierne lux diei" for feasts of the Virgin; "Letabundus" (a contrafact of the Christmas piece) for St. Francis; "Clare sanctorum" or "Cuius laus" for apostles; and for other duplex feasts of saints "Superne matris gaudia," or others that might be suitable.[93] Sequences were not going to be favored by Franciscans as models for vernacular lyrics to use in preaching or meditation, or even as sung contrafacts, because in general they were not a major feature of their liturgical practices in England or anywhere.[94] And this was a major liturgical distinction between Franciscans in England and the Augustinians, Benedictines, Dominicans, and secular churches, where the sequence was a major lyrical genre, highly developed, professionally copied, and clearly beloved by monastics and secular clergy and the cantors who served in their institutions.

When we turn to the lyric and its development in the fourteenth century in Franciscan sources, particularly inasmuch as the nascent carol, too, was involved in the work of the Franciscan friars in England, we encounter a genre that is on the edge between the tactical and the strategic, as were the friars themselves, as Ingrid Nelson notes: "Friars had to navigate between their dual identities as ecstatic or charismatic performers, which linked them to divinity, and as representatives of their institutional orders . . . perhaps more than any other group of lyric readers, writers, and performers, friars had to reconcile the tactics of the lyric genre with their strategic aims for its usage."[95] It seems at least from what survives, that they turned to the Divine Office, especially to hymns and antiphons, in their work.[96] And that they sought ways to use refrains in their preaching and in their religious poetry. The much-studied lyrics of William Herebert are a case in point.[97] He chose his models from not only hymn texts and antiphons but also from two places where the people might sing with a refrain, the Improperia of Good Friday, and the procession of Palm Sunday.

Our overview suggests that the fourteenth century was a time of con-
solidation for the transitional period just before it. The Latin lyrics of the
Sarum sequentiary began to win prominence especially in the south of
England in secular churches; the Benedictines continued to write and incorporate sequences into their liturgies, with the nuns of Barking standing
out as example. At this same time, Franciscans, who may have experimented
with sequences in their early decades, turned to incorporation of lyrics in
the vernacular in their preaching, and worked within their own collections
to translate works from their office liturgy into the vernacular. The popularity of the *conductus* ceased in the later fourteenth century; and the votive
antiphon, so important especially for Marian veneration, became exceedingly
important. It was in the fifteenth century that the carol, the greatest genre
for the production of sung English lyrics, came to the fore. This is a genre
that surely had its impetus from the Franciscans in the fourteenth century.
Franciscans continued to promote carols in monophonic versions that do not
survive and that must have had a lively oral tradition.[98] The expectation for
Franciscans was to preach to the people in open air, and after that, to sing,
and it would seem that at least some Franciscans drew the texts and music
they knew from their office out to the people, with texts they could speak
and sing themselves.[99] Oleg Bychkov says, "Franciscan speculative theology
seems to encourage the arts that use concrete and specific forms that are
both beautiful and relevant precisely in their formal specificity."[100] The vernacular lyrics rising from out of liturgical and festive earlier works fits this
definition quite well, and the hymn collection and office books that survive
from English Franciscan friaries beckon to further study.

The polyphonic carols of the fifteenth century, which survive in six major sources, are art music, designed for the singing of the well trained, and
wrought by musicians who knew their craft, both as composers and as copyists.[101] There is no possibility that this is music to be sung by untutored
people, but surely it was appreciated by them, and in ways that more cultivated music with Latin texts might not, in general, have been. The same
thing happened in Italy with the music of the Franciscan friars, the *lauda*,
which was monophonic and popular at first, but which later in its development became refined and more musically complex.[102] Christmas was the season in which liturgical practices created extra room for the clergy and the
musicians they employed to make merry, and the carol found its place there
in English churches of the fifteenth century, especially, it would seem, as
copied and sung by young choristers.

There are many places to look for ways to read the lyric more deeply as it developed over the centuries from the twelfth to the early sixteenth century in England. The sources for interdisciplinary study are fairly plentiful, once one adds them all up, and the work is ours to do, as we examine both tactics and strategies, from liturgical, musicological, and literary points of view. It would seem that there will be a major shift from the fourteenth to the fifteenth century, and that study of the carol will play a major role in that transformation. But that study awaits another day.

Letabundus: A Case in Point

The Christmas or Epiphany sequence "Letabundus" is one of a few sequences composed in the later eleventh century that was destined for eventual popularity in all regions of Europe, and with a particular melody that, with, certain variations, was apparently always used for this text as well as for its numerous contrafacts.[103] The piece spread throughout Europe in the twelfth century, and so can be found in collections of sequences from many regions and religious affiliations, and was often sung in praise of the Virgin Mary as well. One of the earliest known sources is the troper/proser Cambrai, Bibliothèque Municipale, MS 78 (79), which dates from the late eleventh century. In this collection, "Letabundus" appears as part of an ordered collection, but is an alternate piece for Epiphany, which means that it was seen as a newer work at the time the collection was copied. Other early witnesses are from Monte Cassino or its immediate region (Vatican, Biblioteca Apostolica Vaticana, MS Urb.Lat.602), from around Einsiedeln (Einsiedeln, Stiftsbibliothek, Codex 366), and from Anglo-Norman England (Cambridge, Corpus Christi College, MS 367). The editors of *Analecta hymnica* (vol. 54, no. 3) suggest French origins for the piece.[104]

"Letabundus" appears frequently in studies of the lyric in England and elsewhere, and the text is directly related to the prophets' plays, dramas that became much celebrated in every region of Europe.[105] The plays rose out of a sermon by the fifth-century Quodvultdeus, which was read on Christmas Eve in many medieval liturgies; in this work the prophets of the Old Testament and of pagan antiquity including the Sibyl, are called upon to come forth and speak about the messianic coming, interpreted by Christian exegetes to be examples of the foretelling of Christ. The work is anti-Jewish in its nature, and this aspect of the sermon helps contextualize some related

Christmas texts, including the prophets' plays themselves and also the sequence "Letabundus."[106]

The text and melody of "Letabundus" are quite different from those of
most sequences, early or late, given that the work has a kind of textual refrain,
which is echoed in the music, at least for some of the versicles. The text, as
transcribed and translated here by John Stevens, falls into six double-versicle
strophes and is composed in rhyming, accentual verse.[107] Its popularity, linked
as it was to the readings found in the office liturgy at Christmas and to the
plays of the prophets as well, offers a lyrical view of the theology of Christmas, with every strophe and half strophe providing yet further summaries.
The poem and its music demonstrate the effectiveness of the lyric as a shortcut for teaching within the liturgy, ideas that could be remembered, and
could move readily from inside the church to cloister, home, fields, and for-
ests, playing in the memory and shaping understanding, in this case, both for
good and for the ills of its anti-Judaizing, which infected many of its contrafacts as well. One could make a chart of the way in which this lyric is a distil-
lation, and then the tag-like refrains within its form yet further distillations
of even the shortcut itself to teaching and learning and to remembering. The
summary would look something like this: The sense of messianic prophecy in
the first testament, and Christ as a fulfillment of that prophecy is fundamental. The reams of Christian exegesis on this theme would be the second stage
of interpretation. The sermon by Quodvultdeus as a fifth-century summary of
that exegesis in one treatise provided a useful text. At some point an excerpt
from this sermon text was made for readings in the Night Office, a process that
certainly was ongoing from the Carolingian period forward. As the sermon is
fairly dramatic, and the prophets are called up one by one to speak, the idea
emerged of setting the text dramatically, and this happened in the eleventh
century and spread very quickly.[108] The sequence "Letabundus" is a commentary on the sermon too, and was doubtless created to create a supplement to
this reading and the plays of prophecy within the Mass liturgy; in fact it sometimes became part of the plays themselves.

As one looks down the line of development, the distillations become
shorter and shorter, until the catchy refrains of the sequence become the ulti-
mate summations of this theological complex: "res miranda"; "sol de stella";
"pari forma"; "carne sumpta"; "hec predicta"; "gens misera." In other words, it
is a miracle: the sun comes from a star. Both are incorrupt and both are
human, the divinity of Christ taking on flesh. This event was predicted in our
scriptures and by the Jews themselves, who now are a miserable people because

they refuse to believe in the miracle. Any of these catchy tags could conjure up the whole sequence, and the whole sequence could evoke the multiple meanings of the entire Christmas season and the Virgin Mary's place in the season. How very useful for teaching and polemical preaching such a lyric might have been, with all the power of its music and its rhythmic rhymes. It is no wonder that this was one of the few works recommended for inclusion in the Dominican Mass liturgy, almost always falling at the head of the repertory. As mentioned above, it was one of the few sequences that was regularly sung by Franciscans, and was contrafacted by them as well (see Figure 26).[109]

1.1 Letabundus / exsultet fidelis chorus, / alleluia;
1.2 regem regum / intacte profudit thorus, / res miranda.
(Let the faithful choir exult in gladness—Alleluia;
the womb of a virgin has brought forth the king of kings—a
   marvellous event.)

2.1 Angelus consilii / natus est de virgine, / sol de stella,
2.2 sol occasum nesciens, / stella semper rutilans, / semper clara.
(The angel of counsel is born of a virgin—the sun from a star;
a sun which knows no setting, a star that glows for ever, always
   bright.)

3.1 Sicut sidus radium, / profert virgo filium / pari forma;
3.2 neque sidus radio, / neque mater filio / fit corrupta.
(As the star produces its ray so the virgin her son, alike in nature;
neither is the star corrupted by its ray nor the mother by her son.)

4.1 Cedrus alta Lybani / conformatur ysopo / valle nostra;
4.2 verbum, ens altissimi, / corporari passum est / carne sumpta.
(The high cedar of Lebanon conforms itself to the hyssop in the
   valley of this world;
the Word, the being of the Most High, has suffered itself to be
   embodied in the flesh it has taken.)

5.1 Ysayas cecinit, / synagoga meminit, / numquam tamen desinit
   / esse ceca;
5.2 si non suis vatibus, / credat vel gentilibus / sibillinis versibus /
   hec predicta.

Figure 26. University of Notre Dame, Hesburgh Library, cod. Lat. c.2, fol. 134v.

(Isaiah sang, the synagogue remembers but never ceases to be blind;
if the Jews will not believe their own prophets, let them at least
      believe the Gentiles', the predictions of these things in the
      Sibylline oracles.)

6.1 Infelix propera, /crede vel vetera; / cur damnaberis, / gens
      misera?
6.2 Quem docet litera, / natum considera; / ispum genuit / puerpera.
(Unhappy people, make haste, believe the ancient [writings];
      miserable nation, why should you be damned?
Consider this child of whom scripture teaches us; a maiden gave
      him birth.)

The complexities of the way the piece circulated and its seemingly endless
numbers of contrafacts cannot concern us here; nor can the many parodies,
sacred and secular, and some of them painfully humorous. The most over-
the-top of these jokes is the scene in the Christmas play of the *Carmina
Burana*, wherein the characters Archysinagogus and Augustine debate, using
one of the refrain lines from the sequence. Augustine, who begins to sing
the sequence, arrives at the words "res miranda." Archysinagogus and his
cohort burst in with a parody line, "res neganda." And the stage directions
say they do this many times, making a mock debate. After this, Augustine
continues to sing the sequence through to the end.[110] One of the most cap-
tivating of the parodies was copied in London, British Library, Codex 16.E.viii
in the old Royal collection, folio 103r, a source now presumed lost.[111] The
text is offered here in the original language with an English translation, and
the entire work could be performed today with minor alterations, so nearly
does it fit the original and widely circulating melody.[112]

Parody upon *Letabundus*.

1   Or i parra: Listen hereto:
       la cerveise nos chantera   now the beer will sing for us
         Alleluia.   Hallelujah.

     Qui que en beit,   If the tasting
       se tele seit com estre deit,   prove it as it ought to be,
         Res miranda.   Res miranda.

2   Bevez quant l'avez en poing: Drink while still you've cup in hand,
     bien est droit, car mout est loing,   it is well, for long's the way
          Sol de stella.   Sol de stella.

     Bevez bien e bevez bel: Drink then deep, and drink on long,
     el vos vendra del tonel   while the stream flows from the keg,
          Semper clara.   Semper clara.

3   Bevez bel e bevez bien,   Drink then deep, and drink on long,
     vos le vostre e jo le mien,   drain your beaker, I'll drain mine,
          Pari forma.   Pari forma.

     De ço seit bien porveü: Be assured that this is true:
     qui auques la tient al fu,   what remains within the keg
          Fit corrupta.   Fit corrupta.

4   Se riches genz font lor bruit,   Gentle folks have merry routs,
     faisons nos nostre deduit   we will also have our bout,
          Valle nostra.   Valle nostra.

     Beneit seit le bon veisin   Blessed be the neighbor good
     qui nos done pain e vin,   kindly spending wine and food,
          Carne sumpta.   Carne sumpta.

5   E la dame de l'ostal,   And the hostess of the Inn
     qui nos fait chiere real,   spreading us the cheer around,
     ja ne puisse elle par mal   may misfortune ne'er await
          Esse ceca.   Esse ceca.

     Mout nos done volentiers   Willingly she metes us out
     bons beivres e bons mangiers: good to drink and good to eat:
     mieuz vaut que autres moilliers   worthiest of all her kin
          Hec predicta.   Hec predicta.

6   Or bevons al derain   Finally we now will drain
     par meitiez e par plein,   cups in halves and cups in wholes,
     que ne seions demain   that the morning finds us not
          Gens misera.   Gens misera.

Nostre tone ne vuit,	Empty must our keg not be,
Car pleine est de bon fruit,	fill'd it is with goodly fruit,
e si ert tote nuit	and it will be all the night
Puerpera.	Puerpera.

"Letabundus" is a useful test case for the ways a lyric that originated on the Continent made a home for itself in England. What happened to this famous piece over time, as we examine the three areas broached in this chapter? How does it show up (1) in liturgical collections, (2) in various song collections, and (3) as a model for Middle English lyrics, sung and not sung? I begin with the coming of this late eleventh-century work into English liturgical collections, both in its original form and as a contrafact. An early witness to its presence is in the early twelfth-century troper-proser, a section of London, British Library, Cotton MS Caligula A.xiv (fols. 50v–51r). In this manuscript (which lacks rubrics for the festal occasions in the sequentiary, although room was left for rubrics), "Letabundus" falls between two sequences for Epiphany, "[Epiphaniam domino] Canamus gloriosam," and the sequence "Gaudete vos fideles," a late eleventh-century work usually sung for the Octave of the Epiphany. In several French and English sources, "Letabundus" often is paired with "Gaudete vos fideles," as is the case here in Cotton MS Caligula A.xiv.[113] The chant was in England by the middle of the twelfth century, that much is clear. And if we examine its life in other English sources, we find that it was copied in both Benedictine manuscripts and in sources for the Sarum rite. At Barking, for example, "Letabundus" was sung for Mary after Christmas; in other Benedictine and Sarum graduals, "Letabundus" was sung for one of the three Masses of Christmas. In the sources tabulated by David Hiley, the chant is found in six Benedictine sources at Christmas, and the troper-proser from Dublin (Cambridge, Cambridge University Library, MS Additional 710), and sources from Hereford (London, British Library, Harley MS 3965), York (Oxford, Bodleian Library, MS Lat.liturg.b.5), and the ordinal representing the Gilbertine order (Cambridge, Pembroke College, MS 226). But turning to its use as a Marian piece, there the representation is far greater, with the vast majority of Sarum sources wishing it to be sung for the Virgin. During the fourteenth century it had become part of the great influx of Marian works into English liturgies (referenced above).

It is not a surprise, given the great popularity of this sequence in medieval England, to find contrafacts of it in liturgical sources as well. One of the works most closely tied to its parent is a contrafact crafted for the Feast of the Dedication.[114] The sequence was also used as a model for many saints throughout Europe, although the great majority of these texts did not make their way to England. Some were apparently written in England, however: "Letabundus sit iocundus" is dedicated to Thomas Becket and is found in liturgical order in the later thirteenth-century Sarum gradual Manchester, John Rylands Library, MS Latin 24 (fols. 235v–236r). The Dublin Troper (troper-proser) contains a contrafact of "Letabundus" for St. Patrick, and the sequence "Letabunda" was sung both at Barking and at Durham (London, British Library, Harley MS 5289, from the fourteenth century), apparently an adaptation for St. Agnes; both these sources contain incipits only. "Letabundus Francisco" is one of the most popular contrafacts for the chant on the Continent, but the fifteenth-century Sarum gradual now at Yale's Beinecke Library is the only instance known to me of its presence in late medieval England. This provides another example of a lagging Franciscan influence in English sequentiaries.

The manuscript examples edited by Helen Deeming (and discussed at some length above) contain two witnesses to "Letabundus," in different guises and from different time periods. The earlier copy dates from the late twelfth century and is found as part of a group of six Marian sequences all written in the late eleventh and twelfth centuries on the Continent; the collection is part of Oxford, Trinity College, MS 34, which belonged to the Cistercian abbey of Kingswood, Gloucestershire.[115] This *libellus* is the kind of supplement containing sequences that cantors were preparing all over Europe, and this is by a practiced music scribe, probably a cantor who wanted such a collection for possible liturgical use. The relationship of the hands writing the chant texts to those who copied the major parts of the codex, Berengaudus's commentary on the Apocalypse and the *Institutions* of Cassiodorus, is nowhere discussed, and the manuscript is not available online. But if it was copied by a Cistercian, this would not be completely surprising, as many stray copies of sequences can be found in Cistercian libraries, in spite of the fact that the monks in general did not sing sequences in their liturgies, although there is evidence that some Cistercian nuns may have done so.[116] The *libellus* proves the interest in late twelfth-century England in acquiring sequences, especially Marian sequences.

As demonstrated in discussion above, there were contrafacts being composed for the sequence "Letabundus" in late medieval England.[117] An

example of this creative process is found in Deeming's edition in the form of
a sequence for Mary Magdalene: "Magdalene laudes plene," found in London,
British Library, Arundel MS 248. This late thirteenth-century miscellany
includes a vast array of genres including sermons, proverbs, exempla, verses,
treatises, Albertano of Brescia's *Ars loquendi et tacendi*, Hugh of St. Cher's
Speculum missae, and a small group of songs in Latin, French, and English,
copied into a single fascicle.[118] The poet/composer of this sequence has taken
liberties with the form of the original, dividing each half strophe into four
lines, rather than three, and not making use of any of the well-known Latin
texts of the original refrains.[119] Yet the music works to perpetuate the connection to the parent work, the beginning and ends of each line reflecting the
original more directly. "Magdalene laudes plene" is transformed yet further
in the ways that Magdelene is depicted, praised for her historic witnesses to
Christ. In this work she is Mary of Bethany with whom Jesus wept, and at
the close, she is blessed for her presence with Christ in the garden after the
Resurrection. Concentration on the sensual and direct encounter with Christ,
so important to many late sequence poets as well as to preachers, is central
to this late thirteenth-century work.

    Beloved as it was in late medieval England, "Letabundus" was only rarely
used as model for the works of the three major Franciscan poets, William
Herebert, John of Grimestone, and James Ryman, as indeed were sequences
more generally for reasons explored above. Herebert did not use it, nor was he
particularly interested in sequences; none are cited as models by name in his
works. It is clear, though, that he knew the form: one of his poems could well
be modeled after a sequence: "Þou wommon boute uére."[120] His "Vous pu-
rueez en cete vye" is a translation into Middle English of several stanzas of an
Anglo-French verse sermon by the Franciscan Nicholas Bozon; the work is
in sequence form, with the rhyme scheme *aabaab*, although the *b* lines rhyme in
every stanza and there is also a textual refrain. Both these works come close
in their formal structure to many of the texts set in Deeming edition; however,
they are rare for Herebert, who prefers to use hymns and other office music
for his models, with the occasional processional verse with refrain.[121]

    The most relevant work among these three Franciscan poets is a poem
by James Ryman, the contrafact "Now gladly shall the clergy singe," a work
clearly based on the Franciscan sequence in honor of Francis, itself a contrafact of "Letabundus." This work "Letabundus Francisco," was found, as mentioned above, in the fifteenth century in a liturgical collection, probably
from Norwich (Altstatt). Ryman's text is very closely modeled on the Fran-

ciscan sequence, which itself uses the refrain tags of the original work; without too much stretching, the piece could be sung.

1   Now gladly shall the clergy singe
    To seint Fraunceys, this heuenly thinge,
            Alleluia;

2   Whome Criste hath fixte, that louer true,
    Hert, hande and foote transfourmed new,
            Res miranda.

3   His myende in his flesshe did appere,
    And in new wyse he shone full clere,
            Sol de stella.

4   This man, the whiche this wyse did floure,
    Taught birdes with voice god to honoure
            Semper clara.

5   And, as Crist hath taught, pouerte
    In wille, dede and thought kepe did he
            Pari forma.

6   He wolde, nouther in wille nor dede,
    That his doughter dere shulde possede
            Hec corrupta.

7   Now he ioieth aboue in blisse,
    With tokenes newe shynyng he is
            Valle nostra.

8   Ien with light by hym renewed,
    A chielde with tunge he hath endewed
            Carne sumpta.

9   Sume having speche, sume lyfe agayn,
    Heresy by hym is knowen full playne
            Esse ceca.

10 Dume, blynde and lame taking comforte
    Diuers kingdomes knowing reporte
        Hec predicta.

11 The sawdons fraude he did despise,
    And yet hym hurt hath in no wise
        Gens misera.

12 His woundes sheweth gyftes newe
    Geven of Criste borne of Marie true,
        Puerpera.[122]

It seems appropriate to end this brief case study with a search through the repertory of sung carols in search of "Letabundus." There are two of them, one of which John Stevens edited in two versions: "Alleluia: Now well may we mirthes make."[123] The other, "There is no rose of swych virtu," has become a staple of the early music performance repertory.[124] These are the most free of all adaptations of the original, and in fact only the use of the textual refrain tags identifies the relationship. The association of the sequence with both the Virgin Mary and with the Christmas and Epiphany seasons is borne out, as both works have this as their major complex of themes. In "Alleluia: Now well may we mirthes make," the poet chose refrain texts from strophe 1.1 and 1.2, 2.1 and 2.2, and 3.1 of the original, suiting the rest of his text to make smooth connections. The refrain of 1.1, "Alleluia," becomes a burden, in two-voice and three-voice versions. "There is no rose," on the other hand, includes only the refrains of 1.1, 1.2, and 3.1; the last two strophes close with "gaudeamus" and "transeamus" respectively.

"Letabundus" provides many kinds of materials for a variety of lyrics in medieval England and holds them in a network of relationships that is rich and deep as well as liturgical, musical, and poetic. It is one of a kind, such a dense thicket of works did it produce. But it is far from the only musical/poetic matrix that functioned in this period and region. As this and other chapters in this book demonstrate, the lyric in medieval England provokes not only the study of music, literature, and liturgy; it is also a subject, both in form and substance, that unfolded in the middle of a culture, and that provides a vital way in to this culture, as it changed, and dramatically so, over several centuries.

Chapter 11

Theory of the Fourteenth-Century English Lyric

ANDREW GALLOWAY

What theory suits the fourteenth-century English lyric? In some ways the prospect of answering this question seems closer than ever, since scholars of medieval literature have been reopening the topic of "the lyric" at what seems an auspicious moment in literary criticism generally, when philosophical and figural approaches to poetry often intersect with emphases on more contextual and historically contingent elements. "Theory of the lyric" has unfolded in the wider arena of poetics as a point of that debate, a focus of conferences and critical anthologies. A major exposition by Jonathan Culler elucidates a capacious notion of "lyric," grounded in recurrent elements of poetics across two millennia rather than framed by other historical categories or developments; Culler's study constitutes a much larger and more intricate successor to Northrop Frye's treatment situating "lyric" at the center of the literary, the genre that "most clearly shows the hypothetical core of literature, narrative and meaning in their literal aspects as word-order and word-pattern."[1] Other critics, often scholars of nineteenth-century or later poetry in which Culler's own main expertise lies, have emphasized features of "lyric" in narrower formal terms and wider contexts, dissolving generic unity by pursuing the "social affinities and antagonisms in literary form by comparative description" (to quote a call for papers for a 2014 conference on "Poetic Genre and Social Imagination: Pope to Swinburne").[2]

Amid these debates, scholars of medieval English literature hold a peculiar position. In certain respects the formal, modal, and even "literary" qualifications of their materials raise more questions about the transcendent category of "lyric" than the poetry of Emily Dickinson or poetic theories of Sidney Lanier, both of whom have served as focuses for the issues. At the same time, medieval English literary scholarship regularly collects, names, and discusses short, nonnarrative poetry that, although inevitably peripheral to wider studies of "lyric," can be, and sometimes was, flagged as verse of a distinctive kind: some version of written (or "natural") "song" or *canticus* or "ballad" or "complaint," often reflecting (always to a less specified degree) the labeling and regimen of "fixed form" poetry in French and Italian. The fourteenth-century English versions of such distinctive verse present features that scholars addressing later periods might consider essential for "lyric," if only in partial or unfamiliar ways, including not only "extravagant" displays of figural language—one of Culler's criteria for the genre—but also, at times, narrative framings of reflection or lament, anticipating what Roland Greene calls the merging of "fictional" and "ritual" elements in the Petrarchan sonnet sequence and its followers; a few instances foreshadow what Colin Burrow sees emerging only in the seventeenth century as "Horatian" epistolary postures.[3] Though medieval English lyric is often said to present only a collective or universally adoptable voice, at times it seems up to the critic (and editor) to decide if the poems' enigmatic speakers or addressees are generic and universal, or locally known but historically effaced individuals, *early* early modern individualized subjectivities, anticipating the "effect of singularity" that Ullrich Langer finds possible only after Petrarch.[4] Since the anonymous miscellanies in which we find "poems without contexts" often compel us to decide voice and genre, medieval scholars are often more aware than usual of their own framing and acts of interpretation, their own guesses of where uncertainties about poetic features are our problem or invited (or tolerated) by the writers or scribes.[5] Just how different from surrounding Latin homilies are the English verses that interlard Latin sermons can be a matter both of judgment and degree: some instances are said to be *nearly* "genuine lyric," while other Middle English phrases, including some long considered "lyric," turn out to be prose translations of neighboring Latin.[6] Can this situation—both the historical span and the range of critical judgments—present an even more fundamental challenge to claims for the genre's transhistorical existence, or does it oblige medievalists to adopt principles beyond their typically recalcitrant historicizing? Is it theoretically coherent to imagine a perspective allowing both historical and transhistorical methods and principles?

Some of the most evocative responses by medievalists to the questions surrounding "lyric" as a genre focus less on local effects of "extravagant figurality," still less on line breaks, punctuation, or titles (elements refined and settled only in printed texts), than on the wide networks of imagery and figurality that are necessary for appreciating—and indeed creating—any given instance. Thus Ardis Butterfield, while noting the "great body of verse that was self-consciously defined, highly artful, and anthologized in often beautifully produced *chansonniers*" in Occitan and northern French from the twelfth century on, emphasizes that the partial snatches and often inconsistently shaped forms of short medieval English verse thoroughly defeat twentieth-century New Critical and Structuralist assumptions based on printed, fixed, isolated, and more or less poetically self-sufficient "lyric." The suggestiveness of Butterfield's view for medieval and all lyric studies justifies extended quotation:

> Reading each [short English poem] involves tracing a long (and perhaps always incomplete) textual journey. The journey reveals how the kinds of patterning we now associate with verse—rhyme, a discernible meter, various kinds of repetition—fluctuate along the way, sometimes with a more discrete shape and at others with any kind of shape obscured by continuous lineation, a seemingly careless copying of syllables and sometimes awkward juxtapositions with other languages and other verses. What we have here is something like a poetic core that is realized in different genres, different books, different places and different memories.[7]

This suggests that crafted performances available for close reading and re-reading can be seen as just one kind of performance among many less secure or fixed kinds, all of whose effects are best appreciated by following potential as well as activated "poetic cores" into a wide range of verbal and musical expressions, a web or archive actively constituting any given poem's effects, rather than the inert materials for a sonnet's "pretty rooms" (as Donne puts it).[8] It is not new to assert that medieval lyrics' figural language should be pursued in such wide scope. In 1985, Patrick Diehl emphasized that "European religious lyric" conveyed the "air of fragments washed down from higher and older regions," its images and ideas "pointing out from the text to some external point at which they will meet and marry into meaning, if the reader has the qualifications for ascending to that focus."[9] Diehl found this deferral to "some external point" not a principle of phenomenological flux but an explanation of why "the medieval religious lyric" remained unchanging, along with religious belief itself: "the religious lyric resisted any complication of the old simplicities, for if anything is more conservative than religion, it is lyric poetry." Butterfield's more open-ended view is of constantly dynamic and local reshapings of "poetic cores," centers of figural or metrical or thematic elements that underlie the fragments and languages, glimpsed and indeed existing always in a vestigial state of half-realization.[10]

Yet Diehl is surely right that medieval figurality pervaded religious as well as poetic spheres, to which might be added political, social, institutional, and economic ones, extending beyond the realm of poetics on which Butterfield quite reasonably focuses. The relation between verse and its media, contexts, and official uses is an essential element of the period's poetics, as Ingrid Nelson demonstrates in her cases of "lyric tactics."[11] This is particularly true in the fourteenth century, when rapidly expanding uses of written English, growing numbers of secular readers and writers, and increasingly complex narrative settings for short nonnarrative verse not only encouraged fuller preservation of anonymous, occasional, and oral or musical poetry but also established new possibilities for putting figurality to work. Increasing generic self-consciousness is certainly one result of these transformations, but it does not always confer a stabilizing influence; as late as Chaucer's wittily non-advising advice poem on marriage, "Lenvoy de Chaucer a Bukton," probably from the 1390s since Chaucer ultimately directs his addressee simply to "rede" "the Wyf of Bathe" (29), the poet offers his work only as "this lytel writ, proverbes, or figure" (25). This makes the poem less an occasion for (re)discovery of Horatian epistolary lyric than a declaration of how many uses the word "figure," which starkly summarizes the other options, might serve.

As Chaucer's restless options acknowledge, fourteenth-century England was a mass of proverbial and paralyrical samples and reminders. If we identify in those some of the constituents of "lyric," we should grant that lyric is frequently embedded, if not dissolved, in socially or religiously signifying poetic apparatuses that were far more varied and abundant than at any point earlier, on brasses, rings, front doors, roofs, windows, jugs, even across the front of a castle: all supporting the point that metaphors, for example, signify differently "not just in various contexts but also in diverse modes of thought," as Cristina Maria Cervone remarks in her study of fourteenth- and fifteenth-century metaphors of the Incarnation.[12] In some respects the abundant but vestigial figurality of the fourteenth century offered more widespread possibilities of lyric in the terms on which Culler dwells than the centuries either before or after, although direct embrace of that principle as the goal of poetry was extremely rare. Increasingly captured in writing, fourteenth-century English verse presents more fragmentary, allusive, and nonnarrative modalities than the following century, in spite of the fifteenth century's increasing enshrinement of secular lyric as a rubricated and anthologized entity, not to mention the fifteenth century's generally more thorough exploitation of written poetry, putting into English verse "any kind of information, were it on husbandry, on table manners, on cookery, on alchemy."[13]

Amid these contexts and critical debates, it seems more pertinent than ever to investigate a range of figural and discursive apparatuses involved in making fourteenth-century "lyric," both to assess the emergence of English poetry claiming some connection to a pantheon of "poesie" (a generic noun first appearing in English then), constructed along with its own implied histories, its own isolated and concentrated scope of figural efficacy, and the properties of short "lyric" verse that performed, with equal originality, new variations in the political, religious, and other structures of feeling and meaning.[14] To this end I offer three case studies, including one double-case study, to explore figural poetry's roles in some of the major institutional and ideological domains of late-medieval England—national history and religious ritual—and the emerging domain of English "poesie." In each, the broader contexts contribute elements essential to, indeed part of, the basic figural action and meanings of the poems I consider. Yet all these domains, including "poesie," are also fields of significant social and religious importance. My term "poetic apparatus" thus indicates a debt to Louis Althusser's "ideological state apparatus," which Althusser used so forcefully to define the role of ideology in establishing a culture's ability to reproduce its own mode of production, through a full gamut of modern institutions (especially education, which in his view had replaced the role of the medieval church in creating proper subjects of the modern bourgeois state), but also guides my pursuit of what might be considered the "lyric machinery" that the medieval domains supported, albeit with the paradoxes, innovations, and even self-contradictory features that their uses of figurality often entail.[15]

My heuristic use of case studies, however, is intended to emphasize that my term—in this, quite unlike Althusser's—claims no aspirations to comprehensiveness, nor to establishing any laws of historical or generic development; it is itself merely a tool for advancing literary and cultural inquiry in some of their overt as well as less visible connections. In that sense, my phrase might better recall Martin Heidegger's notion of "gear" or "equipment" (*das Zeug*), whose discrete existence (as Thing) vanishes in the making of whatever work it serves to produce. "The less we just stare at the hammer-Thing," Heidegger observes, "and the more we seize hold of it and use it, the more primordial does our relationship to it become, and the more unveiledly is it encountered as that which it is—as equipment. . . . If we look at Things just 'theoretically,' we can get along without understanding readiness-to-hand. But when we deal with them by using them and manipulating them, this activity is not a blind one; it has its own kind of sight, by which our manipulation is guided and from which it acquires its specific Thingly character."[16] The "lyric-Thing" occupies either visible or invisible status, just as the discursive and institutional apparatus that participates in its creation can be pondered directly or recede into more "primordial" instrumentality, shifting attention to other works and ends.

Deployed across all the domains I sample, Culler's (and others') lyric theory certainly allows us to chart the emergence of more explicitly "poetic" configurations. But I seek to show that that theory may also allow us to see all these configurations as sustaining and opening social and religious possibilities. Yet all these in turn can lead us back, if we shift our focus on the continuum of ends and instrumentality, to the powers of scandalously nontranscendental and material mere language, in "figure."

Rombylogh Rhythms

Amid its accounts of nearly contemporary history, the prose chronicle of England, the *Brut*, composed in Anglo-Norman in the early fourteenth century but soon translated and continued in English (and Latin), includes a series of satirical battle poems, always in English, by both the Scots and the English. As exchanges scattered through the loosely connected narrative of the Anglo-Scottish wars that present commentaries on the battles as well as the supposed historical bases for further conflict, these also constitute in some ways the most popular sequence of secular English lyric before Petrarchism.[17] For with at least 250 surviving copies owned by everyone from gentry to kings, the *Brut*'s lyrics are arguably the most widespread short secular medieval poetry in English. Yet few critics have lingered over them. The account of the battle of Bannockburn of 1314, for example, with its deceptively simple, supposedly Scottish taunting poem, might logically be noted in either Angus

MacDonald's survey of "Lyrics in Middle Scots" or Thorlac Turville-Petre's of "Political Lyrics," both in Thomas Duncan's capacious and highly useful *A Companion to the Middle English Lyric*, though it happens not to be.[18] Julia Marvin's otherwise rhetorically attentive discussion of the *Brut* in its original Anglo-Norman form finds occasion only briefly to mention "passages of English verse." Even treating "Middle English Verse in Chronicles," Julia Boffey and A. S. G. Edwards mention only distantly the *Brut*'s battle poems, although those appear in their English forms even in the Anglo-Norman original.[19]

At least for circumstantial reasons, it is not surprising to find this poem overlooked. In the earliest manuscripts, in which the prose chronicle is in Anglo-Norman, the verse, which was always in Middle English, is often run into the prose, in some cases distinguished neither by size nor rubrication; copies of the Middle English translation of the prose appearing in the late fourteenth century usually lineate the verses and present their refrain beside them linked by lines. From the first insertion of the poem, the poem was intricately part of the *Brut*'s complex historical project, whose popularity certainly contributed to the short poem's appearances in later contexts. Here is the account, using the English translation of the prose:

> Allas þe sorw and losse þat þere was done! for þere was slayn, þe noble Erl Gilbert of Clare, Sire Robert of Clifford, a baroun, and meny oþere; & of oþere peple þat no man couþ nombre; and þere Kyng Edward was scomfitede. And Sir Edmund of Maule, þe kynges stiward, for drede went and drenchede him-self in a fresshe ryuer þat is called Bannokesbourn; þerefore þe Scottes saide, in reprofe and despite of Kyng Edward, foralsemiche as he louede forto go by watere, and also for he was descomfitede at Bannokesbourne, þerfore maidenes made a songe þerof, in þat countre, of Kyng Edward of Engeland and in þis maner þai songe:
>
> Maydenes of Engelande, sare may ʒe morne,
> Fortynt ʒe haue ʒoure lemmans at Bannokesborn
>   wiþ hevalogh.
> What wende þe Kyng of Engeland haue ygete Scotlande
>   wiþ Rombylogh.[20]

Is this "lyric," in any isolable sense? To view in fine grain how such an explicitly ephemeral "songe" relies on narrative and wider contexts for its meanings and what it contributes to those contexts in turn, we may start, paradoxically enough, by applying the terms and tools from discussions where genre and poetics are used exclusively to define the elements of poetry and where the "action" of a nonnarrative poem is its figural effects rather than its provocative insults of the English. Discussion of lyric as the epitome of poetics goes back most prominently to Northrop Frye's premise, noted above, that lyric "most clearly shows the hypothetical core of literature";[21] it is a sign of Frye's foundational utility that his focus not only provides a basis for Butterfield's notion of "poetic cores" but also underwrites the wide range of poetics collected and deployed on "lyric" by Culler.[22] In turn, in spite of Butterfield's skeptical view of the aptness of Culler's approach for medieval lyric, Culler's exposition of what he takes to be the transhistorical "genre" of lyric provides a conspectus of poetics with much to offer investigations of all sorts of short poetry both in and outside the scope and terms he considers proper to "lyric." His focus on "lyric" in *Theory of the Lyric* is offered simply as a matter of priorities for where his concerns might be most fully elaborated, not a matter of classification or ontology, as for deciding whether this or that poem is a lyric. Yet his framing and strategies resist the premises of "historical poetics," with its emphasis on the alterity of media, social uses, subgenres, and other features that the historicists, for their part, consider too fundamental to receive the single genre label "lyric," much less the ahistorical (or rather, distinctly New Critical) Structuralism that such an imposition entails.

The proposition that severely ahistorical and decontextualized analyses of poetic functions could offer much appreciation of situated poetry like the *Brut* poem might seem especially unlikely. But if theory of the medieval English lyric is to develop further, it might risk confronting such poetry with critical focuses from which by several means those poems seem excluded, in order to see how poetic elements were activated by that poetry's very different relation between figurality and contextuality. The chief difficulty that Culler's theory poses to such uses is, perhaps, his view of genre, as a fundamental and recurrent possibility beyond context and history, a position that seems to require models that hardly exist in medieval England, a period that receives only fleeting mention in Culler's study before he moves on to Petrarch.[23] But Culler argues for "lyric" not in order to exclude instances but to posit a distinctive but capacious category, whose properties he takes as his task to investigate both very broadly and in close particularity. These properties especially feature the "extravagant display" of figural and rhythmic language, overshadowing in degree and purpose the rhetorical elements used in nonliterary communication or mimetically functional narratives, like drama or the novel, the application of whose modes to lyric, as in reading lyric "dramatically," Culler takes as a primary mistake of much criticism. Since for Culler, "what happens" in lyric is not reducible to narrative, or to coherent drama of consistently definable personae, or to rationally cogent exposition rather than sheer experience of the poetry's untranslatable "ritualistic" force, then many of the medieval English "lyrics," which often seem to exist between rather than fully in any one persona's voice and with fragments of metamorphosing images that rarely stand clear of their language, might find unexpected assistance from the considerations he advances, even if to find those effects also often requires tracing large apparatuses with wide social or institutional implications, and which might, by sharper focus on the workings of figurality, teach us something new about those implications and medieval poetics itself.

To take up one element, "ritual" has a special status in Culler's study (as it did in Frye's *Anatomy of Criticism*) in that it includes features of lyric that are important precisely because those exceed explanation or interpretation, especially rhythm, repetition, and patterning. Like the Kantian sublime, it works on us in ways that cannot be represented but must simply be experienced and as a pleasure—sometimes the main attractant to a poem, even over "meaning."[24] In many ways the poem at the English defeat at Bannockburn displays with unusual intensity a rhythmic core at the center of its internal as well as the wider narrative elaboration. Yet the narrative's repeated explanations for the poem's particular features, "þerefore . . . foralsemiche as . . . and also . . . þerfore . . . ," show that the chronicler also carefully pondered the logical situating of this rhythmic feature in the poem and thus in his narrative. By his claims, the poem seems carefully calculated to suit the occasion, framed by a political drama that allows the chronicler to give it a narrative one. The historical narrative justifies the poem and gives it further shock value, not only mocking the English for their undignified defeat in a kind of marshy river ("vne riuere marresta," the French says more pointedly), capped by the suicide of the king's steward, Sir Edward of Maule, who threw himself in the river that gave the battle its name, but also the king himself, whose defeat by the river waters is described using a low-caste register in the core refrain.

In fact this enshrines an untraceable, unbounded oral song or chant and sublimates it to a high level of complex wit. The alternating refrain, "wiþ hevalogh, . . . wiþ Rombylogh," divided to close two stanzas, was, as a single phrase, a common rowing song, and, by a further complication in the layered voicings granted to this poem by its contexts, always gendered male.

The refrain's more usual form is first recorded in the late thirteenth-century romance *Richard Coer de Lyon* (possibly based on a lost French source, though the rowing song was likely always in English):

> Kyng Richard bad hem faste rowe:
> "Rowes on faste! Who that is feynt,
> In evel water moot he be dreynt!"
> They roweden harde and sunggen thertoo
> With "hevelow" and "rummeloo."[25]
>
> (2532–36)

The phrase appears in refrains to other nautical or quasi-nautical poems, such as a poem in a late fifteenth-century civic account book at Bristol about "keeping the ship well" since the "Prior of Prickingham" is coming (a bawdy pun?). In his *Bowge of Courte* (1499), John Skelton mentioned a song commemorating the arrival to London by boat of a new mayor, John Norman, "Heve and how, rombelow, row the bote, Norman, rowe" (this is among the repertoire of ballads known to the dubious Hervy Hafter).[26] The basic phrase also appears outside explicitly nautical settings on a range of seals and other jewelry from the later Middle Ages, reduced to "havelow": by synecdoche conveying the whole phrase, and by metonymy, the ethos or family tradition of seafarers. It appears in names of families, presumably with some nautical connection.[27]

All these show this core at its pre-semantic essence. Most narrowly, it "means" a peculiarly elongated treatment of "heave" (OE *hebban*), although the latter never appears as the form used for rowing chants before the sixteenth century. By that later date, the melodically lengthened "heavelow and rummeloo" yield to a brusquer "heave and hoe" (then "heave ho" and later, in a new rhythmical lengthening of that, the current phrase, first recorded in the late eighteenth century, "yo heave ho").[28] As with any work song, matching voice and breathing to bodily rhythm is key. As Culler says, rhythm "is an event without representation" and has "a power to inscribe [itself] in mechanical memory independently of any attempt to remember [it]," one pathway to the social role that poetry plays.[29] Culler finds "this sense of rhythm in the broad sense as something independent of writer or reader may be very strong in lyrics, where language seems to be echoing itself, with words generated by their phonological resemblance to other words."[30] The refrain is itself a common mini-lyric. Its point, however, always depends entirely on its situating, sublimating, and manipulating. In the *Brut* poem, the bodily sympathy that listeners are invited to experience, indeed, told to sing, is suffused with humiliating implications, perhaps further drawing into mind Edward II's particular fondness for heavy exercise and manual labor, which is mentioned openly in other chronicles, to which this narrator faintly but with some precision alludes ("foralsemiche as he louede forto go by watere").[31] The Scots' poem (if it is theirs, which we know only from this chronicler) emphasizes the sublimation of the refrain by splitting it: two short lines enclosing longer verses, and with more long lines of the verse before the first refrain than the second. This implies some native formal theory; while certainly evoking the short, beat-counted lines of much Middle English verse, it also recalls Eustache Deschamps's discussion in his *Art of Poetry* of 1391 of "ver coupe" ("truncated line") used in *ballades*, which should take twice as many full verses before the first *ver coupe* as before the second.[32] Even the meter may show complex structure. Just as Deschamps says that "if there is any truncated line which has five feet, the one following it must have ten," so "Maidens of England" (to give this poem a name qua poem, which it certainly does not have in the chronicle) presents ten syllables in the long lines with four (or possibly five) in the short rowing refrain.

The *Brut* poem's internal framing of maidens writing to rival maidens, a deeply insulting ploy for addressing male English warriors and likely male readers of historical prose, also exploits tropes in ballad traditions. It parallels, for instance, the refrain of the widely disseminated and widely varied Scottish ballad of a tragic sea voyage, "Sir Patrick Spens," which imagines how bereft maidens might or should lament as a way to stir listeners' own empathetic sorrow at the tale:

> O lang, lang may the ladyes sit,
> Wi' their fans into their hand,
> Before they see Sir Patrick Spens
> Come sailing to the strand![33]

The hypothetical address of "Maidens of England," however, does not invite an audience to reflect in sorrow, like ballads, but instead imposes on English reciters and readers a self-humiliating script, using the ballad trope, as it does the rowing song, as a means of luring English recipients into physical and emotional participation in insulting their king and their fellow fallen warriors or compatriots.

Here surely is a large and cleverly invoked poetic apparatus imbedding and indeed creating "lyric," with a smaller dynamic and adaptable vernacular poetic core. How far to extend the necessary scope and essential discursive field to appreciate the full figural efficacy of this poem, with its unmarked but distinctive refrain, remains uncertain. Given the political implications, it is pertinent to ask why the *Brut*'s unknown but certainly English author (though he wrote in French) appreciated and helped hone the Scottish insults so shrewdly. We might speculate that doing so proved an English reader could understand a Scot's insult. Or perhaps keeping alive anger against the Scots was important, confirming the justice of the later English revenge on this defeat. Yet so finessed is this poem, so adroitly used its ever-mobile refrain within the larger poetic apparatus, that it is hard to resist the thought that perfecting the complex poetic event it accomplishes was an end in itself to the chronicler.

Rhythmic and otherwise patterned sounds are always physically affecting, as applications of "sound studies" to lyric demonstrate.[34] The results need not be irenic. It is precisely what is most catchy in songs and lyrics that can be considered not only "compulsory but coercive discourse," as Roland Greene observes in his comments on lyric's "ritual" dimensions—in which he includes the "sounds that serve referential or expressive purposes in nonpoetic contexts, other sounds (such as 'hey-nonny-nonny' or 'oba-la-la') that have no other contexts, and the patterns that organize these sounds in the reader-auditor's experience." Although medieval lyric is often considered to differ from modern lyric in its universalizing rather than particularizing "I," Greene neatly, though perhaps unintentionally, dissolves that cliché period distinction; for Greene concludes that "the nature of lyric's ritual dimension is to superpose the subjectivity of the scripted speaker on the reader" to a degree that "can entail a kind of violence."[35] No more blatant case can be easily imagined of this than a popular refrain offered as a script for a defeated army, recast in its rocking lines as untimely widows.

Although this is very far from "lyric" as the Renaissance would recognize that, its forceful success is probably responsible for its reappearance as a poetic interruption in Christopher Marlowe's *Edward II*. To include the poem, Marlowe had to turn away from his main source, Holinshed's *Chronicle*, where it does not appear, to the *Brut* or a chronicle based on that for just this moment, when the Earl of Lancaster recites the mocking poem to the king himself as part of Lancaster's own diatribe against royal failures:

And thereof came it that the fleering Scots,
To England's high disgrace, have made this jig:
     "Maids of England, sore may you mourn,
For your lemans you have lost at Bannocksbourn,
     With a heave and a ho,
What weeneth the King of England,
So soon to have won Scotland?
     With a rombelow."[36]
                    (2.2.188–95)

In Marlowe's play the poem serves as narrative and resentful recitation. Such uses demote it from "lyric" in Renaissance terms, as does its attribution to the "fleering" Scots. But the poem's reappearance grants it new kinds of power: a vulgar contrast to the more prestigiously classicized English alternatives by then available, which Marlowe himself well knew and wrote. No genre is an island; Marlowe's replication of "Maidens of England" implies some unstated contrasting English military and discursive civility. Marlowe does not, however, imply an economy of genres any simpler than that of the fourteenth century; after all, he chose the story of a homosexual and brutally murdered king as his sole English history play. Even with these purposes, "rombylogh . . . hevalogh" bobs back to the surface of historical narrative, demonstrating Scottish incivility but perhaps also poetic skill, in the guttural vernacularism and self-conflicted poetic pleasures that such efficacious poetry kept alive.

The Chorus of Confession

If an example from the early fourteenth-century Anglo-Scottish wars shows how "lyric" genres were in part at least always social systems, even when recycled in sixteenth-century replications, then religious poetry before the Reformation displays "lyric" within at least as large apparatuses, and before the Reformation more publicly authoritative ones than insult poetry. Religious lyric often evokes more explicit dramatic and historical scenes than Culler would accept as proper to "lyric" (which, for him, should never be read like a "mini-novel"),[37] and sometimes rupture even that much poetic drama with commentary or doctrine. Medieval English religious lyric often finds itself treatable neither by most of Culler's criteria nor by most Renaissance standards of "lyric."

We should be cautious, therefore, before seeing fourteenth-century English religious poetry on a developmental path toward anything familiar. Siegfried Wenzel has been particularly attentive to the ill fit between modern ideas of "lyric" and the verses he has long studied in homiletic contexts. Yet he emphasizes the "expression of feeling and imaginative re-creation of an emotionally powerful scene" in the religious poems collected by the later fourteenth-century Lincolnshire friar, John of Grimestone, which almost "make . . . a genuine lyric poet" out of him.[38] The originality of Grimestone's book as a whole, however, is an indication of the eccentricity of many of the lyrics found within it. With 246 items in English verse, Grimestone's compilation is extraordinary, in a period when English lyric anthologies were unknown. The poems are organized by homiletic topics, but not placed in or subordinated to sermons; instead, they are found in sections including Latin compilations of points about topics that would be apt for preaching or private confession, though the collection has no indication that it was made for anyone but Grimestone himself. The book's display of his lyric collection prioritizes the English poetry, though it presents that as if to epitomize the homiletic and sacramental Latin memoranda; these are sermon notes among verses rather than verses in sermons. As a request for prayers in its colophon shows, Grimestone was at work on his sermon collection around 1372. That colophon, placed early in his volume, also shows that Grimestone considered the compilation itself a significant achievement; he mentions the "great care" he applied to writing "this book" ("qui scripsit istum librum cum magna solicitudine Anno domini 1372").[39] This indicates a commitment to crafted form on large scale; the colophon's early placement indicates he wished to announce this to the reader almost like a title. Latin rubrics on the poems are likewise sometimes prominent, as if those too served as titles, often potent with allusion.

The poems themselves cannot simply be isolated to their English verse, but must be inspected in their settings to appreciate the apparatus that Grimestone most immediately established for them. Grimestone's verses on the Passion are the most numerous, and show, as Wenzel notes, the greatest number "independent" from Latin sources.[40] These are inserted at two orientations in the manuscript (see Figure 27), whether to preserve space or to allow use from different orientations. One is the lyric titled by Carleton Brown "Ecce sto ad hostium et pulso" (Behold, I stand at the door and knock [Rev. 3:20]).[41] With its speech of Christ as a wounded knight outside the hard-hearted beloved's door, the poem has close connections to the tradition of the Song of Songs, as indicated by the title Grimestone offered: "Capud meum plenum est rore [My

Figure 27. John of Grimestone, "Undo Thy Door" ("Ecce, sto ad hostium
et pulso"). Edinburgh, National Library of Scotland,
MS Advocates' 18.7.21, fol. 121v.

Reproduced with permission from the National Library of Scotland.

head is full of dew; Song of Songs 5:2]; Ecce, sto ad hostium et pulso."[42] By
this "title" it more clearly invokes quasi-erotic religious traditions in the *sponsa
Christi*, or "bride of Christ," tradition, like other vernacular poems, sometimes
even secular love poetry, keyed to the Song of Songs.[43]

This poem initially establishes an erotic dialogue, verging on drama,
keyed not only by the English address but also by a Latin speech tag, which
Carleton Brown does not print: *Respondit peccator* ("the sinner replies"). A further rubric in both Latin and English, "*Ideo.* Þerfore," ties the final passage of
the sinner's confession onto the poem. The poem's abrupt shifts of levels between dramatic "voices" and other public or more direct address offers neither
continuous drama nor continuous exposition of sin and confession. The poem's
movement between these forms and postures of address is its most dynamic
and unpredictable feature, invoking mimesis but then stepping away to make
the poem a direct address outside the roles assumed and to a wider implied
audience, in a complicated process of producing intersubjectivity found in

religious medieval lyric in particular.[44] How this might have been exploited as a performance that is many-sided (metaphorically or literally, as the doubled orientation suggests), and whether in a church or private chapel or merely a matter of private reading, is unclear. The use of English in the second half of the midway rubric, "*Ideo.* Þerfore," suggests that the logic of the poem was meant to be at least basically understandable by English-only readers, or perhaps was meant to be used to declare aloud the change in the mode, from dialogue to lament.

It is difficult to imagine the results as only for performance before an audience but also difficult to imagine it as not involving more than one participant, at least as a duet. The result is both a recalled drama of a knight and damsel and a more direct but scripted confession between a penitent and some (Latin reading) confessor. The poem's form and genre are neither drama nor lyric, neither private nor public, neither predominantly homiletic nor theatrical, but with a compact experience of all of these. Presenting these elements as in the manuscript that was crafted "with great care" captures these multiple possibilities best, although no edition has yet printed them all (I silently expand abbreviations):

Capud meum plenum est rore: **Canticum 5;** *Ecce, sto ad hostium et pulso*: **Apocalypsis 3**

> Vndo þi dore, my spuse dere,
> Allas! Wy stond I loken out here?
> Fre am I þi make.
> Loke mi lokkes & ek myn heued
> & al my bodi with blod be-weued
> For þi sake.

Respondet peccator:
> Allas! Allas! Hevel haue i sped.
> For senne iesu is fro me fled.
> Mi trewe fere.
> With-outen my gate he stant alone.
> Sorfuliche he maket his mone
> On his manere.

Ideo. Þerfore:
> Lord, for senne i sike sore,
> Forȝef & i ne wil no more,

With al my mith senne i forsake.
& opne myn herte þe inne to take.
For þin herte is clouen our leue to kecchen,
Þi suete loue to hauen in mende.
Perce myn herte with þi louengge,
Þat in þe I haue my duellingge. Amen.

The textual divisions multiply both the kinds of dialogue and of intellectual or emotional "event." Although the final section clearly implies that the allegorical identity of the speaker of the first two stanzas is Christ, wounded from fighting the devil, this does not erase the dramatic mode of a knight beseeching a resisting beloved.[45] Even a performative style is indicated by the mention that the Christ-knight has spoken "on his manere." The confession that follows this characterologically mannered dialogue is realized in a register different from the dramatic interaction, offered as a logical rather than narrative result, "*Ideo*. Þerefore," the shift to lament made an event created by the narrator's (or rubricator's) guidance to enter a different space and time from what precedes. The logic implies the consequence, the "therefore," that the reader or listener will identify more directly and personally with this script: the final stanza is a prompt for a further, enforced sympathy with the lady's plight by whoever performs or reads this poem.

This is not, therefore, a "narrative" poem, nor is "dialogue" a certain or stable frame for its effects, though it seems to evoke both discursive structures, with a blandly prosaic clarity in spite of the rapid shifts between the modes. Such shifts balance the generic communality of sinful Christians with the distinctly individual reenactment of its cry of conscience, exploiting the social (collective/individual) as well as the temporal (sacred history/ present confession) paradoxes of "lyric time" in ways at least as complex as in the earlier and later secular poems discussed by Culler.[46] And though almost always printed as entirely English, Grimestone's "Undo Thy Door" exists between its languages, never fully incarnate in its words while nonetheless clearly indicating the potential for both guidance and affective identification and self-abjection. Latin guides the poem at each turning point, revealing its changing figural and narrative direction, but the Latin is remade by the English as the poem unfolds. The first dramatic plea draws into its English a typological reuse of the sensuous passage "my head is full of dew" from the Song of Songs: "myn heued . . . with blod be-weued." One change of signification is therefore already accomplished by moving from the scriptural taglines or "title" to the plaint. Although titles granted to medieval poems are not often productive for appreciating works in preprint culture, here such attention is fully justified.[47]

The larger apparatus for the figurality of Grimestone's poem can be followed further, well beyond his book and Lincolnshire. Its figural modes and scripted postures take their full potency and even basic meaning from the wide and shifting English religious network of its core elements. A late thirteenth-century manuscript, London, Lambeth Palace Library, MS 557, with Latin materials for sermons, grouped like Grimestone's ("De ebrietate," "De abstinentia," and so on), apparently compiled by an Irish friar at Cashel, includes a page with Latin passages followed by an English poem with many of the lines and forms of Grimestone's.[48] There, the English verse itself lacks the Latin rubrics and connecting statements that Grimestone's presents, but this lyric is also framed and reinterpreted by its neighboring materials. The leaf on which the poem appears starts with praise of "voluntary poverty" in Latin, credited to "Bernardus de sermone quodam" ("Bernard, from a certain sermon"): such chosen poverty's virtues, this quotation states, produce "a kind of martyrdom" ("Paupertas est genus martyrii, ait; nam sic vere martyrii genus paupertas voluntaria" [fol. 185v]).[49] This topic is central to, and much debated within, the Franciscan order, and the second Latin passage on the leaf speaks in persona of someone confessing failure in that ethic. This passage is a plangent cry based on Job 10:18–19, "Why didst thou bring me forth out of the womb? . . . I should have been as if I had not been," but rendered as a confession of a life of enjoying goods on earth—the opposite of "voluntary poverty" just lauded—and now facing hell after death.

These two sections are followed in the Lambeth manuscript by an English lyric often considered to be like, or even to *be*, though somewhat disarrayed, Grimestone's lyric. Its opening lament "Allas, allas," uses the same verses in different order. But this poem's "Allas, allas" directly repeats in English the final phrase "Heu, heu" with which the Latin lament preceding it in the Lambeth manuscript ends, when that speaker laments his failure to live in virtuous poverty. The English continues with the demand from Jesus knocking and appealing to this new beloved to open the door. Since only the English of this has ever been (inaccurately) transcribed, and the context of this version never appreciated, I present both the preceding Latin plaint and the following English verse.[50]

Quid valet me ab utero concipi? Quid ab eo nasci et postmodo om-
nibus bonis perfrui et denique in infernum descendere? Heu, heu,
melius esset mihi non ab utero concipi nec ab eo nasci.[51]
Allas allas vel yvel y sped
For synne Jesu fro me ys fled
         þat lyvely fere
At my dore he standed all one
And kallys undo yit
         on þis manere.
"Undo, my lef, my dowve dere,
Undo! Wy stond stekyn out here.
         iyk am þi make.
Lo my heued and myne lockys
Ar al by-wevyd wyt blody dropys
         for þyne seke."

There is no indication here of a sermon on the Passion. The larger agenda
seems the declaration of Franciscan voluntary poverty followed by a model
lament for a life led by the opposite inclinations. In this context the English
poem, flagged by "calling" at the door by the sinner's bloodied beloved, serves
to prompt a rather different kind of penitent's lament, here closing with the
Christ-knight's reproof. The final response by the penitent is dissolved into
whatever response the listener or reader might make. This version of the
poem leaves that final moment unscripted altogether, performable perhaps
in actions or further prayer or discussion.

The adaptability yet relative stability of these elements, merging private
with more communal experience, are clear in a simpler version of both in
yet another friar-confessor's miscellany, an early fifteenth-century copy of the
Speculum Vitae, New Haven, CT, Yale University, Beinecke Library, Takamiya MS 15, which includes other poems along with Walter Hilton's prose
commentaries on *Qui habitat* and *Bonum est,* belonging to the Franciscan convent of Lichfield.[52] This closely resembles the English poem in the Lambeth
manuscript, although that one lacks rubricated speech tags; the Takamiya
version, however—in this regard more like Grimestone's—includes Latin
speech tags and explanatory scene directions (see Figure 28).[53] In this adaptation it thus presents the core exchange, reduced to its barest economy of
obligation and repayment, reflected in penance and confession. The Latin

tags here introduce and frame the first English speech ("Allas, allas . . .") as follows:

> Exemplum. Erat quidam bonus homo qui pecavit contra deum, et
>   sic dixit.
> (Illustrative example. There was a certain good man who sinned
>   against God, and he spoke thus.)

A Latin speech tag like that in Grimestone's introduces the second speech, otherwise as in Lambeth ("Behold my body and my heved / With blody dropes is al be-weved"):

> Et respondit Jhesus sic.
> (And Jesus answered thus)

As this shows, the speeches are now cast into a past narrative, lacking any gendering of the sinner as feminine. Using many of the same phrases as Lambeth and Grimestone, the Takamiya version layers the past more distinctly against the present, offering the dialogue as an "exemplum" of "a certain" penitent sinful man who once prayed to Jesus. This distills the elements down to the basic form of a penitent hearing Jesus's appeal, ending rather than beginning with the call "undo þi dore my leve lyfe." The application is more explicit: the present penitent listening or reading should do the same as at one time did this "certain good man who had sinned."

To see all these works as wholly separate is clearly inadequate for appreciating the conventions they invoke and contribute to, but to see them as all simply "witnesses" to the same poem ignores the highly distinctive applications of their similar figures and postures, and of the immediate and larger poetic apparatuses on which they rely.[54] All presume further backgrounds for basic effect: the allegory of Jesus as a "knight" is part of a long tradition of infusions between passion and the Passion, found even when, as in Chrétien de Troyes's *Chevalier de la Charrette*, Lancelot enters and departs from the bedchamber of his beloved "as if before an altar" ("Con s'il fust devant un autel").[55] Whereas the other Franciscan versions of the motifs Grimestone uses make clear their focus on poverty, Grimestone conveys the issue through the wealthy and heroic knight brought to a desperate condition: a figure of sudden and tragic impoverishment to be honored and admitted into the castle and heart, as in as in Philippians 2:5–8, or fulfilled in

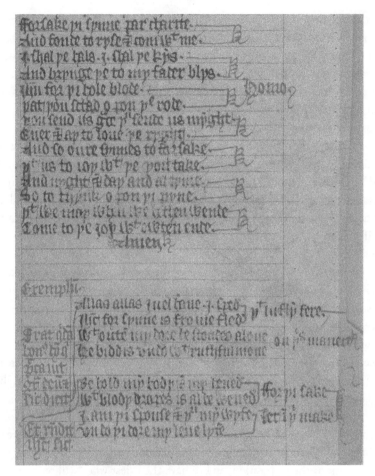

Figure 28. New Haven, CT, Yale University, Beinecke Library,
Takamiya MS 15, fol. 84.

Reproduced courtesy of the Beinecke Rare Book and Manuscript Library, Yale University.

a different, again more spiritual rather than literally economic sense, with
the self-abjection of the penitent who has turned away one thus begging.
The profusion of public as well as private ritual indicates other necessary
apparatuses to these poems or re-poemings by Grimestone and the other
Franciscans. Rosemary Woolf notes an anonymous eleventh-century Latin
poem including many of the features found in these.[56] Although Woolf finds
the earlier Latin poem "much more dogmatic and impersonal" than any of
the English versions, its identification of the speaker as a feminine beloved

draws more directly on the Song of Songs. Beyond that, the trope of knock-ing, and of dialogue with the lord who knocks, has a wider liturgical basis. In the service for consecrating a church, for instance, the bishop is instructed to arrive at a new church—with whatever holy relics will be installed there carried behind him—circling and sprinkling the ground outside the church with holy water, then the bishop is to knock three times on the door ("pul-sat ostium tribus vicibus") to announce the coming of Jesus to inhabit that church. The bishop then uses words from the Gospel of Nicodemus to an-nounce the lord's entry, in a knocking that releases to freedom the souls who died before Jesus's incarnation: "Tollite portas, principes, vestras, et elevamini, portae aeternales, et introibit rex gloriae . . ."[57] At this pounding and an-nouncement, a cleric who has previously remained inside the new church "as if one in hiding" ("quasi latente") opens the door and flees ("quasi fu-giens"), representing the devil being expelled from the church.

The ritual replication of such gestures and the physical participation of so many people in these or similar actions suggest a shared experience of worship, confession, and penitential communion. In several fourteenth- and fifteenth-century examples of Easter church liturgy, the priest or bishop rep-resenting Jesus seizes the cross and uses it to knock on the "door" of an altar space, asking clerics or nuns hidden within to open the doors, representing the Harrowing of Hell. Such *elevationes* became particularly sensational dur-ing Grimestone's period. At Barking Abbey, outside London, in the 1360s and 1370s, Abbess Katherine Sutton, in order to combat the "cooling of devotion in our times" and "excite more fully the devotion of the faith to so great a celebration," rewrote the Easter service to include bathing Jesus in effigy with oil and wine at the Deposition, and to have the priest who "will represent the person of Christ" (*representabit personam Christi*) seize the cross and pound three times with it on the altar chapel door, crying "in a loud voice," "Open the doors," "representing the breaking of the doors of hell." Thereupon all those (here, the entire convent of Barking nuns) who have been waiting in the chapel, representing the souls of the patriarch and fathers born before Jesus, depart from the chapel, "that is, from the limbo of the Fathers."[58]

These liturgical parallels support Wenzel's suggestion that Grimestone's lyrics "de Passione" might have been designed for Good Friday and Easter ser-vices, whose monastic versions Franciscan priories might have imitated. But all these instances of knocking by a beloved, answered by one longing for re-lease, confession, or erotic intimacy, carry echoes, even audibly material ones, of the other uses of this trope, while releasing further meanings from these contexts. In all these cases, the interaction presents as a matter initially in the balance who is in charge and who is subservient, who claims lordship and who yields in submission, who is private and inside, who is taking blows without. A set of shifting positions in relationships of authority and submission seems as central to the "core" of these lyrics and their wider practices as any narrowly discursive or even auditory experience. As Culler suggests, lyric can create "community" even while serving to complain about the status quo.[59] Yet here the core of "lyric" power depends on a much larger and more impersonal scripting than identification with a lone dissenting voice. The range of possible identity positions swinging between lordship and submission is focused on creating sudden accesses of individuation, not simply by the act of making confession but by the shift that each of these poems and religious rituals feature: the abrupt discovery that these each continually enact, that being the person in the castle or in the abbey does not make one the lord or even a male after all, but a submissive and at times feminized figure, forced to repent and open to the truer lord now revealed. The turn from a posture of lordship to exposure as the true subaltern makes each of these part of an apparatus of self-discovery as well as reinscription of hierarchical subject positions, offering social unity in the dramatic proof, "*Ideo.* Þerfore," that no one, however wealthy or fortified, is secure from sudden abjection.

Such an affective and institutional apparatus could not survive a more commercial world or the Reformation. Even the sounds of the poem would lack the contexts that gave them meaning. Before the Reformation, for instance, and except for papal interdictions, continual bells, pounding, processions, and chants of public life allowed "the temporal flow to incorporate the past and the future within the space of the present," as Niall Atkinson describes the "sound culture" of medieval Florence.[60] This parallels lyric time too, though it also suggests the contingent circumstances necessary for the effect of many kinds of individual "lyrics," certainly those with wider resonance in pre-Reformation liturgies. The collapse of what I am calling the poetic apparatus of Grimestone's and the related lyrics is all the more evident when some of the same core features, including the phrase "undo thy [your] door," persist in a sixteenth-century romance, *The Squire of Low Degree*, which Wynkyn de Worde's title shows was originally titled *Undo Your Door*.[61] Its explicitly erotic social drama includes the effort of a lowly squire to rise in wealth and fame so that he might marry a princess; as Nicola McDonald shows, it is haunted by elements of the earlier religious dialogue but transformed into a wholly private erotic obsession. The beloved, finding her suitor dead and mutilated beyond recognition—in fact it is not the suitor as she thought—embalms his corpse and worships it as a relic for seven years.[62]

The gesture of enclosing the body that she thought was the Squire's in a reliquary retraces the history of this "poetic core" itself, passing from wide public currency and devotional expression into a privatized, emotionally personalized, and fetishized form. Echoes of the violence and eroticism of the earlier religious tradition this may carry,[63] but the later romance's compression of such previously widely public elements also offers an implicit theory of "lyric": a discursive and dramatic core of passion and recognition preserved in an urn that transcends time, even if the medieval, feudal past in which those features were generated is now made a relic in a commercial and more socially mobile cosmos.

Venturing Lyric

In both "Hevalogh . . . Rombylogh" and "Undo Thy Door," what I have called poetic apparatuses are both essential and traceable: wide discursive and social fields producing and necessary for the poetics of those short English poems, just as the demotion of both poems at the Renaissance stripped that apparatus (and much of its social and historical significance) from the poems. Even if such later poetry is, therefore, free in some sense from "the logic of historical determination" that Culler demands of lyric, it is free only to the degree that isolated formal replication can be accomplished at will and only by those who have such models available. "We cannot return to the ancient Greek polis or the Renaissance city-state," as Culler remarks, "but poets can revive the lyric practices of those times, as Horace revived Greek meters."[64] But establishing the terms of such a "revival"—not to mention, as Horace's own poetry shows, the distinct status of particular kinds of poetry reemerging in untimely ways—involves major readjustments in the nature and range of poetic apparatuses, and inevitably the circumstances that sustained those.

A fundamentally different world of poetic modality was fully established by the time of Richard Tottel's 1557 *Songes and Sonettes*, whose preface advertises works by those who have "wel written in verse, yea and in small parcelles."[65] Produced nearly four decades before the publication (post mortem) of Sidney's *An Apologie for Poetrie*, Tottel's collection was itself more an indication than a trendsetter. It both nationally and transhistorically defines poetry by means of timeless, decontextualized evaluations of exotic ancient and continental examples against English ones: Tottel's anthology is meant to show that "our tong is able . . . to do as praiseworthely" as "the workes of diuers Latines, Italians, and other" poets.[66] In its bluntly competitive spirit, this casts a classicizing eye on English poetry but promotes and treats English poems as isolable commodities in a marketplace of praiseworthiness. Tottel's metrical homogenizing and thematic depoliticizing of the poems he renders up to the print market is well known, by which, for example, Tottel titled a sonnet by Thomas Wyatt that decries the execution of Thomas Cromwell by Henry VIII as "The lover lamentes the death of his love"; the process of revaluing a wide range of poetry as depoliticized "lyric" has a long genealogy.[67] Unlike manuscript modes of publication, increasingly an elite realm (ironically preferred by the courtly poets Tottel anthologized),[68] the nascent commercial book market provided new opportunities for a consensus of what "lyric" was at a period when commercialism and early capitalism was rapidly spreading, allowing printer-editors like Tottel to chide the "common ears" into achieving a more homogenized level of cultivation.[69] Tottel's preface nods to less-educated readers as if they were eavesdroppers, but it is clear they were his main public. Their implied abjection creates the value of what he offers. His offerings could prompt "the vnlearned, by reding to learne to be more skilfull, and to purge that swinelike grossenesse, that maketh the swete maierome [marjoram] not to smell to their delight."[70] Reading lyric as self-help—a posture or even broad genre that itself proliferated in printing's early decades—has rarely had so vigorous an advocate.[71]

The implicitly select but also mercantile and broadly competitive social values visible in Tottel's project are not irrelevant to the late fourteenth-century experiments in short stand-alone English poems by Geoffrey Chaucer and John Gower, who first adopted such continental and ancient models for "lyric" into English. For one thing, their short poetry often features apostrophe or lament conflating erotic, political, and economic transactions—and not simply in Chaucer's wry lyrical begging poem to the new king, Henry IV, "Complaint to His Purse."[72] But rather than the leveling and crassly competitive outlook of Tottel's preface, comparing one praiseworthy item with others at a time when the classicizing lyric had become familiar, for both Chaucer and Gower, short poems whose "action" is centrally poised on some element of figural language were fraught encounters with otherness, ruptures from the values and figural apparatuses of nationalist history or Christian ritual. From a later perspective it is difficult to appreciate the risks involved. But the prospect of purely figural transactions, however deeply engaged in reestablishing former *auctores* and poetic strategies for the English poets' current readers, appears less like a reassuring repetition than an abandoning of known value on any side of the exchange.

The first *canticus Troili* in Chaucer's *Troilus and Criseyde* presents the origin and ontological status of Troilus's love lament as extravagantly obscure. Chaucer introduces this poem as not only a direct and full presentation of Troilus's love lament but also as fully conveyed by and from his fictional ancient "auctor," save that he cannot offer the original language, nor its music, nor grasp a text on which we might entirely rely, even as we are prompted to read "nexte this verse" to discern what Troilus "seyde" (see Figure 29).

> And of his song naught only the sentence,
> As writ myn auctour called Lollius,
> But pleinly, save oure tonges difference,
> I dar wel seyn, in al, that Troilus
> Seyde in his song, loo, every word right thus
> As I shal seyn; and whoso list it here,
> Loo, next this vers he may it fynden here.
>
> *Canticus Troili.*
> "If no love is, O God, what fele I so?
> And if love is, what thing and which is he?
> If love be good, from whennes cometh my woo?
> If it be wikke, a wonder thynketh me . . ."
>   (1.393–403)

Weaving lyrics into narrative is common in the continental tradition, displayed as early as Jean Renart's early thirteenth-century *Roman de la rose ou de Guillaume de Dole*, which builds its thin plot into a lavish compilation of "biaus chans" ("beautiful lyrics") as people "met la graine / Es dras por avois los et pris" ("put scarlet dye into cloth to earn praise and fame"), embroidering the story "de biaus vers / Que vilains nel porroit savoir" ("with fair verses that an uncultivated man would not recognize"), and examples of mixing lyric in narrative are common through the fourteenth century, in which Guillaume de Machaut's works are a high-water mark.[73] Like Gower, Chaucer certainly knew Machaut's works and used them in other experiments of seeding "lyric" into "narrative" verse (as in the *Book of the Duchess*, modeled in part on Machaut's *Fontaine Amoreuse*). But the narrator's comments in

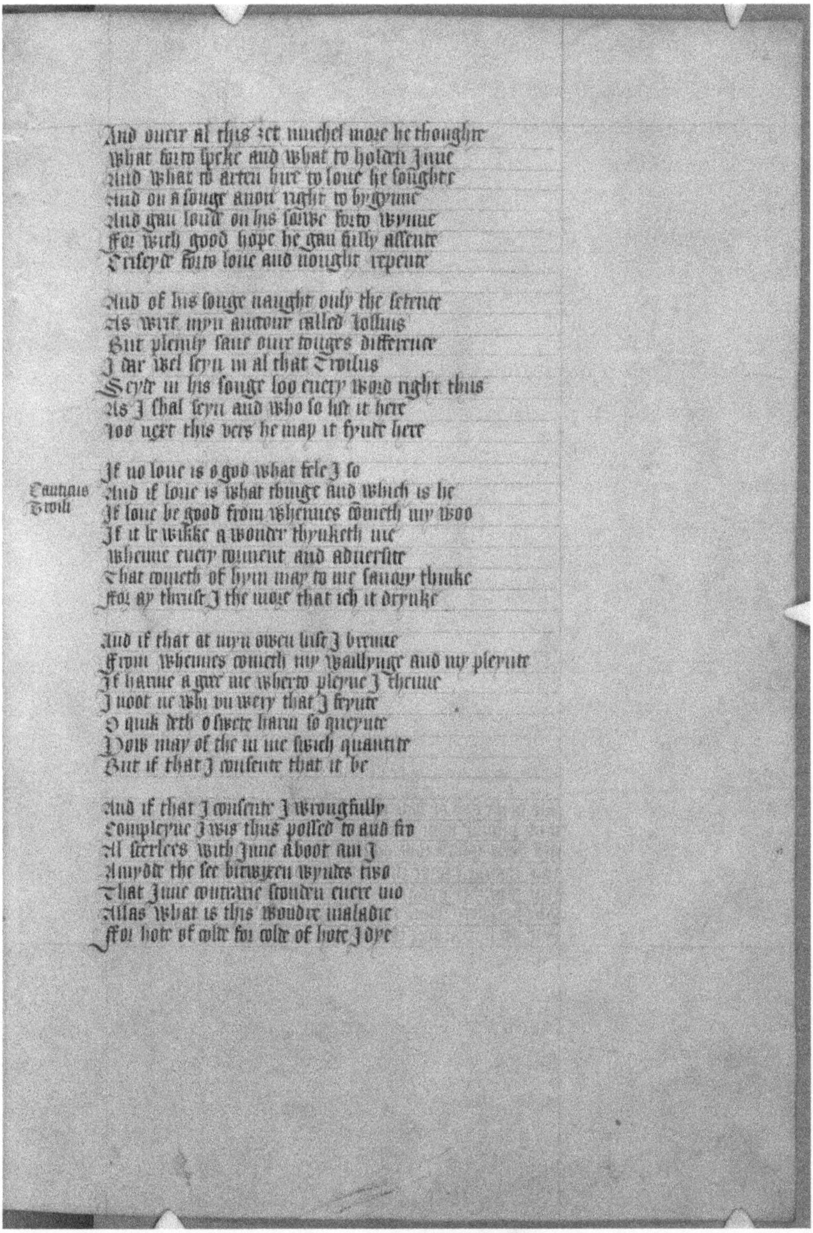

Figure 29. Geoffrey Chaucer, *Troilus and Criseyde*, "Canticus Troili." Cambridge, Corpus Christi College, MS 61, fol. 12.

Troilus show the more fraught encounter with a more intrusive and alien object. Thomas Stillinger shrewdly observes that Troilus's first "song" renders the present tense of "pure lyric," "the expression . . . of a timeless state of mind," whereas Troilus's second (and similarly rubricated) "song" in book 5 expressing his despair at the circumstances taking Criseyde away begins, Stillinger notes, in the "timeless" form of lyric but then collapses into mere narrative, when Troilus turns the second *canticus* into a comment on recent experiences, including the particular day he expects Criseyde to return.[74] These observations capture Chaucer's acute self-consciousness of the effects of a kind of poetry outside time, as, for instance, do the laments of the Black Knight in the *Book of the Duchess*. But both indicate Chaucer's reluctance to authorize such poetry without some paradox, irony, or tragedy. Whereas Chaucer's emphatic and emphatically textual pointing in Troilus's *canticus* directs us to the stark letters we read, Chaucer forces us in the same gesture to defer actually experiencing the song. Chaucer's emphasis on an impossible encounter with *originalia* denies we can hear it or even imagine its original "tongue"; its Real vanishes as elusively as Criseyde herself from Troilus's grasp. As Culler says about "lyrical address," often its "you" is expressed— "the 'you' of the beloved, or God, the wind, a flower. But sometimes it is not, and lingers as a spectral presence, a yearning, something like love."[75]

As *Troilus and Criseyde* proceeds, doubts grow that this *canticus* ever existed, at least in any form we experienced or could repeat. When Pandarus describes the scene to Criseyde he says he found Troilus "complaynynge," nearly a technical term for a *planctus*, or song of lament, but "What that was his mone / Ne wist I nought," Pandarus dismissively adds (2.558–59). The gestures of denying responsibility for the actual lyric we read and the actual steps that produced it begin with Chaucer's introduction to the *canticus*, where his claim to capturing "Lollius" in every word obscures how he there departed from Boccaccio, his main source for *Troilus and Criseyde*, to translate, for the first time into English, one of Petrarch's *canzoni*. Whereas to postmedieval critics this might seem an inevitable prelude to the cult of the Petrarchan sonnet that would thrive in the Renaissance, the first of many "revivals" of lyric from the classicizing Italian world, to medievalists, Chaucer's *canticus* might seem a smooth expansion of the well-established Anglo-Continental courtly lyric network. But the status of Troilus's song appears more alien than either perspective can accommodate. His studious misattribution is one clue. Replacing Petrarch's name with Lollius's suggests something analogous to Troilus's frantic effort to conceal his beloved's name: both mark resistance to acknowledging the historical and material realities of negotiation and acquisition in love or love song. As Criseyde seems too precious to Troilus to turn over to Pandarus, without great pressure, the actual name allowing Pandarus to begin his stalking and delivery of his niece, so the *canticus*, we might conjecture, was too extravagant an indulgence in figural language (oxymorons, rhyme royal, etc.) strictly for its own sake—it was not drawn, for instance, from any source actually tied to the story of Troilus—to allow disclosure of the realities of Chaucer's sourcing and translation of this gem (with all the diplomatic and other labors of his journeys to Italy). In both cases, we are made aware of an elaborate suppression of the actual transactions involved or desired. At this stage in the overall poem, the risk of failure seems too high even to acknowl-edge the pursuit or the object, in poetry or love; "difference" alone seems to sum up both Chaucer's and Troilus's encounters: after all, for Troilus at first sight, but utter love, Criseyde was simply "nevere lasse mannyssh in semynge" (1.284). By the end of the poem, after Criseyde has been exchanged with the Greeks for a Trojan hostage and has abruptly transferred her own loyalties from Troilus to the Greek Diomede, the narrator portrays her (along with Troilus and Diomede) with the coldly specific detail of a particular earthly entity, down to her unibrow (5.813). There is no mistaking the "tragedye" (5.1786) in the poem's transformation of objects of love, desire, hope, and fidel-ity into fungible commodities; less visible is that this process is already under-way in the creation of lyric in the *canticus Troili*. Petrarch no less than Criseyde is the unwitting first object of the poet's and Troilus's transactions.

After sampling the poetic apparatuses in political and religious realms, should we ourselves venture beyond literary history to economic formations and perspectives? We might best do so not by way of "commerce" or "com-mercialization," which had banal but steadily increasing roles in all later me-dieval culture but included only nascent elements of full-bore "capitalism," but as *venturing*, approached as both an economic and philosophical endeavor, embracing extraordinary risk in the hope of unassessable rewards.[76] To re-visit Heidegger, in late writings he posits German elegy (by Friedrich Hölder-lin and, especially, Rainer Maria Rilke) as vehicles for his notion of what he calls "venturing" as an intensely individuating encounter with the world as existential Being, with full awareness of mortality. Referring to Rilke's eighth *Duino Elegy*, Heidegger declares, "Rilke likes to use the term 'the Open' to designate the whole draft to which all beings, as ventured beings, are given over," a condition Heidegger found expressed most clearly by poets in a "des-titute time" after the gods, when such poets venture by willing themselves to will. This captures some of the riskily godless pursuit of the unknown in Chaucer's and Troilus's joint "unsely aventure" (1.35) in the pre-Christian universe, whose values of earthly love and "name" pervade Chaucer's own paradoxical efforts to animate Troilus's lost passion and song. We might even say that Heidegger's claims present a certain idea of "lyric" at its purest: willful individuality in the face of ephemerality and mortality. But Heidegger's elaboration of this as a philosophical and political ideal, it might be, has more sinister implications than Rilke's elegiac yearnings for unthinking presentness.[77] Still less like Heidegger's imperial advances, Chaucer's venturing into Petrarchism was launched within the terms of fourteenth-century English poetic apparatuses as forms of social contracts, offering promises—albeit self-contradictory ones—to deliver to listeners (or only readers?) the genealogically verified evidence of Troilus's passion, even though that, no less than its object of desire, turns out to depend on mere poetic figurality.

If the fragility of such venturing is not clear enough there, a more direct example of the risks involved in social contracts centered on the "action" of figural language appears at the midpoint of *Troilus and Criseyde*. There, the lovers' consummation of their love affair expands into pools of complaint and expressions of longing for endless intimacy, passages suspending all narrative exposition by their hyperbolic figurality. Yet these passages also happen to present the poem's most consequential speech acts. As the end of their first night together approaches, Troilus and Criseyde each utter aubades, dawn songs protesting the coming of day and demanding that night not be so hasty (3.1429–70). This form, already old in Ovid, is directly invoked by Boccaccio not only in the *Filostrato* that Chaucer was directly translating but also in the *Filocolo*, Boccaccio's early prose "novel" version of the love affair between Floris and Blanchfleur (which, as David Wallace notes, Chaucer's *Troilus and Criseyde* evokes in touches throughout).[78] Hints of the aubade form appear in the *Filostrato*'s analogous scene of Troilo's and Criseida's first consummation; but Chaucer takes the opportunity to canvass a wider terrain and slot in many further instances, an overabundance in quantity as well as in figural invocations. Whereas Boccaccio's *Filostrato* has

> Ma poi che' galli presso al giorno udiro
> cantar per l'aurora che surgea,
> dell'abbracciar si raffocò 'l disiro,
> dolendosi dell'ora che dovea
> lor dipartir ed in nuovo martiro

il qual nessun ancor provato avea
porgli

(But when near day they heard the cocks crow because of the dawn
which was rising, the desire of embracing rekindled itself and they
grieved for the hour which must part them and must put them into
new suffering, which neither had yet felt)[79]

Chaucer offers a duet of full laments, starting with Criseyde's. Her aubade,
however, most closely parallels a complaint by Florio's father in the *Filocolo*,
where that character hopes that the night would be *shorter*, an ironic reversal of the genre of aubade that Chaucer's character again reverses:[80]

> O blake nyght, as folk in bokes rede,
> That shapen art by God this world to hide
> . . . .
> Thow doost, allas to shortly thyn office,
> Thow rakle nyght!
> (3.1429–30, 1436–37)

At this, Chaucer's Troilus adds a more traditional (and, as can be seen from
the instances below, more directly Ovidian) address to denounce daylight for
its arrival:

> "O cruel day, accusour of the joie
> That nyght and love han stole and faste iwryen,
> Acorsed be thi comyng into Troye . . ."
> . . . .
> And ek the sonne, Titan, gan he chide
> (3.1450–52, 1464)

It is logical for Chaucer to fill out what he finds in Boccaccio's *Filostrato* with
elements from Boccaccio's *Filocolo*, since the latter shows Boccaccio "experimenting with the tension between lyric and narrative components, meditat-
ing on the relationship between a modern author to his classical forebears and
(a parallel concern) on the relationship of Christendom to the ancient, pagan
world."[81] But Chaucer's florilegium of aubades also emphasizes the risks of
such socially and narratively unmoored figural language. In the next breath,

the lovers merge their aubades with pledges of undying fidelity and "troth," in terms serving to deepen yet complicate the force of figural language both in the aubades and the vows. Having addressed daylight and the sun, Troilus declares to Criseyde that he will be "ded anon" unless he remains with her continually—the very condition that the aubade, with its impossible prayers, has just shown an unlikely wish—and vows he will endure any pain, so long as he could know absolutely ("were it so that I wiste outrely") that she loves him just as he loves her (3.1478–91). This stipulation grounds his vow on a profoundly unstable and unknowable correlative. At a minimum, we have already seen the very different ways in which Troilus and Criseyde approach and assess love. On her side, Criseyde answers Troilus with a vow of her own that is similarly hyperbolic, assuring him that the sun must fall from its orbit ("first shal Phebus fallen fro his speere") before Troilus would depart Criseyde's "herte" (3.1492–98)—itself an oddly passive construction for her ceasing to love him. Emphasizing the risks of such extravagantly figural language still more, Phebus's fall from the skies is exactly what both their aubades, protesting the coming of daylight, have demanded. What lyric joins hyperbolically, the rhetorical excesses of the contractual language dissolve.

The figural language that Chaucer emphasizes in the songs and lyrics in *Troilus and Criseyde* puts more utilitarian or expository language to the test, making the lyrics the more visibly eventful in strictly poetic ways but in turn revealing the fragilities of all speech acts: when are they reliable, or (as J. L. Austin would say) felicitous?[82] We might say, as Eleanor Johnson does, that the moments of "song" found throughout *Troilus and Criseyde* (and elsewhere in *The Canterbury Tales*) are framed to demonstrate the "psychological transformation" they produce in their listeners, instanced by characters' responses.[83] This is certainly supported by moments like Criseyde's overhearing of Antigone's song on the ethical power of love (2.820–903). But Johnson's general conclusion from this might be too optimistic, regarding both the fates of these figures and the powers of extravagantly figural poetry itself. Chaucer's settings, introductions, and responses to those "songs" *create* the sense of encountering figural language as "difference," emphasizing the power of purely figural speech acts in ways that destabilize perceptions of more quotidian speech acts. If all figurality requires an apparatus for its basic efficacy as figural language, such language can also infuse, or co-opt, the discursive field it takes as its apparatus into functioning as yet more hyperbole and specious invocation. The illustrative powers of "lyric" in narrative settings can transform that lyrical discourse's apparatus.

What became English "lyric," therefore, can be seen in Chaucer's most innovative forms to be marked as exotic commerce with unusually grave problems of assimilation and valuation; against the attribution of Troilus's *canticus* to Lollius can be placed the Franklin's sneering remark on Dorigen's complaints: "as doon thise noble wyves whan hem liketh" ("The Franklin's Tale," 818). In his "Retraction" in *The Canterbury Tales*, Chaucer sweepingly repents his "many a song and many a leccherous lay, that Crist for his grete mercy foryeve me the synne" (10.1086); yet it is clear that his lyric experiments occupy some of his most ambitious works and drew the attention of others in his and later literary and social communities, as confirmed by numerous fifteenth-century copies of his poetry that gather his lyrics along with many others by his fifteenth-century successors.[84] By then, the trend of gathering short, nonnarrative, amorous English poetry into dedicated collections was itself a common discursive apparatus, placing fewer demands on poets, scribes, and the poems themselves in defining the genre's value. In his own time, however, Chaucer's experiments with English lyric were paralleled or even anticipated by the lyric ventures of Chaucer's London, Suffolk, and Westminster associate and perhaps competitor for patronage, John Gower, in whose hands the genre already presents less severe self-interrogation but at times at least as bold a display of figural extravagance.

Although Chaucer and Gower often exchanged sources, Gower shows no signs of knowing any of the Italian works Chaucer used so heavily. Nor, so far as we know, did Gower produce any discrete English "songs" as Chaucer did. Gower was, however, the author of two French collections of "balades," the *Traitié selonc les auctours pour essampler les amantz marietz*, and the *Cinkante Balades*.[85] Moreover, possibly guided by Guillaume de Machaut's model, in particular *Le voir dit* (a sequence of *balades* serving as part of a dialogue and love affair between a young woman and an older man), Gower's longest English poem, the *Confessio Amantis*, uses a succession of short poems as "exempla" that his Lover's Confessor, Genius, offers as examples of the various "sins of love" to the poet, who after responding to these as a Lover for some 30,000 lines is finally unmasked as old John Gower.

This resolution shows a safe retreat from the risks of love lyric or other poetry, just as Venus urges old John Gower to make a "beau retret" from her "court" once his age and predilections for reading and writing books on "vertu moral" have returned (8.2416, 2925).[86] Yet perhaps because of this safety, Gower's production of short nonnarrative love poetry in the *Confessio* at times approaches the Petrarchan model of lyric more closely than Chaucer's does. This is clearest in Gower's uses of his most alien but favorite literary source (perhaps the only ancient poet he deeply knew), Ovid.[87] Whereas Gower used Ovid, with great innovation, for social and historical allegory in his Latin *Vox clamantis*, it is only in the *Confessio* that Gower took up Ovid's model of lyric, although regularly framing such Ovidian imitations under moral terms, albeit the rather flexible category of the sins of love.[88]

Genius tells the tale of Cephalus under the sin of "sluggardy in love," itself under "sloth." The "tale" against sluggardy is wittily chosen to be an aubade, not to scold those who are sluggish to love but, as in *Troilus and Criseyde*'s central, third book (which Gower may have had in mind) asking Phebus to slow the coming of dawn to allow lovers to languish in amorous delay. Based on a poem in Ovid's *Amores* (1.13), also the model behind Boccaccio's and ultimately Chaucer's aubades in *Troilus and Criseyde*, this "tale" is unlike most of Gower's more direct uses of Ovid to expand or rebuild in that it builds a wholly new poem out of a figural reading of an antecedent poet's figure. In Ovid's poem, the human narrator asks Aurora, goddess of dawn, to slow her arrival so he can continue to lie with his beloved:

> Quo properas, Aurora? mane!—sic Memnonis umbris
> annua sollemni caede parentet avis!
> nunc iuvat in teneris dominae iacuisse lacertis;
> si quando, lateri nunc bene iuncta meo est.
> nunc etiam somni pingues et frigidus aer,
> et liquidum tenui gutture cantat avis.
> quo properas, ingrata viris, ingrata puellis?
> roscida purpurea supprime lora manu!

> (Whither are you hastening, Aurora? Stay! So may his birds each year make sacrifice to the shades of Memnon their sire in the solemn combat! Now I delight to lie in the tender arms of my love; if ever, now I am happy to have her close by my side. Now, too, slumber is deep and the air is cool, and birds chant liquid song from their slender throats. Where are you hastening, o unwelcome to men, unwelcome to girls? Stop with rosy hand the dewy rein!)[89]

Aurora, Ovid's narrator archly suggests, must be rushing from bed to flee old Tithonus. If she had her young strong Cephalus, she herself would be begging the horses of night to run slowly. That hypothetical speech act merges into the narrator's own:

> Tithono vellem de te narrare liceret;
> fabula non caelo turpior ulla foret.
> illum dum refugis, longo quia grandior aevo,
> surgis ad invisas a sene mane rotas.
> at si, quem mavis, Cephalum conplexa teneres,
> clamares, "lente currite, noctis equi!"

> (I wish Tithonus were free to talk about you; no more shameful scandal would be known in heaven. Flying from him because he is long ages older, you rise early from the old man to the chariot wheels he hates. But if you had in your arms the Cephalus you preferred, you would cry, "Run gently, steeds of night!")[90]

Ovid's address to Aurora not only appeals for delay, it enacts that delay by listing the reasons for the request, implying that Aurora has paused to listen. Lyric temporality is even more complicated than usual here, since it folds the request for delay into an invitation—advanced with a leisure that implies it actually is occurring—for Aurora to dally with false surmise herself. This draws the poem into a series of "nows" that each resist linear time in multiple ways, inviting his addressee and his reader to pause in longing for an impossible lingering consummation.

Ovid's many-layered expansion of the poem's "now" seems to have been the center of Gower's response. Gower poses the case of what Cephalus himself might say if the time for Aurora to rise had come. For on this basis Gower creates Cephalus's own aubade, whose possibility, conjured by Ovid only as a counterfactual desire, is realized in order to create another counterfactual appeal for the sun's and time's delay. So extended and deft is Gower's elaboration of Ovid's brief premise, and so rarely is Gower read as a major English lyric poet, that it merits sustained quotation:

> For love who that list to wake
> Be nyhte, he mai ensample take
> Of Cephalus, whan that he lay
> With Aurora that swete may
> In armes all the longe nyht.

Bot whanne it drogh toward the liht,
That he withinne his herte sih
The dai which was amorwe nyh,
Anon unto the Sonne he preide
For lust of love, and thus he seide:

     "O Phebus, which the daies liht
Governest, til that it be nyht,
And gladest every creature
After the lawe of thi nature,—
Bot natheles ther is a thing,
Which onli to the knouleching
Belongeth as in privete
To love and to his duete,
Which asketh noght to ben apert,
Bot in cilence and in covert
Desireth forto be beschaded:
And thus whan that thi liht is faded
And Vesper scheweth him alofte,
And that the nyht is long and softe,
Under the cloudes derke and stille
Thanne hath this thing most of his wille.
Forthi unto thi myhtes hyhe,
As thou which art the daies yhe,
Of love and myht no conseil hyde,
Upon this derke nyhtes tyde
With al myn herte I thee beseche
That I plesance myhte seche
With hire which lith in min armes.
Withdrawgh the Banere of thin Armes,
And let thi lyhtes ben unborn,
And in the Signe of Capricorn,
The hous appropred to Satorne,
I preie that thou wolt sojorne,
Wher ben the nihtes derke and longe:
For I mi love have underfonge,
Which lith hier be mi syde naked,
As sche which wolde ben awaked,

And me lest nothing forto slepe.
So were it good to take kepe
Nou at this need of mi preiere,
And that the like forto stiere
Thi fyri Carte, and so ordeigne,
That thou thi swifte hors restreigne
Lowe under Erthe in Occident,
That thei towardes Orient
Be Cercle go the longe weie . . ."
                    (4.3187–237)

The address to Phebus might, given Cephalus's mythic setting, stand as a literal invocation, but against the long tradition of the aubade protesting the arrival of daybreak, the address plainly functions as an apostrophe, its addressee fictional.[91] The entire poem flaunts freedom from more prosaic reality: political, religious, and military ideologies, even moral guidance of the kind the *Confessio Amantis* overtly conveys, fall away, or rather into service of "sluggardy." Genius goes on to claim that the tale warns against the "sloth" of those who want to sleep until midday; but in the "tale" this is a feature to luxuriate in, unfolding from Ovid's passing figure of a hypothetical dawn song that Aurora would sing if she had her Cephalus. By granting to Cephalus the longing that Ovid invites Aurora to entertain, Gower uses the strategy on Ovid that Ovid used with Aurora, opening space in linear time by turning hypotheticals into events, albeit purely discursive ones, with a prayer to a god who is not expected to hear or answer.

Gower's poem reveals these elements fully only in relation to Ovid's prior poem, without whose background it is a simpler aubade. Gower's maneuvers build on Ovid's demonstration of the figural power of apostrophe. It is thus no coincidence that Culler's model has more parallels to Gower than to any of the other works considered here. Apostrophe, in Culler's view, is the figure most crucial, even primal, among all forms of "lyrical address," granting lyric its essential claims to self-generativity by conjuring "spirit or meaning" from "the very down-to-earth activity of seducing us with its arrangements of letters, sounds, and silences"; apostrophe makes that capability so visible that, Culler argues, critics and sometimes poets recoil from it as if in "embarrassment."[92] Gower's use of this rhetorical figure, however, follows medieval theory, although into more concentrated and self-perpetuating forms than elsewhere in English verse before the sixteenth century. In Geoffrey of Vinsauf's verse thirteenth-century *Poetria nova*, apostrophe is a source of particularly witty play, including a self-fulfilling address to *Apostropha* herself: "Rise up, apostrophe, before the man whose mind soars too high in prosperity, and rebuke him thus" ("Cui nimis in laetis mens surgit, apostropha, surge, / Et sic castiges ipsum").[93] Geoffrey of Vinsauf's demonstrations of using apostrophe to "amplify" a point are all designed to "let apostrophe be a . . . mode of delay": "by it you may cause the subject to linger on its way, and in it you may stroll for an hour."[94] So too, Cephalus's apostrophizing delays the narrative time of the sun's arrival even as Cephalus prays for the sun to delay his real course, "and so ordeigne, / That thou thi swifte hors restreigne" (4.3233–34), "That thei towardes Orient / Be Cercle go the longe weie" (4.3236–37), lines reusing and answering Ovid's imagining of how Aurora, embracing Cephalus, might herself call out "lente currite, noctis equi!" ("run gently, steeds of night!").

Unlike Chaucer, who indulges in apostrophe in brief or self-mocking ways (Geoffrey of Vinsauf's passages on apostrophe appear, for instance, only in the childish genre of a beast fable of "The Nun's Priest's Tale," and only to exaggerate the bathos of high style against a farmyard in uproar), Gower develops an entire poem from the figure. By inviting apostrophe's full force against the march of narrative and time, Gower unfolds his address by Cephalus and paean to "sloth" not only within but prior to Ovid's hypothetical case. Gower anticipates Ovid's address, with its counterfactual evocation of lost desire, with another, logically prior address, which makes an equally impossible demand: nesting delay within delay, making history linger, even run backward, by inserting a scene that would have occurred (if it could) before the counterfactual scenario Ovid narrates. This is a "now" present only in the poem's hypothetical time, perpetually recreated (*as* hypothetical) by the reader's performance of it.[95] Gower's poem achieves this effect fully, however, only when seen in connection with Ovid's *Amores* 1.13, a necessary intertextual apparatus standing in for the more traditional connections and poetic apparatuses of fourteenth-century England. Sloth, a relic of the otherwise pervasive apparatus of homiletic discourse and its clerical institutions, becomes lyric time.

As a social and economic barometer, such joint ventures in lyric and its frameworks might thus register not only Chaucer's much-lauded diplomatic and literary journeys to Italy but also both Chaucer's and Gower's London, Westminster, and courtly audiences and settings, whose discursive as well as commercial exchanges regularly featured a variety of tongues, goods, fashions, and models difficult to interpret and value.[96] But they were undeniably unusual in the venturing they undertook. Against the more topical or more institutionally leveraged lyrics in English of the period, we may see in both Chaucer and Gower not just a change in poetic fashion but a major shifting and isolating of figural "action," from a range of traditional social and religious horizons and histories to a new and more explicitly exotic context of eventfulness. Chaucer's experiments in such exoteric figurality are more obviously fragile, paradoxical, and (perhaps deliberately) self-defeating. They imply a theory of lyric measured by the losses and costs as much as any more gains of prestigious value and lineage. Gower's emphases on figural and poetic power demonstrate more sanguine redefinitions of classicizing figural language, defining a new basis for community keyed to distinctive claims of his own authority as lay intellectual and "auctor."[97] For both, such reshapings of English poetry affirmed new interpretive communities, implying new kinds of prestige and exclusion, and new kinds of subordination of readers who lack the tools to participate as fully in these figural domains. Tottel's swinelike English readers were already being fashioned by Chaucer's and Gower's elevating discoveries in English figurality.[98] Yet the shifts of figural apparatus in England to classicizing and continental literary traditions also carried a utopian potency, not only diminishing and reordering into new hierarchies the social and historical field but also theorizing a new freedom from political, religious, and institutional history itself, opening new possibilities in the hypothetical "core of literature" precisely as that lost the figurations constituting so much of fourteenth-century literature and life.

Chapter 12

Response: Old Lyric Things

VIRGINIA JACKSON

The editors of this book have asked me to describe some of the ways in which these great earlier chapters respond to the current field of "lyric studies." That is an easy assignment, since the big question that frames *What Kind of a Thing Is a Middle English Lyric?* is, of course, "What kind of a thing is a lyric?" You will have noticed that not everybody contributing to this book has the same answer to that question. In fact, the answers here are so various that one comes to see early and often that what these chapters are talking about is not one thing but many different things. That's not surprising, since the definition of lyric as a "kind" or genre of literature has lately (though not for the first time) become a matter of debate, and I take it that this book marks the entrance of medievalists into the troubled waters of that debate. Welcome! It is time you joined us! Hope you can swim! But of course you can, since medievalists have been asking the serious questions central to lyric studies all along—in fact, medievalists might just be in a position to keep the rest of us from drowning. The conveners' description of the Radcliffe seminar where this all started in 2016 begins so sensibly: "This advanced seminar centers on the study of English short poems written c. 1200–c. 1500 CE."[1] Why study these poems? Because "even more than most vernacular literature of this period, these poems offer special interpretive challenges, including a basic understanding of what they are." I love the canny premise here that even the distinguished scholars assembled for this advanced seminar might not recognize what it is they are reading, and I really admire the implicit acknowledgment that to call these poems "lyric" might make such recognition more rather than less difficult. In fact, calling them lyric may have made the "interpretive challenges" that readers of early poetry continue to face special indeed, since the definition of lyric is and always has been a hot mess.

That is why when I tried to define "lyric" for the most recent edition of *The Princeton Encyclopedia of Poetry and Poetics* (2012), I began by hedging my bets:

> In Western poetics, almost all poetry is now characterized as *lyric*, but this has not always been the case. Over the last three centuries, *lyric* has shifted its meaning from adjective to noun, from a quality in poetry to a category that can seem to include nearly all verse. The ancient, medieval, and early modern verse we now think of as lyric was made up of a variety of songs or short occasional poems. Since the eighteenth century, brevity, subjectivity, passion, and sensuality have been the qualities associated with poems called *lyric*; thus, in modernity, the term is used for a kind of poetry that expresses personal feeling (G. W. F. Hegel) in a concentrated and harmoniously arranged form (E. A. Poe, S. T. Coleridge) and that is indirectly addressed to the private reader (William Wordsworth, John Stuart Mill). A modern invention, this idea of lyric has profoundly influenced how we understand all poetic genres.[2]

The genre of the encyclopedia entry calls for such general claims, but in my version these claims may seem to have more to do with the long and uneven process through which most poetry has become lyric—the historical process I have called "lyricization"—than with *the lyric* as such. That is true. I do think that ideas of lyric are differential and historically contingent, made rather than given, and in the entry I pointed to some of the complexity of those differences and contingencies in various European and especially Anglocentric periods and places, including the English Middle Ages. The lyric has never been just one thing, but what strikes me now is that even though I thought this qualified definition was describing historical contingency, the time frame I attributed to that contingency was pretty absolute, since I insisted that lyric is a *"modern* invention." I even said that "when medievalists such as Zumthor apply the term *lyric* retrospectively to 'a mode of expression entirely and exclusively referring to an I, which, although frequently no more than a grammatical cipher, nonetheless fixes the plane and modalities of discourse to the exclusion of any narrative element,'" that "the modern sense of *lyric* as poetry that is nonnarrative and personally expressive" was being used "to characterize a variety of medieval verse practices" that had little to do with the "modern sense" of the term.[3] After reading the chapters in this book, I would say instead that even if I do think that the solitary, personally expressive lyric is a creature of "the last three centuries," even if it has had its heyday "since the eighteenth century," even if it has thrived "in modernity," even if this sense of lyric is an especially "modern invention," that does not mean that "ancient, medieval, and early modern verse" was simply pre-lyricized, was innocent of or not yet susceptible to the post-eighteenth-century (or, as we shall see, really post-Hegelian) abstraction that turned many different stipulative genres of verse address into one big lyric genre. Thanks to the book you are reading, I see that the process I thought was "modern" had its start much earlier and that it was not just attached to personal and nonnarrative verse. Lyricization has been going on for much longer than I thought, not just because, as Ardis Butterfield writes here, "the *modern* history of Middle English lyrics has been a prime example of what Virginia Jackson has called 'lyricization'" (emphasis mine, not hers),[4] but because, as I have learned from the chapters in this book, the blurring of miscellaneous verse genres into one big idea of poetry as *lyric* did not begin in modernity but was always already happening in "English short poems written c. 1200–c. 1500 CE." This is to say that whatever it was that the poems now called Middle English lyrics once were, they have not only become lyric by being interpreted (and as Butterfield will go to explain, edited) according to post-eighteenth-century protocols of lyric reading (on which more in a moment), but were part and parcel of how and why lyric reading came about in the first place.

Scholars of early literature are used to such snafus, since premodern objects of study rarely fit into modern hermeneutic categories, yet the scholars assembled in that Radcliffe advanced seminar and hence in this book know better than I do that when we read old lyric things, we can't just remove post-1500 ideas from those pre-1500 things themselves as if hermeneutic categories were so many layers of flashy packaging—which is to say that the title of this book may ask the wrong question, if only by making its subject singular rather than plural. What if rather than asking "What Kind of a Thing *Is a* Middle English Lyric?" we asked instead, "What Kind of Things *Were* Middle English Lyrics?" Medievalists are experts on how and why history problems are always wrapped up in theory problems, and on how and why theoretical problems quickly become history. Ideas about a thing aren't so easy to separate from *the* thing itself (especially if you throw in the definite article, *pace* William Carlos Williams), but ideas about things plural always sit at interesting angles to things themselves, especially when those ideas are new and those things are old. I am not a medievalist, but I have learned that much from this book. The first thing I have learned is that yes, lyrics can be many different genres of songs or occasional poems in this period and those genres were called many different things other than "lyric," but even when we describe, say, a troubadour poem as a *chanson, tenso, descort, partimen, alba, pastourelle, dansa, sirventes,* or *cobla,* that does not mean it is not also lyric, and though modern lyrics are supposed to be brief and personal, medieval lyrics can be either brief or long, narrative or nonnarrative, personal or impersonal, musical or graphic, collectively or individually authored or received (or not authored or received at all), sung in church or stamped on a cup, religious or secular (even during a period when that distinction made no sense), public or private, intentional or unintentional, lost or found. If we lyric theorists take the lessons of these chapters to heart, our definitions and debates over what kind of thing "the lyric" is might become less hot and messy and a lot more fun, since these chapters are not as interested in defining one kind of lyric thing as they are in embracing the many kinds of things old lyrics may have been and may even continue to be.

In this sense, it seems to me that these chapters have more to offer current lyric theorists than we have to offer scholars of Middle English lyric, if only because lyric theorists have recently been so divided over a definition of *the* lyric. Honestly, in my experience medievalists have always understood the concept of lyricization before I have a chance to explain it, since the idea that *the lyric* was not really a thing until modern literary critics made it one is hardly news to literary historians working in early periods. But the idea of lyric as a relatively recent hermeneutic category does seem to have come as news to some lyric theorists working in later periods, and there has been a lot of argument about it. In a review of *The Lyric Theory Reader,* a critical anthology of mostly twentieth-century Anglo-American lyric theory I co-edited with Yopie Prins in 2014, Stephanie Burt, the other respondent to *What Kind of a Thing Is a Middle English Lyric?,* made an excellent point about the problem with the binary structure of these arguments. At the end of her review, Burt also called for the corrective that I am suggesting these chapters on the multiplicity and heterogeneity of early lyric might offer to current competing definitions of *the* lyric *tout court.* "Without contraries is no progression," she concluded, turning to invite us all to let the claim "that 'lyric' has almost always been with us in some form, even if it is not called by that name; even if it does not dominate every literary period where it occurs—stand as the contrary, or the antithesis, to the New Lyric Studies' claim that 'lyricization' occludes the categories and the ways of reading of even the recent past. Can we have, now, a synthesis? What could it accomplish?"[5] This response gives you a good idea of at least one view of the two sides of the current debate over what kind of thing the lyric is. Burt portrays these sides as "contraries" by channeling William Blake's line from *The Marriage of Heaven and Hell* (1790)[6] (I love this), but then Blake seems to become Hegel. Since I agree with Steven Shaviro that "Blake's system of Contraries is generated by a movement which is endlessly contradictory, endlessly inadmissible by the standards not only of formal logic but of Hegelian dialectical logic," because "progression . . . has a very special meaning for Blake, implying the continuation of a lived tension of opposites, rather than any sublation or furthering resolution," I think this slide to Hegel is a problem—not Burt's problem, exactly, but the problem with modern lyric theory and thus the problem that the chapters collected in this book are in a position to solve, or at least put in its historical place.[7] Blake is hardly premodern, but his gorgeous thought is never totalizing in the post-Hegelian way modern thought tends to be (and as medieval thought never was, as far as I can tell from these chapters). The words "antithesis" and "synthesis" are enough to seal the Hegelian dialectical deal in this prose, but the benign (and these days common) assertion that seems to me most thoroughly Hegelian is "that 'lyric' has almost always been with us in some form." With *us*? *Always*? Hegel's argument in his *Aesthetics* is that what is at stake in the lyric is the achievement of subjectivity, and that it is this achievement that makes the lyric the little engine that could drive the progress of history. In order for this idealist version of lyric to work, that progressive philosophy of history has to mean the progress of Western civilization, so the idea that lyric has almost always been with "us" in some form depends not so much on any particular version of lyric form as it does on a very particular idea of who *we* are, of who *we* have always been, and of who *we* will continue to be, "always."

I hope I don't need to list the problems with the communitarian impulse of that idea of "our" historical continuity or with the concept of a progressive Western civilization that begins in antiquity and remains "our" own.[8] Again, this lyric-driven narrative of civilizational progress is not Burt's own argument but Burt's accurate echo of the Hegelian basis of all modern lyric theory. On one hand, this basis affirms the idea of a transhistorical lyric form, and, on the other, it seems to mean that my theory of lyricization "occludes" such a continuous generic category. What Burt is describing has become known as the Culler/Jackson debate, and it is not a dialectic, since at least as of this writing, there is no hope of a synthesis between these contraries and no historical progress anywhere in sight. I take it that it is this stalemate that Burt's rhetoric generously attempts to dialectically reanimate, since in her view lyric theory is stuck because once one contrary "occludes" (a word, it turns out, was not available until the late sixteenth century, when it was taken from the Latin *occludere*, to "shut up") the other, the game is up. I *think* that Burt is accusing "the New Lyric Studies," which she associates with our project in *The Lyric Theory Reader*, of not playing fair. In fact, the idea of "the New Lyric Studies" was the late great Patsy Yaeger's, when she was editor of *PMLA* and asked Yopie and me to gather essays for a special "theories and methodologies" section of the journal in 2008.[9] Yopie and I didn't want to invite only scholars who shared our views to contribute to the *PMLA* forum, and we certainly did not want to include only essays that shared our views in *The Lyric Theory Reader*. Our lifelong feminist collaboration is not invested in dialectical conflict or in promoting any one idea of progress, especially not one based on the cultivation of contraries; it's ironic (or just sad) that in retrospect everyone associated with us has been placed on one side or the other of a debate we have wanted to make less agonistic and more indeterminate from the beginning. So, what if the contraries that Burt names designate not a Hegelian dialectic but instead a Blakean "lived tension of opposites" in which the names (as in Blake) keep changing, in which the collectives keep shifting, and what if the endless reiteration of a perceived opposition is what keeps getting us nowhere? That has certainly been my experience. I don't want to dwell on that experience, so I'll just say a little more about current lyric nonstarters before returning to why I think the chapters in this book might start more interesting conversations.

After the publication of *The Lyric Theory Reader* in 2014, Jonathan Culler, whom we invited to contribute both to the *PMLA* forum and to our anthology, published a book he called *Theory of the Lyric* (2015). In that book, rather than engage with our argument (as Burt does), Culler took it upon himself to defend transhistorical Hegelian lyric form from us by doubling down on the definite article. Culler's book is emphatically about *the* lyric and not about lots of different kinds of poems that have been called lyrics for the last several centuries, since the latter idea is something he attributes to "a modern historicist critique of lyric, often known as 'the new lyric studies.'"[10] I hope you are beginning to see a trend here: even though Culler himself was part of the forum that the editor of *PMLA* called "The New Lyric Studies," he, like Burt, attaches the label only to the work that Yopie and I (and especially I) have done. But while Burt's formulation makes it seem as if we were trying to shut everyone else up, Culler's effectively casts us as even more aggressive, since he thinks that "the historicist critique [to which he attaches our names, and especially my name] apparently seeks to dissolve the category of lyric in order to return us to a variety of particular historical practices" (84). I am not sure how any critic, historicist or formalist, could do such a thing even if she wanted to, but dissolving the category of lyric is the last thing I want to do. My point has always been that the modern idea of lyric has kept getting bigger and bigger, more and more abstract and all-encompassing over the last few centuries. Far from dissolving the lyric, I have tried to show how *large* the category has become over the last two hundred years—and I am so pleased to see how many years and how many versions of lyric the chapters in this collection add to my previous understanding of that category. This is not a point attached to Hegel's philosophy of history, even in its more attractive Marxist versions. I do not think that the gradual and ongoing synthesis of a great variety of what Culler calls "particular historical practices" into a genre so capacious that poetry has become another name for it is a sign of "our" civilizational progress, a way of continually reinventing the poetry of the future that will move us all forward, an expanding force that can push the spirit of the age further toward eventual enlightenment or revolution. Even in Adorno's negative dialectic, that Hegelian idea of continuous *lyrik* progress toward a utopian horizon, of the lyric as the mover and shaker of *our* communal horizon—as "the speech of men between whom the barriers have fallen"—is residual.[11] In her review of *Theory of the Lyric*, Marjorie Perloff wrote that Culler's "own theory of the lyric" is "a modified Hegelianism," but I would say that there is not much modification.[12] Consider Culler's first sentence: "Lyric poetry has a long history in the West but an uncertain generic status" (*Theory of the Lyric*, 1). The project of the book is to clarify that generic status so that the Western lyric's long history can continue and can become even more expansive, to do "justice to the possibilities inherent in the tradition" (9). And there is that definite article again, here used to define not only the Western tradition but the lyric tradition. *What Kind of a Thing Is a Middle English Lyric?* would seem to be the kind of book tailor-made to guarantee lyric poetry just such a long and singular and definitive history as a continuous Western genre, as "our" common inheritance of old lyric things, but the thing is, the chapters in this book do not do that at all.

What they do instead is not one thing but a lot of different things, and that is the best thing about this book. The old version of a culturally coherent inheritance of *the* lyric tradition that extends from antiquity to the present is not the story these chapters tell, even when some of them come close. Perhaps it is because medievalists have had to be especially wary of such totalizing narratives that so many of the chapters here avoid the trap of defining Middle English lyric as any one kind of thing. There is a certain homogenizing grandiosity in both Culler's account of the long history and theory of Western lyric *and* in my account of the long history and theory of lyricization. Most of the chapters here cut right through such master narratives in order to think about Middle English lyrics that came before Hegel's doomed versions of civilizational progress turned lyric plurals into the lyric singular, thus turning the lived experience of contraries into a (culturally, racially, historically) unifying dialectic. Most of these chapters take Rosemary Greentree's wise note that when it comes to medieval lyric, "vexation comes from attempts to define the genre, to confine its members within a few descriptive sentences. Every statement can be questioned, every adjective is ambiguous, every category has exceptions."[13] What a relief! The chapters by Ardis Butterfield, Christopher Cannon, and Ingrid Nelson take up some of the current debates in lyric theory I have just sketched (and some others that I have not) in order to show how they fall short of accounting for poems that don't fit into the totalizing Hegelian assumptions that ground those debates (though the point about Hegel is mine, not theirs). We will come back to those chapters in a moment. They tempt me to say that medievalists generally know better than to attach the category of lyric to a progressive philosophy of history, but the chapters by Barbara Zimbalist and Andrew Galloway *are* attached to such philosophies, and at least in Galloway's case, that is because his theory of lyric is basically Structuralist, partly Jonathan Culler's, but also partly Northrop Frye's.

This is to say that not only do these chapters demonstrate the limitations of contemporary lyric theory by multiplying the kinds of lyrics such theories have yet to consider, they also demonstrate those limitations by multiplying the uses of lyric theory. This is true even for the six chapters here that are much less interested in the uses of any theory of lyric than they are in how medieval lyrics were actually used. Cristina Maria Cervone's chapter does not worry about the definition of "lyric" because she has so much to say about what lyrics *do*;[14] Ian Cornelius says explicitly that he "deliberately" takes "lyric" to mean simply a "short composition in verse" so he can turn his attention to an amazing consideration of the "metrical shape of verse lines in Middle English lyric," or really, to a new way of thinking about Middle English prosody;[15] Raymond Gibbs seems less invested in what a Middle English lyric *is* than in what kinds of thinking Middle English lyrics make possible, but it turns out that he does have a theory of lyric, and it is Helen Vendler's now slightly old-fashioned description of a lyric as "a score for performance by the reader," a performance in which "you don't read or overhear the voice in the poem, you are the voice in the poem" (if you hear echoes of Burt's *The Poem Is You* here, you are onto something).[16] I have always thought that although Vendler's method of close reading was once normative classroom practice, it is a diva performance (like singing along with Rihanna in your car but pretending Rihanna is the one singing along with you and you are not in your car), and Gibbs manages to show how dramatic that version of lyric reading really is.

Aden Kumler's chapter goes to the other extreme, like Cornelius ostensibly forswearing any theorizing of lyric in order "to examine what happens to short poems in Middle English when they are integrated into the material form of an object rather than a book," specifically into objects that "convey something: wine, ale, water" and even "lyric."[17] I do think that there is a fascinating theory of lyric-in-use (a close cousin of the concept of language-in-use in linguistic anthropology) in Kumler's wonderful examination of the lyrics inscribed on turned wood bowls, "face-jugs," lavers, ewers, and other everyday vessels, and she betrays as much when she concludes by suggesting "that 'lyric' is productive as a proposition, or a playful question . . . , precisely because as a term of art and an artful practice, "lyric" was not codified, collected, or generically stabilized in late medieval England as it was on the Continent."[18] In other words, rather than worrying about what kind of single thing a Middle English—or any other period's—lyric was or is, Kumler suggests that we learn to appreciate the miscellaneous ways that people in late medieval England worked, encountered, and lived with poetry long before post-Hegelian lyric theorists who wanted to codify, collect, and stabilize poetry as one big genre came along.

Margot Fassler's chapter agrees that "the collection of chapters gathered in this book attempts the necessary work of recontextualizing and repositioning the lyric, not through a greater narrowness, but from the multiplicity of disciplinary viewpoints the subject demands," but her chapter, like Andrew Albin's, needs to hold "the lyric" as stable as a genre in order to survey that multiplicity.[19] While Kumler thinks about vessels of lyric expression as dumb speaking objects, both Albin and Fassler think about lyric sound, about medieval music's infinite variations on a singular lyric idea. Albin does invoke Simon Jarvis's very Hegelian view of lyric as a vessel "for a cognitive content," but again, the song these chapters are interested in is, as Albin puts it, "the lived aural experiences of historical hearers," not the singular, unifying, collective song of ourselves.[20]

This cursory survey certainly does not do these chapters justice, but you have the advantage of being able to read them for yourselves, so you don't need me to summarize them for you. In fact, since what the many different things these chapters have to say about Middle English lyrics are a lot more interesting than anything I have to say, I should just defer to the experts. Briefly, in that case, in conclusion, let me return to the ways in which three of these experts engage with current lyric theory, if only to remark that these scholars make what we lyric theorists say a lot more interesting.

In "Lyric Value," Ingrid Nelson emphasizes the way in which shifting lyric out of its nominal back into its adjectival form takes the pressure off any unified, autonomous definition of lyric's generic stability. Nelson takes my theory of lyricization as a starting point, and she defines it as "the process by which the broad field of poetry has narrowed to comprise only verse writing that conforms to a normalized lyric form."[21] That characterization of lyricization makes sense, but I would say that it might be better to say that the process has actually worked the other way around: "narrow" verse genres have gradually been subsumed into a "broad" idea of poetry as a single, lyricized genre. Nelson is right that this lyricized idea has become the new normal, but of course there are lots of different reasons for norms at lots of different times and in many different places. Her chapter shows how medieval dialogue poems "on their own terms (so far as possible) . . . can serve as the foundation for a mode of lyric reading that promotes certain urgent ethical values" that are at odds with the idea of an autonomous, unified genre, and especially at odds with the post-Hegelian concept of lyric based on the self-sufficiency of the single lyric subject. Instead, "the values of difference, diversity, and plurality, in particular as they are represented and realized through the interactions between subjects" in medieval dialogue poems form the basis for Nelson's anti-Hegelian understanding of what such lyrics are and do.[22] Yet the idea of a progressive history isn't entirely absent from her analysis, since she focuses that analysis on a concept of "value" she derives (in variation) from I. A. Richards. Why go back to Richards? On one hand, Nelson finds in Richards an alternative to what she calls "an anti-totalizing poetics of personhood" that tends to be relentlessly presentist rather than historical in recent literary criticism, and, on the other hand, Nelson wants Richards's now forgotten theory of value to intervene in current lyric debates in order to take the focus off the question of whether lyric is or is not one or many genres, instead insisting that "choosing to value the formal, historical other that is the Middle English dialogue lyric is choosing to value difference, and to recognize the many voices in which it speaks."[23] This is one way to allow one kind of thing Middle English lyrics were to cut through the all-or-nothing, progressive claims of contemporary lyric theory, though I would say that Nelson's tactic is metacritical here, since rather than emphasizing many different kinds of things the Middle English lyric could be, she is thematizing the many over the one, the other over the selfsame as an ethical imperative attached to a stubbornly progressive lyric ideal.

Christopher Cannon's chapter "Lyric Romance" begins by calling the progressive ideals that seem so inseparable from lyric discourse into question by asking a deceptively simple question: "What is the poem usually now called *King Horn* doing in the book now cataloged as London, British Library, Harley MS 2253?"[24] Not only is this poem ten times longer than any of the other Harley lyrics, but it poses problems for the idealist claims made in and for twentieth-century editions of these definitive Middle English lyrics, claims "for the historical significance of these few poems (the 'only substantial body of English secular love-poetry before Chaucer' that survives)," and also claims for their modernity, since "their 'individualized voiced feelings' were praised as the closest Middle English ever got to the 'self-expression of subjective life' that Hegel had said constituted lyricism itself."[25] Cannon, like me, wants to disentangle Middle English lyric from these modernizing ideals, but it's not easy. He frames the Harley lyrics as "a classic instance of what Virginia Jackson has called 'lyricization,' a process whereby 'the notion of lyric [is] enlarged in direct proportion to the diminution of the varieties of poetry' that surround it, and an entirely 'new concept' (the definition of the Harley lyric in this case) is 'artificially treated to appear old,' so that (again, in this case) the poems in booklet 5 of Harley 2253 other than its short poems are never even allowed to register as part of what is still presented as a historical category."[26] By quoting Cannon quoting me, I may seem to be promoting a single theory of lyric (my own), but what Cannon sees so well is that there is no such theory to promote, since what is at stake in the idea of lyricization is indeed a *process*, and historical processes never obey the rules. Since for the last two centuries we have not been able to read the lyric without reading according to Hegel's rules, Cannon does not pretend we can. His brilliant strategy is instead to take two Hegelian truisms about lyric—that lyrics are brief and that they are nonnarrative—and then to use the example of *King Horn* to demonstrate that at least one Middle English lyric was neither. Since literary critics are generic spin artists, Cannon concedes that he could simply suggest that *King Horn* is not simply a lyric but a "lyric romance," but he makes the more difficult and promising choice to explore the term "lyric romance" itself, "not because it newly identifies some kind of Middle English text, but because it provides an analytic category in which we can put the modern distinction between two genres under scrutiny, as well as the characteristics thought to define and distinguish them."[27] This is carefully done: if distinctions between genres are "modern" yet by now unavoidable, even when we talk about old poems, then at least we can examine those distinctions closely. This does not mean that *King Horn* is not a Middle English lyric, but it might mean that, as Cannon writes, "the process of lyricization that began with the term 'Harley lyric' and has since drawn such a firm line between short poems and long, 'nonnarrative' and 'narrative,' has obscured the extent to which we have been pleased to call" almost all poetry "lyric."[28]

If Nelson stretches the question of genre into the question of value and Cannon points out how elastic questions of genre can be, Ardis Butterfield shows us that while literary critics can make choices about how to understand the historicity of literary genres—including the historicity of their misappropriation—literary editors cannot. As Butterfield writes, from her perspective as editor of the new Norton Critical Edition of *Medieval English Lyrics*, she needs to choose what poems make it into the book and which do not (though notice the plural noun in the title). Like several of the scholars in this book, Butterfield begins by emphasizing medieval lyrics' intimate relation to music, and she argues that "lyric studies, and not only in the medieval period, have left music to one side to a degree that has impoverished and indeed misrepresented the object of study."[29] It is such a good point. Whereas I would say, with Kumler, that modern lyric reading has taken most poems out of their lived environments, Butterfield shows that "the modern history of Middle English lyrics"—that is, the *editing* of Middle English lyrics—"has been a prime example of . . . 'lyricization.'"[30] If the modern lyric reading of medieval song entextualized experiences that were not fundamentally textual, then, as Butterfield writes, "to edit the Middle English lyric is to create the Middle English lyric." But if, in this admirably radical view, "the 'thing' of Middle English lyric needs not so much a new definition, or even a new 'new criticism', as a new kind of lyric editing," what would such lyric editing look like?[31] This is where Butterfield's project becomes thrilling, at least for a nonspecialist like me who relies on her editing in order to be able to read these lyric things at all. Rather than attempting to make medieval lyric conform to the Hegelian ideal of brief subjective expression that is formally self-sufficient (or to a Vendleresque version of these songs as ours to sing), Butterfield proposes "paying attention to the 'whole' song: that is, to an object of study that not only includes music where that exists or can be posited, but a contextual landscape that takes account of the linguistic plurality in which Middle English lyric was composed, performed, and copied, and hence also to the many social and cultural environments of musical and poetic production in Britain during these centuries from circa 1150 to 1450."[32] Wow. Butterfield admits that this idea of "the whole song" might be aspirational, but she is acutely interested in what it might mean for lyric studies—and so am I. One thing it means is that not only the archive for medieval lyrics but the archive for all lyrics is vast and uncontrollable, since the lived experience of lyric cannot be reduced to a single, authoritative object called "the lyric." And this is also an admission that the kinds of things medieval lyrics were cannot be so reduced, nor should they ever be. What kind of thing is a lyric? In an earlier essay called "Why Medieval Lyric?" Butterfield writes that she does not think that my accounts of the practice of lyric reading and the process of lyricization need be opposed to Culler's "enduring desire . . . to give ground back to lyric that narrative had long possessed . . . to give credence to the term lyric."[33] I agree. Let's embrace "lyric" as a term capacious enough to contain contraries that, as the chapters here attest, are on endless repeat in a history so long it should be clear by now that it is not getting us anywhere fast, least of all further toward a definition of any one kind of thing a lyric is or was, let alone any one kind of thing "we" ever were or will continue to be.

Chapter 13

Response: Hevy Hameres

STEPHANIE BURT

I'll begin with some tropes familiar to the medievalists who will make up the bulk of the audience for this volume. I consider myself unworthy to relate what I am about to set down; I do so by instruction of my betters, and I am only a translator or an explainer, making the knowledge already available in mine *auctor*—or in this case *auctors*—available in a new, and in this case a modern, English form.

The chapters in this volume reassess, re-present, and find new reasons to admire the body of verse we are used to calling—perhaps miscalling—Middle English lyric: poems secular and religious and both at once, poems "genuinely anonymous," "poems without contexts" and poems by Rolle, Henryson, Chaucer, poems that seem grounded in one person's deep feeling and poems that start and end with other concerns. They make clear what these texts, and their reception, offer people already immersed in medieval letters or in medieval verse.

But what do these texts, and these texts in particular, offer people who spend our imaginative and professional lives with the poetry of later centuries? What can we learn from new scholarly models for them and from new ideas about them?

In one sense the question, like all questions about entire historical periods, ends up too general to permit an answer. A contemporary poet, or a critic, with something to learn from *Sir Orfeo* or *The Parliament of Fowles* may learn it without immersion in the period, just as a contemporary poet may learn from Blake or from Catullus without becoming a Latinist or a Romanticist.

That said, these chapters, together and separately, tell students of later periods two big things. The first is that features of lyric poetry found in later centuries may after all be found in the disorderly, fascinating, and forever incomplete resources of insular lyric (on vellum and on ewers, in English and Latin and French). The second is that many of the features that set off Middle English lyric (or poems called lyric) from a main line of post-Reformation or post-Tudor poems, many of the features that make these Middle English short poems hard to collect, or to fix in print, or to interpret, are features they share, not with later poems in general, but specifically with late twentieth- and twenty-first-century work.

*   *   *

Cristina Maria Cervone points out that medieval lyric, read in our day, may require unfamiliar cognitive frames. But her first example seems familiar: the incarnational logic of paradox became a defining feature of successful lyric poetry for yesterday's canon-makers, today's all-purpose bad guys, the American New Critics. Words in poetry often take us beyond denotation or proposition, into other, nondiscursive effects: Rita Felski has even argued, persuasively, that something like the sense of wonder (she calls it "enchantment") is one of the major reasons why lay, or nonprofessional, readers bother to read what we now call literature. Cervone's set of poems "privileges multiplicity of sense . . . and . . . also makes use of recursion," so that if we ask to whom the *I* refers we end up with questions about how the poem can possibly know what it knows.[1] That's Cervone's point about "Summe men sayoun" but it's also a thing we say—almost a cliché—when introducing the floating pronouns and absent anchors in John Ashbery. Again, there's something about medieval lyric that points directly to our own day: I'll get back to that point soon.

Christopher Cannon and others ask not only (with Cervone) how we take a certain body of Middle English poems, but what that body says about the terms literary historians now use. "Could a Middle English lyric," Cannon asks, "be narrative?"[2] Why not? A modern lyric can: it can tell stories, for example, about the departure of swans from a lake, or about the growth of a poet's mind. The folding and refolding of sounds and events that Cannon describes in *King Horn* also occurs in long modern texts that we tend to call lyric or lyrical, both in verse sequences (such as *In Memoriam A. H. H.* or Langston Hughes's *ASK YOUR MAMA*) and in fiction such as *Mrs. Dalloway*, or John Crowley's *Engine Summer*, or anything you like by Janet Frame. (Refrain, repetition, verbal reuse, and ritual are for Jonathan Culler constitutive, though not necessary, features of "the lyric" throughout history.)

Ingrid Nelson suggests beautifully that lyric is like water, in a riddle from the Exeter Book: "manifold," able to get around various obstacles, and—as Elizabeth Bishop would put it—"historical, flowing and flown." Nelson also shows how Middle English lyric tends not to fit the analytical frames introduced by those New Critics, frames that professed to cherish autonomy and individuality over intersubjectivity, dialogue, and interdependence. More attention to Middle English lyric, among people who do not read a lot of it already, might remedy both any lingering wish to imagine autonomous individuals and freestanding well-wrought urns (on the one hand) and the "relentlessly presentist" counter-canons of a neo-avant-garde, on the other.[3]

She's right. But her way of describing these poems (poems in which "*I* am constituted by not-*I*") can also describe many poems, even hypercanonical poems, that rely on dialogue, or on an implied interlocutor, from later periods, "presenting readers, listeners, and singers with multiple voices," either directly (the listeners/readers hear multiple speakers) or indirectly (the poet hears other voices, but we don't).[4] Consider John Keats's "La Belle Dame sans Merci," with its conscious medievalizing; Robert Browning's "Fra Lippo Lippi"; any number of poems by Langston Hughes, from "Theme for English B" to "Madam and Her Madam"; Bishop's "At the Fishhouses" ("He was a friend of my grandfather. / We talk"); even George Herbert's "Jordan (2)" ("But while I bustled, I might hear a friend").

Aden Kumler examines short inscriptional verse (which might or might not fit the label "lyric") found on cups, mazers, jugs, lavers, and other vessels; sometimes the verse seems to speak for the vessel itself, at others for the drinker, or to the drinker. "What does it do to lyric" (or to a poem, anyway) "to be made of metal?"[5] The corpus of short poems in Middle English includes verse inscribed on physical objects whose meaning should not be severed from those objects' material form. This way of seeing verse from before English print culture does separate it from much of the verse written, printed, or circulated in the time of Donne, or Milton, or Robert Frost (though see Donne's "Of My Name in the Window"). Yet it, too, returns, if not with the verse on eighteenth- and nineteenth-century medallions and statuary ("Give me your tired, your poor . . ."), then certainly with the variety of printing and writing and circulating verse that emerge in the past half-century, the age of cheap duplication, of custom printing, of the internet. We will see some of that verse below.

"Brasses, rings, front doors, roofs, windows, jugs," as Andrew Galloway writes, "even across the front of a castle": fourteenth-century verse in particular saw many short works in verse whose effects and meanings could not or should not be divorced from their unusual inscriptional surface.[6] "Form and lyric substance are inseparable," says Kumler, in the poetry of, on, or in the Robinson Jug,[7] just as they are in those poets, or—if we are not to confine our attention to people primarily labeled as poets—in the neon signs and scrolling digital apothegms of Jenny Holzer: Holzer's slogan "IT IS IN YOUR SELF-INTEREST TO BE VERY TENDER" means more, and means differently, and perhaps means lyrically (it speaks from the soul, to the soul), as a wall stencil or in flashing lights.

The inset lyrics in Richard Rolle's *Ego Dormio*, according to Andrew Albin, instantiate an argument not dependent on genre labels: the argument that sonic patterns in verse are a mode of nonpropositional or nondiscursive thought, guiding readers' experience and affecting cognition. This argument, associated with Simon Jarvis, may not be as new as it seems (the philosopher Suzanne K. Langer argued that musical sounds conveyed nonpropositional meaning back in the 1950s), but it's a good way into the thick description of poets' sonic effects and into the elements of what we now call lyric, whether encountered in verse or in prose. "Textual features . . . generate the impression of authorial vocal presence"; Rolle indeed "uses lyric sound to alter what and how a reader reads, sees, hears, thinks and sings," and "draws our ears into greater attentiveness." So do Bishop and Hughes and Herbert and Auden, at times; they, too, can ask whether "love brings bodies together by means of the lyric."[8]

Rolle's trio of inset poems, with their array of speech acts, their sonic ambition, the final sense of inadequacy before *canor*, show for a particular moment in the history of Christianity a pattern of striving, and demonstrating, and falling short, that we can find elsewhere in lyric history too. They show, moreover, a double-mindedness about whether lyric makes good on its promises about whether mere sound and words can truly bring bodies (author and reader; lover and beloved; living and dead) together.

I have been arguing *not* that Middle English lyric is deeply and wholly the same as lyric, or as poetry in general, from later periods. Indeed, as the chapters here show, "Middle English lyric" is not necessarily the same as itself—various overlapping categories of short poems produce various gen-eralities, some consonant and some dissonant with the meanings that "lyric," the singular noun, now holds. Rather, I argue that Middle English lyric, those understudied and various poems without names, has more in common with lyric from later periods—can say more to and about those later poems—than critics who cover only print cultures assume. In some cases those com-monalities speak to the *longue durée* history of the kinds of writing and hearing and singing that we now call lyric.

In others, they speak to particular commonalities between the thirteenth and fourteenth century and our own time of context-specific inscriptions, rapidly evolving paratexts, digital printing, glowing screens, new media, and technological change.

Medieval lyrics do not have consistent, robust relations to print culture: by definition they arise before modern print and modern books. Often they circulate detached from their original contexts, or with a vexed sense of what those contexts might be. Yet, as Ingrid Nelson argues, we may see these poems "not as relics of an extinct oral culture but as positive evidence of a comprehensive network of lyric practice," of partial preservation, circu-lation, and both oral and written reuse.[9] This body of texts casts light, not only (as several contributors note) to the ongoing debate about the meaning and the historical persistence of the category "lyric," but also on some as-pects that much contemporary poetry shares with a good deal of medieval insular verse, aspects more common before 1490 (or so) and after 1990 (or so) than in the English-language verse written and published during the five centuries in between.

A list of those aspects might combine features long attributed to medi-eval short poems with features newly described, or newly emphasized, by the scholars in the present book. Compared to the verse of the mid-sixteenth through the mid-twentieth centuries, medieval insular short verse, espe-cially the verse historically labeled as lyric, is characterized or typified by the following:

- extreme brevity ("Nou goth sonne under wode")
- multiple speakers, ambiguous speakers, or both, so that we cannot be sure who speaks what lines
- unique, unpredictable or unstable relations to the material surface on which it is written, including nonbook contexts such as jewelry, jugs, drinking glasses, and castle entrances

- verse whose "handwritten form" (as Jessica Brantley puts it) "is a unique object, wedding the text it presents to the form of its presentation less transparently, and more meaningfully, than do the mass productions of print culture"[10]
- a wide variety of potential relations among spoken, written, and especially sung texts
- unclear or variable generic markers—the same text may be taken as sacred or secular, as parodic or as straightforward advice
- complex embedding; lyric verse and lyric genres inset within prose or in verse narrative (Cnut's song, as discussed by Ingrid Nelson in her *Lyric Tactics*; the embedded love lyrics in *Troilus and Criseyde* and in "The Franklin's Tale")[11]
- unstable or unconventional (by later standards) orthography
- polyglot or macaronic construction, "intertextual, multilingual" (Fassler), with multiple languages at work close together
- implied readers who have not read very widely or deeply in English-language verse (because, in the thirteenth and fourteenth century, no deep tradition exists); sometimes they know legends, proverbs, and orature; sometimes they know Latin or continental vernacular verse

Every one of these characteristics *can* be found, if you look, in the verse of every century, even the eighteenth—but as outliers (the exception that proves the rule may be William Blake). Every one is a commonplace either of reading Middle English lyric, or of recent discussions about it (especially Butterfield's and Nelson's). And every one of these characteristics recur, once you look for them, much more commonly in the verse of the twenty-first century; some of that verse seems at once less new, less out-of-nowhere, and more rewarding, when read alongside medieval counterparts.

Here is a page taken almost at random from Aby Kaupang and Matthew Cooperman's *NOS*, their book-length account in verse and prose of their young child's disability and neurodiversity:

husband:
                    who are they that enjoy
          the sun

                                        wife:
                              everyone enjoys the sun

on an outing
> through the glass
>>   Maya doesn't enjoy the sun[12]

Kaupang and Cooperman use the page as a space of composition, almost as a canvas, in a manner originating in the midcentury projective verse of Charles Olson, and far more common now than in Olson's day. They also use conversation and multiple speakers and a vocabulary simpler than most to create (tersely) a scene that aspires to portray these figures in one child's drama and as an arrangement of archetypes—the extrovert, the introvert, the neurotypical parent who makes assumptions about "everyone." It's also unclear how much we should take individual pages of *NOS* as individual poems, or potential excerpts, and how much they work as chapters or scenes or paragraph-like elements in the narrative of the whole, as the parents learn to accept their "atypical . . . spouse / childs / falcon / selves," to see how their nonverbal "daughter is a people" (113–14, 140).

NOS is not only a poem but a life narrative, an essay, a memoir, and a moral argument about the framing of disability and about how we view people (including, perhaps, ourselves) who will never display neurotypical subjectivity, people for whom "it is a violence of pronouns to be / he and I and she" (98). Nor is this generic multiplicity (rooted in, but extending very far beyond, its prosimetrum, or mixed format) unique to *NOS*: similar effects drive Emmalea Russo's *Wave Archive*, at once art criticism, lyric sequence, memoir, and study of epilepsy; Julie Carr's *Real Life: An Installation*, diary and gallery-art criticism; and a series of British book-length twenty-first-century poems from Alice Oswald's *Dart* through Robert Minhinnick's *Diary of the Last Man* and Vahni Capildeo's *Measures of Expatriation*, books of verse and prose that are at once lyric expostulations and nonfiction travel writing. Minhinnick's colorful prose poetry, dominated by alliteration, distinguishes itself both from the expository prose of most other travel writers and fiction writers (even the most lyrical) and from the inset verse:

> This is how freshwater tastes. I breathe in its crowbones and its cressbeds, its phenols and its fennels, its foxbloo and its icemelt. Beneath my feet a sweet aquifer has drawn the boundary with salt. Yes, daily its dew, duly its dew, daily is its duty done.
>   Sleet
> out of sunlight and the day
> losing its identity. Now

rostas of mistlethrushes
are called down to the roosts.

How they burn, those barbarians,
for buckthorn berries in their sunset reefs.[13]

Other poets use short works to take advantage of the adjustable page, the possibilities of handwriting and nonstandard printing, the uses of visual form. This line of poets perhaps begins with the alphabet poems and poem-drawings of the Canadian writer bpNichol, but in the twenty-first century it is less a line than a crowd. Ana Carrete, one of the best of the poets to come from the youthful "alt-lit" publishing circles of the mid-2010s, combines a casual immediacy, a multilingual vocabulary, and a set of pages dependent on visual and material form. She's also conscious of her own place amid cultures whose mores and languages and assumptions are changing fast. A love poem called "french kiss you" begins

you need to come to my house because I need to feed you

i'm going to French kiss you Mexican style

whatever that means.

Carrete then continues with apparently unrelated, equally casual, equally intimate language: "I need you to get this / fucking eyelash out of my eye."[14]

Does this sentence come from the same poem? It's the kind of question we can ask about much earlier vernacular manuscripts, and if Carrete's immediate model for that kind of intimate discoherency might be Bernadette Mayer or Ted Berrigan, she goes beyond them in her use of visual form, of ink on paper and characters and letters (not only whole words):

SOY MEXICANA
SOY MEXIC ANA
SOY MEXI C   ANA
SOY C < ANA
SOY ANA > C
SOY ANA
SOY[15]

The page is a puzzle: can she be "Ana" (herself, with her own name) and "Mexicana" at once, or do people (especially non-Mexican and non-Mexican American people) see her as merely a representative of all Spanish-speaking Mexicans? To become greater than (>) the stereotypes, must Carrete fix herself in print, or move at the speed of light (c)?

"Features of the material text," here as in the London, British Library, Harley MS 2253 lyrics discussed by Nelson, "suggest tactics to the voice of performance."[16] Some are features other periods' written or printed lyric rarely or never use: multiple letter sizes, for example, and nonalphanumeric typography, and, in the case of Harley 2253, "holes in the parchment . . . to remind readers of Christ's wounds."[17] Carrete—though her affect is less beguine than teen Goth—uses Zapf Dingbats to similar effect, filling a page and a half with various crosses (the one on the Swiss flag, a crucifix with shading, a Greek Orthodox doubled gross, a dagger, and more), then using the crosses on the succeeding page: "+EENY †INY ‡EENY ±INY."[18] Such effects depend on print (you can't have Zapf Dingbats without Zapf). But they also depend on a style that makes us aware of the letters as letters, the physical pages, and the parts of the poem that in a more conventional printed work would become invisible: the paratext, the physical book, the ink.

You can find other characteristically medievalizing devices all over the work of another twenty-first-century poet, Douglas Kearney, many of whose most ambitious experiments with typography and visual form cannot be reproduced here. Some of the pages in *The Black Automaton* (2009) and in *Patter* (2014) demand to be read both as post-Olsonian poems whose typography and page layout matters and as works of visual art. Kearney's more recent works include prosimetrum and devotional texts that demand completion by engaged readers, among them this deliberately repetitious prose called "incantation":

incantation

So a call for effect: I ask _____. I ask _____. I ask _____. I ask _____. The repeat entreats, endures out a threshold in its and again and again and again. A really really *really* ask "but not only that," the performance of devotion: *I won't stop* since the source of power, the entreatied, doesn't want me to stop "but not only that," the source is boundless and will only answer if it reckons me for kin.[19]

This "performance of devotion" cannot be identical to any that Middle English texts, in prose or verse, demand of their readers, but the same phrase has been applied to exactly what some of those texts solicit.[20] Their insistence on an ongoing participatory present, "I won't stop," and on blanks the reader must repeatedly fill must seem familiar from the private devotions of a pre-Reformation world: it is not verse, but lyricism, the sonically rich use of language to share an emotional world, that Kearney's prose shares with much older work, and the blanks after "I," the attempt at some kinship with power, suggests what Anna Wilson has called "the self-insert imaginative approach to texts," with its "delicate balance that readers had to maintain between entering the text and distorting it."[21]

Other effects among contemporary poets approach those of prosimetrum and of devotional prose in other ways. Consider the meditations of Erika Meitner in "Vicissitudes," one of several that blur the distinction between meditation and diary, and between long-lined verse and short-paragraph prose:

I've been bitten by something that itches (the vicissitudes of daily life?)

I wash the accidental pee off blue sandals

I wash the red clay dust from yellow rain boots . . .

Rabbi Tarfon said it is not your responsibility to finish the work (the dishes in the sink, the knotted plastic bag from daycare)

He also said you are not free to desist from it

When he said "the work" he meant perfecting the world[22]

These resemblances between the contemporary and the Middle English lyric can be found in British and in American verse, but they do not stop there. To take just one example from elsewhere: Ng Yi-Sheng, one of the rising poets of Singapore, got attention in 2017 for *A Book of Hims*. Ng writes in English, but with sustained attention to the multiple languages and cultures of his nation and upbringing, as well as paying attention to his own place near (not at) the start of a national tradition. Ng's "Seven Deadly Ghazals" introduce themselves as a series of twisted proverbs, pieces of orature, concluding with "Ghazal of Pride": "This is the greatest poem in the world. . . . Throw out your Hanshan, Homer and Hafez. / Their ballads with their charming quirks are nothing." Of course the poem rebukes its speaker's sin: "Yi-Sheng, these words too shall be forgotten."[23]

Ng also pens work whose full effect depends on an education in multiple languages and multiple Asian traditions, as in "Chengyu Haiku," whose English haiku stanzas—despite the Japanese origins of the form—speak to parallel stanzas written in Mandarin, constructed out of Chinese classical proverbs: "Before the butcher / harvests your meat and leather," Ng writes, "I give you this song."[24] Is the Chinese, or the English, the "original"? Does Ng write metaphorically to a friend or to a boyfriend or literally to a cow, a bull, a steer? (Is "Foweles in the frith" about Christ, or about a girl?)

But all these texts' similarity to Middle English ones could be coincidental: indeed any one, in isolation, except perhaps Minhinnick with his alliterations, would seem so. I am arguing not just for individual correspondences but for a pattern. Patterns, however, can be coincidences too (as statisticians regularly explain). What cannot be coincidence is a contemporary poet—one who has attracted attention lately—who clearly and deliberately and self-consciously draws on aspects of Middle English, and on the way that Middle English feels to modern readers, as an effect that drives an entire book. That poet is Jos Charles, and her book is *feeld* (2018), and here are the first lines on the first page:

> thees wite skirtes / & orang
> sweters / i wont / inn the feedynge marte /
> wile mye vegetable partes bloome[25]

Charles encodes all manner of multiple meanings through unconventional, medievalizing orthography: Edmund Spenser, James Joyce, and Russell Hoban have done so too, but Charles's word choice and the density of her alternative spellings, along with her portmanteau words and her uses of etymology, ask us explicitly to look back to pre-Reformation, nonstandardized, or noncourtly insular English.

"Translated," as one translates Chaucer for beginners, Charles might be telling us that she wants white skirts and orange sweaters while in a supermarket, selecting ripe vegetables. But her dense, "tactical" language says much

more than that: the clothes that she wants would be "sweeter" than the
clothes she has. Perhaps her "wit" "skirts" larger issues around biology, reproduction, trans identity, what parts of her body, or anyone's body, can
"bloom." On the next page Charles tries "2 curl myeself / inn / thees the
dreggs / the grl beguines": she imitates a medieval religious, but also begins
to become a girl with drugs that are like doctor's eggs ("dreggs"). On the
page after that Charles takes up the trope by which many poets in Middle
English exhort an auditor to pay attention:

> lisen /
> i daye u wil be all ere /
> a ewe alowne / inn a feeld
> off mare / i am oldre /   & the sayme /
> than the naymes u gave / this
> is the corse / a tran /
> a feeld /   a corpse[26]

One day you will be all here, to listen to me, to hear my names, to learn
about this corpse; is the corpse trans? How does being trans feel? How did
it feel ("feeld," as if some nonstandard English made the past tense of "feel"
that way)? One day you (ewe), you too, will be alone; you will bend a low
knee; I will be able to come in, and will not be left outside in a field, as Joseph and Mary found no room at the inn. To "say me" (to say my true name)
I will have to outlive (become older than) the names you gave, names that
also denied my essence ("nay me").

All of Charles's volume works this way: the deeper you go into her orthography, the farther you see what she has become able to do, by analogy
with the way that we already read Middle English—not Old English, not
continental verse in translation, but English from the period when *lyric* work
had no standard orthography, pronunciations varied vastly from region to
region, and modern readers must scrutinize it for multilingual puns, for effects that crop up anew from page to page, manuscript to manuscript, variant
to variant, as well as from poem to poem.

And Charles knew what she wanted to do. She says in one interview that
in beginning *feeld*, she "thought that it would be cool to have some sort of
language"—for trans and queer experience, in particular—"that didn't seek
to situate itself as corrective, nor did it ironically break into incorrectness":
as she began to seek such a language, she asked herself, "What if the Wife

of Bath was trans?"[27] She cites Spenser, both for his idiosyncratic, self-conscious orthography, and for his place in the English Renaissance as a poet who expected silent reading: respelling the words in "text-speak meets Middle English," Charles "wanted to call attention to the words and how they are read and produced—to put the onus on the reader to be aware of their role as a performer."[28] As of 2021, she is working toward a Ph.D. in medieval studies from the University of California, Irvine.

Contemporary poets, then—not all of them, but far more than a handful—come closer, more often, to the effects and to the conundrums posed by Middle English lyric, and by insular medieval verse practice, than most of the verse in English composed and circulated during the several hundred years in between. That proximity crops up both in poets who seem to have come to it by accident, or by convergent evolution, and in poets (like Charles) who use medieval sources deliberately, consistently, and as a matter of research. And these poets—unlike, say, the Pre-Raphaelites, or the early troubadour-obsessed Ezra Pound—gravitate to the same aspects of Middle English composition and performance that attract critical attention now: its sense of being unfixed, new, not quite canonical, all over the place in terms of its potential genres, split between voices, and aware of its material frames, what Ardis Butterfield calls, in the present book, "copying context."[29]

Why would these contemporary poets want to revive or embrace these kinds of (to reuse Nelson's term) tactics? Some answers may already seem evident: the poets of our era have been taught to value openness, partiality, unfixedness, even "subversiveness" (a word I place in scare quotes because its vernacular use in literary criticism has drifted so far from its other modern meanings). Poets now, especially those from multilingual contexts, with heritage languages other than English, come to adulthood in a space where no single mastery can be taken for granted and no single tradition can plausibly represent us, or them. They, or we, also come to maturity radically unsure about our possible audience; who will recognize what allusion, what bilingual pun, what aureate word? Why not use all of them? And why not—in a time when more people read poetry than ever before, but fewer read it primarily in codex books—write poems that call attention to where and how we write and read them?[30]

Finally—though no period of English verse, not even the Augustan, now seems uniform in what poets and readers expected—the juxtaposition of poetry from the 2010s with poetry in Middle English might remind us, as readers and writers and teachers, of truths essential to any decent pedagogy, as well as to reading pleasure. Whether or not we already know what genre in which to place them, what genre their first readers assigned, or whether those readers agreed with one another, poems differ one from another. What they have in common, sometimes all they have in common, lies in their ability to hold our interest through their patterns and sounds.

The study of Middle English lyric—or of short poems that sometimes get called lyric—gives contemporary readers and poets a chance to show how unalike poems from the same period can feel, and how genre terms may guide but cannot confine our experience of individual texts. Religious and secular, amorous and penitential, freestanding and inset, blazon and chanson and incantation: none of these categories account for all the poems that survive from these days, nor does the metacategory "lyric"—useful as it is, transhistorical as it may be—account for some of the period's best poems. Any comprehensive critical approach, any inclusive pedagogy, will have to draw on such chestnuts as "Nou goth sonne" and on the varieties of religious verse described in the present book by Barbara Zimbalist, Margot Fassler, and others. It might well look at devotional practice, at contrafacts and at the evolution of sung performance, as well as at the interplay among insular languages and dialects of those languages (including Scots—and Welsh).

But it should also look at kinds of verse that "do not readily fit into any of the usually recognized categories," as Thomas Duncan put it fifteen years ago: his example—the "Complaint Against Blacksmiths"—would also be my own.[31] That complaint rewards attention not so much for its subtle interiority, nor for its relation to its (single) manuscript, but for its acoustics, which drive its intense feeling, and which benefit from its own orthography:

Þei spyttyn & spraulyn & spellyn many spelles,
. . . .
Heuy hamerys þey han, þat hard ben handled
Stark strokes þey stryken on a stelyd stokke.[32]

These gloriously annoying blacksmiths' blows and their accompanying imprecations at once include speech, and carry meanings, and require interpretations, and permit many orthographic representations, and defy sense, as if they were magical charms. All these senses of "spelle," attested in the *Middle English Dictionary*, might apply to the incessant noise made by these smiths, who at once demand and defy interpretation, and who won't shut up. "Stark strokes they striken on a stelyd stokke," as if they were engravers inscribing letters and representations, though they are not: they are louder, and harsher, than that, and they are the cause of poems, rather than authors themselves. Those "swarte smekyd smethes" and their disgruntled neighbor are no basis on which to construct a unified theory of the lyric, nor a theory of devotion, nor a model of copying and textuality. And yet they belong in the body of work that we read and teach, the body of work available to con- temporary poets, alongside appeals to Christ, to lovers, to Mary, beside "Summe men sayoun" and Chaucer's complaint to his purse.

They belong in that body—as Ana Carrete and Robert Minhinnick and Jos Charles, to my mind, belong in the body of contemporary poetry that we examine and teach and enjoy—because they arrange sound in ways that form memorable patterns, and also because those arrangements trouble or take apart the categories we may bring to them. Sometimes they are—and I'll end on this point—direct imitations of a material world, with an unpre- dictable relation to the materiality of their own reproduction. The complaint against blacksmiths is, famously, marginalia, and it's tempting—though it may also go too far—to liken the literally marginal status of so much medi- eval lyric to the "marginal" status of poets and poetry, "living on the margin," as Ashbery says self-mockingly in "Soonest Mended," "in our technological society," "always having to be rescued."[33]

Perhaps marginal status lends itself to experiment, or to medium- specificity, since marginal poems do not need to be copied widely, memo- rized, held up as exemplary, in the way that culturally central works (in our time, perhaps Hollywood film; in earlier times, some poems, some sermons) do. This marginal status, too, links Middle English lyric to contemporary printed or written poems and distinguishes both from the poetry of periods (say, the Romantic) when poetry in English seemed, to readers of English, central. What survives, again, is what's unpredictable and yet patterned about the language and its delivery—and what's available, to us and to our future, in distinctively mediated patterns of sound.

New Medieval Lyrics

A Chapbook

Hank McCoy's Complaint Against the Danger Room
Stephanie Burt

Many merry mutants, mauling with metal
Force me to flee their fists and their fights:
Such scraps stop my sleeping and sour my mind.
What voices like villains at vengeful volume!
Telekinetics toss tables and tangle
And our weather worker sends wind against walls.
Snikt snikt! sounds one, snarling; another sends snow
And hail at high speed upon hostile heads;
One goes bamf! and bamf! bouncing on his blue heels.
They skirmish and scrape and they spar and keep score;
They fly and they fling their friends like fastballs
And warn our winged man, "Whoa! out of the way!"
With lasers and leaping and loud metal loads,
They strike and they stretch their strong limbs of steel
And drive into dregs many droids and drones.
The Danger Room doesn't go dark for one day!
Professor X should explain these exertions
Training his tyros at twelve and at ten.
My live-in lab allows me little latitude:
I can't concentrate with their cannonball crashes,
Their blasts and their blams!, great blows that draw blood,
Still slam in my ears. I can't slip back to sleep.
I can't stand such stress. O my stars and garters!
Maybe Magneto can make them go mute.
If those callow kids won't cool off or calm down,
I'll move myself out of the mansion this month
And join the Avengers. Avoid the X-Men!

margerykempething 22
Pattie McCarthy

> your grammar has driven me outdoors   first
> margery kempe told her book to her son
> but it was *neithyr good englysch ne dewch*
> the letters *ne formyd as other letters ben*
> the use of characters no one could read
> no one but her son   one supposes   so
> the son made a beautiful illegible book
> because everyone's mother is incomprehensible
> we shared this mess   a sweet bird's voice in her
> ear singing   the wrong bird in the wrong season
> this creature illiterate did not notice
> her son's strange invented letters   bottom-
> to-top formation   spiegelschrift impatience
> burn what letters you have in my hand

The Word Water
Hunter Keough

evaporates
from the throat
in a breath as hot
as a branding
iron, as desperate
as Hell, arouses
our bodies somewhere
into God. What is
the world waiting for
& what are we?
Purveyors of the flood,
fools among the stars
trapped in buckets
of our own human
beliefs? We always
appear to be kissing
arses in the dark,
searching among
false gods for our
Lord. I beckon
Heaven's glisten
of oceans
from the night.
Perhaps we should
consider a different
view of salvation.
Not being saved
from ruin, but
knowing faith
will find our way.

A Trinity-Riddle
Carter Revard

I spread, descending,   a samite of stars.
White fingers bring me   for breakfast Mont Blanc,
and I develop   on earth's negative
the prints proving   a presence absent.
Rainbow-dancing,   my restless soft-self
teaches the sun at   his summer turn to
reprise in dawn-prisms   the light-praise of plants,
or stars in winter   the still song-homes
with brittle jewels   dropped bright from darkness,
or shifts my shape to   a shimmering self-trap.
NOW Speak, if you spy it,   the spECIal name
I bear in spring when   I baRE TAWdry alleys
to wear till dawn night-diamonds,   till dusk the jewel of time.

when I left my second husband
(*from* "3 poems for Saint Æthelthryth")
Kate Caoimhe Arthur

I did not know where I was going
lost acres where my mind froze
the sun in my eyes while I drove
for miles over sun-buckled roads
not registering the settlements

the haystacks looked like shelter
I couldn't stop   all I know is I drove north

when we first met   he was a boy really
it wasn't the case that as he grew
he wanted me
when he knew he couldn't have me
he wanted me
the more I tried to leave the greater his desire

it wasn't so much that I didn't want him
as I had somewhere else to be
in my own flesh
I wouldn't say it felt good to leave
but I was myself in my own body

what if I had stayed? I'd have been
another good fenland wife and mother

I know that by holding my body back
in life I would be free
in death I would be a dwelling
I kept it for myself

I walked alone for miles
back to the only thing I
wanted for my own   I
never saw a man   I
never saw god   but god saw me

I am a wonder to behold
Bill Manhire

I am a wonder to behold
I lift and hold
I lift and hold

I stand yet move from side to side
I reach you with a single stride

I reach and arch
I reach and arch
I feel the soldiers when they march

I am the hope on which you cross.
if you lose me, you are lost

I swing and sway
I swing and sway
I hear the children when they play

I am the hope on which you cross
if you lose me, you are lost

Notes from March and April 2020
Miller Wolf Oberman

1. Given that lyrics are made up categories, as Virginia Jackson defines them in the Princeton doorstopper, as always already a description of a music we can no longer hear, ghosts of ghosts. And given that so much of it is conventional. I find myself drawn to bits that *sound* lyrical to me. How-to's, recipes. Part of lyric charm is that sense that something is beautiful and meaningful in a way that may reveal itself over time, or is nearly accidental. MS Sloane 73, containing *Early English Artistic Recipes* is a great example of this. Here half-translated by me.

> Folio 138v
> Here it techith how that shalt make good vermyloun to alle
>   manner preves where thu wolt.
>
> Take a pound of quyk silver, and a v. ij of quyk brimstone and put
> it in a pot of earth, and look that the pot have a wide mouth that
> you might see all to the bottom and look that you have a lid of tree,
> upon the pots mouth, well closed, and then set it on a few (coolis?)
> and always have thin y3e(??) into the pot and stir it otherwhile and
> when you see the light (flash of fire!) fly out of the pot, anoon smat
> adoun the lid and hold down the lid ij or iij times.

> Folio 215
> For to make glass nesche (soft) [n.b. I'm translating this but
>   doesn't "nesche" sound so much softer than "soft"? Let's bring
>   this one back]
>
> Take the goat's blood, look, and the juice of senevey (mustard?) and
> boil them well together and with the two matters boil well the glass
> and the glass shall become nesche as past, and if it be cast again it
> shall not break.

2. Some re-ordered and mangled and at times purposeful mis-readings of Harley lyrics. Harley, I just can't with anything about women, with you. No patience for all these fanciful layers of cis-hetness and romance or the possibility of tongue in cheek critique of romance, of women, of the form itself.

Maybe tomorrow I will find something in it, but not today. It is not the April
for courtly love, maybe it never was. This is made like these days, in the brief
silences between sirens. Brief flashes of taking it all head on, long looks away,
salvaging of sound and rhythm, salvaging of the shape of words and the space
they take.

> Erþe toc of erþe erþe wyþ woh.
> Erþe oþer erþe to þe erþe droh.
> Erþe leyde erþe in erþene þroh.
> þo heuede erþe of erþe erþe ynoh

> Earth talk of earth, earth with woe
> Earth other earth to the earth draw
> Earth lead earth in earthen throw/through
> though heaved/heavied earth of earth, earth enough/you know

> When it comes in my thought
> of this world's joys how it goes all to not
> now it is and now it's not.
> Also it near never was

> A whale white as a whale's bone
> a green in gold that goldly shone
> a turtle that my heart is on

> That all the woods ring
> the rose, the rails we rode
> the leaves on the light woods
> the white in the wood is flame

What the Eagle Fan Says

For the Voelkers, the Besses, and all the Dancers.

Carter Revard

> I strung dazzling thrones   of thunder beings
> on a spiraling thread   of spinning flight,
> beading dawn's blood   and blue of noon
> to the gold and dark   of day's leaving,
> circling with Sun   the soaring heaven
> over turquoise eyes   of Earth below,
> her silver veins,   her sable fur,
> heard human relatives   hunting below
> calling me down,   crying their need
> that I bring them closer   to Wakonda's ways,
> and I turned from heaven   to help them then.
> When the bullet came,   it caught my heart,
> the hunter's hands   gave earth its blood,
> loosed our light beings,   let us float
> toward the sacred center   of song in the drum,
> but fixed us first   firm in song-home
> that green light-dancers   gave to men's knives,
> ash-heart in hiding where   deer-heart had beat,
> and a one-eyed serpent   with silver-straight head
> strung tiny rattles   around white softness
> in beaded harmonies   of blue and red—
> lightly I move now   in a man's left hand,
> above dancing feet   follow the sun
> around old songs   soaring toward heaven
> on human breath,   and I help them rise.

Credits

"Hank McCoy's Complaint Against the Danger Room" appears in the chapbook *For All Mutants* (Rain Taxi, 2021) and is printed with the permission of Stephanie Burt.

"margerykempething 22," by Pattie McCarthy, first appeared in *wifthing* (2021). Reprinted with the permission of Apogee Press.

"The Word Water" is printed with the permission of Hunter Keough.

"A Trinity-Riddle" first appeared in *Winning the Dust Bowl* (2001), by Carter Revard. © 2001 Carter Revard. Reprinted by permission of the University of Arizona Press.

"when I left my second husband," by Kate Caoimhe Arthur, first appeared in *Blackbox Manifold* 25 (2020). Reprinted with the permission of Blackbox.

"I am a wonder to behold," by Bill Manhire, first appeared in *Tell Me My Name* (2017). Reprinted with the permission of Victoria University of Wellington Press.

"Notes from March and April 2020" is printed with the permission of Miller Wolf Oberman.

"What the Eagle Fan Says" was first published in *An Eagle Nation*, by Carter Revard. © 1993 Carter C. Revard. Reprinted by permission of the University of Arizona Press.

Notes

1. *Layamon: Brut; Edited from British Museum MS. Cotton Caligula A. IX and British Museum MS. Cotton Otho C. XIII*, ed. G. L. Brook and R. F. Leslie, EETS, o.s., 250 (London: Oxford University Press, 1963), lines 3488–95. Layamon's account draws on Wace's insular French *Roman de Brut* (ca. 1170), which itself draws on Geoffrey of Monmouth's *Historia regum Britanniae* (*History of the Kings of Britain*, ca. 1140). In Geoffrey's mythical history, which was vastly influential well into the modern era, Blæðgabreat (= Blegabret) is fifty-sixth in the line established by Brutus and Ignoge of the royal house of Troy (descendants of Lavinia and Aeneas, respectively), tenth in line before Lud III, founder of London, whose successor, Cassibellaun, is king at the time of Julius Caesar's invasion in 55 BCE. Although the imagined dates are not ascertainable, he therefore lives perhaps five hundred years after King Lear and his three daughters. See the helpful family tree in J. A. Giles, ed., *Galfredi Monumetensis historia Britonum: Nunc primum in Anglia, novem codd. msstis collatis* (London: Nutt, 1844), xix–xxvi.

2. "Gleomen" translates Wace's "jugleors" (rhymed with "chanteurs"), which translates Geoffrey of Monmouth's "ioculatores." See Wace, *Roman de Brut: A History of the British; Text and Translation*, ed. and trans. Judith Weiss (Exeter: Exeter University Press, 1999), lines 3705–6; Geoffrey of Monmouth, *The History of the Kings of Britain*, ed. Michael D. Reeve, trans. Neil Wright (Woodbridge, Suffolk: Boydell Press, 2007), 3.360.

3. Geoffrey Chaucer, *The House of Fame*, lines 1201–13. Quotations from Chaucer are from *The Riverside Chaucer*, gen. ed. Larry D. Benson, 3rd ed. (Boston: Houghton Mifflin, 1987).

4. John Capgrave, *The Life of St. Norbert by John Capgrave, O.E.S.A. (1393–1464)*, ed. Cyril Lawrence Smetana (Toronto: Pontifical Institute of Mediaeval Studies, 1977), p. 36, lines 404–5.

5. See Isidore of Seville, *Etymologies* 8.7.4, on "lyric poets" (written ca. 630 CE): "4. "Lyric (*lyricus*) poets are named after the Greek term ληρεῖν (lit. 'speak trifles') that is, from the variety of their songs. Hence also the lyre (*lyra*) is named"; quoted from *The "Etymologies" of Isidore of Seville*, trans. Stephen A. Barney et al. (Cambridge: Cambridge University Press, 2006), 180.

6. Raymond Gibbs, Jr., "Cognitive Poetics of Middle English Lyric Poetry," this volume (Chapter 6).

7. Chaucer, prologue to "The Reeve's Tale," in *The Canterbury Tales*, frag. 1, lines 3857–58. Although there is some overlap, by "pley" we do not intend a totalizing Bakhtinian or Marxist sense of the "carnivalesque," which undergirds a model of the medieval period as "other" from modernity we are concerned to avoid.

8. Robert Mannyng, *Robert of Brunne's "Handlyng Synne,"* ed. Frederick J. Furnivall, EETS, o.s., 119 (London: Kegan Paul, Trench, Trübner, 1901), p. 287, line 9156.

9. Chaucer, "The Parson's Prologue," *Canterbury Tales*, frag. 10, lines 46–47.

10. Mannyng, *Handlyng Synne*, line 9117. For Mannyng's judgment of the priest's behavior, see lines 10895–912.

11. Some recent ones in Middle English lyric studies are surveyed by Julia Boffey and Christiania Whitehead in the introduction to *Middle English Lyrics: New Readings of Short Poems* (Cambridge: D. S. Brewer, 2018), where they address, in particular: voice, the formal and material turns in medieval literary studies, affect, performativity, figuration, music, and manuscript context (1–11). For a somewhat parallel discussion of the current situation in early Greek lyric, see David Fearn, "Greek Lyric of the Archaic and Classical Periods: From the Past to the Future of the Lyric Subject," *Classical Poetry* 1 (2020): 1–113.

12. The first use of "Middle English lyric" as a categorizing term was by Frederic Ives Carpenter in *An Outline Guide to the Study of English Lyric Poetry* (Chicago: University of Chicago, 1897), 6–9. The phrase became established in the 1920s. It is thus not used directly by John Edwin Wells in his *Manual of the Writings in Middle English, 1050–1400* (New Haven: Connecticut Academy of Arts and Sciences, 1916), whose chapter on short poems is instead entitled "Poems Lyrical in Impulse or in Form" (p. 485). Other ways to think about the process of reading Middle English lyrics are highlighted in this volume: Cristina Maria Cervone, "Wondering Through Middle English Lyric" (Chapter 2); Ingrid Nelson, "Lyric Value" (Chapter 5); Andrew Albin, "The Sound of Rollean Lyric" (Chapter 8); Barbara Zimbalist, "The Lyric Christ" (Chapter 9); and others. Eleanor Johnson's characterization of Middle English lyrics as "a body of poetic works that invite and reward certain mental operations and strategies of thought" is especially apt ("How Middle English Lyrics Make Us Think: Song as Devotional Memory," paper presented at the advanced seminar on "What Kind of a Thing Is a Middle English Lyric?" at the Radcliffe Institute for Advanced Study, Harvard University, December 1, 2016).

13. See Ardis Butterfield, "Lyric Editing," this volume (Chapter 1); Christopher Cannon, "Lyric Romance," this volume (Chapter 3); Nelson, "Lyric Value." The term "close" also began to be used to describe a mode of reading between the 1890s and the 1920s. For the emergence of the pedagogical philosophy underlying the practice, see Jesse Cordes Selbin, "'Read with Attention': John Cassell, John Ruskin, and the History of Close Reading," *Victorian Studies* 58, no. 3 (2016): 493–521.

14. See, e.g., George Puttenham, *The Arte of English Poesie* (London: Richard Field, 1589), STC [Short Title Catalog] 20519.5, 1.11: "Others who more delighted to write songs or ballads of pleasure, to be song with the voice, and to the harpe, lute, or citheron, and such other, musical, instruments, they were called melodious Poets [*melici*] or by a more common name *Lirique* Poets, of which sort was *Pindarus, Anacreon*, and *Callimachus* with others among the Greeks: *Horace* and *Catullus* among the Latines." For a modernized critical edition, see *The Art of English Poesy: A Critical Edition*, ed. Frank Whigham and Wayne A. Rebhorn (Ithaca, NY: Cornell University Press, 2007), quotation at p. 115. Puttenham's sources include Isidore's *Etymologies* (note 5 above).

15. *The Oxford English Dictionary Online* (*OED*), s.v. "lyric, adj. and n." Most of this entry derives from *A New English Dictionary on Historical Principles: Founded Mainly on the Materials Collected by the Philological Society*, vol. 6, part 1, ed. James A. H. Murray and Henry Bradley (Oxford: Clarendon Press, 1908), s.v. "lyric." So, too, does the word's primary definition: "the name for short poems (whether or not intended to be sung), usually divided into

stanzas or strophes, and directly expressing the poet's own thoughts and sentiments." As the examples given in the entry show, in 1908 this meaning of the word, partly developed under the influence of a tripartite division of poetry into lyric, narrative, and dramatic in German Romanticism, was still well under a hundred years old. For the history of this division, see Gérard Genette, *The Architext: An Introduction*, trans. Jane E. Lewin (Berkeley: University of California Press, 1992), 1–72. For ancient and modern genre theory and medieval literature, see Hans Robert Jauss, *Towards an Aesthetic of Reception*, trans. Timothy Bahti (Minneapolis: University of Minnesota Press, 1982), 76–109.

16. See below: Butterfield, "Lyric Editing"; Margot Fassler, "The Religious Lyric in Medieval England (1150–1400): Three Disciplines and a Question," this volume (Chapter 10). See also Ardis Butterfield and Helen Deeming, "Editing Insular Song Across the Disciplines: Worldes Blis," in *Probable Truth: Editing Medieval Texts from Britain in the Twenty-First Century*, ed. Vincent Gillespie and Anne Hudson (Turnhout: Brepols, 2013), 151–66; John Hall and David Prior, "Towards Song: Shaping Spoken Lyric," *Performance Research* 23, no. 2 (2018): 100–106.

17. The quoted positions are taken by Stephanie Burt, Jonathan Culler, and Virginia Jackson, respectively. Stephanie [Stephen] Burt, "What Is This Thing Called Lyric?," *Modern Philology* 113, no. 3 (2016): 422–40; Jonathan Culler, *Theory of the Lyric* (Cambridge, MA: Harvard University Press, 2015); Virginia Jackson, *Dickinson's Misery: A Theory of Lyric Reading* (Princeton: Princeton University Press, 2005), Virginia Jackson, "Lyric," in *The Princeton Encyclopedia of Poetry and Poetics*, 4th ed., ed. Roland Greene and Stephen Cushman (Princeton, NJ: Princeton University Press, 2012), 826–34. See also Ricardo Matthews, "Song in Reverse: The Medieval Prosimetrum and Lyric Theory," *PMLA* 133, no. 2 (2018): 296–313; and Virginia Jackson, "Response: Old Lyric Things," this volume (Chapter 12), who continues the debate and notes the allusion in Burt's title to that of the two Radcliffe seminars from which this book developed, which took place in 2015 and 2016 respectively, at the height of the "New Lyric Studies" controversy.

18. For these terms and their valence, see Sandeep Parmar, "Still Not a British Subject: Race and UK Poetry," *Journal of British and Irish Innovative Poetry* 12, no. 1 (2020), https://doi.org/10.16995/bip.3384, and references there. Parmar's wide-ranging and important essay includes a discussion of some ways in which experiences and concerns of poets and critics of color from the United Kingdom and the United States may differ, including with regard to "the lyric I."

19. See Jahan Ramazani, *Poetry in a Global Age* (Chicago: University of Chicago Press, 2020), esp. 230–50; we extend to the study of Middle English lyric Ramazani's caution that "poetry studies, even if historically and linguistically centered, [should not] be overly restrictive in its scope. Even as it stays attuned to local histories and specific languages, the field also needs to draw inspiration from, and contribute to, world literary studies, global studies, transnational studies, world anglophone studies, and postcolonial studies, if it's to prosper in the coming decades" (249–50).

20. Douglas Mao, "The New Critics and the Text-Object," *English Literary History* 63, no. 1 (1996): 227–54. See also Cleanth Brooks, *The Well Wrought Urn: Studies in the Structure of Poetry* (New York: Reynal and Hitchcock, 1947).

21. The "object/thing" dichotomy here notices but is not closely related to the Heideggerian one made famous by Bill Brown in *The Sense of Things: The Object Matter of American Literature* (Chicago: University of Chicago Press, 2004).

22. Seth Lerer, "The Genre of the Grave and the Origins of the Middle English Lyric," *Modern Language Quarterly* 58, no. 2 (1997): 127–61; Ardis Butterfield, "Why Medieval

Lyric?," *English Literary History* 82, no. 2 (2015): 319–43; Ingrid Nelson, *Lyric Tactics: Poetry, Genre, and Practice in Late Medieval England* (Philadelphia: University of Pennsylvania Press, 2017).

23. Bernard J. Muir, ed., *The Exeter Anthology of Old English Poetry: An Edition of Exeter Dean and Chapter MS 3501*, 2nd ed. (Exeter: University of Exeter Press, 2000). On early song in western continental Europe, see John Haines, *Medieval Song in Romance Languages* (Cambridge: Cambridge University Press, 2010).

24. Karl Breul, ed., *The Cambridge Songs: A Goliard's Songbook of the Eleventh Century* (Cambridge: Cambridge University Press, 1915).

25. The poems of Baudri de Bourgeoil are collected in Vatican City, Biblioteca Apostolica Vaticana, MS Reg.lat. 1351, https://digi.vatlib.it/view/MSS_Reg.lat.1351. See Jean-Yves Tilliette, "Note sur le manuscrit des poèmes de Baudri de Bourgueil (Vatican, Reg. Lat. 1351)," *Scriptorium* 37 (1983): 241–45.

26. Marisa Galvez, *Songbook: How Lyrics Became Poetry in Medieval Europe* (Chicago: Chicago University Press, 2012); Sarah Kay, *Parrots and Nightingales: Troubadour Quotations and the Development of European Poetry* (Philadelphia: University of Pennsylvania Press, 2013); Catherine A. McKenna, *The Medieval Welsh Religious Lyric: Poems of the Gogynfeirdd, 1137–1282* (Belmont, MA: Ford and Bailie, 1991); Howard Mayer Brown, "Chansonnier (i)," *Grove Music Online* (2001), https://doi.org/10.1093/gmo/9781561592630.article.05412. The great Welsh lyric book is Aberystwyth, National Library of Wales, MS 6680B, the Hendregadredd Manuscript (mid-fourteenth century), https://www.library.wales/discover/digital-gallery/manuscripts/the-middle-ages/hendregadredd-manuscript.

27. Edinburgh, National Library of Scotland, MS Advocates' 18.7.21. See Edward Wilson, *A Descriptive Index of the English Lyrics in John of Grimestone's Preaching Book* (Oxford: Basil Blackwell, 1973); Andrew Galloway, "Theory of the Fourteenth-Century English Lyric," this volume (Chapter 11).

28. Susanna Fein, ed. and trans., *The Complete Harley 2253 Manuscript*, with David Raybin and Jan Ziolkowski, 3 vols. (Kalamazoo, MI: Medieval Institute Publications for TEAMS, 2014–15); Carter Revard, "Scribe and Provenance," in *Studies in the Harley Manuscript: The Scribes, Contents, and Social Contexts of British Library MS Harley 2253*, ed. Susanna Fein (Kalamazoo, MI: Medieval Institute Publications, 2000), 21–109. See also Daniel Birkholz, *Harley Manuscript Geographies: Literary History and the Medieval Miscellany* (Manchester: Manchester University Press, 2020).

29. John Frankis, "The Social Context of Vernacular Writing in Thirteenth-Century England: The Evidence of the Manuscripts," in *Thirteenth Century England I: Proceedings of the Newcastle upon Tyne Conference, 1985*, ed. Peter R. Coss and S. D. Lloyd (Woodbridge, Suffolk: Boydell Press, 1986), 175–84. For the collection most similar to Harley, see Susanna Fein, ed., *Interpreting MS Digby 86: A Trilingual Book from Thirteenth-Century Worcestershire* (York: York Medieval Press, 2019).

30. Wendy Scase, ed., *A Facsimile Edition of the Vernon Manuscript: Oxford, Bodleian Library, MS. Eng. Poet. A. 1* (Oxford: Bodleian Library, 2011); Carl Horstmann and F. J. Furnivall, eds., *The Minor Poems of the Vernon MS.*, 2 vols., EETS, o.s., 98 and 117 (London: Kegan Paul, Trench, Trübner, 1892, 1901); Wendy Scase, ed., *The Making of the Vernon Manuscript: The Production and Contexts of Oxford, Bodleian Library, MS Eng. poet. a. 1* (Turnhout: Brepols, 2013). See also the sixteen short poems known as the "Kildare lyrics" (early fourteenth century), in Thorlac Turville-Petre, ed., *Poems from BL MS Harley 913: "The Kildare Manuscript,"* EETS, o.s., 345 (Oxford: Oxford University Press, 2015).

31. Cannon, "Lyric Romance," 88–91.

32. Susanna Greer Fein, "Twelve-Line Stanza Forms in Middle English and the Date of *Pearl*," *Speculum* 72, no. 2 (1997): 367–98.

33. See Matthew Evan Davis, "Lydgate at Long Melford: Reassessing the Testament and 'Quis Dabit Meo Capiti Fontem Lacrimarum,' in Their Local Context," *Journal of Medieval Religious Cultures* 43, no. 1 (2017): 77–114; Cristina Maria Cervone, "John de Cobham and Cooling Castle's Charter Poem," *Speculum* 83, no. 4 (2008): 884–916. See also Cervone, "Wondering Through Middle English Lyric"; Aden Kumler, "Lyric Vessels," this volume (Chapter 7); Galloway, "Theory of the Fourteenth-Century English Lyric."

34. Julia Boffey, "What to Call a Lyric? Middle English Lyrics and Their Manuscript Titles," *Revue belge de philologie et d'histoire* 83, no. 3 (2005): 671–83; Cristina Maria Cervone, "'I' and 'We' in Chaucer's *Complaint unto Pity*," in *Readings in Medieval Textuality: Essays in Honour of A. C. Spearing* (Cambridge: D. S. Brewer, 2016), 195–212.

35. *Songes and Sonettes* (London: Richard Tottel, 1557), STC 13860.

36. Published in Richard Leighton Greene, ed., *The Early English Carols*, 2nd ed., rev. and enl. (Oxford: Clarendon Press, 1977).

37. London, British Library, Harley MS 682, http://www.bl.uk/manuscripts/FullDisplay .aspx?ref=Harley_MS_682. See Mary-Jo Arn, ed., *Fortunes Stabilnes: Charles of Orléans's English Book of Love; A Critical Edition* (Binghamton, NY: Medieval and Renaissance Texts and Studies, 1994).

38. Richard Beadle and A. E. B. Owen, eds., *The Findern Manuscript: Cambridge University Library MS Ff.i.6* (London: Scolar Press, 1978); Sarah McNamer, "Female Authors, Provincial Settings: The Re-versing of Courtly Love in the Findern Manuscript," *Viator* 22 (1991): 279–310; Frederick J. Furnivall, ed., *Political, Religious, and Love Poems*, EETS, o.s., 15 (London: Kegan Paul, Trench, Trübner, 1866; reedited, 1903).

39. Helen Barr, ed., *The Digby Poems: A New Edition of the Lyrics* (Exeter: University of Exeter Press, 2009); John the Blind Audelay, *Poems and Carols (Oxford, Bodleian Library MS Douce 302)*, ed. Susanna Fein (Kalamazoo, MI: Medieval Institute Publications for TEAMS, 2009).

40. See Fassler, "Religious Lyric."

41. Jocelyn Wogan-Browne et al., eds., *Language and Culture in Medieval Britain: The French of England, c.1100–c.1500* (York: York Medieval Press, 2009); Ardis Butterfield, *The Familiar Enemy: Chaucer, Language, and Nation in the Hundred Years War* (Oxford: Oxford University Press, 2009). For an exception, see John Gower, *The French Balades*, ed. and trans. R. F. Yeager (Kalamazoo, MI: Medieval Institute Publications for TEAMS, 2011).

42. Butterfield, *Familiar Enemy*, 269–348; Nicholas Watson, *Balaam's Ass: Vernacular Theology Before the English Reformation*, vol. 2, *French 1100–1400, English 1250–1540* (Philadelphia: University of Pennsylvania Press, forthcoming), chaps. 8 and 9.

43. Richard Foster Jones, *The Triumph of the English Language: A Survey of Opinions Concerning the Vernacular from the Introduction of Printing to the Restoration* (Stanford, CA: Stanford University Press, 1953); David Lawton, "Dullness and the Fifteenth Century," *English Literary History* 54, no. 4 (1987): 761–99; Jocelyn Wogan-Browne, Nicholas Watson, Andrew Taylor, and Ruth Evans, eds., *The Idea of the Vernacular: An Anthology of Middle English Literary Theory, 1280–1520* (University Park: Pennsylvania State University Press, 1999).

44. John Lydgate, *The Siege of Thebes*, ed. Robert R. Edwards (Kalamazoo, MI: Medieval Institute Publications for TEAMS, 2001), line 40; John Dryden, *Fables ancient and modern translated into verse from Homer, Ovid, Boccace, & Chaucer, with Original poems, by Mr. Dryden* (London: Jacob Tonson, 1700), preface, sig. B2r; Megan L. Cook, *The Poet and*

the Antiquaries: Chaucerian Scholarship and the Rise of Literary History, 1532–1635 (Philadelphia: University of Pennsylvania Press, 2019).

45. Thomas Percy, *Reliques of Ancient English Poetry: Consisting of Old Heroic Ballads, Songs, and other Pieces of our Earlier Poets*, 3 vols. (London: J. Dodsley, 1765); Thomas Chatterton, *The Rowley Poems by Thomas Chatterton: Reprinted from Tyrwhitt's Third Edition*, ed. Maurice Evan Hare (Oxford: Clarendon Press, 1911); Maureen N. McLane and Laura M. Slatkin, "British Romantic Homer: Oral Tradition, 'Primitive Poetry' and the Emergence of Comparative Poetics in Britain, 1760–1830," *English Literary History* 78, no. 3 (2011): 687–714; Chris Jones, *Strange Likeness: The Use of Old English in Twentieth-Century Poetry* (Oxford: Oxford University Press, 2006); Chris Jones, *Fossil Poetry: Anglo-Saxon and Linguistic Nativism in Nineteenth-Century Poetry* (Oxford: Oxford University Press, 2018).

46. Elizabeth Fay, *Romantic Medievalism: History and the Romantic Literary Ideal* (New York: Palgrave, 2002).

47. Tom Scott, *Seeven poems o Maister Francis Villon, made owre intil scots bi Tom Scott* (Tunbridge Wells, Kent: Pound Press, 1953); Pattie McCarthy, *bk of (h)rs* (Berkeley, CA: Apogee Press, 2002); Caroline Bergvall, *Meddle English* (New York: Nightboat Books Callicoon, 2011); Julian T. Brolaski, *Gowanus Atropolis* (Brooklyn, NY: Ugly Duckling Presse, 2011); Miller Wolf Oberman, *The Unstill Ones: Poems* (Princeton, NJ: Princeton University Press, 2017); Jos Charles, *feeld* (Minneapolis: Milkweed, 2018); among others.

48. John Lydgate, *Lydgate's Fall of Princes*, ed. Henry Bergen, vol. 1, EETS, e.s. [extra series], 121 (London: Oxford University Press, 1924), book 1, line 252; Frederic Ives Carpenter, *English Lyric Poetry, 1500–1700* (London: Blackie and Son; New York: Charles Scribner's Sons, 1897), xxxii.

49. See Galloway, "Theory of the Fourteenth-Century English Lyric."

50. The point can be extended to poetics, as A. C. Spearing points out: "Chaucer invoked . . . European tradition in a famous passage near the end of *Troilus and Criseyde*, a poem more apostrophic than any earlier work in English, and one that incorporates the first English version of a lyric by Petrarch. Sending his little book out into the world and into posterity, he tells it to be subject to 'alle poesye' (V 1790)—all poetry, the European tradition as he knew and imagined it, stretching back into the classical past and forward into a possible future, 'literature' considered as a single whole" ("Middle English Lyrics, Lyrics in Narratives, and 'Who Made This Song?,'" paper written for the advanced seminar on "What Kind of a Thing Is a Middle English Lyric?" at the Radcliffe Institute for Advanced Study, Harvard University, December 2, 2016).

51. Ian Cornelius, "Language and Meter," this volume (Chapter 4); Eric Weiskott, *English Alliterative Verse: Poetic Tradition and Literary History* (Cambridge: Cambridge University Press, 2016).

52. Chaucer, "Prologue to Sir Thopas," *Canterbury Tales*, frag. 7, lines 694–95, 703.

53. See Stephanie Burt, "Response: Hevy Hameres," this volume (Chapter 13).

54. *Pearl*, ed. Ad Putter and Myra Stokes, in *The Works of the Gawain Poet: Pearl, Cleanness, Patience, Sir Gawain and the Green Knight* (London: Penguin Books, 2014), lines 929 and 749–52.

55. Alastair Minnis, *Medieval Theory of Authorship: Scholastic Literary Attitudes in the Later Middle Ages*, 2nd ed. (Philadelphia: University of Pennsylvania Press, 2012), 16. For the works of Aristotle mentioned in this paragraph and their place within his philosophical system, with bibliography, see Robin Smith, "Aristotle's Logic," *Stanford Encyclopedia of Philosophy* (2000,

rev. 2017: https://plato.stanford.edu/entries/aristotle-logic/). See also *Cicero's Topica*, ed. Tobias Reinhardt (Oxford: Oxford University Press, 2006).

56. Minnis, *Medieval Theory of Authorship*, 9–39; Andrea Falcon, "Aristotle on Causality," *Stanford Encyclopedia of Philosophy* (2006 rev. 2019: https://plato.stanford.edu/entries/aristotle-causality/). F. A. J. de Haas, Mariska Leunissen, and Marije Martijn, eds., *Interpreting Aristotle's "Posterior Analytics" in Late Antiquity and Beyond* (Leiden: Brill, 2011), surveys the early history of textual reception, including the influence of Arabic commentaries on Latin Christian scholarship (pp. x–xx).

57. For the intricacies of the "categories," or "predicaments," in Aristotle's system and medieval scholarship (twelfth to fourteenth centuries), see Paul Studtmann, "Aristotle's Categories" (2007, rev. 2021) and Jorge Gracia and Lloyd Newton, "Medieval Theories of the Categories" (2006, rev. 2012), both in *Stanford Encyclopedia of Philosophy*. (https://plato.stanford.edu/entries/aristotle-categories/; https://plato.stanford.edu/entries/medieval-categories/). Again, Arabic commentaries were an important influence on later Latin Christian scholarship.

58. Kumler, "Lyric Vessels," 217.

59. Hugh of St. Victor, *On the Sacraments of the Christian Faith (De sacramentis)*, trans. Roy J. Deferrari (Cambridge, MA: Medieval Academy of America, 1951), book 1, prol. sect. 2, 3. While the Christian historiographic theory in play here ("supercession") is sometimes used aggressively, even violently, by medieval Christian theologians, Hugh emphasizes the continuity between the Old and New Law. On supercession, see John J. O'Keefe and R. R. Reno, *Sanctified Vision: An Introduction to Early Christian Interpretation of the Bible* (Baltimore: Johns Hopkins University Press, 2005), 69–88.

60. *The Didascalicon of Hugh of Saint Victor: A Medieval Guide to the Arts*, trans. Jerome Taylor, Records of Western Civilization (New York: Columbia University Press, 1961).

61. Burt, "Response: Hevy Hameres," this volume (Chapter 13), 355.

62. It is a suitable symmetry that many of our contributors discuss the medieval carol, a communal ring dance as well as a song.

63. Dante Alighieri, *Paradiso*, ed. Giorgio Petrocchi, trans. Charles S. Singleton (Princeton, NJ: Princeton University Press, 1980), canto 33, line 142.

64. David Burnley, "Lexis and Semantics," in *The Cambridge History of the English Language*, vol. 2, *1066–1476*, ed. Norman Blake (Cambridge: Cambridge University Press, 1992), 409–99.

65. Sue Zemka, "Spiritual Authority and the Life of Thomas Arnold," *Victorian Studies* 38, no. 3 (1995): 429–62.

66. On the poetics, politics, and economics of enclosure, see Raymond Williams, *The Country and the City* (Oxford: Oxford University Press, 1973), 96–107.

67. Minnis, *Medieval Theory of Authorship*, 118–59.

68. *Disticha Catonis*, ed. Marcus Boas (Amsterdam: North Holland, 1952). The most important Middle English derivative is *The Proverbs of Alfred*, ed. Olaf Arngart, 2 vols. (Lund: University of Lund, 1942–55).

69. Serge Lusignan, *La langue des rois au Moyen Âge: Le français en France et en Angleterre* (Paris: Presses universitaires de France, 2004).

70. See Raymond Williams, *Keywords: A Vocabulary of Culture and Society*, rev. ed. (Oxford: Oxford University Press, 1983), although Williams, as always, excludes terms distinctively medieval.

71. However, on stanzas, see Fein, "Twelve-Line Stanza Forms"; on lyrics and image texts, Jessica Brantley, *Reading in the Wilderness: Private Devotion and Public Performance in Late Medieval England* (Chicago: University of Chicago Press, 2007), 121–66; on the macaronic, Ad Putter, "The French of English Letters: Two Trilingual Verse Epistles in Context," in Wogan-Browne et al., *Language and Culture*, 397–408; on insular French, Helen Deeming, "Multilingual Networks in Twelfth- and Thirteenth-Century Song," in *Language in Medieval Britain: Networks and Exchanges*, ed. Mary Carruthers (Donington, Lincolnshire: Shaun Tyas, 2015), 127–43.

72. The Anglo-Norman comes from Layamon's source, Wace's *Roman de Brut*, lines 3707–10.

CHAPTER I

Grateful thanks to Sean Curran, Nicolas Bell, Andy Galloway, and the editors of this book for their comments on an earlier draft of this chapter.

1. I borrow this wonderful phrase from Ian Cornelius, who coined it in an earlier draft of "Language and Meter," this volume (Chapter 3).

2. I would like to acknowledge the invaluable support of the Leverhulme Trust (2008–11) in the initial stages of my research for this edition; and, for their lively interest and helpful comments on specific aspects of the work in progress, the hosts and interlocutors in All Souls College, Oxford (2011), the London Medieval Manuscripts Seminar (2011), the Oxford Medieval English Graduate Seminar (2011), the conference "New Directions in Medieval Manuscript Studies and Reading Practices: A Conference in Honour of Derek Pearsall's Eightieth Birthday" (2011), the Yale Medieval Studies Lecture Series (2013), and the Medieval and Renaissance Music Conference, Birmingham University (2014).

3. For a concise survey, see William Burgwinkle, "The *Chansonniers* as Books," in *The Troubadours: An Introduction*, ed. Simon Gaunt and Sarah Kay (Cambridge: Cambridge University Press, 1999), 246–62.

4. Certain genres of short verse, such as the *arma Christi* and certain books, such as London, British Library, Additional MS 37049, are exceptions to the lack of illumination.

5. As with most modern descriptive terms to do with Middle English manuscripts, "poetic anthology" is not straightforward; I have in mind such examples as John Shirley's compilation Cambridge, Trinity College, MS R.3.20; the Findern Manuscript (Cambridge, Cambridge University Library, MS Ff.1.6); Oxford, Bodleian Library, MS Digby 102; and the three Norfolk carol manuscripts (London, British Library, Sloane MS 2593; Cambridge, St. John's College, MS S.54 (259); and Oxford, Bodleian Library, MS English Poetry e.1). Many more, such as the 126 manuscripts listed by Julia Boffey, *Manuscripts of English Courtly Love Lyrics in the Later Middle Ages* (Cambridge: D. S. Brewer, 1985), app. 2, could be included, though many of these also include prose and other verse genres (as does, for example Shirley's R.3.20). Moreover the notion of "poetic anthology" need not mean "courtly love lyrics": the author collections by John Audelay (Oxford, Bodleian Library, MS Douce 302) and James Ryman (Cambridge, Cambridge University Library, MS Ee.1.12) are a case in point.

6. See the discussion of Carleton Brown and Rossell Hope Robbins below. For a fourteenth-century example of terminological switching, see John Trevisa's translation of Ranulf Higden's *Polychronicon* in Cambridge, St. John's College, MS H.1 (204), *Polychroni-*

con Ranulphi Higden monachi Cestrensis; Together with the English Translations of John Trevisa and of an Unknown Writer of the Fifteenth Century, ed. C. Babington and J. R. Lumby, 9 vols., Rolls Series (Rerum Britannicarum Medii Aevi Scriptores) 41 (1865–86), vol. 5 (1874), p. 321: "Boethius . . . made fifty songes endited comice [*cantus comicos edidit*] þat is as it were schort vers."

7. As Margot Fassler also remarks; see "The Religious Lyric in Medieval England (1150–1400): Three Disciplines and a Question," this volume (Chapter 10).

8. Virginia Jackson, *Dickinson's Misery: A Theory of Lyric Reading* (Princeton, NJ: Princeton University Press, 2005), 6.

9. Virginia Jackson and Yopie Prins, eds., *The Lyric Theory Reader: A Critical Anthology* (Baltimore: Johns Hopkins University Press, 2014), 2.

10. Jackson, *Dickinson's Misery*, 6.

11. I choose these examples as they are case studies in Jonathan D. Culler, *Theory of the Lyric* (Cambridge, MA: Harvard University Press, 2015), 78–81, 115, 339.

12. Maxwell S. Luria and Richard L. Hoffman, eds., *Middle English Lyrics: Authoritative Texts, Critical and Historical Backgrounds, Perspectives on Six Poems* (New York: W. W. Norton, 1974), 325–49 and 317–18 respectively.

13. Key work was generated by British scholars from the mid-1980s. Boffey, *Manuscripts of English Courtly Love Lyrics* (1985) and John J. Thompson, *Robert Thornton and the London Thornton Manuscript: British Library MS Additional 31042* (Cambridge: D. S. Brewer, 1987). From a decade earlier and with an emphasis on politics, see also, V. J. Scattergood, *Politics and Poetry in the Fifteenth Century* (London: Blandford Press, 1971).

14. Peter Dronke, *Medieval Latin and the Rise of European Love-Lyric*, 2 vols. (Oxford: Clarendon Press, 1965–66; 2nd ed., 1968); Dronke, *The Medieval Lyric* (London: Hutchinson, 1968); Rosemary Woolf, *The English Religious Lyric in the Middle Ages* (Oxford: Clarendon Press, 1968); Douglas Gray, *Themes and Images in the Medieval English Religious Lyric* (London: Routledge, 1972); Gray, ed., *A Selection of Religious Lyrics* (Oxford: Clarendon Press, 1975). A wave of new work is beginning to emerge. Alongside (and in some cases emerging from) the collaborations instigated by Helen Deeming and Ardis Butterfield (see note 32), see Marjorie Harrington, "Of Earth You Were Made: Constructing the Bilingual Poem 'Erþ' in British Library, MS Harley 913," *Florilegium* 31 (2014): 103–37; Ingrid Nelson, *Lyric Tactics: Poetry, Genre, and Practice in Later Medieval England* (Philadelphia: University of Pennsylvania Press, 2017); Seeta Chaganti, *Strange Footing: Poetic Form and Dance in the Late Middle Ages* (Chicago: University of Chicago Press, 2018); Julia Boffey and Christiania Whitehead, eds., *Middle English Lyrics: New Readings of Short Poems* (Cambridge: D. S. Brewer, 2018); Ardis Butterfield, ed., *Medieval English Lyrics* (New York: W. W. Norton, 2023 [anticipated]); Ardis Butterfield, *Medieval Songlines* (forthcoming); and this book.

15. David Wallace, ed., *The Cambridge History of Medieval English Literature* (Cambridge: Cambridge University Press, 1999); this was pointed out aggressively in an early review, and yet one might regard the absence of lyric more sympathetically as in some sense a natural decision for a historicist literary history of the late 1990s.

16. I am grateful to the editors for their indulgence in allowing me to refer with a smile to their title in this way.

17. The most recent anthologies that present lyrics in thematic groupings are Thomas G. Duncan, ed., *Late Medieval English Lyrics and Carols, 1400–1530* (London: Penguin, 2000); John C. Hirsh, ed., *Medieval Lyric: Middle English Lyrics, Ballads, and Carols* (Malden, MA: Blackwell, 2005); and Anne L. Klinck, *The Voices of Medieval English Lyric: An Anthology of*

Poems ca. 1150–1530 (Montreal: McGill-Queen's University Press, 2019); though Hirsh's edition takes the valuable pedagogical step of presenting each lyric with a detailed contextual introduction, as does (in part) Klinck. The choice of thematic organization was also commonly made in an earlier generation of anthologies, such as R. T. Davies, ed., *Medieval English Lyrics: A Critical Anthology* (London: Faber and Faber, 1963); Theodore Silverstein, ed., *Medieval English Lyrics* (London: Edward Arnold, 1971); and Gray, *Selection* (1975).

18. As Fassler also notes in "The Religious Lyric," 268–71.

19. Julia Boffey, "Middle English Lyrics and Manuscripts," in *A Companion to the Middle English Lyric*, ed. Thomas Duncan (Cambridge: D. S. Brewer, 2005), 1–18, at p. 1.

20. Christopher Cannon experiments provocatively with thinking of romance as lyric ("Lyric Romance," this volume, Chapter 3); for extended work on form in alliterative poetry, see Susanna Fein's groundbreaking essay on *Pearl* ("Twelve-Line Stanza Forms in Middle English and the Date of *Pearl*," *Speculum* 72, no. 2 [1997]: 367–98); and the reevaluation of notions of form and genre in thirteenth- and early fourteenth-century French poetic writing in Ardis Butterfield, *Poetry and Music in Medieval France: From Jean Renart to Guillaume de Machaut* (Cambridge: Cambridge University Press, 2002), chap. 12 and sect. 5, "Lyric and Narrative," chaps. 13 and 14. Studies that consider the poetic qualities of medieval prose, such as meter and rhyme, include Lois K. Smedick, "Parallelism and Pointing in Rolle's Rhythmical Style," *Mediaeval Studies* 41, no. 1 (1979): 404–67. Other Middle English prose works that editors have represented in linear form include *The Wooing of Our Lord* (and its descendant *A Talking of a Love of God*); instances of rhyme and metrical variation in vernacular material inset in sermons and devotional treatises have been widely discussed by Siegfried Wenzel; see also Cornelius, "Language and Meter," 118–24.

21. Since the focus of this volume is on the Middle English lyric I leave aside the other languages of Britain, such as Welsh, Irish, and Cornish, while signaling that sustained comparative analysis of all medieval Britain's lyric traditions is badly needed.

22. For a standard introduction, see John Stevens, Ardis Butterfield, and Theodore Karp, "Troubadours, Trouvères," *Grove Music Online* (2001), https://doi.org/10.1093/gmo/9781561592630.article.28468; Simon Gaunt and Sarah Kay, *The Troubadours: An Introduction* (Cambridge: Cambridge University Press, 1999); Ardis Butterfield and Elizabeth Hebbard, "Troubadours and Trouvères," *Oxford Bibliographies in Music Online* (Medieval Studies: Oxford University Press, 2021), https://www.oxfordbibliographies.com/view/document/obo-9780199757824/obo-9780199757824-0288.xml. Newer scholarship is drawing attention to the much larger range of copying contexts for troubadour and trouvère lyric than modern editors and critics have traditionally acknowledged (Elizabeth Hebbard, "Manuscripts and the Making of the Troubadour Lyric Tradition" [Ph.D. diss., Yale University, 2017]), but the broader point of comparison stands.

23. The manuscripts of the French poetry of Charles d'Orléans are a telling exception. For a comparative discussion of songbooks (without consideration of the music) in French, German, and Spanish, see Marisa Galvez, *Songbook: How Lyrics Became Poetry in Medieval Europe* (Chicago: University of Chicago Press, 2012).

24. There is no simple way to track these types of manuscript from any one available research tool. The *Digital Index of Middle English Verse* (*DIMEV*) lists manuscripts and catalogs items of verse, but the types of codex or compilation are only partially discernible since only English verse is listed. See note 43 below for further comment on books with music.

25. The still standard bibliography is Lawrence Marshburn Earp, ed., *Guillaume de Machaut: A Guide to Research* (New York: Garland, 1995).

26. One should also mention William Herebert, an Oxford Franciscan (ca. 1270–1333), whose personal, signed trilingual compilation includes nineteen English translations of Latin hymns. Other later author collections, such as the now lost "balades & chancons, / Rondeaulx & laiz" by John Montagu, 3rd Earl of Salisbury (mentioned by Jean Creton, *Metrical History of the Deposition of King Richard II*, ed. J. Webb, *Archaeologia* 20 [1824], 1–423, at p. 314), and the poetry of Charles d'Orléans, widely copied (including an autograph collection Paris, Bibliothèque Nationale, MS Fr. 25458, with English translations in London, British Library, Harley MS 682), are either of French language poetry or, in the case of Harley MS 682, closely cloned from French manuscripts. There are further groupings of French lyrics in Cambridge, Trinity College, MS R.3.20, a John Shirley manuscript that anthologizes (and attributes) poems by Chaucer, Hoccleve, and Lydgate. In short, fifteenth-century practices in author collections are heavily dependent on French models.

27. On Litchfield, see Barbara Zimbalist, "The Lyric Christ," this volume (Chapter 9).

28. Susanna Fein, ed., *Studies in the Harley Manuscript: The Scribes, Contents, and Social Contexts of British Library MS Harley 2253* (Kalamazoo, MI: Medieval Institute Publications, 2000), "Introduction," 5.

29. For further details, see Ardis Butterfield, "The Construction of Textual Form: Cross-Lingual Citation in the Medieval Insular Lyric," in *Citation, Intertextuality and Memory in the Middle Ages and Renaissance*, vol. 1, *Text, Music and Image from Machaut to Ariosto*, ed. Yolanda Plumley, Giuliano Di Bacco, and Stefano Jossa (Exeter: University of Exeter Press, 2011), 41–57, at pp. 45–47. It is a fascinating case of a citation in English that remains in English in all three of the languages in which this treatise was adapted, translated, and retranslated (I have checked some three-quarters of the surviving copies).

30. *NIMEV* 2320.

31. Ruth Dean and Maureen Boulton's *Anglo-Norman Literature* lists only the manuscripts of the French version. See Ruth J. Dean, *Anglo-Norman Literature: A Guide to Texts and Manuscripts*, with the collaboration of Maureen B. M. Boulton, ANTS, O.P., 3 (London: Anglo-Norman Text Society, 1999), no. 692.

32. Pioneering research across the fields of English, French, Latin, and music was begun by John Stevens, though left unfinished at his death in 2002. My own research, in suit, has called for this repeatedly over the years and taken a variety of forms, much of it collaborative in recognition of the scale of research required:

• An international, multidisciplinary scholarly network funded by the Arts and Humanities Research Council (AHRC), cofounded with Helen Deeming—the Medieval Song Network 2010 to 2014 (www.medievalsongnetwork.org). This aimed to tackle the dearth of new thinking and research on insular lyric by holding two London workshops in 2010 and 2011 to encourage cross-disciplinary research and collaboration among scholars working in English, music, modern languages, medieval studies, Latin, history, art history, librarianship, and archives. The network also worked with performers and sponsored two concerts of previously unedited music by the Orlando Consort in 2011 (London) and 2013 (Yale). It was maintained and co-run from 2012 to 2014 by Emma Gorst and Sophie Sawicka-Sykes. Its work has helped shape a range of further research by Deeming and Butterfield, including Deeming's pioneering edition *Songs in British Sources, c. 1150–1300*, Musica Britannica, vol. 95 (London: Stainer & Bell, 2013); and Butterfield and Deeming, "Editing Insular Song Across the Disciplines: Worldes

Blis," in *Probable Truth: Editing Medieval Texts from Britain in the Twenty-First Century*, ed. Vincent Gillespie and Anne Hudson (Turnhout: Brepols, 2013), 151–66.

• Manuscript research toward a new Norton edition of *Medieval English Lyrics*, and a monograph, *Medieval Songlines*, funded initially by a three-year Leverhulme Senior Research Fellowship (2008–11).

• The development of online research resources: (1) "The Digital Troubadour," a pilot project in computer science, music, and literature, with Nicolas Gold and Sangita Ganeesh (University College London, Computer Science) and Helen Deeming (Royal Holloway University of London, Music), funded by the Engineering and Physical Science Research Council (EPSRC); (2) an online Filemaker teaching resource created by Emma Gorst (funded by a postdoctoral award from the Social Sciences and Research Council of Canada (SSHRC); (3) a Yale Digital Humanities Lab Project Grant with Ann Killian, Joe Stadolnik, Anya Adair, Seamus Dwyer, and Melissa Tu for a prototype of the Digital Archive of Medieval Song, https:// web.library.yale.edu/dhlab/medievalsong, a searchable online database of song lyrics in English, French, and Latin, using IIIF/Mirador accompanied by annotated digital surrogates of their manuscript contexts and an index of melodies.

It became clear in the 2010 and 2011 Medieval Song Network workshops that there was then a severe shortage of musicologists working on insular materials: the large majority (including myself) were specialists in continental French song and motet. New work is gradually being accomplished however: see Lisa Colton, *Angel Song: Medieval English Music in History* (London: Routledge, 2017); and the many articles by Deeming. The perspective provided by continental lyric is of course a valuable one to bring to bear, and much fresh research is needed on the relationships and patterns of transmission of song between Britain and the Continent.

33. On this distinction, and some of its implications for meter, see Cornelius, "Language and Meter."

34. It is difficult to find satisfactory terminology for French as a functional language in Britain. "French of England" is awkward to use and potentially problematic. Anglo-French has a useful umbrella application to the cross-channel character of French usage; where relevant one might also use "insular French" or just "French."

35. A start is being made with Base de Français Médiéval (BFM), http://bfm.ens-lyon.fr.

36. Dean and Boulton, *Anglo-Norman Literature*.

37. Rossell Hope Robbins, ed., *Secular Lyrics of the XIVth and XVth Centuries*, 2nd ed. (Oxford: Clarendon Press, 1955; first published 1952), xvii.

38. See Dean and Boulton, *Anglo-Norman Literature*, in particular the mini-section "Songs to the Virgin," nos. 802ff.; the terms "song" and "hymn" are used fairly widely under "devotional."

39. Indices of English verse do not refer to music. For a useful initial listing, see Christopher Page, "A Catalogue and Bibliography of English Song from Its Beginnings to c1300," *RMA Research Chronicle* 13 (1976): 67–83.

40. John Stevens, "Alphabetical Check-List of Anglo-Norman Songs c. 1150–c. 1350," *Plainsong and Medieval Music* 3 (1994): 1–22.

41. Demonstrated notably by Susanna Fein whose editing work in the past decade for the Teaching Association for Middle English Studies (TEAMS) and collaborative essay collections on specific manuscripts has brought the trilingual and generically diverse nature of Middle English verse into the public domain in ways that open up many new prospects for teaching and research: *Moral Love Songs and Laments* (Kalamazoo, MI: Medieval Institute Publications

for TEAMS, 1998); *Studies in the Harley Manuscript* (2000); *My Wyl and My Wrytyng: Essays on John the Blind Audelay* (Kalamazoo, MI: Medieval Institute Publications for TEAMS, 2009); ed. and trans., *The Complete Harley 2253 Manuscript*, with David Raybin and Jan Ziolkowski, 3 vols. (Kalamazoo, MI: Medieval Institute Publications for TEAMS 2014–15); *Robert Thornton and His Books: Essays on the Lincoln and London Thornton Manuscripts* (York: York Medieval Press, 2014); *Interpreting MS Digby 86: A Trilingual Book from Thirteenth-Century Worcestershire* (York: York Medieval Press, 2019).

42. Isabel Stewart Tod Aspin, ed., *Anglo-Norman Political Songs*, ANTS 11 (Oxford: Published for the Anglo-Norman Text Society by B. Blackwell, 1953); David L. Jeffrey and Brian J. Levy, eds., *The Anglo-Norman Lyric: An Anthology Edited from the Manuscripts with Translations and Commentary* (Toronto: Pontifical Institute of Mediaeval Studies, 1990); *Analecta hymnica Medii Aevi*, ed. Guido Maria Dreves et al., 55 vols. (Leipzig, 1866–1922); Ulisse Chevalier, *Repertorium Hymnicum: Catalogue des chants, hymnes, proses, séquences, tropes, en usage dans l'Église latine depuis les origines jusqu'à nos jours* (Brussels: Société des Bollandistes, 1892–1921); Joseph Szövérffy, *Repertorium hymnologicum novum*, Vol. 1 (Turnhout: Brepols, 1983). Online editions of the last three items are now available at www.erwin-rauner.de.

43. Early editions of insular song include, most notably, John Stainer, ed., *Sacred & Secular Songs, Together with Other MS. Compositions in the Bodleian Library, Oxford, Ranging from About A.D. 1185 to About A.D. 1505*, introd. E. W. B. Nicholson, transcriptions into modern musical notation by J. F. R. Stainer and C. Stainer, 2 vols. (London: Novello, 1901). It is hard to give a thorough conspectus of the music for insular song because the distinguished editing and research of such scholars as Frank Harrison, Ernest Sanders, Peter Lefferts, William Summers, and Margaret Bent have tended to pay more attention to polyphony, liturgical chant, *conductus*, and motet than to monophonic song. Furthermore, exact numbers are elusive, since many sources are fragmentary and hard to decipher. Helen Deeming's important edition (*Songs in British Sources*) is a big step forward toward presenting a new view of pre-fourteenth-century surviving and previously unpublished material. For a recent overview of scholarship, see Margaret Bent, "The Absent First Gathering of the Chantilly Manuscript," *Plainsong and Medieval Music* 26, no. 1 (2017): 19–36; Peter M. Lefferts's review of Deeming (*Plainsong and Medieval Music* 23, no. 2 [2014]: 245–51); and hers of his facsimile edition of *English Thirteenth-Century Polyphony* (*Plainsong and Medieval Music* 27, no. 1 [2018]: 90–97). See also Fassler, "The Religious Lyric."

44. William J. Summers and Peter M. Lefferts, *English Thirteenth-Century Polyphony: A Facsimile Edition*, foreword by Magnus Williamson (London: Stainer & Bell for the British Academy, 2016); Deeming, review of *English Thirteenth-Century Polyphony*, 92.

45. Deeming, *Songs in British Sources*. Deeming excludes what she calls "liturgical" pieces.

46. David Fallows, ed., *Secular Polyphony, 1380–1480*, Musica Britannica, vol. 97 (London: Stainer & Bell, 2014).

47. An important exception is Monika Otter, "Godric of Finchale's *Canora Modulatio*: The Auditory and Visionary Worlds of a Twelfth-Century Hermit," *Haskins Society Journal* 24 (2012): 127–44.

48. See John Stevens, review of *Medieval English Songs*, by E. J. Dobson and F. Ll. Harrison, *Music and Letters* 62, nos. 3–4 (1981): 461–66; and David Wulstan, review in *Journal of the Plainsong and Mediaeval Music Society* 3 (1980): 59–61. Also Butterfield and Deeming, "Editing Insular Song"; Ardis Butterfield, "Poems without Form? *Maiden in the mor lay* Revisited," in *Readings in Medieval Textuality: Essays in Honour of A. C. Spearing*, ed. Cristina Maria Cervone and D. Vance Smith (Cambridge: D. S. Brewer, 2016), 169–94.

49. Stevens, review of *Medieval English Songs*, 461.

50. This is not the place to go into detail about the editorial controversies, but for some specific discussion, see Butterfield and Deeming, "Editing Insular Song"; and Butterfield, "Poems without Form?," 182–85, 192.

51. The *Oxford English Dictionary Online* (*OED*) cites Puttenham (1589) as the first English adjectival usage of "lyric" as applied to "short poem meant to be sung," and Sidney (1586) of "lyric" as poem. However, Colin Burrow in an unpublished paper points out that the notes to Edmund Spenser's *Shepheardes Calender* of 1579 had referred to "that famous Lyrick poet Pindarus." I am grateful to him for sharing the paper with me.

52. The best example, ironically, is Charles d'Orléans, see note 26 above.

53. Such as Fein, *Complete Harley 2253 Manuscript*.

54. Brown followed in the footsteps of Frederick J. Furnivall, Hilda M. R. Murray, and other editors in the Early English Text Society, who published material from specific manuscripts (including London, Lambeth Palace Library, MS 306; London, British Library, Harley MS 7322; and London, Lambeth Palace Library, MS 853); or, in the case of Murray, made the pioneering decision to print all the known versions of "Erthe upon erthe" (Hilda M. R. Murray, ed., *The Middle English Poem, Erthe upon Erthe, Printed from Twenty-Four Manuscripts*, EETS, o.s., 141 [London: Oxford University Press, 1911]). E. K. Chambers and F. Sidgwick's *Early English Lyrics: Amorous, Moral, Divine and Trivial* (London: A. H. Bullen, 1907) was one of the earliest anthologies of English poems; by contrast, Thomas Wright's *The Political Songs of England* (London: J. B. Nichols and Son for the Camden Society, 1839) was trilingual; Laurence Minot's poems were edited by Joseph Hall probably for their nationalistic character (Oxford: Clarendon Press, 1887).

55. They came out in nonchronological order (Brown explains this project in the preface to the fifteenth-century volume): Carleton Brown, ed., *Religious Lyrics of the XIVth Century* (Oxford: Clarendon Press, 1924); *English Lyrics of the XIIIth Century* (Oxford: Clarendon Press, 1932); and *Religious Lyrics of the XVth Century* (Oxford: Clarendon Press, 1939).

56. Rossell Hope Robbins, ed., *Historical Poems of the XIVth and XVth Centuries* (New York: Columbia University Press, 1959); Robbins, *Secular Lyrics*.

57. Like Brown before him, Robbins undercuts his own sharp division by discussing how fully the discourse of love is shared by poems addressed to the Virgin and to so-called secular "mistresses" (*Secular Lyrics*, xix).

58. Richard Leighton Greene, ed., *The Early English Carols*, 2nd ed., rev. and enl. (Oxford: Clarendon Press, 1977), xxxiii. Greene prints 474 carols, plus ten "fragments" in an Appendix (292–96), all pre-1550, but gives the discrepant figure of 502 as his total.

59. Thomas Duncan mixes carols with lyrics in his interesting collection *Late Medieval English Lyrics and Carols* (2000); partially reprinted in Thomas G. Duncan, ed., *Medieval English Lyrics and Carols* (Cambridge: D. S. Brewer, 2013), but with only brief commentary on his choices; since Greene, there has been remarkably little work on carols as a genre, apart from my former student Kathleen Palti's thesis and some summarizing articles (see Karl Reichl, "The Middle English Carol," in Duncan, *Companion to the Middle English Lyric*, 150–70). The most recent reinvestigation of the genre is on musical grounds by David Fallows (*Henry V and the Earliest English Carols: 1413–1440* [London: Routledge, 2018]), who revisits the work of John Stevens (*Words and Music in the Middle Ages: Song, Narrative, Dance and Drama, 1050–1350* [Cambridge: Cambridge University Press, 1986]).

60. According to Greene, 210 carols "include Latin lines and phrases" (*Early English Carols*, lxxxi).

61. Cornelius, "Language and Meter," 115–17, 124.

62. One might want to include items that are *not* verse; see Andrew Albin, "The Sound of Rollean Lyric," this volume (Chapter 8).

63. It is worth noting that Chambers and Sidgwick use the term "lyric" in their anthology title, and Wright, without reference to music, the term "song," in keeping with a desire to interpret such material for a Victorian market.

64. On value, see Ingrid Nelson's comments on Brown's and Robbins's contemporary I. A. Richards: "Lyric Value," this volume (Chapter 5), 140–45.

65. Consonant with his left-wing politics, and especially those of his wife, Helen Ann Mims, who worked closely with him on the lyric editions. I am grateful to Richard Firth Green for his correspondence on this point via his acquaintance with Robbins.

66. See Rosemary Greentree's survey, *The Middle English Lyric and Short Poem* (Cambridge: D. S. Brewer, 2001).

67. Luria and Hoffman, *Middle English Lyrics*; Hirsh, *Medieval Lyric*; Duncan, *Medieval English Lyrics and Carols*.

68. Robbins, *Secular Lyrics*, no. 33. For a discussion of this poem, including this title, see Cristina Maria Cervone, "Wondering Through Middle English Lyric," this volume (Chapter 2).

69. Robbins, *Secular Lyrics*, nos. 43 and 44.

70. Carleton Brown, *English Lyrics of the XIIIth Century*, no. 79.

71. For specifics, see note 17.

72. See Cristina Maria Cervone, "John de Cobham and Cooling Castle's Charter Poem," *Speculum* 83, no. 4 (2008): 884–916; and Aden Kumler, "Lyric Vessels," this volume (Chapter 7).

73. Plans are in place to create an online resource to support the edition: see note 32.

74. Marjorie Perloff and Craig Dworkin, "The Sound of Poetry / The Poetry of Sound: The 2006 MLA Presidential Forum," *PMLA* 123 (2008): 749–61, at p. 751.

75. Ardis Butterfield, "Why Medieval Lyric?," *English Literary History* 82, no. 2 (2015): 319–43.

76. In some ways this idea merely restates old adages about editing, but I am restating them to bring them into conversation with current notions of "lyric reading."

77. Cædmon's seventh-century Northumbrian world was also multilingual in English, Latin, and Brittonic (his name appears to be British); with lingering cultural influence from Roman rule (the circulation of the harp at the feast he avoids recalls that at a Roman-style banquet).

78. Daniel Paul O'Donnell, "Bede's Strategy in Paraphrasing 'Cædmon's Hymn,'" *Journal of English and Germanic Philology* 103, no. 4 (2004): 417–32.

79. Until the late twentieth century, research on Godric's songs was based on the foundational work by the German scholar Julius Zupitza ("Cantus beati Godrici," *Englische Studien* 11 [1888]: 401–32), with specific attention first paid to the music by J. B. Trend ("The First English Songs," *Music and Letters* 9, no. 2 [1928]: 111–28). Dobson and Harrison's edition followed in 1979; then the new discovery of the Paris Mazarine manuscript by Alexandra Barratt, "The Lyrics of St. Godric: A New Manuscript," *Notes and Queries* 230 (1985): 439–45. Helen Deeming revisited the music of the songs in an important article, "The Songs of St. Godric: A Neglected Context," *Music and Letters* 86, no. 2 (2005): 169–85. Subsequently, see discussion of the music and text of the songs in the context of Reginald's *Vita* by Monika Otter, "Godric of Finchale's *Canora Modulatio*"; specific comments on "Welcome, Simund," an additional song described but not quoted by Reginald, in Butterfield, "Why Medieval

Lyric?," 337–39; and, on Reginald's remarks on musical performance more broadly, Margaret Coombe, "What a Performance: The Songs of St Godric of Finchale," in *Saints of North-East England, 600–1500*, ed. Margaret Coombe, Anne Mouron, and Christiania Whitehead (Turnhout: Brepols, 2017), 219–42. Heather Blurton, most recently, has proposed that the songs are a form of "vernacular liturgy" and has also looked again at the Paris manuscript, in "The Songs of Godric of Finchale: Vernacular Liturgy and Literary History," *New Medieval Literatures* 18 (2018): 75–104; and "Godric of Finchale's 'Jerusalem Song' in Bibliothèque Mazarine MS 1716," *Notes and Queries* 66, no. 2 (2019): 183–92.

80. For more detail on these lives, including a now lost twelfth-century account by Germanus, see Coombe, "What a Performance," 224–26.

81. Deeming's account of the complex manuscript tradition (based on Joseph Stevenson's edition: Reginald [of Durham], *Libellus de vita et miraculis S. Godrici, heremitae de Finchale* [London: J. B. Nichols and Son, 1847]) should now be supplemented by the additional information in Coombe, "What a Performance." I follow here Deeming's figures given in her table "The Songs of St. Godric," 171, which Coombe also cites. For a new edition and translation of Reginald's *Libellus*, see *Reginald of Durham: "The Life and Miracles of Saint Godric, Hermit of Finchale,"* ed. and trans. by Margaret Coombe (Oxford: Oxford University Press, 2022).

82. Blurton suggests the placing could be "right"—or at least deliberate ("The Songs of Godric of Finchale," 98). This is worth considering but does not solve the complications of how to proceed editorially.

83. See detailed discussion by Deeming, "The Songs of St. Godric."

84. The spaces for staves in the Mazarine manuscript are common in manuscripts of French romances containing inset songs (see Butterfield, *Poetry and Music*, chap. 10 and appendix).

85. Barratt, "The Lyrics of St. Godric," 445.

86. Barratt urged the primacy of the Paris manuscript, but see now Anne Mouron, "'Help Thin Godric in Francrice': An Old French Life of St Godric," in *Translation and Authority—Authorities in Translation*, ed. Pieter De Leemans and Michèle Goyens (Turnhout: Brepols, 2016), 215–28, cited in Coombe; and Blurton's "Godric of Finchale's 'Jerusalem Song.'"

87. Further research is required on the presentation of the song texts in all the surviving manuscripts. There are further intriguing parallels here with Cædmon. Twenty-one surviving manuscripts of Bede's *Historia* (they range in date from the eighth to the fifteenth century) are mostly in Latin prose with the "Hymn" in Old English, but four are full translations rendering the prose into Old English as well. Debate about the status of the "Hymn" as a record of what Cædmon is said to have composed is intense and unresolved. In ten of the Latin manuscripts the Old English is added in the margin rather than in the main body of the text; this and other factors have prompted the inference that the Old English version of the "Hymn" was not in fact the "original" song as Cædmon composed it, but a translation into Old English from Bede's Latin. See Benjamin Slade, "Bede's Story of Cædmon: Text and Facing Translation," app. 2, https://heorot.dk/bede-caedmon-i.html.

88. I am grateful to Tony Hunt for kindly sharing pre-publication the relevant pages of the fascimile and transcription of this manuscript: *Reginald of Durham's Life of St Godric: An Old French Version*, ed. Margaret Coombe, Tony Hunt, and Anne Mouron, ANTS, O.P., 9 (Oxford: Anglo-Norman Text Society, 2019).

89. Cited in Deeming, "The Songs of St. Godric," 179, from Zupitza, "Cantus beati Godrici," 420.

90. Coombe rejects the surviving music as irrelevant since it postdates Reginald's account, but given the vagaries of musical transmission in English sources (indeed in musical sources in general in medieval copying practices), I take a less severe view.

91. British Library, Harley MS 322, fol. 74v. The form "onfong" (as a past tense) is strange in context, and only the Harley manuscript has that form both times; the other two manuscripts have "on fo" and "onfang" (Cambridge University Library, MS Mm.4.28, fol. 149r); "onfo" with "onfong" written above it and "onfang" (British Library, Royal MS 5.F.vii, fol. 85r). Dobson, who provides a lengthy commentary, regards "onfang" as "a new imper[ative] s[in]g[ular] modelled on the ME infinitive 'onfangen'" (Dobson and Harrison, *Medieval English Songs*, 106–7). Most editors choose "onfo" (imperative), and I have translated it as such. For suggestions of other meanings in play, see below.

92. Reginald, *Libellus*, 118. This recalls Christ's question to Mary after the Resurrection (John 20:15–16).

93. Reginald, *Libellus*, 118; for this translation and further discussion, see Otter, "Godric of Finchale's *Canora Modulatio*." See also Reginald, *Libellus*, 119 and 144.

94. Butterfield, 'Why Medieval Lyric?," 337–39.

95. Mary J. Carruthers, *The Experience of Beauty in the Middle Ages* (Oxford: Oxford University Press, 2013), 89–91 and passim.

96. This passage has shades of incantation or wordless vocality, especially as Reginald uses the word *iubilatio*, which has a textual history relating to wordless outpourings of joy. See Helen Deeming, "Music and Contemplation in the Twelfth-Century *Dulcis Jesu memoria*," *Journal of the Royal Musical Association* 139, no. 1 (2014): 1–39.

97. On the sequence, see Fassler, "The Religious Lyric," especially 270–76. For comment on melodic differences between the Royal and Harley versions, see Deeming, "The Songs of St. Godric," 184.

98. Cambridge University Library, MS Mm.4.28, fol. 149r. The Royal MS also has a Latin version of this song, but underlaid beneath the English line by line, rather than as here added on a new line at the end of the song.

99. *Onfon* is used with all these meanings and more (see *Middle English Dictionary* [*MED*], s.v. "onfon, v.") but not all of them work grammatically with these lines of verse where the verb form required is imperative. In the sense "to receive a name, be named," *MED*'s examples are associated with the phrase *onfang nome*, rather than the verb on its own. However, the wordplay on Godric's name clearly indicates that naming is in the poet's mind. It seems likely that transmission has been garbled. I am grateful to Roberta Frank for discussing these lines with me.

100. There is a ^ in the manuscript here and "to" is written above "winne."

101. British Library, Royal MS 5.F.vii, fol. 85r. The interpretation of "with" on this line is ambiguous; I have offered two possibilities. Deeming emends "selfd" to "self."

102. This is not to suggest that this is a "whole" edition. But it can stand as an indication or sense of potential.

CHAPTER 2

My thanks to the participants in our seminars at the Radcliffe Institute for Advanced Study for their attention and comments, which helped to shape this chapter. I am especially grateful to Nicholas Watson for valuable suggestions, particularly in the last stages of editing.

Epigraphs: "A God and yet a man?," in Carleton Brown, ed., *Religious Lyrics of the XVth Century* (Oxford: Clarendon Press, 1939), no. 120, p. 187; Oxford, Bodleian Library, MS Rawlinson B.332, fol. ii verso (flyleaf); *Digital Index of Middle English Verse (DIMEV)*, no. 51. D. Nurkse, "Anonymous Lyrics from Medieval Spain," *Literary Review* 45, no. 3 (2002): 509–11, at p. 509. Cord J. Whitaker, *Black Metaphors: How Modern Racism Emerged from Medieval Race-Thinking* (Philadelphia: University of Pennsylvania Press, 2019), 11.

1. For problems that ensue because "the category 'verse' is not self-evident in Middle English," see Ian Cornelius, "Language and Meter," this volume (Chapter 4), 116–18, quotation from p. 116.

2. Cristina Maria Cervone, *Poetics of the Incarnation: Middle English Writing and the Leap of Love* (Philadelphia: University of Pennsylvania Press, 2013), 211–12.

3. Some useful explorations of medieval interest in wonder include Emily Steiner, "Encyclopedic Verse and Vernacular Science: The Book of Sydrac," in her *John Trevisa's Information Age: Knowledge and the Pursuit of Literature, c. 1400* (Oxford: Oxford University Press, 2021), 177–209; Michelle Karnes, "Wonder, Marvels, and Metaphor in the *Squire's Tale*," *English Literary History* 82, no. 2 (2015): 461–90; and Karnes, "Marvels in the Medieval Imagination," *Speculum* 90, no. 2 (2015): 327–65; Patricia Dailey, "Riddles, Wonder, and Responsiveness in Anglo-Saxon Literature," in *The Cambridge History of Early Medieval English Literature*, ed. Clare A. Lees (Cambridge: Cambridge University Press, 2013), 451–72; and Caroline Walker Bynum, *Metamorphosis and Identity* (New York: Zone Books, 2001), 37–75.

4. Augustine, *De civitate Dei* 21.8, quoted in Bynum, *Metamorphosis and Identity*, 48.

5. Aristotle, *Metaphysics* 1.2, quoted in Karnes, "Wonder, Marvels, and Metaphor," 462.

6. Aquinas, *Metaphysicorum* 3.55, quoted in Karnes, "Wonder, Marvels, and Metaphor," 463.

7. *Analecta hymnica Medii Aevi*, ed. Guido Maria Dreves, Clemens Blume, and Henry M. Bannister, 55 vols. (Leipzig, 1866–1922), vol. 50, p. 586; translated in Hugh Henry, "Pange Lingua Gloriosi," in *The Catholic Encyclopedia*, vol. 11 (New York: Robert Appleton, 1911), http://www.newadvent.org/cathen/11441c.htm, as: "The Word-(made)-Flesh makes by (His) word true bread into flesh; and wine becomes Christ's blood; and if the (unassisted) intellect fails (to recognize all this), faith alone suffices to assure the pure heart."

8. Cervone, *Poetics of the Incarnation*.

9. On close reading, see Cristina Maria Cervone and Nicholas Watson, "Why stonde we? why go we no3t?," this volume (Introduction), 6–7; Ingrid Nelson, "Lyric Value," this volume (Chapter 5), 137–39, 142.

10. Personal communication, April 2009.

11. This idea resonates with critical thought on the Old English Exeter Book riddles, which "take mundane objects and transform them into strange and wondrous beings" (Peter Ramey, "Crafting Strangeness: Wonder Terminology in the Exeter Book Riddles and the Anglo-Latin Enigmata," *Review of English Studies* 69, no. 289 [2017]: 201–15).

12. *DIMEV* 3486; Cambridge, Pembroke College, MS 258, fol. 141v; transcribed from the manuscript. This poem would be worth considering alongside "As I me rode this ender day" (*DIMEV* 614), which Nelson discusses (as "Now springes the spray") in "Lyric Value," 153–57.

13. Jean Leclercq, *The Love of Learning and the Desire for God: A Study of Monastic Culture*, trans. Catharine Misrahi (New York: Fordham University Press, 1961); Duncan Robertson, *"Lectio Divina": The Medieval Experience of Reading* (Collegeville, MN: Cistercian Publications, 2011).

14. *DIMEV* 3486.5; Oxford, Bodleian Library, MS Rawlinson G.22, fol. 1v.

15. Some Middle English lyrics as we find them may not necessarily be complete in themselves. Ardis Butterfield, "Why Medieval Lyric?," *English Literary History* 82, no. 2 (2015): 319–43; "Poems Without Form? *Maiden in the mor lay* Revisited," in *Readings in Medieval Textuality: Essays in Honour of A. C. Spearing*, ed. Cristina Maria Cervone and D. Vance Smith (Cambridge: D. S. Brewer, 2016), 169–94; J. A. Burrow, "Poems Without Contexts," *Essays in Criticism* 29, no. 1 (1979): 6–32.

16. Montague Rhodes James, *A Descriptive Catalogue of the Manuscripts in the Library of Pembroke College Cambridge, with a Hand List of the Printed Books to the Year 1500 by Ellis H. Minns, M.A., Fellow and Librarian* (Cambridge: Cambridge University Press, 1905), 233.

17. *DIMEV* 3742; I have quoted Pembroke College, MS 258, fol. 129, from *DIMEV*, but I emend "sunne" to "sonne" to keep the pun salient.

18. Quoted from C. Horstman, ed., *Yorkshire Writers: Richard Rolle of Hampole, an English Father of the Church, and His Followers*, 2 vols. (London: Swan Sonnenschein; New York: Macmillan, 1895–96), 1:256. The lines seem to have been added when Edmund's original Latin version (there are several) was translated into French in the mid-thirteenth century; Nicholas Watson, "The Original Audience and Institutional Setting of Edmund Rich's *Mirror of Holy Church*: The Case for the Salisbury Canons," in *Medieval and Early Modern Religious Cultures: Essays Honouring Vincent Gillespie on His Sixty-Fifth Birthday*, ed. Laura Ashe and Ralph Hanna (Cambridge: D. S. Brewer, 2019), 21–42. Ardis Butterfield briefly discusses Edmund's *Mirror* and "Nou goth sonne" in "Lyric Editing," this volume (Chapter 1), 35–36. See also Cornelius, "Language and Meter," 111.

19. Frederick Holweck, "The Feast of the Annunciation," in *The Catholic Encyclopedia*, vol. 1 (New York: Robert Appleton, 1907), http://www.newadvent.org/cathen/01542a.htm. See also my discussion of simultaneous narration in the visual topos of the Lily Crucifixion in *Poetics of the Incarnation*, 17, 197–208.

20. Horstman, *Yorkshire Writers*, 1:256–57; emphasis mine.

21. A. D. Wilshere, ed., *Mirour de seinte eglyse: St Edmund of Abingdon's "Speculum ecclesiae,"* ANTS 40 (London: Anglo-Norman Text Society, 1982), 68–69; emphasis mine.

22. Biblical quotations are from *The Holy Bible, Douay Rheims Version* (Baltimore: John Murphy, 1899; reprint Rockford, Ill.: Tan Books, 1971).

23. *Middle English Dictionary* (*MED*), s.v. "blo, adj."

24. It is a pleasure to thank Nicholas Watson for drawing my attention to Edmund's use of "Nou goth sonne" as well as the Song of Songs connotation of the *Mirror* and for prompting me to think more deeply about "Nou goth sonne."

25. On communities and riddles, see Andrew Galloway, "The Rhetoric of Riddling in Late-Medieval England: The 'Oxford' Riddles, the *Secretum philosophorum*, and the Riddles in *Piers Plowman*," *Speculum* 70, no. 1 (1995): 68–105, at p. 72; Curtis A. Gruenler, *"Piers Plowman" and the Poetics of Enigma: Riddles, Rhetoric, and Theology* (Notre Dame, IN: University of Notre Dame Press, 2017).

26. Dailey, "Riddles, Wonder, and Responsiveness," 452, 451. Scholarship on Old English riddles readily recognizes that, as Tiffany Beechy puts it, "the solution to the riddle is only part of what the riddle 'is' or 'does'" (*The Poetics of Old English* [Farnham, Surrey: Ashgate, 2010], 91).

27. Cf. Bynum on the category of "wonder" writing she terms "a literature of entertainment": "In such tales and accounts, wonder is, moreover, deeply perspectival. It is a reaction of a particular 'us' to an 'other' that is 'other' only *relative* to the particular 'us'" (*Metamorphosis and Identity*, 43, 55).

28. See Aden Kumler, "Lyric Vessels," this volume (Chapter 7), 190; Nelson, "Lyric Value,";
139 Barbara Zimbalist, "The Lyric Christ," this volume (Chapter 9), 263.

29. In this respect, Middle English lyric might betray a commonality of purpose with the desire to open a place for nontotalizing subjectivity of the sort that underlies present-day post-lyric impulses to "[critique] the supposed homogeny of lyricism" and "make space for the unique experiments and challenges posed by poets of color," where "lyricism" imposes "homogeny" because critics and others may presume a "lyric I" of a sort that excludes the experiences of some (Sandeep Parmar, "Still Not a British Subject: Race and UK Poetry" *Journal of British and Irish Innovative Poetry* 12, no. 1 [2020]). For a related conversation within medieval studies, see Sierra Lomuto, "Becoming Postmedieval: The Stakes of the Global Middle Ages," *postmedieval* 11, no. 4 (2020): 503–12, where Lomuto "explores and cautions against a global turn that makes diversity and inclusivity its focal point" by "argu[ing] for a 'Global Middle Ages' that exceeds curricular diversification and confronts how whiteness inheres within the 'medieval'" (504).

30. Cristina Maria Cervone, "'I' and 'We' in Chaucer's *Complaint unto Pity*," in Cervone and Smith, *Readings in Medieval Textuality*, 195–212. The previous two sentences replicate some of my wording there (198). A nonlyric example of collective subjectivity would be the doubleness of the servant in the fourteenth-century visionary Julian of Norwich's example of the lord and servant; see my discussion in *Poetics of the Incarnation*, 138–55.

31. *DIMEV* gives the first line as "Sume men sayonne þat i am blac," apparently over-looking the abbreviation on "Sum*me*" and reading an abbreviated final *e* on "sayou*n*," although final *e* is written out, not abbreviated, throughout the rest of the poem. Whether the word as written should be rendered as "sayou*n*" or "sayon*n*" is debatable; neither is standard. For "sayou*n*," read "sayen."

32. Montague Rhodes James, *A Descriptive Catalogue of the Manuscripts in the Library of Gonville and Caius* (Cambridge: Cambridge University Press, 1907–8), 435–47; Richard Leighton Greene, ed., *The Early English Carols*, 2nd ed., rev. and enl. (Oxford: Clarendon Press, 1977), 324–25. James's description makes clear that he was not sure what the manuscript's contents were, beyond identifying their language. Incipits to the Latin grammar texts are listed in G. L. Bursill-Hall, *A Census of Medieval Latin Grammatical Manuscripts*, Grammatica speculativa 4 (Stuttgart: Frommann-Holzboog, 1981), 50.

33. Rossell Hope Robbins, ed., *Secular Lyrics of the XIVth and XVth Centuries*, 2nd ed. (Oxford: Clarendon Press, 1955), no. 33, pp. 30–31. While Robbins's text is largely reliable, I quote from a digitized image of the manuscript. Expansions of abbreviations are indicated by italics. Variant translations are given in square brackets. The poem also appears in Celia Sisam and Kenneth Sisam, eds., *The Oxford Book of Medieval English Verse* (Oxford: Clarendon Press, 1970), 455–56 (the editors channel their inner Shakespeare by titling the poem "The Dark Lady"); Maxwell S. Luria and Richard L. Hoffman, eds., *Middle English Lyrics: Authoritative Texts, Critical and Historical Backgrounds, Perspectives on Six Poems* (New York: W. W. Norton, 1974), no. 139, p. 129; and Thomas G. Duncan, ed., *Late Medieval English Lyrics and Carols, 1400–1530* (London: Penguin, 2000), no. 108, pp. 137–38.

34. Stephanie M. H. Camp, "Black Is Beautiful: An American History," *Journal of Southern History* 81, no. 3 (2015): 675–90; Paul C. Taylor, *Black Is Beautiful: A Philosophy of Black Aesthetics* (Chichester, West Sussex: John Wiley and Sons, 2016).

35. All editors have followed Robbins in "emending" the manuscript reading from "þrow" to "prow" (*MED*, "prou [n.]," "benefit," "advantage," "profit"). To me, the letter looks a bit more like a *p* than a *þ*, so perhaps this is no emendation at all. Yet, *þrow* (*MED*, "throu [n. 2]," "suffering," "contraction of the uterus while giving birth," "anguish," "emotional distress"),

being the *difficilio lector*, has much to recommend it. Its homophonic relationship with *MED* "throu (n. 1)" ("a moment in time," "an instant") extends its resonance. As Ian Cornelius pointed out to me, *prou* and *þou* are true rhymes while *þrou* has a dipthong, so rhyme would also favor *prou*. Surprisingly, the *DIMEV* records "trow," perhaps a typo?

36. This word is unclear. Robbins reads "þer yse" ("where is the black is all my delight"), which is syntactically odd but makes a certain sense. As with the last word on line 2, the character looks more like a *p* than a thorn; however, here on line 15 an infinitive would be expected ("to preyse"). If Robbins is correct ("þer yse"), the *p* for thorn here might help explain *p* for thorn in line 2, *þrow* (as against *prow*). If the character really should be a *p* here, then the scribe must have accidentally omitted the "to" of "to preyse." Could this indicate he was copying the poem from some written source? My thanks to Ian Cornelius for suggesting this idea.

37. Interlinear insertion.

38. The final stanza might be a later addition; see further below.

39. When I first encountered this poem, I was looking for readings to include in my early British literature survey course at the University of Memphis. My students happily embrace skin color as central to the meaning of the poem. "Summe men sayoun" teaches well at all levels; I hope the edition offered here will be of use to others in the classroom.

40. The *MED* places this line under "broun (adj.)," sense 3a: "Of persons: brown, sunburnt, brunet; prob. also, brown-haired; swarthy or sallow (from the effects of love or Mars' wrath); of a brown-skinned race." The skin-based example offered under 3a is from John Trevisa's translation of Bartholomaeus Anglicus's *De Proprietatibus Rerum*: "In hote londes comeþ forþ blake men & browne as among þe Moores." For "hod," see *MED*, s.v. "hōd(e, n." ("rank, condition, status"), and/or *MED*, s.v. "hōd, n." (hood). The poem may be drawing on both. Geoffrey Chaucer, *The Book of the Duchess*, in *The Riverside Chaucer*, gen. ed. Larry D. Benson, 3rd ed. (Boston: Houghton Mifflin, 1987).

41. *MED*, s.v. "bord, n.," sense 5(d), where the examples include: "His Biddyng to folfulle, In Bedde and at Borde" (William Langland, *Piers Plowman* A-text); "He bryngiþ his spouse . . . and makeþ hire felawe in bedde and at bourde" (John Trevisa, translation of Bartholomaeus Anglicus's *De Proprietatibus Rerum*); "Here I take ye to my wedded housband, to hald and to haue at bed and at borde" (*Manuale et processionale ad usum insignis ecclesiae Eboracensis*).

42. *Sir Gawain and Green Knight* is an obvious example and there are many others. See Richard Firth Green, *A Crisis of Truth: Literature and Law in Ricardian England* (Philadelphia: University of Pennsylvania Press, 1999); George Kane, *The Liberating Truth: The Concept of Integrity in Chaucer's Writings* (London: Athlone Press, 1980).

43. *MED*, s.v. "broun," sense 5, as in "He took in honde a rede pensel, Wiþ a soket of broun stel" (*King Alexander*) and, for a nonsword example, "Þe cercle watz . . . Of diamauntez . . . Þat boþe were briȝt and broun" (*Sir Gawain and the Green Knight*).

44. The crux centering on "but" or "and" has long complicated interpretations of this verse: "but" casts blackness as undesirable while "and" champions blackness. For a useful and brief sketch of the issue, see Jacqueline de Weever, *Sheba's Daughters: Whitening and Demonizing the Saracen Woman in Medieval French Epic* (New York: Garland, 1998), xii–xvi.

45. In *Eros and Allegory: Medieval Exegesis of the Song of Songs* (Kalamazoo, MI: Cistercian Publications, 1995), Denys Turner compiles and translates a few commentaries on the text; among these, the following discuss the Bride's blackness: Gregory the Great, 238–42; Alcuin of York, 261–62; Alan of Lille, 300–2; Thomas Gallus (Vercellensis), 331; and Nicholas of Lyra, 389, 399–400. The most well known and influential interpretation was Bernard of Clairvaux's *Sermons on the Song of Songs*.

46. "In a valley of this restless mind" (*DIMEV* 2464; sometimes called "Quia amore langueo"), in Susanna Greer Fein, ed., *Moral Love Songs and Laments* (Kalamazoo, MI: Medieval Institute Publications for TEAMS, 1998), 71. See further my examination of this stanza in *Poetics of the Incarnation*, 60–61. Barbara Zimbalist also discusses this poem in "The Lyric Christ." On the motherhood of Christ, see Caroline Walker Bynum, *Jesus as Mother: Studies in the Spirituality of the High Middle Ages* (Berkeley: University of California Press, 1982); Ritamary Bradley, "Mysticism in the Motherhood Similitude of Julian of Norwich," *Studia Mystica* 8, no. 2 (1985): 4–14.

47. If the final stanza in the manuscript truly belongs with the rest; see below.

48. The Bride's work was variously interpreted; the commentators in Turner, *Eros and Allegory*, give some idea of the range (see note 45, above).

49. *MED*, s.v. "blak, adj.," senses 1a ("Of a black color, black") and 6 ("Confused with *blok*; ?also *bleik, blo*: [a] pale, livid; [b] white; [c] clear, limpid")"; "broun, adj.," senses 2a ("Of a brown color; brown") and 5 ("Of steel, weapons, armor, glass, etc.: shining, polished, bright"); "blo, adj.," senses 1a ("Of the body: dark, discolored, black-and-blue, livid"), 3 ("Of persons: black or blackish in color, dark-skinned"), 2b ("tawny; of hair: blond"), and 1c ("pale, ashen").

50. "The terms of engagement between sacred and secular before the early modern shift" that made the concept of "secular" normative is the topic of Barbara Newman's wonderful *Medieval Crossover: Reading the Secular Against the Sacred* (Notre Dame, IN: University of Notre Dame Press, 2013).

51. As also in the colloquial expression "that's mighty white of you," perhaps originally intended as a compliment (although its history is unclear) but now certainly considered racist and offensive. In its latter use, this expression may be similarly tinged with a put-down to someone who thinks they are more virtuous or just all around better than they actually are, and who is likely to misinterpret the criticism as praise. The *Oxford English Dictionary Online* (*OED*), s.v. "white man, n.," sense 3, and "white, adj.," sense 5c.

52. Among a growing body of work on race and ethnicity in medieval studies, I have found the following especially helpful: Carolyn Dinshaw, "Pale Faces: Race, Religion, and Affect in Chaucer's Texts and Their Readers," *Studies in the Age of Chaucer* 23 (2001): 19–41; the essays in *Journal of Medieval and Early Modern Studies* 31, no. 1 (2001); the essays in *postmedieval* 6, no. 1 (2015); Nahir Otaño Gracia and Daniel Armenti, "Constructing Prejudice in the Middle Ages and the Repercussions of Racism Today," *Medieval Feminist Forum* 53, no. 1 (2017): 176–201; Matthew X. Vernon, *The Black Middle Ages: Race and the Construction of the Middle Ages* (Cham, Switzerland: Palgrave Macmillan, 2018); the essays in *postmedieval* 10, vol. 2 (2019); Dorothy Kim, introduction to *Literature Compass* special cluster on "Critical Race and the Middle Ages," *Literature Compass* 16, nos. 9–10 (2019); and the essays in this cluster, especially Shokoofeh Rajabzadeh, "The Depoliticized Saracen and Muslim Erasure."

53. Suggestively and intriguingly, the *MED* attests to "the broun and the blak" as a phrase for "everyone," where hair color is specifically indicated. The only quotations supporting this definition, however, come from a single work, the romance *Havelok the Dane. MED*, s.v. "blak, n.," 1c.

54. Robert Bartlett, "Medieval and Modern Concepts of Race and Ethnicity," *Journal of Medieval and Early Modern Studies* 31, no. 1 (2001): 39–56, esp. 45–48; Thomas Hahn, "The Difference the Middle Ages Makes: Color and Race Before the Modern World," *Journal of Medieval and Early Modern Studies* 31, no. 1 (2001): 1–37; Joseph Ziegler, "Skin and Character in Medieval and Early Renaissance Physiognomy," in "La pelle umana/The Human Skin," ed. Agostino Paravicini Bagliani, special issue, *Micrologus* 13 (2005): 511–35. Citing the work of V.

Groebner ("Haben Hautfarben eine Geschichte? Personenbeschreibungen und ihre Kate-gorien zwischen dem 13. und dem 16. Jahrhundert," *Zeitschrift für historische Forschung* 30 [2003]: 1–18), Ziegler notes that "Groebner shows how only in the sixteenth century did skin colour gradually emerge as an essential category for distinguishing ethnic identities, thus altering the concept of complexion from a tool describing individual physiological and mental characteristics to a tool describing collectivities" and warns that "generally, blackness in physiognomic texts denotes dark rather than black skin, and thus cannot be automatically used for reconstructing medieval attitudes to black people" (534 and n. 83). Bartlett further shows that "a race can . . . be specified by reference to its language. The intimate relationship between the two is reflected in the fact that in many medieval languages, including Latin, there were terms that could be translated either as 'people' or as 'language.' For some medi-eval thinkers languages were indeed even more permanent parts of the human dispensation than races" ("Medieval and Modern Concepts," 48–49).

55. Bartlett, "Medieval and Modern Concepts," 47.

56. Whitaker, *Black Metaphors*; Suzanne Conklin Akbari, *Idols in the East: European Representations of Islam and the Orient, 1100–1450* (Ithaca, NY: Cornell University Press, 2009), 189–99; Geraldine Heng, *Empire of Magic: Medieval Romance and the Politics of Cultural Fantasy* (New York: Columbia University Press, 2003), 226–37; de Weever, *Sheba's Daughters*; Steven F. Kruger, "Conversion and Medieval Sexual, Religious, and Racial Categories," in *Constructing Medieval Sexuality*, ed. Karma Lochrie, Peggy McCracken, and James A. Schultz (Minneapolis: University of Minnesota Press, 1997), 158–79; and (for gendered examples) Val-entina Jones-Wagner, "The Body of the Saracen Princess in *La Belle Hélène de Constantinople*," *Bucknell Review* 47, no. 2 (2004): 82–89.

For early modern examples of female standards of beauty "whitewashing" a black woman, see Elizabeth McGrath, "The Black Andromeda," *Journal of the Warburg and Courtauld Insti-tutes* 55 (1992): 1–18. On broader racial themes in *The King of Tars*, beyond the now commonly discussed black-to-white transformation of the Sultan, see Sierra Lomuto, "The Mongol Princess of Tars: Global Relations and Racial Formation in *The King of Tars* (c. 1330)," *Exem-plaria* 31, no. 3 (2019): 171–92.

57. For Bernard, the blackness of Christ becomes personal; as Ann Astell puts it, "To Bernard Jesus appears in the form of Bernard: 'I am you'" (*Eating Beauty: The Eucharist and the Spiritual Arts of the Middle Ages* [Ithaca, NY: Cornell University Press, 2006], 82–85). But for a contrasting reading of Bernard's black Christ, see Bruce Holsinger, "The Color of Salvation: Desire, Death, and the Second Crusade in Bernard of Clairvaux's *Sermons on the Song of Songs*," in *The Tongue of the Fathers: Gender and Ideology in Twelfth-Century Latin*, ed. David Townsend and Andrew Taylor (Philadelphia: University of Pennsylvania Press, 1998), 156–86.

58. Bruce Holsinger points out that "in sermons 25 through 29, male homosocial rela-tions are grounded specifically in a *black* female body," linking Bernard's thought to a history of misogyny associated with blackness ("The Color of Salvation," 163, 165). Examples from other authors may be found in Hahn, "The Difference the Middle Ages Makes"; and Geral-dine Heng, "The Invention of Race in the European Middle Ages," 2 pts., *Literature Com-pass* 8, no. 5 (2011): 315–31, 332–50. Misogynistic ideas about black sexuality, notably female sexuality, unfortunately have a long afterlife, as well.

59. Cord Whitaker, "Race-ing the Dragon: The Middle Ages, Race and Trippin' into the Future," *postmedieval* 6, no. 1 (2015): 3–11, at p. 5; Holsinger, "The Color of Salvation," 178. In a continental example probably contemporaneous to the poem, Núria Silleras-Fernández em-phasizes that black slaves at the Aragonese court were valued more for their beauty than for

their blackness (nevertheless, they were slaves, displayed as exotica); *"Nigra Sum Sed Formosa*: Black Slaves and Exotica in the Court of a Fourteenth-Century Aragonese Queen," *Medieval Encounters* 13, no. 3 (2007): 546–65. The slaves cited by name—Sofia, Rosa, Dominica, and Caterina—are all black *women*. Slavery had died out in England long before, by circa 1200; see John Gillingham, *Conquests, Catastrophe and Recovery: Britain and Ireland, 1066–1485* (London: Vintage, 2014), 23; David A. E. Pelteret, *Slavery in Early Mediaeval England from the Reign of Alfred Until the Twelfth Century* (Woodbridge, Suffolk: Boydell Press, 1995), 253.

60. Whitaker, *Black Metaphors*, 38.

61. Greene, *Early English Carols*, 325; A. B. Emden, *A Biographical Register of the University of Oxford to A.D. 1500*, vol. 2 (Oxford: Clarendon Press, 1958), 1158a. "Wymundus london" is written at the top of the page of Gonville and Caius MS 383/603 containing "Summe man sayoun" (with fancy, rubricated ascenders) and also below the left column of the poem (see Figure 8). "Wymundus" is also written in the right margin at the fifth line, among test letters, and "Wymund" is to the left of and below the "Wymundus london" written below the poem.

62. Nicholas Orme, *Education in Early Tudor England: Magdalen College Oxford and Its School, 1480–1540*, Magdalen College Occasional Paper 4 (Oxford: Magdalen College, 1998), 4.

63. G. R. M. Ward, trans., *Statutes of Magdalen College, Oxford* (Oxford: Henry Alden; London: Jackson and Walford, 1840), 23–24.

64. John N. Miner dates the manuscript to "a little before or after 1400," on the basis of unspecified "internal evidence" (*The Grammar Schools of Medieval England: A. F. Leach in Historiographical Perspective* [Montreal: McGill-Queen's University Press, 1990], 138).

65. Christopher Cannon, *From Literacy to Literature: England, 1300–1400* (Oxford: Oxford University Press, 2016), 68; Miner, *Grammar Schools*, 138–39, 171.

66. Their first lines are as follows (in all cases, where I note a refrain, it is copied before the verses are):

p. 41	*refrain begins "Wybbe ne rele ne spynne ye ne may"*	
	"Al þis day ic han sought"	*DIMEV* 393 ("The Serving Maid's Holiday"; female *I*)
	refrain begins "Alas alas þe wyle"	
	"Ladd y þe dance a myssomur day"	*DIMEV* 3044 ("Jack and the Dancing Maid"; female *I*)
	"Alone i lyue alone"	*DIMEV* 451; this is a fragment before the following verse, here seemingly indicating the music to which the verse is to be sung
	"Wan ic wente by3onde þe see"	*DIMEV* 6343 ("Fare Far and Have Little")
p. 68	"Alle 3e mouwen of ioye synge"	*DIMEV* 410 (a Marian carol)
	refrain begins: "A. a. a. a. nun gaudet ecclesia"	
	"Herkennd lordingus grete & smale"	*DIMEV* 3113 ("Listeneth lordings both great and small," a carol about St. Thomas of Canterbury) (this carol carries over onto page 69)
	refrain begins: "Care away away away murnynge away"	
	"y am for sake an oþer ys take"	*DIMEV* 2130 ("I am sorry for her sake")
p. 190	"Summe men sayoun"	the only verse on the page, between a Latin grammatical text and French letter specimens

p. 210 the words "Bryd on brer," together   *DIMEV* 853
      with some of its music, written to
      indicate the tune for the following verse, which is
    "y louede a child of þis cuntre"   *DIMEV* 2222 (female *I*)
     refrain begins: "Þei y synge & murþ I make"
    "Myn owne dere ladi fair & f[re]"   *DIMEV* 3516 (a lover's plea)
     refrain begins: "Aue uirgo regina"
    "vous qui nostre dame aymez"   a carol in the English manner, in French
     refrain begins: "Now þis 3ol"
    "Mari milde haþ boren a chylde"   *DIMEV* 3422 (fragmentary)

For discussion of the music and the manuscript's layout of Gonville and Caius MS 383/603, see Butterfield, "Why Medieval Lyric?"

67. James (*A Descriptive Catalogue*, 436–37) indicates that while two copyists are responsible for the contents of this manuscript, the poetry (the carols plus "Summe men sayoun") is all in the same hand. Greene, *Early English Carols*, 324, says the same of the carols (following James?). However, James does not seem to have done a concerted study of the handwriting, so this attribution is provisional.

68. Bartlett Jere Whiting, "A Collection of Proverbs in BM Additional MS 37075," in *Franciplegius: Medieval and Linguistic Studies in Honor of Francis Peabody Magoun, Jr.*, ed. Jess B. Bessinger, Jr., and Robert P. Creed (New York: New York University Press, 1965), 274–89, at p. 278. Whiting offers the following additional instances (I have found others too):

c1450 *Rylands MS. 394* 105.28: Thawgh peper be blac, it hath a good smak. c1470 *Harley MS. 3362* f. 5a: Thaw pepyr be blac *(no more). Est peper sapidum quamvis sit corpore nigrum.* a1500 Hill 128.9: Thowgh peper be blak, it hath a good smak, 130.17: Thowgh peper be blake, hit hath a good smakke. *Est piper nigrum, quod gratum prestat odorem.* 1508 (1519) John Stanbridge, *Vulgaria*, ed. Beatrice White (EETS 187, 1932) 23.1: Though peper be blacke it hathe a good smacke. *Tamen si piper nig[ri] coloris sit bene sapit tamen.* 1546 Heywood D 68.66: Pepper is blacke And hath a good smacke And every man doth it bye *(in a multiple saying with snow, milk and ink).* Apperson 584.7; *Oxford* 496; Tilley S593. (286–87)

69. If "Summe men sayoun" evolved even partially from *latinitates*, it would not be the only work of its time to have done so. Nicholas Orme points to two that explicitly imitate sentence translation exercises and notes that there are likely more (*English School Exercises, 1420–1530* [Toronto: Pontifical Institute of Mediaeval Studies, 2013], 5). Moreover, he says *latinitates* and *vulgaria* were used to teach Latin grammar and vocabulary but also were framed to school students in ethics and behavior, and were often drawn from everyday life (Orme, "Latin and English Sentences in Fifteenth-Century Schoolbooks," *Yale University Library Gazette* 60, no. 1/2 [1985]: 47–57, at p. 51). On proverbs as a basis for some lyrics, see Helen E. Wicker, "Between Proverbs and Lyrics: Customization Practices in Late Medieval English Moral Verse," *English* 59, no. 224 (2010): 3–24. The variability Wicker notes in development of such poems might be relevant to the materially instantiated lyrics Aden Kumler discusses in Chapter 7 of the present book, too; Christopher Cannon also notes the presence of "proverbs" or "sententia" among the *progymnasmata* ("elementary exercises") of early grammatical

training in his "Proverbs and the Wisdom of Literature: *The Proverbs of Alfred* and Chaucer's *Tale of Melibee*," *Textual Practice* 24, no. 3 (2010): 407–34.

70. "Smack" does not come to mean "a sharp noise or sound made by separating the lips quickly, esp. in kissing, and in tasting or anticipating food or liquor" (*OED*, s.v. "smack, n.2," sense 1a), or "a loud or sounding kiss" (1b), or "a sounding blow delivered with the flat of the hand or something having a flat surface; a slap" (3a), until the sixteenth, seventeenth, and eighteenth centuries, respectively. While in this stanza, as in the proverbs, *smac* clearly means "taste," in the context of this poem its alternate sense of "taint, stigma" may also be in play (*MED*, s.v. "smak[ke] [n.]," sense 3); however, the *MED* only offers one example of this sense, which is not picked up by the *OED*. The sense of "taint" seems to be an extension of "smell," as in *MED*, s.v. "smaken," sense 3, e.g., "Suche beggynge moste smake synne, ouþer in hym þat begges or in hym þat first schulde helpe hym" (*De Blasphemia, contra Fratres* [Wycliffite tract]).

71. For example, "& þerfore late us pike of þe rou3 bark, & fede us of þe swete kyrnel," *Cloud of Unknowing* 59.37–38; Phyllis Hodgson, ed., *The Cloud of Unknowing and Related Treatises on Contemplative Prayer* (Salzburg: Institut für Anglistik und Amerikanistik, Universität Salzburg; Exeter: Catholic Records Press, 1982).

72. Rita Copeland, *Rhetoric, Hermeneutics, and Translation in the Middle Ages: Academic Traditions and Vernacular Texts* (London: Cambridge University Press, 1991), esp. 221–29; Lisa Cooper, "The Poetics of Practicality," in *Middle English*, ed. Paul Strohm, Oxford Twenty-First Century Approaches to Literature (Oxford: Oxford University Press, 2007), 491–505; Peter W. Travis, *Disseminal Chaucer: Rereading "The Nun's Priest's Tale"* (Notre Dame, IN: University of Notre Dame Press, 2010), 51–117; Cannon, *From Literacy to Literature*, 74–124.

73. Elizabeth Salter, "A Complaint Against Blacksmiths," *Literature and History* 5, no. 2 (1979): 194–215, at p. 207. Stephanie Burt discusses "A Complaint Against Blacksmiths" in this volume, "Response: Hevy Hameres" (Chapter 13), and then riffs off of it in her poem, "Hank McCoy's Complaint Against the Danger Room," this volume (New Medieval Lyrics: A Chapbook), 371–72.

74. "Þer to" in line 8 is vague—belonging to what? The *I*? Clothing? Skin? Livery? Similar issues exist for lines 11 and 12 (stanza 3) and 16 (stanza 4), exacerbated by a shift of the word's meaning between lines 11 ("moreover") and 12 ("to that"). In stanza 3, the parallelism set up by the escalating repetition of "& þer to" makes it seem like we should know what is being said—I feel intuitively I should—and yet when you seek to pin it down, it slips away. What, or who, is "treu in dede" (and in what deed, or, indeed?), and in the service of whom, or what, is the *I* pledging his or her life? The punchy "& þer tos" double down on an amplified intensity of a claim for the value of blackness. Why is amplification needed?

Again, in stanza 4, as in stanza 2, the "þer to" of line 16 is remarkably unmoored, though it upholds the sentiment of line 15, something along the lines of "being faithful to reason requires me to think," or, more emphatically, "that's my story and I'm sticking to it!" This use of "þer to" is similar to Julian of Norwich's technique of using anaphoric pronouns in linguistic dilations (Cervone, *Poetics of the Incarnation*, 117–23).

75. A similar effect occurs in "Erþe toc of erþe," where "earth" seems to be everywhere, all around, and inescapable:

Erþe toc of erþe erþe wyþ woh	*took from; woe*
Erþe oþer erþe to þe erþe droh	*dragged/enticed*
Erþe leyde erþe in erþene þroh	*tomb*
Þo heuede erþe of erþe erþe ynoh.	*had; enough*

Hilda M. R. Murray, *The Middle English Poem, Erthe upon Erthe, Printed from Twenty-Four Manuscripts*, EETS, o.s., 141 (London: Oxford University Press, 1911), 1. See also Miller Wolf Oberman's poem, "Notes from March and April 2020," this volume (New Medieval Lyrics: A Chapbook), 378–79.

76. Cannon, "Lyric Romance," this volume (Chapter 3).

77. Langston Hughes, "Dream Variation," in *The Weary Blues* (New York: Knopf, 1926).

78. *DIMEV* 5582; no. 173 in Greene, *Early English Carols*, p. 116; printed with its music and modernized words in John Stevens, ed., *Mediaeval Carols*, Musica Britannica, vol. 4 (London: Stainer & Bell, for the Royal Music Association, 1952), 10–11. Margot Fassler notes that "Ther is no rose" is one of the contrafacts of "Letabundus." See Fassler, "The Religious Lyric in Medieval England (1150–1400): Three Disciplines and a Question," this volume (Chapter 10), 302.

79. Seamus Heaney, "Voices Behind a Door: Robert Frost," *Poetry Review* 83, no. 4 (Winter 1993–94): 31–32, at p. 32; quoted by Stephen James, "Verbal Fixities and the 'Law of Increasing Returns': Uses of the Refrain in Poetry," *Imaginaires* 9 (2003): 343–52, at p. 345.

80. Andrew Albin considers communal aspects of the *carole* with respect to the second lyric of Richard Rolle's *Ego dormio* in "The Sound of Rollean Lyric," this volume (Chapter 8), 232. See also Cervone and Watson, "Why stonde we?," 5; Nelson, "Lyric Value," 155–56.

81. Joyce Coleman, *Public Reading and the Reading Public in Late Medieval England and France* (Cambridge: Cambridge University Press, 1996), xii. While Coleman makes a distinction between the solitary reading of "scholarly-professional readers" (91) or writers and the communal enjoyment of audiences (she sums up her argument at pp. 221–22), the shared enjoyment of riddles and puzzles sent by one member of a learned community to another creates another sort of community for Coleman's "scholarly-professional reader." See also Anne Middleton, "The Idea of Public Poetry in the Reign of Richard II," *Speculum* 53, no. 1 (1978): 94–114; Daniel Donoghue, *How the Anglo-Saxons Read Their Poems* (Philadelphia: University of Pennsylvania Press, 2018), chap. 1. Increasing attention to performance and community in medieval English lyric studies is relevant as well; see, e.g., Jessica Brantley, *Reading in the Wilderness: Private Devotion and Public Performance in Late Medieval England* (Chicago: University of Chicago Press, 2007), esp. 1–25 and 269–305; and, from a different stance, Ingrid Nelson, *Lyric Tactics: Poetry, Genre, and Practice in Later Medieval England* (Philadelphia: University of Pennsylvania Press, 2017).

82. *DIMEV* 1241; no. 29 in Greene, *Early English Carols*, 16.

83. This would put the working of Middle English lyric in line with broader trends of other writing contemporaneous to it—not only the "gyre" Cannon notes in *King Horn*, but also, for example, the "eddies whirling counter to the main current . . . musings [that] slow the reader's progress and offset the passage of linear time with a cyclical or spiral motion" that Barbara Newman sees as common to William Langland's *Piers Plowman* and Julian of Norwich's *A Revelation of Love* ("Redeeming the Time: Langland, Julian, and the Art of Lifelong Revision," *Yearbook of Langland Studies* 23 [2009]: 1–32, at p. 8); or the "chiastic structures [that] resist purely linear reading" that Ryan McDermott discerns in the inner workings of *Piers Plowman* ("Practices of Satisfaction and *Piers Plowman*'s Dynamic Middle," *Studies in the Age of Chaucer* 36, no. 1 (2014): 169–207, at p. 173); or the "completeness that refuses to privilege the end, a way of moving forward that draws much of its energy from the middle" that Claire M. Waters perceives in Chaucer's work ("*Makyng* and Middles in Chaucer's Poetry," in Cervone and Smith, *Readings in Medieval Textuality*, 31–44, at p. 44).

84. Also relevant are notions of causation in the Aristotelian systems discussed in Cervone and Watson, "Why stonde we?," 14–15.

CHAPTER 3

1. It is now possible to read all of these contents, in their mutually informing context, in the recent edition and translation of all the texts in the manuscript: Susanna Fein, ed. and trans., *The Complete Harley 2253 Manuscript*, with David Raybin and Jan Ziolkowski, 3 vols. (Kalamazoo, MI: Medieval Institute Publications for TEAMS, 2014–15). I will cite texts from this collection by volume and page number from this edition.

2. See Joseph Ritson, *Ancient Songs, from the Time of King Henry the Third, to the Revolution* (London, 1790), 24–26 and 26–44; and Carleton Brown, ed., *English Lyrics of the XIIIth Century* (Oxford: Clarendon Press, 1932). The anthologizing of the "lyrics" of Harley 2253 began with four poems in Carleton Brown's *Religious Lyrics of the XIVth Century* (Oxford: Clarendon Press, 1924); and continued when another twenty concluded Brown, *English Lyrics of the XIIIth Century*, 131–63. Although Brown seems to define the "lyric" as a poem that was accompanied by music or could have been (see *English Lyrics*, xi–xvi), his selections in these two volumes effectively defined the lyric "as any short poem," as Rossell Hope Robbins noted in 1952 (Robbins, ed., *Secular Lyrics of the XIV and XV Centuries*, 2nd ed. [Oxford: Clarendon Press, 1955; first published 1952], v). On this process of genre formation, see Ardis Butterfield, "Lyric Editing," this volume (Chapter 1), 39–43; and Ingrid Nelson, *Lyric Tactics: Poetry, Genre and Practice in Later Medieval England* (Philadelphia: University of Pennsylvania Press, 2017), 18–21.

3. G. L. Brook, ed., *The Harley Lyrics*, 2nd ed. (Manchester: Manchester University Press, 1956; first published 1948). Brook's edition came between those of Brown and Robbins (see previous note), and the work it did can be seen by comparing the descriptions of the poems in the manuscripts. Brown sees a certain chaos ("no arrangement is discernible in the contents of the book," *English Lyrics*, xxxvi) and notes the book's breadth ("representing the attempt of a collector with an unusually catholic interest in literature" [*English Lyrics*, xxxvii]). By the time we reach Robbins in 1952, however, the lyrics of Harley 2253 (along with those of Oxford, Bodleian Library, MS Digby 86) are "the greatest achievement of all Middle English poetry" (*Secular Lyrics*, xviii). Brook also defines the "lyric" as a short poem: "A characteristic of all the earliest English secular lyrics that have survived is that they are very short" (*Harley Lyrics*, 5).

4. Derek Pearsall, *Old English and Middle English Poetry* (London: Routledge & Kegan Paul, 1977), 125; Seth Lerer, "Old English and Its Afterlife," in *The Cambridge History of Medieval English Literature*, ed. David Wallace (Cambridge: Cambridge University Press, 1999), 7–34, at p. 30 ("individualized"); G. W. F. Hegel, *Aesthetics: Lectures on Fine Art*, trans. T. M. Knox, 2 vols. (Oxford: Oxford University Press, 1975), 2:1038.

5. Susanna Fein, "The Lyrics of MS Harley 2253," in *A Manual of the Writings in Middle English, 1050–1500*, vol. 11, ed. Peter G. Beidler (New Haven: Connecticut Academy of Arts and Sciences, 2005), 4168–206 and 4317–61.

6. It has been customary, since Neil Ker's analysis in the facsimile of the manuscript, to divide the fifteen quires that Harley 2253 comprises into seven "independent blocks" (see Neil Ker, "Introduction," *Facsimile of British Museum MS. Harley 2253*, EETS, o.s., 255 [London: Oxford University Press, for the Early English Text Society, 1965], xvi). "Booklet" is the term that Fein uses in her edition to identify these gatherings (see Fein, *Complete Harley 2253*, pp. 4–8 in each volume), and she also analyzes the book's quires in this form in the appendix to her article in the valuable collection she edited, *Studies in the Harley Manuscript: The Scribes, Contents, and Social Contexts of British Library MS Harley 2253* (Kalamazoo, MI: Medieval Institute Publications, 2000), 371–76. Brook took twenty-six of the thirty-two

poems in his collection from booklet 5 (which concludes with *King Horn*), as well as items 1–2 from booklet 4 and items 29–32 from booklet 6.

7. The whole of the first volume of the *Manual* was devoted to "romances." For *King Horn*, see Charles Dunn, "Romances Derived from English Legends," in *A Manual of the Writings in Middle English, 1050–1500*, vol. 1, ed. J. Burke Severs (New Haven: Connecticut Academy of Arts and Sciences, 1967), 17–37, at pp. 18–20. "Written in the last part of the thirteenth century, *King Horn* is probably the oldest surviving Middle English romance," introduction to Ronald B. Herzman, Graham Drake, and Eve Salisbury, eds., *King Horn*, in *Four Romances of England: King Horn, Havelok the Dane, Bevis of Hampton, Athelston* (Kalamazoo, MI: Medieval Institute Publications for TEAMS, 1997), 11, http://d.lib.rochester.edu/teams/text/salisbury-king-horn-introduction. Unless otherwise indicated I will cite *King Horn* from this edition by line number in the text.

8. See Gisela Guddat-Figge, *Catalogue of Manuscripts Containing Middle English Romances* (Munich: W. Fink, 1976), 283. For a more detailed analysis of the placement of *King Horn* alongside the saint's legends in Laud Misc. 108, see Diane Speed, "A Text for Its Time: The *Sanctorale* of the Early *South English Legendary*," in *The Texts and Contexts of Oxford, Bodleian Library, MS Laud Misc. 108*, ed. Kimberly K. Bell and Julie Nelson Crouch (Leiden: Brill, 2011), 117–36, at pp. 122–23. For a reading of *Horn* in the context of saint's life, see, in the same volume, Kimberly K. Bell, "'Holie Mannes Liues': England and Its Saints in Oxford Bodleian Library, MS Laud Misc. 108," 251–74.

9. Child called the ballad version "Hind Horn." For these ballads and his characterization, see Francis J. Child, *English and Scottish Popular Ballads*, ed. Helen Child Sargent and George Lyman Kittredge (Cambridge, MA: Houghton Mifflin, 1904), 31–33. On this ballad, see also James R. Hurt, "The Texts of *King Horn*," *Journal of the Folklore Institute* 7 (1970): 47–59, at p. 49.

10. For the association of lyric and song (stemming, of course, from the presumption that early lyrics were accompanied by music, and more specifically, music played on a "lyre"), see Jonathan Culler, *Theory of the Lyric* (Cambridge, MA: Harvard University Press, 2015), 49–51. For instances of Middle English *singen* as "to chant or recite verse" or "to relate . . . a story . . . in song or verse," see the *Middle English Dictionary* (*MED*), s.v. "singen, v.," 4a–b. For medieval English lyrics and their music, see Butterfield, "Lyric Editing"; Margot Fassler, "The Religious Lyric in Medieval England (1150–1400): Three Disciplines and a Question," this volume (Chapter 10).

11. Brook, *Harley Lyrics*, 10–11.

12. Ibid., 1. Brook says that he had 20,000 volumes before he began to cull them but recognized from the start that "for a collection to approach anywhere near completeness considerable subdivision is necessary" (*Books and Book-Collecting* [London: Andre Deutsch, 1980], 27 ["for"] and 160 [on the number of books in his collection]). Marisa Galvez has described the "dual quality of the songbook" and demonstrated how collections of lyrics can be, at once, a "collection of discrete units" and "a coherent corpus" (*Songbook: How Lyrics Became Poetry in Medieval Europe* [Chicago: University of Chicago Press, 2012], 9). On the role of manuscript layout in soliciting particular reading practices, see Andrew Albin, "The Sound of Rollean Lyric," this volume (Chapter 8).

13. Virginia Jackson, *Dickinson's Misery: A Theory of Lyric Reading* (Princeton, NJ: Princeton University Press, 2005), 8. On the tendency in literary history to reduce all poetry to lyric, see Mark Jeffreys, "Ideologies of Lyric: A Problem of Genre in Contemporary Anglophone Poetics," *PMLA* 110, no. 2 (1995): 196–205, at p. 200, cited by Jackson, 8.

14. Virginia Jackson, "Lyric," in *The Princeton Encyclopedia of Poetry and Poetics*, 4th ed., ed. Roland Greene and Stephen Cushman (Princeton, NJ: Princeton University Press, 2012), 826–34, at p. 832.

15. For a digitized image of folio 83r, which contains the rubric, see http://www.bl.uk /manuscripts/Viewer.aspx?ref=harley_ms_2253_f083r. For this meaning of "geste," see *MED*, s.v. "geste, n.(1)," 1(a). The romance also survives in Oxford, Bodleian Library, MS Bodley 1486 (fols. 219v–28r); and Cambridge, Cambridge University Library, MS Gg.4.27 (II) (fols. 6r–13v).

16. Hegel, *Aesthetics*, 2:1038; M. H. Abrams, *A Glossary of Literary Terms* (New York: Holt, Rinehart and Winston, 1971; first published 1957), 89.

17. Sylvia Huot, *From Song to Book: The Poetics of Writing in Old French Lyric and Lyrical Narrative Poetry* (Ithaca, NY: Cornell University Press, 1987), 83.

18. Paul Zumthor, *Essai de poétique médiévale* (Paris: Seuil, 1972), 287 ("chant narratif" and "récit chanté"), 288 ("cadres"), 312 (on epic). See also the whole of Zumthor's chapter on "chant et récit" (286–338).

19. Jean Dufournet, ed., *Aucassin et Nicolette* (Paris: Flammarion, 1984), 41.24. On this poem and its form, see Ardis Butterfield, *Poetry and Music in Medieval France: From Jean Renart to Guillaume de Machaut* (Cambridge: Cambridge University Press, 2002), 191–99.

20. Andrew Galloway, "Theory of the Fourteenth-Century English Lyric," this volume (Chapter 11).

21. Derek Pearsall, "The Development of Middle English Romance," *Mediaeval Studies* 27 (1965): 91–116, at pp. 105–6.

22. Ardis Butterfield, "Why Medieval Lyric?," *English Literary History* 82, no. 2 (2015): 319–43, at p. 327.

23. Paul de Man, "Lyrical Voice in Contemporary Theory," in *Lyric Poetry: Beyond New Criticism*, ed. Chaviva Hošek and Patricia Parker (Ithaca, NY: Cornell University Press, 1985), 55–72, at p. 55.

24. *Horn Childe & Maiden Rimnild*, lines 1–6, https://auchinleck.nls.uk/mss/horn.html.

25. *Havelok the Dane*, lines 1–4, http://d.lib.rochester.edu/teams/text/salisbury-four -romances-of-england-havelok-the-dane. For *Havelok the Dane* as a "romance," see Severs, *Manual of the Writings*, 1:22–25.

26. Joyce Coleman, *Public Reading and the Reading Public in Late Medieval England and France* (Cambridge: Cambridge University Press, 1996), 82–85.

27. Ibid., 52–63.

28. For these claims (the first by Laura Hibbard, the second by Julius Zupitza), see Andrew Taylor, "The Myth of the Minstrel Manuscript," *Speculum* 66, no. 1 (1991): 43–73, at pp. 54–55. Taylor thinks it is more likely that this part of Laud Misc. 108 was copied from a minstrel's book. For this book and its contents, see also *The Texts and Contexts of Oxford, Bodleian Library, MS Laud Misc. 108: The Shaping of English Vernacular Narrative*, ed. Kimberly K. Bell and Julie Nelson Couch (Leiden; Boston: Brill, 2011).

29. Ruth Crosby, "Oral Delivery in the Middle Ages," *Speculum* 11, no. 1 (1936): 88–110, at p. 102. For examples, see Crosby at p. 101; and for examples in English and in the Italian *canterini*, see David Wallace, *Chaucer and the Early Writings of Boccaccio* (Cambridge: D. S. Brewer, 1985), 78–81.

30. Robert Mannyng, *Chronicle*, ed. Idelle Sullens (Binghamton, NY: Binghamton University, 1996), line 75. On the "disour" as a "story-teller or minstrel," see Derek Pearsall, "The Auchinleck Manuscript 40 Years On," in *The Auchinleck Manuscript: New Perspectives*, ed. Susanna Fein (York: York Medieval Press, 2016), 11–25, at pp. 18–19.

31. John Gower, *Confessio Amantis*, ed. Russell A. Peck (Kalamazoo, MI: Medieval Institute Publications for TEAMS, 2004), 7.2423–24.

32. William Langland, *The Vision of Piers Plowman: A Critical Edition of the B-Text*, ed. A. V. C. Schmidt, 2nd ed. (London: J. M. Dent, 1995), 10.31 (for more such references see P.35, 13.173 and 13.224); Geoffrey Chaucer, *The House of Fame*, line 1198 ("gestiours"), and *The Canterbury Tales*, 7.846 ("geestours"), in *The Riverside Chaucer*, gen. ed. Larry D. Benson, 3rd ed. (Boston: Houghton Mifflin, 1987).

33. *Emaré*, in Anne Laskaya and Eve Salisbury, eds., *The Middle English Breton Lays* (Kalamazoo, MI: Medieval Institute Publications for TEAMS, 1995), lines 13 ("menstrelles") and 24 ("As I").

34. Andrew Taylor, "Myth of the Minstrel Manuscript," 59.

35. Albert Baugh, "Improvisation in the Middle English Romance," *Proceedings of the American Philosophical Society* 103, no. 3 (1959): 418–54, esp. pp. 420–31.

36. Ibid., 432.

37. See Ad Putter, "Middle English Romances and the Oral Tradition," in *Medieval Oral Literature*, ed. Karl Reichl (Berlin: De Gruyter, 2012), 335–51; and Richard Trachsler, "Orality, Literacy and Performativity of Arthurian Texts," in *Handbook of Arthurian Romance: King Arthur's Court in Medieval European Literature*, ed. Leah Tether and Johnny McFadyen (Berlin: De Gruyter, 2017), 273–92.

38. I take these examples from Baugh, "Improvisation," 436.

39. Ibid., 437.

40. Hurt, "Texts of *King Horn*," 50.

41. Joseph Hall, ed., *King Horn: A Middle English Romance* (Oxford: Clarendon Press, 1901), xiv.

42. Hurt, "Texts of *King Horn*," 56.

43. Rosamund Allen attempted to harmonize all three texts in an edition by recension because she also believed that *King Horn* once had a "fixed, authorial form" that could be retrieved, although she acknowledged that some of the divergences between the three witnesses resembled "corruptions which might have been introduced into the tradition by oral transmission." For her method, see Allen, ed., *King Horn: An Edition Based on Cambridge University Library MS Gg.4.27 (2)* (New York: Garland, 1984). For the phrases I quote, see Allen's introduction, pp. 34 ("fixed") and 35 ("corruptions"). Nicolas Jacobs argued, in a review of this edition, that it was difficult for Allen to determine original readings in the many cases where the manuscripts used synonyms and the direction of substitution could therefore never be determined (see *Medium Aevum* 57, no. 2 [1988]: 301–3).

44. The text here and in subsequent comparisons of the versions of *Horn* is taken from Hall's edition and cited by his line numbers for each version.

45. George Kane, "Introduction," in William Langland, *Piers Plowman: The A Version*, ed. George Kane (London: Athlone Press, 1960), 1–172, at p. 144. To compression, expansion, and dislocation, and unevenness in accuracy of reproduction Kane added "omissions . . . from defect of memory." All of these criteria were advanced by way of claiming that the manuscripts of the A text show no such characteristics, although it is hard not to point out that these are exactly the distinctions that differentiate the A text from the B and C texts.

46. I take these figures from Hurt, "Texts of *King Horn*," 50.

47. Mildred K. Pope, ed., *The Romance of Horn by Thomas*, 2 vols., ANTS 9–10, 12–13 (Oxford: Published for the Anglo-Norman Text Society by B. Blackwell, 1955–64), lines 1–2. Michael Clanchy suggests that this passage understands the parchment as a "substitute for a

jongleur; it speaks and is heard," like a charter (*From Memory to Written Record: England, 1066–1307*, 2nd ed. [Oxford: Blackwell, 1993], 263).

48. On "lyric insertion," see Huot, *From Song to Book*, 106–34; Jacqueline Cerquiglini, "Pour une typologie de l'insertion," *Perspectives médiévales* 3 (1977): 9–14; and Jane H. M. Taylor, "The Lyric Insertion: Towards a Functional Model," in *Courtly Literature: Culture and Context*, ed. Keith Busby and Erik Kooper (Amsterdam: John Benjamins, 1990), 539–48.

49. Butterfield, *Poetry and Music*, 225–26.

50. Culler, *Theory of the Lyric*, 115 (on dramatic monologue) and 123 ("lyric sequence").

51. Sharon Cameron, *Lyric Time: Dickinson and the Limits of Genre* (Baltimore: Johns Hopkins University Press, 1979), 240–41.

52. Culler, *Theory of the Lyric*, 28; on the "lyric present," see also pp. 283–95.

53. Jacques Lacan, "Logical Time and the Assertion of Anticipated Certainty: A New Sophism," in *Écrits: The First Complete Edition in English*, trans. Bruce Fink, with Héloïse Fink and Russell Grigg (New York: W. W. Norton, 2002), 161–75, at p. 166 (and, on the simultaneity of the "time for comprehending," the "time of meditation," and the "moment for concluding," see 168–69). Lacan imagines a situation in which three subjects, faced with a set of rules about the color of the disks placed on each of their backs, guess rightly the color of the disk they are wearing by noticing the hesitation that more or less overlaps with the resolute action of the other two subjects.

54. Sarah Kay, "The 'Changeful Pen': Paradox, Logical Time and Poetic Spectrality in the Poems Attributed to Chrétien de Troyes," in *Thinking Through Chrétien de Troyes*, by Zrinka Stahuljak et al. (Cambridge: D. S. Brewer, 2011), 36.

55. Gérard Genette, *Narrative Discourse: An Essay in Method*, trans. Jane E. Lewin (Ithaca, NY: Cornell University Press, 1980), 86–88.

56. Wayne C. Booth, *The Rhetoric of Fiction*, 2nd ed. (Chicago: University of Chicago Press, 1983), 19 ("durational"); and (as cited here in Booth) Jean-Paul Sartre, "Situation of the Writer in 1947," in *What Is Literature?*, trans. Bernard Frechtman (London, 1967; first published 1950), 128–229, at p. 176.

57. Genette, *Narrative Discourse*, 114.

58. See, especially, ibid., 94.

59. On "iterative" narration, see ibid., 116.

60. On "tempo" in the novel, see ibid., 94–95.

61. Butterfield, *Poetry and Music*, 294.

62. This term is also Butterfield's (see ibid.).

63. James A. Snead, "Repetition as a Figure of Black Culture," in *Black Literature and Literary Theory*, ed. Henry Louis Gates, Jr. (New York: Routledge, 1990), 59–79, at p. 67.

64. I count inversions of these pairings too, so honde/londe is equivalent to londe/honde.

65. I take my text from *Sir Orfeo*, in Laskaya and Salisbury, *Middle English Breton Lays*, 15–59. On the oral transmission of *Sir Orfeo*, see Nancy Mason Bradbury, *Writing Aloud: Storytelling in Late Medieval England* (Urbana: University of Illinois Press, 1998), 19; and Murray McGillivray, *Memorization in the Transmission of the Middle English Romances* (New York: Garland, 1990), 90–91.

66. Oakden cataloged 1,415 recurrent alliterative phrases in the "non-rhyming poems of the alliterative revival," a further 261 in the "alliterative works with end rhyme," and 820 in the romances. See J. P. Oakden, *Alliterative Poetry in Middle English: A Survey of the Traditions* (Manchester: Manchester University Press, 1935), 263, 312, and 314 (for these tabulations) and 267–312, 315–43, and 344–63 (for lists of these phrases).

67. Butterfield, "Why Medieval Lyric?," 325.

68. See *MED*, s.vv. "lai, n.(2)" and "song, n."; Nicolette Zeeman, "Imaginative Theory," in *Middle English*, ed. Paul Strohm, Oxford Twenty-First Century Approaches to Literature (Oxford: Oxford University Press, 2007), 222–40.

69. See *Oxford English Dictionary Online* (*OED*), s.v. "refrain, n.1"; and *Dictionnaire du Moyen Français (1330–1500)* (*DMF*), s.v. "refrain, subst. masc.," http://www.atilf.fr/dmf/definition/refrain.

70. "A refrain is not something that can be defined once: its range of functions is so diverse that it needs constant redefinition within each context" (Ardis Butterfield, "Repetition and Variation in the Thirteenth-Century Refrain," *Journal of the Royal Musical Association* 116, no. 1 [1991]: 1–23, at p. 3).

71. Butterfield, *Poetry and Music*, 43 and 57.

72. Ibid., 268.

73. This is an observation Butterfield makes about the rondeaux of Guillaume d'Amiens (ibid., 48–49).

74. Gilles Deleuze and Félix Guattari, *A Thousand Plateaus: Capitalism and Schizophrenia,* trans. Brian Massumi (London: Continuum, 1987), 349; John Hollander, "Breaking into Song: Some Notes on Refrain," in *Lyric Poetry: Beyond New Criticism,* ed. Chaviva Hošek and Patricia Parker (Ithaca, NY: Cornell University Press, 1985), 73–89, at p. 75.

75. Eleanor Johnson, "*Reddere* and Refrain: A Meditation on Poetic Procedure in *Piers Plowman*," *Yearbook of Langland Studies* 30 (2016): 3–27, at p. 13.

76. Hollander, "Breaking into Song," 76.

77. See Brook, *Harley Lyrics*, 70–72; and the poems "Lutel wot hit any mon hou love hym haveth ybounde" (3:240–41) and "Lutel wot hit any mon hou derne love may stonde" (3:242–43) in Fein's collection.

78. Johnson, "*Reddere* and Refrain," 6.

79. Susanna Greer Fein, "Twelve-Line Stanza Forms in Middle English and the Date of *Pearl*," *Speculum* 72, no. 2 (1997), 367–98 (see esp. pp. 373–75).

80. Simon Jarvis, "Prosody as Cognition," *Critical Quarterly* 40, no. 4 (1998): 3–15. See also Simon Jarvis, "For a Poetics of Verse," *PMLA* 125, no. 4 (2010): 931–35.

81. Jarvis, "Prosody as Cognition," 12.

CHAPTER 4

I acknowledge with gratitude the volume editors and fellow participants in the Radcliffe seminars; audiences in St. Louis, Chicago, and Kalamazoo, 2016–17; and conversations with colleagues and students at Yale University, 2010–16, especially Ardis Butterfield and Eric Weiskott. As always, errors are mine.

1. See, for two perspectives, Virginia Jackson, "Lyric," in *The Princeton Encyclopedia of Poetry and Poetics*, 4th ed., ed. Roland Greene and Stephen Cushman (Princeton, NJ: Princeton University Press, 2012), 826–34; and Jonathan Culler, *Theory of the Lyric* (Cambridge, MA: Harvard University Press, 2015).

2. For this way of stating relations between lyric and meter, I adapt the non-Aristotelian logic of "prototype theory": see John R. Taylor, *Linguistic Categorization: Prototypes in Linguistic Theory* (Oxford: Clarendon Press, 1989).

3. Brown remarks on meter only in exceptional circumstances in his first anthology volume: see, for examples, Carleton Brown, ed., *Religious Lyrics of the XIVth Century* (Oxford:

Clarendon Press, 1924), 267, 278 (notes to items 69 and 103, respectively). Comments on English meter remain rare in later volumes except where an English poem may be compared with the meter of its Latin source, usually a hymn. For examples, see Carleton Brown, ed., *English Lyrics of the XIIIth Century* (Oxford: Clarendon Press, 1932), xviii–xix, xxv, and the notes to items 45 and 47. The only summative treatment occurs in Rossell Hope Robbins, *Secular Lyrics of the XIVth and XVth Centuries*, 2nd ed. (Oxford: Clarendon Press, 1955), xlvii–li, based on a 1932 dissertation by Beatrice Geary. Brown and Robbins's *Index of Middle English Verse* (New York: Columbia University Press, 1943) will be the target of sustained critique later in this chapter.

4. Salient among recent studies of poetic meter in Middle English lyric are Thomas Cable, "Foreign Influence, Native Continuation, and Metrical Typology in Alliterative Lyrics," in *Approaches to the Metres of Alliterative Verse*, ed. Judith Jefferson and Ad Putter (Leeds: Leeds Studies in English, 2009), 219–34; Thomas G. Duncan, "Middle English Lyrics: Metre and Editorial Practice," in *A Companion to the Middle English Lyric*, ed. Thomas G. Duncan (Cambridge: D. S. Brewer, 2005), 19–38; and Thomas G. Duncan, ed., *Medieval English Lyrics and Carols* (Cambridge: D. S. Brewer, 2013), 40–45, 454–56. I dissent from Duncan's syllabic interpretation of Middle English meters, but the editorial reconstructions detailed in his 2005 essay are illuminating.

5. Brown and Robbins adopt a similarly capacious definition. See Robbins, *Secular Lyrics of the XIVth and XVth Centuries*, v, where Robbins states that he has "accepted Brown's definition of a lyric as any short poem." For comment, see Rosemary Greentree, *The Middle English Lyric and Short Poem* (Cambridge: D. S. Brewer, 2001), 5–13, 32–35.

6. Lynda Mugglestone, ed., *The Oxford History of English*, updated ed. (Oxford: Oxford University Press, 2012), is a good introduction. For Middle English, see R. D. Fulk, *An Introduction to Middle English: Grammar; Texts* (Peterborough, Ontario: Broadview Press, 2012).

7. Multilingualism has received much attention in the past two decades. See Judith A. Jefferson and Ad Putter, eds., *Multilingualism in Medieval Britain (c. 1066–1520): Sources and Analysis* (Turnhout: Brepols, 2013); for general orientation, see John Burrow, "The Languages of Medieval England," in *The Oxford History of Literary Translation in English*, vol. 1, *To 1550*, ed. Roger Ellis (Oxford: Oxford University Press, 2008), 7–28; and Elaine Treharne, "The Vernaculars of Medieval England, 1170–1350," in *The Cambridge Companion to Medieval English Culture*, ed. Andrew Galloway (Cambridge: Cambridge University Press, 2011), 217–36.

8. On this assessment, the massive influence of Norse on the English language becomes evident in written records around the time that Norse ceased to be a discrete, living language in Britain. See Matthew Townend, *Language and History in Viking Age England: Linguistic Relations Between Speakers of Old Norse and Old English* (Turnhout: Brepols, 2002), 189, 201–10, and references there.

9. See, for a fifteenth-century English lyric in a traditional Welsh meter, E. J. Dobson, "The Hymn to the Virgin," in *Transactions of the Honourable Society of Cymmrodorion* (1954): 70–124.

10. This assessment is hard-won and not uncontroversial: see William Rothwell, "A quelle époque a-t-on cessé de parler français en Angleterre?," in *Mélanges de philologie romane offerts à Charles Camproux* (Montpellier: Université Paul-Valéry, 1978), 2:1075–89; and Ian Short, *Manual of Anglo-Norman*, ANTS, O.P., 7 (London: Anglo-Norman Text Society, 2007), 12–17, 21–28. Compare Hugh M. Thomas, *The English and the Normans: Ethnic Hostility, Assimilation, and Identity, 1066–c.1220* (Oxford: Oxford University Press, 2003), 377–88.

11. See Ralph Hanna, *Patient Reading/Reading Patience: Oxford Essays on Medieval English Literature* (Liverpool: Liverpool University Press, 2017), 21–23, 34–40; Ralph Hanna, "Lambeth Palace Library, MS 260, and the Problem of English Vernacularity," *Studies in Medieval and Renaissance History*, 3rd ser., 5 (2008): 131–99, at pp. 163–73; and, for reassessment of fourteenth-century evidence, Christopher Cannon, *From Literacy to Literature: England, 1300–1400* (Oxford: Oxford University Press, 2016).

12. Sheldon Pollock, *The Language of the Gods in the World of Men: Sanskrit, Culture, and Power in Premodern India* (Berkeley: University of California Press, 2006), 26 (emphasis in original). Two other of Pollock's concepts are worth noticing here. Pollock proposes the term "literization" for the process by which a language comes to be committed to writing and "literarization" for the process by which a language comes to be employed in literary composition. Vernacularization of literary culture and literarization of a vernacular language are linked processes, but they are asymmetrical: one and the same text may constitute a significant event in the literarization of English without constituting a significant event in the vernacularization of the cultural space to which it belongs.

13. See Derek Pearsall, *Old English and Middle English Poetry* (London: Routledge & Kegan Paul, 1977); Jakob Schipper, *A History of English Versification* (Oxford: Clarendon Press, 1910); Max Kaluza, *A Short History of English Versification from the Earliest Times to the Present Day: A Handbook for Teachers and Students*, trans. A. C. Dunstan (London: George Allen, 1911); and George Saintsbury, *A History of English Prosody from the Twelfth Century to the Present Day*, vol. 1, *From the Origins to Spenser*, 2nd ed. (London: Macmillan, 1923).

14. Thomas Cable, "English Prosody," *Oxford Bibliographies*, Medieval Studies (Oxford University Press, 2010), http://dx.doi.org/10.1093/OBO/9780195396584-0035.

15. Martin J. Duffell, *A New History of English Metre* (London: Legenda, 2008). Duffell is not recommendable on alliterative verse. On that, see Thomas Cable, *The English Alliterative Tradition* (Philadelphia: University of Pennsylvania Press, 1991); and Geoffrey Russom, *The Evolution of Verse Structure in Old and Middle English Poetry: From the Earliest Alliterative Poems to Iambic Pentameter* (Cambridge: Cambridge University Press, 2017). Eric Weiskott, *Meter and Modernity in English Verse, 1350–1650* (Philadelphia: University of Pennsylvania Press, 2021), which appeared after this chapter was written, is a valuable new survey of major verse types in Middle English and their postmedieval legacies. See note 27, below.

16. See Duffell, *A New History of English Metre*, 35–46 (surveying "Foreign Influences on English Metre"), 75–77 ("Versifying in Insular French"), and 83–92 (on fourteenth-century Francien *vers de dix*, Italian *endecasillabo*, and the verse of Chaucer and Gower).

17. On the prosodic system of continental French, see Alfred Ewert, *The French Language* (New York: Macmillan, 1941), 104–8; and Ernst Pulgram, "Prosodic Systems: French," *Lingua* 13 (1965): 125–44.

18. See P. H. Matthews, *The Concise Oxford Dictionary of Linguistics*, 3rd ed. (Oxford: Oxford University Press, 2014), s.v. "substratum."

19. Short, *Manual of Anglo-Norman*, 24.

20. Duffell, *A New History of English Metre*, 77. See too Roger Pensom, "Pour la versification anglo-normande," *Romania: Revue trimestrielle consacré a l'étude des langues et des littératures romanes* 124, no. 1 (2006): 50–65, showing that insular French alexandrine verse exhibits patterns of avoidance consistent with an accentual construction.

21. My account omits the influences of Latin hymns on vernacular versification. See Margot Fassler, "The Religious Lyric in Medieval England (1150–1400): Three Disciplines and a Question," this volume (Chapter 10); and the summary account in M. L. Gasparov, *A History*

of European Versification, ed. G. S. Smith and Leofranc Holford-Strevens, trans. G. S. Smith and Marina Tarlinskaja (Oxford: Clarendon Press, 1996), 125–29, 179–80. For commentary (not prosodic) on some Middle English translations of Latin hymns, see Siegfried Wenzel, *Preachers, Poets, and the Early English Lyric* (Princeton, NJ: Princeton University Press, 1986), chap. 2.

22. Marina Tarlinskaja, "Meter and Rhythm of Pre-Chaucerian Rhymed Verse," *Linguistics* 12, no. 121 (1974): 65–87; Marina Tarlinskaja, *English Verse: Theory and History* (The Hague: Mouton, 1976); Marina Tarlinskaja, *Strict Stress-Meter in English Poetry Compared with German and Russian* (Calgary: University of Calgary Press, 1993). Duffell summarizes Tarlinskaja's contributions and analyzes Middle English dolnik at *A New History of English Metre*, 24–25, 65–66, 79–80, 85.

23. I quote G. V. Smithers, "The Scansion of *Havelok* and the Use of ME -*en* and -*e* in *Havelok* and by Chaucer," in *Middle English Studies: Presented to Norman Davis in Honour of His Seventieth Birthday*, ed. Douglas Gray and E. G. Stanley (Oxford: Clarendon Press, 1983), 195–234, at p. 196.

24. Derek Attridge, "An Enduring Form: The English Dolnik," in *Moving Words: Forms of English Poetry* (Oxford: Oxford University Press, 2013), 147–87. On "Nou goth sonne," see also Ardis Butterfield, "Lyric Editing," this volume (Chapter 1), 32, 35–36; Cristina Maria Cervone, "Wondering Through Middle English Lyric," this volume (Chapter 2), 68–71; Stephanie Burt, "Response: Hevy Hameres," this volume (Chapter 13), 359, 368.

25. Carleton Brown, *English Lyrics of the XIIIth Century*, 1. I impose modern English capitalization. For the manuscript context of this lyric, see Brown's notes at pp. 165–66.

26. Attridge, "An Enduring Form," 151.

27. See Duffell, *A New History of English Metre*, 90–91. Weiskott, *Meter and Modernity in English Verse*, 74–89, subsumes "dolnik" within "tetrameter" (for him a big-tent category).

28. These are "Ich herde men vpo mold make muche mon" (*DIMEV* 2198); "Ichot a burde in a bour ase beryl so bryht" (*DIMEV* 2324); "Mon in þe mone stond ant strit" (*DIMEV* 3362); "Ne mai no lewed lued libben in londe" (*DIMEV* 3683); and "Of rybaudȝ y ryme ant rede o my rolle" (*DIMEV* 4202).

29. See Cable, "Foreign Influence"; Eric Weiskott, *English Alliterative Verse: Poetic Tradition and Literary History* (Cambridge: Cambridge University Press, 2016), 103–6; Ian Cornelius, *Reconstructing Alliterative Verse: The Pursuit of a Medieval Meter* (Cambridge: Cambridge University Press, 2017), chap. 5; and Ian Cornelius, "The Text of the *ABC of Aristotle* in the 'Winchester Anthology,'" *Anglia* 139, no. 2 (2021): 400–18.

30. A concise overview is Thomas Cable, "Progress in Middle English Alliterative Metrics," *Yearbook of Langland Studies* 23 (2009): 243–64.

31. For stylistic developments in late Old English poetry, see Emily V. Thornbury, *Becoming a Poet in Anglo-Saxon England* (Cambridge: Cambridge University Press, 2014), 223–37.

32. Aspects of oral performance are explored by Ad Putter, "Middle English Romances and the Oral Tradition," and Karin Boklund-Lagopoulou, "Popular Song and the Middle English Lyric," both in *Medieval Oral Literature*, ed. Karl Reichl (Berlin: De Gruyter, 2012), 335–51, 555–80.

33. See, for a technical exposition of this historical condition, Thomas Cable, "Philology: Analysis of Written Records," in *Research Guide on Language Change*, ed. Edgar C. Polomé (Berlin: Mouton de Gruyter, 1990), 97–106.

34. Spenser's *Faerie Queene*, 1.2.44.7 and 1.2.24.3, respectively, from Early English Books Online (EEBO)'s images of the first edition: Edmund Spenser, *The Faerie Queene Disposed into twelue books, Fashioning XII. Morall vertues* (London: Printed for William Ponsonbie, 1590),

sig. C1r and B6r, respectively, https://www.proquest.com/books/faerie-queene-disposed-into
-twelue-books/docview/2240874158/se-2. See the list of "words and word groups sometimes
reduced, sometimes used in full, in sixteenth- and seventeenth-century English verse," printed
as an appendix to Edward R. Weismiller, "Triple Threats to Duple Rhythm," in *Phonetics and
Phonology*, vol. 1, *Rhythm and Meter*, ed. Paul Kiparsky and Gilbert Youmans (San Diego: Academic Press, 1989), 288–89, and discussion at pp. 269–71, 275 n. 15, and 276–78.

35. The principal reference source for Middle English dialects is M. Benskin et al., *An
Electronic Version of "A Linguistic Atlas of Late Mediaeval English"* (Edinburgh: University of
Edinburgh, 2013–), http://www.lel.ed.ac.uk/ihd/elalme/elalme.html (hereafter *eLALME*),
revising Angus McIntosh, M. L. Samuels, and Michael Benskin, *A Linguistic Atlas of Late
Mediaeval English*, 4 vols. (Aberdeen: Aberdeen University Press, 1986). For "without(en),"
see *eLALME*'s maps of survey item 295; the form with *-n* is comparatively infrequent in the
southwest, while the form without *-n* is comparatively infrequent north of the Humber.
Some other survey items exhibiting syllabic variants are 70 ("about"), 206–9 (negative particles in contracting position), 212 ("never"), 221 ("or"), and 238 ("self"). For final *-e* see the
next notes. A good introduction to Middle English dialectology is Fulk, *An Introduction to
Middle English*, 112–28.

36. See *eLALME*'s dot maps for survey items 61-30 (3sg. pres. ind., contracted) and 160-
40 ("has" 3sg., variants with syllabic inflexions).

37. See M. L. Samuels, "Chaucerian Final '-*e*,'" *Notes and Queries* 19, no. 12 (1972): 445–
48; Cable, *English Alliterative Tradition*, 76–78; and Robert McColl Millar, "Language,
Genre, and Register: Factors in the Use of Simple Demonstrative Forms in the South-West
Midlands of the Thirteenth Century," in *Laʒamon: Contexts, Language, and Interpretation*,
ed. Rosamund Allen, Lucy Perry, and Jane Roberts (London: King's College London, Centre for Late Antique and Medieval Studies, 2002), 227–39.

38. On weak final *-e* in Middle English poetry, excluding alliterative, see Donka Minkova,
The History of Final Vowels in English: The Sound of Muting (Berlin: Mouton de Gruyter, 1991),
esp. 75–80; Samuels, "Chaucerian Final '-*e*'"; Smithers, "Scansion of *Havelok*"; and E. Talbot
Donaldson, "Chaucer's Final *-e*," *PMLA* 63, no. 4 (1948): 1101–24, esp. 1110–16. On final *-e* in
Middle English alliterative poetry see Cable, *English Alliterative Tradition*, chap. 3; Ad Putter,
Judith Jefferson, and Myra Stokes, *Studies in the Metre of Alliterative Verse* (Oxford: Society
for the Study of Medieval Languages and Literature, 2007), 19–117; Nicolay Yakovlev, "On
Final *-e* in the B-Verses of *Sir Gawain and the Green Knight*," in Jefferson and Putter, *Ap-
proaches to the Metres of Alliterative Verse*, 135–57. Hoyt N. Duggan, "The End of the Line," in
Medieval Alliterative Poetry: Essays in Honour of Thorlac Turville-Petre, ed. John A. Burrow
and Hoyt N. Duggan (Dublin: Four Courts Press, 2010), 67–79, attempts to reconcile con-
flicting data from the two poetic traditions.

39. See note 6 above.

40. See the studies in note 38.

41. See the argument of Hoyt N. Duggan, "Libertine Scribes and Maidenly Editors:
Meditations on Textual Criticism and Metrics," in *English Historical Metrics*, ed. C. B. Mc-
Cully and J. J. Anderson (Cambridge: Cambridge University Press, 1996), 219–37.

42. For a survey of the manuscript record, see Julia Boffey, "Middle English Lyrics and
Manuscripts," in Duncan, *Companion to the Middle English Lyric*, 1–18. Greentree, *Middle
English Lyric*, emphasizes the importance of the Index as a research tool: see pp. 1, 19, 21, 37.

43. For examples and references, see Ruth Kennedy, "'A Bird in Bishopswood': Some
Newly-Discovered Lines of Alliterative Verse from the Late Fourteenth Century," in *Medieval

Literature and Antiquities: Studies in Honour of Basil Cottle, ed. Myra Stokes and T. L. Burton (Cambridge: D. S. Brewer, 1987), 71–87; Susanna Greer Fein, "A Thirteen-Line Alliterative Stanza on the Abuse of Prayer from the Audelay MS," *Medium Aevum* 63, no. 1 (1994): 61–74; and Weiskott, *English Alliterative Verse*, 84–85.

44. Saintsbury, *History of English Prosody*, 41, 49. Emphasis in the original. These passages are unchanged from the first edition, published in 1906. The pages between these two quotations are of first importance.

45. Andrew Albin discusses this lyric in "The Sound of Rollean Lyric," this volume (Chapter 8), 226–28; see also Derek Pearsall, "The Origins of the Alliterative Revival," in *The Alliterative Tradition in the Fourteenth Century*, ed. Bernard S. Levy and Paul E. Szarmach (Kent, OH: Kent State University Press, 1981), 5; for analysis of the meter, see Weiskott, *English Alliterative Verse*, 96–97. The fundamental bibliographical treatment of Middle English alliterative verse, with special reference to the cataloging efforts of the Index, is Ralph Hanna, "Defining Middle English Alliterative Poetry," in *The Endless Knot: Essays on Old and Middle English in Honor of Marie Borroff*, ed. M. Teresa Tavormina and R. F. Yeager (Cambridge: D. S. Brewer, 1995), 43–64. See also Eric Weiskott, "A Checklist of Short and Fragmentary Unrhymed English Alliterative Poems, 1300–1600," *Notes and Queries* 67, no. 3 (2020): 340–47.

46. So far as I can see, the *DIMEV* has yet to make any public statement regarding its procedures.

47. Alan J. Fletcher, "The Lyric in the Sermon," in Duncan, *Companion to the Middle English Lyric*, 189–209, is a good introduction. For the procedures of Brown and Robbins when faced with sermon materials, see Hanna, *Patient Reading*, 58 n. 9 (reporting conversation with Robbins). Hanna's studies supply instructive illustrations, often leveraged towards criticism of the Index. See *Patient Reading*, 56–63, 66–91; Ralph Hanna, "The Verses of Bodleian Library, MS Laud Misc. 77," *Notes and Queries* 63, no. 3 (2016): 361–70; and Ralph Hanna, "Verses in Sermons Again: The Case of Cambridge, Jesus College, MS Q.A.13," *Studies in Bibliography* 57 (2005–6): 63–83 (esp. pp. 71–74). The most intrepid navigator of mixed-language preachers' materials is Siegfried Wenzel. See his *Macaronic Sermons: Bilingualism and Preaching in Late-Medieval England* (Ann Arbor: University of Michigan Press, 1994), esp. 13–28; and Wenzel's earlier treatments: *Verses in Sermons: "Fasciculus Morum" and Its Middle English Poems* (Cambridge, MA: Mediaeval Academy of America, 1978), chap. 2; and *Preachers*, chaps. 1 and 3.

48. See Siegfried Wenzel, *Medieval "Artes Praedicandi": A Synthesis of Scholastic Sermon Structure* (Toronto: University of Toronto Press, 2015), 73; and Karl Polheim, *Die lateinische Reimprosa* (Berlin: Weidmann, 1925), 456–57. The thema is the sermon's principal reference passage, usually taken from the Bible and quoted at the beginning of the sermon.

49. Wenzel, *Verses in Sermons*. Wenzel has also edited and translated the full text: *Fasciculus Morum: A Fourteenth-Century Preacher's Handbook* (University Park: Pennsylvania State University Press, 1989).

50. This is Wenzel's item C, printed as two lines at *Verses in Sermons*, 205, with commentary on p. 191. The line is recorded as verse in *IMEV* (4151) and *DIMEV* (6647), but regarded as prose in *NIMEV*.

51. Kumler, "Lyric Vessels," this volume (Chapter 7), 202–16.

52. Despite appearances, the spellings "spare" and "spend" probably do not represent an inconsistent graphic registration of verbal inflection. The *-e* in "spare" indicates that the preceding vowel is long; on this interpretation, both spellings are graphic monosyllables. The words acquire grammatically justified inflectional syllables in vocal enunciation, if at all.

53. Bartlett Jere Whiting, *Proverbs, Sentences, and Proverbial Phrases from English Writings Mainly Before 1500* (Cambridge, MA: Belknap Press, 1968), 537, 642–43. Parenthetical references in the main text are Whiting's alphanumeric identifiers.

54. Quoting Kumler, "Lyric Vessels," 212. The poem "Summe men sayoun," discussed by Cristina Maria Cervone elsewhere in this book, supplies another instance of a versified Middle English proverb. See Cervone, "Wondering Through Middle English Lyric," 82.

55. "Þe wel ne deð, þe hwile he mai, ne scal he wenne he walde." This is line 35 in the text of London, Lambeth Palace Library, MS 487; I quote from Fulk, *An Introduction to Middle English*, 167, but print *w* in place of the letter wynn.

56. The other nonverse items are Wenzel's numbers 18 (*DIMEV* 3521), 44 (*DIMEV* 4516), and 46 (*DIMEV* 6592). For discussion of the "signs of death," see Wenzel, *Verses in Sermons*, 197–99; Rossell Hope Robbins, "Signs of Death in Middle English," *Mediaeval Studies* 32 (1970): 282–98; and Rosemary Woolf, *The English Religious Lyric in the Middle Ages* (Oxford: Clarendon Press, 1968), 78–82.

57. Gasparov's capacious perspective is helpful here: "Readers accustomed to the classic European literature of modern times usually imagine that the main feature opposing prose to verse is the absence of rhyme. This is not true. The main distinctive feature is . . . the fact that verse is segmented into equivalent and commensurable segments independent of syntax, and prose only in relation to syntax." Gasparov, *A History of European Versification*, 97.

58. Wenzel, *Verses in Sermons*, 198; Wenzel, *Fasciculus Morum*, 718.

59. John of Garland, *Parisiana poetria*, ed. and trans. Traugott Lawler (Cambridge, MA: Harvard University Press, 2020), 178–81, 474.

60. Christine Mohrmann, *Études sur le latin des chrétiens*, vol. 2, *Latin chrétien et médiéval* (Rome: Edizioni di storia e letteratura, 1961), 351–67; Polheim, *Die lateinische Reimprosa*, 389–90.

61. See the discussions of Cecily Clark, "As Seint Austin Seith . . . ," *Medium Aevum* 46, no. 2 (1977): 212–18; and Elizabeth Salter, *English and International: Studies in Literature, Art and Patronage of Medieval England*, ed. Derek Pearsall and Nicolette Zeeman (Cambridge: Cambridge University Press, 1988), 70–74.

62. Wenzel, *Verses in Sermons*, 47–49.

63. Qualifications in this sentence register the nuanced treatment of the language of preaching in Wenzel, *Macaronic Sermons*, 119–23; compare Wenzel, *Verses in Sermons*, 86–88. For evidence that *Fasciculus Morum* was intended to support preaching to a lay audience, see Wenzel, *Verses in Sermons*, 50.

64. Hanna, *Patient Reading*, 87–91, analyzes a sermon script consisting of "notes awaiting fuller performative enactment" (87). For the intricacies of scholastic sermon structure, see the sermon analyzed at Wenzel, *Medieval "Artes Praedicandi,"* 89–103; and discussion at Wenzel, *Macaronic Sermons*, 74–79. A good account of *inventio, dispositio*, and *elocutio* may be found in Heinrich Lausberg, *Handbook of Literary Rhetoric: A Foundation for Literary Study*, ed. David E. Orton and R. Dean Anderson, trans. Matthew T. Bliss, Annemiek Jansen, and David E. Orton (Leiden: Brill, 1998).

65. Wenzel reports English verses noticed but not recorded, or recorded incompletely, in Latin sermons (*Verses in Sermons*, 84 and 94). And see the examples discussed at Wenzel, *Macaronic Sermons*, 97–98; and Hanna, *Patient Reading*, 60 (two lines of verse in triple time), 89–90. Ardis Butterfield, "Poems Without Form? *Maiden in the mor lay* Revisited," in *Readings in Medieval Textuality: Essays in Honour of A. C. Spearing*, ed. Cristina Maria Cervone and

D. Vance Smith (Cambridge: D. S. Brewer, 2016), 169–94, at p. 189, illustrates similar problems of inscription and performance.

66. Holly Johnson, *The Grammar of Good Friday: Macaronic Sermons of Late Medieval England* (Turnhout: Brepols, 2012), xxiii. Similarly, Wenzel likens such sermon texts to the notes "of an experienced lecturer who usually speaks extempore and requires only a brief outline, yet who will jot down his best jokes verbatim to make sure that he gets them right." Siegfried Wenzel, "Poets, Preachers, and the Plight of Literary Critics," *Speculum* 60, no. 2 (1985): 343–63, at p. 350.

67. Wenzel, *Macaronic Sermons*, 218–21. On this sermon, see Wenzel's discussion; and Holly Johnson, *Grammar of Good Friday*, 61–66. The quality of language-mixing instanced in *Amore langueo* is unusual and its relation to oral performance disputed. For discussion and a variety of opinions, see Wenzel, *Macaronic Sermons*, 65–129; Alan J. Fletcher, "Written versus Spoken Macaronic Discourse in Late Medieval England: The View from a Pulpit," in Jefferson and Putter, *Multilingualism in Medieval Britain*, 137–51; Herbert Schendl, "Code-Switching in Late Medieval Macaronic Sermons," in Jefferson and Putter, *Multilingualism in Medieval Britain*, 153–69; and Ardis Butterfield, "Fuzziness and Perceptions of Language in the Middle Ages," part 3, "Translating Fuzziness: Countertexts," *Common Knowledge* 19, no. 3 (2013): 446–73, at pp. 455–62. For the particular English item I discuss, see Carleton Brown, *English Lyrics of the XIIIth Century*, 113; Wenzel, *Verses in Sermons*, 128, 131; and Woolf, *English Religious Lyric*, 20–21, 370–71, 373.

68. On the meter of these two poems, see Hanna, "Defining Middle English Alliterative Poetry," 46–47. Compare Cable, "Foreign Influence," 230–31.

69. The best candidate for alternating rhythm in the second half-lines of "Ich herde men" is "nou wereþ ragges" (36). This half-line could be scanned "nou **wereþ ragges**" (xSxSx), except that contrastive stress probably throws the first beat to the adverb *nou* ("now"). (The first half of the line reads "Þat er werede robes.") I quote from Thorlac Turville-Petre, ed., *Alliterative Poetry of the Later Middle Ages: An Anthology* (Washington, DC: Catholic University of America Press, 1989).

70. On the manuscript, see Wenzel, *Macaronic Sermons*, 43–44, 177–80; and Hanna, *Patient Reading*, 57. I thank librarians at Balliol College Oxford, Trinity College Dublin, and the British Library for images of manuscripts in their collections.

71. Delete "with his blode" (at line 639 in Wenzel's ed.) and "Lord" (line 656); both are pleonastic.

72. See William Langland, *Piers Plowman: The A Version; Will's Visions of Piers Plowman and Do-Well, an Edition in the Form of Trinity College Cambridge MS R.3.14 Corrected from Other Manuscripts, with Variant Readings*, ed. George Kane, rev. ed. (London: Athlone Press; and Berkeley: University of California Press, 1988), 122, for remarks on small grammatical variants in Middle English poetry.

73. See *MED*, s.v. "forleten, v.," sense 6(a). The reading in Cambridge, Cambridge University Library, MS Kk.4.24 (Wenzel's sigil B) is also metrical.

74. Trinity's spelling is distinctive of northern dialects, but disyllabic forms are geographically unrestricted. See *eLALME*'s dot maps for item 16, "much."

75. Weak final -*e* separates the third and fourth beats on only four other occasions: 73, "swete" (< OE *swēte*); 545, "alle" (pl. adj.); 635, "new" (< OE *nēowe*); and 769, "wythoute"(< OE *wiþūtan*). I count weak final -*e* only where that syllable is justified by grammar or derivation and stands alone between beats. The relevant instances, in addition to those just listed, are

59, "hyme" (infinitive); 68, "loue" (< OE *lufu*); 201 and 716, "hert" (< OE *heorte*); 480, "serue" (infinitive); 717 and 747, "swete" (< OE *swēte*).

76. At least one other scribe had the same idea, for the other two witnesses have "ful" for Trinity's "so."

77. The other instances are (the Balliol reading precedes the bracket, Trinity follows): 69, "deye"] "drery"; 200, "tokenes"] "tokynys gret"; 479, "As"] "for as"; 544, "no"] "noght a"; 557, "þe"] *om*; 635, "we"] "to owre lorde"; 657, "þi"] *om* (*also* T); B and T are Wenzel's sigla for Cambridge University Library, MS Kk.4.24, and Oxford, Magdalen College, MS 93, respectively (these copies do not supply independent improvements, except for B at line 655). To this list one could add Trinity's rewritten lines at 654–55 and the following: 558, "Ioy"] "þe ioye"; 718, "me"] "me þi."

78. These are 194, *198, 201, *337, *635, 657, *767, *769, and *DIMEV* 1367.2. An asterisk marks lines interpretable as having initial stress inversion.

79. These are 73, 184, 196, 197, 336, 337, 478, 569, 636, 655, 747, and *DIMEV* 1367.3.

80. On stress clash, see Tarlinskaja, *English Verse*, 92–93; and Smithers, "Scansion of *Havelok*," 218.

81. For a sophisticated foot-based scansion of Middle English materials, see the chapter "The Birth of Iambic Meter," in Russom, *The Evolution of Verse Structure*, 259–71.

82. I use the Oxford Text Archive's digital text of *Pearl*, ed. E. V. Gordon (Oxford: Clarendon Press, 1953).

83. This is the interpretation favored by Duggan, "Libertine Scribes and Maidenly Editors," 228–31, with reference specially to *Pearl*.

84. See Russom, *Evolution of Verse Structure*, 20; Cable, "Progress in Middle English Alliterative Metrics," 257 n. 15 and references there.

85. My count of unambiguous monosyllabic intervals (81 percent of the total) treats final -*e* as elided when followed by a vowel or *h*-. In an additional 4 percent of lines, the final interval may be contracted to one syllable (e.g., *euer* > *er*; *trendeled* > *trendel'd*; *precios* with consonantal *i*). In a further 9 percent of lines, election of a form without final -*e* would yield a monosyllabic final interval. Duggan likewise finds that the interval between the third and fourth beats is monosyllabic in "over 90 per cent" of lines in *Pearl* ("Libertine Scribes and Maidenly Editors," 223).

86. See Richard Bauman and Charles L. Briggs, "Poetics and Performance as Critical Perspectives on Language and Social Life," *Annual Review of Anthropology* 19 (1990): 72–78; and Michael Silverstein and Greg Urban, eds., *Natural Histories of Discourse* (Chicago: University of Chicago Press, 1996), 1–14.

87. Wenzel, *Verses in Sermons*, 102.

88. Nos. 2, 3, 5, 6, 8, 9, 12, 17, 19, 20, 22, 23, 24A, 28, 29, 30, 31, 33, 35, 36, 38, 41A, 42A, 43, 47, 50, 51, 53, 56, 58, 59, 61. I take "Now" to be extrametrical at the head of 58.1. For 17.1, "executors," the meter calls for the aphetic and contracted form *sectores*. Contraction is represented in the spelling of one witness to this lyric, receives confirmation from meter in the *Cursor Mundi* (quoted in *MED*, s.v. "secutour, n."), and accords with well-established patterns of sound change in trisyllabic words of Romance origin. The spelling "executors," which is the form transmitted in most copies of *Fasciculus Morum* 17, might have been favored as graphically unambiguous.

89. I find only five instances among the lyrics in the previous note: 9.4, 31.1, 43.1, 43.2, 50.2. At 31.1 two copies preserve a metrically regular variant.

90. In *FM* 27.1 I take "man" to be extrametrical or an intrusion. *FM* 34A.3 might be regularized by reading "þat þou" for "þou." In *FM* 48.1 and 48.3 there is stress clash between the first two beats; these lines return to regularity in their second half.

91. *FM* 45 has suffered textual corruption in all copies of *Fasciculus Morum* and all sixteen witnesses for which the *DIMEV* supplies transcriptions (*DIMEV* 3167).

92. Compare 2.4 "a" (absent from most copies including Wenzel's base text prior to correction) and 15.2 "in."

93. Wenzel, *Verses in Sermons*, 121. *FM* 26B is an unsuccessful and aborted effort to rewrite 26A in alternating-stress lines.

CHAPTER 5

1. I. A. Richards, *Principles of Literary Criticism*, ed. John Constable (London: Routledge, 2001; first published 1924 by Kegan Paul, Trench, Trübner), 31.

2. Cleanth Brooks, *The Well Wrought Urn: Studies in the Structure of Poetry* (New York: Harcourt, Brace, Jovanovich, 1975).

3. Horace, *Ars poetica*, in *Satires, Epistles, and Ars Poetica*, ed. and trans. H. Rushton Fairclough (Cambridge, MA: Harvard University Press, 1955); Sir Philip Sidney, "The Defence of Poesy," in *Sidney's "The Defence of Poesy" and Select Renaissance Literary Criticism*, ed. Gavin Alexander (New York: Penguin, 2004), 1–54.

4. Virginia Jackson, *Dickinson's Misery: A Theory of Lyric Reading* (Princeton, NJ: Princeton University Press, 2005), 6, 7.

5. Jahan Ramazani, *Poetry and Its Others: News, Prayer, Song, and the Dialogue of Genres* (Chicago: University of Chicago Press, 2014), 1–62.

6. Thomas Percy, *Reliques of Ancient English Poetry: Consisting of Old Heroic Ballads, Songs, and Other Pieces of Our Earlier Poets (Chiefly of the Lyric Kind)*, 3 vols. (London, 1765), vol. 1; David Matthews, *The Making of Middle English, 1765–1910* (Minneapolis: University of Minnesota Press, 1999).

7. For a history of close reading, see Barbara Hernstein Smith, "What Was 'Close Reading'? A Century of Methods in Literary Studies," *Minnesota Review* 87 (2016): 57–75. As a measure of the critical neglect of premodern poetry, we might note that there are twenty-nine Middle English lyric poems out of a total of 883 in Arthur Quiller-Couch, ed., *The Oxford Book of English Verse, 1250–1900* (Oxford: Clarendon Press, 1908). The most recent edition of the *Norton Anthology of Poetry* contains only twenty-four Middle English lyric poems out of a total of 1,871. Among the numerous critical works that aspire to represent lyric poetry as a transhistorical and transnational genre, two examples serve as representative. Chaviva Hošek and Patricia Parker, eds., *Lyric Poetry: Beyond New Criticism* (Ithaca, NY: Cornell University Press, 1985), omits any discussion of Middle English lyric. Jonathan Culler, *Theory of the Lyric* (Cambridge, MA: Harvard University Press, 2015), discusses Middle English lyric in a cursory manner, citing primarily one critic. More inclusive, Virginia Jackson and Yopie Prins, eds., *The Lyric Theory Reader: A Critical Anthology* (Baltimore: Johns Hopkins University Press, 2014), offers an essay on Middle English lyric.

8. Mark Jeffreys, "Ideologies of Lyric: A Problem of Genre in Contemporary Anglophone Poetics," *PMLA* 110, no. 2 (1995): 196–205.

9. Text from Maxwell S. Luria and Richard L. Hoffman, eds., *Middle English Lyrics: Authoritative Texts, Critical and Historical Backgrounds, Perspectives on Six Poems* (New York:

W. W. Norton, 1974), pp. 215–17, no. 226; *Digital Index of Middle English Verse* (*DIMEV*) 5030. I have altered the punctuation (which is editorial). On the musical setting of this poem, see Margot Fassler, "The Religious Lyric in Medieval England (1150–1400): Three Disciplines and a Question," this volume (Chapter 10), 282–83. For the work's narrative strategies, see Barbara Zimbalist, "The Lyric Christ," this volume (Chapter 9).

   10. Exeter Book Riddle K–D 84.

An wiht is on eorþan   wundrum acenned,
hreoh ond reþe   hafað ryne strongne,
grimme grymetað,   ond be grunde fareð.
Modor is monigra   mærra wihta.
Fæger ferende   fundað æfre;
neol is nearograp.   Nænig oþrum mæg
wlite ond wisan   wordum gecyþan,
hu mislic biþ   mægen þara cynna.

   Original text Craig Williamson, ed., *The Old English Riddles of the "Exeter Book"* (Chapel Hill: University of North Carolina Press, 1977), 113; translation Paull F. Baum, *Anglo-Saxon Riddles of the Exeter Book* (Durham, NC: Duke University Press, 1963), 8–9.

   11. "Perhaps I might say it [scripture] is like a river both shallow and deep, in which a lamb walks and an elephant swims" (Quasi quidam quippe est fluvius ut ita dixerim planus et altus in quo et agnus ambulet, et elephas natet) (Gregory the Great, *Moralia in Job*, ed. Marcus Adriaen, Corpus Christianorum, Series Latina 143 [Turnhout: Brepols, 1979], inscr. 4; translation from Gregory the Great, *Moral Reflections on the Book of Job*, trans. Brian Kerns, 3 vols. [Collegeville, MN: Liturgical Press, 2014], 1:53); "Imitating the action of the swiftest of rivers, Holy Scripture fills up the depths of the human mind and yet always overflows, quenches the thirsty and yet remains inexhaustible. Bountiful streams of spiritual sense gush out from it and, merging into others, make still others spring up—or rather (since 'wisdom is undying') they do not merge but *emerge* and, showing their beauty to others, cause these others not to replace them as they fail but to succeed them as they remain" (Scriptura sacra, morem rapidissimi fluminis tenens, sic humanarum mentium profunda replet ut semper exundet, sic haurientes satiat ut inexhausta permaneat. Profluunt ex ea spiritualium sensuum gurgites abundantes, et transeuntibus aliis alii surgunt, immo non transeuntibus, quia sapientia immortalis est, sed, emergentibus et decorem suum ostendentibus aliis, alii non defitientibus succedunt, sed manentes subsequuntur) (Gilbert of Stanford, *Tractatus super Cantica canticorum*, ed. Rossana Guglielmetti [Florence: Edizioni del Galluzzo, 2002], 2; quoted also in Umberto Eco, *Semiotics and the Philosophy of Language* [Bloomington: Indiana University Press, 1984], 150; translation from Nicholas Watson, "The Trinitarian Hermeneutic in Julian of Norwich's *Revelation of Love*," in *The Medieval Mystical Tradition in England: Exeter Symposium V*, ed. Marion Glasscoe [Cambridge: D. S. Brewer, 1992], 79–100, at p. 92). I thank Nicholas Watson for these references.

   12. For an introduction to this theory, see Jackson and Prins, *The Lyric Theory Reader*. For a recent summa, see Culler, *Theory of the Lyric*.

   13. On the lyric as "whole," see, e.g., Brooks, *The Well Wrought Urn*; John Paul Russo, *I. A. Richards: His Life and Work* (Baltimore: Johns Hopkins University Press, 1989); Caroline Levine, *Forms: Whole, Rhythm, Hierarchy, Network* (Princeton, NJ: Princeton University Press, 2015), 24–48.

   14. For example, John Guillory, "Close Reading: Prologue and Epilogue," *ADE Bulletin* 149, no. 3 (2010): 8–14, compares Richards's methods to N. Katherine Hayles's media theory.

Frances Ferguson, "Our I. A. Richards Moment: The Machine and Its Adjustments," in *Theory Aside*, ed. Jason Potts and Daniel Stout (Durham, NC: Duke University Press, 2014), 261–79, demonstrates the commonality between Richards's approach and Jacques Rancière's idea of *dissensus*.

15. Thomas L. Reed, *Middle English Debate Poetry and the Aesthetics of Irresolution* (Columbia: University of Missouri Press, 1990).

16. Ralph Barton Perry, "Economic Value and Moral Value," *Quarterly Journal of Economics* 30, no. 3 (1916): 443–85, at p. 445.

17. Ralph Barton Perry, *General Theory of Value: Its Meaning and Basic Principles Construed in Terms of Interest* (New York: Longmans, Green, 1926), 115.

18. *Oxford English Dictionary Online (OED)*, s.v. "value," esp. 6d.

19. *Middle English Dictionary (MED)*, s.v. "valu(e) n.," 2 and 4.

20. Russo, *I. A. Richards*, 43–46.

21. Richards, *Principles of Literary Criticism*, 31–34.

22. See, e.g., ibid., 232: "The extent to which reference is interfered with by needs and desires is underestimated even by those who, not having yet forgotten the events of 1914–1918, are most sceptical as to the independence of opinions and desires."

23. I. A. Richards, *Practical Criticism: A Study of Literary Judgment*, ed. John Constable (New York: Routledge, 2001), 308–9.

24. Richards, *Principles of Literary Criticism*, 43.

25. Ibid., 52–53.

26. Ibid., 53.

27. For a discussion of this training, see Paul H. Fry, "I. A. Richards," in *The Cambridge History of Literary Criticism*, ed. A. Walton Litz, Louis Menand, and Lawrence Rainey (Cambridge: Cambridge University Press, 2000), 179–99, at pp. 183–84; Murray Krieger, *The New Apologists for Poetry* (Minneapolis: University of Minnesota Press, 1956), 57–58; Russo, *I. A. Richards*, 177–202.

28. Richards, *Principles of Literary Criticism*, 255.

29. Ibid., 177.

30. Ibid., 178.

31. Ibid., 235. Compare and contrast the contemporary theory of language discussed by Raymond W. Gibbs, Jr., "Cognitive Poetics of Middle English Poetry," this volume (Chapter 6).

32. Brooks, *The Well Wrought Urn*, 3, 195. In drawing this connection, I do not mean to suggest that the New Critics accorded with Richards's theory in all respects. For a perceptive discussion of their differences, see Ferguson, "Our I. A. Richards Moment."

33. William Empson, *Seven Types of Ambiguity* (London: Chatto and Windus, 1930); Brooks, *The Well Wrought Urn*.

34. I. A. Richards, *Poetries: Their Media and Ends; A Collection of Essays*, ed. Trevor Eaton (The Hague: Mouton, 1974), 80.

35. Helen Vendler, *Soul Says: On Recent Poetry* (Cambridge, MA: Harvard University Press, 1995), 6–7.

36. Rosemary Woolf, *The English Religious Lyric in the Middle Ages* (Oxford: Clarendon Press, 1968), 4–7; Judson Boyce Allen, "Grammar, Poetic Form, and the Lyric Ego: A Medieval *A Priori*," in *Vernacular Poetics in the Middle Ages*, ed. Lois Ebin (Kalamazoo, MI: Medieval Institute Publications, 1984), 199–226.

37. See, for example, Sarah Kay, "Desire and Subjectivity," in *The Troubadours: An Introduction*, ed. Simon Gaunt and Sarah Kay (Cambridge: Cambridge University Press, 1999), 212–27; Eugene Vance, "Greimas, Freud, and the Story of Trouvère Lyric," in Hošek and Parker, *Lyric Poetry*, 93–105.

38. Theodor Adorno, "Lyric Poetry and Society," trans. Bruce Mayo, *Telos* 20 (1974): 52–71.

39. Charles Altieri, "What Is Living and What Is Dead in American Postmodernism: Establishing the Contemporaneity of Some American Poetry," in Jackson and Prins, *The Lyric Theory Reader*, 477–87, at p. 477.

40. Ibid., 482.

41. Here, I am somewhat in accord with the general line of reasoning laid out in Marjorie Perloff, "Can(n)on to the Right of Us, Can(n)on to the Left of Us: A Plea for Difference," *New Literary History* 18, no. 3 (1987): 633–56. But I challenge her assumption that this reasoning pertains only to twentieth-century poetry.

42. *MED*, s.v. "valu(e), n.," 1(c).

43. Peter Biller, *The Measure of Multitude: Population in Medieval Thought* (Oxford: Oxford University Press, 2000), 1–16.

44. Robert Meyer-Lee, *Literary Value and Social Identity in the "Canterbury Tales"* (Cambridge: Cambridge University Press, 2019).

45. Ingrid Nelson, *Lyric Tactics: Poetry, Genre, and Practice in Later Medieval England* (Philadelphia: University of Pennsylvania Press, 2017), 6–12; Ardis Butterfield, "The Construction of Textual Form: Cross-Lingual Citation in the Medieval Insular Lyric," in *Citation, Intertextuality and Memory in the Middle Ages and Renaissance*, vol. 1: *Text, Music and Image from Machaut to Ariosto*, ed. Yolanda Plumley, Giuliano Di Bacco, and Stefano Jossa (Exeter: University of Exeter Press, 2011), 41–57; Julia Boffey, "Middle English Lyrics and Manuscripts," in *A Companion to the Middle English Lyric*, ed. Thomas G. Duncan (Cambridge: D. S. Brewer, 2005), 1–18.

46. Ardis Butterfield, "Why Medieval Lyric?," *English Literary History* 82, no. 2 (2015): 319–43, at p. 334.

47. Joseph Sung-Yul Park and Mary Bucholtz, "Introduction: Public Transcripts: Entextualization and Linguistic Representation in Institutional Contexts," *Text and Talk* 29, no. 5 (2009): 485–502, at p. 485. See also the discussion in Ian Cornelius, "Language and Meter," this volume (Chapter 4), 130.

48. A. C. Spearing, *Textual Subjectivity: The Encoding of Subjectivity in Medieval Narratives and Lyrics* (Oxford: Oxford University Press, 2005); A. C. Spearing, *Medieval Autographies: The "I" of the Text* (Notre Dame, IN: University of Notre Dame Press, 2012); Julie Orlemanski, "Literary Persons and Medieval Fiction in Bernard of Clairvaux's *Sermons on the Song of Songs*," *Representations* 153 (2021): 29–50.

49. Elizabeth Fowler, "The Proximity of the Virtual: A. C. Spearing's Experientiality (or, Roaming with Palamon and Arcite)," in *Readings in Medieval Textuality: Essays in Honour of A. C. Spearing*, ed. Cristina Maria Cervone and D. Vance Smith (Cambridge: D. S. Brewer, 2016), 15–30.

50. Cristina Maria Cervone, "Wondering Through Middle English Lyric," this volume (Chapter 2), 72–73, 76, 87; David Lawton, "Voice and Public Interiorities: Chaucer, Orpheus, Machaut," in *Answerable Style: The Idea of the Literary in Medieval England*, ed. Frank Grady and Andrew Galloway (Columbus: Ohio State University Press, 2013), 284–306; see also

Cristina Maria Cervone, "'I' and 'We' in Chaucer's *Complaint unto Pity*," in Cervone and Smith, *Readings in Medieval Textuality*, 195–212.

51. Aden Kumler, "Lyric Vessels," this volume (Chapter 7).

52. This summary draws on Edmund Husserl, *Cartesian Meditations: An Introduction to Phenomenology*, trans. Dorion Cairns (The Hague: M. Nijhoff, 1960), 89–177; Nick Crossley, *Intersubjectivity: The Fabric of Social Becoming* (London: SAGE, 1996), 1–7; A. D. Smith, *Routledge Philosophy Guidebook to Husserl and the Cartesian Meditations* (New York: Routledge, 2003), 229–35.

53. Maurice Merleau-Ponty, *Phenomenology of Perception*, trans. Donald A. Landes (New York: Routledge, 2012), 364–80.

54. Ibid., 370–71.

55. Frank J. Macke, "Body, Liquidity and Flesh: Bachelard, Merleau-Ponty, and the Elements of Interpersonal Communication," *Philosophy Today* 51, no. 4 (2007): 401–15, at p. 411.

56. Nick Crossley, "Mead, Merleau-Ponty and Embodied Communication," *Journal of Pragmatics* 58 (2013): 46–48; Crossley, *Intersubjectivity*, 73–74.

57. Butterfield, "Why Medieval Lyric?," 336.

58. Ardis Butterfield, "Afterwords: Forms of Death," *Exemplaria* 27, nos. 1–2 (2015): 167–82. It is also worth considering Rosemary Woolf's comments on the anonymity of medieval lyric in this context: "most medieval lyrics can be called genuinely anonymous, for they were written by self-effacing poets, who did not obtrude peculiarities of style and thought between the subject matter and the audience" (Woolf, *English Religious Lyric*, 5).

59. Nelson, *Lyric Tactics*, 35–44.

60. Isidore of Seville, *The "Etymologies" of Isidore of Seville*, trans. Stephen A. Barney et al. (Cambridge: Cambridge University Press, 2006), 74.

61. This formulation comes originally from John Stuart Mill's dictum, "Eloquence is *heard*, poetry is *overheard*" (Mill, *Essays on Poetry*, ed. F. Parvin Sharpless [Columbia: University of South Carolina Press, 1976], 12). Northrop Frye develops this into a definition of lyric as "preeminently the utterance that is overheard" (Frye, *Anatomy of Criticism: Four Essays* [Princeton, NJ: Princeton University Press, 1957], 249). For an analysis of how dramatic monologues complicate the idea of an "overheard" lyric, see Herbert Tucker, "Dramatic Monologue and the Overhearing of Lyric," in *Lyric Poetry*, ed. Hošek and Parker, 226–43.

62. See, e.g., Geoffrey of Vinsauf, *Poetria Nova of Geoffrey of Vinsauf*, trans. Margaret F. Nims (Toronto: Pontifical Institute of Mediaeval Studies, 1967); Siegfried Wenzel, *Verses in Sermons: "Fasciculus Morum" and Its Middle English Poems* (Cambridge, MA: Mediaeval Academy of America, 1978).

63. Sarah McNamer, *Affective Meditation and the Invention of Medieval Compassion* (Philadelphia: University of Pennsylvania Press, 2010), 150–73.

64. Sarah Stanbury, "Gender and Voice in Middle English Religious Lyrics," in Duncan, *A Companion to the Middle English Lyric*, 227–41, at p. 240.

65. I thank Cristina Maria Cervone for suggesting this reading to me.

66. On Middle English lyrics in sermons, see Siegfried Wenzel, *Preachers, Poets, and the Early English Lyric* (Princeton, NJ: Princeton University Press, 1986).

67. Oxford, Bodleian Library, MS Digby 86, fol. 127. For a descriptive list of manuscript witnesses, see Karen Saupe, ed., *Middle English Marian Lyrics* (Kalamazoo, MI: Medieval Institute Publications for TEAMS, 1998), note to §33.

68. Jacques Derrida, *Voice and Phenomenon: Introduction to the Problem of the Sign in Husserl's Phenomenology*, trans. Leonard Lawlor (Evanston, IL: Northwestern University Press, 2011), 60–74.

69. Anne Middleton, "The Idea of Public Poetry in the Reign of Richard II," *Speculum* 53, no. 1 (1978): 94–114; Lawton, "Voice and Public Interiorities."

70. The music appears in Cambridge, St. John's College, MS E.8 (111), fol. 106v; and London, British Library, Royal MS 12.E.i, fol. 193.

71. Helen Estabrook Sandison, *The "Chanson d'Aventure" in Middle English* (Bryn Mawr, PA: Bryn Mawr College, 1913), 5–8; Carissa Harris, *Obscene Pedagogies: Transgressive Talk and Sexual Education in Late Medieval Britain* (Ithaca, NY: Cornell University Press, 2018), 103–49.

72. Harris, *Obscene Pedagogies*, 147.

73. Text and translation from Susanna Greer Fein, ed. and trans., *The Complete Harley 2253 Manuscript*, with David B. Raybin and Jan M. Ziolkowski, vol. 2 (Kalamazoo, MI: Medieval Institute Publications for TEAMS, 2014), 150–51; *DIMEV* 2446.

74. Nicolette Zeeman, "Imaginative Theory," in *Middle English*, ed. Paul Strohm, Oxford Twenty-First Century Approaches to Literature (Oxford: Oxford University Press, 2007), 222–40, at p. 231.

75. Harris, *Obscene Pedagogies*, 103–49.

76. Luria and Hoffman, *Middle English Lyrics*, p. 16, no. 16 (*DIMEV* 614); again, I have changed the (editorial) punctuation.

77. Edmund Reiss, *The Art of the Middle English Lyric: Essays in Criticism* (Athens: University of Georgia Press, 1972), 45–49.

78. I thank Cristina Maria Cervone for suggesting this reading to me.

79. Merleau-Ponty, *Phenomenology of Perception*, 370.

80. John Hollander, "Breaking into Song: Some Notes on Refrain," in Hošek and Parker, *Lyric Poetry*, 73–89, at pp. 74–75 (emphasis in original).

81. Lori Ann Garner, "Contexts of Interpretation in the Burdens of Middle English Carols," *Neophilologus* 84, no. 3 (2000): 467–83; Richard Leighton Greene, ed., *The Early English Carols*, 2nd ed., rev. and enl. (Oxford: Clarendon Press, 1977), xliv–xlvi.

82. Seeta Chaganti, "Choreographing Mouvance: The Case of the English Carol," *Philological Quarterly* 87, nos. 1–2 (2008): 77–103, at p. 78. See also Seeta Chaganti, "Dance in a Haunted Space: Genre, Form, and the Middle English Carol," *Exemplaria* 27, nos. 1–2 (2015): 129–49.

83. Lee Patterson, "Chaucer's Pardoner on the Couch: Psyche and Clio in Medieval Literary Studies," *Speculum* 76, no. 3 (2001): 638–80; L. O. Aranye Fradenburg, *Sacrifice Your Love: Psychoanalysis, Historicism, Chaucer* (Minneapolis: University of Minnesota Press, 2002), 43–78.

84. Fradenburg, *Sacrifice Your Love*, 45.

85. See discussion in Nelson, *Lyric Tactics*, 18–26.

86. This concept of *erlebnis* appears in Käte Hamburger, *The Logic of Literature*, trans. Marilyn J. Rose, 2nd ed. (Bloomington: Indiana University Press, 1973). For a summary, see René Wellek, "Genre Theory, the Lyric, and *Erlebnis*," in Jackson and Prins, *The Lyric Theory Reader*, 40–52; and more recently, Derek Attridge, *The Experience of Poetry* (Oxford: Oxford University Press, 2019).

87. A significant critical literature exists on this topic. Of special relevance to medieval studies are Maura Nolan, "Historicism After Historicism," in *The Post-Historical Middle*

Ages, ed. Elizabeth Scala and Sylvia Federico (New York: Palgrave Macmillan, 2009), 63–85; Carolyn Dinshaw, *How Soon Is Now? Medieval Texts, Amateur Readers, and the Queerness of Time* (Durham, NC: Duke University Press, 2012). Essays addressing historicism and lyric include Eric Hayot, "Against Historicist Fundamentalism," *PMLA* 131, no. 5 (2016): 1414–22; John Michael, "Lyric History: Temporality, Rhetoric, and the Ethics of Poetry," *New Literary History* 48, no. 2 (2017): 265–84.

88. Michael, "Lyric History," 265.

89. George Edmondson calls this "extimacy," and discusses it as an approach to the Middle Ages in George Edmondson, "Naked Chaucer," in Scala and Federico, *The Post-Historical Middle Ages*, 139–60.

CHAPTER 6

1. For a different kind of discussion of the relationship between language and "human embodied action," involving language inscribed on physical objects, see Aden Kumler, "Lyric Vessels," this volume (Chapter 7).

2. Peter Stockwell, *Cognitive Poetics: An Introduction* (London: Routledge, 2002); Reuven Tsur, *Toward a Theory of Cognitive Poetics* (Amsterdam: Elsevier, 1992).

3. Classic references include George Lakoff and Mark Turner, *More Than Cool Reason: A Field Guide to Poetic Metaphor* (Chicago: University of Chicago Press, 1989); and Mark Turner, *The Literary Mind: The Origins of Language and Thought* (New York: Oxford University Press, 1996).

4. George Lakoff and Mark Johnson, *Metaphors We Live By* (Chicago: University of Chicago Press, 1980); Eve Sweetser, *From Etymology to Pragmatics: Metaphorical and Cultural Aspects of Semantic Structure* (New York: Cambridge University Press, 1990); Raymond W. Gibbs, Jr., *The Poetics of Mind: Figurative Thought, Language, and Understanding* (New York: Cambridge University Press, 1994), 154–57; Edward Slingerland, *Effortless Action: Wu-wei as Conceptual Metaphor and Spiritual Ideal in Early China* (New York: Oxford University Press, 2003); Zoltán Kövecses, *Language, Mind and Culture: A Practical Introduction* (New York: Oxford University Press, 2010).

5. Maxwell S. Luria and Richard L. Hoffman, eds., *Middle English Lyrics: Authoritative Texts, Critical and Historical Backgrounds, Perspectives on Six Poems* (New York: W. W. Norton, 1974), p. 23, no. 27; *Digital Index of Middle English Verse* (*DIMEV*) 842. Also see Christopher Cannon, "Lyric Romance," this volume (Chapter 3), 98–99, quoting a different edition from the one used here.

6. I. A. Richards, *The Philosophy of Rhetoric* (Oxford: Oxford University Press, 1936); Max Black, *Models and Metaphors: Studies in Language and Philosophy* (Ithaca, NY: Cornell University Press, 1962); Samuel R. Levin, *The Semantics of Metaphor* (Baltimore: Johns Hopkins University Press, 1977).

7. Conceptual metaphors are, by convention, presented in underlined small caps to distinguish them from linguistic or verbal metaphors.

8. Yakov Malkiel, *Etymology* (Cambridge: Cambridge University Press, 1993); Steven Pinker, *The Stuff of Thought: Language as a Window into Human Nature* (New York: Basic Books, 2007).

9. For examples of cognitive poetics informing the study of history as well as, more specifically, of Old and Middle English literary texts, see Daniel Lord Smail, *On Deep His-*

tory and the Brain (Berkeley: University of California Press, 2007); Juliana Dresvina and Victoria Blud, eds., *Cognitive Science and Medieval Studies: An Introduction* (Cardiff: University of Wales Press, 2020); Daniel Donoghue, *How the Anglo-Saxons Read Their Poems* (Philadelphia: University of Pennsylvania Press, 2018); Antonina Harbus, *Cognitive Approaches to Old English Poetry* (Cambridge: D. S. Brewer, 2012); Cristina Maria Cervone, *Poetics of the Incarnation: Middle English Writing and the Leap of Love* (Philadelphia: University of Pennsylvania Press, 2013).

10. George Lakoff and Mark Johnson, *Philosophy in the Flesh* (Chicago: University of Chicago Press, 1999), 3–122; Raymond W. Gibbs, Jr., *Metaphor Wars: Conceptual Metaphor in Human Life* (New York: Cambridge University Press, 2017), 222–61.

11. Turner, *The Literary Mind.*

12. See Gibbs, *The Poetics of Mind*, 120–207.

13. Lakoff and Johnson, *Metaphors We Live By.*

14. For summary of development of systematic evidence for conceptual metaphor, see Zoltán Kövecses, *Metaphor: A Practical Introduction* (New York: Oxford University Press, 2002).

15. Gibbs, *The Poetics of Mind*, 265–318.

16. Richard Trim, *Metaphor and the Historical Evolution of Conceptual Mapping* (Houndmills, Basingstoke, Hampshire, UK: Palgrave Macmillan, 2011).

17. Sweetser, *From Etymology to Pragmatics.*

18. In *Robert of Brunne's "Handlyng Synne,"* ed. Frederick J. Furnivall, EETS, o.s., 119 (London: Kegan Paul, Trench, Trübner, 1901), p. 287, line 9156; *DIMEV* 1283. The exemplum is also discussed briefly in Cristina Maria Cervone and Nicholas Watson, "Why stonde we? why go we no3t?," this volume (Introduction), 5, 6.

19. Raymond W. Gibbs, Jr., et al., "Taking a Stand on the Meanings of *Stand*: Bodily Experience as Motivation for Polysemy," *Journal of Semantics* 11, no. 4 (1994): 231–51.

20. Lakoff and Turner, *More Than Cool Reason.*

21. Thomas G. Duncan, ed., *Medieval English Lyrics and Carols* (Cambridge: D. S. Brewer, 2013), p. 69, no. 1.20 (*DIMEV* 3050).

22. Raymond W. Gibbs, Jr., and Solange Nascimento, "How We Talk When We Talk About Love: Metaphorical Concepts and Understanding Love Poetry," in *Empirical Approaches to Literature and Aesthetics*, ed. Roger J. Kreuz and Mary Sue MacNealy (Norwood, NJ: Ablex, 1996), 291–308.

23. Raymond W. Gibbs, Jr., ed., *Cambridge Handbook of Metaphor and Thought* (New York: Cambridge University Press, 2008).

24. Gibbs, *Metaphor Wars.*

25. Joseph Grady, "A Typology of Motivation for Conceptual Metaphor: Correlation vs. Resemblance," in *Metaphor in Cognitive Linguistics: Selected Papers from the Fifth International Cognitive Linguistics Conference, Amsterdam, July 1997*, ed. Raymond W. Gibbs, Jr., and Gerard J. Steen (Amsterdam: John Benjamins, 1999), 79–100.

26. Zoltán Kövecses, "Language, Figurative Thought, and Cross-Cultural Comparison," *Metaphor and Symbol* 18 (2003): 311–20.

27. Gregory Murphy, "On Metaphoric Representation," *Cognition* 60, no. 2 (1996): 173–204.

28. Gibbs, *The Poetics of Mind*; see also Gibbs, *Metaphor Wars.*

29. Raymond W. Gibbs, Jr., "What Do Idioms Really Mean?," *Journal of Memory and Language* 31, no. 4 (1992): 485–506.

30. Raymond W. Gibbs, Jr., Paula Lima, and Edson Francuzo, "Metaphor Is Grounded in Embodied Experience," *Journal of Pragmatics* 36, no. 7 (2004): 1189–210.

31. Paul Thibodeau and Frank H. Durgin, "Productive Figurative Communication: Conventional Metaphors Facilitate the Comprehension of Related Novel Metaphors," *Journal of Memory and Language* 58, no. 2 (2008): 521–40.

32. Shari Robins and Richard E. Mayer, "The Metaphor Framing Effect: Metaphorical Reasoning About Text-Based Dilemmas," *Discourse Processes* 30, no. 1 (2000): 57–86.

33. Alan Cienki and Cornelia Müller, eds., *Metaphor and Gesture* (Amsterdam: John Benjamins, 2006); Charles J. Forceville and Eduardo Urios-Aparisi, eds., *Multimodal Metaphor* (Berlin: Mouton de Gruyter, 2009).

34. Alan Cienki, "Metaphoric Gestures and Some of Their Relations to Verbal Metaphoric Expressions," in *Discourse and Cognition: Bridging the Gap*, ed. Jean-Pierre Koenig (Stanford, CA: CSLI Publications, 1998), 189–204.

35. María J. Ortiz, "Visual Manifestations of Primary Metaphors Through *Mise-en-scène* Techniques," *Image & Narrative* 15, no. 1 (2014): 5–16.

36. Mark Landau, *Conceptual Metaphor in Social Psychology: The Poetics of Everyday Life* (Washington, DC: Psychology Press, 2016).

37. Lakoff and Johnson, *Metaphors We Live By*.

38. Brian P. Meier and Michael D. Robinson, "Why the Sunny Side Is Up: Associations Between Affect and Vertical Position," *Psychological Science* 15, no. 4 (2004): 243–47.

39. Brian P. Meier et al., "What's 'Up' with God? Vertical Space as a Representation of the Divine," *Journal of Personality and Social Psychology* 93, no. 5 (2007): 699–710.

40. Nils B. Jostmann, Daniël Lakens, and Thomas W. Schubert, "Weight as an Embodiment of Importance," *Psychological Science* 20, no. 9 (2009): 1169–74.

41. Lawrence E. Williams and John A. Bargh, "Experiencing Physical Warmth Influences Interpersonal Warmth," *Science* 322, no. 5901 (2008): 606–7.

42. Raymond W. Gibbs, Jr., *Embodiment and Cognitive Science* (New York: Cambridge University Press, 2006); Benjamin K. Bergen, *Louder Than Words: The New Science of How the Mind Makes Meaning* (New York: Basic Books, 2012). Also Gibbs, *Metaphor Wars*, 199–204.

43. Scott T. Grafton, "Embodied Cognition and the Simulation of Action to Understand Others," *Annals of the New York Academy of Sciences* 1156 (2011): 97–117.

44. Arthur Glenberg and Michael Kaschak, "Grounding Language in Action," *Psychonomic Bulletin & Review* 9, no. 3 (2002): 558–65.

45. Quoted from *The Riverside Chaucer*, gen. ed. Larry D. Benson, 3rd ed. (Boston: Houghton Mifflin, 1987); *DIMEV* 4375.

46. Cristina Maria Cervone, "'I' and 'We' in Chaucer's *Complaint unto Pity*," in *Readings in Medieval Textuality: Essays in Honour of A. C. Spearing*, ed. Cristina Maria Cervone and D. Vance Smith (Cambridge: D. S. Brewer, 2016), 195–212, at p. 198.

47. Raymond W. Gibbs, Jr., "The Allegorical Impulse," *Metaphor and Symbol* 26, no. 2 (2011): 121–30.

48. Lakoff and Turner, *More Than Cool Reason*, 72.

49. Pain has been studied within cognitive poetics in terms of the varying metaphoric ways in which it can be conceived and is thought, not surprisingly, to be understood via common embodied simulation processes. See Elena Semino, "Descriptions of Pain, Metaphor and Embodied Simulation," *Metaphor and Symbol* 25, no. 4 (2010): 205–26. Moreover, studies on Middle English medical narratives also show some of the complex metaphoric ways in

which pain is described and treated. This work adds additional evidence of the conventional metaphoric ways that pain was thought of in Middle English, with Chaucer tapping into some of these metaphors in "The Complaint unto Pity." See Javier E. Díaz Vera, "When Pain Is Not a Place: Pain and Its Metaphors in Late Middle English Medical Texts," *Onomazein* 26, no. 2 (2012): 279–308.

50. See Bruno Galantucci, Carol A. Fowler, and M. T. Turvey, "The Motor Theory of Speech Perception Reviewed," *Psychonomic Bulletin & Review* 13, no. 2 (2006): 361–77.

51. Raymond W. Gibbs, Jr., and Natalia Blackwell, "Climbing the Ladder to Literary Heaven: A Case Study of Allegorical Interpretation of Fiction," *Scientific Study of Literature* 2, no. 2 (2012): 199–217; Maja Djikic and Keith Oatley, "The Art in Fiction: From Indirect Communication to Changes of the Self," *Psychology of Aesthetics, Creativity, and the Arts* 8, no. 4 (2014): 498–505; Jana Lüdtke, Burkhard Meyer-Sickendieck, and Arthur M. Jacobs, "Immersing in the Stillness of an Early Morning: Testing the Mood Empathy Hypothesis of Poetry Reception," *Psychology of Aesthetics, Creativity, and the Arts* 8, no. 3 (2014): 363–77.

52. Cervone, "'I' and 'We' in Chaucer's *Complaint unto Pity*," 205–6.

53. A. C. Spearing, *Textual Subjectivity: The Encoding of Subjectivity in Medieval Narratives and Lyrics* (Oxford: Oxford University Press, 2005).

54. Raymond W. Gibbs, Jr., and Lacey Okonski, "Cognitive Poetics of Allegorical Experience," in *Expressive Minds and Artistic Creations: Studies in Cognitive Poetics*, ed. Szilvia Csábi (New York: Oxford University Press, 2018), 33–53.

55. Helen Vendler, "The Art of Criticism No. 3," interview by Henri Cole, *Paris Review* 141 (1996), https://www.theparisreview.org/interviews/1324/the-art-of-criticism-no-3-helen -vendler.

56. Ibid.

CHAPTER 7

1. My thinking in this chapter has been informed and enriched, from start to finish, by the lively exchanges that animated the "WKOAT?" (What Kind of a Thing?) seminars convened by Cristina Maria Cervone and Nicholas Watson. It was a great privilege and great fun to take part in the rich "pley" of those discussions and in the development of this book, so thoughtfully and skillfully choreographed by Cristina and Nicholas. I am also grateful to participants in the Workshop in the History of Material Texts at the University of Pennsylvania, the Medieval Studies Workshop at the University of Chicago, and to this book's anonymous peer reviewers for insightful critical responses to earlier states of this chapter. Finally, it is a pleasure to thank my research assistants, past and present, for their help: Alexis Wells, Vanessa Gonzalvez, and Simon Bühler.

2. Rosemary Greentree, "Lyric," in *A Companion to Medieval English Literature and Culture, c. 1350–c. 1500*, ed. Peter Brown (Malden, MA: Blackwell, 2007), 387–405, at p. 387.

3. Julia Boffey, "Middle English Lyrics and Manuscripts," in *A Companion to the Middle English Lyric*, ed. Thomas G. Duncan (Cambridge: D. S. Brewer, 2005), 1–18, at p. 1. For further discussion of the taxonomic vexations posed by Middle English lyric, see Rosemary Greentree, *The Middle English Lyric and Short Poem* (Cambridge: D. S. Brewer, 2001), esp. 5–13; Greentree, "Lyric"; Michael P. Kuczynski, "Theological Sophistication and the Middle English Religious Lyric: A Polemic," *Chaucer Review* 45, no. 3 (2011): 321–39. My thinking about the imbrication of lyric, object, and occasion has benefited from Ingrid Nelson, *Lyric*

Tactics: Poetry, Genre, and Practice in Later Medieval England (Philadelphia: University of Pennsylvania Press, 2017), 1–30.

4. From an ever-growing body of scholarship, see Seeta Chaganti, "Vestigial Signs: Inscription, Performance and *The Dream of the Rood*," *PMLA* 125, no. 1 (2010): 48–72; Catherine E. Karkov, "Art and Writing: Voice, Image, Object," in *The Cambridge History of Early Medieval English Literature*, ed. Clare A. Lees (Cambridge: Cambridge University Press, 2012), 73–98; Catherine E. Karkov, *The Art of Anglo-Saxon England* (Woodbridge, Suffolk: Boydell Press, 2011), 135–78; Thomas Bredehoft, "Multiliteralism in Anglo-Saxon Verse Inscriptions," in *Conceptualizing Multilingualism in England, c. 800–c. 1250*, ed. Elizabeth Tyler (Turnhout: Brepols, 2011), 15–32; Thomas Bredehoft, "First-Person Inscriptions and Literacy," *Anglo-Saxon Studies in Archaeology and History* 9 (1996): 103–10; Benjamin Tilghman, "On the Engimatic Nature of Things in Anglo-Saxon Art," *Different Visions* 4 (2014): 1–43; Elizabeth Okasha, "Literacy in Anglo-Saxon England: The Evidence from Inscriptions," *Anglo-Saxon Studies in Archaeology and History* 8 (1995): 69–74; Elizabeth Okasha, "The Commissioners, Makers and Owners of Anglo-Saxon Inscriptions," *Anglo-Saxon Studies in Archaeology and History* 7 (1994): 71–77.

5. Anthony S. G. Edwards, "Middle English Inscriptional Verse Texts," in *Texts and Their Contexts: Papers from the Early Book Society*, ed. John Scattergood and Julia Boffey (Dublin: Four Courts Press, 1997), 26–43; Michael van Dussen, "Tourists and *Tabulae* in Late-Medieval England," in *Truth and Tales: Cultural Mobility and Medieval Media*, ed. Fiona Somerset and Nicholas Watson (Columbus: Ohio State University Press, 2015), 238–54; Cristina Maria Cervone, "John de Cobham and Cooling Castle's Charter Poem," *Speculum* 83, no. 4 (2008): 884–916; Cristina Maria Cervone, *Poetics of the Incarnation: Middle English Writing and the Leap of Love* (Philadelphia: University of Pennsylvania Press, 2013); Ralph Hanna, "The Bridges at Abingdon: An Unnoticed Alliterative Poem," in *Yee? Baw for Bokes: Essays on Medieval Manuscripts and Poetics in Honor of Hoyt N. Duggan*, ed. Michael Calabrese and Stephen H. A. Shepherd (Los Angeles: Marymount Institute Press, 2013), 31–44; Ashby Kinch, "Image, Ideology, and Form: The Middle English *Three Dead Kings* in Its Iconographic Context," *Chaucer Review* 43, no. 1 (2008): 48–81.

6. Jennifer Floyd, "Writing on the Wall: John Lydgate's Architectural Verse," Ph.D. diss., Stanford University, 2008; Jennifer Floyd, "St. George and the 'Steyned Halle': Lydgate's Verse for the London Armourers," in *Lydgate Matters: Poetry and Material Culture in the Fifteenth Century*, ed. Lisa Cooper and Andrea Denny-Brown (New York: Palgrave Macmillan, 2008), 139–64; Amy Appleford, "The Dance of Death in London: John Carpenter, John Lydgate, and the *Daunce of Poulys*," *Journal of Medieval and Early Modern Studies* 38, no. 2 (2008): 285–314; Seeta Chaganti, "*Danse macabre* and the Virtual Churchyard," *postmedieval* 3 (2012): 7–26; Matthew Evan Davis, "Lydgate at Long Melford: Reassessing the *Testament* and 'Quis Dabit Meo Capiti Fontem Lacrimarum' in Their Local Context," *Journal of Medieval Religious Cultures* 43, no. 1 (2017): 77–114.

7. A point also made by Boffey, "Middle English Lyrics," 18.

8. The single best treatment of medieval mazers remains W. H. St. John Hope, "On the English Medieval Drinking Bowls Called Mazers," *Archaeologia* 50 (1887): 129–93. On mazers and poetry, see Rosemond Tuve, "Spenser and Mediaeval Mazers, with a Note on Jason in Ivory," in *Essays by Rosemond Tuve: On Spenser, Herbert and Milton*, ed. Thomas P. Roche, Jr. (Princeton, NJ: Princeton University Press, 1970), 102–11.

9. Hope, "On the English Medieval Drinking Bowls," 149–50. For the Victoria and Albert Museum (V&A)'s online cataloging and a brief notice of the mazer, see http://

collections.vam.ac.uk/item/O103993/mazer-unknown/ and http://www.vam.ac.uk/content /articles/m/mazer.

10. On the intersection of proverbs and lyrics, with emphasis on proverbs treating good and bad speech, see Helen E. Wicker, "Between Proverbs and Lyrics: Customization Practices in Late Medieval English Moral Verse," *English* 59, no. 224 (2010): 3–24.

11. See Andrew Albin, "The Sound of Rollean Lyric," this volume (Chapter 8), 444 n. 19.

12. The only publication of the Cloisters Mazer known to me is Timothy B. Husband and Jane Hayward, eds., *The Secular Spirit: Life and Art at the End of the Middle Ages* (New York: E. P. Dutton, in association with The Metropolitan Museum of Art, 1975), 43–44 (no. 37).

13. Transcription (also employed in the *DIMEV* [4448]) from Husband and Hayward, *The Secular Spirit*, 44.

14. Husband and Hayward, *The Secular Spirit*, 44.

15. It is a pleasure to thank Cristina Maria Cervone and Nicholas Watson for their helpful comments on this inscription.

16. For further discussion, see Frederick J. Furnivall, *Early English Meals and Manners* (London: N. Trübner, 1868); Sheila Lindenbaum, "London Texts and Literate Practice," in *The Cambridge History of Medieval English Literature*, ed. David Wallace (Cambridge: Cambridge University Press, 1999), 284–309, at pp. 305–9; D. Vance Smith, "The Silence of Langland's Study: Matter, Invisibility, Instruction," in *Answerable Style: The Idea of the Literary in Medieval England*, ed. Frank Grady and Andrew Galloway (Columbus: Ohio State University Press, 2013), 263–83, at pp. 279–83; Wicker, "Between Proverbs and Lyrics."

17. It is tempting to attribute the inscription's "I" to its artificer-inscriber, but this does not seem to have been a common practice; only three mazers in Hope's catalog bear a patron's and/or maker's name: Hope, "On the English Medieval Drinking Bowls," 162 (no. 27), 168 (no. 37), 171–72 (no. 40). A number of the cataloged mazers feature goldsmiths' marks; I think it unlikely that most beholders could have "decoded" these quasi-pictographic makers' marks.

18. The British Museum's cataloging of this object is available at https://www .britishmuseum.org/collection/object/H_1855-1029-11. For further discussion of English medieval face-jugs, see Brian Spencer, "Medieval Face-Jug (The London Museum)," *Burlington Magazine* 111, no. 794 (1969): 302–3; Ben Jervis, *Pottery and Social Life in Medieval England: Towards a Relational Approach* (Oxford: Oxbow Books, 2014); Kelly Green, "Constructing Masculinity Through the Material Culture of Dining and Drinking in Later Medieval England: A Study of the Production and Consumption of Anthropomorphic Pottery in Selected Sites from Eastern England, the Midlands, and the South West, c. 1250–1450," Ph.D. diss., University of Sheffield, 2015. On the nexus of body and vessel, with brief consideration of English face jugs, see Juliet Fleming, "Pots," in *Graffiti and the Writing Arts of Early Modern England* (Philadelphia: University of Pennsylvania Press, 2001), 113–64.

19. Published in Hope, "On the English Medieval Drinking Bowls," 176–81. For further discussion, see Sheila Sweetinburgh, "Remembering the Dead at Dinner-Time," in *Everyday Objects: Medieval and Early Modern Material Culture and Its Meanings*, ed. Tara Hamling and Catherine Richardson (Farnham, Surrey: Ashgate, 2010), 257–66.

20. Hope, "On the English Medieval Drinking Bowls," 177, 179; I list here only the relevant examples from the inventory (which groups them according to a taxonomy of size and value).

21. Ibid., 185.

22. Ibid., 186.

23. Ibid., 187.

24. My thinking about the conflation of human bodies with vessels and conceptions of poetry as a "container" for the human voice is indebted to Fleming, "Pots"; Barbara Johnson, "Muteness Envy," in *The Feminist Difference: Literature, Psychoanalysis, Race, and Gender* (Cambridge, MA: Harvard University Press, 1998); and Barbara Johnson, *Persons and Things* (Cambridge, MA: Harvard University Press, 2008). I'm grateful to Julie Orlemanski for bringing the last to my attention and for generously sharing the syllabus for a seminar she taught on prosopopoeia in 2015.

25. The significance of the "CF" that concludes the laver's epigraphy remains a topic of discussion; the question of whether these may be the maker's initials has yet to be settled. A laver in the Swansea Museum (Reg. no. A 879.1) inscribed "IE SUI LAWR GILEBERT KI MEMBLERA MAL I DEDERT" is an analogous case; for further discussion of these lavers, see Michael Finlay, "British Late Medieval Inscribed Bronze Jugs: A Stylistic Study," *Journal of the Antique Metalware Society* 4 (1996): 1–10, at pp. 4–5; John Cherry, "A Medieval Bronze Laver," *British Museum Yearbook* 2 (1977): 199–201; J. M. Lewis, R. Brownsword, and E. E. H. Pitt, "Medieval 'Bronze' Tripod Ewers from Wales," *Medieval Archaeology* 31 (1987): 80–93, at p. 83. For the British Museum's online cataloging of the laver discussed above (1975, 1001.1), see https://www.britishmuseum.org/collection/object/H_1975-1001-1.

26. National Museums Liverpool, Nelson Collection, 53.113; see sources cited in n. 25 above. A further laver (exhibited at Norwich in 1847 and published in 1856, current location unknown to me) with the text "+ VENEZ LAVER" would seem to belong to this tradition, although its use of the imperative is distinct; see Cherry, "A Medieval Bronze Laver," 200, 201 n. 5; Weston Walford and Albert Way, "Examples of Mediaeval Seals," *Archaeological Journal* 13 (1856): 62–76, at pp. 73–74.

27. Reportedly found in a Norfolk manor house in 1879, the Robinson Jug has received considerable attention, often in connection with the Wenlok Jug (acquired in 2006 by the Luton Museum) and the Asante Ewer (discussed at length below). No serious analysis has yet been undertaken of the Robinson Jug's epigraphic text. See Marian Campbell, "An English Medieval Jug," in *Tributes to Nigel Morgan: Contexts of Medieval Art; Images, Objects and Ideas*, ed. Julian M. Luxford and M. A. Michael (London: Harvey Miller, 2010), 187–96; Malcolm Vale, "From the Court of Richard II to the Court of Prempeh I: The Problem of the 'Asante' Ewers," in *Soldiers, Nobles and Gentlemen: Essays in Honour of Maurice Keen*, ed. Peter R. Coss and Christopher Tyerman (Woodbridge, Suffolk: Boydell Press, 2009), 335–53 at pp. 351–52; Jonathan Alexander and Paul Binski, eds., *Age of Chivalry: Art in Plantagenet England, 1200–1400* (London: Royal Academy of Arts, 1987), pp. 524–25 (cat. no. 727) (hereafter *Age of Chivalry*); Finlay, "British Late Medieval Inscribed Bronze Jugs," 8; Roger Brownsword and Ernest Pitt, "British Late-Medieval Inscribed Bronze Jugs: A Technical Study," *Journal of the Antique Metalware Society* 4 (1996): 11–13; Anna-Elisabeth Theuerkauff-Liederwald, *Mittelalterliche Bronze- und Messinggefässe: Eimer, Kannen, Lavabokessel* (Berlin: Deutscher Verlag für Kunstwissenschaft, 1988), 241–42 (no. 280); Paul Williamson, ed., *The Medieval Treasury: The Middle Ages in the Victoria and Albert Museum* (London: Victoria and Albert Museum, 1986), 223; J. Romilly Allen, "Inscribed Bronze Flagon of the Fourteenth Century in the South Kensington Museum," *Reliquary and Illustrated Archaeologist*, n.s., 2 (1896): 103–6; C. H. Read, "Bronze Jug," *Proceedings of the Society of Antiquaries of London*, 2nd ser., 17 (1898): 82–87.

28. Vale, "From the Court of Richard II," 351–52; John Cherry and Neil Stratford, "The Ashanti Ewers," in *Westminster Kings and the Medieval Palace of Westminster*, British Museum Occasional Paper 115 (London: British Museum, 1995), 98–100 at p. 98. Scientific analyses

have shown that the Robinson Jug and the Asante Ewer were made from a heavily leaded bronze with much higher levels of antimony, arsenic, and nickel than other contemporary copper-alloy vessels, and both vessels preserve distinctive bronze "spacers" (left over from the casting process), lending further support to the hypothesis that the two vessels were produced by a single workshop, perhaps as a "set"; see Brownsword and Pitt, "British Late-Medieval Inscribed Bronze Jugs," 11–13; Susan La Niece, "Asante Ewer," in *Richard II's Treasure: The Riches of a Medieval King*, Institute of Historical Research and Royal Holloway, University of London (2017), http://www.history.ac.uk/richardII/asante.html.

29. J. Romilly Allen, "Inscribed Bronze Flagon," 105.

30. *Age of Chivalry*, 524 (cat. no. 727).

31. *Digital Index of Middle English Verse* (*DIMEV*) 5028.

32. Victoria and Albert Museum's online collection catalog entry, http://collections.vam .ac.uk/item/O97902/robinson-jug-jug-unknown/.

33. Referencing the *Age of Chivalry* catalog entry as the only "edition" of the "inscription," the *DIMEV* does not acknowledge its own editorial reorganization of the text. As I will discuss, the text presented in the *DIMEV* is perhaps the most misleadingly "emended" of all of the published transcriptions examined here. For discussion of the *DIMEV*'s use of rhyme as a proxy for "verse," inattention to metrical structure, and the implications of this "undertheorization of verse" for our conceptions of Middle English lyric, see Ian Cornelius, "Language and Meter," this volume (Chapter 4), 116–18, quotation at p. 117.

34. *Age of Chivalry*, 524–25.

35. This comment continues: "and probably indicate illiterate craftsmen" ("Summary" section of the online cataloging, http://collections.vam.ac.uk/item/O97902/robinson-jug-jug -unknown/).

36. This *S* is also rotated ninety degrees to the right.

37. As Andrew Albin notes, the nonlineated lyric poetry embedded within the prose of Rolle's *Ego Dormio* upon the material surfaces of manuscript pages also "asks us to read and listen in order to detect its poems and their sonorous forms" ("The Sound of Rollean Lyric," 221).

38. For further details concerning the casting of copper alloy vessels in late medieval England, see Roger Brownsword, "Medieval Metalwork: An Analytical Study of Copper-Alloy Objects," *Historical Metallurgy* 38, no. 2 (2004): 84–105; Claude Blair and John Blair, "Copper Alloys," in *English Medieval Industries*, ed. John Blair and Nigel Ramsay (London: Hambledon Press, 2001), 81–106 (with a technical appendix by Roger Brownsword); Alison Goodall, "The Medieval Bronzesmith and His Products," in *Medieval Industry*, ed. D. W. Crossley, Research Report no. 40 (London: Council for British Archaeology, 1981), 63–71.

39. For further discussion, see Kim M. Phillips, "The Invisible Man: Body and Ritual in a Fifteenth-Century Noble Household," *Journal of Medieval History* 31 (2005): 143–62; C. M. Woolgar, *The Senses in Late Medieval England* (New Haven, CT: Yale University Press, 2006), 132–36 et passim; Peter Barnet and Pete Dandridge, eds., *Lions, Dragons, and Other Beasts: Aquamanilia of the Middle Ages, Vessels for Church and Table* (New Haven, CT: Yale University Press for the Bard Graduate Center, 2006), esp. 2–17; John Steane, *The Archaeology of the British Monarchy* (London: Routledge, 1999), 134–41.

40. My attention to the role of deixis in this lyric (and following) was catalyzed by Cristina Maria Cervone, "John de Cobham and Cooling Castle's Charter Poem" and *Poetics of the Incarnation*.

41. I owe Nicholas Watson thanks for the phrase "language of command" and for drawing my attention to the "if/then" logic that implicitly integrates the ewer's two lyrics.

42. For Froissart's remark, see *Oeuvres de Froissart*, ed. M. le baron Kervyn de Letten-hove (1867–77; repr., Osnabrück: Biblio Verlag, 1967), 15:167. On French as a "royal language" in England, see Serge Lusignan, *La langue des rois au Moyen Âge: Le français en France et en Angleterre* (Paris: Presses universitaires de France, 2004); Christopher Fletcher, "Langue et nation en Angleterre à la fin du moyen âge," *Revue Française d'Histoire des Idées Politiques* 36, no. 2 (2012): 233–52.

43. Andrew Galloway, "Theory of the Fourteenth-Century English Lyric," this volume (Chapter 11).

44. Sometimes designated as the "Ashante" or "Ashanti" Ewer (or Jug), the vessel's conventional names derive from its provenance: almost certainly made in London for Rich-ard II's household, this ewer and another ewer (now on loan to the Leeds City Museum: LEEDM.FLI.1984) were seized by British forces in 1896 from the Asante royal mausoleum at Bantama or, perhaps, the palace of the King Prempeh I (Kwaku Dua III) in Kumasi (modern-day Ghana). A third ewer (British Museum, 1896,0727.1; *olim* Af1896,0727.1) was subsequently taken from the Asante, likely in 1900. For further discussion, see Richard Firth Green, *A Crisis of Truth: Literature and Law in Ricardian England* (Philadelphia: Uni-versity of Pennsylvania Press, 1999), 381–92; Vale, "From the Court of Richard II"; Mal-colm D. McLeod, "Art and Archaeology in Asante," in *Dall'archeologia all'arte tradizionale africana/De l'archéologie à l'art traditionnel africain/From Archaeology to Traditonal African Art*, ed. Gigi Pezzoli (Milan: Centro Studi Archeologia Africana, 1992), 65–81; David Ekserdjian, ed., *Bronze* (London: Royal Academy of the Arts, 2012), 265 (cat. no. 67); Ray-mond Silverman, "Red Gold: Things Made of Copper, Bronze, and Brass," in *Caravans of Gold, Fragments in Time: Art, Culture, and Exchange Across Medieval Saharan Africa*, ed. Kathleen Berzock (Princeton, NJ: Princeton University Press, 2019), 257–67, at pp. 263–66; Raymond Silverman, "Material Biographies: Saharan Trade and the Lives of Objects in Fourteenth and Fifteenth-Century West Africa," *History in Africa* 42 (2015): 375–95; Da-vid A. Hinton, *Gold & Gilt, Pots & Pins: Possessions and People in Medieval Britain* (Oxford: Oxford University Press, 2005), 234; Antonia Lovelace, "War Booty: Changing Contexts, Changing Displays; Asante 'Relics' from Kumasi, Acquired by the Prince of Wales's Own Regiment of Yorkshire in 1896," *Journal of Museum Ethnography* 12 (2000): 147–60; Malcolm McLeod, "Richard II, Part 3, at Kumase," in *West African Economic and Social History: Stud-ies in Memory of Marion Johnson*, ed. David Henige and T. C. McCaskie (Madison: African Studies Program at the University of Wisconsin, 1990), 171–74; Steane, *Archaeology of the British Monarchy*, 123–45; Cherry and Stratford, "The Ashanti Ewers," 98–100; Martin Bai-ley, "Two Kings, Their Armies and Some Jugs: The Ashanti Ewer," *Apollo Magazine* 138 (1993): 387–90; *Age of Chivalry*, p. 524 (cat. no. 726); Finlay, "British Late Medieval In-scribed Bronze Jugs," 7–8; Brownsword and Pitt, "British Late-Medieval Inscribed Bronze Jugs," 11–13; Theuerkauff-Liederwald, *Mittelalterliche Bronze- und Messinggefässe*, 241 (cat. no. 279); Read, "Bronze Jug."

45. *Age of Chivalry*, 524 (cat. no. 727). For scientific analyses relevant to this hypothesis, see note 28 above. The Wenlok Jug (acquired by the Luton Museum in 2006) is thought to have been produced in the same London workshop for the "Lord Wenlok" mentioned in its epigraphy; on this jug (with further bibliography), see Marian Campbell, "An English Medi-eval Jug," 187–96.

46. Although most commentators have described these avian forms as falcons, Marian Campbell identifies them as eagles and has remarked that they, together with the lion motif,

belong to the repertoire of devices employed by Edward III ("An English Medieval Jug," 187–96).

47. As Kay Staniland has noted, Richard seems to have first publicly displayed the hart device on the Feast of the Purification of the Virgin in 1386; but most scholars identify the Smithfield Tournament of 1390 as the motif's major public debut: Kay Staniland, "Extravagance or Regal Necessity? The Clothing of Richard II," in *The Regal Image of Richard II and the Wilton Diptych*, ed. Dillian Gordon, Lisa Monnas, and Caroline Elam (London: Harvey Miller, 1997), 85–93, at p. 91. For further discussion of the hart couchant and Richard's unprecedented expansion of the royal affinity starting in the second half of 1390, see Nigel Saul, "The Commons and the Abolition of Badges," *Parliamentary History* 9 (1990): 302–15; Nigel Saul, *Richard II* (New Haven, CT: Yale University Press, 1997), 265–69; Chris Given-Wilson, "Richard II and the Higher Nobility," in *Richard II: The Art of Kingship*, ed. Anthony Goodman and James Gillespie (Oxford: Clarendon Press, 1999), 107–28, esp. 123–27; Chris Given-Wilson, *The Royal Household and the King's Affinity: Service, Politics and Finance in England, 1360–1413* (New Haven, CT: Yale University Press, 1986), 212–16, 238–40.

48. From the British Museum's online collections catalog, https://britishmuseum.org /collection/object/H_1896-0727-1 (*DIMEV* 1911, 1112). On "Who-so woll no3t when he may / he schall no3t when he wolde," see Cornelius, "Language and Meter," 119–20.

49. Marian Campbell, "An English Medieval Jug," 190.

50. It is a pleasure to thank Andreas Böhmig for his work on this diagram of the Asante Ewer's epigraphy.

51. Invoking Daniel Tiffany's conception of "lyric substance," I wish to stress how lyrics encountered beyond the limits of the page require us to attend to nonmetaphoric substance (in ways Tiffany does not engage). See Daniel Tiffany, "Lyric Substance: On Riddles, Materialism, and Poetic Obscurity," *Critical Inquiry* 28 (2001): 72–98; Daniel Tiffany, *Toy Medium: Materialism and Modern Lyric* (Berkeley: University of California Press, 2000). As Andrew Albin's chapter in this book explores, the "sonorous matter" of Middle English lyric also rewards close consideration (Albin, "The Sound of Rollean Lyric," 218).

52. William Langland, *The Vision of Piers Plowman: A Critical Edition of the B-Text*, ed. A. V. C. Schmidt, 2nd ed. (London: J. M. Dent, 1995), 10.96–102; emphasis added.

53. For further discussion of this passage, see D. Vance Smith, "The Silence of Langland's Study."

54. As Ian Cornelius discusses, a more generalized version of this couplet, circulating relatively widely, may well have been verbally (and semantically) "recast" for use in the Asante Ewer; see, with further bibliography, Cornelius, "Language and Meter," 119–20.

55. Yet more speculatively: the alternative sense of "spillen" as "despoil" or "lay waste" may have rendered the prescribed decorous handling of the ewer's contents a performative figure for the (much contested) exercise of royal prerogative; see *MED*, s.v. "spillen (v.)." Critique of the royal court's extravagance is attested as early as 1386 and continued after Richard's deposition and death; on critiques of Richard II's wasteful extravagance, see Patricia Eberle, "The Politics of Courtly Style at the Court of Richard II," in *The Spirit of the Court: Selected Proceedings of the Fourth Congress of the International Courtly Literature Society (Toronto 1983)*, ed. Glyn S. Burgess and Robert A. Taylor (Cambridge: D. S. Brewer, 1985), 168–78; Stephanie Trigg, "The Rhetoric of Excess in *Winner and Waster*," *Yearbook of Langland Studies* 3 (1989): 91–108; Eleanor Johnson, "The Poetics of Waste: Medieval English Ecocriticsm,"

PMLA 127, no. 1 (2012): 460–76. Kay Staniland has persuasively argued that such invective has been read too credulously ("Extravagance or Regal Necessity?"). Nonetheless, an accumulation of evidence indicates that ceremonial protocols at court became increasingly elaborate in the 1390s; see Saul, *Richard II*, 339–58 et passim.

56. Marian Campbell, "An English Medieval Jug," 190; Campbell has tentatively proposed that the jug could have been used as an "alms pot" rather than as a vessel for liquids; were this true, it would necessarily have important implications for how we construe the import of the Asante Ewer's poetry.

57. On Richard II's subscription to the widely held view that lavish display "bore visible witness to wisdom," see Saul, *Richard II*, 355–58, at p. 356. See also the discussion in Christopher Fletcher, *Richard II: Manhood, Youth, and Politics, 1377–99* (Oxford: Oxford University Press, 2008), 45–59.

58. Livery badges were a cause for complaint and parliamentary petition as of 1384, and they continued to provoke acute concern and parliamentary legislation over the course of Richard II's reign, culminating in the statute of 1399's drastic restrictions. For further discussion, see Saul, "The Commons and the Abolition of Badges"; Given-Wilson, *The Royal Household*, 236–42; Given-Wilson, "Richard II and the Higher Nobility," 123–27.

59. Helen Barr, *Socioliterary Practice in Late Medieval England* (Oxford: Oxford University Press, 2001), 63–79; Helen Barr, *Signes and Sothe: Language in the Piers Plowman Tradition*, (Cambridge: D. S. Brewer, 1994), 72–80.

60. Cristina Maria Cervone, "Wondering Through Middle English Lyric," this volume (Chapter 2), 85; see also Barbara Zimbalist's exploration of how "Christ's speech . . . consistently creates a devotional community, both in the poem as well as beyond it" ("The Lyric Christ," this volume [Chapter 9], 255); and Galloway's analysis of how medieval "'lyric' genres" as "social systems" could be enlisted in politically charged disparagement, just as well as for "merging private with more communal experience" ("Theory of the Fourteenth-Century English Lyric," 315, 321).

61. Ingrid Nelson, "Lyric Value," this volume (Chapter 5), 156.

62. *DIMEV* 1112. The manuscript entries that follow are quoted from the *DIMEV* entry.

63. Finlay independently noted the distich's presence on the Asante Ewer and in this manuscript: Finlay, "British Late Medieval Inscribed Bronze Jugs," 8. For detailed discussion of the contents and collation of Rawlinson C.86, see Jeremy J. Griffiths, "A Re-examination of Oxford, Bodleian Library, MS Rawlinson C.86," *Archiv für das Studium der neueren Sprachen und Literaturen* 219 (1982): 381–88. The manuscript is also included in Daniel W. Mosser, *A Digital Catalogue of the Pre-1500 Manuscripts and Incunables of the Canterbury Tales*, 2nd ed., http://mossercatalogue.net/record.php?recID=Ra4.

64. As the *DIMEV* notes, this expanded setting of the couplet is seamlessly prefaced by *DIMEV* 6594 ("Whose conscience be cumbered and be not clean"); in Cambridge University Library MS Ii.3.26, therefore, we might think of the couplet as an "embedded" proverb, but it lacks the "voice change" markers that Nancy Mason Bradbury argues are constitutive of the proverb as an "embedded microgenre" (Bradbury, "The Proverb as Embedded Microgenre in Chaucer and *The Dialogue of Solomon and Marcolf*," *Exemplaria* 27 [2015]: 55–72). For stimulating discussion of proverbs in relation to other poetic forms, including lyric, see Wicker, "Between Proverbs and Lyrics"; Christopher Cannon, "Proverbs and the Wisdom of Literature: *The Proverbs of Alfred* and Chaucer's *Tale of Melibee*," *Textual Practice* 24, no. 3 (2010): 407–34.

65. The so-called "Henry VIII Manuscript," this volume of polyphonic music has been dated to 1510–20 CE and associated with a member of Henry VIII's court; for further details

and bibliography, see *Census-Catalogue of Manuscript Sources of Polyphonic Music, 1400–1550*, 5 vols. ([Rome]: American Institute of Musicology; Neuhausen-Stuttgart: Hänssler Verlag, 1979–88), 2:64; and the Digital Image Archive of Medieval Music (DIAMM) record (with full digital surrogate available to registered users), http://www.diamm.ac.uk/sources/1238/#/.

66. Malcolm Vale, in my view, underestimates the Asante Ewer when he writes that it "communicated few (if any) symbolic . . . meanings" and characterizes its poetry as devoid of "evidently symbolic" meaning (Vale, "From the Court of Richard II," 337).

67. Terminological distinction of "bronze" and "brass" was not observed in the medieval period. For further discussion of the making and working of copper alloys in the Middle Ages, see Blair and Blair, "Copper Alloys"; Goodall, "The Medieval Bronzesmith"; Ittai Weinryb, *The Bronze Object in the Middle Ages* (Cambridge: Cambridge University Press, 2016).

68. For recent arguments for the production of brass "from scratch" in late medieval England, see Claude Blair, John Blair, and R. Brownsword, "An Oxford Brasiers' Dispute of the 1390s: Evidence for Brass-making in Medieval England," *Antiquaries Journal* 66 (1986): 82–90; Blair and Blair, "Copper Alloys," 82–85; David Dungworth and Matthew Nicholas, "Caldarium? An Antimony Bronze Used for Medieval and Post-Medieval Cast Domestic Vessels," *Historical Metallurgy* 38, no. 1 (2004): 24–34.

69. Henry Thomas Riley, ed. and trans., *Memorials of London and London Life, in the XIIIth, XIVth, and XVth Centuries: Being a Series of Extracts, Local, Social, and Political, from the Early Archives of the City of London, A.D. 1276–1419* (London: Longmans, Green, 1868), 118.

70. Ibid.

71. *Middle English Dictionary (MED)*, s.v. "trien (v.)." Although I cannot pursue this point here, it bears noting that the phrase "trien a truthe" also has strong legal (and literary) resonances; for further discussion, see Barr, *Signes and Sothe*, 137–38. I thank Cristina Maria Cervone and Nicholas Watson for directing me to Barr's work.

72. On the 1388 "Merciless Parliament" and chivalric falsity, see E. Amanda McVitty, "False Knights and True Men: Contesting Chivalric Masculinity in English Treason Trials, 1388–1415," *Journal of Medieval History* 40, no. 4 (2014): 458–77. For a magisterial account of how intensively the concept of truth was itself interrogated and transformed during Richard's reign, see Richard Firth Green, *A Crisis of Truth*. As Cristina Maria Cervone has suggested (personal communication), "deme" and its variants play a critical role in both *Pearl* and *Patience*; the resonance—both consonant and dissonant—between the polyvalence of the activity of "deming" in these poems and the Asante Ewer merits more consideration than I can give it here. For discussion of "deming" in *Pearl*, with further bibliography, see James C. Staples, "'Mercy Schal Hyr Craftez Kyþe': Learning to Perform Re-Deeming Readings of Materiality in *Pearl*," *Glossator* 9 (2015): 109–31.

73. On Ricardian "public poetry," see the seminal article by Anne Middleton, "The Idea of Public Poetry in the Reign of Richard II," *Speculum* 53, no. 1 (1978): 94–114.

74. For further discussion, see Nelson, *Lyric Tactics*, 1–30.

75. The single best point of departure for further forays in this direction remains Edwards, "Middle English Inscriptional Verse Texts." Lamentably, Anglo-French and Latin inscriptions and epigraphy produced in late medieval England have yet to attract much scholarly interest, with the notable exceptions of David Griffith, "A Living Language of the Dead? French Commemorative Inscriptions from Late Medieval England," *Mediaeval Journal* 3, no. 2 (2013): 69–136; and David Griffith, "English Commemorative Inscriptions: Some Literary Dimensions," in *Memory and Commemoration in Medieval England: Proceedings of*

the 2008 Harlaxton Symposium, ed. Caroline M. Barron and Clive Burgess (Donington, Lincolnshire: Shaun Tyas, 2010), 251–70.

CHAPTER 8

Epigraph: Paul Zumthor, "Considérations sur les valeurs de la voix," *Cahiers de civilisation médiévale* 25, no. 99 (1982): 233–38, at p. 238.

1. Some 470 manuscripts of Rolle's works survive today, an otherwise unheard of sum for a late medieval English author.

2. Rosemary Woolf attests to Rolle's immense impact on English vernacular devotional writing in the later Middle Ages: "the name of Rolle, at least by the fifteenth century . . . was used with the same indiscriminate reverence as that of St. Bernard had been, and a credulous attentiveness to the attributions of fifteenth-century manuscripts would lead one to suppose that nearly all devotional prose had been written by Rolle and nearly all didactic prose by Wycliffe" (*The English Religious Lyric in the Middle Ages* [Oxford: Clarendon Press, 1968], 381).

3. Musicologists have debated the role of verbal sound in medieval performance practice, musical audition, and related intellectual contexts, usually as an adjunct to pitched musical sound or music notation as the proper sites of scholarly interest. See, for example, John Stevens, *Words and Music in the Middle Ages: Song, Narrative, Dance and Drama, 1050–1350* (Cambridge: Cambridge University Press, 1986); Christopher Page, "Around the Performance of a 13th-Century Motet," *Early Music* 28, no. 3 (2000): 343–57; Elizabeth Eva Leach, *Sung Birds: Music, Nature, and Poetry in the Later Middle Ages* (Ithaca, NY: Cornell University Press, 2007); Anna Zayaruznaya, "Intelligibility Redux: Motets and the Modern Medieval Sound," *Music Theory Online* 23, no. 2 (2017), https://mtosmt.org/issues/mto.17.23.2/mto.17.23.2.zayaruznaya.html.

4. My project thus overlaps with Aden Kumler's study of the disposition of Middle English lyric in materialities beyond the book; "Lyric Vessels," this volume (Chapter 7).

5. Richard Rolle, *Richard Rolle: Prose and Verse Edited from the MS Longleat 29 and Related Manuscripts*, ed. S. J. Ogilvie-Thomson, EETS, o.s. 293 (Oxford: Oxford University Press, 1988), p. 26, lines 1–3. Hereafter, I cite Ogilvie-Thomson's edition parenthetically in text by page and line number. Although its non-Northern dialect does not reflect Rolle's regional idiom, Ogilvie-Thomson prefers MS Longleat 29 for her base text; I emend (with indication in notes) where Longleat's readings are uniquely eccentric. I adopt Ogilvie-Thomson's sigla for manuscripts (see her pp. xvi–xvii) as follows: Ad = British Library, Additional MS 37790; Dd = Cambridge University Library, MS Dd.v.64.III; G = Bibliothèque Sainte-Geneviève, MS 3390; Lt = Longleat House, MS Longleat 29; R and R¹= Bodleian Library, MS Rawlinson A.389 (there are two copies of the text in this manuscript); S = British Library, Additional MS 22283; V = Bodleian Library, MS English Poetry a.1; W = Westminster School, MS 3. Ogilvie-Thomson's Bradfer-Lawrence 10 (Br) is now Beinecke Library, MS Takamiya 66, which I represent as "Tk" for clarity's sake. While worthy of study in their own right, British Library, Arundel MS 507 (Ar), Magdalene College, MS Pepys 2125 (P), and Trinity College Dublin, MS 155 (Tr) do not figure into this chapter's manuscript considerations: P alters *Ego Dormio*'s second lyric substantially and lacks the third lyric; Tr splits and expands the second lyric, inserts a new lyric at 31.235, and lacks the third lyric; Ar is deficient, terminating at 29.124, and thus only contains the first lyric (xliv–xlv). I extend sincere gratitude to Nicholas Courtney, S.J., for his assistance with manuscript research for this chapter.

6. LtR's "lust" appears as the more Northerly "lyste" in R¹WGDdAd. See the *Middle English Dictionary* (*MED*), s.v. "listen v.(1)" and "listen v.(2)."

7. This sentence's slightly "awkward" or "tortuous" self-authorizing thrust has drawn the attention of at least two other critics. See Annie Sutherland, "Biblical Text and Spiritual Experience in the English Epistles of Richard Rolle," *Review of English Studies* 56, no. 227 (2005): 695–711, at pp. 703–4; and Nicholas Watson, *Richard Rolle and the Invention of Authority* (Cambridge: Cambridge University Press, 1991), 230.

8. Jesse Gellrich accounts compellingly for this spell as an "ideology of writing" in chapter 1 of *Discourse and Dominion in the Fourteenth Century: Oral Contexts of Writing in Philosophy, Politics, and Poetry* (Princeton, NJ: Princeton University Press, 1995), 3–36. Denis Renevey traces how mystical authors including Rolle adapted the letter and spirit of the Song of Songs to their authorial projects in *Language, Self and Love: Hermeneutics in Richard Rolle and the Commentaries of the Song of Songs* (Cardiff: University of Wales Press, 2001).

9. Simon Jarvis, "Prosody as Cognition," *Critical Quarterly* 40, no. 4 (1998): 3–15, at pp. 6, 4.

10. Simon Jarvis, "The Melodics of Long Poems," *Textual Practice* 24, no. 4 (2010): 607–21, at p. 612.

11. Jarvis, "Prosody as Cognition," 11.

12. Vincent Gillespie goes so far as to say that *Ego Dormio* provides us with a "hierarchy of lyric writing" in "Mystic's Foot: Rolle and Affectivity," in *Looking in Holy Books: Essays on Late Medieval Religious Writing in England* (Turnhout: Brepols, 2012), 243–76, at p. 266.

13. While rubrication and pointing reflect the lyrics' formal design in a number of manuscripts, similar marking habits in the surrounding prose make this feature visually unremarkable. Rather, one must read the text in order to discover the poetic line, even when the lyrics are signaled with initials (as in MSS SV; see note 28), paraphs, or other forms of *ordinatio*. Deliberate scribal preservation of prose layout is most conspicuous in R¹, on folio 99r, where *Ego Dormio*'s third lyric concludes in prose layout at the top of the folio and the same scribal hand lineates the lyric "Almighty God in Trinity" (*Digital Index of Middle English Verse* [*DIMEV*] 422) immediately underneath. At the end of the fourteenth century, to which *Ego Dormio*'s earliest manuscripts are dated, the presentation of verse in prose format would have been atypical, especially when that verse was metered and rhymed, as with *Ego Dormio*'s second and third lyrics. As Eric Weiskott writes, though "some English poetry, especially alliterative poetry, continued to be laid out as prose" after 1250, "the final decades of the thirteenth century mark the end of the older, prose format as the standard for poetry in English" (*English Alliterative Verse: Poetic Tradition and Literary History* [Cambridge: Cambridge University Press, 2016], 84–85, also 98). Exceptions to this general rule can of course be found: in his chapter in the present book, Ian Cornelius points out the common prose format presentation of short vernacular lyrics embedded in Latin preaching manuals ("Language and Meter," this volume [Chapter 4], 118).

14. This interactive discovery of lyric in *Ego Dormio* resonates with haptic detection of lyric in the Robinson Jug Kumler describes in "Lyric Vessels."

15. For medieval prosimetrum, see Eleanor Johnson, *Practicing Literary Theory in the Middle Ages: Ethics and the Mixed Form in Chaucer, Gower, Usk, and Hoccleve* (Chicago: University of Chicago Press, 2013).

16. For the romance narrative, see Ardis Butterfield, *Poetry and Music in Medieval France: From Jean Renart to Guillaume de Machaut* (Cambridge: Cambridge University Press, 2002). For the long romance as a lyric form, see Christopher Cannon, "Lyric Romance," this volume (Chapter 3).

17. Responding to Hope Emily Allen, *Writings Ascribed to Richard Rolle, Hermit of Hampole* (London: Oxford University Press, 1927), 250, Ogilvie-Thomson speculates about the identity and facticity of the nun of Yedingham; see *Prose and Verse*, lxvi–lxvii. Watson, McIlroy, and Sutherland each respond in turn. See Watson, *Invention*, 227–28; Claire Elizabeth McIlroy, *The English Prose Treatises of Richard Rolle* (Cambridge: D. S. Brewer, 2004), 62–64; Sutherland, "Biblical Text," 703.

18. Scholars have sought to align these three degrees of love with Richard of St. Victor's four degrees of violent love, in part because Rolle applies the Victorine's terminology to his own mystical theology in the *Form of Living*. The alignment does not fit especially well.

19. Ingrid Nelson discusses the flexible uses to which medieval lyrics can be put, in relation to and independent of the material texts in which they are recorded, in *Lyric Tactics: Poetry, Genre, and Practice in Later Medieval England* (Philadelphia: University of Pennsylvania Press, 2017). That *Ego Dormio*'s lyrics were detached, broken apart, and creatively used by late medieval readers is apparent when we consider their reconstituted appearance as Rollean speech bubbles and image-text devotions in the Carthusian miscellany London, British Library, Additional MS 37049. See Jessica Brantley, *Reading in the Wilderness: Private Devotion and Public Performance in Late Medieval England* (Chicago: University of Chicago Press, 2007), chap. 4. Katherine Zieman's account of the modular, recombinatory poetics at work in Add. 37049's Rollean imitations dovetails with the poetics of sound I describe here; Zieman, "Compiling the Lyric: Richard Rolle, Textual Dynamism and Devotional Song in London, British Library, Additional MS 37049," in *Middle English Lyrics: New Readings of Short Poems*, ed. Julia Boffey and Christiania Whitehead (Cambridge: D. S. Brewer, 2018), 158–72.

20. I discuss the Rollean notion of *canor* at greater length in Andrew Albin, "Listening for *Canor* in Richard Rolle's *Melos amoris*," in *Voice and Voicelessness in Medieval Europe*, ed. Irit Ruth Kleiman (New York: Palgrave Macmillan, 2015), 177–97.

21. Watson, *Invention*, 231.

22. Patrick S. Diehl, *The Medieval European Religious Lyric: An Ars Poetica* (Berkeley: University of California Press, 1985). Diehl connects these literary developments with fraternal vernacular preaching, a new theological emphasis on Christ's humanity, and lay-oriented affective pieties.

23. Rebecca Krug, "Jesus' Voice: Dialogue and Late-Medieval Readers," in *Form and Reform: Reading Across the Fifteenth Century*, ed. Shannon Gayk and Kathleen Tonry (Columbus: Ohio State University Press, 2011), 110–29, at p. 111. Barbara Zimbalist examines the intensity of Christ's lyric speech, particularly its ability to motivate devotional response in a future moment of reading, in "The Lyric Christ," this volume (Chapter 9). The effect of Rolle's speaking voice in *Ego Dormio* must owe something to this tradition.

24. Watson elaborates on the "special tone" Rolle uses in *Ego Dormio* to "bathe this work in as much intimacy as he can" and "contribute to our sense of Rolle's personal presence in the work": "Rolle himself . . . is always to be heard 'speaking' the words he has written" (*Invention,* 228–29). McIlroy surmises an "oral context" for Rolle's vernacular epistles in which "the work will be both read and heard" (*English Prose Treatises*, 173, also 66). For the predominance of vocalized reading practices in late medieval England, even as literacy apparently increased in the later Middle Ages, see Joyce Coleman, *Public Reading and the Reading Public in Late Medieval England and France* (Cambridge: Cambridge University Press, 1996).

25. Though arrived at independently, the virtual space I describe here agrees well with the one Elizabeth Fowler describes in "The Proximity of the Virtual: A. C. Spearing's Experientiality (or, Roaming with Palamon and Arcite)," in *Readings in Medieval Textuality: Essays*

in Honour of A. C. Spearing, ed. Cristina Maria Cervone and D. Vance Smith (Cambridge: D. S. Brewer, 2016), 15–30. Though Spearing's notion of "textual subjectivity" is not incompatible with Rolle's vernacular epistles, their cultivation of Rolle's present and sounding voice does complicate the Derridean disarticulations that underlie Spearing's approach. See A. C. Spearing, *Textual Subjectivity: The Encoding of Subjectivity in Medieval Narratives and Lyrics* (Oxford: Oxford University Press, 2005), esp. chap. 1.

26. This turn of phrase has received no shortage of critical attention. See Ann W. Astell, "Feminine Figurae in the Writings of Richard Rolle: A Register of Growth," *Mystics Quarterly* 15, no. 3 (1989): 117–24; Watson, *Invention*, 229–32; McIlroy, *English Prose Treatises*, 67–72; Sutherland, "Biblical Text," 704; Barry Windeatt, "Love," in *A Companion to Medieval English Literature and Culture, c.1350–c.1500*, ed. Peter Brown (Malden, MA: Blackwell, 2007), 322–38, at p. 329; Sarah McNamer, *Affective Meditation and the Invention of Medieval Compassion* (Philadelphia: University of Pennsylvania Press, 2010), 121; and Christopher M. Roman, *Queering Richard Rolle: Mystical Theology and the Hermit in Fourteenth-Century England* (Cham, Switzerland: Palgrave Macmillan, 2017), 69.

27. Ogilvie-Thomson does not lineate the first lyric. I follow the lineation of Hope Emily Allen in *English Writings of Richard Rolle: Hermit of Hampole* (Oxford: Clarendon Press, 1931), 64; and Rosamund Allen in *Richard Rolle: The English Writings* (New York: Paulist Press, 1988), 135. Only Rolle's first modern editor, Carl Horstmann, reflects the manuscript presentation of all three lyrics as prose, in C. Horstman [Horstmann], ed., *Yorkshire Writers: Richard Rolle of Hampole, an English Father of the Church, and His Followers*, 2 vols. (London: Swan Sonnenschein; New York: Macmillan, 1895–96), 1:49–61, 415–16.

28. S marks off all major divisions of the text, including the three lyrics, with decorated initials, without distinction. V is the only manuscript that draws deliberate attention to the three lyrics by marking only them and *Ego Dormio*'s first word with decorated initials.

29. VRLtW all mark the end of the lyric after line 8 with a paraph. Ad excises the lyric altogether, but retains lines 9–10, indicating that the scribe understood the lyric to end at line 8. Of the remaining copies, R¹ and G mark the end of the lyric after line 10 with a rubricated paraph, Dd marks it with rubrication, and STk make no indication.

30. Paraphs, rubrication, and a marginal *nota* in LtWGDd indicate this earlier beginning to the lyric. RSVWAd indicate the lyric's beginning as above; R¹ and Tk make no indication.

31. Ogilvie-Thomson places a colon here, but in no manuscript—including Longleat—does scribal pointing indicate a major medial pause.

32. Rolle indicates distrust of visuality across his writings, connected to his anxieties around accusations that his spiritual sensations are imaginative overindulgence. See Andrew Albin, *Richard Rolle's Melody of Love: A Study and Translation with Manuscript and Musical Context* (Toronto: Pontifical Institute of Mediaeval Studies, 2018), 8–9, 87–90.

33. Gillespie, "Mystic's Foot," 248–49.

34. Lt is the only witness to include the demonstrative pronoun "þis" here, directing the reader to the second lyric instead of inviting her more abstractly into the activity of thought.

35. The gesture also echoes and reenergizes the virtual vocality *Ego Dormio* has sponsored from the start by eliding speech, thought, and the work of reading into a single cognitive endeavor.

36. On the role of the imagination and affect in Passion meditations, see Robert Worth Frank, Jr., "*Meditationes Vitae Christi*: The Logistics of Access to Divinity," in *Hermeneutics*

and Medieval Culture, ed. Patrick Gallacher and Helen Damico (Albany: State University of New York Press, 1989), 39–50; Niklaus Largier, "Inner Senses–Outer Senses: The Practice of Emotions in Medieval Mysticism," in *Emotion and Sensibilities in the Middle Ages*, ed. C. Stephen Jaeger and Ingrid Kasten (Berlin: Walter de Gruyter, 2003), 3–15; McNamer, *Affective Meditation*; and Michelle Karnes, *Imagination, Meditation, and Cognition in the Middle Ages* (Chicago: University of Chicago Press, 2011).

37. Rolle authored a pair of freestanding vernacular Passion meditations; see Ogilvie-Thomson, *Prose and Verse*, 64–83; and Hope Emily Allen, *English Writings*, 17–36. Another appears in chapter 30 of the *Melos amoris*; see Albin, *Melody of Love*, 227–31. For a meditation on the work of wonder in the Middle English lyric, see Cristina Maria Cervone's "Wondering Through Middle English Lyric," this volume (Chapter 2).

38. Only R^1ArTk do not mark the lyric's beginning in some fashion. Scribal attention to lineation is greater here: where only VGDd mark line endings for the first lyric, RR^1S-VWGDdArTk mark line endings and LtR^1WDd mark rhymes for the second lyric with either pointing or rubrication. That said, this greater attention generally does not distinguish itself from the treatment of the surrounding prose in frequency or type of scribal marks.

39. Spearing explores the inhabitable, subjectless subjectivity of the *I* of medieval lyric discourse in *Textual Subjectivity*, esp. chap. 6. Diehl discusses the comparable function of the *I* in the religious lyric as it pertains to rhetorical figures of apostrophe, prosopopoeia, and dialogue in *Medieval European Religious Lyric*, 135ff. In these accounts, the anonymous authorship of devotional literature assists readerly entry into the textual *I* and the communities to which that *I* belongs: "As with medieval religious texts in the tradition of affective spirituality, the first person, which functions as the source of 'thoughts and sentiments,' can readily be identified with the author precisely because it lacks most characterizing features, and can therefore also be taken over without difficulty by any likely reader" (Spearing, *Textual Subjectivity*, 189). By contrast, Rolle's *I* in *Ego Dormio* can hardly be called anonymous; the hermit employs a highly characterized first person for distinct aims.

40. In *Giving Voice to Love: Song and Self-Expression from the Troubadours to Guillaume de Machaut* (Oxford: Oxford University Press, 2011), Judith Peraino examines a similar construction of hybrid subjectivity in the medieval performance of song, in terms that profit the study of medieval lyric more broadly. David Lawton's consideration of revoicing antecedent texts in *Voice in Later Medieval English Literature: Public Interiorities* (Oxford: Oxford University Press, 2017) bears comparison. Ingrid Nelson's account of Merleau-Pontian intersubjectivity in the medieval lyric dialogue is pertinent here; see "Lyric Value," this volume (Chapter 5).

41. Butterfield, *Poetry and Music*, 45. Butterfield contests this classic description of the *rondet*, arguing that it was the conventional strophic sections of *rondets* that remains constant, the refrain that "provid[ed] individual point to the songs . . . [and] act[ed] as the distinguishing semantic feature of each *rondet*" (48). This, she argues, is why it is soloists who so often sing the refrains, not the strophes, of *rondets* embedded in romances. Ingrid Nelson also discusses the *carole* as a dance form and its relation to the lyric ("Lyric Value," 153–56), as does Cervone ("Wondering Through Middle English Lyric," 86).

42. Cristina Maria Cervone writes that this collective subjectivity "is characteristic of Middle English lyric or carols that emphasize 'each of us' and 'all of us.'" See "'I' and 'We' in Chaucer's *Complaint unto Pity*," in Cervone and Smith, *Readings in Medieval Textuality*, 195–212, at p. 198.

43. V's scribal marks match these closely, and those manuscripts that mark *ordinatio* within the body of the second lyric generally mark the interlude and the longing petition, though not uniformly.

44. Denis Renevey considers *Ego Dormio* as an enactable mystical script from the perspective of Jerzy Grotowski's poor theater in "Mystical Texts or Mystical Bodies? Peculiar Modes of Performance in Late Medieval England," *Swiss Papers in English Language and Literature* 11 (1998): 89–104.

45. Rhyme scheme type 2 seems to mirror the spread of wonder: it too extends from the end of the Passion meditation, across the interlude, and into the love complaint.

46. Retained within this structure of affect is the delay of affective onset from the first reading: the trace of readerly encounter. That fresh act of first reading thus becomes incorporated into the meditation, reinscribing Rolle's hybrid authorial voice, and the text that hosts that voice, into the reader's spiritual devotions. This unexpectedly Derridean configuration figures well into Rolle's project of self-authorization, amply documented in Watson, *Invention*.

47. Chapter 31 of the *Incendium amoris* or chapters 45 and 47 of the *Melos amoris*, for example. See Albin, *Melody of Love*, 79, 105, 120.

48. See *MED*, s.vv. "seien v.(1)" and "sīghen v."

49. For a complementary reading that instead locates Rollean *canor* in the worldly noisemaking of *Ego Dormio*'s lyrics, see Adin Lears, *World of Echo: Noise and Knowing in Late Medieval England* (Ithaca, NY: Cornell University Press, 2020), esp. 57–61.

50. Alliteration in the second lyric is largely relegated to the Passion meditation and interlude. Given alliteration's association in the first lyric with worldliness and visuality, its more frequent use in the third lyric might be taken as a nod to the future redemption of visuality through the divine face-to-face, or as the retention of the third lyric within earthbound frames of experience.

51. The "-ynge" *a* rhyme receives prominent enough emphasis at opening and close and recurs frequently enough throughout the poem for it to sustain over the poem's full length, reiterating the third lyric's stalled momentum with a grammatical suffix that hangs between verbal process and substantive stasis.

52. See Catherine A. Carsley, "Devotion to the Holy Name: Late Medieval Piety in England," *Princeton University Library Chronicle* 53 (1992): 156–72; and Denis Renevey, "Name Above Names: The Devotion to the Name of Jesus from Richard Rolle to Walter Hilton's *Scale of Perfection I*," in *The Medieval Mystical Tradition: England, Ireland and Wales; Exeter Symposium VI; Papers Read at Charney Manor, July 1999*, ed. Marion Glasscoe (Cambridge: D. S. Brewer, 1999), 103–21.

53. Where most other manuscripts use pointing, rubrication, or other marks to indicate the third lyric's versification, rhyme scheme, or both, Ad points versification with comparative unevenness. By contrast, the emphasis on the Holy Name is unmistakable: every appearance is underlined, and its triple repetitions in large red script leap off the page.

54. Ogilvie-Thomson's quotation marks surrounding "I slepe and my hert waketh. Who shal to my leman say, for his loue me longeth ay?" are modern editorial intervention and do not appear in manuscript.

55. For more on Rolle's imbrication of his own writing with scripture, the Song of Songs in particular, see Albin, *Melody of Love*, 118–24.

56. *DIMEV* 2286.

57. We might see the rogue lyric's unexpected emergence from Rolle's description of the third degree of love to occur in symmetric counterpoint with the first lyric's emergence from its prose surrounds.

58. For medieval sound studies, see the bibliography in Susan Boynton et al., "Sound Matters," *Speculum* 91, no. 4 (2016): 998–1039. Of special importance are Bruce Holsinger, *Music, Body, and Desire in Medieval Culture: Hildegard of Bingen to Chaucer* (Stanford, CA: Stanford University, 2001); Leach, *Sung Birds*; Emma Dillon, *The Sense of Sound: Musical Meaning in France, 1260–1330* (Oxford: Oxford University, 2012); and Andrew Hicks, *Composing the World: Harmony in the Medieval Platonic Cosmos* (Oxford: Oxford University, 2017).

59. Andrew Albin, "Theorizing Richard Rolle's Sound Art," forthcoming.

60. *MED*, s.v. "hōlden v.(1)," definitions 1 and 14a.

CHAPTER 9

1. Rosemary Woolf, *The English Religious Lyric in the Middle Ages* (Oxford: Clarendon Press, 1968).

2. In his anthology of Middle English lyrics, R. T. Davies claims that poems in the tradition of affective piety "do not appeal to the intellect through theological elaborations and subtleties but inflame the heart through a contemplation of the physical Passion and poignant consideration of its implications for a sinner" (Davies, ed., *Medieval English Lyrics: A Critical Anthology* [London: Faber and Faber, 1963], 22). More recently, Vincent Gillespie has traced the long connection between the affective tradition and vernacular devotional poetry; and Sarah McNamer has argued that the types of devotion encouraged by such affective poetry promoted explicitly gendered emotional performance. See Gillespie, "Mystic's Foot: Rolle and Affectivity," in *The Medieval Mystical Tradition in England: Papers Read at Dartington Hall, July 1982*, ed. Marion Glasscoe (Exeter: University of Exeter Press, 1982), 199–230; and McNamer, *Affective Meditation and the Invention of Medieval Compassion* (Philadelphia: University of Pennsylvania Press, 2010).

3. My attention to the effects of the Middle English lyric other than—or in addition to—the affective responds especially to the work of David Aers and Nicholas Watson. Aers argues that entirely affective identification with Christ's suffering can ultimately reinscribe its practitioners within discourses of patriarchal and ecclesiastic control; Watson cautions that limited focus on Christ's suffering humanity can generate a narrow view of medieval devotional experience as solely imagined through the Passion, thus neglecting other modes of Christ-centered devotion or piety. See Aers, "The Humanity of Christ: Reflections on Orthodox Late Medieval Representations," in *Powers of the Holy: Religion, Politics, and Gender in Late Medieval English Culture*, David Aers and Lynn Staley (University Park: Pennsylvania State University Press, 1996), 15–42; and Watson, "Desire for the Past," *Studies in the Age of Chaucer* 21 (1991): 59–97.

4. Ingrid Nelson, *Lyric Tactics: Poetry, Genre, and Practice in Later Medieval England* (Philadelphia: University of Pennsylvania Press, 2017), 6.

5. Cervone describes collective subjectivity as "a medieval mode of metaphysical poetry that considers abstract concepts in light of shared human experience," which prompts readers "to consider collective subjectivity, through both the collectivity of personified abstraction (a 'we' that in lived experience would abide within a unified 'I'), and the collectivity of how 'we' readers can nevertheless identify with the 'I' of the narrative"; Cristina Maria Cervone, "'I' and 'We' in Chaucer's *Complaint unto Pity*," in *Readings in Medieval Textuality: Es-*

says in Honour of A. C. Spearing, ed. Cristina Maria Cervone and D. Vance Smith (Cambridge: D. S. Brewer, 2016), 195–212, at pp. 196–97.

6. Stock defines "textual communities" as "microsocieties organized around the common understanding of a script" that both "model the way a text is interpreted and influence behavior." He describes the relationship between the text and the community as "the interpenetration of written structures with reality"; a text that elicits interpretation, in his view, "influences behavior: the members of the group, having imbibed the message, go forth into the world—not the world of language, or of speech acts, but the world of events—and carry out actions based on their textually informed beliefs"; Brian Stock, *Listening for the Text: On the Uses of the Past* (Philadelphia: University of Pennsylvania Press, 1996), 23, 108–9.

7. James Simpson, "Not Yet: Chaucer and Anagogy," *Studies in the Age of Chaucer* 37 (2015): 31–54. Simpson describes an anagogic text as a narrative that "not only predicts, or desires, a future in which that which has been lost will be found, that which has been divided united. Additionally, [such narratives] help *bring that transformed community into being*, by changing the consciousness of their own readers" (34). He sees the anagogic impulse as a transhistorical literary mode with particular prophetic shape in pre-Reformation England.

8. Nicholas Watson and Jacqueline Jenkins, eds., *The Writings of Julian of Norwich: "A Vision Showed to a Devout Woman" and "A Revelation of Love"* (University Park: Pennsylvania State University Press, 2006).

9. Stephanie Burt has suggested that recent theoretical attention to lyric has overlooked earlier, pre-Romantic modalities of the genre. See Stephanie [Stephen] Burt, "What Is This Thing Called Lyric?," *Modern Philology* 113, no. 3 (2016): 422–40. Jonathan Culler's call to "bring poetry back into literary studies" advocates for the historically attenuated study of lyric traditions, "emphasizing features that can become the basis of new typologies." See Culler, "Why Lyric?," *PMLA* 123, no 1 (2008): 201–6, at p. 205; and more recently, *Theory of the Lyric* (Cambridge, MA: Harvard University Press, 2015).

10. As Virginia Jackson and Jonathan Culler (among others) have shown, post-Romantic ideas of the lyric as fundamentally expressive, personal, and individual continue to shape narratives of lyric development. For extended discussion of the tradition of lyric as the expression of individual subjectivity see Culler, "Why Lyric?" and *Theory of the Lyric*; for a history of the critical tradition understanding lyric as a short form, see Jackson, "Lyric," *The Princeton Encyclopedia of Poetry and Poetics*, 4th ed., ed. Roland Greene and Stephen Cushman (Princeton, NJ: Princeton University Press, 2012), 826–34. Jackson in particular cautions that "our notion of subjectivity, emotion, and compassion in poetry—in sum, the personal lyric— did not match ideas about poetry (or persons) in antiquity" ("Lyric," 828).

11. Christopher Cannon, "Lyric Romance," this volume (Chapter 4).

12. *Digital Index of Middle English Verse* (*DIMEV*) 5030. Carleton Brown dated the poem to the last quarter of the thirteenth century; more recently, Susanna Fein has dated the poem to the late thirteenth century, based on E. J. Dobson and F. Ll. Harrison's edition. Carleton Brown, *English Lyrics of the XIIIth Century* (Oxford: Oxford University Press, 1932); Susanna Fein, "Stond wel, moder, under rode: Introduction," in Susanna Fein, ed. and trans., *The Complete Harley 2253 Manuscript*, with David Raybin and Jan Ziolkowski (Kalamazoo, MI: Medieval Institute Publications for TEAMS, 2014), vol. 2, art. 60; E. J. Dobson and F. Ll. Harrison, eds., *Medieval English Songs* (London: Faber and Faber; New York: Cambridge University Press, 1979).

13. For discussion of the poem as dream vision, see George Kane, who terms it a "special mode of courtly vision poetry" (*Middle English Literature: A Critical Study of the Romances, the*

Religious Lyrics, Piers Plowman [London: Methuen, 1951], 158); James Wimsatt, who terms the poem a "dream realm" ("The Canticle of Canticles, Two Latin Poems, and 'In a valey of this restles mynde,'" *Modern Philology* 75, no. 4 [1978]: 327–45, at p. 336); Susanna Fein, who describes the poem's setting as "a visionary place" (Fein, ed., *Moral Love Songs and Laments* [Kalamazoo, MI: Medieval Institute Publications for TEAMS, 1998], 57); and Cristina Maria Cervone, who describes it as "an interior landscape, within the self" (*Poetics of the Incarnation: Middle English Writing and the Leap of Love* [Philadelphia: University of Pennsylvania Press, 2013], 61).

14. The repeated refrain "quia amore langueo" is a direct quotation from the Song of Songs 2:5 and 5:8. For extensive analysis of the poem's use of the Song of Songs tradition, see Ann Astell, *The Song of Songs in the Middle Ages* (Ithaca, NY: Cornell University Press, 1990), 133–43. For discussion of the blending of courtly love conventions and mystical devotion, see Barbara Newman, *From Virile Woman to WomanChrist: Studies in Medieval Religion and Literature* (Philadelphia: University of Pennsylvania Press, 1995), 137–67.

15. The *Index of Middle English Verse* (*IMEV*) and the *DIMEV* erroneously catalog the poem as two different poems: *DIMEV* 5704, "This is Christ's own complaint, 'The Complaint of Christ to Man and Man's Answer'"; and *DIMEV* 5707, "This is God's own complaint, 'The Complaint of God.'" This confusion results from the omission of a single stanza in two manuscript versions: Oxford, Bodleian Library, MS Douce 78; and Cambridge, Trinity College, MS R.3.20. All ten versions of the "Complaint" are united formally by the repeated refrain and monologue-and-answer structure. Moreover, the dual catalog identity results not only from the absence of a single stanza but also from the unattributed editorial decision to designate the shorter version the utterance of "Christ" and the longer version the utterance of "God." The "Complaint of Christ" appears in the following two manuscripts with ten stanzas: (1) Oxford, Bodleian Library, MS Douce 78, fols. 5–7v; (2) Cambridge, Trinity College, MS R.3.20 (600), pp. 234–35; and these eight with eleven stanzas: (1) Oxford, Bodleian Library, MS Bodley 596, fols. 12–14; (2) Oxford, Bodleian Library, MS Rawlinson C.86, fols. 67–69; (3) London, British Library, Additional MS 39574, fols. 54–57; (4) London, British Library, Harley MS 2380, fols. 71v–72v; (5) Edinburgh, National Library of Scotland, MS Advocates' 34.7.3, fols. 75–76v, 77–77v; (6) London, Lambeth Palace Library, MS 306, fols. 145–47; (7) London, Lambeth Palace Library, MS 853, pp. 81–88; (8) Cambridge, MA, Harvard University, Houghton Library, MS Eng. 530, fols. 1ra–4.

16. *DIMEV* 4312. See R. M. Ball, "Lichefeld, William," *Oxford Dictionary of National Biography* (online ed.). Oxford University Press, https://doi.org/10.1093/ref:odnb/16638. There is almost no scholarship on Litchfield and his work, with the exception of Amy Appleford and Nicholas Watson, "Merchant Religion in Fifteenth-Century London: The Writings of William Litchfield," *Chaucer Review* 46, nos. 1–2 (2011): 203–22.

17. Three manuscripts preserve eleven stanzas: London, British Library, Harley MS 2253; London, British Library, Royal MS 12.E.i (with music); and Dublin, Trinity College, MS 201. Three others contain excerpts: Oxford, Bodleian Library, MS Digby 86 (stanzas 1–7); Cambridge, St. John's College, MS E.8 (111) (stanzas 1–5, partial, presented bilingually, with music); and London, British Library, Royal MS 8.F.II (stanza 1 only).

18. *DIMEV* 2464. "Valley" occurs in Cambridge, University Library, MS Hh.4.12; and London, Lambeth Palace Library, MS 853. Carleton Brown included the poem in his 1924 collection *Religious Lyrics of the XIVth Century*; Felicity Riddy dated it to the last half of the fourteenth century; most recently, Susanna Fein assigns the poem to the late fourteenth century based on the poem's similarity to "In a Tabernacle of a Tower," a fourteenth-century

poem that shares the Latin refrain of "Valley," but not its speaker. Both Brown and Riddy understood "Valley" and "Tabernacle" as versions of the same poem; the two poems have since been identified as separate lyrics with a shared refrain, and the *DIMEV* now separates the two poems and their manuscripts into discrete records, allowing for a more precise dating. Brown, *Religious Lyrics of the XIVth Century* (Oxford: Clarendon Press, 1924), no. 132, at pp. 234–37; Riddy, "The Provenance of *Quia amore langueo*," *Review of English Studies* 18, no. 72 (1967): 429–33; Fein, *Moral Love Songs*, 61.

19. *DIMEV* 4312; Oxford, Corpus Christi College, MS 237, fols. 137v–46; Cambridge, Cambridge University Library, MS Ff.2.38, fols. 3ra–6ra; Cambridge, Gonville and Caius College MS 174/95, pp. 469–80; Cambridge, Magdalene College, MS Pepys 1584, fols. 1v–13v; Cambridge, Trinity College, MS R.3.21 (601), fols. 182–89; London, British Library, Harley MS 2339, fols. 82–100v; London, British Library, Additional MS 36983, fols. 275rb–79va; Edinburgh, National Library of Scotland, Advocates' 19.3.1, fols. 158–70v; London, Lambeth Palace Library, MS 306, fols. 147–52; London, Lambeth Palace Library, MS 853, pp. 193–225; Cambridge, MA, Harvard University, Houghton Library, MS Eng. 530, fol. 1; San Marino, CA, Huntington Library, MS HM 144, fols. 1–9v; William Lichfield [Litchfield], *The remors of conscyence* [London: Wynkyn de Worde, ca. 1510], STC 20881.3, fols. 2–6v; and [Enprynted at London]: [In Fletestrete at ye sygne of ye Sonne by me Wynkyn de Worde], [1534?], STC 20882.

20. Ingrid Nelson and Margot Fassler both discuss "Stond wel," in "Lyric Value," this volume (Chapter 5), 137–38, 145, 149–52, and "The Religious Lyric in Medieval England (1150–1400): Three Disciplines and a Question," this volume (Chapter 10), 282–83, respectively.

21. Readings of the poem as primarily affective often point to Mary as the most important figure in the lyric, which has led to a neglect of Christ's speech and its lyric effects. Rosemary Woolf, for example, identified the poem as a "lyric on the compassion of the virgin" and compared it favorably to its Latin precursor, the *Stabat iuxta Christi crucem*, with praise it for its "warmth not characteristic of Latin hymns" (*English Religious Lyric*, 245). Siegfried Wenzel describes the poem as "an appeal to the audience's emotions" (*Preachers, Poets, and the Early English Lyric* [Princeton, NJ: Princeton University Press, 1986], 48).

22. All quotations from "Stond wel" are taken from Fein, *Complete Harley 2253*, http://d .lib.rochester.edu/camelot/text/fein-harley2253-volume-2-article-60.

23. As Cervone has suggested, the medieval lyric creates collective subjectivity through a "thought process [that] opens outward socially just where we might most expect it to narrow in self-interest" ("'I' and 'We'," 202).

24. All quotations are from "In a valley of this restless mind," in Fein, *Moral Love Songs*.

25. Fein argues that Christ's shifting subjectivity "implicitly identif[ies] him with both the masculine, love-seeking wooer *and* the feminized love object, Mannis Soule . . . the poet's seemingly bizarre blurring of gender lines can be seen to belong to a larger, anthropomorphized expression of God's relationship to humankind" (*Moral Love Songs*, 59–60).

26. On subjectivity and community, see Cristina Maria Cervone, "Wondering Through Middle English Lyric," this volume (Chapter 2), 71–73, 76.

27. As Eleanor Johnson has explained, "In order to experience refrains as refrains, one must hold the memory of the previous refrains in the poem in one's mind. In order to experience refrains that are quotations embedded into a narrative as such, one must hold—at once—the memory of the previous instantiations of the repetition in the poem *and* the memory of the quotation's sources" ("*Reddere* and Refrain: A Meditation on Poetic Procedure in *Piers Plowman*," *Yearbook of Langland Studies* 30 [2016]: 3–27, at p. 13).

28. Astell, *Song of Songs*, 149.

29. Ardis Butterfield, "Repetition and Variation in the Thirteenth-Century Refrain," *Journal of the Royal Musical Association* 116, no. 1 (1991): 1–23.

30. See note 18.

31. I use the version of the "Complaint of Christ" preserved in London, Lambeth Palace Library, MS 853, as edited by Frederick J. Furnivall, *Political, Religious, and Love Poems*, EETS, o.s., 15 (London: Kegan Paul, Trench, Trübner, 1866, re-edited 1903), 190–99, ending with line 132 (line 133 begins Litchfield's "Complaint of God").

32. Jonathan Culler posits the shift of tenses inherent in a poem's report of a particular persona's speech as one of the fundamental qualities of the lyric: "the sliding between reported speech and direct discourse creates the remarkable effect of an appearance by [the speaker] *in the present*. . . . The speech event narrated happens not only then but also now—in every instance of 'this time' as the poem is performed" (*Theory of the Lyric*, 14, emphasis in original).

33. Wenzel argues that "Stond wel" occupies an important place in the history of Middle English lyric precisely because "in it an English poet has utilized the dialogue form in lyric poetry in order to create two different personae whose different characters he explores as well as the intellectual and emotional tension between them. The use of the dialogue form for such a purpose is not unique in medieval lyric poetry, but it seems to have held a special place in the vernacular religious lyric of medieval England." While Wenzel is of course more interested in how the lyric interacted with sermons, his observations throw the formal significance of the poem into relief (Wenzel, *Preachers*, 50).

34. Quoted from London, Lambeth Palace Library, MS 853, as edited by Furnivall, *Political, Religious, and Love Poems*, 198–232, beginning at line 133 (line 132 being the end of "Complaint of Christ").

35. Wenzel notes that "within the dialogue proper it is not at all clear whether or not Mary comes to understand and accept the need for her son's death" (*Preachers*, 50); I suggest that this lack of clarity augments the poem's devotional function.

36. As Fein notes, these final stanzas "expound for Mary the joyous outcome of the Passion, and the poem ends with the narrator petitioning for mercy" (Fein, *Complete Harley 2253*).

37. Wenzel terms this poetic quality "expandable": "the number and sequence of stanzas do not really matter. This is what I would call the 'expandable lyric,' whose structural features are confined to the repetition of a chosen stanza form" (*Preachers*, 53).

38. The *DIMEV* notes that Oxford, Bodleian Library, MS Digby 86 contains only the first nine stanzas; Cambridge, St. John's College, MS E.8 (111) contains four and a half; and London, British Library, Royal MS 8.F.2 contains one stanza.

39. Mary-Ann Stouck describes the poem's movement from narrative frame to quoted speech as a "merging": "during the first ten stanzas, the narrative 'I' merges rather with the 'I' of the second speaker, Christ, and it is part of the emphatic recreation of Christ's feelings: Christ is the intimate object of the narrator's contemplation, as the Soul is the object of Christ's" (Stouck, "'In a valey of þis restles mynde': Contexts and Meaning," *Modern Philology* 85, no. 1 [1987]: 1–11, at p. 9).

40. As Susanna Fein puts it, "Christ the Bridegroom here makes love to the reader, approaching first through the distanced figure of Mannis Soule, then through the drawn-in narrator, and finally through direct address to 'thow,' the reader" (*Moral Love Songs*, 58).

41. Sarah Stanbury, "The Virgin's Gaze: Spectacle and Transgression in Middle English Lyrics of the Passion," *PMLA* 106, no. 5 (1991): 1083–93.

42. This type of subjective multiplicity functions in a similar way to the type of mutually referential presence of Christ and Mary that Cristina Maria Cervone has shown to be at work within the Truelove tradition in Middle English poetry—what she describes as "an imperceptible gliding over from one site of reference to another" that results from the poem's reticence to distinguish between its holy speakers (*Poetics of the Incarnation*, 187).

43. As Rebecca Krug has shown, during the fifteenth century, "dialogues in which the reader might 'speak' with Jesus were attractive because they offered audiences the opportunity to enter into direct conversation with the divine" ("Jesus' Voice: Dialogue and Late Medieval Readers," in *Form and Reform: Reading Across the Fifteenth Century*, ed. Shannon Gayk and Kathleen Tonry [Columbus: Ohio State University Press, 2011], 110–29, at p. 111).

44. This process—of inhabiting one or both positions of dialogic subjectivity through the process of reading—functions devotionally, allowing readers to experience a verbal subjectivity through rhetorical inhabitation and identification. Jessica Brantley has shown how private devotional reading elicits devotional habitus; see Brantley, *Reading in the Wilderness: Private Devotion and Public Performance in Late Medieval England* (Chicago: University of Chicago Press, 2007).

45. As Christopher Cannon observes in his discussion of *King Horn*, in Middle English poetry repetition fosters a sense of recursivity that even in longer poetry functions lyrically (Cannon, "Lyric Romance," this volume [Chapter 3]).

46. For extended discussion of the process of applying reading to individual circumstance, see Jennifer Bryan, *Looking Inward: Devotional Reading and the Private Self in Late Medieval England* (Philadelphia: University of Pennsylvania Press, 2007).

47. As Jonathan Culler puts it, from ancient lyric poetry on, the "deictic apparatus of the here-and-now of enunciation . . . creates for us effects of presence that will henceforth be one of the fundamental possibilities of lyric" (*Theory of the Lyric*, 16).

48. Nelson, *Lyric Tactics*, 6.

CHAPTER 10

Epigraph: Susanna Fein, "BL MS Harley 2253: The Lyrics, the Facsimile, the Book," in *Studies in the Harley Manuscript: The Scribes, Contents and Social Contexts of the BL MS Harley 2253*, ed. Susanna Fein (Kalamazoo, MI: Medieval Institute for TEAMS, 2000), 1–19, at p. 7.

1. Seth Lerer, "'Dum ludis floribus:' Language and Text in the Medieval English Lyric," *Philological Quarterly* 87, nos. 3 and 4 (2008): 237–55.

2. Thomas C. Moser, "'And I Mon Waxe Wod': The Middle English 'Foweles in the Frith,'" *PMLA* 102, no. 3 (1987): 326–37, at p. 326.

3. See Helen Deeming, "The Song and the Page: Experiments with Form and Layout in Manuscripts of Medieval Latin Song," *Plainsong and Medieval Music* 15, no. 1 (2006): 1–27.

4. Ardis Butterfield and Helen Deeming, "Editing Insular Song Across the Disciplines: Worldes Blis," in *Probable Truth: Editing Medieval Texts from Britain in the Twenty-First Century*, ed. Vincent Gillespie (Turnhout: Brepols, 2013), 151–66; Ingrid Nelson, *Lyric Tactics: Poetry, Genre, and Practice in Later Medieval England* (Philadelphia: University of Pennsylvania Press, 2017).

5. The importance of bringing these disciplines together is underscored by looking at the scholarship and how poorly referenced the work of one discipline is in the work of another. As an example, the *Digital Index of Middle English Verse* (*DIMEV*), an online go-to

site, has an extensive bibliography: https://www.dimev.net. But as of December 2021, neither Helen Deeming nor Ardis Butterfield are present in it; John Stevens, *Words and Music in the Middle Ages: Song, Narrative, Dance and Drama, 1050–1350* (Cambridge: Cambridge University Press, 1986), is not found there either (although his edition of carols is there). *A New Index of Middle English Verse* (*NIMEV*), ed. Julia Boffey and A. S. G. Edwards (London: British Library, 2005), is not currently online, except through libraries that own a digital copy, but the results of a search are the same. English songs are cataloged separately in Christopher Page, "A Catalogue and Bibliography of English Song from Its Beginnings to c1300," *RMA Research Chronicle* 13 (1976): 67–83, now updatable through Helen Deeming, ed., *Songs in British Sources, c. 1150–1300*, Musica Britannica, vol. 95 (London: Stainer & Bell, 2013); and the accompanying website, http://www.diamm.ac.uk/resources/sbs. Subsequent citations of Deeming refer to item number in this edition, unless otherwise specified.

6. John Scahill, "Trilingualism in Early Middle English Miscellanies: Languages and Literature," *Yearbook of English Studies* 33 (2003): 18–32; Laura Wright, "The Languages of Medieval Britain," in *A Companion to Medieval English Literature and Culture*, ed. Peter Brown (Oxford: Blackwell, 2007), 143–58; several essays in *The French of Medieval England: Essays in Honour of Jocelyn Wogan-Browne*, ed. Thelma Fenster and Carolyn P. Collette (Cambridge: D. S. Brewer, 2014); and Helen Deeming, "Multilingual Networks in Twelfth- and Thirteenth- Century Song," in *Language in Medieval Britain: Networks and Exchanges*, ed. Mary Carruthers (Donnington, Lincolnshire: Shaun Tyas, 2015), 127–43.

7. Ardis Butterfield, "The Construction of Textual Form: Cross-Lingual Citation in the Medieval Insular Lyric," in *Citation, Intertextuality and Memory in the Middle Ages and Renaissance*, vol. 1, *Text, Music and Image from Machaut to Ariosto*, ed. Yolanda Plumley, Guiliano di Bacco, and Stefano Jossa (Exeter: University of Exeter Press, 2011), 41–57, at p. 55.

8. Nelson, *Lyric Tactics*, 59–60.

9. On the sources, see Helmut Gneuss, "Liturgical Books in Anglo-Saxon England and Their Old English Terminology," in *Books and Libraries in Early England* (Aldershot: Variorum, 1996), 91–141; reprinted with original pagination from *Learning and Literature in Anglo-Saxon England: Studies Presented to Peter Clemoes on the Occasion of His Sixty-Fifth Birthday*, ed. Michael Lapidge and Helmut Gneuss (Cambridge: Cambridge University Press, 1985).

10. On offices for Becket, see Kay Brainerd Slocum, "Office for the Feast Day of St Thomas Becket, 29 December," in *Liturgies in Honour of Thomas Becket* (Toronto: University of Toronto Press, 2004), 129–238; and Sherry L. Reames, "Reconstructing and Interpreting a Thirteenth-Century Office for the Translation of Thomas Becket," *Speculum* 80, no. 1 (2005): 118–70. A variety of English offices and their developments over time are discussed in Andrew Hughes, "British Rhymed Offices: A Catalogue and Commentary," in *Music in the Medieval English Liturgy: Plainsong & Mediaeval Music Society Centennial Essays*, ed. Susan Rankin and David Hiley (Oxford: Clarendon Press, 1993), 239–84; David Hiley, "The Music of Prose Offices in Honour of English Saints," *Plainsong and Medieval Music* 10 (2001): 23–37; and his "The Saints Venerated in Medieval Peterborough as Reflected in the Antiphoner Cambridge, Magdalene College, F.4.10," in *Essays on the History of English Music in Honour of John Caldwell: Sources, Style, Performance, Historiography*, ed. Emma Hornby and David Maw (Woodbridge, Suffolk: Boydell Press, 2010), 22–46; Margot Fassler, "Shaping the Historical Dunstan: Many Lives and a Musical Office," in *Medieval Cantors and Their Craft: Music, Liturgy and the Shaping of History, 800–1500*, ed. Katie Bugyis, A. B. Kraebel, and Margot Fassler (York: York Medieval Press, 2017), 125–50; Catherine Sanok, "Exemplarity

and England in Native Saints' Lives," in *Her Life Historical: Exemplarity and Female Saints' Lives in Late Medieval England* (Philadelphia: University of Pennsylvania Press, 2007), 83–115; and Henry Parkes, "St. Edmund Between Liturgy and Hagiography," in *Bury St Edmunds and the Norman Conquest*, ed. Tom Licence (Woodbridge, Suffolk: Boydell Press, 2014), 131–59.

11. On the hymn, see especially the work of Helmut Gneuss, including his monumental *Hymnar und Hymnen im englischen Mittelalter* (Tübingen: M. Niemeyer, 1968); and David Hiley, "Zur englischen Hymnenüberlieferung," in *Der lateinische Hymnus im Mittelalter: Überlieferung–Ästhetik–Ausstrahlung*, ed. Andreas Haug, Christoph März, and Lorenz Welker, Monumenta Monodica Medii Aevi, Subsidia 4 (Kassel: Bärenreiter, 2004), 199–214.

12. Alejandro Enrique Planchart, "On the Nature of Transmission and Change in Trope Repertories," *Journal of the American Musicological Society* 41, no. 2 (1988): 215–49; and Planchart, *The Repertory of Tropes at Winchester* (Princeton, NJ: Princeton University Press, 1977). Recent work on the liturgical practices of Anglo-Saxon England provides useful context for the study of hymns and sequences: see Helen Gittos and M. Bradford Bedingfield, eds., *The Liturgy of the Late Anglo-Saxon Church* (Woodbridge, Suffolk: Boydell Press for the Henry Bradshaw Society, 2005); and Helen Gittos, *Liturgy, Architecture, and Sacred Places in Anglo-Saxon England* (Oxford: Oxford University Press, 2013); for a collection that emphasizes rituals that stand outside and yet are related to the Mass and Office, see Helen Gittos and Sarah Hamilton, *Understanding Medieval Liturgy: Essays in Interpretation* (Burlington, VT: Ashgate, 2016). Many of these essays describe Anglo-Saxon practices.

13. Latin text as found in Deeming, *Songs in British Sources*, no. 66a, p. 88, from Cambridge, St. John's College, MS E.8, fol. 106v; English translation modified from Deeming, 90.

14. The grammarian John of Garland, writing in the thirteenth century, praises the salutary nature of rhymed poetry, calling it a branch of the art of music. He says, "A rhymed poem is a harmonious arrangement of words with like endings, regulated not by quantity, but by number of syllables. . . . 'Regulated' indicates that the words in a rhymed poem should fall in a regular cadence." See Traugott Lawler, ed. and trans., *The "Parisiana Poetria" of John of Garland* (New Haven, CT: Yale University Press, 1974), 161. This passage is discussed at length in Nelson, *Lyric Tactics*, 68–69.

15. Calvin M. Bower, ed. and trans., *The "Liber Ymnorum" of Notker Balbulus*, Henry Bradshaw Society 121 and 122 (London: Henry Bradshaw Society, 2016). For study of the West Frankish tradition, see Richard L. Crocker, *The Early Medieval Sequence* (Berkeley: University of California Press, 1977).

16. See especially Margot Fassler, *Gothic Song: Victorine Sequences and Augustinian Reform in Twelfth-Century Paris* (Notre Dame, IN: University of Notre Dame Press, 2011); and Heinrich Husmann, "Notre-Dame und Saint-Victor: Repertoire-Studien zur Geschichte der gereimten Prosen," *Acta Musicologica* 36 (1964): 98–123.

17. Susan Boynton and Margot Fassler, "The Language, Form, and Performance of Monophonic Liturgical Chants," in *The Oxford Handbook of Medieval Latin Literature*, ed. Ralph J. Hexter and David Townsend (New York: Oxford University Press, 2012), 686–730.

18. David Hiley, "The Rhymed Sequence in England—a Preliminary Survey," in *Musicologie médiévale: Notations et séquences; Actes de la table ronde du C.N.R.S. à l'Institut de Recherche et d'Histoire des Textes, 6–7 septembre 1982*, ed. Michel Huglo (Paris: H. Champion, 1987), 227–46; Hiley, "The Repertory of Sequences at Winchester," in *Essays on Medieval Music in Honor of David G. Hughes*, ed. Graeme M. Boone (Cambridge, MA: Harvard University Department of Music, distr. Harvard University Press, 1995), 153–93; Hiley, "The

English Background to the Nidaros Sequences," in *The Sequences of Nidaros: A Nordic Repertory and Its European Context*, ed. Lori Kruckenberg and Andreas Haug (Trondheim: Tapir Academic Press, 2006), 63–117.

19. Hiley, "The English Background," 70–71.

20. Hiley, "Repertory of Sequences at Winchester," 157.

21. Ibid.; Hiley breaks down the fifty-nine melodies as follows: nineteen widespread on the Continent; twenty-five well known only in West Francia; two from East Francia; four only in English and Northern French sources; three found only at Winchester; and six problematic melodies he does not categorize. See Hiley, "Repertory of Sequences at Winchester," 157.

22. Hiley is preparing a critical edition of the Winchester sequences.

23. Hiley, "Repertory of Sequences at Winchester," 161.

24. For a case study of the difficulties of one predominantly Anglo-Saxon community in the acceptance of the liturgical reforms of the Normans in the years after the conquest, see David Hiley, "Thurstan of Caen and Plainchant at Glastonbury: Musicological Reflections on the Norman Conquest," *Proceedings of the British Academy* 72 (1986): 57–59. An overview of the liturgical situation in the century after the Conquest is Richard Pfaff, *The Liturgy in Medieval England: A History* (Cambridge: Cambridge University Press, 2009), 101–99. Susan K. Rankin will give the Lyell Lectures at Oxford University in 2022 on the subject of English liturgical books up to 1150, with an emphasis on manuscripts with music notation.

25. For a related overview of the situation in Ireland, see Frank Lawrence, "What Did They Sing at Cashel in 1172? Winchester, Sarum and Romano-Frankish Chant in Ireland," *Journal of the Society for Musicology in Ireland* 3 (2008): 111–25.

26. Pfaff, *Liturgy in Medieval England*, 378.

27. Hiley, "Rhymed Sequence in England," 235.

28. Ibid., 235–36.

29. See especially the tables in Hiley, "The English Background."

30. René-Jean Hesbert, ed., *Le Tropaire-Prosaire de Dublin: Manuscrit add. 710 de l'Université de Cambridge (vers 1360)* (Rouen: Imprimerie Rouennaise, 1966). For further discussion of this source, see Hiley, "Rhymed Sequence in England," 232.

31. See, for example, Deeming, *Songs in British Sources*, no. 13, "Missus Gabriel de celis." This sequence has five strophes, each consisting of a double versicle, with the scheme 8p + 8p+ 8p+ 7pp.

32. J. B. L. Tolhurst, ed., *The Ordinale and Customary of the Benedictine Nuns of Barking Abbey (University College, Oxford, Ms. 169)*, 2 vols., Henry Bradshaw Society vols. 65–66 (London: Henry Bradshaw Society, 1927–28). For more detailed study of the Barking repertory, see Anne Bagnall Yardley, "Liturgy as the Site of Creative Engagement: Contributions of the Nuns of Barking," in *Barking Abbey and Medieval Literary Culture: Authorship and Authority in a Female Community*, ed. Jennifer N. Brown and Donna Alfano Bussell (York: York Medieval Press, 2012), 267–82; and Margot Fassler, "Women and Their Sequences: An Overview and a Case Study," *Speculum* 94, no. 3 (2019): 625–73, which includes a table of the Barking repertory and comparison to other English sources.

33. See Hiley, "Rhymed Sequence in England," 235.

34. The most complete listing of English manuscripts in David Hiley's scholarship is found in his early study, "The Norman Chant Traditions: Normandy, Britain, Sicily," *Proceedings of the Royal Musical Association* 107 (1980–81): 1–33. There are new sources that could profitably be added to this list, including New Haven, CT, Yale University, Beinecke Library, Ege 1026.1988, the subject of a forthcoming study by Alison Altstatt.

35. Now dated to the 1020s and 1030s and shown to be the earlier of the two collections from Winchester: see Susan Rankin, ed., *The Winchester Troper* (London: Stainer & Bell, 2007), for discussion of the nature of both of these eleventh-century books from Winchester.

36. The sequences break off; there seems to be a missing quire. The manuscript is digitized with notes and bibliography: http://www.bl.uk/manuscripts/FullDisplay.aspx?ref=Harley _MS_2961. See especially Susan Rankin, "From Memory to Record: Musical Notations in Manuscripts from Exeter," *Anglo-Saxon England* 13 (1984): 97–112; and Pfaff, *Liturgy in Medieval England*, 132–36. Exeter, Exeter Cathedral Library and Archives MS 3515 is a twelfth-century source that has incipits for sequences; see Anne Mannion, "*Missale Vetus*: Liturgy, Palaeography and Repertories in the Notated Missal EXc.3515," Ph.D. diss., University of Limerick, 2012.

37. K. D. Hartzell, "An Unknown English Benedictine Gradual of the Eleventh Century," *Anglo-Saxon England* 4 (1975): 131–44, with a facsimile of folio 40 at plate IIIa. This eleventh-century gradual has been assigned by Susan K. Rankin and Michael Gullick to Canterbury and dated to the late 1080s or 1090s but before 1096 (the death of William of St. Calais); the sequences were added in Durham in the course of the early twelfth century. See Susan Rankin and Michael Gullick, Review of *Catalogue of Manuscripts Written or Owned in England up to 1200 Containing Music* by K. D. Hartzell, *Early Music History* 28 (2009): 262–85.

38. K. D. Hartzell, *Catalogue of Manuscripts Written or Owned in England up to 1200 Containing Music* (Woodbridge, Suffolk: Boydell Press, 2006), no. 171, 308–16.

39. Elizabeth Cover Teviotdale, "The Cotton Troper (London, British Library, Cotton MS Caligula A.xiv, ff. 1–36): A Study of an Illustrated English Troper of the Eleventh Century," Ph.D. diss., University of North Carolina at Chapel Hill, 1991. The origin of this complex book was once contested, but it has recently been firmly established as Worcester (see the notes to the digitized manuscript: http://www.bl.uk/manuscripts/FullDisplay.aspx?ref =Cotton_MS_Caligula_A_XIV and Susan Rankin's forthcoming study of the manuscript in her Lyell lectures). The folios studied for this table are 37 to 92, which contain sequences and date from the mid-twelfth century.

40. Digitized description at http://www.bl.uk/catalogues/illuminatedmanuscripts/record .asp?MSID=7322.

41. Studied and cataloged in Bradford Lee Eden, "The Thirteenth-Century Sequence Repertory of the Sarum Use," Ph.D. diss., University of Kansas, 1991. Richard Pfaff dates this manuscript to the third quarter of the thirteenth century (*The Liturgy in Medieval England*, 395).

42. Studied and cataloged in Eden, "Thirteenth-Century Sequence Repertory."

43. E. J. Dobson and F. Ll. Harrison, eds., *Medieval English Songs* (New York: Cambridge University Press, 1979).

44. Deeming, *Songs in British Sources*; and the accompanying website, http://www .diamm.ac.uk/resources/sbs.

45. Susan Rankin, "Taking the Rough with the Smooth: Melodic Versions and Manuscript Status," in *The Divine Office in the Latin Middle Ages: Methodology and Source Studies, Regional Developments, Hagiography*, ed. Margot E. Fassler and Rebecca A. Baltzer (Oxford: Oxford University Press, 2000), 213–33; John Stevens, ed. *The Later Cambridge Songs: An English Song Collection of the Twelfth Century* (Oxford: Oxford University Press, 2005).

46. Deeming, *Songs in British Sources*, xxxi.

47. It is possible to follow the edition and arguments along with the website, DIAMM (https://www.diamm.ac.uk), which is free and to which access is implied in this discussion of

Deeming's analyses. For suggestions about another possible way to organize the material, see the review by Peter Lefferts in *Plainsong and Medieval Music* 23, no. 2 (2014): 245–51.

48. For an introduction to various aspects of the late medieval sequence, see Fassler, *Gothic Song*; and the three chapters on sequences in Jeffrey Hamburger et al., *Liturgical Life and Latin Learning at Paradies bei Soest, 1300–1425: Inscription and Illumination in the Choir Books of a North German Dominican Convent* (Munster: Aschendorff Verlag, 2016) 1:211–84.

49. Stevens, *Words and Music*, 140–55.

50. Helen Deeming, "The Songs of St. Godric: A Neglected Context," *Music and Letters* 86, no. 2 (2005): 169–85. See also Ardis Butterfield, "Why Medieval Lyric?," *English Literary History* 82, no. 2 (2015): 319–43; and Butterfield, "Lyric Editing," this volume (Chapter 1), 45–58.

51. On "little books" and their taxonomies, see Peter Jeffery, "Libelli: Quires, Pieces, and Fascicles, or: What Do You Call a Little Book?," in *Décrire le manuscrit liturgique: Méthodes, problématiques, perspectives*, ed. Laura Albiero and Eleonora Celora (Turnhout: Brepols, 2021), 41–55.

52. Helen Deeming, "Music and Contemplation in the Twelfth-Century *Dulcis Jesu memoria*," *Journal of the Royal Musical Association* 139, no. 1 (2014): 1–39.

53. Dobson and Harrison, *Medieval English Songs*, 298. See also Helen Deeming, "Observations on the Habits of Twelfth- and Thirteenth-Century Music Scribes," *Scriptorium* 60 (2006): 38–59; for the scribe of "Man mai longe," see p. 46.

54. Several recorded performances of the work (both vocal and instrumental) highlight the lugubrious nature of the text.

55. Dobson and Harrison, *Medieval English Songs*, 123.

56. Yet another example of work with setting lyrics to melodies that seem to fit them is the complex of seemingly interrelated lyrics "Bryd on brer," "Maiden in the mor lay," and its Latin contrafact "Peperit virgo, virgo regia," this found in Ledrede's *Red Book of Ossory*; see Dobson and Harrison, *Medieval English Songs*, 183–93. Some difficulties with the lynchpin to the grouping, "Maiden in the mor lay," are explored in Ardis Butterfield, "Poems without Form? *Maiden in the mor lay* Revisited," in *Readings in Medieval Textuality: Essays in Honour of A. C. Spearing*, ed. Cristina Maria Cervone and D. Vance Smith (Cambridge: D. S. Brewer, 2016), 169–94. Butterfield has new comments to make regarding "Bryd on brer" in "Why Medieval Lyric?"

57. On a section of an earlier Latin lament, with notated French and English versions (Deeming 92a and b), see Monika Otter, "Contrafacture and Translation: The Prisoner's Lament," in Fenster and Collette, *The French of Medieval England*, 55–81.

58. *Analecta hymnica Medii Aevi*, ed. Guido Maria Dreves, Clemens Blume, and Henry M. Bannister, 55 vols. (Leipzig, 1866–1922), vol. 8, no. 58, p. 55.

59. See Deeming's edition of the piece in *Songs in British Sources*, no. 90, pp. 133–34.

60. Hiley, "The English Background," 63–117.

61. For bibliography and a full digital copy of the manuscript, see http://luna.manchester .ac.uk/luna/servlet/detail/Man4MedievalVC-4-4-990033-142732.

62. Siegfried Wenzel discusses this complex of material in *Preachers, Poets, and the Early English Lyric* (Princeton, NJ: Princeton University Press, 1986), 42–54; he says, "The significant feature of 'Stond wel, moder' is that in it an English poet has utilized the dialogue form in lyric poetry in order to create two different personae whose different characters he explores as well as the intellectual and emotional tension between them. The use of the dialogue form for such a purpose is not unique in medieval lyric poetry, but it seems to have

held a special place in the vernacular religious lyric of medieval England" (50). The relationship of the dialogue to both preaching and to the drama is not to be ignored either. On the lyric's dialogue form, see Ingrid Nelson, "Lyric Value," this volume (Chapter 5), and Barbara Zimbalist, "The Lyric Christ," this volume (Chapter 9).

63. See Wenzel, *Preachers, Poets*; for an overview of the Franciscans and their preaching, see Timothy J. Johnson, ed., *Franciscans and Preaching: Every Miracle from the Beginning of the World Came About Through Words* (Leiden: Brill, 2012).

64. For discussion of the lai and the *planctus*, see Stevens, *Words and Music*, 110–55, with a detailed analysis of "Omnis caro peccaverat" (Deeming 65).

65. Peter M. Lefferts, "Cantilena and Antiphon: Music for Marian Services in Late Medieval England," *Current Musicology* 45–47 (1990): 247–82, at p. 249.

66. John Caldwell, "Relations Between Liturgical and Vernacular Music in Medieval England," in *Music in Medieval English Liturgy*, ed. Susan Rankin and David Hiley (Oxford: Clarendon Press, 1993), 285–93.

67. At this point, yet another section should be presented concerning texts for motets and cantilenas, as well as other genres; such a study would doubtless be worthwhile and revealing. Foundational studies for such work are Peter M. Lefferts, *The Motet in England in the Fourteenth Century* (Ann Arbor, MI: UMI Research Press, 1986); and Andrew Hughes and Margaret Bent, eds., *The Old Hall Manuscript*, 2 vols. in 3 ([Rome]: American Institute of Musicology, 1969–73).

68. Ernest H. Sanders, ed., *English Music of the Thirteenth and Fourteenth Centuries*, Polyphonic Music of the Fourteenth Century 14 (Monaco: Éditions de l'Oiseau-Lyre, 1979); Frank Ll. Harrison, ed., *Motets of English Provenance*, Polyphonic Music of the Fourteenth Century 15 (Monaco: Éditions de l'Oiseau-Lyre, 1980); and Frank Ll. Harrison, Ernest H. Sanders, and Peter M. Lefferts, eds., *English Music for Mass and Offices*, 2 vols., Polyphonic Music of the Fourteenth Century 16 and 17 (Monaco: Éditions de l'Oiseau-Lyre, 1983–86).

69. For an overview of the *cantilena*, the votive antiphon, and the motet, both in England and on the Continent, see David Rothenberg, *The Flower of Paradise: Marian Devotion and Secular Song in Medieval and Renaissance Music* (Oxford: Oxford University Press, 2011), 97–105.

70. Julia Boffey, "Middle English Lyrics and Manuscripts," in *A Companion to the Middle English Lyric*, ed. Thomas G. Duncan (Cambridge: D. S. Brewer, 2005), 1–18.

71. Another useful list of sources, this in alphabetical order, is that provided in Emma Gorst, "Middle English Lyrics: Lyric Manuscripts 1200–1400 and Chaucer's Lyric" (Ph.D. diss., University of Toronto, 2013), 244–71.

72. See Grace Newcombe, "Britain's Cleric Composers: Poetic Stress and Ornamentation in *Worldes blis*," in *Ars Antiqua: Music and Culture in Europe c. 1150–1330*, ed. Gregorio Bevilacqua and Thomas Payne (Turnhout: Brepols, 2020), 143–62.

73. A classic exception is Stevens, *Words and Music*.

74. Especially useful to this study is Butterfield's clear articulation of the idea that the medieval English lyric must be "read" both deeply and broadly, drawing parallels with studies of the lyrics of Emily Dickinson and work by Jonathan Culler. See her "Why Medieval Lyric?" and "Lyric Editing."

75. The study of the manuscripts and of their scripts and makeups have been the most fruitful and exciting aspects of research in the last twenty years. Much of the bibliography cited here is of this nature. Kathryn Kerby-Fulton's work is an example: Kathryn Kerby-Fulton, Maidie Hilmo, and Linda Olson, *Opening Up Middle English Manuscripts: Literary*

and Visual Approaches (Ithaca, NY: Cornell University Press, 2012) (a digital supplement is in preparation); and Kerby-Fulton, John J. Thompson, and Sarah Baechle, eds., *New Directions in Medieval Manuscript Studies and Reading Practices: Essays in Honour of Derek Pearsall* (Notre Dame, IN: University of Notre Dame Press, 2014). That these works are collaborative helps to make the point that many literary scholars are engaged with this kind of study at present.

76. Susanna Fein, ed., *The Auchinleck Manuscript: New Perspectives* (York: York Medieval Press, 2016).

77. A. G. Rigg, "Review: The Red Book of Ossory," *Medium Aevum* 46, no. 2 (1977): 269–78. For an overview of the period and authors, including a discussion of Ledrede, see A. B. Scott, "Latin Learning and Literature in Ireland, 1169–1500," in *A New History of Ireland*, vol. 1, *Prehistoric and Early Ireland*, ed. Dáibhí Ó Cróinín (Oxford: Clarendon Press, 2005), 934–95.

78. At the bottom of the first page of the collection (fol. 70r), the bishop stated his purpose: "Nota: attende lector quod episcopus Ossoriensis fecit istas cantilenas pro vicariis ecclesie cathedralis sacerdotibus et clericis suis ad cantandum in magnis festis et solaciis, ne guttura eorum et ora Deo sanctificata polluantur cantilenis teatralibus turpibus et secularibus, et cum sint cantatores prouideant sibi de notis conuenientibus secundum quod dictamina requirunt" (as transcribed in *The Latin Poems of Richard Ledrede, O.F.M.: Bishop of Ossory, 1317–1360*, ed. Edmund Colledge [Toronto: Pontifical Institute of Mediaeval Studies, 1974], p. xl). The text is translated by Ardis Butterfield in "Poems without Form?" as follows: "Be advised, reader, that the Bishop of Ossory has made these songs for the vicars of the cathedral church, for the priests, and for his clerks, to be sung on the important holidays and at celebrations (*solaciis*) in order that their throats and mouths, consecrated to God, may not be polluted by songs which are lewd, secular, and associated with revelry (*teatralibus*), and, since they are trained singers (*cantatores*), let them provide themselves with suitable tunes (*notis*) according to what these sets of words (*dictamina*) require" (182).

79. Kathleen Rose Palti, "'Synge we now alle and sum': Three Fifteenth-Century Collections of Communal Song; A Study of British Library, Sloane MS 2593; Bodleian Library, MS Eng. poet. e.1; and St John's College, Cambridge, MS S.54" (Ph.D. diss, University College London, 2008), 1:51; also see Karl Reichl, "The Middle English Carol," in *A Companion to the Middle English Lyric*, ed. Thomas G. Duncan (Cambridge: D. S. Brewer, 2005), 150–70; and the standard theories on the subject, all of which are much discussed by Palti: Richard Leighton Greene, ed., *The Early English Carols*, 2nd ed., rev. and enl. (Oxford: Clarendon Press, 1977); several discussions by Rossell Hope Robbins, who believed the carol evolved from singing in processions ("The Earliest Carols and the Franciscans," *Modern Language Notes* 53, no. 4 [1938]: 239–45; "Friar Herebert and the Carol," *Anglia* 75 [1957]: 194–98; "Middle English Carols as Processional Hymns," *Studies in Philology* 56, no. 4 [1959]: 559–82; and "The Bradshaw Carols," *PMLA* 81, no. 3 [1966]: 308–10) and who makes a case for the development of the carol at the hands of the friars. David L. Jeffrey advocates for a major role for the friars in *The Early English Lyric and Franciscan Spirituality* (Lincoln: University of Nebraska Press, 1975). Another theory about the development of the carol (from the *Benedicamus* trope) has been developed extensively by Frank Ll. Harrison (and carries weight today), *Music in Medieval Britain* (London: Routledge and Paul, 1958), 354–424.

80. Reichl, "The Middle English Carol."

81. From John Stevens, ed., *Mediaeval Carols*, Musica Britannica, vol. 4 (London: Stainer & Bell, for the Royal Music Association, 1952).

82. Butterfield and Deeming, "Editing Insular Song."

83. Nigel J. Morgan, "The Liturgical Manuscripts of the English Franciscans c.1250–1350," in *The English Province of the Franciscans (1224–c.1350)*, ed. Michael J. P. Robson (Leiden: Brill, 2017), 214–44. For more detailed discussion of the English situation over time, see Andrew G. Little, *Studies in English Franciscan History* (Manchester: University of Manchester, 1917), app. 6, "List of Franciscan Custodies and Houses in the Province of England," 235–38.

84. I have examined only those books available digitally.

85. Pfaff, *Liturgy in Medieval England*, 326.

86. S. J. P. van Dijk, "Some Manuscripts of the Earliest Franciscan Liturgy," *Franciscan Studies* 14, no. 3 (1954): 225–64, at p. 227.

87. Pfaff, *Liturgy in Medieval England*, 324–25.

88. Otto Pächt and J. J. G. Alexander, *Illuminated Manuscripts in the Bodleian Library Oxford*, vol. 1 (Oxford: Clarendon Press, 1966), 72. This missal apparently had three sequences for the Virgin Mary added.

89. Victor Leroquais, *Les sacramentaires et les missels manuscrits des bibliothèques publiques de France* (Paris, 1924), 2:218–19.

90. Nigel Morgan, "A French Franciscan Breviary in Lisbon and the Breviaries by Jean Pucelle and His Followers," in *Quand la peinture était dans les livres: Mélanges en l'honneur de François Avril*, ed. M. Hofmann and C. Zöhl (Turnhout: Brepols: Turnhout, 2007), 211–19; Sean L. Field, "Marie of Saint-Pol and Her Books," *English Historical Review* 125, no. 513 (2010): 255–78.

91. There are exceptions, which include Paris, Bibliothèque Nationale, MS Lat. 1339, a fourteenth-century sequentiary, incomplete at the beginning and end.

92. S. J. P. van Dijk, ed., *Sources of the Modern Roman Liturgy: The Ordinals by Haymo of Faversham and Related Documents, 1243–1307*, 2 vols. (Leiden: Brill, 1963).

93. Ibid., 2:414–15.

94. In the later Middle Ages sequences generally were songs written for singing within the choirs of religious communities, and as through-composed works, sometimes of considerable length, might not have been deemed appropriate for abbreviated books meant for individuals to take on the road. The liturgical practices of the Dominicans developed in thirteenth-century Paris, where sequences were highly favored, both at the Cathedral of Notre Dame and by the Victorines and other religious orders. See Fassler, *Gothic Song*. The practices of the Franciscans, on the other hand, developed in Rome, where sequences did not play major roles.

95. Nelson, *Lyric Tactics*, 60.

96. Timothy J. Johnson, "Choir Prayer as the Place of Formation and Identity Definition," *Miscellanea Francescana* 111 (2011): 123–35.

97. Nelson, *Lyric Tactics*, 59–87; Domenico Pezzini, "Versions of Latin Hymns in Medieval England: William Herebert and the English Hymnal," *Mediaevistik* 4 (1991): 297–315; Robbins, "Friar Herebert"; Steven R. Reimer, ed., *The Works of William Herebert, OFM* (Toronto: PIMS, 1987).

98. "There is ample testimony to the existence of a large repertory of popular melodies to which carols could be sung." From John Stevens and Dennis Libby, "Carol," in *Grove Music Online* (2001), https://doi.org/10.1093/gmo/9781561592630.article.04974.

99. The place of music in the life of Francis and of his early followers is explored in Peter Loewen, *Music in Early Franciscan Thought* (Leiden: Brill, 2014), 17–60.

100. Oleg Bychkov, "The Place of Aesthetics and the Arts in Medieval Franciscan Theology," in *Beyond the Text: Franciscan Art and the Construction of Religion*, ed. Xavier Seubert

and Oleg Bychkov (St. Bonaventure, NY: Franciscan Institute Publications, 2012), 196–209, at p. 209.

101. John Stevens, *Mediaeval Carols*, Musica Britannica, vol. 4, 2nd ed., rev. (London: Stainer & Bell, for the Royal Music Association, 1958); review of earlier edition by Manfred F. Bukofzer and Richard L. Greene, *Journal of the American Musicological Society* 7, no. 1 (1954): 63–82. For a more detailed discussion of these major six sources, and of other sources that contain music for carols, see Palti, "'Synge we now alle and sum,'" 196–208.

102. For an excellent overview, see Blake Wilson, "Lauda," *Grove Music Online* (2001) https://doi.org/10.1093/gmo/9781561592630.article.43313.

103. Christian Meyer's online database of sequence melodies shows many sources with the sequence and with many contrafacts, but only one melody: "Catalogue thématique des Séquences" (CthS), at Catalogue des manuscrits notés (CMN) (2017), http://www.musmed.fr/CMN/proseq/proseq_proses.htm.

104. For analysis of text-music relationships in the work, see especially Wulf Arlt, "Sequence and 'Neues Lied,'" in *La sequenza medievale: Atti del Convegno internazionale, Milano, 7–8 aprile 1984*, ed. Agostino Ziino (Lucca: Libreria musicale italiana, 1992), 3–18.

105. The role of the plays in the rise of the drama has been much emphasized in the scholarship: Marius Sepet, *Les prophètes du Christ: Étude sur les origines du théâtre au moyen âge* (Paris, 1878; repr., Geneva: Slatkine, 1974); Robert Lagueux, "Sermons, Exegesis, and Performance: The Laon *Ordo Prophetarum* and the Meaning of Advent," *Comparative Drama* 43 (2009): 197–220; William Hodapp, "Performing Prophecy: The Advents of Christ in Medieval Latin Drama," in *Prophet Margins: The Medieval Vatic Impulse and Social Stability*, ed. E. L. Risden, Karen Moranski, and Stephen Yardell (New York: Peter Lang, 2004), 101–22.

106. Regula Meyer Evitt, "Anti-Judaism and the Medieval Prophet Plays: Exegetical Contexts for the 'Ordines Prophetarum'" (Ph.D. diss., University of Virginia, 1992).

107. Stevens took his transcription from London, British Library, Royal MS 2.B.iv, fol. 177 (the so-called St. Albans troper); *Words and Music,* 91–100.

108. For a sense of the geographical range, see Clyde Brockett, "A Previously Unknown Ordo Prophetarum in a Manuscript Fragment in Zagreb," *Comparative Drama* 27 (1993): 114–27.

109. For the opening music of "Letabundus," see Figure 26, Notre Dame, IN, University of Notre Dame, Hesburgh Library, cod. Lat. c.2, fol. 134v, a Franciscan gradual from the convent of the Annunciata in Ventimiglia, dated to the first half of the sixteenth century. The book is described in David T. Gura, *A Descriptive Catalogue of the Medieval and Renaissance Manuscripts of the University of Notre Dame and Saint Mary's College* (Notre Dame, IN: University of Notre Dame Press, 2016), 239–41.

110. The text of the play is edited in Karl Young, *The Drama of the Medieval Church*, vol. 2 (Oxford: Clarendon Press, 1933), 172–96; see pp. 178–79, lines 200–230.

111. Carla Rossi, "A Clue to the Fate of the Lost MS. Royal 16 E VIII, Copy of the Voyage de Charlemagne," *Romania* 126 (2008): 245–52.

112. Angul Hammerich, ed., *Mediaeval Musical Relics of Denmark*, trans. Margaret Williams Hamerik (Leipzig: Breitkopf & Härtel, 1912), 59.

113. For the "Gaudete," see *Analecta hymnica*, vol. 54, no. 3, pp. 8–9.

114. The contrafact is edited in *Analecta hymnica* 8:41, and the earliest of two sources cited is a fifteenth-century Sarum gradual now found in the Vatican (in the Rossi collection, but without a number in the *Analecta hymnica* citation).

115. Deeming, *Songs in British Sources*, 174.

116. See Fassler, "Women and Their Sequences."

117. The way the contrafact relates to the original chant is discussed in Helen Deeming's essay "Music, Memory and Mobility: Citation and Contrafactum in Thirteenth-Century Sequence Repertories," in *Citation, Intertextuality and Memory in the Middle Ages and Renaissance*, vol. 2, *Cross-Disciplinary Perspectives on Medieval Cultures*, ed. Giuliano Di Bacco and Yolanda Plumley (Liverpool: Liverpool University Press, 2013), 67–81.

118. Deeming, *Songs in British Sources*, 197.

119. Deeming, "Music, Memory and Mobility," includes a chart of the verses demonstrating this form.

120. Reimer, *The Works of William Herebert*, 118–20; *DIMEV* 5865.

121. See especially Pezzini, "Versions of Latin Hymns."

122. Julius Zupitza, "Die Gedichte des Franziskaners Jacob Ryman," *Archiv für das Studium der neueren Sprachen und Literaturen* 89 (1892): 167–338, at pp. 237–38; *DIMEV* 3736, https://www.dimev.net/record.php?recID=3736.

123. Stevens, *Mediaeval Carols*, no. 20, p. 14; no. 105, p. 94; *DIMEV* 3817, https://www.dimev.net/record.php?recID=3817.

124. Ardis Butterfield, "Fuzziness and Perceptions of Language in the Middle Ages," part 3, "Translating Fuzziness: Countertexts," *Common Knowledge* 19, no. 3 (2013): 446–73, at p. 451. The piece is set in two parts and was copied on the Trinity Carol Roll (Cambridge, Trinity College, MS O.3.58) (Stevens, *Mediaeval Carols*, no. 14, pp. 10–11).

CHAPTER 11

1. Northrop Frye, *Anatomy of Criticism: Four Essays* (Princeton, NJ: Princeton University Press, 1957), 271; Jonathan Culler, *Theory of the Lyric* (Cambridge, MA: Harvard University Press, 2015). See also Virginia Jackson and Yopie Prins, eds., *The Lyric Theory Reader: A Critical Anthology* (Baltimore: Johns Hopkins University Press, 2014). The "First Biennial Conference of the International Network for the Study of Lyric" was held June 7–11, 2017, at Boston University; a second was held June 4–7, 2019, at the University of Lausanne. Other studies are noted below.

2. Quoted in Yopie Prins, "What Is Historical Poetics?," *Modern Language Quarterly* 77, no. 1 (2016): 13–40, at p. 14. See especially Virginia Jackson, *Dickinson's Misery: A Theory of Lyric Reading* (Princeton, NJ: Princeton University Press, 2005); and Yopie Prins, "Historical Poetics, Dysprosody, and *The Science of English Verse*," *PMLA* 123, no. 1 (2008): 229–34.

3. Roland Greene, *Post-Petrarchism: Origins and Innovations of the Western Lyric Sequence* (Princeton: Princeton University Press, 1991); Colin Burrow, "Horace at Home and Abroad: Wyatt and Sixteenth-Century Horatianism," in *Horace Made New: Horatian Influences on British Writing from the Renaissance to the Twentieth Century*, ed. Charles Martindale and David Hopkins (Cambridge: Cambridge University Press, 1993), 27–49. For Chaucer's translation of Petrarch, see below.

4. The lyrics in Cambridge, Cambridge University Library MS Ff.1.6, the Findern Manuscript, are among the many that seem created within a close and mutually recognized group, in this case family members, including many women; whether that licenses scholars and editors to identify the lyrics added to this anthology of texts by Chaucer, Gower, and others, as written by those women, or even in some cases whether they definitively speak from female positions, is less answerable: for the case that they were and do, see Sarah McNamer,

"Female Authors, Provincial Setting: The Re-versing of Courtly Love in the Findern Manuscript," *Viator* 22 (1991): 279–310. For "effect of singularity," see Ullrich Langer, *Lyric in the Renaissance: From Petrarch to Montaigne* (Cambridge: Cambridge University Press, 2015), 2; see also Stephen Regan, *The Sonnet* (Oxford: Oxford University Press, 2019). For Culler's views, see below. For medieval pedagogical uses and understandings of Horace, see Suzanne Reynolds, *Medieval Reading: Grammar, Rhetoric and the Classical Text* (Cambridge: Cambridge University Press, 2004); these bear little resemblance to seventeenth-century poetic "Horatianism," but Chaucer's "Lenvoy de Chaucer a Scogan" and "Lenvoy de Chaucer a Bukton" offer important anticipations of what Burrow describes. Further back, Alcuin of York's widely copied Latin lyrics from the eighth century directly emulate Horace's epistolary lyrics and elegiac posture, and Alcuin in fact adopted Horace's cognomen, "Flaccus," although Alcuin goes unmentioned even by scholars treating the "Horatian" lyric traditions.

5. John Burrow, "Poems without Contexts," *Essays in Criticism* 29, no. 1 (1979): 6–32; reprinted in *Essays on Medieval Literature* (Oxford: Oxford University Press, 1984), 1–26.

6. Siegfried Wenzel, *Preachers, Poets, and the Early English Lyric* (Princeton, NJ: Princeton University Press, 1986), see p. 144 for "genuine lyric"; Siegfried Wenzel, "Poets, Preachers, and the Plight of Literary Critics," *Speculum* 60, no. 2 (1985): 343–63. See also Ian Cornelius, "Language and Meter," this volume (Chapter 4), 118–24.

7. Ardis Butterfield, "Why Medieval Lyric?," *English Literary History* 82, no. 2 (2015): 319–43, at p. 334; the comparison with the Continent is on p. 326.

8. John Donne, *The Complete Poems of John Donne*, ed. Robin Robbins, rev. ed. (Harlow: Longman, 2010), 147–55.

9. Patrick S. Diehl, *The Medieval European Religious Lyric: An Ars Poetica* (Berkeley: University of California Press, 1985), 14.

10. For a somewhat parallel emphasis focusing on the uncertainties in the "cognitive and affective" processing of the meter of the lyrics in London, British Library, Harley MS 2253, see Nicholas Mykelbust, "Rhythmic Cognition in Late Medieval Lyrics: BL MS Harley 2253," in *The Palgrave Handbook of Affect Theory and Textual Criticism*, ed. Donald R. Wehrs and Thomas Blake (New York: Palgrave, 2017), 587–608, where Mykelbust notes the uncertainty of what genre or tradition the meter and rhythm these lyrics display: "The approximation of contrasting prosodic modes among the vernacular lyrics promotes exemplars of contradictory types for classifying and identifying the poems" (584).

11. Ingrid Nelson, *Lyric Tactics: Poetry, Genre, and Practice in Later Medieval England* (Philadelphia: University of Pennsylvania Press, 2017).

12. Cristina Maria Cervone, *Poetics of the Incarnation: Middle English Writing and the Leap of Love* (Philadelphia: University of Pennsylvania Press, 2013), 33, a study that has been essential to my thinking about the topic of this chapter. For close study of "lyric" inscribed in bronze jugs and what it accomplishes, see Aden Kumler, "Lyric Vessels," this volume (Chapter 7); a list, surely incomplete, of Middle English examples is at http://www.dimev.net/Inscriptions.php. A notable example of a castle, from shortly after 1381, is discussed by Cristina Maria Cervone, "John de Cobham and Cooling Castle's Charter Poem," *Speculum* 83, no. 4 (2008): 884–916.

13. See Julia Boffey, *Manuscripts of English Courtly Love Lyrics in the Later Middle Ages* (Cambridge: D. S. Brewer, 1985); for the comment, Eleanor Prescott Hammond, *English Verse Between Chaucer and Surrey* (Durham, NC: Duke University Press, 1927), 243.

14. See *Middle English Dictionary* (*MED*), s.v., "poesi(e), noun," which offers instances from the 1380s on, from Geoffrey Chaucer, John Trevisa, Thomas Usk, and others.

15. "Ideology and Ideological State Apparatuses (Notes Towards an Investigation)," in Louis Althusser, *Lenin and Philosophy and Other Essays* (New York: Monthly Review Press, 1971), 127–86.

16. Martin Heidegger, *Being and Time*, trans. John Macquarrie and Edward Robinson (New York: Harper, 1962), 98. Given Heidegger's early support for Hitler and the Nazi party, extreme caution is needed when redeploying any of his ideas, intriguing as they always are; see also below for his views on lyric.

17. This temporally specific frame is not, of course, in the wholly poetic and implied form of what Roland Greene considers the distinguishing use of "fiction" of the Petrarchan and post-Petrarchan lyric sequence (*Post-Petrarchism*, esp. chaps. 1 and 2).

18. A. A. MacDonald, "Lyrics in Middle Scots," and Thorlac Turville-Petre, "Political Lyrics," in *A Companion to the Middle English Lyric*, ed. Thomas G. Duncan (Cambridge: D. S. Brewer, 2005), 243–61, 171–88 (respectively).

19. Julia Marvin, *The Construction of Vernacular History in the Anglo-Norman Prose Brut Chronicle: The Manuscript Culture of Late Medieval England* (York: University of York Press, 2017), 202; Julia Boffey and A. S. G. Edwards, "Middle English Verse in Chronicles," in *New Perspectives on Middle English Texts: A Festschrift for R. A. Waldron*, ed. Susan Powell and Jeremy J. Smith (Cambridge: D. S. Brewer, 2000), 119–28, cf. p. 122, "the Middle English prose *Brut* remains the most variegated source for the incorporation of Middle English verse." For some treatment of the *Brut*'s English satiric verses, see Andrew Galloway, "The Borderlands of Satire: Linked, Opposed, and Exchanged Political Poetry During the Scottish and English Wars of the Early Fourteenth Century," in *The Anglo-Scottish Border and the Shaping of Identity, 1300–1600*, ed. Mark Bruce and Katherine Terrell (New York: Palgrave, 2012), 15–31.

20. The Middle English prose is from Friedrich W. D. Brie, ed., *The Brut, or The Chronicles of England, edited from Ms. Rawl. B 171, Bodleian Library, &c.*, EETS, o.s., 131 (London: Oxford University Press, 1906), 208. After "haue" is "lost" in Brie's edition, but in brackets, presumably showing the need to omit a word that crept in as a lexical gloss on "fortynt." A copy of the Anglo-Norman "long version" in London, British Library, Cotton MS Cleopatra D.3, fol. 152, does not distinguish the English verse visually from the surrounding Anglo-Norman; for an edition, see Marcia Lusk Maxwell, "The Anglo-Norman Prose 'Brut': An Edition of British Library MS Cotton Cleopatra D. III" (Ph.D. diss., Michigan State University, 1995).

21. Frye, *Anatomy of Criticism*, 271.

22. Culler, *Theory of the Lyric*. His views are briefly anticipated in "Why Lyric?," *PMLA* 123, no. 1 (2008): 201–6, to which Butterfield's chapter title refers, just as Butterfield notes in passing Culler's focus elsewhere on the effects of visual as well as aural properties, features that, as she observes, are more proper to print than manuscript culture ("Why Medieval Lyric?," 337).

23. Culler, *Theory of the Lyric*, 70. For Culler's establishment of his category via a set of poetic "prototypes" across time and languages, see pp. 10–38. The features establishing the genre are, essentially, "lyrical address" (whose postures are most clearly visible in avoiding a more mimetic "fiction of a speaker and [of] explicit address," 34); poetic eventfulness (accomplished by many other strategies that resist the mimetic claims of narrative); and "ritualistic" power, elaborated in due course in such matters as rhythm and untranslatability, the means by which lyric poetry's language imposes experience rather than offering something to decode or translate or allegorize. Finding similarity across the vast temporal and cultural expanses he takes up the basis of his results, as when he defends the "argument for lyric as a

genre" on the grounds that "we have no better alternatives" (87). But the genre is also defended on the grounds of allowing more visible difference and particularity. Culler refuses, for instance, to use locally named subgenres as frameworks, since those might deceptively seem to offer repeatable genres when in fact it is better to avow openly that any generic label is "a slippery, even dubious category." It is enough to say that "it is blatantly obvious that the lyric changes" (87). This dual use of similarity and difference to sustain his inductive category has some circularity: it presumes "the lyric" established by the properties described can remain a permanent imagined modality (though one so abstract that few narrowly formal rules apply) while remaining overtly open to major "change," at least to a certain limit. So long as that limit defines itself against something, something like "lyric tradition," the inductive approach sustains the category. When short, nonnarrative poetry neither defines itself within or against such a "tradition" or "model," the category tends to omit whole stretches of poetry, as it generally does medieval English.

24. Ibid., 168–71.

25. Peter Larken, ed., *Richard Coer de Lyon* (Kalamazoo, MI: Medieval Institute Publications for TEAMS, 2015).

26. Line 252, in John Skelton, *Poems*, ed. Robert S. Kinsman (Oxford: Clarendon Press, 1969), 19. Kinsman mentions a further example (he thinks the specific song Skelton mentions) from *Cocke Lorelle's Bote* (ca. 1508), "sung by his boatmen as they sail from 'garyke hed' to 'knaues in,'" at p. 140.

27. K. Hinds, "NMS1606: A Medieval Seal Matrix" (2003), https://finds.org.uk/database/artefacts/record/id/39051; for the poem see R. M. Wilson, *The Lost Literature of Medieval England* (London: Metheun, 1952), 178. My thanks to Cristina Maria Cervone and Nicholas Watson for these and some other trackings as well as much else. See also the discussion of the surname "Rumbelow" at the Surname Database, http://www.surnamedb.com/Surname/Rumbelow.

28. *Oxford English Dictionary Online* (*OED*), s.v. "heave, v.," def. 10, 19; "heave ho, int. and n."

29. Culler, *Theory of the Lyric*, 138, 142.

30. Ibid., 136.

31. See Amanda Richardson, "'Hedging, Ditching and Other Improper Occupations': Royal Landscapes and Their Meaning Under Edward II and Edward III," in *Fourteenth Century England IV*, ed. J. S. Hamilton (Woodbridge, Suffolk: Boydell, 2006), 26–42.

32. Eustache Deschamps, *L'art de dictier*, ed. and trans. Deborah M. Sinnreich-Levi (East Lansing, MI: Colleagues Press, 1994), 70–71. For the short, beat-counted lines in Middle English see Cornelius, "Language and Meter."

33. Quoted from Bertrand Harris Bronson, ed., *The Traditional Tunes of the Child Ballads, with Their Texts, According to the Extant Records of Great Britain and America* (Princeton, NJ: Princeton University Press, 1962), 2:34, stanza 24; Child ballad no. 58.

34. See Andrew Albin, "The Sound of Rollean Lyric," this volume (Chapter 8).

35. Roland Greene, *Post-Petrarchism*, 5–6.

36. Christopher Marlowe, *Edward the Second*, ed. W. Moelwyn Merchant (London: A. and C. Black, 1987).

37. Culler, *Theory of the Lyric*, 111.

38. Wenzel, *Preachers, Poets*, 144.

39. Edward Wilson, *A Descriptive Index of the English Lyrics in John of Grimestone's Preaching Book* (Oxford: Basil Blackwell, 1973), xiii.

40. Wenzel, *Preachers, Poets*, 144.

41. Carleton Brown, ed., *Religious Lyrics of the XIVth Century* (Oxford: Clarendon Press, 1924), no. 68; no. 3825 in Julia Boffey and A. S. G. Edwards, *A New Index of Middle English Verse* (London: The British Library, 2005). For convenience I generally cite the poem by Boffey and Edward's title, "Undo Thy Door"; but for Grimestone's Latin headnote at its intended title, see below.

42. Edward Wilson, *Descriptive Index,* 39.

43. For an example written for beguines in the Low Countries, see Tony Hunt, ed., *Les Cantiques Salemon: The Song of Songs in MS Paris BNF Fr. 14966* (Turnhout: Brepols, 2006).

44. For this effect, see generally Cristina Maria Cervone, "Wondering Through Middle English Lyric," this volume (Chapter 2), and Ingrid Nelson, "Lyric Value," this volume (Chapter 5); and for the specific use of the kinds of devotional communities created by Jesus speaking, Barbara Zimbalist, "The Lyric Christ," this volume (Chapter 9).

45. For general background to the motif, see Rosemary Woolf, "The Theme of Christ the Lover-Knight in Medieval English Literature," *Review of English Studies* 13, no. 49 (1962): 1–16.

46. See Culler, *Theory of the Lyric,* 225–26. Culler's one mention of medieval English lyric, however, observes that its "meditative and penitential poetry" invites each reader (as he quotes another critic) "to perfect or universalize himself by occupying that language as his own" (68).

47. For poetics of titles based explicitly on the period of print, see Anne Ferry, *The Title to the Poem* (Stanford, CA: Stanford University Press, 1996). For the model of the Song of Songs in particular, see Cervone, "Wondering Through Middle English Lyric."

48. See the online catalog based on the print catalog of M. R. James, *A Descriptive Catalogue of the Manuscripts in the Library of Lambeth Palace* (Cambridge: Cambridge University Press, 1930–32), http://archives.lambethpalacelibrary.org.uk/CalmView/Record.aspx?src=CalmView.Catalog&id=MSS%2f557&pos=236.

49. The passage is derived from Bernard of Clairvaux's sermon 1, "In festivitate omnium sanctorum," section 15, e.g., "*Beati* enim *qui persecutionem patiuntur propter iustitiam, quoniam ipsorum est regnum caelorum:* Verumtamen quid sibi vult, quod eadem promissio facta est pauperibus et martyribus, nisi quia vere martyrii genus paupertas voluntaria est?" (For *blessed are those who suffer for the sake of justice, for theirs will be the kingdom of heaven* [Matt. 5:10]: wherefore what else does he mean when saying that the same promise is made to pauper as to martyrs, except indeed that voluntary poverty is a species of martyrdom?") (*Sermones II,* vol. 5 of *Sancti Bernardi Opera,* ed. J. Leclercq and H. M. Rochais [Rome: Editiones Cistercienses, 1968], p. 341; my translation).

50. I clarify where *u* is *v* and undotted *y* is *þ*.

51. "What good was it for me to be conceived by the womb? Why be born from it, and then enjoy all goods, and finally descend into hell? Alas, alas, it would have been better for me not to have been conceived by the womb nor born from it."

52. See the online catalog entry for the Beinecke, with a full scan of the manuscript: https://brbl-dl.library.yale.edu/vufind/Record/4281593.

53. Although the Beinecke catalog description calls this a "dialogue," no scholar who discusses it mentions the Latin speech-tags. See, e.g., Ralph Hanna, "Verses in Sermons Again: The Case of Cambridge, Jesus College MS Q.A.13," *Studies in Bibliography* 57 (2005–6): 63–83, at p. 70.

54. Rosemary Woolf speaks of the Lambeth poem as the same poem as Grimestone's "but with the stanzas in the reverse order, and with an addition in different metre" (*The English Religious Lyric in the Middle Ages* [Oxford: Clarendon Press, 1968], 51 n. 2). Ralph Hanna, "Verses

in Sermons Again," 70, states that the Takamiya 15 lyric is "a reproduction" of Grimestone's, and thus misleadingly claims that this is a "unique" instance of any copy of Grimestone's lyrics outside his notebook. The *Digital Index of Middle English Verse* (*DIMEV*) lists all three of these poems as "witnesses" to the same poem (it also mistakenly quotes a two-line poem immediately after "Undo Thy Door" as if it were the latter's explicit): http://www.dimev.net/record.php ?recID=6108. It is a sign of the elusiveness of defining medieval English lyric that if the Takamiya poem is "a reproduction" of Grimestone's, then so is Lambeth 557; if it is not, then there are no instances of Grimestone's lyrics outside his notebook.

55. E.g., Chrétien de Troyes, *Le Chevalier de la Charrette (Lancelot)*, ed. A. Foulet and Karl D. Uitti (Paris: Bordas, 1989), lines 4670–71, 4735–36. For this phenomenon generally, see Barbara Newman, *Medieval Crossover: Reading the Secular Against the Sacred* (Notre Dame, IN: University of Notre Dame Press, 2013).

56. Woolf, *English Religious Lyric*, 51–52; the Latin lyric is edited in F. J. E. Raby, ed., *The Oxford Book of Medieval Latin Verse* (Oxford: Clarendon Press, 1959), no. 115, p. 158.

57. In David Bevington, ed., *Medieval Drama* (Boston: Houghton Mifflin, 1975), 12–13.

58. Karl Young, *The Drama of the Medieval Church* (London: Oxford University Press, 1933), 1:164–70. My translation. Young presents versions from Ireland as well. For the remarkable Easter liturgy at Barking, see Jill Stephenson, "Rhythmic Liturgy, Embodiment and Female Authority in Barking's Easter Plays," in Jennifer N. Brown and Donna Alfano Bussell, eds., *Barking Abbey and Medieval Literary Culture: Authorship and Authority in a Female Community* (York: York Medieval Press, 2002), 245–66; and for a longer view of the musical liturgy there and other nunneries, Anne Bagnall Yardley, *Performing Piety: Musical Culture in Medieval English Nunneries* (New York: Palgrave MacMillan, 2006), esp. 179–202.

59. Culler, *Theory of the Lyric*, 301.

60. Niall Atkinson, *The Noisy Renaissance: Sound, Architecture, and Florentine Urban Life* (University Park: Pennsylvania State University Press, 2016), 149.

61. *The Squire of Low Degree*, in *Sentimental and Humorous Romances*, ed. Erik Kooper (Kalamazoo, MI: Medieval Institute Publications for TEAMS, 2005).

62. Nicola McDonald, "Desire Out of Order and *Undo Your Door*," *Studies in the Age of Chaucer* 34 (2012): 247–75.

63. Ibid.

64. Culler, *Theory of the Lyric*, 89–90; see also his chapter on "lyric address," 186–243.

65. *Tottel's Miscellany: Songes and Sonnets by Henry Howard, Earl of Surrey, Sir Thomas Wyatt the Elder, Nicholas Grimald, and Uncertain Authors*, ed. Edward Arber (London: Bloomsbury, 1870), 2.

66. Ibid. Sir Philip Sidney, *An Apologie for poetrie* (London: William Ponsonby, 1595) [STC (Short Title Catalogue) 22534.5].

67. See Nelson, "Lyric Value," and Virginia Jackson, "Response: Old Lyric Things," this volume (Chapter 12). For Wyatt in particular, see David R. Carlson, "Manuscripts After Printing: Affinity, Dissent, and Display in the Texts of Wyatt's Psalms," in *Prestige, Authority and Power in Late-Medieval Manuscripts and Texts*, ed. Felicity Riddy (York: York Medieval Press, 2000), 171–88.

68. See, e.g., H. R. Woudhuysen, *Sir Philip Sidney and the Circulation of Manuscripts, 1558–1640* (Oxford: Clarendon Press, 1996).

69. For a brief summary of the print industry's rapid growth, see Robert S. Duplessis, *Transitions to Capitalism in Early Modern Europe* (Cambridge: Cambridge University Press, 1997), 92.

70. *Tottel's Miscellany*, 2.

71. For the rise of "self-help" books in the early years of printing, see Elizabeth L. Eisenstein, *The Printing Press as an Agent of Change: Communications and Cultural Transformations in Early-Modern Europe*, 2 vols. in 1 (Cambridge: Cambridge University Press, 1979; repr., 1985), 230, 244–46.

72. Citations of Chaucer are from *The Riverside Chaucer*, gen. ed. Larry D. Benson, 3rd ed. (Boston: Houghton Mifflin, 1987).

73. Jean Renart, *The Romance of the Rose or of Guillaume de Dole*, ed. and trans. Regina Psaki (New York: Garland, 1995), lines 9–10, 14–15. For useful discussion of the tradition categorizing its instances and presenting summaries of the major examples, see Maureen Barry McCann Boulton, *The Song in the Story: Lyric Insertions in French Narrative Fiction, 1200–1400* (Philadelphia: University of Pennsylvania Press, 1993).

74. Thomas C. Stillinger, *The Song of Troilus: Lyric Authority in the Medieval Book* (Philadelphia: University of Pennsylvania Press, 1992).

75. Culler, *Theory of the Lyric*, 243.

76. See generally John Hatcher and Mark Bailey, *Modelling the Middle Ages: The History and Theory of England's Economic Development* (Oxford: Oxford University Press, 2001); Christopher Dyer, *An Age of Transition? Economy and Society in England in the Later Middle Ages* (Oxford: Oxford University Press, 2005); and Martha C. Howell, *Commerce Before Capitalism in Europe, 1300–1600* (Cambridge: Cambridge University Press, 2010).

77. Martin Heidegger, "What Are Poets For?," in *Poetry, Language, Thought*, trans. Albert Hofstadter (New York: Harper and Row, 1971), 89–142, at p. 115. Heidegger's lecture was originally given on the twentieth anniversary of Rilke's death, i.e., 1946, when Heidegger's earlier interest in Hitler and the Nazi party were not known but might have informed both his sense of existential, self-created willing and his views, expressed in a linked lecture on "The Origin of the Work of Art," that the "clearing of and establishing of the Open" can include not only certain foundational works of art but also "the act that founds a political state," and "the essential sacrifice" (in *Poetry, Language, Thought*, 62). Both claims possess chilling associations with the Nazi doctrine of Lebensraum.

78. See David Wallace, "Chaucer and Boccaccio's Early Writings," in *Chaucer and the Italian Trecento*, ed. Piero Boitani (Cambridge: Cambridge University Press, 1983), 141–62, at p. 155; other examples at 150–51, 156–57.

79. Giovanni Boccaccio, *Il Filostrato*, in *Opere*, ed. Cesare Segre (Milan: Mursia, 1966), 3.42, p. 836; translation from Geoffrey Chaucer, *Troilus and Criseyde*, ed. Stephen A. Barney (New York: W. W. Norton, 2006), 198.

80. See *Filocolo* 2.50, in *Tutte le Opere di Giovanni Boccaccio*, gen. ed. Vittore Branca, vol. 1 (Verona: Arnoldo Mondadorni, 1967), 204–5; trans. Donald Cheney with the collaboration of Thomas G. Bergin, *Giovanni Boccaccio: Il Filocolo* (New York: Garland, 1985), 107–9.

81. Wallace, "Chaucer and Boccaccio's Early Writings," 148.

82. J. L. Austin, *How to Do Things with Words* (Oxford: Clarendon Press, 1962). Austin's notorious dismissal of performative utterances in fictional or dramatic contexts as "*in a peculiar way* hollow or void" (22, his emphasis) has long fostered further discussion.

83. Eleanor Johnson, *Practicing Literary Theory in the Middle Ages: Ethics and the Mixed Form in Chaucer, Gower, Usk, and Hoccleve* (Chicago: University of Chicago Press, 2013), 127.

84. See Boffey, *Manuscripts of English Courtly Love Lyrics*.

85. John Gower, *The French Balades*, ed. and trans. R. F. Yeager (Kalamazoo, MI: Medieval Institute, 2011).

86. Citations are from *The English Works of John Gower*, ed. G. C. Macaulay, 2 vols., EETS, e.s., 81–82 (Oxford: Oxford University Press, 1900).

87. See Andrew Galloway, "Gower's Ovids," in *The Oxford History of Classical Reception in English Literature, Volume 1, 800–1558*, ed. Rita Copeland (Oxford: Oxford University Press, 2016), 435–64.

88. John Burrow argues that the *Confessio* should be seen in its "overall genre" as a *dit* like Machaut's or Froissart's: "Gower's *Confessio Amantis* and Chaucer's *Canterbury Tales* as Dits," in *Readings in Medieval Textuality: Essays in Honour of A. C. Spearing*, ed. Cristina Maria Cervone and D. Vance Smith (Cambridge: D. S. Brewer, 2016), 157–68.

89. Text and translation from *Heroides; Amores*, trans. Grant Showerman, 2nd ed., rev. G. P. Goold (Cambridge, MA: Harvard University Press, 1977) 1:368–69, no. 13, lines 3–10. Translation modified.

90. Ibid., 370–71, no. 13, lines 35–40. Translation modified.

91. For the genre, see Peter Dronke, *The Medieval Lyric*, 3rd ed. (Cambridge: D. S. Brewer, 1996), 167–85.

92. Culler, *Theory of the Lyric*, 352, 350, 190, 229. This focus, as Culler notes (vii–viii), began Culler's project on lyric (in an essay from 1977, "Apostrophe," *Diacritics* 7, no. 4 [1977]: 59–69; reprinted [with revisions] in *The Pursuit of Signs: Semiotics, Literature, Deconstruction*, [Ithaca, NY: Cornell University Press, 1981, 135–54]).

93. Edmond Faral, ed., *Les arts poétiques des XIIe et XIIIe siècle: Recherches et documents sur la technique littéraire du moyen âge* (Paris: Champion, 1962), lines 276–78; Geoffrey of Vinsauf, *Poetria Nova of Geoffrey of Vinsauf*, trans. Margaret F. Nims (Toronto: Pontifical Institute of Mediaeval Studies, 1967), 26. John Hollander offers a similar self-fulfilling definition of apostrophe in *Rhyme's Reason: A Guide to English Verse* (New Haven, CT: Yale University Press, 2014), 48, of which Culler takes note (*Theory of the Lyric*, 212–13); neither Culler nor Hollander mentions Geoffrey of Vinsauf's prior display of this witticism. Chaucer's uses of Geoffrey of Vinsauf are most evident in *Troilus and Criseyde* (e.g., 1.1065–71), and "The Nun's Priest's Tale."

94. Geoffrey of Vinsauf, *Poetria nova*, 25.

95. For "heaped and layered" poetic temporalities in relation to "lyric romance," see also Christopher Cannon, "Lyric Romance," this volume (Chapter 3).

96. See especially Jonathan Hsy, *Trading Tongues: Merchants, Multilingualism, and Medieval Literature* (Columbus: Ohio State University Press, 2013).

97. See David Carlson, "The Invention of the Anglo-Latin Public Poetry (circa 1367–1402) and Its Prosody, Especially in John Gower," *Mittellateinisches Jahrbuch* 39 (2004): 389–406; Andrew Galloway, "Gower in His Most Learned Role and the Peasants' Revolt of 1381," *Mediaevalia* 16 (1993 for 1990): 329–47.

98. Lynn Arner, *Chaucer, Gower, and the Vernacular Rising: Poetry and the Problem of the Populace After 1381* (University Park: Pennsylvania State University Press, 2013).

CHAPTER 12

1. Editors' note: the first (exploratory) seminar was in 2015, but Virginia Jackson joined our discussion in 2016.

2. Virginia Jackson, "Lyric," in *The Princeton Encyclopedia of Poetry and Poetics*, 4th ed., ed. Roland Greene and Stephen Cushman (Princeton, NJ: Princeton University Press, 2012), 826–34, at p. 826.

3. Ibid., 827. See also Paul Zumthor, *Toward a Medieval Poetics*, trans. Philip Bennett (Minneapolis: University of Minnesota Press, 1991).

4. Ardis Butterfield, "Lyric Editing," this volume (Chapter 1), 31, my emphasis.

5. Stephanie [Stephen] Burt, "What Is This Thing Called Lyric?," *Modern Philology* 113, no. 3 (2016): 422–40, at p. 440. It is actually not surprising that Burt's title echoes the title of the Radcliffe seminar and this book and that her review also echoes some of these chapters' affordances, since she had attended the first meeting of the seminar before she wrote the review. I attended the second meeting at Radcliffe and also learned so much.

6. "Without Contraries is no progression. Attraction and Repulsion, Reason and Energy, Love and Hate, are necessary to Human existence." William Blake, *The Marriage of Heaven and Hell* (London, 1790), plate 3, William Blake Archive, http://www.blakearchive .org/work/mhh.

7. Steven Shaviro, "'Striving with Systems': Blake and the Politics of Difference," *boundary 2* 10, no. 3 (1982): 229–50, at p. 231.

8. On the ongoing "appropriation of faux-medieval culture by modern racists" attached to narratives of Western civilizational progress, see, for example, Jo Livingstone, "Racism, Medievalism, and the White Supremacists of Charlottesville," *New Republic*, August 15, 2017, https://newrepublic.com/article/144320/racism-medievalism-white-supremacists -charlottesville.

9. "The New Lyric Studies," *PMLA* 123, no. 1 (2008): 181–234. When Yopie and I invited Brent Hayes Edwards, Rei Terada, Jonathan Culler, Robert Kaufman, Oren Izenberg, and Stathis Gourgouris to contribute to a forum on lyric, we did not know that Patsy Yaeger was going to call these theories and methodologies "The New Lyric Studies," and none of the contributors agreed then or would agree now on a singular definition of lyric or on a single way of studying lyric. Culler, Izenberg, and Kaufman have since disagreed with the ways in which Yopie and I have thought about lyric, and Terada, Edwards, and Gourgouris don't so much reject our idea of lyricization as they just don't care about it. So, not only is the lyric not a thing, but "The New Lyric Studies" is not a thing beyond how it was framed in that journal issue—unless critics make it one.

10. Jonathan Culler, *Theory of the Lyric* (Cambridge, MA: Harvard University Press, 2015), 83.

11. See Theodor W. Adorno, "On Lyric Poetry and Society" (1957), in *The Lyric Theory Reader*, ed. Virginia Jackson and Yopie Prins (Baltimore: Johns Hopkins University Press, 2014), 339–50.

12. Marjorie Perloff, review of *Theory of the Lyric* by Jonathan Culler, *Nineteenth-Century Literature* 71, no. 2 (2016): 256–61, at p. 257.

13. Rosemary Greentree, "Lyric," in *A Companion to Medieval English Literature and Culture, c. 1350–c. 1500*, ed. Peter Brown (Malden, MA: Blackwell, 2007), 387–405, at p. 387.

14. Cristina Maria Cervone, "Wondering Through Middle English Lyric," this volume (Chapter 2).

15. Ian Cornelius, "Language and Meter," this volume (Chapter 4), 107.

16. Helen Vendler, "The Art of Criticism No. 3," interview by Henri Cole, *Paris Review* 141 (1996), as quoted in Raymond W. Gibbs, Jr., "Cognitive Poetics of Middle English Lyric Poetry," this volume (Chapter 6), 181; Stephanie [Stephen] Burt, *The Poem is You: 60 Contemporary American Poems and How to Read Them* (Cambridge, MA: Harvard University Press, 2016). Stephanie Burt was Vendler's student, and her theory of lyric reading owes a lot to Vendler's radical phenomenology of performance.

17. Aden Kumler, "Lyric Vessels," this volume (Chapter 7), 182.

18. Ibid, 217. For an introduction to the concept of "language-in-use," see Michael Lucey and Tom McEnaney, "Language-in-Use and Literary Fieldwork," *Representations* 137, no. 1 (2017): 1–22.

19. Margot Fassler, "The Religious Lyric in Medieval England (1150–1400): Three Disciplines and a Question," this volume (Chapter 10), 269.

20. Andrew Albin, "The Sound of Rollean Lyric," this volume (Chapter 8), 220. See Simon Jarvis, "Prosody as Cognition," *Critical Quarterly* 40, no. 4 (1998): 3–15.

21. Ingrid Nelson, "Lyric Value," this volume (Chapter 5), 136.

22. Ibid, 137.

23. Ibid, 144, 158.

24. Christopher Cannon, "Lyric Romance," this volume (Chapter 3), 88.

25. Ibid., 88, quoting Derek Pearsall and Seth Lerer, respectively.

26. Cannon, "Lyric Romance," 90.

27. Ibid., 91.

28. Ibid., 105.

29. Ardis Butterfield, "Lyric Editing," 31.

30. Ibid., 31.

31. Ibid., 33.

32. Ibid., 33.

33. Ardis Butterfield, "Why Medieval Lyric?," *English Literary History* 82, no. 2 (2015): 319–43, at p. 324.

CHAPTER 13

1. Cristina Maria Cervone, "Wondering Through Middle English Lyric," this volume (Chapter 2), 84.

2. Christopher Cannon, "Lyric Romance," this volume (Chapter 3), 90.

3. Ingrid Nelson, "Lyric Value," this volume (Chapter 5), 138, 144.

4. Ibid, 139.

5. Aden Kumler, "Lyric Vessels," this volume (Chapter 7), 190.

6. Andrew Galloway, "Theory of the Fourteenth-Century English Lyric," this volume (Chapter 11), 306.

7. Kumler, "Lyric Vessels," 195.

8. Andrew Albin, "The Sound of Rollean Lyric," this volume (Chapter 8), 225.

9. Ingrid Nelson, *Lyric Tactics: Poetry, Genre, and Practice in Later Medieval England* (Philadelphia: University of Pennsylvania Press, 2017), 7.

10. Jessica Brantley, *Reading in the Wilderness: Private Devotion and Public Performance in Late Medieval England* (Chicago: University of Chicago Press, 2007), 2.

11. Nelson, *Lyric Tactics*.

12. Aby Kaupang and Matthew Cooperman, *NOS (disorder, not otherwise specified)* (New York: Futurepoem, 2018), 50.

13. Robert Minhinnick, *Diary of the Last Man* (Manchester: Carcanet, 2019), 30.

14. Ana Carrete, *Baby Babe* (Arlington, VA: Civil Coping Mechanisms, 2012), 110.

15. Ibid., 111.

16. Nelson, *Lyric Tactics*, 52.

17. Ibid.

18. Carrete, *Baby Babe*, 65.

19. Douglas Kearney, "Repetition and Revulsion," *Jacket2*, February 5, 2016, http:// jacket2.org/article/repetition-and-revulsion; italics in original.

20. Shannon Gayk, review of *Reading in the Wilderness*, by Jessica Brantley, *Medieval Review* 9, no. 1 (2015).

21. Anna Wilson, "The Role of Affect in Fan Fiction," *Transformative Works and Cultures* 21 (2016), https://doi.org/10.3983/twc.2016.0684, at 2.1.

22. Erika Meitner, *Holy Moly Carry Me* (Rochester, NY: BOA, 2018), 73.

23. Ng Yi-Sheng, *A Book of Hims* (Singapore: Math Paper, 2017), 72.

24. Ibid., 61.

25. Jos Charles, *feeld* (Minneapolis: Milkweed, 2018), 1.

26. Ibid., 3.

27. Brad Trumpfheller, "Groundshift: A Conversation with Jos Charles," *Adroit* 26 (2018), https://theadroitjournal.org/2018/08/30/jos-charles-poetry-interview/.

28. S. Yarberry, "Standardizing the Vernacular: An Interview with Jos Charles," *BOMB* (August 2018), https://bombmagazine.org/articles/jos-charles/.

29. Ardis Butterfield, "Lyric Editing," this volume (Chapter 1), 44.

30. Sunil Iyengar, "Taking Note: Poetry Reading Is Up—Federal Survey Results," National Endowment for the Arts blog, June 7, 2018, https://www.arts.gov/stories/blog/2018 /taking-note-poetry-reading-federal-survey-results.

31. Thomas Duncan, ed., *A Companion to the Middle English Lyric* (Cambridge: D. S. Brewer, 2005), xviii.

32. Edited by Elizabeth Salter from London, British Library MS Arundel 292 in "A Complaint Against Blacksmiths," *Literature and History* 5, no. 2 (1979), 194–215, at 194.

33. John Ashbery, *Selected Poems* (New York: Penguin, 1982), 87.

References

MANUSCRIPTS AND ARTIFACTS

Aberystwyth, National Library of Wales, MS 6680B (Hendregadredd Manuscript).
Cambrai, Bibliothèque Municipale, MS 78 (79).
Cambridge, Cambridge University Library, MS Additional 710 (Dublin Troper).
Cambridge, Cambridge University Library, MS Dd.v.64.III.
Cambridge, Cambridge University Library, MS Ee.1.12.
Cambridge, Cambridge University Library, MS Ff.1.6 (Findern Manuscript).
Cambridge, Cambridge University Library, MS Ff.2.38.
Cambridge, Cambridge University Library, MS Gg.4.27.
Cambridge, Cambridge University Library, MS Hh.4.12.
Cambridge, Cambridge University Library, MS Ii.3.26.
Cambridge, Cambridge University Library, MS Kk.4.24.
Cambridge, Cambridge University Library, MS Mm.4.23.
Cambridge, Cambridge University Library, MS Mm.4.28.
Cambridge, Corpus Christi College, MS 61.
Cambridge, Corpus Christi College, MS 253.
Cambridge, Corpus Christi College, MS 367.
Cambridge, Gonville and Caius College, MS 174/95.
Cambridge, Gonville and Caius College, MS 383/603.
Cambridge, Magdalene College, MS Pepys 1584.
Cambridge, Pembroke College, MS 226.
Cambridge, Pembroke College, MS 258.
Cambridge, St. John's College, MS D.27.
Cambridge, St. John's College, MS E.8 (111).
Cambridge, St. John's College, MS H.1 (204).
Cambridge, St. John's College, MS S.54 (259).
Cambridge, Trinity College, MS O.3.58 (Trinity Carol Roll).
Cambridge, Trinity College, MS R.3.20 (600).
Cambridge, Trinity College, MS R.3.21 (601).
Cambridge, MA, Harvard University, Houghton Library, MS Eng. 530.
Dublin, Trinity College, MS 201.
Dublin, Trinity College, MS 277.
Dublin, Trinity College, MS 501.
Edinburgh, National Library of Scotland, MS Advocates' 18.7.21.

Edinburgh, National Library of Scotland, MS Advocates' 19.2.1 (Auchinleck).
Edinburgh, National Library of Scotland, MS Advocates' 19.3.1.
Edinburgh, National Library of Scotland, MS Advocates' 34.7.3.
Einsiedeln, Stiftsbibliothek, Codex 366.
Liverpool, National Museums Liverpool, Nelson Collection, 53.113 (laver).
London, British Library, Additional MS 22283.
London, British Library, Additional MS 31922.
London, British Library, Additional MS 36983.
London, British Library, Additional MS 37049.
London, British Library, Additional MS 37790.
London, British Library, Additional MS 39574.
London, British Library, Arundel MS 248.
London, British Library, Arundel MS 507.
London, British Library, Cotton MS Caligula A.ix.
London, British Library, Cotton MS Caligula A.xiv.
London, British Library, Cotton MS Cleopatra D.3.
London, British Library, Harley MS 322.
London, British Library, Harley MS 682.
London, British Library, Harley MS 1587.
London, British Library, Harley MS 2253.
London, British Library, Harley MS 2339.
London, British Library, Harley MS 2380.
London, British Library, Harley MS 3965.
London, British Library, Harley MS 5289.
London, British Library, Harley MS 7322.
London, British Library, Royal MS 2.B.iv (St. Albans troper).
London, British Library, Royal MS 5.F.vii.
London, British Library, Royal MS 8.F.II.
London, British Library, Royal MS 12.E.1.
London, British Library, Sloane MS 2593.
London, British Museum, 1855,1029.11 (Kingston-type ware face-jug).
London, British Museum, 1896,0727.1 (Asante Ewer).
London, British Museum, 1975,1001.1 (tripod laver).
London, Lambeth Palace Library, MS 306.
London, Lambeth Palace Library, MS 487.
London, Lambeth Palace Library, MS 557.
London, Lambeth Palace Library, MS 853.
London, Victoria and Albert Museum, 217–1879 (Robinson Jug).
London, Victoria and Albert Museum, M.165-1914 (Rokewode Mazer).
London, Westminster School, MS 3.
Luton, Luton Museum, Stockwood Discovery Centre, Wenlok Jug.
Maidstone, Kent, Maidstone Museum and Art Gallery, MS MA.13.
Manchester, John Rylands Library, MS Latin 24.
New Haven, CT, Yale University, Beinecke Library, MS Ege 1026.1988.
New Haven, CT, Yale University, Beinecke Library, Takamiya MS 15.
New Haven, CT, Yale University, Beinecke Library, Takamiya MS 66.
New York, Metropolitan Museum of Art, Cloisters Collection, 55.25 (Cloisters Mazer).

Notre Dame, IN, Hesburgh Library, cod. Lat. c.2.

Oxford, Balliol College, MS 149.

Oxford, Bodleian Library, MS Bodley 596.

Oxford, Bodleian Library, MS Bodley 1486.

Oxford, Bodleian Library, MS Digby 86.

Oxford, Bodleian Library, MS Digby 102.

Oxford, Bodleian Library, MS Douce 78.

Oxford, Bodleian Library, MS Douce 228.

Oxford, Bodleian Library, MS Douce 302.

Oxford, Bodleian Library, MS English Poetry a.1 (Vernon).

Oxford, Bodleian Library, MS English Poetry e.1.

Oxford, Bodleian Library, MS Lat.liturg.b.5.

Oxford, Bodleian Library, MS Laud Misc. 108.

Oxford, Bodleian Library, MS Laud Misc. 471.

Oxford, Bodleian Library, MS Rawlinson A.389.

Oxford, Bodleian Library, MS Rawlinson B.332.

Oxford, Bodleian Library, MS Rawlinson C.86.

Oxford, Bodleian Library, MS Rawlinson G.22.

Oxford, Bodleian Library, MS Tanner 169*.

Oxford, Corpus Christi College, MS 237.

Oxford, Jesus College, MS 29.

Oxford, Magdalen College, MS 93.

Oxford, Trinity College, MS 34.

Oxford, University College, MS 169.

Paris, Bibliothèque de l'Arsenal, MS 135.

Paris, Bibliothèque Mazarine, MS 1716.

Paris, Bibliothèque Nationale, MS Fr. 25458.

Paris, Bibliothèque Nationale, MS Lat. 1339.

Paris, Bibliothèque Sainte-Geneviève, MS 3390.

San Marino, CA, Huntington Library, MS HM 144.

Somerset, Longleat House, MS Longleat 29.

Swansea, Swansea Museum, Reg. no. A 879.1 (laver).

Vatican City, Biblioteca Apostolica Vaticana, MS Reg.lat. 1351.

Vatican City, Biblioteca Apostolica Vaticana, MS Urb.Lat.602.

PRIMARY SOURCES

Allen, Rosamund, ed. *King Horn: An Edition Based on Cambridge University Library MS Gg.4.27 (2)*. New York: Garland, 1984.

Analecta hymnica Medii Aevi. Edited by Guido Maria Dreves, Clemens Blume, and Henry M. Bannister. 55 vols. Leipzig: Reisland, 1866–1922.

Arn, Mary-Jo, ed. *Fortunes Stabilnes: Charles of Orléans's English Book of Love; A Critical Edition*. Binghamton, NY: Medieval and Renaissance Texts and Studies, 1994.

Ashbery, John. *Selected Poems*. New York: Penguin, 1982.

Aspin, Isabel Stewart Tod, ed. *Anglo-Norman Political Songs*. ANTS 11. Oxford: Published for the Anglo-Norman Text Society by B. Blackwell, 1953.

Audelay, John the Blind. *Poems and Carols (Oxford, Bodleian Library MS Douce 302)*. Edited by Susanna Fein. Kalamazoo, MI: Medieval Institute Publications for TEAMS, 2009.

Barr, Helen ed. *The Digby Poems: A New Edition of the Lyrics*. Exeter: University of Exeter Press, 2009.

Beadle, Richard, and A. E. B. Owen, eds. *The Findern Manuscript: Cambridge University Library MS Ff.i.6*. London: Scolar Press, 1978.

Bergvall, Caroline. *Meddle English*. New York: Nightboat Books Callicoon, 2011.

Bernard of Clairvaux. "Sermo 1: In festivitate omnium sanctorum." In *Sermones II*, vol. 5 of *Sancti Bernardi Opera*, edited by J. Leclercq and H. M. Rochais, 327–70. Rome: Editiones Cistercienses, 1968.

Bevington, David, ed. *Medieval Drama*. Boston: Houghton Mifflin, 1975.

Blake, William. *The Marriage of Heaven and Hell*. London, 1790. William Blake Archive. http://www.blakearchive.org/work/mhh.

Boccaccio, Giovanni. *Il Filocolo*. In *Tutte le Opere di Giovanni Boccaccio*, edited by Vittore Branca, vol. 1, pp. 47–970. Verona: Arnoldo Mondadorni, 1967.

———. *Il Filostrato*. In *Opere*, edited by Cesare Segre, 771–942. Milan: Mursia, 1966.

———. *Giovanni Boccaccio: Il Filocolo*. Translated by Donald Cheney, with the collaboration of Thomas G. Bergin. New York: Garland, 1985.

Bower, Calvin M., ed. and trans. *The "Liber Ymnorum" of Notker Balbulus*. Henry Bradshaw Society 121 and 122. London: Henry Bradshaw Society, 2016.

Breul, Karl, ed. *The Cambridge Songs: A Goliard's Songbook of the Eleventh Century*. Cambridge: Cambridge University Press, 1915.

Brie, Friedrich W. D., ed. *The Brut, or The Chronicles of England, edited from MS. Rawl. B 171, Bodleian Library, &c.* 2 vols. EETS, o.s., 131–32. London: Oxford University Press, 1906–8.

Brolaski, Julian T. *Gowanus Atropolis*. Brooklyn, NY: Ugly Duckling Presse, 2011.

Bronson, Bertrand Harris, ed. *The Traditional Tunes of the Child Ballads: With Their Texts, According to the Extant Records of Great Britain and America*. 4 vols. Princeton, NJ: Princeton University Press, 1959–72.

Brook, G. L., ed. *The Harley Lyrics*. 2nd ed. Manchester: Manchester University Press, 1956. First published 1948.

Brown, Carleton, ed. *English Lyrics of the XIIIth Century*. Oxford: Clarendon Press, 1932.

———. *Religious Lyrics of the XIVth Century*. Oxford: Clarendon Press, 1924.

———. *Religious Lyrics of the XVth Century*. Oxford: Clarendon Press, 1939.

Butterfield, Ardis, ed. *Medieval English Lyrics*. A Norton Critical Edition. New York: W. W. Norton, 2023 (anticipated).

Capgrave, John. *The Life of St. Norbert by John Capgrave, O.E.S.A. (1393–1464)*. Edited by Cyril Lawrence Smetana. Toronto: Pontifical Institute of Mediaeval Studies, 1977.

Carrete, Ana. *Baby Babe*. Arlington, VA: Civil Coping Mechanisms, 2012.

Chambers, E. K., and F. Sidgwick, eds. *Early English Lyrics: Amorous, Divine, Moral and Trivial*. London: A. H. Bullen, 1907.

Charles, Jos. *feeld*. Minneapolis: Milkweed, 2018.

Chatterton, Thomas. *The Rowley Poems by Thomas Chatterton: Reprinted from Tyrwhitt's Third Edition*. Edited by Maurice Evan Hare. Oxford: Clarendon Press, 1911.

Chaucer, Geoffrey. *The Riverside Chaucer*. Gen. ed. Larry D. Benson. 3rd ed. Boston: Houghton Mifflin, 1987.

———. *Troilus and Criseyde*. Edited by Stephen A. Barney. New York: W. W. Norton, 2006.

Chevalier, Ulisse. *Repertorium Hymnicum: Catalogue des chants, hymnes, proses, séquences, tropes, en usage dans l'Église latine depuis les origines jusqu'à nos jours.* 6 vols. Brussels: Société des Bollandistes, 1892–1921. www.erwin-rauner.de.

Child, Francis J. *English and Scottish Popular Ballads.* Edited by Helen Child Sargent and George Lyman Kittredge. Cambridge, MA: Houghton Mifflin, 1904.

Chrétien de Troyes. *Le Chevalier de la Charrette (Lancelot).* Edited by A. Foulet and Karl D. Uitti. Paris: Bordas, 1989.

Cicero. *Cicero's Topica.* Edited by Tobias Reinhardt. Oxford: Oxford University Press, 2006.

Creton, Jean. *Metrical History of the Deposition of King Richard II.* Edited by J. Webb. *Archaeologia* 20 (1824): 1–423.

Dante Alighieri. *Paradiso.* Edited by Giorgio Petrocchi, translated by Charles S. Singleton. Princeton, NJ: Princeton University Press, 1980.

Davies, R. T., ed. *Medieval English Lyrics: A Critical Anthology.* London: Faber and Faber, 1963.

Deeming, Helen, ed. *Songs in British Sources, c. 1150–1300.* Musica Britannica, vol. 95. London: Stainer & Bell, 2013. Supplemented by http://www.diamm.ac.uk/resources/sbs.

Deschamps, Eustache. *L'art de dictier.* Edited and translated by Deborah M. Sinnreich-Levi. East Lansing, MI: Colleagues Press, 1994.

Disticha Catonis. Edited by Marcus Boas. Amsterdam: North Holland, 1952.

Dobson, E. J., and F. Ll. Harrison, eds. *Medieval English Songs.* London: Faber and Faber; New York: Cambridge University Press, 1979.

Donne, John. *The Complete Poems of John Donne.* Edited by Robin Robbins. Rev. ed. Harlow: Longman, 2010.

Dryden, John. *Fables ancient and modern translated into verse from Homer, Ovid, Boccace, & Chaucer, with Original poems, by Mr. Dryden.* London: Jacob Tonson, 1700.

Dufournet, Jean, ed. *Aucassin et Nicolette.* Paris: Flammarion, 1984.

Duncan, Thomas G., ed. *Late Medieval English Lyrics and Carols, 1400–1530.* London: Penguin, 2000.

———, ed. *Medieval English Lyrics and Carols.* Cambridge: D. S. Brewer, 2013.

Fallows, David, ed. *Secular Polyphony, 1380–1480.* Musica Britannica, vol. 97. London: Stainer & Bell, 2014.

Faral, Edmond, ed. *Les arts poetiques des XIIe et XIIIe siècle: Recherches et documents sur la technique littéraire du moyen âge.* Paris: Champion, 1962.

Fein, Susanna, ed. and trans. *The Complete Harley 2253 Manuscript.* With David Raybin and Jan Ziolkowski. 3 vols. Kalamazoo, MI: Medieval Institute Publications for TEAMS, 2014–15.

———, ed. *Interpreting MS Digby 86: A Trilingual Book from Thirteenth-Century Worcestershire.* York: York Medieval Press, 2019.

———, ed. *Moral Love Songs and Laments.* Kalamazoo, MI: Medieval Institute Publications for TEAMS, 1998.

Froissart, Jean. *Oeuvres de Froissart.* Edited by M. le baron Kervyn de Lettenhove. 25 vols. in 26. Osnabrück: Biblio Verlag, 1967. Reprint of 1867–77 edition.

Furnivall, Frederick J., ed. *Political, Religious, and Love Poems.* EETS, o.s., 15. London: Kegan Paul, Trench, Trübner, 1866, reedited 1903.

Geoffrey of Monmouth. *The History of the Kings of Britain.* Edited by Michael D. Reeve. Translated by Neil Wright. Woodbridge, Suffolk: Boydell Press, 2007.

Geoffrey of Vinsauf. *Poetria Nova of Geoffrey of Vinsauf.* Translated by Margaret F. Nims. Toronto: Pontifical Institute of Mediaeval Studies, 1967.

Gilbert of Stanford. *Tractatus super Cantica canticorum.* Edited by Rossana Guglielmetti. Florence: Edizioni del Galluzzo, 2002.

Giles, J. A., ed. *Galfredi Monumetensis historia Britonum: Nunc primum in Anglia, novem codd. msstis collatis.* London: Nutt, 1844.

Gower, John. *Confessio Amantis.* Edited by Russell A. Peck. Kalamazoo, MI: Medieval Institute Publications for TEAMS, 2004.

———. *The English Works of John Gower.* Edited by G. C. Macaulay. 2 vols. EETS, e.s. 81–82. Oxford: Oxford University Press, 1900.

———. *The French Balades.* Edited and translated by R. F. Yeager. Kalamazoo, MI: Medieval Institute for TEAMS, 2011.

Gray, Douglas, ed. *A Selection of Religious Lyrics.* Oxford: Clarendon Press, 1975.

Greene, Richard Leighton, ed. *The Early English Carols.* 2nd ed., rev. and enl. Oxford: Clarendon Press, 1977.

Gregory the Great. *Moralia in Job.* Edited by Marcus Adriaen. Corpus Christianorum, Series Latina 143. Turnhout: Brepols, 1979.

———. *Moral Reflections on the Book of Job.* Translated by Brian Kerns. 3 vols. Collegeville, MN: Liturgical Press, 2014.

Hall, Joseph, ed. *King Horn: A Middle English Romance.* Oxford: Clarendon Press, 1901.

Hammerich, Angul, ed. *Mediaeval Musical Relics of Denmark.* Translated by Margaret Williams Hamerik. Leipzig: Breitkopf & Härtel, 1912.

Harrison, Frank Ll., ed. *Motets of English Provenance.* Polyphonic Music of the Fourteenth Century 15. Monaco: Éditions de l'Oiseau-Lyre, 1980.

Harrison, Frank Ll., Ernest H. Sanders, and Peter M. Lefferts, eds. *English Music for Mass and Offices.* 2 vols. Polyphonic Music of the Fourteenth Century 16 and 17. Monaco: Éditions de l'Oiseau-Lyre, 1983–86.

Havelok the Dane. In Herzman, Drake, and Salisbury. *Four Romances of England.*

Herzman, Ronald B., Graham Drake, and Eve Salisbury, eds. *Four Romances of England: King Horn, Havelok the Dane, Bevis of Hampton, Athelston.* Kalamazoo, MI: Medieval Institute Publications for TEAMS, 1997. https://d.lib.rochester.edu/teams/publication /salisbury-four-romances-of-england.

Hesbert, René-Jean, ed., *Le Tropaire-Prosaire de Dublin: Manuscrit add. 710 de l'Université de Cambridge (vers 1360).* Rouen: Imprimerie Rouennaise, 1966.

Higden, Ranulf. *Polychronicon Ranulphi Higden monachi Cestrensis; Together with the English Translations of John Trevisa and of an Unknown Writer of the Fifteenth Century.* Edited by C. Babington and J. R. Lumby. 9 vols. Rolls Series (Rerum Britannicarum Medii Aevi Scriptores) 41 (1865–86).

Hirsh, John C., ed. *Medieval Lyric: Middle English Lyrics, Ballads, and Carols.* Malden, MA: Blackwell, 2005.

Hodgson, Phyllis, ed. *The Cloud of Unknowing and Related Treatises on Contemplative Prayer.* Salzburg: Institut für Anglistik und Amerikanistik, Universität Salzburg; Exeter: Catholic Records Press, 1982.

Holy Bible, Douay Rheims Version, The. Baltimore: John Murphy, 1899; reprint Rockford, Ill.: Tan Books, 1971.

Horace. *Ars poetica.* In *Satires, Epistles, and Ars Poetica,* edited and translated by H. Rushton Fairclough. Cambridge, MA: Harvard University Press, 1955.

Horn Childe & Maiden Rimnild. In *The Auchinleck Manuscript,* edited by David Burnley and
    Alison Wiggins. National Library of Scotland. Version 1.1, March 15, 2004. https://
    auchinleck.nls.uk/mss/horn.html.

Horstman, C., ed. *Yorkshire Writers: Richard Rolle of Hampole, an English Father of the
    Church, and His Followers.* 2 vols. London: Swan Sonnenschein; New York: Macmil-
    lan, 1895–96.

Horstmann, Carl, and F. J. Furnivall, eds. *The Minor Poems of the Vernon MS.* 2 vols. EETS,
    o.s., 98 and 117. London: Kegan Paul, Trench, Trübner, 1892, 1901.

Hugh of St. Victor. *The Didascalicon of Hugh of Saint Victor: A Medieval Guide to the Arts.*
    Translated by Jerome Taylor. New York: Columbia University Press, 1961.

———. *On the Sacraments of the Christian Faith (De sacramentis).* Translated by Roy J. Defer-
    rari. Cambridge, MA: Medieval Academy of America, 1951.

Hughes, Langston. *The Weary Blues.* New York: Knopf, 1926.

Hunt, Tony, ed. *Les Cantiques Salemon: The Song of Songs in MS Paris BNF Fr. 14966.* Turn-
    hout: Brepols, 2006.

Isidore of Seville. *The "Etymologies" of Isidore of Seville.* Translated, with introduction and
    notes, by Stephen A. Barney, W. J. Lewis, J. A. Beach, and Oliver Berghof. Cambridge:
    Cambridge University Press, 2006.

Jeffrey, David L., and Brian J. Levy, eds. *The Anglo-Norman Lyric: An Anthology Edited from
    the Manuscripts with Translations and Commentary.* Toronto: Pontifical Institute of Me-
    diaeval Studies, 1990.

John of Garland. *Parisiana Poetria.* Edited and translated by Traugott Lawler. Cambridge,
    MA: Harvard University Press, 2020.

Kaupang, Aby, and Matthew Cooperman. *NOS (disorder not otherwise specified).* New York:
    Futurepoem, 2018.

Kearney, Douglas. "Repetition and Revulsion." *Jacket2,* February 5, 2016. http://jacket2.org
    /article/repetition-and-revulsion.

Klinck, Anne L. *The Voices of Medieval English Lyric: An Anthology of Poems ca. 1150–1530.*
    Montreal: McGill-Queen's University Press, 2019.

Langland, William. *Piers Plowman: The A Version; Will's Visions of Piers Plowman and Do-
    Well, an Edition in the Form of Trinity College Cambridge MS R.3.14 Corrected from
    Other Manuscripts, with Variant Readings.* Edited by George Kane. Rev. ed. London:
    Athlone Press; and Berkeley: University of California Press, 1988.

———. *The Vision of Piers Plowman: A Critical Edition of the B-Text.* Edited by A. V. C
    Schmidt. 2nd ed. London: J. M. Dent, 1995.

Larken, Peter, ed. *Richard Coer de Lyon.* Kalamazoo, MI: Medieval Institute Publications for
    TEAMS, 2015.

Laskaya, Anne, and Eve Salisbury, eds. *The Middle English Breton Lays.* Kalamazoo, MI:
    Medieval Institute Publications for TEAMS, 1995.

Layamon. *Layamon: Brut; Edited from British Museum Ms. Cotton Caligula A. IX and British
    Museum Ms. Cotton Otho C. XIII.* Vol. 1, *Text (Lines 1–8020).* Edited by G. L. Brook
    and R. F. Leslie. EETS, o.s., vol. 250. London: Oxford University Press, 1963.

Ledrede, Richard. *The Latin Poems of Richard Ledrede, O.F.M.: Bishop of Ossory, 1317–
    1360.* Edited by Edmund Colledge. Toronto: Pontifical Institute of Mediaeval Studies,
    1974.

Lichfield [Litchfield], William. *The remors of conscyence.* London: Wynkyn de Worde, ca.
    1510. STC 20881.3.

———. *The remors of conscyence*. [Enprynted at London]: [In Flete-strete at ye sygne of ye Sonne by me Wynkyn de Worde], [1534?]. STC 20882.

Luria, Maxwell S., and Richard L. Hoffman, eds. *Middle English Lyrics: Authoritative Texts, Critical and Historical Backgrounds, Perspectives on Six Poems*. New York: W. W. Norton, 1974.

Lydgate, John. *Lydgate's Fall of Princes*. Edited by Henry Bergen. Vol. 1. EETS, e.s., 121. London: Oxford University Press, 1924.

———. *The Siege of Thebes*. Edited by Robert R. Edwards. Kalamazoo, MI: Medieval Institute Publications for TEAMS, 2001.

Mannyng, Robert. *Chronicle*. Edited by Idelle Sullens. Binghamton, NY: Binghamton University, 1996.

———. *Robert of Brunne's "Handlyng Synne."* Edited by Frederick J. Furnivall. EETS, o.s., vol. 119. London: Kegan Paul, Trench, Trübner, 1901.

Marlowe, Christopher. *Edward the Second*. Edited by W. Moelwyn Merchant. London: A. and C. Black, 1987.

Maxwell, Marcia Lusk. "The Anglo-Norman Prose 'Brut': An Edition of British Library MS Cotton Cleopatra D. III." Ph.D. diss., Michigan State University, 1995.

McCarthy, Pattie. *bk of (h)rs*. Berkeley, CA: Apogee Press, 2002.

McDonough, Christopher J., ed. and trans. *The Arundel Lyrics: The Poems of Hugh Primas*. Cambridge, MA: Harvard University Press, 2010.

Meitner, Erika. *Holy Moly Carry Me*. Rochester, NY: BOA, 2018.

Minhinnick, Robert. *Diary of the Last Man*. Manchester: Carcanet, 2019.

Minot, Laurence. *The Poems of Laurence Minot*. Edited by Joseph Hall. Oxford: Clarendon Press, 1887.

Muir, Bernard J., ed. *The Exeter Anthology of Old English Poetry: An Edition of Exeter Dean and Chapter MS 3501*. 2nd ed. 2 vols. Exeter: University of Exeter Press, 2000.

Murray, Hilda M. R., ed. *The Middle English Poem, Erthe upon Erthe, Printed from Twenty-Four Manuscripts*. EETS, o.s., no. 141. London: Oxford University Press, 1911.

Ng Yi-Sheng. *A Book of Hims*. Singapore: Math Paper, 2017.

Oberman, Miller. *The Unstill Ones: Poems*. Princeton, NJ: Princeton University Press, 2017.

Ovid. *Heroides; Amores*. Translated by Grant Showerman. 2nd ed. Revised by G. P. Goold. Cambridge, MA: Harvard University Press, 1977.

Pearl. Edited by E. V. Gordon. Oxford: Clarendon Press, 1953.

Pearl. Edited by Ad Putter and Myra Stokes. In *The Works of the Gawain Poet: Pearl, Cleanness, Patience, Sir Gawain and the Green Knight*, 3–81. London: Penguin Books, 2014.

Percy, Thomas. *Reliques of Ancient English Poetry: Consisting of Old Heroic Ballads, Songs, and Other Pieces of Our Earlier Poets (Chiefly of the Lyric Kind)*. 3 vols. London: J. Dodsley, 1765.

Pope, Mildred K., ed. *The Romance of Horn by Thomas*. 2 vols. ANTS 9–10, 12–13. Oxford: Published for the Anglo-Norman Text Society by B. Blackwell, 1955, 1964.

The Proverbs of Alfred. Edited by Olaf Arngart. 2 vols. Lund: University of Lund, 1942–55.

Puttenham, George. *The Arte of English Poesie*. London: Richard Field, 1589. STC 20519.5.

———. *The Art of English Poesy: A Critical Edition*. Edited by Frank Whigham and Wayne A. Rebhorn. Ithaca, NY: Cornell University Press, 2007.

Quiller-Couch, Arthur, ed. *The Oxford Book of English Verse, 1250–1900*. Oxford: Clarendon Press, 1908.

Raby, F. J. E., ed. *The Oxford Book of Medieval Latin Verse*. Oxford: Clarendon Press, 1959.

Rankin, Susan, ed. *The Winchester Troper*. London: Stainer & Bell, 2007.

Reginald [of Durham]. *Libellus de vita et miraculis S. Godrici, heremitae de Finchale*. Edited by Joseph Stevenson. London: J. B. Nichols and Son, 1847.

———. *Reginald of Durham: "The Life and Miracles of Saint Godric, Hermit of Finchale."* Edited and translated by Margaret Coombe. Oxford: Oxford University Press, 2022.

———. *Reginald of Durham's Life of St Godric: An Old French Version*. Edited by Margaret Coombe, Tony Hunt, and Anne Mouron. ANTS, O.P., 9. Oxford: Anglo-Norman Text Society, 2019.

Reimer, Steven R., ed. *The Works of William Herebert, OFM*. Toronto: PIMS, 1987.

Renart, Jean. *The Romance of the Rose or of Guillaume de Dole*. Edited and translated by Regina Psaki. New York: Garland, 1995.

Riley, Henry Thomas, ed. and trans. *Memorials of London and London Life, in the XIIIth, XIVth, and XVth Centuries: Being a Series of Extracts, Local, Social, and Political, from the Early Archives of the City of London, A.D. 1276–1419*. London: Longmans, Green, 1868.

Ritson, Joseph. *Ancient Songs, from the Time of King Henry the Third, to the Revolution*. London, 1790.

Robbins, Rossell Hope, ed. *Historical Poems of the XIVth and XVth Centuries*. New York: Columbia University Press, 1959.

———, ed. *Secular Lyrics of the XIVth and XVth Centuries*. 2nd ed. Oxford: Clarendon Press, 1955. First published 1952.

Rolle, Richard. *English Writings of Richard Rolle: Hermit of Hampole*. Edited by Hope Emily Allen. Oxford, Clarendon Press, 1931.

———. *Richard Rolle: The English Writings*. Translated, edited, and introduced by Rosamund Allen. New York: Paulist Press, 1988.

———. *Richard Rolle: Prose and Verse Edited from the MS Longleat 29 and Related Manuscripts*. Edited by S. J. Ogilvie-Thomson. EETS, o.s., 293. Oxford: Oxford University Press, 1988.

Sanders, Ernest H., ed. *English Music of the Thirteenth and Fourteenth Centuries*. Polyphonic Music of the Fourteenth Century 14. Monaco: Éditions de l'Oiseau-Lyre, 1979.

Saupe, Karen, ed. *Middle English Marian Lyrics*. Kalamazoo, MI: Medieval Institute Publications for TEAMS, 1998.

Scase, Wendy, ed. *A Facsimile Edition of the Vernon Manuscript: Oxford, Bodleian Library, MS. Eng. Poet. A. 1*. Oxford: Bodleian Library, 2011.

Scott, Tom. *Seeven poems o Maister Francis Villon, made owre intil scots bi Tom Scott*. Tunbridge Wells, Kent: Pound Press, 1953.

Sidney, Philip, Sir. *An Apologie for poetrie*. London: William Ponsonby, 1595. STC (Short Title Catalogue) 22534.5.

———. "The Defence of Poesy." In *Sidney's "The Defence of Poesy" and Select Renaissance Literary Criticism*, edited by Gavin Alexander, 1–54. New York: Penguin, 2004.

Silverstein, Theodore, ed. *Medieval English Lyrics*. London: Edward Arnold, 1971.

Sir Orfeo. In *The Middle English Breton Lays*, edited by Anne Laskaya and Eve Salisbury, 15–59. Kalamazoo, MI: Medieval Institute Publications for TEAMS, 1995.

Sisam, Celia, and Kenneth Sisam, eds. *The Oxford Book of Medieval English Verse*. Oxford: Clarendon Press, 1970.

Skelton, John. *Poems*. Edited by Robert S. Kinsman. Oxford: Clarendon Press, 1969.

Songes and Sonettes. London: Richard Tottel, 1557. STC 13860.

Szövérffy, Joseph. *Repertorium hymnologicum novum*. Turnhout: Brepols, 1983. www.erwin-rauner.de.

Spenser, Edmund. *The Faerie Queene Disposed into twelue books, Fashioning XII. Morall vertues*. London: Printed for William Ponsonbie, 1590.

The Squire of Low Degree. In *Sentimental and Humorous Romances*, edited by Erik Kooper. Kalamazoo, MI: Medieval Institute Publications for TEAMS, 2005.

Stainer, John, ed. *Sacred & Secular Songs, Together with Other MS. Compositions in the Bodleian Library, Oxford, Ranging from About A.D. 1185 to About A.D. 1505*. Introduction by E. W. B. Nicholson. Transcriptions into modern musical notation by J. F. R. Stainer and C. Stainer. 2 vols. London: Novello, 1901.

Stevens, John, ed. *The Later Cambridge Songs: An English Song Collection of the Twelfth Century*. Oxford: Oxford University Press, 2005.

———. *Mediaeval Carols*. Musica Britannica, vol. 4. London: Stainer & Bell, for the Royal Music Association, 1952; 2nd ed., rev., 1958.

Summers, William J., and Peter M. Lefferts. *English Thirteenth-Century Polyphony: A Facsimile Edition*. Foreword by Magnus Williamson. London: Stainer & Bell for the British Academy, 2016.

Tolhurst, J. B. L., ed. *The Ordinale and Customary of the Benedictine Nuns of Barking Abbey (University College, Oxford, Ms. 169)*. 2 vols. Henry Bradshaw Society, vols. 65–66. London: Henry Bradshaw Society, 1927–28.

Tottel's Miscellany: Songes and Sonnets by Henry Howard, Earl of Surrey, Sir Thomas Wyatt the Elder, Nicholas Grimald, and Uncertain Authors. Edited by Edward Arber. London: Bloomsbury, 1870.

Turville-Petre, Thorlac, ed. *Alliterative Poetry of the Later Middle Ages: An Anthology*. Washington, DC: Catholic University of America Press, 1989.

———. *Poems from BL MS Harley 913: "The Kildare Manuscript."* EETS, o.s., 345. Oxford: Oxford University Press, 2015.

Wace. *Roman de Brut: A History of the British; Text and Translation*. Edited and translated by Judith Weiss. Exeter: Exeter University Press, 1999.

Ward, G. R. M., trans. *Statutes of Magdalen College, Oxford*. Oxford: Henry Alden; London: Jackson and Walford, 1840.

Watson, Nicholas, and Jacqueline Jenkins, eds. *The Writings of Julian of Norwich: "A Vision Showed to a Devout Woman" and "A Revelation of Love."* University Park: Pennsylvania State University Press, 2006.

Wenzel, Siegfried, ed. and trans. *Fasciculus Morum: A Fourteenth-Century Preacher's Handbook*. University Park: Pennsylvania State University Press, 1989.

Wilshere, A. D., ed. *Mirour de seinte eglyse: St. Edmund of Abingdon's "Speculum ecclesiae."* ANTS 40. London: Anglo-Norman Text Society, 1982.

Wogan-Browne, Jocelyn, Nicholas Watson, Andrew Taylor, and Ruth Evans, eds. *The Idea of the Vernacular: An Anthology of Middle English Literary Theory, 1280–1520*. University Park: Pennsylvania State University Press, 1999.

Wright, Thomas, trans. and ed. *The Political Songs of England: From the Reign of John to That of Edward II.* Camden Society, no. 6. London: J. B. Nichols and Son for the Camden Society, 1839.

Young, Karl. *The Drama of the Medieval Church.* 2 vols. London: Oxford University Press, 1933.

SECONDARY SOURCES

Abrams, M. H. *A Glossary of Literary Terms.* New York: Holt, Rinehart and Winston, 1971. First published 1957.

Adorno, Theodor. "Lyric Poetry and Society." Translated by Bruce Mayo. *Telos* 20 (1974): 52–71.

———. "On Lyric Poetry and Society" (1957). In *The Lyric Theory Reader: A Critical Anthology*, edited by Virginia Jackson and Yopie Prins, 339–50. Baltimore: Johns Hopkins University Press, 2014.

Aers, David. "The Humanity of Christ: Reflections on Orthodox Late Medieval Representations." In *The Powers of the Holy: Religion, Politics, and Gender in Late Medieval English Culture*, by David Aers and Lynn Staley, 15–42. University Park: Pennsylvania State University Press, 1996.

Akbari, Suzanne Conklin. *Idols in the East: European Representations of Islam and the Orient, 1100–1450.* Ithaca, NY: Cornell University Press, 2009.

Albin, Andrew. "Listening for *Canor* in Richard Rolle's *Melos amoris.*" In *Voice and Voicelessness in Medieval Europe*, edited by Irit Ruth Kleiman, 177–97. New York: Palgrave Macmillan, 2015.

———. *Richard Rolle's Melody of Love: A Study and Translation with Manuscript and Musical Context.* Toronto: Pontifical Institute of Mediaeval Studies, 2018.

———. "Theorizing Richard Rolle's Sound Art." Forthcoming.

Alexander, Jonathan, and Paul Binski, eds. *Age of Chivalry: Art in Plantagenet England, 1200–1400.* London: Royal Academy of Arts, 1987.

Allen, Hope Emily. *Writings Ascribed to Richard Rolle, Hermit of Hampole.* London: Oxford University Press, 1927.

Allen, J. Romilly. "Inscribed Bronze Flagon of the Fourteenth Century in the South Kensington Museum." *Reliquary and Illustrated Archaeologist*, n.s., 2 (1896): 103–6.

Allen, Judson Boyce. "Grammar, Poetic Form, and the Lyric Ego: A Medieval *A Priori.*" In *Vernacular Poetics in the Middle Ages*, edited by Lois Ebin, 199–226. Kalamazoo, MI: Medieval Institute Publications, 1984.

Althusser, Louis. "Ideology and Ideological State Apparatuses (Notes Towards an Investigation." In Louis Althusser, *Lenin and Philosophy and Other Essays*, 127–86. New York: Monthly Review Press, 1971.

Altieri, Charles. "What Is Living and What Is Dead in American Postmodernism: Establishing the Contemporaneity of Some American Poetry." In *The Lyric Theory Reader: A Critical Anthology*, edited by Virginia Jackson and Yopie Prins, 477–87. Baltimore: Johns Hopkins University Press, 2014.

Appleford, Amy. "The Dance of Death in London: John Carpenter, John Lydgate, and the *Daunce of Poulys.*" *Journal of Medieval and Early Modern Studies* 38, no. 2 (2008): 285–314.

Appleford, Amy, and Nicholas Watson. "Merchant Religion in Fifteenth-Century London: The Writings of William Litchfield." *Chaucer Review* 46, nos.1–2 (2011): 203–22.

Arlt, Wulf. "Sequence and 'Neues Lied.'" In *La sequenza medievale: Atti del Convegno internazionale, Milano, 7–8 aprile 1984*, edited by Agostino Ziino, 3–18. Lucca: Libreria musicale italiana, 1992.

Arner, Lynn. *Chaucer, Gower, and the Vernacular Rising: Poetry and the Problem of the Populace After 1381*. University Park: Pennsylvania State University Press, 2013.

Astell, Ann W. *Eating Beauty: The Eucharist and the Spiritual Arts of the Middle Ages*. Ithaca, NY: Cornell University Press, 2006.

———. "Feminine Figurae in the Writings of Richard Rolle: A Register of Growth." *Mystics Quarterly* 15, no. 3 (1989): 117–24.

———. *The Song of Songs in the Middle Ages*. Ithaca, NY: Cornell University Press, 1990.

Atkinson, Niall. *The Noisy Renaissance: Sound, Architecture, and Florentine Urban Life*. University Park: Pennsylvania State University Press, 2016.

Attridge, Derek. "An Enduring Form: The English Dolnik." In *Moving Words: Forms of English Poetry*, 147–87. Oxford: Oxford University Press, 2013.

———. *The Experience of Poetry*. Oxford: Oxford University Press, 2019.

Austin, J. L. *How to Do Things with Words*. Oxford: Clarendon Press, 1962.

Bailey, Martin. "Two Kings, Their Armies and Some Jugs: The Ashanti Ewer." *Apollo Magazine* 138 (1993): 387–90.

Ball, R. M. "Lichefeld, William." *Oxford Dictionary of National Biography* (online ed.). Oxford University Press. https://doi.org/10.1093/ref:odnb/16638.

Barnet, Peter, and Pete Dandridge, eds. *Lions, Dragons, and Other Beasts: Aquamanilia of the Middle Ages, Vessels for Church and Table*. New Haven, CT: Yale University Press for the Bard Graduate Center, 2006.

Barr, Helen. *Signes and Sothe: Language in the Piers Plowman Tradition*. Cambridge: D. S. Brewer, 1994.

———. *Socioliterary Practice in Late Medieval England*. Oxford: Oxford University Press, 2001.

Barratt, Alexandra. "The Lyrics of St. Godric: A New Manuscript." *Notes and Queries* 230 (1985): 439–45.

Bartlett, Robert. "Medieval and Modern Concepts of Race and Ethnicity." *Journal of Medieval and Early Modern Studies* 31, no. 1 (2001): 39–56.

Base de Français Médiéval (BFM). http://bfm.ens-lyon.fr.

Baugh, Albert. "Improvisation in the Middle English Romance." *Proceedings of the American Philosophical Society* 103, no. 3 (1959): 418–54.

Baum, Paull F. *Anglo-Saxon Riddles of the Exeter Book*. Durham, NC: Duke University Press, 1963.

Bauman, Richard, and Charles L. Briggs. "Poetics and Performance as Critical Perspectives on Language and Social Life." *Annual Review of Anthropology* 19 (1990): 59–88.

Beechy, Tiffany. *The Poetics of Old English*. Farnham, Surrey: Ashgate, 2010.

Bell, Kimberly K. "'Holie Mannes Liues': England and Its Saints in Oxford Bodleian Library, MS Laud Misc. 108." In *The Texts and Contexts of Oxford, Bodleian Library, MS Laud Misc. 108*, edited by Kimberly K. Bell and Julie Nelson Crouch, 251–74. Leiden: Brill, 2011.

Bell, Kimberly K., and Julie Nelson Crouch, eds. *The Texts and Contexts of Oxford, Bodleian Library, MS Laud Misc. 108*. Leiden: Brill, 2011.

Benskin, M., M. Laing, V. Karaiskos, and K. Williamson. *An Electronic Version of "A Linguistic Atlas of Late Mediaeval English."* Edinburgh: University of Edinburgh, 2013–. http://www.lel.ed.ac.uk/ihd/elalme/elalme.html.

Bent, Margaret. "The Absent First Gathering of the Chantilly Manuscript." *Plainsong and Medieval Music* 26, no. 1 (2017): 19–36.

Bergen, Benjamin K. *Louder Than Words: The New Science of How the Mind Makes Meaning.* New York: Basic Books, 2012.

Biller, Peter. *The Measure of Multitude: Population in Medieval Thought.* Oxford: Oxford University Press, 2000.

Birkholz, Daniel. *Harley Manuscript Geographies: Literary History and the Medieval Miscellany.* Manchester: Manchester University Press, 2020.

Black, Max. *Models and Metaphors: Studies in Language and Philosophy.* Ithaca, NY: Cornell University Press, 1962.

Blair, Claude, and John Blair. "Copper Alloys." With a technical appendix by Roger Brownsword. In *English Medieval Industries,* edited by John Blair and Nigel Ramsay, 81–106. London: Hambledon Press, 2001.

Blair, Claude, John Blair, and R. Brownsword. "An Oxford Brasiers' Dispute of the 1390s: Evidence for Brass-Making in Medieval England." *Antiquaries Journal* 66 (1986): 82–90.

Blurton, Heather. "Godric of Finchale's 'Jerusalem Song' in Bibliothèque Mazarine MS 1716." *Notes and Queries* 66, no. 2 (2019): 183–92.

———. "The Songs of Godric of Finchale: Vernacular Liturgy and Literary History." *New Medieval Literatures* 18 (2018): 75–104.

Boffey, Julia. *Manuscripts of English Courtly Love Lyrics in the Later Middle Ages.* Cambridge: D. S. Brewer, 1985.

———. "Middle English Lyrics and Manuscripts." In *A Companion to the Middle English Lyric,* ed. Thomas G. Duncan, 1–18. Cambridge: D. S. Brewer, 2005.

———. "What to Call a Lyric? Middle English Lyrics and Their Manuscript Titles." *Revue belge de philologie et d'histoire* 83, no. 3 (2005): 671–83.

Boffey, Julia, and A. S. G. Edwards. "Middle English Verse in Chronicles." In *New Perspectives on Middle English Texts: A Festschrift for R. A. Waldron,* edited by Susan Powell and Jeremy J. Smith, 119–28. Cambridge: D. S. Brewer, 2000.

———, eds. *A New Index of Middle English Verse.* London: British Library, 2005.

Boffey, Julia, and Christiania Whitehead, eds. *Middle English Lyrics: New Readings of Short Poems.* Cambridge: D. S. Brewer, 2018.

Boklund-Lagopoulou, Karin. "Popular Song and the Middle English Lyric." In *Medieval Oral Literature,* edited by Karl Reichl, 555–80. Berlin: De Gruyter, 2012.

Booth, Wayne C. *The Rhetoric of Fiction.* 2nd ed. Chicago: University of Chicago Press, 1983.

Boulton, Maureen Barry McCann. *The Song in the Story: Lyric Insertions in French Narrative Fiction, 1200–1400.* Philadelphia: University of Pennsylvania Press, 1993.

Boynton, Susan, and Margot Fassler. "The Language, Form, and Performance of Monophonic Liturgical Chants." In *The Oxford Handbook of Medieval Latin Literature,* edited by Ralph J. Hexter and David Townsend, 686–730. New York: Oxford University Press, 2012.

Boynton, Susan, Sarah Kay, Alison Cornish, and Andrew Albin. "Sound Matters." *Speculum* 91, no. 4 (2016): 998–1039.

Bradbury, Nancy Mason. "The Proverb as Embedded Microgenre in Chaucer and *The Dialogue of Solomon and Marcolf.*" *Exemplaria* 27 (2015): 55–72.

————. *Writing Aloud: Storytelling in Late Medieval England*. Urbana: University of Illinois Press, 1998.

Bradley, Ritamary. "Mysticism in the Motherhood Similitude of Julian of Norwich." *Studia Mystica* 8, no. 2 (1985): 4–14.

Brantley, Jessica. *Reading in the Wilderness: Private Devotion and Public Performance in Late Medieval England*. Chicago: University of Chicago Press, 2007.

Bredehoft, Thomas. "First-Person Inscriptions and Literacy." *Anglo-Saxon Studies in Archaeology and History* 9 (1996): 103–10.

————. "Multiliteralism in Anglo-Saxon Verse Inscriptions." In *Conceptualizing Multilingualism in England, c. 800–c. 1250*, edited by Elizabeth Tyler, 15–32. Turnhout: Brepols, 2011.

British Museum. "The Asante Jug." https://research.britishmuseum.org/research/collection_online/collection_object_details.aspx?objectId=43862&partId=1.

Brockett, Clyde. "A Previously Unknown Ordo Prophetarum in a Manuscript Fragment in Zagreb." *Comparative Drama* 27 (1993): 114–27.

Brook, G. L. *Books and Book-Collecting*. London: Andre Deutsch, 1980.

Brooks, Cleanth. *The Well Wrought Urn: Studies in the Structure of Poetry*. New York: Harcourt, Brace, 1975. First published 1947 by Reynal and Hitchcock (New York).

Brown, Bill. *The Sense of Things: The Object Matter of American Literature*. Chicago: University of Chicago Press, 2004.

Brown, Carleton, ed. *A Register of Middle English Religious and Didactic Verse*. 2 vols. Oxford: Oxford University Press, 1916–20.

Brown, Carleton, and Rossell Hope Robbins, eds. *The Index of Middle English Verse [IMEV]*. New York: Columbia University Press, 1943.

Brown, Howard Mayer. "Chansonnier (i)." *Grove Music Online*. 2001. https://doi.org/10.1093/gmo/9781561592630.article.05412.

Brownsword, Roger. "Medieval Metalwork: An Analytical Study of Copper-Alloy Objects." *Historical Metallurgy* 38, no. 2 (2004): 84–105.

Brownsword, Roger, and Ernest Pitt. "British Late-Medieval Inscribed Bronze Jugs: A Technical Study." *Journal of the Antique Metalware Society* 4 (1996): 11–13.

Bryan, Jennifer. *Looking Inward: Devotional Reading and the Private Self in Late Medieval England*. Philadelphia: University of Pennsylvania Press, 2007.

Bukofzer, Manfred F., and Richard L. Greene. Review of *Mediaeval Carols*, edited by John Stevens. *Journal of the American Musicological Society* 7, no. 1 (1954): 63–82.

Burgwinkle, William. "The Chansonniers as Books." In *The Troubadours: An Introduction*, edited by Simon Gaunt and Sarah Kay, 246–62. Cambridge: Cambridge University Press, 1999.

Burnley, David. "Lexis and Semantics." In *The Cambridge History of the English Language*, vol. 2, *1066–1476*, edited by Norman Blake, 409–99. Cambridge: Cambridge University Press, 1992.

Burrow, Colin. "Horace at Home and Abroad: Wyatt and Sixteenth-Century Horatianism." In *Horace Made New: Horatian Influences on British Writing from the Renaissance to the Twentieth Century*, edited by Charles Martindale and David Hopkins, 27–49. Cambridge: Cambridge University Press, 1993.

Burrow, John. "Gower's *Confessio Amantis* and Chaucer's *Canterbury Tales* as Dits." In *Readings in Medieval Textuality: Essays in Honour of A. C. Spearing*, edited by Cristina Maria Cervone and D. Vance Smith, 157–68. Cambridge: D. S. Brewer, 2016.

———. "The Languages of Medieval England." In *The Oxford History of Literary Translation in English*, vol. 1, *To 1550*, edited by Roger Ellis, 7–28. Oxford: Oxford University Press, 2008.

———. "Poems Without Contexts." *Essays in Criticism* 29, no. 1 (1979): 6–32. Reprinted in *Essays on Medieval Literature*, 1–26. Oxford: Oxford University Press, 1984.

Bursill-Hall, G. L. *A Census of Medieval Latin Grammatical Manuscripts*. Grammatica speculativa 4. Stuttgart: Frommann-Holzboog, 1981.

Burt, Stephanie [Stephen]. *The Poem Is You: 60 Contemporary American Poems and How to Read Them*. Cambridge, MA: Harvard University Press, 2016.

———. "What Is This Thing Called Lyric?" *Modern Philology* 113, no. 3 (2016): 422–40.

Butterfield, Ardis. "Afterwords: Forms of Death." *Exemplaria* 27, nos. 1–2 (2015): 167–82.

———. "The Construction of Textual Form: Cross-Lingual Citation in the Medieval Insular Lyric." In *Citation, Intertextuality and Memory in the Middle Ages and Renaissance*, vol. 1, *Text, Music and Image from Machaut to Ariosto*, edited by Yolanda Plumley, Giuliano Di Bacco, and Stefano Jossa, 41–57. Exeter: University of Exeter Press, 2011.

———. *The Familiar Enemy: Chaucer, Language, and Nation in the Hundred Years War*. Oxford: Oxford University Press, 2009.

———. "Fuzziness and Perceptions of Language in the Middle Ages." Part 3, "Translating Fuzziness: Countertexts." *Common Knowledge* 19, no. 3 (2013): 446–73.

———. *Medieval Songlines*. Forthcoming.

———. "Poems without Form? *Maiden in the mor lay* Revisited." In *Readings in Medieval Textuality: Essays in Honour of A. C. Spearing*, edited by Cristina Maria Cervone and D. Vance Smith, 169–94. Cambridge: D. S. Brewer, 2016.

———. *Poetry and Music in Medieval France: From Jean Renart to Guillaume de Machaut*. Cambridge: Cambridge University Press, 2002.

———. "Repetition and Variation in the Thirteenth-Century Refrain." *Journal of the Royal Musical Association* 116, no. 1 (1991): 1–23.

———. "Why Medieval Lyric?" *English Literary History* 82, no. 2 (2015): 319–43.

Butterfield, Ardis, and Helen Deeming. "Editing Insular Song Across the Disciplines: Worldes Blis." In *Probable Truth: Editing Medieval Texts from Britain in the Twenty-First Century*, edited by Vincent Gillespie and Anne Hudson, 151–66. Turnhout: Brepols, 2013.

Butterfield, Ardis, and Elizabeth Hebbard. "Troubadours and Trouvères." *Oxford Bibliographies in Music Online*. Medieval Studies. Oxford University Press, 2021. https://www .oxfordbibliographies.com/view/document/obo-9780199757824/obo-9780199757824 -0288.xml.

Bychkov, Oleg. "The Place of Aesthetics and the Arts in Medieval Franciscan Theology." In *Beyond the Text: Franciscan Art and the Construction of Religion*, edited by Xavier Seubert and Oleg Bychkov, 196–209. St. Bonaventure, NY: Franciscan Institute Publications, 2012.

Bynum, Caroline Walker. *Jesus as Mother: Studies in the Spirituality of the High Middle Ages*. Berkeley: University of California Press, 1982.

———. *Metamorphosis and Identity*. New York: Zone Books, 2001.

———. "Wonder." *American Historical Review* 102, no. 1 (1997): 1–26.

Cable, Thomas. *The English Alliterative Tradition*. Philadelphia: University of Pennsylvania Press, 1991.

———. "English Prosody." *Oxford Bibliographies*. Medieval Studies. Oxford University Press, 2010. http://dx.doi.org/10.1093/OBO/9780195396584-0035.

———. "Foreign Influence, Native Continuation, and Metrical Typology in Alliterative Lyrics." In *Approaches to the Metres of Alliterative Verse*, edited by Judith Jefferson and Ad
Putter, 219–34. Leeds: Leeds Studies in English, 2009.

———. "Philology: Analysis of Written Records." In *Research Guide on Language Change*,
edited by Edgar C. Polomé, 97–106. Berlin: Mouton de Gruyter, 1990.

———. "Progress in Middle English Alliterative Metrics." *Yearbook of Langland Studies* 23
(2009): 243–64.

Caldwell, John. "Relations Between Liturgical and Vernacular Music in Medieval England."
In *Music in Medieval English Liturgy*, edited by Susan Rankin and David Hiley, 285–93.
Oxford: Clarendon Press, 1993.

Cameron, Sharon. *Lyric Time: Dickinson and the Limits of Genre.* Baltimore: Johns Hopkins
University Press, 1979.

Camp, Stephanie M. H. "Black Is Beautiful: An American History." *Journal of Southern History* 81, no. 3 (2015): 675–90.

Campbell, Bruce M. S. *The Great Transition: Climate, Disease and Society in the Late-
Medieval World.* Cambridge: Cambridge University Press, 2016.

Campbell, Marian. "An English Medieval Jug." In *Tributes to Nigel Morgan: Contexts of Medieval Art; Images, Objects and Ideas*, edited by Julian M. Luxford and M. A. Michael,
187–96. London: Harvey Miller, 2010.

Cannon, Christopher. *From Literacy to Literature: England, 1300–1400.* Oxford: Oxford University Press, 2016.

———. "Proverbs and the Wisdom of Literature: *The Proverbs of Alfred* and Chaucer's *Tale of
Melibee*." *Textual Practice* 24, no. 3 (2010): 407–34.

Carlson, David. "The Invention of the Anglo-Latin Public Poetry (circa 1367–1402) and Its
Prosody, Especially in John Gower." *Mittellateinisches Jahrbuch* 39 (2004): 389–406.

———. "Manuscripts After Printing: Affinity, Dissent, and Display in the Texts of Wyatt's
Psalms." In *Prestige, Authority and Power in Late-Medieval Manuscripts and Texts*, edited
by Felicity Riddy, 171–88. York: York Medieval Press, 2000.

Carpenter, Frederic Ives, ed. *English Lyric Poetry, 1500–1700.* London: Blackie and Son; New
York: Charles Scribner's Sons, 1897.

———. *An Outline Guide to the Study of English Lyric Poetry.* Chicago: University of Chicago,
1897.

Carruthers, Mary J. *The Experience of Beauty in the Middle Ages.* Oxford: Oxford University
Press, 2013.

Carsley, Catherine A. "Devotion to the Holy Name: Late Medieval Piety in England." *Princeton University Library Chronicle* 53 (1992): 156–72.

Census-Catalogue of Manuscript Sources of Polyphonic Music, 1400–1550. 5 vols. [Rome]:
American Institute of Musicology; Neuhausen-Stuttgart: Hänssler Verlag, 1979–88.

Cerquiglini, Jacqueline. "Pour une typologie de l'insertion." *Perspectives médiévales* 3 (1977):
9–14.

Cervone, Cristina Maria. "'I' and 'We' in Chaucer's *Complaint unto Pity*." In *Readings in Medieval Textuality: Essays in Honour of A. C. Spearing*, edited by Cristina Maria Cervone
and D. Vance Smith, 195–212. Cambridge: D. S. Brewer, 2016.

———. "John de Cobham and Cooling Castle's Charter Poem." *Speculum* 83, no. 4 (2008):
884–916.

———. *Poetics of the Incarnation: Middle English Writing and the Leap of Love.* Philadelphia:
University of Pennsylvania Press, 2013.

Cervone, Cristina Maria, and D. Vance Smith, eds. *Readings in Medieval Textuality: Essays in Honour of A. C. Spearing.* Cambridge: D. S. Brewer, 2016.

Chaganti, Seeta. "Choreographing Mouvance: The Case of the English Carol." *Philological Quarterly* 87, nos. 1–2 (2008): 77–103.

———. "Dance in a Haunted Space: Genre, Form, and the Middle English Carol." *Exemplaria* 27, nos. 1–2 (2015): 129–49.

———. "*Danse macabre* and the Virtual Churchyard." *postmedieval* 3 (2012): 7–26.

———. *Strange Footing: Poetic Form and Dance in the Late Middle Ages.* Chicago: University of Chicago Press, 2018.

———. "Vestigial Signs: Inscription, Performance and *The Dream of the Rood.*" *PMLA* 125, no. 1 (2010): 48–72.

Cherry, John. "A Medieval Bronze Laver." *British Museum Yearbook* 2 (1977): 199–201.

Cherry, John, and Neil Stratford. "The Ashanti Ewers." In *Westminster Kings and the Medieval Palace of Westminster*, 98–100. British Museum Occasional Paper 115. London: British Museum, 1995.

Cienki, Alan. "Metaphoric Gestures and Some of Their Relations to Verbal Metaphoric Expressions." In *Discourse and Cognition: Bridging the Gap*, edited by Jean-Pierre Koenig, 189–204. Stanford, CA: CSLI Publications, 1998.

Cienki, Alan, and Cornelia Müller, eds. *Metaphor and Gesture.* Amsterdam: John Benjamins, 2006.

Clanchy, Michael. *From Memory to Written Record: England, 1066–1307.* 2nd ed. Oxford: Blackwell, 1993.

Clark, Cecily. "As Seint Austin Seith . . ." *Medium Aevum* 46, no. 2 (1977): 212–18.

Cohen, Jeffrey Jerome. "On Saracen Enjoyment: Some Fantasies of Race in Late Medieval France and England." *Journal of Medieval and Early Modern Studies* 31, no. 1 (2001): 113–46.

———. "Race." In *A Handbook of Middle English Studies*, edited by Marion Turner, 109–22. Chichester: Wiley Blackwell, 2013.

Coleman, Joyce. *Public Reading and the Reading Public in Late Medieval England and France.* Cambridge: Cambridge University Press, 1996.

Colton, Lisa. *Angel Song: Medieval English Music in History.* London: Routledge, 2017.

Cook, Megan L. *The Poet and the Antiquaries: Chaucerian Scholarship and the Rise of Literary History, 1532–1635.* Philadelphia: University of Pennsylvania Press, 2019.

Coombe, Margaret. "What a Performance: The Songs of St Godric of Finchale." In *Saints of North-East England, 600–1500*, edited by Margaret Coombe, Anne Mouron, and Christiania Whitehead, 219–42. Turnhout: Brepols, 2017.

Cooper, Lisa H. "The Poetics of Practicality." In *Middle English*, edited by Paul Strohm, 491–505. Oxford Twenty-First Century Approaches to Literature. Oxford: Oxford University Press, 2007.

Copeland, Rita. *Rhetoric, Hermeneutics, and Translation in the Middle Ages: Academic Traditions and Vernacular Texts.* London: Cambridge University Press, 1991.

Cornelius, Ian. *Reconstructing Alliterative Verse: The Pursuit of a Medieval Meter.* Cambridge: Cambridge University Press, 2017.

———. "The Text of the *ABC of Aristotle* in the 'Winchester Anthology.'" *Anglia* 139, no. 2 (2021): 400–418.

Crocker, Richard L. *The Early Medieval Sequence.* Berkeley: University of California Press, 1977.

Crosby, Ruth. "Oral Delivery in the Middle Ages." *Speculum* 11, no. 1 (1936): 88–110.

Crossley, Nick. *Intersubjectivity: The Fabric of Social Becoming.* London: SAGE, 1996.

———. "Mead, Merleau-Ponty and Embodied Communication." *Journal of Pragmatics* 58 (2013): 46–48.

Culler, Jonathan. "Apostrophe." *Diacritics* 7, no. 4 (1977): 59–69. Reprinted (with revisions) in *The Pursuit of Signs: Semiotics, Literature, Deconstruction*, 135–54. Ithaca, NY: Cornell University Press, 1981.

———. *Theory of the Lyric.* Cambridge, MA: Harvard University Press, 2015.

———. "Why Lyric?" *PMLA* 123, no. 1 (2008): 201–6.

Dailey, Patricia. "Riddles, Wonder, and Responsiveness in Anglo-Saxon Literature." In *The Cambridge History of Early Medieval English Literature*, edited by Clare A. Lees, 451–72. Cambridge: Cambridge University Press, 2013.

Davis, Matthew Evan. "Lydgate at Long Melford: Reassessing the *Testament* and 'Quis Dabit Meo Capiti Fontem Lacrimarum' in Their Local Context." *Journal of Medieval Religious Cultures* 43, no. 1 (2017): 77–114.

Dean, Ruth J. *Anglo-Norman Literature: A Guide to Texts and Manuscripts.* With the collaboration of Maureen B. M. Boulton. ANTS, O.P., 3. London: Anglo-Norman Text Society, 1999.

Deeming, Helen. "Multilingual Networks in Twelfth- and Thirteenth-Century Song." In *Language in Medieval Britain: Networks and Exchanges*, edited by Mary Carruthers, 127–43. Donnington, Lincolnshire: Shaun Tyas, 2015.

———. "Music and Contemplation in the Twelfth-Century *Dulcis Jesu memoria*." *Journal of the Royal Musical Association* 139, no. 1 (2014): 1–39.

———. "Music, Memory and Mobility: Citation and Contrafactum in Thirteenth-Century Sequence Repertories." In *Citation, Intertextuality and Memory in the Middle Ages and Renaissance*, vol. 2, *Cross-Disciplinary Perspectives on Medieval Culture*, edited by Giuliano Di Bacco and Yolanda Plumley, 67–81. Liverpool: Liverpool University Press, 2013.

———. "Observations on the Habits of Twelfth- and Thirteenth-Century Music Scribes." *Scriptorium* 60 (2006): 38–59.

———. Review of *English Thirteenth-Century Polyphony: A Facsimile Edition*, by William J. Summers and Peter M. Lefferts. *Plainsong and Medieval Music* 27, no. 1 (2018): 90–97.

———. "The Song and the Page: Experiments with Form and Layout in Manuscripts of Medieval Latin Song." *Plainsong and Medieval Music* 15, no. 1 (2006): 1–27.

———. "The Songs of St. Godric: A Neglected Context." *Music and Letters* 86, no. 2 (2005): 169–85.

de Haas, F. A. J., Mariska Leunissen, and Marije Martijn, eds. *Interpreting Aristotle's "Posterior Analytics" in Late Antiquity and Beyond.* Leiden: Brill, 2011.

Deleuze, Gilles, and Félix Guattari. *A Thousand Plateaus: Capitalism and Schizophrenia.* Translated by Brian Massumi. London: Continuum, 1987.

de Man, Paul. "Lyrical Voice in Contemporary Theory." In *Lyric Poetry: Beyond New Criticism*, edited by Chaviva Hošek and Patricia Parker, 55–72. Ithaca, NY: Cornell University Press, 1985.

Derrida, Jacques. *Voice and Phenomenon: Introduction to the Problem of the Sign in Husserl's Phenomenology.* Translated by Leonard Lawlor. Evanston, IL: Northwestern University Press, 2011.

de Weever, Jacqueline. *Sheba's Daughters: Whitening and Demonizing the Saracen Woman in Medieval French Epic.* New York: Garland, 1998.

Díaz Vera, Javier E. "When Pain Is Not a Place: Pain and Its Metaphors in Late Middle English Medical Texts." *Onomazein* 26, no. 2 (2012): 279–308.

Dictionnaire du Moyen Français (1330–1500). ATILF–CNRS and Université de Lorraine, 2015. http://www.atilf.fr/dmf.

Diehl, Patrick S. *The Medieval European Religious Lyric: An Ars Poetica*. Berkeley: University of California Press, 1985.

Digital Archive of Medieval Song (DAMS). https://web.library.yale.edu/dhlab/medievalsong.

Digital Index of Middle English Verse (*DIMEV*). Published online as *The DIMEV: An Open-Access, Digital Edition of the Index of Middle English Verse*. Compiled, edited, and supplemented by Linne R. Mooney, Daniel W. Mosser, and Elizabeth Solopova, with Deborah Thorpe, David Hill Radcliffe, and Len Hatfield. http://www.dimev.net. Based on the *Index of Middle English Verse* (1943) and its *Supplement* (1965).

Dillon, Emma. *The Sense of Sound: Musical Meaning in France, 1260–1330*. Oxford: Oxford University Press, 2012.

Dinshaw, Carolyn. *How Soon Is Now? Medieval Texts, Amateur Readers, and the Queerness of Time*. Durham, NC: Duke University Press, 2012.

———. "Pale Faces: Race, Religion, and Affect in Chaucer's Texts and Their Readers." *Studies in the Age of Chaucer* 23 (2001): 19–41.

Djikic, Maja, and Keith Oatley. "The Art in Fiction: From Indirect Communication to Changes of the Self." *Psychology of Aesthetics, Creativity, and the Arts* 8, no. 4 (2014): 498–505.

Dobson, E. J. "The Hymn to the Virgin." *Transactions of the Honourable Society of Cymmrodorion* (1954): 70–124.

Donaldson, E. Talbot. "Chaucer's Final -*e*." *PMLA* 63, no. 4 (1948): 1101–24.

Donoghue, Daniel. *How the Anglo-Saxons Read Their Poems*. Philadelphia: University of Pennsylvania Press, 2018.

Dresvina, Juliana, and Victoria Blud, eds. *Cognitive Science and Medieval Studies: An Introduction*. Cardiff: University of Wales Press, 2020.

Dronke, Peter. *Medieval Latin and the Rise of European Love-Lyric*. 2 vols. Oxford: Clarendon Press, 1965–66; 2nd ed., 1968.

———. *The Medieval Lyric*. London: Hutchinson, 1968. 3rd ed., Cambridge: D. S. Brewer, 1996.

Duffell, Martin J. *A New History of English Metre*. London: Legenda, 2008.

Duggan, Hoyt N. "The End of the Line." In *Medieval Alliterative Poetry: Essays in Honour of Thorlac Turville-Petre*, edited by John A. Burrow and Hoyt N. Duggan, 67–79. Dublin: Four Courts Press, 2010.

———. "Libertine Scribes and Maidenly Editors: Meditations on Textual Criticism and Metrics." In *English Historical Metrics*, edited by C. B. McCully and J. J. Anderson, 219–37. Cambridge: Cambridge University Press, 1996.

Duncan, Thomas G., ed. *A Companion to the Middle English Lyric*. Cambridge: D. S. Brewer, 2005.

———. "Middle English Lyrics: Metre and Editorial Practice." In *A Companion to the Middle English Lyric*, edited by Thomas G. Duncan, 19–38. Cambridge: D. S. Brewer, 2005.

Dungworth, David, and Matthew Nicholas. "Caldarium? An Antimony Bronze Used for Medieval and Post-Medieval Cast Domestic Vessels." *Historical Metallurgy* 38, no. 1 (2004): 24–34.

Dunn, Charles. "Romances Derived from English Legends." In *A Manual of the Writings in Middle English, 1050–1500*, vol. 1, edited by J. Burke Severs, 17–37. New Haven: Connecticut Academy of Arts and Sciences, 1967.

Duplessis, Robert S. *Transitions to Capitalism in Early Modern Europe*. Cambridge: Cambridge University Press, 1997.

Dyer, Christopher. *An Age of Transition? Economy and Society in England in the Later Middle Ages*. Oxford: Oxford University Press, 2005.

Earp, Lawrence Marshburn, ed. *Guillaume de Machaut: A Guide to Research*. New York: Garland, 1995.

Eberle, Patricia. "The Politics of Courtly Style at the Court of Richard II." In *The Spirit of the Court: Selected Proceedings of the Fourth Congress of the International Courtly Literature Society (Toronto 1983)*, edited by Glyn S. Burgess and Robert A. Taylor, 168–78. Cambridge: D. S. Brewer, 1985.

Eco, Umberto. *Semiotics and the Philosophy of Language*. Bloomington: Indiana University Press, 1984.

Eden, Bradford Lee. "The Thirteenth-Century Sequence Repertory of the Sarum Use." Ph.D. diss., University of Kansas, 1991.

Edmondson, George. "Naked Chaucer." In *The Post-Historical Middle Ages*, edited by Elizabeth Scala and Sylvia Federico, 139–60. New York: Palgrave Macmillan, 2009.

Edwards, Anthony S. G. "Middle English Inscriptional Verse Texts." In *Texts and Their Contexts: Papers from the Early Book Society*, edited by John Scattergood and Julia Boffey, 26–43. Dublin: Four Courts Press, 1997.

Eisenstein, Elizabeth L. *The Printing Press as an Agent of Change: Communications and Cultural Transformations in Early-Modern Europe*. 2 vols. in 1. Cambridge: Cambridge University Press, 1979. Reprinted, 1985.

Ekserdjian, David, ed. *Bronze*. London: Royal Academy of the Arts, 2012.

Emden, A. B. *A Biographical Register of the University of Oxford to A.D. 1500*. Vol. 2. Oxford: Clarendon Press, 1958.

Empson, William. *Seven Types of Ambiguity*. London: Chatto and Windus, 1930.

Evitt, Regula Meyer. "Anti-Judaism and the Medieval Prophet Plays: Exegetical Contexts for the 'Ordines Prophetarum.'" Ph.D. diss., University of Virginia, 1992.

Ewert, Alfred. *The French Language*. New York: Macmillan, 1941.

Falcon, Andrea. "Aristotle on Causality." *Stanford Encyclopedia of Philosophy*. 2006, rev. 2019. https://plato.stanford.edu/entries/aristotle-causality/.

Fallows, David. *Henry V and the Earliest English Carols: 1413–1440*. London: Routledge, 2018.

Fassler, Margot. *Gothic Song: Victorine Sequences and Augustinian Reform in Twelfth-Century Paris*. Notre Dame, IN: University of Notre Dame Press, 2011.

———. "Shaping the Historical Dunstan: Many Lives and a Musical Office. In *Medieval Cantors and Their Craft: Music, Liturgy and the Shaping of History, 800–1500*, edited by Katie Bugyis, A. B. Kraebel, and Margot Fassler, 125–50. York: York Medieval Press, 2017.

———. "Women and Their Sequences: An Overview and a Case Study." *Speculum* 94, no. 3 (2019): 625–73.

Fay, Elizabeth. *Romantic Medievalism: History and the Romantic Literary Ideal*. New York: Palgrave, 2002.

Fearn, David. "Greek Lyric of the Archaic and Classical Periods: From the Past to the Future of the Lyric Subject." *Classical Poetry* 1 (2020): 1–113.

Fein, Susanna, ed. *The Auchinleck Manuscript: New Perspectives.* York: York Medieval Press, 2016.

———. "BL MS Harley 2253: The Lyrics, the Facsimile, the Book." In *Studies in the Harley Manuscript: The Scribes, Contents, and Social Contexts of British Library MS Harley 2253,* edited by Susanna Fein, 1–19. Kalamazoo, MI: Medieval Institute Publications, 2000.

———, ed. *Interpreting MS Digby 86: A Trilingual Book from Thirteenth-Century Worcestershire.* York: York Medieval Press, 2019.

———. "The Lyrics of MS Harley 2253." In *A Manual of the Writings in Middle English, 1050–1500,* vol. 11, edited by Peter G. Beidler, 4168–4206 and 4317–61. New Haven: Connecticut Academy of Arts and Sciences, 2005.

———, ed. *My Wyl and My Wrytyng: Essays on John the Blind Audelay.* Kalamazoo, MI: Medieval Institute Publications for TEAMS, 2009.

———, ed. *Robert Thornton and His Books: Essays on the Lincoln and London Thornton Manuscripts.* York: York Medieval Press, 2014.

———, ed. *Studies in the Harley Manuscript: The Scribes, Contents, and Social Contexts of British Library MS Harley 2253.* Kalamazoo, MI: Medieval Institute Publications, 2000.

———. "A Thirteen-Line Alliterative Stanza on the Abuse of Prayer from the Audelay MS." *Medium Aevum* 63, no. 1 (1994): 61–74.

———. "Twelve-Line Stanza Forms in Middle English and the Date of *Pearl.*" *Speculum* 72, no. 2 (1997): 367–98.

Fenster, Thelma, and Carolyn P. Collette, eds. *The French of Medieval England: Essays in Honour of Jocelyn Wogan-Browne.* Cambridge: D. S. Brewer, 2014.

Ferguson, Frances. "Our I. A. Richards Moment: The Machine and Its Adjustments." In *Theory Aside,* edited by Jason Potts and Daniel Stout, 261–79. Durham, NC: Duke University Press, 2014.

Ferry, Anne. *The Title to the Poem.* Stanford, CA: Stanford University Press, 1996.

Finlay, Michael. "British Late Medieval Inscribed Bronze Jugs: A Stylistic Study." *Journal of the Antique Metalware Society* 4 (1996): 1–10.

Fleming, Juliet. "Pots." In *Graffiti and the Writing Arts of Early Modern England,* 113–64. Philadelphia: University of Pennsylvania Press, 2001.

Fletcher, Alan J. "The Lyric in the Sermon." In *A Companion to the Middle English Lyric,* edited by Thomas G. Duncan, 189–209. Cambridge: D. S. Brewer, 2005.

———. "Written Versus Spoken Macaronic Discourse in Late Medieval England: The View from a Pulpit." In *Multilingualism in Medieval Britain (c. 1066–1520): Sources and Analysis,* edited by Judith A. Jefferson and Ad Putter, 137–51. Turnhout: Brepols, 2013.

Fletcher, Christopher. "Langue et nation en Angleterre à la fin du moyen âge." *Revue Française d'Histoire des Idées Politiques* 36, no. 2 (2012): 233–52.

———. *Richard II: Manhood, Youth, and Politics, 1377–99.* Oxford: Oxford University Press, 2008.

Floyd, Jennifer. "St. George and the 'Steyned Halle': Lydgate's Verse for the London Armourers." In *Lydgate Matters: Poetry and Material Culture in the Fifteenth Century,* edited by Lisa Cooper and Andrea Denny-Brown, 139–64. New York: Palgrave Macmillan, 2008.

———. "Writing on the Wall: John Lydgate's Architectural Verse." Ph.D. diss., Stanford University, 2008.

Forceville, Charles J., and Eduardo Urios-Aparisi, eds. *Multimodal Metaphor*. Berlin: Mouton de Gruyter, 2009.

Fowler, Elizabeth. "The Proximity of the Virtual: A. C. Spearing's Experientiality (or, Roaming with Palamon and Arcite)." In *Readings in Medieval Textuality: Essays in Honour of A. C. Spearing*, edited by Cristina Maria Cervone and D. Vance Smith, 15–30. Cambridge: D. S. Brewer, 2016.

Fradenburg, L. O. Aranye. *Sacrifice Your Love: Psychoanalysis, Historicism, Chaucer*. Minneapolis: University of Minnesota Press, 2002.

Frank, Robert Worth, Jr. "*Meditationes Vitae Christi*: The Logistics of Access to Divinity." In *Hermeneutics and Medieval Culture*, edited by Patrick Gallacher and Helen Damico, 39–50. Albany: State University of New York Press, 1989.

Frankis, John. "The Social Context of Vernacular Writing in Thirteenth-Century England: The Evidence of the Manuscripts." In *Thirteenth Century England I: Proceedings of the Newcastle upon Tyne Conference, 1985*, edited by Peter R. Coss and S. D. Lloyd, 175–84. Woodbridge, Suffolk: Boydell Press, 1986.

Fry, Paul H. "I. A. Richards." In *The Cambridge History of Literary Criticism*, edited by A. Walton Litz, Louis Menand, and Lawrence Rainey, 179–99. Cambridge: Cambridge University Press, 2000.

Frye, Northrop. *Anatomy of Criticism: Four Essays*. Princeton, NJ: Princeton University Press, 1957.

Fulk, R. D. *An Introduction to Middle English: Grammar; Texts*. Peterborough, Ontario: Broadview Press, 2012.

Furnivall, Frederick J. *Early English Meals and Manners*. London: N. Trübner, 1868.

Galantucci, Bruno, Carol A. Fowler, and M. T. Turvey. "The Motor Theory of Speech Perception Reviewed." *Psychonomic Bulletin & Review* 13, no. 3 (2006): 361–77.

Galloway, Andrew. "The Borderlands of Satire: Linked, Opposed, and Exchanged Political Poetry During the Scottish and English Wars of the Early Fourteenth Century." In *The Anglo-Scottish Border and the Shaping of Identity, 1300–1600*, edited by Mark Bruce and Katherine Terrell, 15–31. New York: Palgrave, 2012.

———. "Gower in His Most Learned Role and the Peasants' Revolt of 1381." *Mediaevalia* 16 (1993 for 1990): 329–47.

———. "Gower's Ovids." In *The Oxford History of Classical Reception in English Literature, Volume 1, 800–1558*, edited by Rita Copeland, 435–64. Oxford: Oxford University Press, 2016.

———. "The Rhetoric of Riddling in Late-Medieval England: The 'Oxford' Riddles, the *Secretum philosophorum*, and the Riddles in *Piers Plowman*." *Speculum* 70, no. 1 (1995): 68–105.

Galvez, Marisa. *Songbook: How Lyrics Became Poetry in Medieval Europe*. Chicago: University of Chicago Press, 2012.

Garner, Lori Ann. "Contexts of Interpretation in the Burdens of Middle English Carols." *Neophilologus* 84, no. 3 (2000): 467–83.

Gasparov, M. L. *A History of European Versification*. Edited by G. S. Smith and Leofranc Holford-Strevens. Translated by G. S. Smith and Marina Tarlinskaja. Oxford: Clarendon Press, 1996.

Gaunt, Simon, and Sarah Kay. *The Troubadours: An Introduction*. Cambridge: Cambridge University Press, 1999.

Gayk, Shannon. Review of *Reading in the Wilderness*, by Jessica Brantley. *Medieval Review* 9, no. 1 (2015).

Gellrich, Jesse. *Discourse and Dominion in the Fourteenth Century: Oral Contexts of Writing in Philosophy, Politics, and Poetry*. Princeton, NJ: Princeton University Press, 1995.

Genette, Gérard. *The Architext: An Introduction*. Translated by Jane E. Lewin. Berkeley: University of California Press, 1992.

———. *Narrative Discourse: An Essay in Method*. Translated by Jane E. Lewin. Ithaca, NY: Cornell University Press, 1980.

Gibbs, Raymond W., Jr. "The Allegorical Impulse." *Metaphor and Symbol* 26, no. 2 (2011): 121–30.

———, ed. *Cambridge Handbook of Metaphor and Thought*. New York: Cambridge University Press, 2008.

———. *Embodiment and Cognitive Science*. New York: Cambridge University Press, 2006.

———. *Metaphor Wars: Conceptual Metaphor in Human Life*. New York: Cambridge University Press, 2017.

———. *The Poetics of Mind: Figurative Thought, Language, and Understanding*. New York: Cambridge University Press, 1994.

———. "What Do Idioms Really Mean?" *Journal of Memory and Language* 31, no. 4 (1992): 485–506.

Gibbs, Raymond W., Jr., Dinara Beitel, Michael Harrington, and Paul Sanders. "Taking a Stand on the Meanings of *Stand*: Bodily Experience as Motivation for Polysemy." *Journal of Semantics* 11, no. 4 (1994): 231–51.

Gibbs, Raymond W., Jr., and Natalia Blackwell. "Climbing the Ladder to Literary Heaven: A Case Study of Allegorical Interpretation of Fiction." *Scientific Study of Literature* 2, no. 2 (2012): 199–217.

Gibbs, Raymond W., Jr., Paula Lima, and Edson Francuzo. "Metaphor Is Grounded in Embodied Experience." *Journal of Pragmatics* 36, no. 7 (2004): 1189–210.

Gibbs, Raymond W., Jr., and Solange Nascimento. "How We Talk When We Talk About Love: Metaphorical Concepts and Understanding Love Poetry." In *Empirical Approaches to Literature and Aesthetics*, edited by Roger J. Kreuz and Mary Sue MacNealy, 291–308. Norwood, NJ: Ablex, 1996.

Gibbs, Raymond W., Jr., and Lacey Okonski. "Cognitive Poetics of Allegorical Experience." In *Expressive Minds and Artistic Creations: Studies in Cognitive Poetics*, edited by Szilvia Csábi, 33–53. New York: Oxford University Press, 2018.

Gillespie, Vincent. "Mystic's Foot: Rolle and Affectivity." In *The Medieval Mystical Tradition in England: Papers Read at Dartington Hall, July 1982*, edited by Marion Glasscoe, 199–230. Exeter: University of Exeter Press, 1982. Reprinted in *Looking in Holy Books: Essays on Late Medieval Religious Writing in England*. Turnhout: Brepols, 2012.

Gillingham, John. *Conquests, Catastrophe and Recovery: Britain and Ireland, 1066–1485*. London: Vintage, 2014.

Gittos, Helen. *Liturgy, Architecture, and Sacred Places in Anglo-Saxon England*. Oxford: Oxford University Press, 2013.

Gittos, Helen, and M. Bradford Bedingfield, eds. *The Liturgy of the Late Anglo-Saxon Church*. Woodbridge, Suffolk: Boydell Press for the Henry Bradshaw Society, 2005.

Gittos, Helen, and Sarah Hamilton. *Understanding Medieval Liturgy: Essays in Interpretation*. Burlington, VT: Ashgate, 2016.

Given-Wilson, Chris. "Richard II and the Higher Nobility." In *Richard II: The Art of Kingship*, edited by Anthony Goodman and James Gillespie, 107–28. Oxford: Clarendon Press, 1999.

———. *The Royal Household and the King's Affinity: Service, Politics and Finance in England, 1360–1413*. New Haven, CT: Yale University Press, 1986.

Glenberg, Arthur, and Michael Kaschak. "Grounding Language in Action." *Psychonomic Bulletin & Review* 9, no. 3 (2002): 558–65.

Gneuss, Helmut. *Books and Libraries in Early England*. Aldershot: Variorum, 1996.

———. *Hymnar und Hymnen im englischen Mittelalter*. Tübingen: M. Niemeyer, 1968.

———. "Liturgical Books in Anglo-Saxon England and Their Old English Terminology." In *Learning and Literature in Anglo-Saxon England: Studies Presented to Peter Clemoes on the Occasion of His Sixty-Fifth Birthday*, edited by Michael Lapidge and Helmut Gneuss, 91–141. Cambridge: Cambridge University Press, 1985.

Goodall, Alison. "The Medieval Bronzesmith and His Products." In *Medieval Industry*, edited by D. W. Crossley, Research Report no. 40, pp. 63–71. London: Council for British Archaeology, 1981.

Gorst, Emma. "Middle English Lyrics: Lyric Manuscripts 1200–1400 and Chaucer's Lyric." Ph.D. diss., University of Toronto, 2013.

Gracia, Jorge, and Lloyd Newton. "Medieval Theories of the Categories." *Stanford Encyclopedia of Philosophy*. 2006, rev. 2012. https://plato.stanford.edu/entries/medieval-categories/.

Grady, Joseph. "A Typology of Motivation for Conceptual Metaphor: Correlation vs. Resemblance." In *Metaphor in Cognitive Linguistics: Selected Papers from the Fifth International Cognitive Linguistics Conference, Amsterdam, July 1997*, edited by Raymond W. Gibbs, Jr., and Gerard J. Steen, 79–100. Amsterdam: John Benjamins, 1999.

Grafton, Scott T. "Embodied Cognition and the Simulation of Action to Understand Others." *Annals of the New York Academy of Sciences* 1156 (2011): 97–117.

Gray, Douglas. *Themes and Images in the Medieval English Religious Lyric*. London: Routledge, 1972.

Green, Kelly. "Constructing Masculinity Through the Material Culture of Dining and Drinking in Later Medieval England: A Study of the Production and Consumption of Anthropomorphic Pottery in Selected Sites from Eastern England, the Midlands, and the South West, c. 1250–1450." Ph.D. diss., University of Sheffield, 2015.

Green, Richard Firth. *A Crisis of Truth: Literature and Law in Ricardian England*. Philadelphia: University of Pennsylvania Press, 1999.

Greene, Roland. *Post-Petrarchism: Origins and Innovations of the Western Lyric Sequence*. Princeton, NJ: Princeton University Press, 1991.

Greentree, Rosemary. "Lyric." In *A Companion to Medieval English Literature and Culture, c. 1350–c. 1500*, edited by Peter Brown, 387–405. Malden, MA: Blackwell, 2007.

———. *The Middle English Lyric and Short Poem*. Cambridge: D. S. Brewer, 2001.

Griffith, David. "English Commemorative Inscriptions: Some Literary Dimensions." In *Memory and Commemoration in Medieval England: Proceedings of the 2008 Harlaxton Symposium*, edited by Caroline M. Barron and Clive Burgess, 251–70. Donington, Lincolnshire: Shaun Tyas, 2010.

———. "A Living Language of the Dead? French Commemorative Inscriptions from Late Medieval England." *Mediaeval Journal* 3, no. 2 (2013): 69–136.

Griffiths, Jeremy J. "A Re-examination of Oxford, Bodleian Library, MS Rawlinson C.86." *Archiv für das Studium der neueren Sprachen und Literaturen* 219 (1982): 381–88.

Gruenler, Curtis A. *"Piers Plowman" and the Poetics of Enigma: Riddles, Rhetoric, and Theology.* Notre Dame, IN: University of Notre Dame Press, 2017.

Guddat-Figge, Gisela. *Catalogue of Manuscripts Containing Middle English Romances.* Munich: W. Fink, 1976.

Guillory, John. "Close Reading: Prologue and Epilogue." *ADE Bulletin* 149, no. 3 (2010): 8–14.

Gura, David T. *A Descriptive Catalogue of the Medieval and Renaissance Manuscripts of the University of Notre Dame and Saint Mary's College.* Notre Dame, IN: University of Notre Dame Press, 2016.

Hahn, Thomas. "The Difference the Middle Ages Makes: Color and Race Before the Modern World." *Journal of Medieval and Early Modern Studies* 31, no. 1 (2001): 1–37.

Haines, John. *Medieval Song in Romance Languages.* Cambridge: Cambridge University Press, 2010.

Hall, John, and David Prior. "Towards Song: Shaping Spoken Lyric." *Performance Research* 23, no. 2 (2018): 100–106.

Hamburger, Jeffrey, Eva Schlotheuber, Susan Marti, and Margot Fassler. *Liturgical Life and Latin Learning at Paradies bei Soest, 1300–1425: Inscription and Illumination in the Choir Books of a North German Dominican Convent.* 2 vols. Munster: Aschendorff Verlag, 2016.

Hamburger, Käte. *The Logic of Literature.* Translated by Marilyn J. Rose. 2nd ed. Bloomington: Indiana University Press, 1973.

Hammond, Eleanor Prescott. *English Verse Between Chaucer and Surrey.* Durham, NC: Duke University Press, 1927.

Hanna, Ralph. "The Bridges at Abingdon: An Unnoticed Alliterative Poem." In *Yee? Baw for Bokes: Essays on Medieval Manuscripts and Poetics in Honor of Hoyt N. Duggan*, edited by Michael Calabrese and Stephen H. A. Shepherd, 31–44. Los Angeles: Marymount Institute Press, 2013).

———. "Defining Middle English Alliterative Poetry." In *The Endless Knot: Essays on Old and Middle English in Honor of Marie Borroff*, edited by M. Teresa Tavormina and R. F. Yeager, 43–64. Cambridge: D. S. Brewer, 1995.

———. "Lambeth Palace Library, MS 260, and the Problem of English Vernacularity." *Studies in Medieval and Renaissance History*, 3rd ser., 5 (2008): 131–99.

———. *Patient Reading/Reading Patience: Oxford Essays on Medieval English Literature.* Liverpool: Liverpool University Press, 2017.

———. "Verses in Sermons Again: The Case of Cambridge, Jesus College, MS Q.A.13." *Studies in Bibliography* 57 (2005–6): 63–83.

———. "The Verses of Bodleian Library, MS Laud Misc. 77." *Notes and Queries* 63, no. 3 (2016): 361–70.

Harbus, Antonina. *Cognitive Approaches to Old English Poetry.* Cambridge: D. S. Brewer, 2012.

Harrington, Marjorie. "Of Earth You Were Made: Constructing the Bilingual Poem 'Erþ' in British Library, MS Harley 913." *Florilegium* 31 (2014): 103–37.

Harris, Carissa. *Obscene Pedagogies: Transgressive Talk and Sexual Education in Late Medieval Britain.* Ithaca, NY: Cornell University Press, 2018.

Harrison, Frank Ll. *Music in Medieval Britain.* London: Routledge and Paul, 1958.

Hartzell, K. D. *Catalogue of Manuscripts Written or Owned in England up to 1200 Containing Music.* Woodbridge, Suffolk: Boydell Press, 2006.

———. "An Unknown English Benedictine Gradual of the Eleventh Century." *Anglo-Saxon England* 4 (1975): 131–44.

Hatcher, John, and Mark Bailey. *Modelling the Middle Ages: The History and Theory of England's Economic Development.* Oxford: Oxford University Press, 2001.

Hayot, Eric. "Against Historicist Fundamentalism." *PMLA* 131, no. 5 (2016): 1414–22.

Hebbard, Elizabeth. "Manuscripts and the Making of the Troubadour Lyric Tradition." Ph.D. diss., Yale University, 2017.

Hegel, G. W. F. *Aesthetics: Lectures on Fine Art.* Trans. T. M. Knox. 2 vols. Oxford: Oxford University Press, 1975.

Heidegger, Martin. *Being and Time.* Translated by John Macquarrie and Edward Robinson. New York: Harper, 1962.

———. *Poetry, Language, Thought.* Translated by Albert Hofstadter. New York: Harper and Row, 1971.

Heng, Geraldine. *Empire of Magic: Medieval Romance and the Politics of Cultural Fantasy.* New York: Columbia University Press, 2003.

———. "The Invention of Race in the European Middle Ages." 2 parts. *Literature Compass* 8, no. 5 (2011): 315–31, 332–50.

Henry, Hugh. "Pange Lingua Gloriosi." In *The Catholic Encyclopedia*, vol. 11. New York: Robert Appleton, 1911. http://www.newadvent.org/cathen/11441c.htm.

Hicks, Andrew. *Composing the World: Harmony in the Medieval Platonic Cosmos.* Oxford: Oxford University Press, 2017.

Hiley, David. "The English Background to the Nidaros Sequences." in *The Sequences of Nidaros: A Nordic Repertory and Its European Context,* edited by Lori Kruckenberg and Andreas Haug, 63–117. Trondheim: Tapir Academic Press, 2006.

———. "The Music of Prose Offices in Honour of English Saints." *Plainsong and Medieval Music* 10 (2001): 23–37.

———. "The Norman Chant Traditions: Normandy, Britain, Sicily." *Proceedings of the Royal Musical Association* 107 (1980–81): 1–33.

———. "The Repertory of Sequences at Winchester." In *Essays on Medieval Music in Honor of David G. Hughes,* ed. Graeme M. Boone, 153–93. Cambridge, MA: Harvard University Department of Music, distributed by Harvard University Press, 1995.

———. "The Rhymed Sequence in England—a Preliminary Survey," in *Musicologie médiévale: Notations et séquences; Actes de la table ronde du C.N.R.S. àl'Institut de Recherche et d'Histoire des Textes, 6–7 septembre 1982,* edited by Michel Huglo, 227–46. Paris: H. Champion, 1987.

———. "The Saints Venerated in Medieval Peterborough as Reflected in the Antiphoner Cambridge, Magdalene College, F.4.10." In *Essays on the History of English Music in Honour of John Caldwell: Sources, Style, Performance, Historiography,* edited by Emma Hornby and David Maw, 22–46. Woodbridge, Suffolk: Boydell Press, 2010.

———. "Thurstan of Caen and Plainchant at Glastonbury: Musicological Reflections on the Norman Conquest." *Proceedings of the British Academy* 72 (1986): 57–59.

———. "Zur englischen Hymnenüberlieferung." In *Der lateinische Hymnus im Mittelalter: Überlieferung–Ästhetik–Ausstrahlung,* edited by Andreas Haug, Christoph März, and Lorenz Welker, 199–214. Monumenta Monodica Medii Aevi, Subsidia 4. Kassel: Bärenreiter, 2004.

Hinds, K. "NMS1606: A Medieval Seal Matrix," 2003. https://finds.org.uk/database/artefacts /record/id/39051.

Hinton, David A. *Gold & Gilt, Pots & Pins: Possessions and People in Medieval Britain.* Oxford: Oxford University Press, 2005.

Hodapp, William. "Performing Prophecy: The Advents of Christ in Medieval Latin Drama." In *Prophet Margins: The Medieval Vatic Impulse and Social Stability,* edited by E. L. Risden, Karen Moranski, and Stephen Yardell, 101–22. New York: Peter Lang, 2004.

Hollander, John. "Breaking into Song: Some Notes on Refrain." In *Lyric Poetry: Beyond New Criticism,* edited by Chaviva Hošek and Patricia Parker, 73–89. Ithaca, NY: Cornell University Press, 1985.

———. *Rhyme's Reason: A Guide to English Verse.* New Haven, CT: Yale University Press, 2014.

Holsinger, Bruce. "The Color of Salvation: Desire, Death, and the Second Crusade in Bernard of Clairvaux's *Sermons on the Song of Songs.*" In *The Tongue of the Fathers: Gender and Ideology in Twelfth-Century Latin,* edited by David Townsend and Andrew Taylor, 156–86. Philadelphia: University of Pennsylvania Press, 1998.

———. *Music, Body, and Desire in Medieval Culture: Hildegard of Bingen to Chaucer.* Stanford, CA: Stanford University Press, 2001.

Holweck, Frederick. "The Feast of the Annunciation." In *The Catholic Encyclopedia,* vol. 1. New York: Robert Appleton, 1907. http://www.newadvent.org/cathen/01542a.htm.

Hope, W. H. St. John. "On the English Medieval Drinking Bowls Called Mazers." *Archaeologia* 50 (1887): 129–93.

Hošek, Chaviva, and Patricia Parker, eds. *Lyric Poetry: Beyond New Criticism.* Ithaca, NY: Cornell University Press, 1985.

Howell, Martha C. *Commerce Before Capitalism in Europe, 1300–1600.* Cambridge: Cambridge University Press, 2010.

Hsy, Jonathan. *Trading Tongues: Merchants, Multilingualism, and Medieval Literature.* Columbus: Ohio State University Press, 2013.

Hughes, Andrew. "British Rhymed Offices: A Catalogue and Commentary." In *Music in the Medieval English Liturgy: Plainsong & Mediaeval Music Society Centennial Essays,* edited by Susan Rankin and David Hiley, 239–84. Oxford: Clarendon Press, 1993.

Hughes, Andrew, and Margaret Bent, eds. *The Old Hall Manuscript.* 2 vols. in 3. [Rome]: American Institute of Musicology, 1969–73.

Huot, Sylvia. *From Song to Book: The Poetics of Writing in Old French Lyric and Lyrical Narrative Poetry.* Ithaca, NY: Cornell University Press, 1987.

Hurt, James R. "The Texts of *King Horn.*" *Journal of the Folklore Institute* 7 (1970): 47–59.

Husband, Timothy B., and Jane Hayward, eds. *The Secular Spirit: Life and Art at the End of the Middle Ages.* New York: E. P. Dutton, in association with the Metropolitan Museum of Art, 1975.

Husmann, Heinrich. "Notre-Dame und Saint-Victor: Repertoire-Studien zur Geschichte der gereimten Prosen." *Acta Musicologica* 36 (1964): 98–123.

Husserl, Edmund. *Cartesian Meditations: An Introduction to Phenomenology.* Translated by Dorion Cairns. The Hague: M. Nijhoff, 1960.

Iyengar, Sunil. "Taking Note: Poetry Reading Is Up—Federal Survey Results." National Endowment for the Arts blog, June 7, 2018. https://www.arts.gov/stories/blog/2018/taking -note-poetry-reading-federal-survey-results.

Jackson, Virginia. *Dickinson's Misery: A Theory of Lyric Reading.* Princeton, NJ: Princeton University Press, 2005.

———. "Lyric." In *The Princeton Encyclopedia of Poetry and Poetics*, 4th ed., edited by Roland Greene and Stephen Cushman, 826–34. Princeton, NJ: Princeton University Press, 2012.

Jackson, Virginia, and Yopie Prins, eds. *The Lyric Theory Reader: A Critical Anthology*. Baltimore: Johns Hopkins University Press, 2014.

Jacobs, Nicolas. Review of *King Horn: An Edition Based on Cambridge University Library MS Gg.4.27*, edited by Rosamund Allen. *Medium Aevum* 57, no. 2 (1988): 301–3.

James, Montague Rhodes. *A Descriptive Catalogue of the Manuscripts in the Library of Gonville and Caius*. Cambridge: Cambridge University Press, 1907–8.

———. *A Descriptive Catalogue of the Manuscripts in the Library of Lambeth Palace*. Cambridge: Cambridge University Press, 1930–32.

———. *A Descriptive Catalogue of the Manuscripts in the Library of Pembroke College Cambridge, with a Hand List of the Printed Books to the Year 1500 by Ellis H. Minns, M.A., Fellow and Librarian*. Cambridge: Cambridge University Press, 1905.

James, Stephen. "Verbal Fixities and the 'Law of Increasing Returns': Uses of the Refrain in Poetry." *Imaginaires* 9 (2003): 343–52.

Jarvis, Simon. "For a Poetics of Verse." *PMLA* 125, no. 4 (2010): 931–35.

———. "The Melodics of Long Poems." *Textual Practice* 24, no. 4 (2010): 607–21.

———. "Prosody as Cognition." *Critical Quarterly* 40, no. 4 (1998): 3–15.

Jauss, Hans Robert. *Towards an Aesthetic of Reception*. Translated by Timothy Bahti. Minneapolis: University of Minnesota Press, 1982.

Jefferson, Judith A., and Ad Putter, eds. *Approaches to the Metres of Alliterative Verse*. Leeds: Leeds Studies in English, 2009.

———. *Multilingualism in Medieval Britain (c. 1066–1520): Sources and Analysis*. Turnhout: Brepols, 2013.

Jeffrey, David L. *The Early English Lyric and Franciscan Spirituality*. Lincoln: University of Nebraska Press, 1975.

Jeffreys, Mark. "Ideologies of Lyric: A Problem of Genre in Contemporary Anglophone Poetics." *PMLA* 110, no. 2 (1995): 196–205.

Jervis, Ben. *Pottery and Social Life in Medieval England: Towards a Relational Approach*. Oxford: Oxbow Books, 2014.

Johnson, Barbara. *The Feminist Difference: Literature, Psychoanalysis, Race, and Gender*. Cambridge, MA: Harvard University Press, 1998.

———. *Persons and Things*. Cambridge, MA: Harvard University Press, 2008.

Johnson, Eleanor. "How Middle English Lyrics Make Us Think: Song as Devotional Memory." Unpublished paper, for "What Kind of a Thing Is a Middle English Lyric?" Advanced Seminar, Radcliffe Institute for Advanced Study, Harvard University, December 1, 2016.

———. "The Poetics of Waste: Medieval English Ecocriticsm." *PMLA* 127, no. 1 (2012): 460–76.

———. *Practicing Literary Theory in the Middle Ages: Ethics and the Mixed Form in Chaucer, Gower, Usk, and Hoccleve*. Chicago: University of Chicago Press, 2013.

———. "*Reddere* and Refrain: A Meditation on Poetic Procedure in *Piers Plowman*." *Yearbook of Langland Studies* 30 (2016): 3–27.

Johnson, Holly. *The Grammar of Good Friday: Macaronic Sermons of Late Medieval England*. Turnhout: Brepols, 2012.

Johnson, Timothy J. "Choir Prayer as the Place of Formation and Identity Definition." *Miscellanea Francescana* 111 (2011): 123–35.

————, ed. *Franciscans and Preaching: Every Miracle from the Beginning of the World Came About Through Words*. Leiden: Brill, 2012.

Jones, Chris. *Fossil Poetry: Anglo-Saxon and Linguistic Nativism in Nineteenth-Century Poetry*. Oxford: Oxford University Press, 2018.

————. *Strange Likeness: The Use of Old English in Twentieth-Century Poetry*. Oxford: Oxford University Press, 2006.

Jones, Richard Foster. *The Triumph of the English Language: A Survey of Opinions Concerning the Vernacular from the Introduction of Printing to the Restoration*. Stanford, CA: Stanford University Press, 1953.

Jones-Wagner, Valentina. "The Body of the Saracen Princess in *La Belle Hélène de Constantinople*." *Bucknell Review* 47, no. 2 (2004): 82–89.

Jostmann, Nils B., Daniël Lakens, and Thomas Schubert. "Weight as an Embodiment of Importance." *Psychological Science* 20, no. 9 (2009): 1169–74.

Kaluza, Max. *A Short History of English Versification from the Earliest Times to the Present Day: A Handbook for Teachers and Students*. Translated by A. C. Dunstan. London: George Allen, 1911.

Kane, George. "Introduction." In William Langland, *Piers Plowman: The A Version*, edited by George Kane, 1–172. London: Athlone Press, 1960.

————. *The Liberating Truth: The Concept of Integrity in Chaucer's Writings*. London: Athlone Press, 1980.

————. *Middle English Literature: A Critical Study of the Romances, the Religious Lyrics, Piers Plowman*. London: Methuen, 1951.

Karkov, Catherine E. "Art and Writing: Voice, Image, Object." In *The Cambridge History of Early Medieval English Literature*, edited by Clare A. Lees, 73–98. Cambridge: Cambridge University Press, 2012.

————. *The Art of Anglo-Saxon England*. Woodbridge, Suffolk: Boydell Press, 2011.

Karnes, Michelle. *Imagination, Meditation, and Cognition in the Middle Ages*. Chicago: University of Chicago Press, 2011.

————. "Marvels in the Medieval Imagination." *Speculum* 90, no. 2 (2015): 327–65.

————. "Wonder, Marvels, and Metaphor in the *Squire's Tale*." *English Literary History* 82, no. 2 (2015): 461–90.

Kay, Sarah. "The 'Changeful Pen': Paradox, Logical Time and Poetic Spectrality in the Poems Attributed to Chrétien de Troyes." In *Thinking Through Chrétien de Troyes*, by Zrinka Stahuljak, Virginie Greene, Sarah Kay, Sharon Kinoshita, and Peggy McCracken, 15–40. Cambridge: D. S. Brewer, 2011.

————. "Desire and Subjectivity." In *The Troubadours: An Introduction*, edited by Simon Gaunt and Sarah Kay, 212–27. Cambridge: Cambridge University Press, 1999.

————. *Parrots and Nightingales: Troubadour Quotations and the Development of European Poetry*. Philadelphia: University of Pennsylvania Press, 2013.

Kennedy, Ruth. "'A Bird in Bishopswood': Some Newly-Discovered Lines of Alliterative Verse from the Late Fourteenth Century." In *Medieval Literature and Antiquities: Studies in Honour of Basil Cottle*, edited by Myra Stokes and T. L. Burton, 71–87. Cambridge: D. S. Brewer, 1987.

Ker, Neil. "Introduction." In *Facsimile of British Museum MS. Harley 2253*. EETS, o.s., 255. London: Oxford University Press, for the Early English Text Society, 1965.

Kerby-Fulton, Kathryn, Maidie Hilmo, and Linda Olson. *Opening Up Middle English Manuscripts: Literary and Visual Approaches*. Ithaca, NY: Cornell University Press, 2012

Kerby-Fulton, Kathryn, John J. Thompson, and Sarah Baechle, eds. *New Directions in Medieval Manuscript Studies and Reading Practices: Essays in Honour of Derek Pearsall*. Notre Dame, IN: University of Notre Dame Press, 2014.

Kim, Dorothy. Introduction to *Literature Compass* special cluster on "Critical Race and the Middle Ages." *Literature Compass* 16, nos. 9–10 (2019), n.p. (16 pp.).

Kinch, Ashby. "Image, Ideology, and Form: The Middle English *Three Dead Kings* in Its Iconographic Context." *Chaucer Review* 43, no. 1 (2008): 48–81.

Kövecses, Zoltán. "Language, Figurative Thought, and Cross-Cultural Comparison." *Metaphor and Symbol* 18 (2003): 311–20.

———. *Language, Mind and Culture: A Practical Introduction*. New York: Oxford University Press, 2010.

———. *Metaphor: A Practical Introduction*. New York: Oxford University Press, 2002.

Krieger, Murray. *The New Apologists for Poetry*. Minneapolis: University of Minnesota Press, 1956.

Krug, Rebecca. "Jesus' Voice: Dialogue and Late-Medieval Readers." In *Form and Reform: Reading Across the Fifteenth Century*, edited by Shannon Gayk and Kathleen Tonry, 110–29. Columbus: Ohio State University Press, 2011.

Kruger, Steven F. "Conversion and Medieval Sexual, Religious, and Racial Categories." In *Constructing Medieval Sexuality*, edited by Karma Lochrie, Peggy McCracken, and James A. Schultz, 158–79. Minneapolis: University of Minnesota Press, 1997.

Kuczynski, Michael P. "Theological Sophistication and the Middle English Religious Lyric: A Polemic." *Chaucer Review* 45, no. 3 (2011): 321–39.

Lacan, Jacques. "Logical Time and the Assertion of Anticipated Certainty: A New Sophism." In *Écrits: The First Complete Edition in English*, translated by Bruce Fink, with Héloïse Fink and Russell Grigg, 161–75. New York: W. W. Norton, 2002.

Lagueux, Robert. "Sermons, Exegesis, and Performance: The Laon *Ordo Prophetarum* and the Meaning of Advent." *Comparative Drama* 43 (2009): 197–220.

Lakoff, George, and Mark Johnson. *Metaphors We Live By*. Chicago: University of Chicago Press, 1980.

———. *Philosophy in the Flesh*. Chicago: University of Chicago Press, 1999.

Lakoff, George, and Mark Turner. *More Than Cool Reason: A Field Guide to Poetic Metaphor*. Chicago: University of Chicago Press, 1989.

Landau, Mark J. *Conceptual Metaphor in Social Psychology: The Poetics of Everyday Life*. Washington, DC: Psychology Press, 2016.

Langer, Ullrich. *Lyric in the Renaissance: From Petrarch to Montaigne*. Cambridge: Cambridge University Press, 2015.

La Niece, Susan. "Asante Ewer." In *Richard II's Treasure: The Riches of a Medieval King*. Institute of Historical Research and Royal Holloway, University of London, 2017. http://www.history.ac.uk/richardII/asante.html.

Largier, Niklaus. "Inner Senses–Outer Senses: The Practice of Emotions in Medieval Mysticism." In *Emotion and Sensibilities in the Middle Ages*, ed. C. Stephen Jaeger and Ingrid Kasten, 3–15. Berlin: Walter de Gruyter, 2003.

Lausberg, Heinrich. *Handbook of Literary Rhetoric: A Foundation for Literary Study*. Edited by David E. Orton and R. Dean Anderson. Translated by Matthew T. Bliss, Annemiek Jansen, and David E. Orton. Leiden: Brill, 1998.

Lawrence, Frank. "What Did They Sing at Cashel in 1172? Winchester, Sarum and Romano-Frankish Chant in Ireland." *Journal of the Society for Musicology in Ireland* 3 (2008): 111–25.

Lawton, David. "Dullness and the Fifteenth Century." *English Literary History* 54, no. 4 (1987): 761–99.

———. "Voice and Public Interiorities: Chaucer, Orpheus, Machaut." In *Answerable Style: The Idea of the Literary in Medieval England*, edited by Frank Grady and Andrew Galloway, 284–306. Columbus: Ohio State University Press, 2013.

Leach, Elizabeth Eva. *Sung Birds: Music, Nature, and Poetry in the Later Middle Ages.* Ithaca, NY: Cornell University Press, 2007.

Lears, Adin. *World of Echo: Noise and Knowing in Late Medieval England.* Ithaca, NY: Cornell University Press, 2020.

Leclercq, Jean. *The Love of Learning and the Desire for God: A Study of Monastic Culture.* Translated by Catharine Misrahi. New York: Fordham University Press, 1961.

Lefferts, Peter M. "Cantilena and Antiphon: Music for Marian Services in Late Medieval England." *Current Musicology* 45–47 (1990): 247–82.

———. *The Motet in England in the Fourteenth Century.* Ann Arbor, MI: UMI Research Press, 1986.

———. Review of *Songs in British Sources, c. 1150–1300*, edited by Helen Deeming. *Plainsong and Medieval Music* 23, no. 2 (2014): 245–51.

Lerer, Seth. "'Dum ludis floribus:' Language and Text in the Medieval English Lyric." *Philological Quarterly* 87, nos. 3 and 4 (2008): 237–55.

———. "The Genre of the Grave and the Origins of the Middle English Lyric." *Modern Language Quarterly* 58, no. 2 (1997): 127–61.

———. "Old English and Its Afterlife." In *The Cambridge History of Medieval English Literature*, edited by David Wallace, 7–34. Cambridge: Cambridge University Press, 1999.

Leroquais, Victor. *Les sacramentaires et les missels manuscrits des bibliothèques publiques de France.* Paris, 1924.

Levin. Samuel R. *The Semantics of Metaphor.* Baltimore: Johns Hopkins University Press, 1977.

Levine, Caroline. *Forms: Whole, Rhythm, Hierarchy, Network.* Princeton, NJ: Princeton University Press, 2015.

Lewis, J. M., R. Brownsword, and E. E. H. Pitt. "Medieval 'Bronze' Tripod Ewers from Wales." *Medieval Archaeology* 31 (1987): 80–93.

Lindenbaum, Sheila. "London Texts and Literate Practice." In *The Cambridge History of Medieval English Literature*, edited by David Wallace, 284–309. Cambridge: Cambridge University Press, 1999.

Little, Andrew G. *Studies in English Franciscan History.* Manchester: University of Manchester, 1917.

Livingstone, Jo. "Racism, Medievalism, and the White Supremacists of Charlottesville." *New Republic*, August 15, 2017. https://newrepublic.com/article/144320/racism-medievalism -white-supremacists-charlottesville.

Loewen, Peter. *Music in Early Franciscan Thought.* Leiden: Brill, 2014.

Lomuto, Sierra. "Becoming Postmedieval: The Stakes of the Global Middle Ages." *postmedieval* 11, no. 4 (2020): 503–12.

———. "The Mongol Princess of Tars: Global Relations and Racial Formation in *The King of Tars* (c. 1330)." *Exemplaria* 31, no. 3 (2019): 171–92.

Lovelace, Antonia. "War Booty: Changing Contexts, Changing Displays; Asante 'Relics' from Kumasi, Acquired by the Prince of Wales's Own Regiment of Yorkshire in 1896." *Journal of Museum Ethnography* 12 (2000): 147–60.

Lucey, Michael, and Tom McEnaney. "Language-in-Use and Literary Fieldwork." *Representations* 137, no. 1 (2017): 1–22.

Lüdtke, Jana, Burkhard Meyer-Sickendieck, and Arthur M. Jacobs. "Immersing in the Stillness of an Early Morning: Testing the Mood Empathy Hypothesis of Poetry Reception." *Psychology of Aesthetics, Creativity, and the Arts* 8, no. 3 (2014): 363–77.

Lusignan, Serge. *La langue des rois au Moyen Âge: Le français en France et en Angleterre*. Paris: Presses universitaires de France, 2004.

MacDonald, A. A. "Lyrics in Middle Scots." In *A Companion to the Middle English Lyric*, edited by Thomas G. Duncan, 243–61. Cambridge: D. S. Brewer, 2005.

Macke, Frank J. "Body, Liquidity and Flesh: Bachelard, Merleau-Ponty, and the Elements of Interpersonal Communication." *Philosophy Today* 51, no. 4 (2007): 401–15.

Malkiel, Yakov. *Etymology*. Cambridge: Cambridge University Press, 1993.

Mannion, Anne. "*Missale Vetus*: Liturgy, Palaeography and Repertories in the Notated Missal EXc.3515." Ph.D. diss., University of Limerick, 2012.

Mao, Douglas. "The New Critics and the Text-Object." *English Literary History* 63, no. 1 (1996): 227–54.

Marvin, Julia. *The Construction of Vernacular History in the Anglo-Norman Prose Brut Chronicle: The Manuscript Culture of Late Medieval England*. York: University of York Press, 2017.

Matthews, David. *The Making of Middle English, 1765–1910*. Minneapolis: University of Minnesota Press, 1999.

Matthews, P. H. *The Concise Oxford Dictionary of Linguistics*. 3rd ed. Oxford: Oxford University Press, 2014.

Matthews, Ricardo. "Song in Reverse: The Medieval Prosimetrum and Lyric Theory." *PMLA* 133, no. 2 (2018): 296–313.

McDermott, Ryan. "Practices of Satisfaction and *Piers Plowman*'s Dynamic Middle." *Studies in the Age of Chaucer* 36, no. 1 (2014): 169–207.

McDonald, Nicola. "Desire Out of Order and *Undo Your Door*." *Studies in the Age of Chaucer* 34 (2012): 247–75.

McGillivray, Murray. *Memorization in the Transmission of the Middle English Romances*. New York: Garland, 1990.

McGrath, Elizabeth. "The Black Andromeda." *Journal of the Warburg and Courtauld Institutes* 55 (1992): 1–18.

McIlroy, Claire Elizabeth. *The English Prose Treatises of Richard Rolle*. Cambridge: D. S. Brewer, 2004.

McIntosh, Angus, M. L. Samuels, and Michael Benskin. *A Linguistic Atlas of Late Mediaeval English*. 4 vols. Aberdeen: Aberdeen University Press, 1986.

McKenna, Catherine A. *The Medieval Welsh Religious Lyric: Poems of the Gogynfeirdd, 1137–1282*. Belmont, MA: Ford and Bailie, 1991.

McLane, Maureen N., and Laura M. Slatkin. "British Romantic Homer: Oral Tradition, 'Primitive Poetry' and the Emergence of Comparative Poetics in Britain, 1760–1830." *English Literary History* 78, no. 3 (2011): 687–714.

McLeod, Malcolm D. "Art and Archaeology in Asante." In *Dall'archeologia all'arte tradizionale africana/De l'archéologie à l'art traditionnel africain/From Archaeology to Traditonal African Art*, edited by Gigi Pezzoli, 65–81. Milan: Centro Studi Archeologia Africana, 1992.

———. "Richard II, Part 3, at Kumase." In *West African Economic and Social History: Studies in Memory of Marion Johnson*, edited by David Henige and T. C. McCaskie, 171–74. Madison: African Studies Program at the University of Wisconsin, 1990.

McNamer, Sarah. *Affective Meditation and the Invention of Medieval Compassion.* Philadelphia: University of Pennsylvania Press, 2010.

———. "Female Authors, Provincial Settings: The Re-versing of Courtly Love in the Findern Manuscript." *Viator* 22 (1991): 279–310.

McVitty, E. Amanda. "False Knights and True Men: Contesting Chivalric Masculinity in English Treason Trials, 1388–1415." *Journal of Medieval History* 40, no. 4 (2014): 458–77.

Medieval Song Network. http://www.medievalsongnetwork.org.

Meier, Brian P., David J. Hauser, Michael D. Robinson, Chris Kelland Friesen, and Katie Schjeldahl. "What's 'Up' with God? Vertical Space as a Representation of the Divine." *Journal of Personality and Social Psychology* 93, no. 5 (2007): 699–710.

Meier, Brian P., and Michael D. Robinson. "Why the Sunny Side Is Up: Associations Between Affect and Vertical Position." *Psychological Science* 15, no. 4 (2004): 243–47.

Merleau-Ponty, Maurice. *Phenomenology of Perception.* Translated by Donald A. Landes. New York: Routledge, 2012.

Meyer, Christian. "Catalogue thématique des Séquences" (CthS). Catalogue des manuscrits notés (CMN). 2017. http://www.musmed.fr/CMN/proseq/proseq_proses.htm.

Meyer-Lee, Robert. *Literary Value and Social Identity in the "Canterbury Tales."* Cambridge: Cambridge University Press, 2019.

Michael, John. "Lyric History: Temporality, Rhetoric, and the Ethics of Poetry." *New Literary History* 48, no. 2 (2017): 265–84.

Middle English Dictionary (*MED*). Edited by Robert E. Lewis et al. Ann Arbor: University of Michigan Press, 1952–2001. Online edition in Middle English Compendium. Edited by Frances McSparran et al. Ann Arbor: University of Michigan Library, 2000–2018. http://quod.lib.umich.edu/m/middle-english-dictionary.

Middleton, Anne. "The Idea of Public Poetry in the Reign of Richard II." *Speculum* 53, no. 1 (1978): 94–114.

Mill, John Stuart. *Essays on Poetry.* Edited by F. Parvin Sharpless. Columbia: University of South Carolina Press, 1976.

Millar, Robert McColl. "Language, Genre, and Register: Factors in the Use of Simple Demonstrative Forms in the South-West Midlands of the Thirteenth Century." In *Laȝamon: Contexts, Language, and Interpretation,* edited by Rosamund Allen, Lucy Perry, and Jane Roberts, 227–39. London: King's College London, Centre for Late Antique and Medieval Studies, 2002.

Miner, John N. *The Grammar Schools of Medieval England: A. F. Leach in Historiographical Perspective.* Montreal: McGill–Queen's University Press, 1990.

Minkova, Donka. *The History of Final Vowels in English: The Sound of Muting.* Berlin: Mouton de Gruyter, 1991.

Minnis, Alastair. *Medieval Theory of Authorship: Scholastic Literary Attitudes in the Later Middle Ages.* 2nd ed. Philadelphia: University of Pennsylvania Press, 2012.

Mohrmann, Christine. *Études sur le latin des chrétiens.* Vol. 2, *Latin chrétien et médiéval.* Rome: Edizioni di storia e letteratura, 1961.

Mooney, Linne R., Daniel W. Mosser, and Elizabeth Solopova, eds. *The "DIMEV": An Open-Access, Digital Edition of the "Index of Middle English Verse."* http://www.dimev.net/.

Morgan, Nigel J. "A French Franciscan Breviary in Lisbon and the Breviaries by Jean Pucelle and His Followers." In *Quand la peinture était dans les livres: Mélanges en l'honneur de François Avril,* edited by M. Hofmann and C. Zöhl, 211–19. Turnhout: Brepols, 2007.

———. "The Liturgical Manuscripts of the English Franciscans c. 1250–1350." In *The English Province of the Franciscans (1224–c. 1350)*, edited by Michael J. P. Robson, 214–44. Leiden: Brill, 2017.

Moser, Thomas C. "'And I Mon Waxe Wod': The Middle English 'Foweles in the Frith.'" *PMLA* 102, no. 3 (1987): 326–37.

Mosser, Daniel W. *A Digital Catalogue of the Pre-1500 Manuscripts and Incunables of the Canterbury Tales.* 2nd ed. http://mossercatalogue.net/.

Mouron, Anne. "'Help Thin Godric in Francrice': An Old French Life of St Godric." In *Translation and Authority—Authorities in Translation*, edited by Pieter De Leemans and Michèle Goyens, 215–28. Turnhout: Brepols, 2016.

Mugglestone, Lynda, ed. *The Oxford History of English.* Updated ed. Oxford: Oxford University Press, 2012.

Murphy, Gregory. "On Metaphoric Representation." *Cognition* 60, no. 2 (1996): 173–204.

Mykelbust, Nicholas. "Rhythmic Cognition in Late Medieval Lyrics: BL MS Harley 2253." In *The Palgrave Handbook of Affect Theory and Textual Criticism*, edited by Donald R. Wehrs and Thomas Blake, 587–608. New York: Palgrave, 2017.

Nelson, Ingrid. *Lyric Tactics: Poetry, Genre, and Practice in Later Medieval England.* Philadelphia: University of Pennsylvania Press, 2017.

Newcombe, Grace. "Britain's Cleric Composers: Poetic Stress and Ornamentation in *Worldes blis.*" In *Ars Antiqua: Music and Culture in Europe c. 1150–1330*, edited by Gregorio Bevilacqua and Thomas Payne, 143–62. Turnhout: Brepols, 2020.

A New English Dictionary on Historical Principles: Founded Mainly on the Materials Collected by the Philological Society. Vol. 6, part 1. Edited by James A. H. Murray and Henry Bradley. Oxford: Clarendon Press, 1908.

"The New Lyric Studies." *PMLA* 123, no. 1 (2008): 181–234.

Newman, Barbara. *From Virile Woman to WomanChrist: Studies in Medieval Religion and Literature.* Philadelphia: University of Pennsylvania Press, 1995.

———. *Medieval Crossover: Reading the Secular Against the Sacred.* Notre Dame, IN: University of Notre Dame Press, 2013.

———. "Redeeming the Time: Langland, Julian, and the Art of Lifelong Revision." *Yearbook of Langland Studies* 23 (2009): 1–32.

Nichols, Stephen G., and Siegfried Wenzel, eds. *The Whole Book: Cultural Perspectives on the Medieval Miscellany.* Ann Arbor: University of Michigan Press, 1996.

Nolan, Maura. "Historicism After Historicism." In *The Post-Historical Middle Ages*, edited by Elizabeth Scala and Sylvia Federico, 63–85. New York: Palgrave Macmillan, 2009.

Nurkse, D. "Anonymous Lyrics from Medieval Spain." *Literary Review* 45, no. 3 (2002): 509–11.

Oakden, J. P. *Alliterative Poetry in Middle English: A Survey of the Traditions.* Manchester: Manchester University Press, 1935.

O'Donnell, Daniel Paul. "Bede's Strategy in Paraphrasing 'Caedmon's Hymn.'" *Journal of English and Germanic Philology* 103, no. 4 (2004): 417–32.

OED Online. Oxford University Press. http://www.oed.com.

Okasha, Elizabeth. "The Commissioners, Makers and Owners of Anglo-Saxon Inscriptions." *Anglo-Saxon Studies in Archaeology and History* 7 (1994): 71–77.

———. "Literacy in Anglo-Saxon England: The Evidence from Inscriptions." *Anglo-Saxon Studies in Archaeology and History* 8 (1995): 69–74.

O'Keefe John J., and R. R. Reno. *Sanctified Vision: An Introduction to Early Christian Interpretation of the Bible.* Baltimore: Johns Hopkins University Press, 2005.

Orlemanski, Julie. "Literary Persons and Medieval Fiction in Bernard of Clairvaux's *Sermons on the Song of Songs*." *Representations* 153 (2021): 29–50.

Orme, Nicholas. *Education in Early Tudor England: Magdalen College Oxford and Its School, 1480–1540*. Magdalen College Occasional Paper 4. Oxford: Magdalen College, 1998.

———. *English School Exercises, 1420–1530*. Toronto: Pontifical Institute of Mediaeval Studies, 2013.

———. "Latin and English Sentences in Fifteenth-Century Schoolbooks." *Yale University Library Gazette* 60, no. 1/2 (1985): 47–57.

Ortiz, María J. "Visual Manifestations of Primary Metaphors Through *Mise-en-scène* Techniques." *Image & Narrative* 15, no. 1 (2014): 5–16.

Otaño Gracia, Nahir, and Daniel Armenti. "Constructing Prejudice in the Middle Ages and the Repercussions of Racism Today." *Medieval Feminist Forum* 53, no. 1 (2017): 176–201.

Otter, Monika. "Contrafacture and Translation: The Prisoner's Lament." In *The French of Medieval England: Essays in Honour of Jocelyn Wogan-Browne*, ed. Thelma Fenster and Carolyn P. Collette, 55–81. Cambridge: D. S. Brewer, 2014.

———. "Godric of Finchale's *Canora Modulatio*: The Auditory and Visionary Worlds of a Twelfth-Century Hermit." *Haskins Society Journal* 24 (2012): 127–44.

Pächt, Otto, and J. J. G. Alexander. *Illuminated Manuscripts in the Bodleian Library Oxford*. Vol. 1. Oxford: Clarendon Press, 1966.

Page, Christopher. "Around the Performance of a 13th-Century Motet." *Early Music* 28, no. 3 (2000): 343–57.

———. "A Catalogue and Bibliography of English Song from Its Beginnings to c1300." *RMA Research Chronicle* 13 (1976): 67–83.

Palti, Kathleen Rose. "'Synge we now alle and sum': Three Fifteenth-Century Collections of Communal Song; A Study of British Library, Sloane MS 2593; Bodleian Library, MS Eng. poet. e.1; and St John's College, Cambridge, MS S.54." Ph.D. diss., University College, London, 2008.

Park, Joseph Sung-Yul, and Mary Bucholtz. "Introduction: Public Transcripts: Entextualization and Linguistic Representation in Institutional Contexts." *Text and Talk* 29, no. 5 (2009): 485–502.

Parkes, Henry. "St. Edmund Between Liturgy and Hagiography." In *Bury St Edmunds and the Norman Conquest*, edited by Tom Licence, 131–59. Woodbridge, Suffolk: Boydell Press, 2014.

Parmar, Sandeep. "Still Not a British Subject: Race and UK Poetry." *Journal of British and Irish Innovative Poetry* 12, no. 1 (2020). https://doi.org/10.16995/bip.3384.

Patterson, Lee. "Chaucer's Pardoner on the Couch: Psyche and Clio in Medieval Literary Studies." *Speculum* 76, no. 3 (2001): 638–80.

Pearsall, Derek. "The Auchinleck Manuscript 40 Years On." In *The Auchinleck Manuscript: New Perspectives*, edited by Susanna Fein, 11–25. York: York Medieval Press, 2016.

———. "The Development of Middle English Romance." *Mediaeval Studies* 27 (1965): 91–116.

———. *Old English and Middle English Poetry*. London: Routledge & Kegan Paul, 1977.

———. "The Origins of the Alliterative Revival." In *The Alliterative Tradition in the Fourteenth Century*, edited by Bernard S. Levy and Paul E. Szarmach, 1–24. Kent, OH: Kent State University Press, 1981.

Pelteret, David A. E. *Slavery in Early Mediaeval England from the Reign of Alfred Until the Twelfth Century.* Woodbridge, Suffolk: Boydell Press, 1995.

Pensom, Roger. "Pour la versification anglo-normande." *Romania: Revue trimestrielle consacré a l'étude des langues et des littératures romanes* 124, no. 1 (2006): 50–65.

Peraino, Judith. *Giving Voice to Love: Song and Self-Expression from the Troubadors to Guillaume de Machaut.* Oxford: Oxford University Press, 2011.

Perloff, Marjorie. "Can(n)on to the Right of Us, Can(n)on to the Left of Us: A Plea for Difference." *New Literary History* 18, no. 3 (1987): 633–56.

———. Review of *Theory of the Lyric* by Jonathan Culler. *Nineteenth-Century Literature* 71, no. 2 (2016): 256–61.

Perloff, Marjorie, and Craig Dworkin. "The Sound of Poetry / The Poetry of Sound: The 2006 MLA Presidential Forum." *PMLA* 123 (2008): 749–61.

Perry, Ralph Barton. "Economic Value and Moral Value." *Quarterly Journal of Economics* 30, no. 3 (1916): 443–85.

———. *General Theory of Value: Its Meaning and Basic Principles Construed in Terms of Interest.* New York: Longmans, Green, 1926.

Pezzini, Domenico. "Versions of Latin Hymns in Medieval England: William Herebert and the English Hymnal." *Mediaevistik* 4 (1991): 297–315.

Pfaff, Richard. *The Liturgy in Medieval England: A History.* Cambridge: Cambridge University Press, 2009.

Phillips, Kim M. "The Invisible Man: Body and Ritual in a Fifteenth-Century Noble Household." *Journal of Medieval History* 31 (2005): 143–62.

Pinker, Steven. *The Stuff of Thought: Language as a Window into Human Nature.* New York: Basic Books, 2007.

Planchart, Alejandro Enrique. "On the Nature of Transmission and Change in Trope Repertories." *Journal of the American Musicological Society* 41, no. 2 (1988): 215–49.

———. *The Repertory of Tropes at Winchester.* Princeton, NJ: Princeton University Press, 1977.

Polheim, Karl. *Die lateinische Reimprosa.* Berlin: Weidmann, 1925.

Pollock, Sheldon. *The Language of the Gods in the World of Men: Sanskrit, Culture, and Power in Premodern India.* Berkeley: University of California Press, 2006.

Prins, Yopie. "Historical Poetics, Dysprosody, and *The Science of English Verse.*" *PMLA* 123, no. 1 (2008): 229–34.

———. "What Is Historical Poetics?" *Modern Language Quarterly* 77, no. 1 (2016): 13–40.

Pulgram, Ernst. "Prosodic Systems: French." *Lingua* 13 (1965): 125–44.

Putter, Ad. "The French of English Letters: Two Trilingual Verse Epistles in Context." In *Language and Culture in Medieval Britain: The French of England, c. 1100–c. 1500,* ed. Jocelyn Wogan-Browne et al., 397–408. York: York Medieval Press, 2009.

———. "Middle English Romances and the Oral Tradition." In *Medieval Oral Literature,* edited by Karl Reichl, 335–51. Berlin: De Gruyter, 2012.

Putter, Ad, Judith Jefferson, and Myra Stokes. *Studies in the Metre of Alliterative Verse.* Oxford: Society for the Study of Medieval Languages and Literature, 2007.

Rajabzadeh, Shokoofeh. "The Depoliticized Saracen and Muslim Erasure." *Literature Compass* 16, nos. 9–10 (2019).

Ramazani, Jahan. *Poetry and Its Others: News, Prayer, Song, and the Dialogue of Genres.* Chicago: University of Chicago Press, 2014.

———. *Poetry in a Global Age.* Chicago: University of Chicago Press, 2020.

Ramey, Peter. "Crafting Strangeness: Wonder Terminology in the Exeter Book Riddles and the Anglo-Latin Enigmata." *Review of English Studies* 69, no. 289 (2017): 201–15.

Rankin, Susan. "From Memory to Record: Musical Notations in Manuscripts from Exeter." *Anglo-Saxon England* 13 (1984): 97–112.

———. "Taking the Rough with the Smooth: Melodic Versions and Manuscript Status." In *The Divine Office in the Latin Middle Ages: Methodology and Source Studies, Regional Developments, Hagiography*, edited by Margot E. Fassler and Rebecca A. Baltzer, 213–33. Oxford: Oxford University Press, 2000.

Rankin, Susan, and Michael Gullick. Review of *Catalogue of Manuscripts Written or Owned in England up to 1200 Containing Music* by K. D. Hartzell. *Early Music History* 28 (2009): 262–85.

Read, C. H. "Bronze Jug." *Proceedings of the Society of Antiquaries of London*, 2nd ser., 17 (1898): 82–87.

Reames, Sherry L. "Reconstructing and Interpreting a Thirteenth-Century Office for the Translation of Thomas Becket." *Speculum* 80, no. 1 (2005): 118–70.

Reed, Thomas L. *Middle English Debate Poetry and the Aesthetics of Irresolution*. Columbia: University of Missouri Press, 1990.

Regan, Stephen. *The Sonnet*. Oxford: Oxford University Press, 2019.

Reichl, Karl, ed. *Medieval Oral Literature*. Berlin: De Gruyter, 2012.

———. "The Middle English Carol." In *A Companion to the Middle English Lyric*, edited by Thomas G. Duncan, 150–70. Cambridge: D. S. Brewer, 2005.

Reiss, Edmund. *The Art of the Middle English Lyric: Essays in Criticism*. Athens: University of Georgia Press, 1972.

Renevey, Denis. *Language, Self and Love: Hermeneutics in Richard Rolle and the Commentaries of the Song of Songs*. Cardiff: University of Wales Press, 2001.

———. "Mystical Texts or Mystical Bodies? Peculiar Modes of Performance in Late Medieval England." *Swiss Papers in English Language and Literature* 11 (1998): 89–104.

———. "Name Above Names: The Devotion to the Name of Jesus from Richard Rolle to Walter Hilton's *Scale of Perfection I*." In *The Medieval Mystical Tradition: England, Ireland and Wales; Exeter Symposium VI; Papers Read at Charney Manor, July 1999*, edited by Marion Glasscoe, 103–21. Cambridge: D. S. Brewer, 1999.

Revard, Carter. "Scribe and Provenance." In *Studies in the Harley Manuscript: The Scribes, Contents, and Social Contexts of British Library MS Harley 2253*, ed. Susanna Fein, 21–109. Kalamazoo, MI: Medieval Institute Publications, 2000.

Reynolds, Suzanne. *Medieval Reading: Grammar, Rhetoric and the Classical Text*. Cambridge: Cambridge University Press, 2004.

Richards, I. A. *The Philosophy of Rhetoric*. Oxford: Oxford University Press, 1936.

———. *Poetries: Their Media and Ends; A Collection of Essays*. Edited by Trevor Eaton. The Hague: Mouton, 1974.

———. *Practical Criticism: A Study of Literary Judgment*. Edited by John Constable. New York: Routledge, 2001.

———. *Principles of Literary Criticism*. Edited by John Constable. London: Routledge, 2001. First published 1924 by Kegan Paul, Trench, Trübner.

Richardson, Amanda. "'Hedging, Ditching and Other Improper Occupations': Royal Landscapes and Their Meaning Under Edward II and Edward III." In *Fourteenth Century England IV*, edited by J. S. Hamilton, 26–42. Woodbridge, Suffolk: Boydell, 2006.

Riddy, Felicity. "The Provenance of *Quia amore langueo*." *Review of English Studies* 18, no. 72 (1967): 429–33.

Rigg, A. G. "Review: The Red Book of Ossory." *Medium Aevum* 46, no. 2 (1977): 269–78.

Robertson, Duncan. *"Lectio Divina": The Medieval Experience of Reading*. Collegeville, MN: Cistercian Publications, 2011.

Robbins, Rossell Hope. "The Bradshaw Carols." *PMLA* 81, no. 3 (1966): 308–10.

———. "The Earliest Carols and the Franciscans." *Modern Language Notes* 53, no. 4 (1938): 239–45.

———. "Friar Herebert and the Carol." *Anglia* 75 (1957): 194–98.

———. "Middle English Carols as Processional Hymns." *Studies in Philology* 56, no. 4 (1959): 559–82.

———. "Signs of Death in Middle English." *Mediaeval Studies* 32 (1970): 282–98.

Robbins, Rossell Hope, and John L. Cutler, eds. *Supplement to the Index of Middle English Verse*. Lexington: University of Kentucky Press, 1965.

Robins, Shari, and Richard E. Mayer. "The Metaphor Framing Effect: Metaphorical Reasoning About Text-Based Dilemmas." *Discourse Processes* 30, no. 1 (2000): 57–86.

Roman, Christopher M. *Queering Richard Rolle: Mystical Theology and the Hermit in Fourteenth-Century England*. Cham, Switzerland: Palgrave Macmillan, 2017.

Rossi, Carla. "A Clue to the Fate of the Lost MS. Royal 16 E VIII, Copy of the Voyage de Charlemagne." *Romania* 126 (2008): 245–52.

Rothenberg, David. *The Flower of Paradise: Marian Devotion and Secular Song in Medieval and Renaissance Music*. Oxford: Oxford University Press, 2011.

Rothwell, William. "À quelle époque a-t-on cessé de parler français en Angleterre?" In *Mélanges de philologie romane offerts à Charles Camproux*, 2:1075–89. Montpellier: Université Paul-Valéry, 1978.

Russo, John Paul. *I. A. Richards: His Life and Work*. Baltimore: Johns Hopkins University Press, 1989.

Russom, Geoffrey. *The Evolution of Verse Structure in Old and Middle English Poetry: From the Earliest Alliterative Poems to Iambic Pentameter*. Cambridge: Cambridge University Press, 2017.

Sadie, Stanley, and John Tyrrell, eds. *The New Grove Dictionary of Music and Musicians*. 2nd ed. London: New York, 2001. http://www.grovemusic.com/index.html.

Saintsbury, George. *A History of English Prosody from the Twelfth Century to the Present Day*. Vol. 1, *From the Origins to Spenser*. 2nd ed. London: Macmillan, 1923.

Salter, Elizabeth. "A Complaint Against Blacksmiths." *Literature and History* 5, no. 2 (1979): 194–215.

———. *English and International: Studies in Literature, Art and Patronage of Medieval England*. Edited by Derek Pearsall and Nicolette Zeeman. Cambridge: Cambridge University Press, 1988.

Samuels, M. L. "Chaucerian Final '-e.'" *Notes and Queries* 19, no. 12 (1972): 445–48.

Sandison, Helen Estabrook. *The "Chanson d'Aventure" in Middle English*. Bryn Mawr, PA: Bryn Mawr College, 1913.

Sanok, Catherine. *Her Life Historical: Exemplarity and Female Saints' Lives in Late Medieval England*. Philadelphia: University of Pennsylvania Press, 2007.

Sartre, Jean-Paul. "Situation of the Writer in 1947." In *What Is Literature?*, translated by Bernard Frechtman, 128–229. London, 1967. First published 1950.

Saul, Nigel. "The Commons and the Abolition of Badges." *Parliamentary History* 9 (1990): 302–15.

———. *Richard II*. New Haven, CT: Yale University Press, 1997.

Scahill, John. "Trilingualism in Early Middle English Miscellanies: Languages and Literature." *Yearbook of English Studies* 33 (2003): 18–32.

Scala, Elizabeth, and Sylvia Federico, eds. *The Post-Historical Middle Ages*. New York: Palgrave Macmillan, 2009.

Scase, Wendy, ed., *The Making of the Vernon Manuscript: The Production and Contexts of Oxford, Bodleian Library, MS Eng. poet. a. 1*. Turnhout: Brepols, 2013.

Scattergood, V. J. *Politics and Poetry in the Fifteenth Century*. London: Blandford Press, 1971.

Schendl, Herbert. "Code-Switching in Late Medieval Macaronic Sermons." In *Multilingualism in Medieval Britain (c. 1066–1520): Sources and Analysis*, edited by Judith A. Jefferson and Ad Putter, 153–69. Turnhout: Brepols, 2013.

Schipper, Jakob. *A History of English Versification*. Oxford: Clarendon Press, 1910.

Scott, A. B. "Latin Learning and Literature in Ireland, 1169–1500." In *A New History of Ireland*, vol. 1, *Prehistoric and Early Ireland*, edited by Dáibhí Ó Cróinín, 934–95. Oxford: Clarendon Press, 2005.

Selbin, Jesse Cordes. "'Read with Attention': John Cassell, John Ruskin, and the History of Close Reading." *Victorian Studies* 58, no. 3 (2016): 493–521.

Semino, Elena. "Descriptions of Pain, Metaphor and Embodied Simulation." *Metaphor and Symbol* 25, no. 4 (2010): 205–26.

Sepet, Marius. *Les prophètes du Christ: Étude sur les origines du théâtre au moyen âge*. Paris, 1878. Reprint, Geneva: Slatkine, 1974.

Severs, J. Burke, ed. *A Manual of the Writings in Middle English, 1050–1500*. Vol. 1. New Haven: Connecticut Academy of Arts and Sciences, 1967.

Shaviro, Steven. "'Striving with Systems': Blake and the Politics of Difference." *boundary 2* 10, no. 3 (1982): 229–50.

Short, Ian. *Manual of Anglo-Norman*. ANTS, O.P., 7. London: Anglo-Norman Text Society, 2007.

Silleras-Fernández, Núria. "*Nigra Sum Sed Formosa*: Black Slaves and Exotica in the Court of a Fourteenth-Century Aragonese Queen." *Medieval Encounters* 13, no. 3 (2007): 546–65.

Silverman, Raymond. "Material Biographies: Saharan Trade and the Lives of Objects in Fourteenth and Fifteenth-Century West Africa." *History in Africa* 42 (2015): 375–95.

———. "Red Gold: Things Made of Copper, Bronze, and Brass." In *Caravans of Gold, Fragments in Time: Art, Culture, and Exchange Across Medieval Saharan Africa*, edited by Kathleen Berzock, 257–67. Princeton, NJ: Princeton University Press, 2019.

Silverstein, Michael, and Greg Urban, eds. *Natural Histories of Discourse*. Chicago: University of Chicago Press, 1996.

Simpson, James. "Not Yet: Chaucer and Anagogy." *Studies in the Age of Chaucer* 37 (2015): 31–54.

Slade, Benjamin. "Bede's Story of Caedmon: Text and Facing Translation." Appendix 2. http://heorot.dk/bede-caedmon.html#appendix-2.

Slingerland, Edward. *Effortless Action: Wu-wei as Conceptual Metaphor and Spiritual Ideal in Early China*. New York: Oxford University Press, 2003.

Slocum, Kay Brainerd. *Liturgies in Honour of Thomas Becket*. Toronto: University of Toronto Press, 2004.

Smail, Daniel Lord. *On Deep History and the Brain*. Berkeley: University of California Press, 2007.

Smedick, Lois K. "Parallelism and Pointing in Rolle's Rhythmical Style." *Mediaeval Studies* 41, no. 1 (1979): 404–67.

Smith, A. D. *Routledge Philosophy Guidebook to Husserl and the Cartesian Meditations*. New York: Routledge, 2003.

Smith, Barbara Hernstein. "What Was 'Close Reading'? A Century of Methods in Literary Studies." *Minnesota Review* 87 (2016): 57–75.

Smith, D. Vance. "The Silence of Langland's Study: Matter, Invisibility, Instruction." In *Answerable Style: The Idea of the Literary in Medieval England*, edited by Frank Grady and Andrew Galloway, 263–83. Columbus: Ohio State University Press, 2013.

Smith, Robin. "Aristotle's Logic." *Stanford Encyclopedia of Philosophy*. 2000, rev. 2017. https://plato.stanford.edu/entries/aristotle-logic/.

Smithers, G. V. "The Scansion of *Havelok* and the Use of ME *-en* and *-e* in *Havelok* and by Chaucer." In *Middle English Studies: Presented to Norman Davis in Honour of His Seventieth Birthday*, edited by Douglas Gray and E. G. Stanley, 195–234. Oxford: Clarendon Press, 1983.

Snead, James A. "Repetition as a Figure of Black Culture." In *Black Literature and Literary Theory*, edited by Henry Louis Gates, Jr., 59–79. New York: Routledge, 1990.

Spearing, A. C. *Medieval Autographies: The "I" of the Text*. Notre Dame, IN: University of Notre Dame Press, 2012.

———. "Middle English Lyrics, Lyrics in Narratives, and 'Who made this song?'" Unpublished Paper for "What Kind of a Thing Is a Middle English Lyric?" Advanced Seminar, Radcliffe Institute for Advanced Study, Harvard University, December 2, 2016.

———. *Textual Subjectivity: The Encoding of Subjectivity in Medieval Narratives and Lyrics*. Oxford: Oxford University Press, 2005.

Speed, Diane. "A Text for Its Time: The *Sanctorale* of the Early *South English Legendary*." In *The Texts and Contexts of Oxford, Bodleian Library, MS Laud Misc. 108*, edited by Kimberly K. Bell and Julie Nelson Crouch, 117–36. Leiden: Brill, 2011.

Spencer, Brian. "Medieval Face-Jug (The London Museum)." *Burlington Magazine* 111, no. 794 (1969): 302–3.

Stanbury, Sarah. "Gender and Voice in Middle English Religious Lyrics." In *A Companion to the Middle English Lyric*, edited by Thomas G. Duncan, 227–41. Cambridge: D. S. Brewer, 2005.

———. "The Virgin's Gaze: Spectacle and Transgression in Middle English Lyrics of the Passion." *PMLA* 106, no. 5 (1991): 1083–93.

Staniland, Kay. "Extravagance or Regal Necessity? The Clothing of Richard II." In *The Regal Image of Richard II and the Wilton Diptych*, edited by Dillian Gordon, Lisa Monnas, and Caroline Elam, 85–93. London: Harvey Miller, 1997.

Staples, James C. "'Mercy Schal Hyr Craftez Kyþe': Learning to Perform Re-Deeming Readings of Materiality in *Pearl*." *Glossator* 9 (2015): 109–31.

Steane, John. *The Archaeology of the British Monarchy*. London: Routledge, 1999.

Steiner, Emily. *John Trevisa's Information Age: Knowledge and the Pursuit of Literature, c. 1400*. Oxford: Oxford University Press, 2021.

Stephenson, Jill. "Rhythmic Liturgy, Embodiment and Female Authority in Barking's Easter Plays." In *Barking Abbey and Medieval Literary Culture: Authorship and Authority in a Female Community*, edited by Jennifer N. Brown and Donna Alfano Bussell, 245–66. York: York Medieval Press, 2002.

Stevens, John. "Alphabetical Check-List of Anglo-Norman Songs c. 1150–c. 1350." *Plainsong and Medieval Music* 3 (1994): 1–22.

———. Review of *Medieval English Songs*, edited by E. J. Dobson and F. Ll. Harrison. *Music and Letters* 62, nos. 3–4 (1981): 461–66.

———. *Words and Music in the Middle Ages: Song, Narrative, Dance and Drama, 1050–1350*. Cambridge: Cambridge University Press, 1986.

Stevens, John, Ardis Butterfield, and Theodore Karp. "Troubadours, Trouvères." *Grove Music Online*. 2001. https://doi.org/10.1093/gmo/9781561592630.article.28468.

Stevens, John, and Dennis Libby. "Carol." *Grove Music Online*. 2001. https://doi.org/10.1093/gmo/9781561592630.article.04974.

Stillinger, Thomas C. *The Song of Troilus: Lyric Authority in the Medieval Book*. Philadelphia: University of Pennsylvania Press, 1992.

Stock, Brian. *Listening for the Text: On the Uses of the Past*. Philadelphia: University of Pennsylvania Press, 1996.

Stockwell, Peter. *Cognitive Poetics: An Introduction*. London: Routledge, 2002.

Strohm, Paul, ed. *Middle English*. Oxford Twenty-First Century Approaches to Literature. Oxford: Oxford University Press, 2007.

Stouck, Mary-Ann. "'In a valey of þis restles mynde': Contexts and Meaning." *Modern Philology* 85, no. 1 (1987): 1–11.

Studtmann, Paul. "Aristotle's Categories." *Stanford Encyclopedia of Philosophy*. 2007, rev., 2021. https://plato.stanford.edu/entries/aristotle-categories.

Sutherland, Annie. "Biblical Text and Spiritual Experience in the English Epistles of Richard Rolle." *Review of English Studies* 56, no. 227 (2005): 695–711.

Sweetinburgh, Sheila. "Remembering the Dead at Dinner-Time." In *Everyday Objects: Medieval and Early Modern Material Culture and Its Meanings*, edited by Tara Hamling and Catherine Richardson, 257–66. Farnham, Surrey: Ashgate, 2010.

Sweetser, Eve. *From Etymology to Pragmatics: Metaphorical and Cultural Aspects of Semantic Structure*. New York: Cambridge University Press, 1990.

Tarlinskaja, Marina. *English Verse: Theory and History*. The Hague: Mouton, 1976.

———. "Meter and Rhythm of Pre-Chaucerian Rhymed Verse." *Linguistics* 12, no. 121 (1974): 65–87.

———. *Strict Stress-Meter in English Poetry Compared with German and Russian*. Calgary: University of Calgary Press, 1993.

Taylor, Andrew. "The Myth of the Minstrel Manuscript." *Speculum* 66, no. 1 (1991): 43–73.

Taylor, Jane H. M. "The Lyric Insertion: Towards a Functional Model." In *Courtly Literature: Culture and Context*, edited by Keith Busby and Erik Kooper, 539–48. Amsterdam: John Benjamins, 1990.

Taylor, John R. *Linguistic Categorization: Prototypes in Linguistic Theory*. Oxford: Clarendon Press, 1989.

Taylor, Paul C. *Black Is Beautiful: A Philosophy of Black Aesthetics*. Chichester, West Sussex: John Wiley and Sons, 2016.

Teviotdale, Elizabeth Cover. "The Cotton Troper (London, British Library, Cotton MS Caligula A.xiv, ff. 1–36): A Study of an Illustrated English Troper of the Eleventh Century." Ph.D. diss., University of North Carolina at Chapel Hill, 1991.

Theuerkauff-Liederwald, Anna-Elisabeth. *Mittelalterliche Bronze- und Messinggefässe: Eimer, Kannen, Lavabokessel*. Berlin: Deutscher Verlag für Kunstwissenschaft, 1988.

Thibodeau, Paul, and Frank H. Durgin. "Productive Figurative Communication: Conventional Metaphors Facilitate the Comprehension of Related Novel Metaphors." *Journal of Memory and Language* 58, no. 2 (2008): 521–40.

Thomas, Hugh M. *The English and the Normans: Ethnic Hostility, Assimilation, and Identity, 1066–c. 1220.* Oxford: Oxford University Press, 2003.

Thompson, John J. *Robert Thornton and the London Thornton Manuscript: British Library MS Additional 31042.* Cambridge: D. S. Brewer, 1987.

Thornbury, Emily V. *Becoming a Poet in Anglo-Saxon England.* Cambridge: Cambridge University Press, 2014.

Tiffany, Daniel. "Lyric Substance: On Riddles, Materialism, and Poetic Obscurity." *Critical Inquiry* 28 (2001): 72–98.

———. *Toy Medium: Materialism and Modern Lyric.* Berkeley: University of California Press, 2000.

Tilghman, Benjamin. "On the Engimatic Nature of Things in Anglo-Saxon Art." *Different Visions* 4 (2014): 1–43.

Tilliette, Jean-Yves. "Note sur le manuscrit des poèmes de Baudri de Bourgueil (Vatican, Reg. Lat. 1351)." *Scriptorium* 37 (1983): 241–45.

Townend, Matthew. *Language and History in Viking Age England: Linguistic Relations Between Speakers of Old Norse and Old English.* Turnhout: Brepols, 2002.

Trachsler, Richard. "Orality, Literacy and Performativity of Arthurian Texts." In *Handbook of Arthurian Romance: King Arthur's Court in Medieval European Literature*, edited by Leah Tether and Johnny McFadyen, 273–92. Berlin: De Gruyter, 2017.

Travis, Peter W. *Disseminal Chaucer: Rereading "The Nun's Priest's Tale."* Notre Dame, IN: University of Notre Dame Press, 2010.

Treharne, Elaine. "The Vernaculars of Medieval England, 1170–1350." In *The Cambridge Companion to Medieval English Culture*, edited by Andrew Galloway, 217–36. Cambridge: Cambridge University Press, 2011.

Trend, J. B. "The First English Songs." *Music and Letters* 9, no. 2 (1928): 111–28.

Trigg, Stephanie. "The Rhetoric of Excess in *Winner and Waster*." *The Yearbook of Langland Studies* 3 (1989): 91–108.

Trim, Richard. *Metaphor and the Historical Evolution of Conceptual Mapping.* Houndmills, Basingstoke, Hampshire, UK: Palgrave Macmillan, 2007.

Trumpfheller, Brad. "Groundshift: A Conversation with Jos Charles." *Adroit* 26 (2018). https://theadroitjournal.org/2018/08/30/jos-charles-poetry-interview/.

Tsur, Reuven. *Toward a Theory of Cognitive Poetics.* Amsterdam: Elsevier, 1992.

Tucker, Herbert. "Dramatic Monologue and the Overhearing of Lyric." In *Lyric Poetry: Beyond New Criticism*, edited by Chaviva Hošek and Patricia Parker, 226–43. Ithaca, NY: Cornell University Press, 1985.

Turner, Denys. *Eros and Allegory: Medieval Exegesis of the Song of Songs.* Kalamazoo, MI: Cistercian Publications, 1995.

Turner, Mark. *The Literary Mind: The Origins of Language and Thought.* New York: Oxford University Press, 1996.

Turville-Petre, Thorlac. "Political Lyrics." In *A Companion to the Middle English Lyric*, edited by Thomas G. Duncan, 171–88. Cambridge: D. S. Brewer, 2005.

Tuve, Rosemond. "Spenser and Mediaeval Mazers, with a Note on Jason in Ivory." In *Essays by Rosemond Tuve: On Spenser, Herbert and Milton*, edited by Thomas P. Roche, Jr., 102–11. Princeton, NJ: Princeton University Press, 1970.

Vale, Malcolm. "From the Court of Richard II to the Court of Prempeh I: The Problem of the 'Asante' Ewers." In *Soldiers, Nobles and Gentlemen: Essays in Honour of Maurice Keen*, edited by Peter R. Coss and Christopher Tyerman, 335–53. Woodbridge, Suffolk: Boydell Press, 2009.

Vance, Eugene. "Greimas, Freud, and the Story of Trouvère Lyric." In *Lyric Poetry: Beyond New Criticism*, edited by Chaviva Hošek and Patricia Parker, 93–105. Ithaca, NY: Cornell University Press, 1985.

van Dijk, S. J. P. "Some Manuscripts of the Earliest Franciscan Liturgy." *Franciscan Studies* 14, no. 3 (1954): 225–64.

——, ed. *Sources of the Modern Roman Liturgy: The Ordinals by Haymo of Faversham and Related Documents, 1243–1307*. 2 vols. Leiden: Brill, 1963.

van Dussen, Michael. "Tourists and *Tabulae* in Late-Medieval England." In *Truth and Tales: Cultural Mobility and Medieval Media*, edited by Fiona Somerset and Nicholas Watson, 238–54. Columbus: Ohio State University Press, 2015.

Vendler, Helen. "The Art of Criticism No. 3." Interview by Henri Cole. *Paris Review* 141 (1996). https://www.theparisreview.org/interviews/1324/the-art-of-criticism-no-3-helen -vendler.

——. *Soul Says: On Recent Poetry*. Cambridge, MA: Harvard University Press, 1995.

Vernon, Matthew X. *The Black Middle Ages: Race and the Construction of the Middle Ages*. Cham, Switzerland: Palgrave Macmillan, 2018.

Victoria and Albert Museum. "Robinson Jug." http://collections.vam.ac.uk/item/O97902 /robinson-jug-jug-unknown/.

Walford, Weston, and Albert Way. "Examples of Mediaeval Seals." *Archaeological Journal* 13 (1856): 62–76.

Wallace, David, ed. *The Cambridge History of Medieval English Literature*. Cambridge: Cambridge University Press, 1999.

——. "Chaucer and Boccaccio's Early Writings." In *Chaucer and the Italian Trecento*, edited by Piero Boitani, 141–62. Cambridge: Cambridge University Press, 1983.

——. *Chaucer and the Early Writings of Boccaccio*. Cambridge: D. S. Brewer, 1985.

Waters, Claire M. "*Makyng* and Middles in Chaucer's Poetry." In *Readings in Medieval Textuality: Essays in Honour of A. C. Spearing*, edited by Cristina Maria Cervone and D. Vance Smith, 31–44. Cambridge: D. S. Brewer, 2016.

Watson, Nicholas. *Balaam's Ass: Vernacular Theology Before the English Reformation*. Vol. 2, *French 1100–1400, English 1250–1530*. Philadelphia: University of Pennsylvania Press, forthcoming.

——. "Desire for the Past." *Studies in the Age of Chaucer* 21 (1991): 59–97.

——. "The Original Audience and Institutional Setting of Edmund Rich's *Mirror of Holy Church*: The Case for the Salisbury Canons." In *Medieval and Early Modern Religious Cultures: Essays Honouring Vincent Gillespie on His Sixty-Fifth Birthday*, edited by Laura Ashe and Ralph Hanna, 21–42. Cambridge: D. S. Brewer, 2019.

——. *Richard Rolle and the Invention of Authority*. Cambridge: Cambridge University Press, 1991.

——. "The Trinitarian Hermeneutic in Julian of Norwich's *Revelation of Love*." In *The Medieval Mystical Tradition in England: Exeter Symposium V*, edited by Marion Glasscoe, 79–100. Cambridge: D. S. Brewer, 1992.

Weinryb, Ittai. *The Bronze Object in the Middle Ages*. Cambridge: Cambridge University Press, 2016.

Weiskott, Eric. "A Checklist of Short and Fragmentary Unrhymed English Alliterative Poems, 1300–1600." *Notes and Queries* 67, no. 3 (2020): 340–47.

———. *English Alliterative Verse: Poetic Tradition and Literary History.* Cambridge: Cambridge University Press, 2016.

———. *Meter and Modernity in English Verse, 1350–1650.* Philadelphia: University of Pennsylvania Press, 2021.

Weismiller, Edward R. "Triple Threats to Duple Rhythm." In *Phonetics and Phonology*, vol. 1, *Rhythm and Meter*, edited by Paul Kiparsky and Gilbert Youmans, 261–90. San Diego: Academic Press, 1989.

Wellek, René. "Genre Theory, the Lyric, and Erlebnis." In *The Lyric Theory Reader: A Critical Anthology*, edited by Virginia Jackson and Yopie Prins, 40–52. Baltimore: Johns Hopkins University Press, 2014.

Wells, John Edwin. *Manual of the Writings in Middle English, 1050–1400.* New Haven: Connecticut Academy of Arts and Sciences, 1916.

Wenzel, Siegfried. *Macaronic Sermons: Bilingualism and Preaching in Late-Medieval England.* Ann Arbor: University of Michigan Press, 1994.

———. *Medieval "Artes Praedicandi": A Synthesis of Scholastic Sermon Structure.* Toronto: University of Toronto Press, 2015.

———. "Poets, Preachers, and the Plight of Literary Critics." *Speculum* 60, no. 2 (1985): 343–63.

———. *Preachers, Poets, and the Early English Lyric.* Princeton, NJ: Princeton University Press, 1986.

———. *Verses in Sermons: "Fasciculus Morum" and Its Middle English Poems.* Cambridge, MA: Mediaeval Academy of America, 1978.

Whitaker, Cord J. *Black Metaphors: How Modern Racism Emerged from Medieval Race-Thinking.* Philadelphia: University of Pennsylvania Press, 2019.

———. "Black Metaphors in the *King of Tars*." *Journal of English and Germanic Philology* 112, no. 2 (2013): 169–93.

———. "Race-ing the Dragon: The Middle Ages, Race and Trippin' into the Future." *postmedieval* 6, no. 1 (2015): 3–11.

Whiting, Bartlett Jere. "A Collection of Proverbs in BM Additional MS 37075." In *Franciplegius: Medieval and Linguistic Studies in Honor of Francis Peabody Magoun, Jr.*, edited by Jess B. Bessinger, Jr., and Robert P. Creed, 274–89. New York: New York University Press, 1965.

———. *Proverbs, Sentences, and Proverbial Phrases from English Writings Mainly Before 1500.* Cambridge, MA: Belknap Press, 1968.

Wicker, Helen E. "Between Proverbs and Lyrics: Customization Practices in Late Medieval English Moral Verse." *English* 59, no. 224 (2010): 3–24.

Williams, Lawrence E., and John A. Bargh. "Experiencing Physical Warmth Influences Interpersonal Warmth." *Science* 322 (2008): 606–7.

Williams, Raymond. *The Country and the City.* Oxford: Oxford University Press, 1973.

———. *Keywords: A Vocabulary of Culture and Society.* Rev. ed. Oxford: Oxford University Press, 1983.

Williamson, Craig, ed. *The Old English Riddles of the Exeter Book.* Chapel Hill: University of North Carolina Press, 1977.

Williamson, Paul, ed. *The Medieval Treasury: The Middle Ages in the Victoria and Albert Museum.* London: Victoria and Albert Museum, 1986.

Wilson, Anna. "The Role of Affect in Fan Fiction." *Transformative Works and Cultures* 21 (2016). https://doi.org/10.3983/twc.2016.0684.

Wilson, Blake. "Lauda." *Grove Music Online*. 2001. https://doi.org/10.1093/gmo/9781561592630 .article.43313.

Wilson, Edward. *A Descriptive Index of the English Lyrics in John of Grimestone's Preaching Book*. Oxford: Basil Blackwell, 1973.

Wilson, R. M. *The Lost Literature of Medieval England*. London: Metheun, 1952.

Wimsatt, James. "The Canticle of Canticles, Two Latin Poems, and 'In a valey of this restles mynde.'" *Modern Philology* 75, no. 4 (1978): 327–45.

Windeatt, Barry. "Love." In *A Companion to Medieval English Literature and Culture, c. 1350– c. 1500*, edited by Peter Brown, 322–38. Malden, MA: Blackwell, 2007.

Wogan-Browne, Jocelyn, et al., eds. *Language and Culture in Medieval Britain: The French of England, c. 1100–c. 1500*. York: York Medieval Press, 2009.

Woolf, Rosemary. *The English Religious Lyric in the Middle Ages*. Oxford: Clarendon Press, 1968.

———. "The Theme of Christ the Lover-Knight in Medieval English Literature." *Review of English Studies* 13, no. 49 (1962): 1–16.

Woolgar, C. M. *The Senses in Late Medieval England*. New Haven, CT: Yale University Press, 2006.

Woudhuysen, H. R. *Sir Philip Sidney and the Circulation of Manuscripts, 1558–1640*. Oxford: Clarendon Press, 1996.

Wright, Laura. "The Languages of Medieval Britain." In *A Companion to Medieval English Literature and Culture*, edited by Peter Brown, 143–58. Oxford: Blackwell, 2007.

Wulstan, David. Review of *Medieval English Songs*, edited by E. J. Dobson and F. Ll. Harrison. *Journal of the Plainsong and Mediaeval Music Society* 3 (1980): 59–61.

Yakovlev, Nicolay. "On Final -e in the B-Verses of *Sir Gawain and the Green Knight*." In *Approaches to the Metres of Alliterative Verse*, edited by Judith Jefferson and Ad Putter, 135–57. Leeds: Leeds Studies in English, 2009.

Yarberry, S. "Standardizing the Vernacular: An Interview with Jos Charles." *BOMB*, August 2018. https://bombmagazine.org/articles/jos-charles/.

Yardley, Anne Bagnall. "Liturgy as the Site of Creative Engagement: Contributions of the Nuns of Barking." In *Barking Abbey and Medieval Literary Culture: Authorship and Authority in a Female Community*, edited by Jennifer N. Brown and Donna Alfano Bussell, 267–82. York: York Medieval Press, 2012.

———. *Performing Piety: Musical Culture in Medieval English Nunneries*. New York: Palgrave MacMillan, 2006.

Zayaruznaya, Anna. "Intelligibility Redux: Motets and the Modern Medieval Sound." *Music Theory Online* 23, no. 2 (2017). https://mtosmt.org/issues/mto.17.23.2/mto.17.23.2 .zayaruznaya.html.

Zeeman, Nicolette. "Imaginative Theory." In *Middle English*, edited by Paul Strohm, 222–40. Oxford Twenty-First Century Approaches to Literature. Oxford: Oxford University Press, 2007.

Zemka, Sue. "Spiritual Authority and the Life of Thomas Arnold." *Victorian Studies* 38, no. 3 (1995): 429–62.

Ziegler, Joseph. "Skin and Character in Medieval and Early Renaissance Physiognomy." In "La pelle umana/The Human Skin," edited by Agostino Paravicini Bagliani. Special issue, *Micrologus* 13 (2005): 511–35.

Zieman, Katherine. "Compiling the Lyric: Richard Rolle, Textual Dynamism and Devotional Song in London, British Library, Additional MS 37049." In *Middle English Lyrics: New Readings of Short Poems*, edited by Julia Boffey and Christiania Whitehead, 158–72. Cambridge: D. S. Brewer, 2018.

Zumthor, Paul. "Considérations sur les valeurs de la voix." *Cahiers de civilisation médiévale* 25, no. 99 (1982): 233–38.

———. *Essai de poétique médiévale.* Paris: Seuil, 1972.

———. *Toward a Medieval Poetics.* Translated by Philip Bennett. Minneapolis: University of Minnesota Press, 1991.

Zupitza, Julius. "Cantus beati Godrici." *Englische Studien* 11 (1888): 401–32.

———. "Die Gedichte des Franziskaners Jacob Ryman." *Archiv für das Studium der neueren Sprachen und Literaturen* 89 (1892): 167–338.

Contributors

EDITORS

Cristina Maria Cervone is Associate Professor of English at the University of Memphis. Among her books is *Poetics of the Incarnation: Middle English Writing and the Leap of Love* (2013). Her current project, a sister book to the first, is provisionally entitled *Vernacular Poetics of Metaphor: Middle English and the Corporate Subject* and explores interrelationships among metaphor, poetics, and Middle English in light of modern theories of cognition.

Nicholas Watson is Henry B. and Anne M. Cabot Professor of English at Harvard University. Among his books is *Balaam's Ass: Vernacular Theology Before the English Reformation, Volume 1: Frameworks, Arguments, English to 1250*, from the University of Pennsylvania Press (2022), the first in a trilogy. He is presently completing the second volume, subtitled *French 1100–1400, English 1250–1540*, and working on the third.

SCHOLARS

Andrew Albin is Associate Professor of English and Medieval Studies at Fordham University. He is author of *Richard Rolle's Melody of Love: A Study and Translation with Manuscript and Musical Contexts* (2018). He is presently at work on a monograph titled "The Manuscript Is an Instrument and We Must Play."

Stephanie Burt is Professor of English at Harvard University. Her recent books include *Don't Read Poetry: A Book About How to Read Poems* (2019) and *After Callimachus* (2020), a collection of adaptations, imitations, and free translations from the ancient Greek (2019). Her next book of poems will appear from Graywolf Press in 2022.

Ardis Butterfield is the Marie Borroff Professor of English and Professor of French and Music at Yale University. Among her books is *The Familiar Enemy: Chaucer, Language and the Nation in the Hundred Years War* (2009). She is also editor of the forthcoming *Norton Medieval English Lyrics* (2023) and is completing her monograph *Medieval Songlines*.

Christopher Cannon is Bloomberg Distinguished Professor of English and Classics at Johns Hopkins University. He is the author of *From Literacy to Literature: England, 1300–1400* (2016), and, with James Simpson, editor of the *Oxford Chaucer* (2022).

Ian Cornelius is Associate Professor of English at Loyola University Chicago. He is author of *Reconstructing Alliterative Verse: The Pursuit of a Medieval Meter* (2017). His current projects include a digital edition of a unique sixteenth-century translation of the Middle English poem *Piers Plowman*.

Margot Fassler is Keough-Hesburgh Professor of Music History and Liturgy at the University of Notre Dame and the Tangeman Professor of Music History, emerita, Yale University. Among her books is *The Virgin of Chartres: Making History Through Liturgy and the Arts* (2010); her study of Hildegard's Illuminated *Scivias* is in press.

Andrew Galloway is James John Professor of Medieval Studies at Cornell University. Among his books is *The Penn Commentary on "Piers Plowman, Volume 1"* (2006). Forthcoming contributions include a survey of medieval poetic and literary theory for *The Oxford History of Poetry in English* and a survey of ideas of poverty in medieval economic theory for the *Bloomsbury Cultural History of Poverty*.

Raymond W. Gibbs, Jr., is a cognitive scientist and former Distinguished Professor of Psychology, University of California, Santa Cruz. Among his books is *Metaphor Wars: Conceptual Metaphors in Human Life* (2017).

Virginia Jackson is UCI Endowed Chair of Rhetoric and Critical Theory in the Departments of English and Comparative Literature at UC Irvine. Among her books are *Dickinson's Misery: A Theory of Lyric Reading* (2005) and *The Lyric Theory Reader: A Critical Anthology* (2014).

Aden Kumler is Professor of Ältere Kunstgeschichte at the University of Basel. She is author of *Translating Truth: Ambitious Images and Religious Knowledge in Late Medieval France and England* (2011).

Ingrid Nelson is Associate Professor of English at Amherst College. She is author of *Lyric Tactics: Poetry, Genre, and Practice in Later Medieval England* (2017) and is currently completing a book on premodern media.

Barbara Zimbalist is Associate Professor of English at University of Texas El Paso. She is author of *Translating Christ in the Middle Ages: Gender, Authorship and the Visionary Text* (University of Notre Dame Press, 2022).

POETS

Kate Caoimhe Arthur's poems have been published in *The Best New British and Irish Poets, 2018.*

Hunter Keough earned his M.F.A. in poetry/creative writing from the University of Memphis. He is the founder and lead editor of the online literary journal *Gemstone Piano Review.*

Bill Manhire was New Zealand's first poet laureate. His most recent collection is *Wow* (2020).

Pattie McCarthy is the author of seven books of poems, most recently *wifthing* (Apogee Press, 2021), which includes the poem in this volume. She is a non-tenure-track associate professor at Temple University, where she teaches literature and creative writing.

Miller Wolf Oberman is author of *The Unstill Ones: Poems* (2017), a collection of poems, including translations from Old English.

† **Carter Revard** was Professor Emeritus of English at Washington University, St. Louis. A critic, medievalist, and poet, his books of poems include, most recently, *From the Extinct Volcano, A Bird of Paradise* (2014).

Index

Acknowledgments

The editors and contributors owe a deep debt of gratitude to the Radcliffe Institute for Advanced Study, both for generously funding the seminars out of which this book emerged and for the care and professionalism that went into their planning and execution. The Institute's emphasis on "risk taking and creativity" and the nonhierarchic and open-ended atmosphere the format of its seminars encourages did much to shape our conversations.

We acknowledge with gratitude the aid of librarians and staff of the British Library; the British Museum, London; the Cambridge University Library; Gonville and Caius College, Pembroke College, and the Parker Library of Corpus Christi College, Cambridge; the Cloisters Collection of the Metropolitan Museum of Art, New York; the Museum of London; Hesburgh Library, the University of Notre Dame; the Victoria and Albert Museum, London; and the Beinecke Library, Yale University. We appreciate the kind permission to reprint granted us by Apogee Press, Blackbox, Stainer & Bell, the University of Arizona Press, and Victoria University of Wellington Press. Thanks also to the University of Pennsylvania Press for taking on this long book; the two anonymous press readers for their helpful and encouraging reports; Vidyan Ravinthiran for reading the Introduction and for his thought-provoking comments; Sarah Star for her work on the notes and bibliography; Lawrence Revard for his kind assistance; and Jennifer Shenk, Erin Davis and Kimberly Giambattisto for their painstaking and imaginative copyediting.

The editors also wish to thank all those who participated in the two Radcliffe "WKOAT" ("What Kind of a Thing?") seminars for their collegiality, good humor and thoughtfulness. These include the four who did not contribute chapters but from whom we learned so much: Kevin L. Hughes, Eleanor Johnson, A. C. Spearing, and Jerome E. Singerman. Special thanks are due to A. C. Spearing, whose perspective was of great value to us; to Jerome E. Singerman, former senior editor at University of Pennsylvania Press, for his advice and encouragement; to our two respondents, Virginia

Jackson and Stephanie Burt, for their enthusiastic engagement with the project and many insights; to Stephanie Burt, again, for her help in soliciting and selecting the poems in the chapbook at the end of this book; and to the poets whose poems are gathered there, for extending the project so meaningfully. We also thank the other contributors to this book for their wonderful chapters, their dedication to the project, their willingness to draft and redraft with one another's work in mind, and their patience as all were safely gathered in.

Finally, the editors and contributors acknowledge the recent passing of one of our number, Carter Revard, with grief at his death but also with deep gratitude for his life, scholarship, and poetry. It has long seemed fitting that he should offer the last words, poetic ones, in the book proper, given the permanent importance of his work on Harley 2253 (the "Harley lyrics" manuscript), as well as the skill with which his poetry captures the "pley" this book especially associates with the Middle English lyric. Now we all the more appreciate that "What the Eagle Fan Says" here speaks to the liveliness of the dance, the human breath voicing the old songs, and the soaring power of spirit.

CPSIA information can be obtained
at www.ICGtesting.com
Printed in the USA
JSHW022150010722
27784JS00001B/1

9 780812 253900